Contextualized Language Intervention

Scaffolding PreK–12 Literacy Achievement

Teresa A. Ukrainetz, PhD

Editor

Teaching students with language impairments the language needed for academic success through scaffolding explicit skills in purposeful contexts

An International Publisher

8700 Shoal Creek Boulevard
Austin, Texas 78757-6897
800/897-3202   Fax 800/397-7633
www.proedinc.com

Library of Congress Cataloging-in-Publication Data

Contextualized language intervention: scaffolding K–12 literacy achievement /
Teresa A. Ukrainetz, editor.
   p. cm.
Includes bibliographical references and index.
ISBN 1-932054-47-2 (pbk.—original)
ISBN 978-1-4164-0413-2 (new)
ISBN 978-1-4164-0623-5 (e-book PDF)
   1. Language arts—Remedial teaching. 2. Language disorders—Treatment. I. Ukrainetz,
Teresa A. date

LB1576.C65 2005
428.4'071—dc22   2005053855

Printed in the United States of America

Cover design by Debbie Olson

Trademarks: PowerPoint and Word are registered trademarks of Microsoft Corporation. EmPower
                is a trademark of Innovative Learning Partners. Cuisinaire is a registered trademark of
                ETA/Cuisinaire. All other brand names and product names used in this book are trade
                names, service marks, trademarks, or registered trademarks of their respective owners.

Previously published by Thinking Publications®

Printed in the United States of America

9 10 11 12 13 14 15 16 17   21 20 19 18 17

To Jerry L. Starr

Contents

Contributors

Editor: Teresa A. Ukrainetz, PhD, S-LP(C)
Associate Professor, Graduate Advisor, and Distance Coordinator
Division of Communication Disorders
University of Wyoming
Laramie, WY

Anthony S. Bashir, PhD, CCC-SLP
Coordinator
Academic and Disability Services
Emerson College
Boston, MA

Bonnie Brinton, PhD, CCC-SLP
Professor and Dean of Graduate Studies
Audiology and Speech-Language Pathology
Brigham Young University
Provo, UT

Sarita Eisenberg, PhD, CCC-SLP
Assistant Professor
Department of Communication Sciences and Disorders
Montclair State University
Montclair, NJ

Helen Ezell, PhD, CCC-SLP
Research Associate—Reading First Evaluation Project
Department of Instruction and Learning
University of Pittsburgh
Pittsburgh, PA

Martin Fujiki, PhD, CCC-SLP
Professor
Audiology and Speech-Language Pathology
Brigham Young University
Provo, UT

Ronald B. Gillam, PhD, CCC-SLP
Professor and Graduate Program Director
Department of Communication Sciences and Disorders
University of Texas at Austin
Austin, TX

Laura M. Justice, PhD, CCC-SLP
Assistant Professor
Curry School of Education
University of Virginia
Charlottesville, VA

Susan B. Leahy, EdD
Assistant Professor
Department of Educational Studies
Radford University
Radford, VA

Nickola Wolf Nelson, PhD, CCC-SLP
Charles Van Riper Professor of Speech Pathology and Audiology
Director, PhD in Interdisciplinary Health Studies
Western Michigan University
Kalamazoo, MI

Catherine L. Ross, MS, CCC-SLP
Speech-Language Pathologist
Teton County School District
Jackson, WY

Bonnie Singer, PhD, CCC-SLP
Executive Director
Architects for Learning
Wellesley, MA

Lori Skibbe, MA
Doctoral Candidate
Risk and Prevention in Education Sciences
University of Virginia
Charlottesville, VA

Adelia Van Meter, MS, CCC-SLP
Faculty Specialist II and Coordinator
Van Riper Language, Speech, and Hearing Clinic
Western Michigan University
Kalamazoo, MI

Carol Westby, PhD
Albuquerque, NM

Preface

This is a book about language intervention for school-age students. The authors in this book have attempted to respond to Judith Johnston's call so many years ago:

> The challenge of intervention with the language-disordered student is to simplify the language learning task without changing its basic character. Language learning must remain integrated with intellect, motivated by communication, actively inductive, and self-directed…But language learning must also be facilitated in specific, well-calculated ways. The challenge for educators is to manage this tension between the common and the extraordinary. What sort of intervention programme can maintain the essence of language learning and yet accelerate it? (Johnston, 1985, p. 128)

This book is part of a long journey begun while I was working as a school speech-language pathologist. Charlann Simon's (1985) book *Communication Skills and Classroom Success* (reprinted in 1991 by Thinking Publications) was one of the few to address language intervention in the school years. SLPs were determining how to address pragmatics, narrative, communicative competence, and word finding. Collaborative and curriculum-based service delivery were beginning. We were encountering whole language and literature-based instruction in the schools and determining how they applied to oral language intervention.

I was fortunate to work in a country (Canada) and a province (British Columbia) at a time when great freedom in service delivery was allowed. We were experimenting with continuous progress through ungraded primary classes, inclusive service delivery, and anecdotal reporting. There were no high-stakes testing nor standardized curricula. SLPs were not required to have speech-language IEPs. We set our own eligibility standards, caseload size, and waiting lists. We could vary between pull-out and inclusive intervention, individual and group, as many times a week as we each saw fit—so long as we could satisfy principals, teachers, and parents in our assigned six to eight schools. The atmosphere, rather than that of educational crisis, was brimming with possibility.

During this time, I explored the possibilities of language intervention. Connecting to teachers, classrooms, and classwork helped me make sense of what I was doing and made me feel part of a team. I heard Margaret Lahey speak on narrative development, based on her then newly published text (Lahey, 1988). I then developed and co-taught narrative intervention units in regular and resource classrooms, using literature and storymaking to target story grammar skills in a developmental order. These classroom experiences were rewarding. However, they also revealed to me the challenges of inclusive service delivery as I struggled to provide explicit, supportive attention to my caseload students while co-teaching the rest of the class.

During my doctoral education, I sought out experiences in psychology, speech-language pathology, speech communication, and education to better understand how to carry out and investigate literate language intervention. As a professor, I have continued to develop ways of intervening in context; of balancing the need for direct, explicit skill instruction with the need for meaning and purpose. This book is a culmination of thinking to this point. It is not a final answer.

I would like to thank my clinical colleagues, Lynda Coyle, Marcia Kelley, and Christiane Dechert, at the University of Wyoming, and Cathy Ross, of Teton County School District. These talented speech-language pathologists are dedicated to the education of clinicians and improvement of clinical practice in the university and the field. They are continual sources of support and learning. My annual class of graduate students must also be acknowledged. Each class's efforts to understand my conceptualizations and postulations, and the students' willingness to share their own clinical efforts with their triumphs and hiccups, perpetually lead me back to my desk to clarify and develop my own thinking and writing.

I would also like to acknowledge two mentors: Anne van Kleeck, who set me on the long road of transformational writing; and Ron Gillam, who has been a mentor and collaborator since my doctoral student days. Another important mentor and model is Patricia Ukrainetz, a retired teacher and a mother of six very verbal children. Her life lessons are many, but perhaps can be exemplified by the time she told parents of a child she tutored that the best way they could help motivate their son to read was to make reading a part of their own lives.

I would like to acknowledge the staff of Thinking Publications. Linda Schreiber was my initial contact. I thank her for her confidence in my ability to collect this group of impressive scholars and create this book. Joyce Olson, my production editor, must be complimented for an excellent job of editing. She is a careful reader who seeks to understand the author's perspective, and endeavors to make it understandable to everyone else. Finally, I acknowledge Nancy McKinley, founder of Thinking Publications and a great contributor to the profession, who passed away in 2005, long before her time.

This book is directed to clinicians and graduate students. I hope that the contents are helpful in guiding creative and generative interventions that provide the extraordinary within the common. Returning to the words of Judith Johnston (1983):

> Clinical proficiency likewise requires an infinite range of intervention acts. If our knowledge of language intervention is abstract, or theoretic, in nature, we can be productive and creative therapists. No longer stuck with formulas, no longer hopeful imitators, we can use our intervention "rules" to generate activities that are thoroughly responsive to the client and the moment. (p. 56)

Introduction

What This Book Is About

This book is primarily for speech-language pathologists (SLPs), but a spectrum of educators will find helpful ideas for teaching. It is about how to teach students with language impairments the many facets of literate language needed for academic success. This is an intervention book, focused primarily on how to help students. Descriptions of disorders and assessment procedures are provided as the need arises. The interventions presented are not simply a compendium of possibilities, but a selective array from a particular theoretical framework. That framework is social interactionism, which purports that language is learned:

- By active, goal-directed, self-regulated learners
- Through internalization of the language of more competent others
- Via scaffolded interactions with those more competent others
- Within meaningful contexts

This book presents a theoretical framework and methodologies for analyzing, amplifying, supporting, and measuring skills embedded in meaningful activities. The term *contextualized skill intervention* is used to describe this social-interactionist approach, known variously as *hybrid, activity-based, naturalistic, functional,* or *curriculum-based.* The intervention guidance can be applied to any aspect of language. The therapeutic component of this normal language learning process is the provision of RISE:

Repeated opportunities for
Intense interaction with
Systematic support of
Explicitly targeted skills.

The Challenge of Language Intervention in Schools

Language is a huge domain, divisible in many ways, and overlapping with other domains such as speech, perception, cognition, and literacy. Language intervention is the intentional act of accelerating or changing language that is below, or different from, that expected for chronological age (Fey, 1986).

1

Language intervention can occur in many ways (Johnston, 1983; Ukrainetz, 2005).

Understanding of what language involves and for what SLPs are responsible has expanded continuously for several decades (Rees, 1983; Ukrainetz, 2005; Ukrainetz & Fresquez, 2003). The explosion of morphology, syntax, and semantics knowledge in the 1960s, combined with the emergence of age and stage descriptions, led to a period Rees described as, "exciting for the language professional but still simple" (p. 310), with clear goals for language intervention and structured ways of teaching language. The situation became much more complicated, however, with the addition of topics such as pragmatics, reading, learning, and cognition. Rees stated that the problem facing the SLP in 1983 was to make sense out of all this information and apply it to principles and procedures of language intervention. Twenty years later, this continues to be a challenge. The field of school language intervention has become diverse and encompassing, ranging from traditional topics of vocabulary and grammar to newer domains of reading, executive function, social-emotional functioning, and limited English proficiency (American Speech-Language- Hearing Association; ASHA; 1999, 2001).

In addition to myriad intervention target possibilities, service has extended into the secondary grades, and service delivery options have expanded. SLPs may provide intervention in pull-out individual or small groups, in a variety of in-class arrangements, or on a consulting or curriculum-modification basis. Various degrees of collaboration with general and other special education teachers can occur. With a focus on reading and curriculum-based instruction, SLPs may provide services much like resource teachers (Ukrainetz & Fresquez, 2003).

The possibilities of intervention methods have also increased. Discrete skill instruction continues to be an option for language skills that can be shaped within tightly controlled, hierarchically structured tasks and generalized to daily life activities. At the same time, for most language objectives, SLPs must know how to systematically scaffold learning within whole, purposeful, complicated activities (Nelson, 1995; Ukrainetz, 1998). The task of language intervention has become truly daunting.

Overview

Contributing authors for this book are scholars who: (a) come from a speech-language pathology background, (b) have a primary interest in intervention rather than in descriptions of disorders or ways of assessing disorders, and (c) partake in the vision of contextualized skill intervention. In addition, each contributor has a particular domain of interest, such as vocabulary, morphosyntax, or peer interaction. All of us strive to provide quality skill instruction within purposeful, meaningful contexts. All of us recognize students as self-directed learners. All of us recognize clinicians as facilitators who strategically scaffold the internalization and automatization process. We each come to the task with our own views of how contextualized skill intervention can best occur, but all fit within a larger social-interactionist view of learning. Examples of interactions are taken from our work with students. We use pseudonyms for these students, who also are important contributors to this work.

The first section of the book, *The Intervention Approach,* describes contextualized skill intervention. Chapter 1 sets out the framework of contextualized skill intervention. In Chapter 2, Gillam and Ukrainetz detail how to carry out such intervention within literature-based units. The section on *Building Language into Discourse* examines the building blocks of language and how to combine them into purposeful discourse. Nelson and Van Meter provide guidance in Chapter 3 on teaching vocabulary within self-motivated writing activities. Eisenberg addresses how to teach the later acquired aspects of morphosyntax to school-age students (Chapter 4). At the discourse level, a chapter is devoted to narrative structure (Chapter 5) and another to expository structure (Chapter 6). The *Classroom Discourse* section addresses the social-interactional factors involved in acquiring literate language. Brinton and Fujiki address peer interactions (Chapter 7) and Westby addresses classroom discourse (Chapter 8). Westby's chapter includes some important cultural considerations.

The *Language in Print* section addresses ways of directly teaching some parts of the reading process. Justice, Skibbe, and Ezell discuss in Chapter 9 how to introduce preschoolers with language impairment to print concepts within storybook activities. Chapter 10 deals with teaching phonemic awareness, a language skill needed for alphabetic literacy, in a contextualized skill manner. Leahy and Justice present a novel approach to reading fluency through the dramatic activities of Readers Theatre in Chapter 11. In the final section, *Thinking and Learning,* Ukrainetz and Ross (Chapter 12) address text comprehension and bridge it to language in print and the processes involved in thinking and learning. Chapter 13, by Bashir and Singer, considers the self-regulatory processes that underlie and complicate learning difficulties. Students who do not organize, direct, and reflect on their own learning are at risk in all areas of language.

Two literacy areas not specifically addressed in this book are word decoding and spelling. The vocabulary, print awareness, phonemic awareness, and reading fluency chapters provide some information on word decoding, but for detailed attention, additional sources will be required. An excellent analysis of the development of word recognition and the need for intense, systematically supported, explicit instruction are found in Catts and Kamhi (2005). Two good intervention articles for later word decoding and spelling are Apel and Swank (1999), and Apel and Masterson (2001).

In conclusion, I hope that in our efforts to be centrally located in the high visibility area of reading, we SLPs consider the cost to other aspects of communication. Although there are conceptual reasons for extending our attention into reading instruction, we can provide intervention that is sufficiently intense for only a few language needs for any particular student. There is also a limit to how many areas in which we can be skilled interventionists. Focusing on word recognition and spelling will unavoidably occur at a cost of diminished focus to our distinctive areas of service provision (Ukrainetz & Fresquez, 2003). I hope that SLPs make efforts to retain their unique, specialized niches, even if those niches are in lower visibility areas of communication.

References

American Speech-Language-Hearing Association. (1999). *Guidelines for the roles and responsibilities of the school-based speech-language pathologist.* Rockville, MD: Author.

American Speech-Language-Hearing Association. (2001). *Roles and responsibilities of speech-language pathologists with respect to reading and writing in children and adolescents.* Rockville, MD: Author.

Apel, K., & Swank, L. K. (1999). Second chances: Improving decoding skills in the older student. *Language, Speech, and Hearing Services in Schools, 30,* 231–242.

Apel, K., & Masterson, J. J. (2001). Theory-guided spelling assessment and intervention: A case study. *Language, Speech, and Hearing Services in Schools, 32,* 182–196

Catts, H. W., & Kamhi, A. G. (2005). *Language and reading disabilities.* Boston: Pearson.

Fey, M. (1986). *Language intervention with young children.* Boston: College-Hill.

Johnston, J. R. (1983). What is language intervention? The role of theory. In J. Miller, D. Yoder, & R. Schiefelbusch (Eds.), *Contemporary issues in language intervention* (pp. 52–57). Rockville, MD: ASHA.

Johnston, J. R. (1985). Fit, focus, and functionality: An essay on early language intervention. *Child Language Teaching and Therapy, 1*(2), 125–134.

Lahey, M. (1988). *Language development and language disorders.* New York: Macmillan.

Nelson, N. W. (1995). Scaffolding in the secondary schools: A tool for curriculum-based language intervention. In D. F. Tibbits (Ed.), *Language intervention beyond the primary grades* (pp. 375–420). Austin, TX: Pro-Ed.

Rees, N. S. (1983). Language intervention with children. In J. Miller, D. Yoder, & R. Schiefelbusch (Eds.), *Contemporary issues in language intervention* (pp. 309–316). Rockville, MD: ASHA.

Simon, C. S. (1985). *Communication skills and classroom success: Therapy methodologies for language learning disabled students.* San Diego, CA: College-Hill.

Ukrainetz, T. A. (1998). Beyond Vygotsky: What Soviet activity theory offers naturalistic language intervention. *Journal of Speech-Language Pathology and Audiology, 22,* 122–133.

Ukrainetz, T. A. (2005). What to work on how: An examination of the practice of school-age language intervention. *Contemporary Issues in Communication Sciences and Disorders, 32,* 108–119.

Ukrainetz, T. A., & Fresquez, E. F. (2003). What isn't language? A qualitative study of the role of the school speech-language pathologist. *Language, Speech, and Hearing Services in Schools, 34,* 284–298.

Chapter 1

Assessment and Intervention within a Contextualized Skill Framework

Teresa A. Ukrainetz

Introduction

Current approaches to language intervention emphasize improving form, content, and use through purposeful, functional activities. Intervention reflects the understanding that, "language serves communication ends and is learned in the course of communicative events" (Johnston, 1985, p. 126). Such an approach is fundamentally different from teaching discrete skills within tightly controlled, hierarchically structured tasks. Rather than breaking down a task and training on simple components, the speech-language pathologist (SLP) works within whole, real, complicated activities. The intent is to be therapeutic; amplifying language patterns and facilitating language learning within purposeful activities. This naturalistic approach to intervention has been considered best practice for some years, but is difficult to execute effectively. The clinician must maneuver the tightrope between therapeutic and natural, seeking the balance that allows but accelerates normal learning:

> The challenge of intervention with the language-disordered child is to simplify the language learning task without changing its basic character. Language learning must remain integrated with intellect, motivated by communication, actively inductive, and self-directed…But language learning must also be facilitated in specific, well-calculated ways. The challenge for educators is to manage this tension between the common and the extraordinary. What sort of intervention programme can maintain the essence of language learning and yet accelerate it? (Johnston, 1985, p. 128)

This dilemma is intensified when the focus of intervention changes from preschool social communication to school-aged academic communication. Educators are perpetually challenged to provide learning situations that teach skills within contexts that make sense and are motivating to students. Adding the need to accelerate learning for the student with special needs makes the task of the school SLP daunting.

In this chapter and throughout the book, the term *contextualized skill* is used to emphasize the key element of this intervention approach. Labels such as *naturalistic, activity-based, holistic,* or *curriculum-based intervention* all focus on the context. This appropriately moves away from contrived and controlled activities, but runs the risk of losing the "skill" part of the therapy. Bricker, Pretti-Frontczak, and McComas (1998) voiced concern about the conflation of context with procedures in discussions of naturalistic intervention, and the need to keep a focus on facilitative procedures. Contextualized skill intervention maintains such a focus. It is contrasted in this chapter with *discrete skill intervention,* which is also termed *trainer-oriented, structured,* or *skill-based.*

This chapter details how contextualized skill intervention can be carried out on literate language goals with school-age students. A framework is provided for analyzing significant life activities and determining intervention objectives in a way that is consistent with intervening in context. Scaffolding is presented as the support system for aiding the student's internalization of the skills and strategies. Scaffolding support provides one of the four critical elements of intervention that keep a therapeutic focus in intervention: repeated opportunities, intensity, systematic support, and an explicit skill focus (RISE) within purposeful activities.

Contextualized Skill Intervention

Intervening in Early Conversational Language

Contextualized skill and naturalistic interventions are the predominant language intervention approaches for toddlers and preschoolers (Cole, 1995; Pretti-Frontczak & Bricker, 2004). Contextualized skill intervention across developmental domains for preschool children has grown due to inclusion practices, parental involvement, developmentally appropriate practices, and, most importantly, the lack of generalization of adult-directed, highly structured training regimes (Cole; Fey, 1986; Pretti-Frontczak & Bricker). Likewise, a large corpus of efficacy and effectiveness studies has empirically validated naturalistic procedures and contexts for teaching conversational language (e.g., Camarata, Nelson, & Camarata, 1994; Fey, Cleave, Long, & Hughes, 1993; Nelson, Camarata, Welsh, Butkovsky, & Camarata, 1996; Yoder, Kaiser, Alpert, & Fischer, 1993).

Fey (1986) suggested that intervention should be considered on a continuum of control. At one end are interventions in which the child is considered a passive recipient of carefully structured conditioning *(adult-oriented).* At the other end are *child-directed* interventions in which the child is provided rich daily life experiences and expected to implicitly induce language rules and patterns. Child-directed intervention primarily provides a rich language environment with motivating communicative opportunities, little participation structure, and supportive adult interactions (e.g., Manolson, 1983).

Fey (1986) proposed a blend of child and adult orientations, called *hybrid interventions*. Focused stimulation, involving rich language modeling of specific language structures in daily life contexts and no demand for child productions; and milieu teaching, involving following the child's lead within daily life contexts, but employing structured steps for eliciting specific language objectives, are two examples of hybrid interventions. In these interventions, the SLP sets objectives, plans activities to provide motivating communication opportunities, elicits responses, and employs techniques in which targets are presented and elicited in particularly salient ways such as language modeling of expansions and recasts. Teaching follows the child's lead or interest; multiple, naturally occurring examples are used; the child's language productions are prompted; consequences that are natural to the teaching context are used; and teaching episodes are embedded in ongoing interactions (Kaiser, Yoder, & Keetz, 1992). Intervention schedules vary from frequent brief interactions embedded in daily life events to extended interactions in engineered, but purposeful activities. These include routine daily self-care activities, child-initiated play, and planned activities that should interest children and be developed in ways that children find appealing. This approach avoids contrived situations or formal lessons designed exclusively to practice a target skill (Pretti-Frontczak & Bricker, 2004).

Both child-directed and hybrid interventions are typically referred to as *naturalistic interventions;* both involve facilitating active use of language within meaningful daily life contexts. However, only hybrid interventions can also be termed *contextualized skill interventions,* because they provide explicit, systematic attention to specific language objectives.

The Challenge of Intervention with Literate Language

Methods for hybrid or contextualized skill intervention are well-specified for the conversational language of younger children. However, much less is known about working on literate language skills within purposeful academic contexts for older students.

School-age language intervention should be contextually based, educationally relevant, and collaborative (Whitmire, 2002). In addition, the intervention objectives should be related to state and district achievement standards and benchmarks. This means that the SLP considers the curricula and activities of the classroom; teaches language skills closely linked to literacy and academic success; and plans, teaches, and assesses in close communication with teachers.

These are excellent starting points for literate language intervention. However, within these general guidelines, there is tremendous variation in how naturalistic intervention is formulated and executed.

Some naturalistic intervention frameworks are limited primarily to use of purposeful contexts and language assistance, like the child-directed interventions for younger children. For example, language may be taught using literature, thematic units, or classroom activities. A large number of language and literacy skills may be targeted in these rich, meaningful contexts, but with little systematic attention to facilitating learning (e.g., Merritt & Culatta, 1998; Strong & North, 1996). Instruction may be little different from that provided in the regular classroom (Ehren, 2000). For instance, Merritt and Culatta provide a thematic intervention unit for the primary grades. The unit includes activities, expectations for students of differing levels, guidance for how to scaffold individual responses, and 39 intervention objectives. There is no discussion of critical intervention features such as: (1) identifying a specific and limited number of skill targets, (2) supporting practice and learning over repeated opportunities, and (3) including an explicit skill focus. Such an approach could be considered language enrichment rather than language intervention.

Even within the learning disabilities literature, there has been little close investigation of academically oriented intervention that is both contextualized and skill-focused (Palincsar, 1998; Stone, 1998). Notable exceptions within education are scaffolding research on reading comprehension (Palincsar, 1986; Palincsar & Brown, 1984), and writing composition (Englert, 1990, 1992; Englert, Berry, & Dunsmore, 2001). However, even Englert's work on motivating students to write meaningful compositions has been criticized for a lack of explicit skill development (Isaacson, 1992).

In addition, with the No Child Left Behind Act (2002), there is an increasing pressure within special education to have high and uniform standards, which means using achievement benchmarks with grade-level expectations as intervention objectives. The unintended consequence of this is a movement toward task assistance over therapeutic intervention. While assistance allows a student to perform at grade level for a specific assignment, it is imperative that SLPs attend to the underlying skills and processes required for a student to become a better, more independent learner.

It is difficult to be both therapeutic and natural. This is a struggle for many SLPs—regardless of whether they are primarily skill-focused or context-focused. In a qualitative study examining the language intervention practices of five SLPs (Ukrainetz, in press), all the clinicians engaged in task assistance at some times when they were intending to be therapeutic. This meant that the clinician and student were focused on accomplishing the task rather than developing competence within the student. Interestingly, this applied to both the SLPs who favored discrete skill approaches and those who favored more contextualized approaches. When each moved out of her skill instruction comfort zone into more natural activities, the task became less therapeutic. The discrete skill clinicians were accustomed to providing massed practice on isolated skills in a hierarchical task format. When they provided more meaningful activities such as making a zoo display or sharing photos of a trip to Central America, the activity was entertaining and many skills were present, but there was no explicit skill focus as would be evidenced by repeated opportunities, systematic support, or data collection. For the more contextualized clinicians, this loss of therapeutic focus occurred when working with students on teacher-prescribed science and social studies reports. These SLPs, who could maintain a therapeutic focus during an activity such as discussing a shared story, became intent on helping the student generate or fix the assignment so an acceptable grade would result.

This situation in which SLPs provide a therapeutic focus within purposeful contexts is the subject of this chapter and the rest of this book. The contributing authors are all clinical researchers who describe contextualized skill interventions that can assist clinicians in working with many literate language skills. The interventions come in a variety of flavors, but all are intended to provide explicit skill instruction in ways that are meaningful and purposeful to the student.

Theoretical Bases for Contextualized Skill Intervention

Contextualized skill instruction is based on a social-interactionist and cognitivist view of learning. In this view, learning and development occur through active exploration of an organized environment with social mediation from adults. The social-interactionist and cognitivist theories of Vygotsky and Piaget are the theoretical bases for this approach. Functional theories of language acquisition (e.g., Bates, 1976; Bates & MacWhinney, 1987; Bruner, 1983; Nelson, 1986; Ninio & Snow, 1996), which emphasize the effects of social and physical contexts on language learning, also support contextualized skill intervention.

This chapter focuses on the social context of intervention for literate language. (For an excellent consideration of cognitive aspects of intervention that is still highly relevant, see the seminal article by Judith Johnston, 1985.) The importance and inseparability of the social context to learning has three manifestations: (1) consideration of the activity rather than the skill as a basic unit of learning (Leontiev, 1981; Zinchenko & Davydov, 1985), (2) the internalization of social voices (Vygotsky, 1978), and (3) a mediation or scaffolding process that facilitates internalization (Vygotsky; Wood, Bruner, & Ross, 1976).

The Relation between Skill and Activity

A theory that has not been widely disseminated in the field of language intervention is Soviet activity theory. This theory provides a helpful framework for analyzing, supporting, and measuring skills in context. Activity theory was developed in the post-Vygotsky years by his former students Luria and Leontiev (Zinchenko & Davydov, 1985). Following the Vygotskian idea that individual thought and language have their source within inter-individual activity, "internal organizational units for performing a mental function arise out of practical, external, organizational units for performing that function" (Cole, 1981, p. viii). In this view, how we think reflects the social conditions in which the thinking was initially acquired.

Soviet activity theory has been incorporated into Western social-interactionist thinking in terms of the inseparability of skills and activities (e.g., Cole, 1981; Rogoff, 1990; Rogoff & Gardner, 1984; Wertsch, 1981). In situated learning, an individual's skills must be understood in terms of both the immediate situation and the larger sociocultural motivations. Skill acquisition involves not only what is learned, but how it was learned and how it will be used (Brown, Collins, & Duguid, 1989). This theory elevates *activity* over *skill* as the basis of development. Soviet activity theory leads to a framework for analyzing activities so that skills can be taught as integral and functional parts of daily life activities.

The activity analysis arising out of Soviet activity theory requires any consideration of a skill to start with the larger activity or context. As shown in Table 1.1 on page 14, there are five components that comprise any purposeful activity: motive, goal, condition, action, and operation.

The primary, underlying, energizing force is the motive to initiate an activity. Maslow's (1970) hierarchy of needs is a useful organizing list of motivations: physiological (hunger, shelter), safety (from physical or emotional

Table 1.1   **Components of a Purposeful Activity**

Component	Definition
Motive	Basic underlying force
Goal	Purpose of the activity
Condition	Facilitating and constraining features of the context
Action	Conscious behaviors or strategies
Operation	Unconscious processes or skills

Sources: Leontiev (1981); Wertsch (1981)

harm), social (affection, belonging), esteem (autonomy, recognition), and self-actualization (improvement, learning). These underlying motivations must be considered in understanding how an individual will accomplish an activity.

Goals are the specific, conscious aims to satisfy motives. Goals direct the person's selection and orchestration of actions and operations within an activity. Conditions set the contextual boundaries of the activity. Conditions both constrain and facilitate the achievement of goals by determining what actions and operations can be carried out.

Actions are the conscious *behaviors* or *strategies* taken to achieve the goal, and the operations are the unconscious *skills* and *processes*. Operations derive from actions: as a new skill is acquired, it is initially a conscious action, but with practice, it becomes an automatized background operation. Operations can re-emerge as actions if conscious attention and modification are required.

Learning to drive (although currently outside the purview of SLPs) is an excellent example of the relationship between actions and operations. For the novice driver, every act is a conscious action and the many actions required are overwhelming. Initially, the only unconscious operations or skills are those previously acquired as a passenger—putting on a seat belt perhaps. As competence is gained, an action is downgraded to a more automatic level: braking and accelerating, once conscious tentative actions, become fluent, unconscious operations. Attention then shifts to other yet unmastered actions, such as gear shifting or merging onto a freeway. Ultimately, the goal-directed action of gear shifting becomes an unconscious, almost automatic operation, which, under normal circumstances, does not even appear to exist for the driver. However, given a stressful situation, such as start-and-stop traffic on a steep hill, competent drivers may again have to devote conscious attention to the task of shifting gears.

These five components of an activity are defined functionally rather than structurally (Leontiev, 1981). The most important feature that distinguishes one activity from another is the end goal. So the same behaviors may have very different goals. For example, a driver slowly braking on an icy hill and a mechanic slowly braking in a parking lot appear to be performing the same action, but for very different reasons: preventing sliding versus diagnosing mechanical problems. Thus, they are employing very different mental processes. Likewise, two behaviors that appear superficially different may be used interchangeably in achieving one goal: for example, the goal of maintaining a slow, downhill descent can be addressed through the different actions of braking or downshifting. This functional view of activity components (i.e., looking beyond the surface to the underlying reason and mental processes) helps account for both the limited learning transfer seen between superficially similar situations, and the diverse experiences learners actually draw on to solve new problems (Rogoff & Gardner, 1984).

Activity theory provides three major guidelines for intervention: (1) working within purposeful activities that activate all five components, (2) skilled execution of an activity as the goal-directed orchestration of all five components, and (3) facilitating generalization of competence between activities by considering how the goals affect the activity components (Ukrainetz, 1998). Application of activity theory to assessment and intervention will be illustrated following consideration of the other two theoretical underpinnings of contextualized skill intervention.

The Internalization of Social Voices

For development to occur, strategies and skills must move from the interpsychological plane, which is between a more competent other and the student, to the intrapsychological plane, which is within the student's mind (Vygotsky, 1978). The words and actions of more competent others are internalized by the student, becoming inner speech and thought.

Internalization involves the movement and transformation of talk and action from the adult to the student. The internalization process is apparent as students initially consciously, and even externally, guide themselves. With repetition, the words go underground, and task execution becomes smooth, integrated, and removed from the conscious level. Figure 1.1 presents this three-phase movement from other to self and conscious to unconscious for the mastery of an activity, with the possibility of a return to a conscious focus in times of challenge.

An excerpt from a five-year-old child's self-commentary during picture drawing is presented below. Child self-talk is clearly apparent. It is easy to see how the child's language was borrowed from the directions given by adults. With practice, the child will no longer need to talk aloud or carefully think about his drawing. However, should he attempt a more difficult drawing, the regulatory words from the adult can resurface and guide him again.

> *Now I'm gonna draw me with a big head (draws legs) [dwɪt]/[dwɪt]. Wrong ways. Now we need some eyes. And we need a nose. Now I need a mouth. Now I need some green for a*

Figure 1.1   **Internalization Process from Initial Adult Control to Child Mastery of a Purposeful Activity**

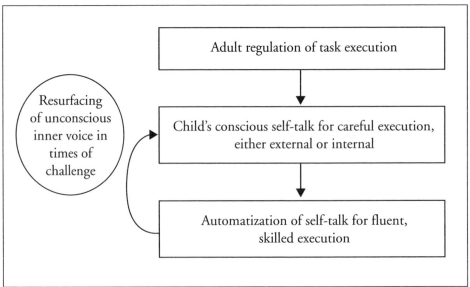

Source: Tharp & Gallimore (1988)

froggie. Whoa, that too little bit. That the froggie's head. Now we need the little eye. Better give him two eyes. He doesn't have enough head. Now need some leg. Here's one, two, three, four.

The process of learning, or internalization, occurs within a range of assistance, called the *zone of proximal development* (Vygotsky, 1978). The zone of proximal development is a region of sensitivity to learning: the distance between independent problem solving and the level of potential development demonstrated by assisted performance. When an adult provides temporary consciousness that allows the student to perform an activity, the student is being provided the learning opportunity in advance of his independent developmental level. The student is observing, participating, and puzzling out what is expected. Learning is occurring during the co-achievement of a task. Development, however, is not considered to have occurred until the student can show a gain in independent performance. Also, according to Vygotsky, each successive opportunity results in more learning, which ultimately results in an advance in development. In this way, *learning occurs in advance of development and carries development forward.*

The concept of the size of a zone of proximal development is particularly helpful for assessment. Two students who show equal failure in an independent task may show very different learning and participation performance when given assistance. For example, Wood et al. (1976) compared the performance of three- and five-year-olds who did not perform a puzzle construction task independently. At age three, children required step-by-step assistance through the task, while five-year-olds made leaps in understanding with only a few prompts. Thus, the older children showed larger zones of proximal development.

In this view of development, students are active participants within their zone of proximal development. Students cannot be blindly copying adult actions. Rather, the student and adult must have some degree of common understanding of what is being achieved (Wertsch, 1984; Wood et al., 1976). For internalization to occur, the student must not only perform particular behaviors independently, but he or she must become aware of the functional significance of the guided behaviors and how they are the means to reach a particular goal (Wertsch & Hickmann, 1987). Sometimes, the learner may be an active force in the learning situation, cuing the instructor to give needed guidance (e.g., *I don't understand what to do).*

The evaluation approach of examining assisted performance is called *dynamic assessment* (Lidz & Peña, 1996; Ukrainetz, Harpell, Walsh, & Coyle, 2000). Instead of identifying students' independent performance level, dynamic assessment reveals how students learn and what they can achieve with varied degrees of assistance or mediation. Dynamic assessment is particularly helpful for answering questions about whether a student has an inherent learning difficulty, or is an effective learner but has missed out on relevant life experiences. The assistance provided during both dynamic assessment and language intervention is considered next.

Scaffolding the Internalization Process

Internalization of the skills required to achieve activities occurs through the mediating support provided by more competent others such as parents, teachers, and peers. This support process is called *scaffolding*. Scaffolding involves working on an emerging skill within purposeful, complex contexts, while incorporating strategic support from the instructor and active involvement from the student (Greenfield, 1984; Nelson, 1995; Wood et al., 1976). This intentional movement of a skill from the adult to the student has been called *handover* for young students (Bruner, 1983) or *question transplant* for older students (Nelson). The handover image emphasizes the active role of the student: the adult proffers the skill to the student and the student reaches out to take it. The question transplant emphasizes the self-talk in which the older student must engage.

The provision of temporary support by a more competent other allows the student to perform an activity that is beyond his or her independent performance level (Vygotsky, 1978; Wood et al., 1976). Competence develops as skills are transferred to the learner and, as the competence develops, the scaffold can be gradually withdrawn. With scaffolding, the student stays within the purposeful context for the entire dependence-to-independence continuum, akin to the guided participation or apprenticing occurring in daily life activities such as learning to tie one's shoe or change the oil in a car (Rogoff, 1990).

Scaffolding can involve a wide range of supportive moves before, during, and after the student's actions. These may include structuring the activity, modeling, prompting, or evaluative commenting. Scaffolding can involve peers. For example, when two students work cooperatively without an adult, they scaffold each other (but not at an adult's level of intentionality and strategic application). The active engagement can be reciprocal. Englert et al. (2001) provide a case study demonstrating how a first grader with a learning disability benefited both from (1) the teacher's facilitation during directive, organized instruction and during less structured cooperative learning situations, and from (2) actively cuing his second grade peer to provide him needed learning support. When the younger boy was in the ideas role, he asked for confirmation and clarification of his word map interpretation on ant ontogeny. When he was put in the writing role, he asked for word spelling and sounding out guidance. The older student appeared to recognize that this arrangement worked—he declined to take over the writing role despite the younger boy's difficulties and continued to offer invented spelling and sounding guidance instead. Scaffolding can even involve more distal sociocultural supports, such as classroom arrangements or family interactions (Rogoff, 1990; Stone, 1998). Scaffolding, then, is how adults or other social partners facilitate the internalization of skills within meaningful, goal-directed activities.

Activity Analysis as a Guide to Intervention

The preceding section described the three main considerations for contextualized skill intervention: (1) teaching component strategies and skills as part of larger goal-directed activities, (2) being aware of the student's degree of internalization of skills, and (3) intentionally and strategically scaffolding the internalization process. Each of these aspects will now be applied to language intervention. Contextualized skill intervention focuses on competence within coherent, meaningful, purposeful, everyday activities, rather than practicing isolated skills independent of context. To plan intervention, activities must be selected and then analyzed in terms of the five component elements—motive, goal, condition, action, and operation.

Activity Selection

Assessment for intervention starts with understanding how the student functions in context. Context can be viewed as frequently occurring, significant life activities that have purpose beyond instructional objectives (Harris-Schmidt & McNamee, 1986; Pretti-Frontczak & Bricker, 2004). In this approach, standardized test results provide little useful intervention information on a student's strengths and weaknesses outside of the test-taking context.

The SLP needs a good understanding of school activities and how students successfully perform them. Discourse genres such as classroom conversation, narration, exposition, and persuasion are starting points for contextualized assessment and intervention. School activities often involve discourse tasks such as understanding the main idea of a text, following a procedure, describing an image, composing an imaginative story, or following a scientific process.

Generalized information on how students are expected to perform is only part of the picture. In addition to any formal normative expectations, there are the many layers of explicit and implicit curricula, including the official district curriculum, the implicit classroom curriculum, the hidden teacher-expectations curriculum, and the underground peer-expectations curriculum (Nelson, 1989; Westby, 1997; see Chapter 8). Determining basic activities for a particular student might involve classroom observation and discussion with the teacher and student about what is important for the student to accomplish during the day, and how frequently the activities occur. Observation, document review, interview, and discourse assessment help identify individual significant life activities and the student's performance within them. A problem-solving perspective is important for evaluating a student's language-learning difficulties (Kratcoski, 1998). This involves hypothesizing, collecting evidence, evaluating the evidence, and determining a course of remediation suited to the particular student.

School activities often lack relationship to eventual real-life adult competencies (Brown et al., 1989; Scribner, 1984). However, the protracted period students are in school and the social significance ascribed to academic success mean that "school life" can be considered "real life" by the SLP. As such, intervention activities should be based on the demands of schooling, in addition to desired ultimate competencies in social and work life.

Experiential and holistic curricula, rather than "back to the basics" skill-driven curricula, provide a better fit for contextualized skill intervention, but the clinician will have to deal with whatever curriculum organization exists in the given situation. In research examining how to teach writing to students with learning disabilities, Palincsar (1998) commented that her efforts to teach writing were initially problematic because the wider school context involved using writing for low-level skills such as matching and copying rather than for communication. Palincsar guided the teachers to change classroom activities to include a class newspaper, a new class member handbook, and letters to family and book authors, so the students had a larger, purposeful literacy environment in which to learn.

For older students, personal life goals become important in selecting activities for assessment and intervention. For example, a graduate student clinician consulted this author about selecting intervention targets for a 19 year-old deaf student in a juvenile facility. From a contextualized skill perspective, the starting point for this client was vocational planning. This would uncover the individual's motivations and specify concrete goals for language intervention. Specific activities could then be devised, in partnership with the student, that fitted the student's immediate and future communication needs. Unfortunately, there had been little discussion of what came next for this individual beyond a vague desire to "attend college." Until more specific plans were formulated, the best route was to work on expression and comprehension in expository contexts—a type of discourse that would be a likely form for any academic or job setting. Personal interests, such as cars and their workings, could be tapped. If college became a firm plan, typical classroom texts, projects, and essay assignments might be a good source of expository objectives.

Assessment through Activity Analysis

An activity analysis is helpful for identifying student difficulties. The aim of an activity analysis is to identify problematic components and how they affect performance of a basic life activity. This analysis leads directly into intervention.

An activity analysis of a student's performance will reveal strengths and weaknesses across components. Intervention will address the components that affect the student's success in the basic life activity. For example, any of the following might be revealed:

- Problematic motivations
- Discordant goals between student and teacher
- Conditions that increase or maintain problems
- Absent behaviors and strategies that need to be acquired as conscious choices
- Conscious steps and strategies that need to be automatized to free up mental space
- Maladaptive or weak skills and processes that need to be brought to conscious attention and modified

Motivation may be a primary concern for older learners with histories of academic failure and perceptions of learned helplessness (Nelson, 1995). For example, in Chapter 13, Bashir and Singer describe how an adolescent had a tendency to give up that prevented him from even attempting to succeed in challenging situations. Such a motivation will sabotage the clinician's efforts to achieve change.

In school, the activity and its goal are most often imposed by adults, rather than selected by students. Students may have a choice of topic, but the activity itself fits the educational requirements of the teacher or curriculum. The SLP should examine whether the student recognizes the goal of an activity, or whether the student has another agenda with a goal operating at cross-purposes to the official activity goal. For example, if the goal of a reading activity is to maximize text comprehension, but because of the influence of a school-wide book-reading competition, the student perceives the goal to be reading as many books as possible, the reading performance will suffer. Instead of decoding accuracy and active comprehension strategies, the student will employ maximum rate and gist-comprehension strategies. Recognizing that the student is operating with a different activity goal helps to explain why the student is doing (or not doing) what is expected.

Part of the student's difficulties may arise from problematic conditions. A student with good comprehension, but word-finding and utterance-formulation difficulties, will appear less competent in a busy, fast-paced classroom in which quick responses are required. The same student may also perform at less than his or her ability level if the pace of instruction must accommodate many students with poor comprehension. Multiple repetitions of instructions and comprehension checks may lead to boredom and distraction in the linguistically more able student. As a result, it is important to examine the conditions of the classroom, both in terms of the immediate interactional features and the larger social environment.

Once the motivation, goal, and condition have been evaluated, the SLP must consider the conscious behaviors and strategies (i.e., actions), and unconscious skills and processes (i.e., operations) that work together toward a goal. Does the student possess the needed skills and processes at an automatic level? For example, in assessing reading comprehension, the SLP or reading teacher must determine whether a third-grade boy is a fluent word decoder. Next, is the student able to consciously employ newly acquired behaviors and strategies? For example, does he know how to read for the main idea in a passage? In a difficult task, can the student focus conscious attention on what are normally automatic achievements? To continue the example, can this same boy, who decodes 3rd grade material fluently, stop at a difficult but desired word, like *velociraptor,* and sound it out? Finally, does the student show maladaptive unconscious skills, such as only sounding out the first grapheme of a word, then guessing from context?

An activity analysis guides the clinician to examine all relevant aspects of significant life situations. An activity analysis of writing a classroom Halloween story is provided in Table 1.2 on page 24. The motive, goal, major facilitating and constraining conditions, and many of the actions and operations required to accomplish the task are listed. Strengths and weaknesses for an individual student, and how classroom conditions affect the student's performance, are determined. By examining the five components and how they interact, the SLP gains a good understanding of what the student does, why, how, and when.

Box 1.1 on page 26 includes a sample summary of the activity analysis for a fourth grader. Sally's motive and goal are satisfactory. She demonstrates both strengths and weaknesses in the actions and operations of story composition, for which the classroom provides sufficient support. (Actions and operations can be difficult to differentiate. The rule of thumb is new versus old; actions are conscious or recently acquired performance, and operations are unconscious or well-established performance.) The aspects that are newer to Sally, and for which she shows some awareness, are providing a lengthy monologic account, sequencing the story, and using pronoun reference. The aspects for which Sally is fluent and automatic (even if weak) are vocabulary, sentence structure, spelling, and handwriting.

Intervention Objectives

Language and literacy are immense domains from which to sample, and even basic activities are complex, with a multitude of possible actions and operations. Students with language-learning disabilities may be deficient in many of these aspects. One way of structuring objectives is along communicative competence lines: pragmatics, discourse structure, grammar, lexicon, word-finding, self-regulation, or metalinguistics. The activity choice can be organized by genre type (along with goals and conditions): exposition, persuasion, narration, conversation, classroom discourse, or poetic. Basic activities in which the discourse can be elicited are selected. Then, objectives for building mastery of the genre are based on the activity component analysis. Table 1.3 on page 27 shows various discourse types with sample language skills and activities.

For the case example of Sally, the assessment information summarized in the present level of performance could lead to three intervention objectives:

Activity Analysis of a Student's Performance in a Classroom Writing Task

Table 1.2

Component	Example
Purposeful Activity • Activity that exists for more than instructional purposes	• To compose a Halloween story during small group instruction to be orally shared with peers at the classroom Halloween party
Motive • Energizing force	• To please parents and teachers • To be considered entertaining by peers
Goal • Purpose of the activity • Assigned by the educator, understood by the student	• To tell a well-formed, correctly written, entertaining, scary (but in good taste) story appropriate to the grade level of the student
Conditions • Social, emotional, physical, and discourse supports and constraints	• Written in the classroom with 24 other students of a range of abilities • Composed as a rough draft and a good draft • Allowed two class periods and homework time • Using a model story previously read and discussed • Using vocabulary words previously discussed • Using an interesting topic • Receiving periodic attention from the teacher when requested • Receiving feedback on all errors in final draft

Table 1.2—*Continued*

Component	Example
Actions (Behaviors and Strategies) • Conscious, goal-directed behaviors • Conscious strategic moves	• Think about how the scary idea could happen in a different way from the story read • Remember to begin the story with setting information • Decide who will be in the story • Decide on the problem • Use previously discussed adjectives to develop a scary atmosphere • Use words other than *and* to link sentences • Write the first draft by hand • Do own corrections • Use the computer to type the good copy • Remember not to worry about spelling in the first draft
Operations (Skills and Processes) • Parts that are automatized • Skills that may or may not be desirable	• Know how to sound out words, but use weak spelling • Use conversational grammar and vocabulary • Use appropriate layout: title, double spacing, name, and date • Use funny and scary ideas • Write the story in the order in which it is conceived • Show a weak understanding of episodic structure • Show a weak understanding of clear pronoun reference • Produce errors in complex sentence construction • Revise only for spelling, with few errors caught

Box 1.1   **Present Level of Performance for Sally**

Sally's expressive (7th percentile) and receptive (14th percentile) oral language scores on the Test of Narrative Language are significantly low. Her language sample shows weak narrative and expository language, which is further supported by the written work samples provided by her teacher. An activity analysis shows that Sally has a good motivation concerning school assignments. In the narrative activity observed, Sally recognizes that the goal of the activity is to tell an entertaining and understandable story. She knows that she often is hard to understand and this bothers her. Sally has trouble organizing her story in both oral and written modalities. She jumps around, misses parts of the story, has abbreviated and incomplete episodes, and uses unclear cohesion pronominal reference. Sally has some entertaining ideas and interesting vocabulary. Her simple sentence and compound sentence structure is good, as are her expanded noun phrases, but she has errors in sentences with relative clauses. Sally is willing to try to spell hard words and her spelling is phonetic. However, there are many incorrect spellings. Sally shows appropriate classroom behavior and completes tasks on time. The classroom is a positive emotional context but provides an insufficient amount of individualized support for Sally's needs.

use of episodic structure, pronoun reference, and relative clauses. All three objectives could be addressed within a series of activities organized around narrative discourse. Rather than providing a list of unrelated objectives, the objectives work towards achieving a single functional activity. The activity is significant, occurs frequently in the student's daily life, and is functionally similar to written narrative compositions expected in the classroom.

Sally's goal and objectives are tied to a state academic standard. Table 1.4 on page 28 summarizes Sally's program plan. The standard is provided from the Wyoming state standards and benchmarks (Wyoming Department of Education, 2003). Matching goals and objectives to state or district standards is appropriate. However, clinicians should not confuse the uniform normative standard set for typically achieving students with the individualized intervention goals required for students who have individualized education programs (IEPs).

Table 1.3

Example Skills and Activity for Various Discourse Genres

Discourse	Language Skills	Activity
Expository Expression	• Procedural structure • Word finding • Expanded noun phrases	Science experiments
Expository Comprehension	• Main and supporting ideas • Curricular vocabulary • Key word note taking	History text comprehension
Imaginative Narrative	• Episodic structure • Character motivation • Feeling vocabulary • Pronoun reference	Story creation
Classroom Discourse	• Verbal interaction structure • Behavior self-regulation • Conditional verbs	Cooperative learning task
Persuasion	• Argument structure • Fact versus opinion • Causal and adversative conjunctions	Letter asking leader to take an action

In each objective, the discourse context is listed. This recognizes that skills are not learned in isolation from the activity and that a skill is not deployed in the same way across different activities. It also better reveals to parents and other teachers what is being taught in speech-language services. For example, for a student who is being taught chronological event organization, recounting sequenced steps from a personally experienced event is more difficult than describing the steps depicted on sequenced picture cards. Likewise, using post-modified noun phrases in a report about birds seen on a field trip (e.g., *I saw*

Table 1.4   **Intervention Goal and Objectives for Sally**

Target	Example
Standard	4th grade students will use listening and speaking skills for a variety of purposes and audiences.
Goal	Sally will increase her score by .5 standard deviation on the expressive scale of the Test of Narrative Language.
Objectives	Sally will independently provide a complex **episodic structure** with 4 elements (complication, internal response, attempt, consequence) in oral narratives. **Criterion:** All 4 elements in each of 3 consecutive narratives.
	Sally will provide clear **pronoun reference** in oral narratives with no more than 1 prompt per narrative. **Criterion:** 90 percent correct over 2 narratives.
	Sally will provide **relative clauses** in oral narratives with no more than 1 prompt. **Criterion:** 3 relative clauses in each of 3 consecutive narratives.

a heron with long, stiff legs) is very different from making up a series of unrelated sentences with expanded noun phrases from an adjective list.

Expected performance on Sally's goal is an overall increase in expressive narrative quality. The criterion could be measured through the achievement of all objectives, or it could use a more global measure of progress provided by a normative reference (if a relevant test is available). In this case, the expressive scale of the Test of Narrative Language (Gillam & Pearson, 2004) would be an applicable tool. A change of .5 standard deviation is greater than the standard error of measure and would indicate a substantive overall improvement in performance.

Sally's objectives are also measurable. Single skills are listed along with quantitative expectations. A sizeable number of pronoun reference opportunities are possible for a single story, but the number cannot be specified in advance and might vary widely, so tallying across two narratives allows for this unpredictability. Two objectives do not state the standard percentage criterion because the number of opportunities within a single event are expected to be very low. For example, a well-formed story may only have one complete episode, so only one opportunity within the story is possible (resulting in either 0 or 100 percent correct). Stating the episode requirement as being three of four elements alleviates this, but mastery would not be reflected in one independently created complex episode. As a result, for the skills that are likely to have five or fewer opportunities within a single discourse event, two to three narratives may be required.

Another example of intervention objectives comes from plans for Millie, a 16 year-old girl with Down syndrome. A colleague, Cathy Ross, developed this IEP after an activity analysis showed the areas of need. Millie's motivations were her enjoyment of shopping and of pleasing the clinician. The activity goal was to engage in successful shopping transactions, which was a goal Millie herself would understand and accept. The intervention goal and objectives listed in Table 1.5 on page 30 target the behaviors and skills involved in the purposeful activity of shopping. Ross and the occupational therapist planned to combine money and comparative shopping skills with vocabulary, critical thinking, and social skills. Ross planned to work on expanding oral language within the context of shopping activities involving appropriate use of money. She planned to use actual shopping, advance planning, and post-shopping reflections as therapeutic activities. Ross recognized functional equivalence by accepting a variety of ways of demonstrating successful payment and social skills. This IEP was welcomed by the team and parents as a collaborative endeavor that involved a meaningful activity using skills that were widely applicable, in a way that was age-appropriate.

Intervention through Activity Analysis

An activity analysis moves from performing assessment into designing intervention. Based on the objectives, a purposeful activity is selected that will make sense beyond the intervention objectives, be motivating, and allow attention to the student's individual needs. SLPs have long capitalized upon students' enjoyment of playing games for the pleasure of the play. But activities go much further beyond games. Reading a good story, composing a dinosaur report, creating a magazine article, enacting a play, and reporting on a field trip are all examples of purposeful activities that make sense in and out of school. There are many possible purposeful activities across conversation,

Embedded Skill Objectives toward Mastery of Communication for Shopping

Table 1.5

IEP Component	Example
Goal	Millie will improve oral communication skills during functional math activities, with 80% performance on critical thinking, sequencing, calculating, writing checks, and social interacting.
Objectives	Millie will improve critical thinking skills by planning, reviewing, and evaluating each shopping experience through a combination of oral, pictured, and written information. **Criterion:** 80% accuracy on a task checklist.
	Millie will explain comparative shopping decisions using correctly sequenced explanations and vocabulary. **Criterion:** 80% accuracy in response to 5 questions.
	Millie will independently participate in purchasing activities by determining the amount of currency needed to purchase an item using the "dollar more" strategy and waiting for change. **Criterion:** Accurate on 4 of 5 shopping trips.
	Millie will independently participate in purchasing activities by writing checks in amounts over $10.00. **Criterion:** All details accurate on 4 of 5 checks.
	Millie will demonstrate appropriate social skills towards other customers and store personnel during shopping activities: respond actively, use eye contact, take turns, and keep appropriate personal space. **Criterion:** 80% accuracy on checklist.

Source: C. Ross, personal communication, February 10, 1999

narrative, expository, and even poetic genres, such as the examples provided in Table 1.6. Comprehension tasks can be demonstrated with minimal verbal output. Expressive tasks require extended conversational turns or monologues. However, it should be kept in mind that there is no clear modality division: comprehension is generally demonstrated through expressive acts, and expression without comprehension reflects rote imitation or confusion.

Purposeful Activity Possibilities
for Discourse Intervention Contexts

Genre	Comprehension	Expression
Conversation	• Understanding a classroom's allowed discourse patterns • Resolving disagreements by understanding others' perspectives	• Expressing your view of a school talent performance • Participating productively in cooperative learning groups
Narrative	• Remembering the plot of a story • Understanding character motivations in children's literature	• Composing an imaginative story • Recounting a personal event
Expository	• Understanding a factual science article • Following the directions for a science experiment • Understanding the main idea of a nature article	• Writing a persuasive letter • Explaining an experiment procedure • Advertising an event
Poetic	• Understanding a metaphoric poem • Understanding the oath of allegiance	• Composing an adjectives poem • Composing a school song with parallel cohesive structure

In addition, oral versus print modalities are not separated in the activity possibilities—in school-age language intervention, it is expected that both speaking and writing activities will occur in support of each other. The service delivery constraints of speech-language services often mean there is insufficient time to work directly on writing, and frequently, the decoding deficits of students preclude rapid independent reading. As a result, the majority of the intervention may take place through oral interactions around print. The SLP's role is to maximize literate language development, working through whatever modalities possible.

The SLP needs to plan for repeated learning opportunities. This may require more than one purposeful activity. The activities should be chosen based on similarity of goals and other components. Two expository activities that involve the goal of procedural competence for entertainment are explaining how to fold origami and explaining how to access a video game. Two expository activities that involve persuasion (position and justification) are explaining to a peer why the student can't go to an unsupervised party and explaining to a peer why the student is saving his or her allowance. Both procedure and persuasion types of talk involve multiple steps, logical organization, precise vocabulary, and endophoric reference, but they fall into two different functional categories.

Purposeful activities do not demand in-classroom situations. While inclusive intervention provides maximum curriculum relevance, it is less amenable to therapeutic control. If the opportunity can be created to provide repeated, explicit, supported intervention within the classroom, it should be seized. Ehren (2000) provides a valuable framework for keeping a therapeutic focus in inclusive service delivery. However, pull-out individual and small groups, or self-contained classrooms, allow more individualization and attention to problematic actions and operations with less pressure for completing assignments, passing tests, and keeping up with the curriculum schedule. Activities are linked to the general curriculum topically, through similarity of activity goal, or through continuity of skills and strategies. This planning of purposeful activities results in a simulation, but one that still presents the functional components of the activity. Purposeful therapeutic activities are thus both engineered and natural.

The clinician selects objectives and plans a functionally similar activity based on an understanding of how a student functions in the classroom. The objectives receive targeted, intentional mediation during intervention. (NOTE: Confusion may arise between terms used in activity analysis and in writing intervention plans. In an activity analysis, *goal* refers to the purpose of performing the meaningful activity. In planning, a student's *intervention goal* [or objectives] will be to acquire the actions and operations necessary to achieve the goal of the purposeful activity.)

Intervention targets for Sally's discourse organization difficulties included episodic structure, pronoun reference, and relative clause construction. Table 1.7 on page 34 sets out an intervention plan for Sally based on the activity analysis in Table 1.2 on page 24. The activity will be engineered to bring targeted objectives into conscious awareness for remediation at particular points in the process. All other actions and operations involved in this complex activity will occur without intentional mediation. Weak, nontarget actions and operations will occur without support (e.g., poor spelling might be accepted) or the SLP will allow compensation (e.g., pictographic sketching, described in Chapter 5, may be used to avoid writing). The remediation process will involve cycling between the larger, whole, purposeful activity of composing a story and the focused-skill activities that target episodic structure, pronoun reference, and relative clauses. Activities will culminate with sharing the story with an audience and reflecting with Sally on her progress on the intervention objectives (see Chapter 2 on intervention units).

Students with language-learning disabilities have multiple areas of weakness, but only a few can be targeted within a student's attentional resources and the limited time available for intervention. As a result, the SLP will select a few components that can be remediated fairly quickly (e.g., learning basic story grammar structure to allow for the action of plot development), will have significant effects in the classroom (e.g., teaching the student comprehension-monitoring strategies), can be used during functionally equivalent activities for generalization (e.g., oral reporting has a common classroom companion in the form of science reports), or will provide solutions for other, longer term problems (e.g., teaching independent use of pictography to plan story ideas if the operation of writing is too laborious). For older students, it is important that they are not only aware of, but play a role in selecting, the intervention objectives (Larson & McKinley, 2004; Nelson, 1995).

The process of intervention involves teaching new actions or modifying old operations. For older students, awareness of one's own cognition and language (metacognition and metalinguistics) are required to achieve change. As a result, old operations will have to be raised to the action level so they can be consciously addressed (e.g., *I know you have been doing this for a long time, but we need to make it better. Let's think about how to do this. I am going to talk aloud to show what I think about when I do this. Then I want you to talk aloud as you do it).* For example, if a student's written complex sentence errors are being

Intervention Plan for Sally Based on a Classroom Activity Analysis

Table 1.7

Component	Example
Objectives	To improve the episodic structure, pronoun reference, and relative clauses of Sally's narratives.
Motive	Same as in classroom.
Goal	Same as in classroom.
Actions	Same as in classroom, minus writing demands, plus: • Provide a complex episode in the story • Use clear pronoun reference for characters • Describe characters using relative clauses
Operations	Same as in classroom except for three operations brought to conscious awareness (see above Actions)
Conditions during Intervention	• In the speech-language room with one other peer • With the story read and vocabulary discussed previously in classroom • With the SLP giving explicit attention to target objectives • By cycling through a complete writing process incorporating multiple, focused skill activities • With the SLP addressing only one action (i.e., episodic structure, pronoun reference, or relative clauses) during each focused activity • With systematic scaffolding for objectives • With compensation for nontargeted actions and operations (e.g., poor spelling avoided through pictography)

remediated, intervention will involve helping the student be aware of grammatical weaknesses, how sentences in familiar books are composed, and how more appropriate complex sentences can be constructed to better transmit desired meaning (see Chapter 4).

Once an action has been modified or newly acquired, the focus of intervention may turn to other objectives, but continued opportunities are needed to automatize the action into an operation. Turning a newly acquired strategy into an unconscious, fluent skill is important—students cannot move on to new learning challenges if recent acquisitions use up their attentional resources. For example, at some point, reading comprehension practices should stop being conscious, considered strategies and become automatic processes. They may become conscious again when the student is faced with difficult reading material, but should generally operate without conscious attention.

Finally, activity components are not unvarying sets of skills, but an array of possibilities that can be flexibly employed to achieve a goal based on reigning conditions. This means that knowing why and when to use a skill is part of the skill. Knowing how to sketch a graphic organizer is of limited help unless the student knows why the organizer is helpful, when to employ it within the classroom lesson structure, and what other alternatives are available if the graphic organizer is not suitable. This is the functional equivalence element of an activity analysis: having more than one way to achieve a goal for varying activity conditions. Sally should be prepared to mentally rehearse, pictographically sketch, or make key word notes to help organize her narrative discourse in classroom situations. SLPs must be cognizant of how students can apply new learning within the variations present in the daily life of classrooms.

Considering Generalization

Ideally, skills are taught within their contexts of use, obviating the need to guide generalization from the therapy room to daily life. Typically, SLPs create activities that have larger purpose and meaning so that generalization concerns are eased, but not erased. In either case, contextualized skill intervention does not require the SLP to teach many different activities. Generalization from one situation to another is expected if the goals of the activities are similar and appropriate mediation is provided.

The tight link between skills and activities does *not* mean that cognitive activities are tied to the episode in which they were originally learned. Instead, "in order to function, people must be able to generalize some aspects of knowledge and skills to new situations" (Rogoff, 1984, p. 3). Skills do not generalize across all settings equally—the more similar the activities, the more likely the skill will generalize between them. Similar activities are determined functionally: the participants' interpretation of the events, the goals of the activities, and the conditions of the activity are considered. For example, raising one's hand, going up to the teacher's desk, or asking a peer would be considered equivalent actions if all are used toward the goal of obtaining instruction clarification. Raising one's hand to request clarification may have limited generalization to raising one's hand to be counted in attendance, because of the differing goals. Further, activities that are similar in topic may have very different goals and thus limited generalization. For example, a classroom report of a field trip may be used to demonstrate new learning (e.g., *What I learned when I visited the zoo).* Little generalization of component actions and operations would be expected to a topically similar, but functionally different social conversation told to maintain social closeness (e.g., *You won't believe what Sam did at the zoo yesterday).*

Within this view of generalization, the Halloween storywriting example would be expected to be functionally related to some activities and not to others. The act of event sequencing is expected to transfer to other event recounts in which the goal is sharing an entertaining and understandable story. Less transfer would be expected to writing a procedure for a science experiment in which the goal is having others accurately follow your directions.

A Close Look at Scaffolding Learning

The social world scaffolds students' learning. Each time a conversational partner demonstrates a step, explains an idea, or prompts a behavior, a little bit of the social world goes inside the student. This internalization is learning, and is followed by an increase in development. Students can learn a lot simply from observing, participating, and receiving occasional cues and directions (Wood et al., 1976). However, within language intervention, this support of daily life learning must be intentionally provided, and even amplified, to guide and accelerate learning. The more closely this mediation or scaffolding matches a student's needs, the more efficiently learning will occur.

Scaffolding is part of intervention, but can also be viewed as a window into ongoing assessment. The SLP is observing, hypothesizing, testing, and judging as intervention happens. The ongoing assessment results affect the course of intervention, both over time and on a moment-by-moment basis.

This dynamic interplay between intervention and assessment is the art of scaffolding—determining the kind and amount of help needed for the student to both achieve a goal-directed task, and to internalize the strategies and skills needed for better future performance. A close examination of the many ways that scaffolding can occur is presented next, concluding with a contrastive analysis of the scaffolding that occurs in contextualized skill intervention versus the shaping that occurs in discrete skill intervention.

Structural Scaffolds

Structural scaffolds are somewhat static features of the context that can often be preplanned. They are the ways that the SLP provides facilitating conditions. They include an engineered context and a skill routine. An engineered context is an activity that is purposeful, but which has been manipulated to maximize the use and desirability of the target skill, to provide a certain internal predictability, and to allow a number of repeated opportunities for the skill to be employed. A skill routine is the predictable order of steps within an activity. Predictability allows the student to focus attention on the skills to be acquired, rather than on the unfolding of the event.

SLPs can provide structural scaffolds through careful selection of materials, order of presentation, tools, and modifying environmental conditions. In Chapter 2, thematic units are described. In these, intervention is organized by opening with a complex, purposeful activity of sharing a piece of literature; then following with a series of focused skill activities; and closing with another complex, purposeful activity of creating a parallel story that integrates strategies and skills learned. Linking a thematic unit to a classroom topic or to the personal interest of a student means that the SLP does not have to take time to present content information. Structural scaffolds include using tools such as pictographic sketching, semantic webbing, audio recording, or computer typing to assist in achieving a purposeful task and its accompanying intervention objective. In terms of environmental modifications, possibilities include teaching the student (and gaining permission from the teacher) to use these compensatory tools in the classroom. Demonstrating to a teacher how to embed phonemic awareness lessons in word-decoding lessons is a way of changing the larger classroom instruction. In pull-out instruction, limiting group size to four or fewer students, keeping the developmental level similar among students, and grouping by disorder type are all ways of providing structural scaffolds.

Interactive Scaffolds

The other broad category of scaffolds contains interactive scaffolds. Interactive scaffolds involve the intentional, dynamic, responsive moves on the part of the instructor during the intervention activity. Considerable interactive scaffolding is expected initially, with a systematic withdrawal as the student internalizes the skills demonstrated by the clinician.

Scaffolding aims at managing the task complexity so the learner can be actively successful. Wood et al. (1996) list the following scaffolding moves:

- Recruit attention, interest, and adherence to task requirements.
- Provide structure to reduce task variability to manageable limits.
- Direct attention to solving a problem.
- Encourage movement beyond previously successful actions.
- Mark critical features to contrast what has been done with what ought to be done.
- Control frustration by providing adequate assistance (in a face-saving way, if necessary).
- Demonstrate solutions when the learner can recognize them.

In addition to this list of scaffolding moves, the literature reveals three general types of interactive scaffolding, which are presented in Table 1.8. One type is response facilitations, such as those used in milieu teaching (e.g., Kaiser, Yoder, & Keetz, 1992). Another is linguistic facilitations, used in interactive versions of focused stimulation (e.g., Camarata et al., 1994; Fey et al., 1993; Girolametto, Pearce, & Weitzman, 1996; Nelson et al., 1996). A third type is regulatory facilitations, such as those used in dynamic assessment and mediated learning (Feuerstein, 1980; Lidz, 1991).

Peers as Structural and Interactive Scaffolds

Peer models could be considered structural scaffolds in that the SLP designs the group in advance to provide social supports. However, in the dynamic interplay of intervention, peer models are also part of the social interactive process.

SLPs can employ peers as informal models or as formal parts of the teaching/learning process. Peer models involve more capable others demonstrating responses at a level slightly above that of the student. They can also

Types of Facilitative Moves Used in Interactive Scaffolding

Table 1.8

Response Facilitations	Linguistic Facilitations	Regulatory Facilitations
• Wait for a response • Model the response • Repeat and emphasize • Cue through physical signals • Pause before providing the answer • Provide part of the answer • Provide the answer and have the student repeat it	• Model (provide in advance) • Expand (add adult syntactic/semantic element) • Extend (add to topic) • Recast (change the syntactic structure) • Use vertical structuring (combine two student utterances) • Use build-up/break-down (model both telegraphic and complete sentences) • Use focused contrast (pair the error and correction) • Redirect (show student how to ask or tell another person)	• Maintain awareness and acceptance of the goal • Highlight importance of content • Relate content to past knowledge • Comment on student performance • Inhibit impulsive responses • Aid selective and sustained attention • Help student manage challenge • Review cumulative performance • Comment on task similarities

Sources: Camarata et al. (1994); Feuerstein (1980); Fey et al. (1993); Girolametto, et al. (1996); Kaiser et al. (1992); Lidz (1991); Nelson et al. (1996)

involve less skilled students demonstrating, with support, the desired skill. Peer models increase the number of opportunities for observation and show the student how other students enact the activity, which is often a more salient model than the clinician's skilled performance.

A method of instruction called Reciprocal Teaching (see Chapter 12), formally involves the learner as teacher for improving text comprehension (Palincsar & Brown, 1984). Students take turns being teacher to other students for material they are themselves still in the process of acquiring. This approach closely follows Vygotsky's (1978) model of how the social world is internalized as students' thoughts. In challenging learning situations, students are aided in their performance by talking themselves through the activity, using the words the adult previously used to guide them. In a situation where students can be the teacher, a real opportunity for "talking aloud" is provided through the student-teacher role. The clinician prompts and supports students to "be teacher," not primarily to teach the other students, but to provide an avenue for students to talk their way through the activity. The words of the clinician become the students' words, externally as speech at first, then internally as the students' own thoughts.

How Much Help When—Staying in the Zone

One of the challenges of scaffolding is knowing how much help to provide the student, in other words, how to stay within the student's zone of proximal development as the student learns and improves. Scaffolding possibilities are preplanned, but enactment is dynamic and responsive to student needs. Scaffolding levels can vary within a group, tailored to each student's abilities and moment-by-moment needs. For example, the SLP may flexibly provide linguistic facilitations (e.g., pragmatic, discourse, grammatical, or lexical support) during an event retell of a field trip. Grammatical support comments might focus on increased detail in noun phrases, such as, *Which boy saw the warbler? Use a description word to identify the boy. Stop and think about how you are describing the students you don't know. You could say, the tall boy with red hair.* As another example, the SLP may provide response facilitations on the phonemic awareness task of first sound isolation, by elongating or repeating the first phoneme of a word (/k/-/k/-/k/-/æt/). Examples of regulatory facilitations include asking students what skill they are learning or telling students to think before responding.

Schneider and Watkins (1996) provide a good description of the degree and types of scaffolds for narrative instruction. In their example, they provide the structural scaffold of a written cue card, which lists and defines story grammar elements. They also provide multiple interactive scaffolds of questioning, partial answers, cloze responses, and response feedback. The interactive scaffolds are classified as high, medium, or low.

High mediations require step-by-step support from the clinician with very little student responsibility, including questions such as, *Who was in the story?* and *How did he feel about that?* For these mediations, the student does not have to consider the overall task to respond correctly. Mid-level mediations involve the clinician cuing the student to attend to the story grammar card with questions such as, *And in this story, what was the problem?* or *How could you find out what is the next part in this story?* Low mediations consist of general guiding questions from the clinician, such as, *What comes first (or next)?,* with the student required to provide both the story grammar unit and the content, such as, *Setting—there was a little boy and he loved riding his bike.*

The elicitation procedures from milieu teaching (Fey, 1986; Kaiser, et al., 1992) can be helpful in judging the prompting needed. In milieu teaching, the student is asked the question, allowed time to respond, then prompted twice. If the second prompt fails to result in the correct answer, the answer is given. Scaffolding needs can then be rated as high, consisting of two prompts and an imitated answer; medium, consisting of two prompts; or low, consisting of one prompt. For example, to teach phonemic awareness (e.g., *sit* starts with /s/), low support could be an elicitation that involves extending the first sound once with an advance reminder to listen (e.g., *Listen.* [points to ear] *What is the first sound in /s/-/s/-/sɪt/?*). If the student requires additional focusing (e.g., *Look at my mouth)* and the word is repeated and extended again, that would be medium support. If the student responds incorrectly and the clinician requests a direct imitation of the answer, support would be high. Progress toward independence can then be measured by tallying the number of scaffolds at each level that were needed for a correct response.

Efficient scaffolding requires the skill of knowing how much is needed and when it is needed. Students must be taught within their zone of proximal development. Too much help leads to boredom and little learning, while too little scaffolding leads to frustration and, again, little learning. Schneider and Watkins (1996) taught graduate-student clinicians to provide scaffolded assistance, and reported that, "there is a tendency to retain responsibility and to keep the student's role at a low level, at which he or she attains consistent success" (p. 161). This common error, providing too much help, focuses on task completion as an end in itself, rather than on revealing to the student the underlying goal and processes needed for independent task completion.

One way of organizing scaffolded support is provided through dynamic assessment mediation lessons (Peña, 1993; Peña, Quinn, & Iglesias, 1992; Ukrainetz et al., 2000). Lidz's (1991) list of mediation principles (summarized

Table 1.9   **Lidz's Mediation Principles**

Principle	Explanation
Intentionality	A conscious attempt by the mediator to influence the behavior of the student (It includes communication to the student of the purpose for the interaction.)
Meaning	Moving the content from neutral to a position of value and importance (It may be done by affective emphasis or by stating that the object or aspect of focus is important.)
Transcendence	Promotion of cognitive bridges between the task or activity and related, but not currently present, experiences of the student
Sharing of Regard	Looking and/or commenting on an object of focus initiated by the student
Sharing of Experience	Communication to the student of an experience or thought the mediator had that the student had not previously shared or experienced with the mediator
Competence through Task Regulation	Manipulation of the task to facilitate mastery by the student
Competence through Praise/ Encouragement	Verbal or nonverbal communication to the student that he or she did a good job
Competence through Challenge	Maintenance of the activity or task so the student is challenged to reach beyond his or her current level of functioning, but is not overwhelmed

Table 1.9—*Continued*

Principle	Explanation
Psychological Differentiation	Maintenance of the idea that the role of the mediator is to facilitate the learning of the student, not to have a learning experience for oneself
Contingent Responsivity	Ability to read the student's cues and signals relating to learning, affective, and motivational needs, and then respond in a timely and appropriate way
Affective Involvement	Communication of a sense of caring about and enjoyment of the student
Change	Communication to the student that he or she has profited in a positive direction from the experience
Reciprocity (by the Student)	The demands exerted by the student's behavior and its effect on the clinician's success in using the mediating strategies

Source: Lidz (1991)

in Table 1.9) sounds complicated, but is really just a list of good instructional practices. To start an intervention session, students are given a goal (e.g., *We're going to learn about how to put things together in a group*) and a general principle for learning the target goal (e.g., *What if you called the teacher a kindergartner instead of a teacher? Would the teacher understand? No, because she is in a different group*). This introduction addresses the mediation principles of intentionality, meaning, and transcendence. During the task, the SLP shares regard and experiences. The SLP keeps the task challenging but possible (task regulation), and provides praise and encouragement. The student gains a sense of competence as challenges are met. Throughout the activity, the clinician keeps the focus on the student's active involvement and learning, continuously reads the student's cues for needed learning support, and communicates caring and enjoyment. In closing this sample activity, the clinician reviews the activity goal (intentionality) and the objective of the task (meaning), and guides the student to recognize changes in the student's ability to categorize, plan, and self-regulate.

The SLP's use of these mediating strategies will be affected by each student's behavior. Lidz (1991) warns that *reciprocity*, or how the student's behavior changes the clinician's behavior, must always be taken into consideration when examining how well the clinician scaffolded a student's learning.

Internalizing Words and Actions

Students participate before they fully understand; they only succeed because others are helping. This guided interaction leads to learning and then to development, which is manifested by a change in independent performance. However, this vital change only happens if the assistance is internalized. How does one plan and measure inner change? Progress within contextualized skill intervention is not achieved through making the task more complex or increasing the number of correct responses. Instead, progress is determined by the student's degree of independence within the meaningful task, and the degree to which the child adopts and applies the behaviors and strategies that are modeled.

Scaffolding *enables* a student to achieve a task. However, the aim of scaffolding is not to *aid* the student to complete the task. The aim of scaffolded support is to aid the handover of the skill to the student; the clinician and student jointly perform the task to develop the student's subsequent ownership of the skill. This distinction between handover and helping is critical. The focus of scaffolding must be on the student's active participation in the task. This enables the student to acquire the knowledge about task goals, behaviors, and strategies that will lead to increased independence in subsequent occurrences of the task. Each assistance move must be directed *toward the student, not the task*. For example, if the intervention is focused on summarization skills, scaffolding would not simply provide some graduated portion of the main idea and supporting details (e.g., *I will say half of the main idea sentence and you finish it*). Effective scaffolding would model competent self-talk and provide self-regulatory questions that the student can use the next time, such as, *I am looking for the main idea* (goal). *How do I find the main idea in this long paragraph? I will look at the beginning. I will see if that is a bigger idea than the next two sentences* (strategy). *Maybe I will have to infer or guess the main idea from those details* (strategy).

As the student learns and improves, the clinician notes the increasing internalization of skills formerly provided by the clinician, as evidenced both by the behaviors the student executes along with the decreased need for support. A graduate student, Kate—who was also a swimming instructor—illustrated this. Kate said when she teaches a student to float, the student is in the pool, attempting to float in water for the full dependence-to-independence continuum. The progression is two-hand support to one-hand support to degrees of standing by, ready with verbal prompts *(belly up)*, and physical prompts. By her touch and comments, she guides the student to move his or her own body into floating position and resistance. She knows when to move from one support level to another from the student's behavior, such as the degree of floppiness in the body, the arch of the back, and the facial expression. Kate looks for indicators of growing physical, mental, and emotional mastery of the skill of floating.

Table 1.10 on page 46 illustrates the plan for developing internalization and independent performance of sequencing skills within the context of a narrative activity. The hierarchical plan reflects scaffolding within an unchanging task complexity. Levels of support decrease, while student competence increases over repeated performance opportunities. The scaffolding provided for preparing a report is fairly heavy initially: advance discussion and practice followed by picture cues and prompting every two to three actions. Another report would follow fairly soon after, with increased expectations. By the fifth opportunity to give a verbal report, the student is expected to use the degree of independence expected for a typical student of that age. An additional expectation would be evidence that the student has transferred support away from the clinician to become independent. The first four steps might be completed during pull-out sessions with the SLP, culminating in the fifth step completed in the classroom at the same level of independence as the student's peers.

Scaffolding versus Shaping

Scaffolding is a form of systematic learning support. The final discussion of scaffolding will be in considering what it is *not*. Scaffolding is a fundamentally different support system from the shaping provided in traditional discrete skill intervention.

Discrete skill intervention involves breaking down the final desired activity into a series of individual tasks that are taught and mastered sequentially. Difficulty level is strictly controlled to yield high rates of correct responding

Table 1.10

Graduated Steps and Achievements for Objective of Actions in Sequential Order

Steps	Scaffolded Support	Achievement in Internalization
Report 1	• Clinician leads advance discussion of what and how • Clinician guides practice • Clinician sketches picture cues • Clinician provides verbal prompting during presentation • Clinician reviews performance	• Student knows to look to clinician for support throughout
Report 2	• Clinician guides advance discussion • Clinician guides practice • Clinician guides student sketching • Clinician reviews performance	• Student is led through advance discussion and practice, but knows to look at sketches
Report 3	• Clinician prompts advance discussion • Clinician guides practice • Clinician reviews performance	• Student conducts advance practice aloud and sketches with prompting
Report 4	• Clinician schedules advance discussion • Clinician observes practice • Clinician reviews performance	• Student is reminded but conducts advance discussion, silent practice, and sketching
Report 5	• Clinician schedules practice time • Clinician reviews performance	• Desired level of independence • Student prepares independently in advance

(Greenfield, 1984; Nelson, 1995). Movement to the next task occurs only when independent mastery is achieved on preceding tasks. Nelson explains that lack of progress through the sequence means the student is never considered competent to participate in the desired purposeful life activity.

In contrast, scaffolding involves working on the emerging behavior or strategy within the purposeful life activity, with support from the clinician and active involvement from the student (Greenfield, 1984; Nelson, 1995; Wood et al., 1976). The student gradually acquires the necessary behaviors and strategies to complete more and more of the task independently. The student stays within the purposeful context for the entire dependence to independence continuum. Scaffolding into competence means that the student can achieve functional goals even when his or her competence is extremely limited. In this way, Nelson concludes, all students can participate in daily life activities with support of a more competent adult or peer.

The contrast between shaping and scaffolding is evident in the following two SLPs' analyses of their intervention techniques (Ukrainetz, 2005). Marla's intervention approach was primarily discrete skill (shaping): teaching phonemic awareness through nonsense syllables, block representation, and a strict task hierarchy. Dana's intervention approach was primarily contextualized skill (scaffolding): teaching language through literature units and science projects.

Each clinician was observed in a session in which a student was introduced to new material and had significant difficulty accomplishing the task. During a phonemic awareness lesson, Marla provided about a half-dozen prompts to one third grader in a 20-minute period. In a story grammar lesson, Dana provided more than a dozen prompts to a fifth grader in the same period of time. After the session, Marla commented that she had provided too much help and that she would use an easier task in the next session. In contrast, Dana commented that she had provided a lot of help, but this was the student's first time and it would get easier with increased familiarity in subsequent lessons. The two clinicians structured their supports consistent with their intervention approach: discrete skills teaching involves structuring the task to allow near-mastery at each level, while contextualized skill teaching involves gradually decreasing the available social support while accomplishing a complex task.

Both shaping and scaffolding involve task simplification. Both involve reducing the task demands on the student by simplifying the purposeful activity. For example, a student may be learning to write with effective word choice. In either intervention approach, the SLP may decide that a full descriptive paragraph is too much writing, so the student may be required to write only a sentence.

In a shaping approach, the student may practice writing individual sentences with descriptive words. He or she may practice 10 times with 10 different sentences in a worksheet format with minimal clinician prompting. If extensive prompting is required, the task may be reduced to a noun phrase or a single word. If successful, the student will move into writing a longer sentence using connectives and descriptive words concurrently. Eventually, if sufficient progress occurs, the concept of word choice to achieve a purpose will be introduced and the student will be allowed to write a descriptive passage.

In contrast, in contextualized skill intervention, the SLP teaches within the context of a purposeful activity. Sentences and phrases only make sense within a discourse unit. In this approach, the descriptive passage and the goal of transmitting images in words is present from the start. Published passages that exemplify word choice may be examined. The student's five sentences will be composed with the intent of placing them within a larger descriptive passage. The SLP may write the passage or may select a passage from literature, but there is a place within the passage for each of the student's descriptive sentences. The student is thus an apprentice in the writing task, assisting the more competent other, but observing and learning the purposeful activity (Rogoff, 1990). In this way, the larger activity purpose is constantly present. It is clear how the student's contribution is orchestrated with the larger whole to provide voice in writing, without unduly stressing the student's writing resources.

Both scaffolding and shaping are well-reasoned ways of supporting learning. Shaping, as part of discrete skill intervention, was the predominant framework in the early years of language intervention (Fey, 1986). Research demonstrates gains in the contrived intervention context, but persistent difficulties with generalization into daily life activities. Scaffolding within contextualized skill intervention is an attempt to bridge this generalization gap, providing both systematic support of explicit objectives and naturalistic contexts. Scaffolding is the recommended practice for acquiring both a skill and an understanding of how, when, and why the skill should be deployed. However, at times, the elements of massed practice, single-skill contrived tasks, and task hierarchy may be used briefly to develop automaticity within the larger contextualized skill approach (Isaacson, 1992). For example, Chapter 4 includes some sentence-combining drills for complex syntax and Chapter 10 employs some phoneme-segmentation tasks for phonemic awareness.

Being Therapeutic in Context: RISE

Activity analysis provides the five components needed for effective mediation during contextualized skill intervention. Scaffolding the internalization of behaviors and strategies is the way to support learning. This therapeutic focus within purposeful activities is what Johnston (1985) terms the "extraordinary" within the "common" (p. 128) and Rice (1995) calls "the concentrated-normative model" (p. 28). This section presents a way of constructing and evaluating language intervention for its therapeutic quality.

Individual clinicians find it difficult to demonstrate the effectiveness of their daily intervention practices. Clinical practice does not lend itself easily to experimental validation and many factors beyond the intervention itself can affect outcome. One way of providing an indication of likely program effectiveness is through demonstration of quality indicators (Duncan, 2003). If a particular program shows evidence of best practice or effective features, then there is some assurance that the intervention is causing positive outcomes. The following four therapy elements could be considered in that light:

- Repeated opportunities
- Intensity
- Systematic support
- Explicit skill focus

These elements, which compose the mnemonic acronym RISE, should occur *regardless* of intervention approach. They are increasingly recognized as critical features of intervention across a variety of specific methods (Berninger et al., 2003; Gillam, Loeb, & Friel-Patti, 2001; O'Shaughnessy & Swanson, 2000; Torgesen et al., 2001; Torgesen, Al Otaiba, & Grek, 2005). Whether the intervention follows a discrete skill framework or a contextualized skill framework, effective intervention is marked by the four elements of RISE.

Repeated Opportunities

For learning to occur, there must be repeated opportunities to practice. Repeated opportunities are easy to provide in discrete skill instruction, by presenting and scoring a certain number of items. Naturalistic interventions have been criticized for the lack of opportunities for practice (Pretti-Frontczak & Bricker, 2004). This is a valid, but surmountable, concern. Structure must be provided, both within and across activities, to allow for repeated learning opportunities. As a result, activities are *naturalistic* rather than fully natural. They still have larger purpose, but the clinician uses some structural and interactive engineering to ensure sufficient learning opportunities. In addition, although the number of opportunities may be fewer than in discrete skill instruction, the systematic mediation makes key elements more salient and more likely to be used in a needed context.

Repeated opportunities should occur within the context of an activity. The close succession of opportunities along with modeling, guidance, and explanation is important for students to internalize a new behavior or strategy. For example, listening to a well-written adventure tale allows multiple models and discussions (i.e., mediation) of expanded pre- and postmodified noun phrases as the explorers are described in many ways (e.g., ***The intrepid explorers** started out on **their great adventure. All the men** were **truly men of stout heart. These first men** to brave **the rigors of the South Pole** would come back to tell **a tale never equaled**). Retelling of the tale allows for repeated work on sequencing actions. Planning a reenactment allows for multiple descriptions of outfits and gear. Interviewing the explorer actors allows for multiple use of conditional verbs (e.g., *Would you do it again? Could you explain? Why wouldn't you...*).

Repeated opportunities should also occur across activities. There should be several opportunities to observe the targeted structure or behavior in use, as well as opportunities to practice, integrate, and use it to achieve the desired level of independence. For example, in teaching conditional verbs, the SLP can provide practice identifying verb use in a story, inserting conditional verbs into blanks within a parallel story, and composing an "I Would If I Could" poem with conditionals.

Some scripting of the sessions, or a familiarity with how the session typically runs, allows for an approximate quantification of number of opportunities. Even if the naturalistic intervention is pull-out and somewhat contrived, the number of opportunities will be lower than in massed-practice, discrete skill intervention. The use of purposeful contexts spreads the repeated opportunities over a longer time period with more distracters. For example, embedding 10 phoneme-segmentation comments while reading aloud a verse book may take 15 minutes, whereas 10 drill items on phoneme-segmentation may take 3 minutes. The tradeoff is that the meaningfulness and active engagement in the learning is expected to improve internalization, spontaneous use, and generalization; and the complexity of the activity allows for multiple objectives to be addressed. In addition, the purposeful activities are inherently interesting, so a student's attention can be maintained for 20 minutes on phoneme segmentation within book reading. As a result, contextualized skill practice to establish initial understanding and judgment of how and when to use a behavior can be combined with a period of discrete skill massed practice to automatize the behavior. Chapter 2 describes how to organize intervention in this whole and part manner.

Intensity

Intensity is the frequency of encounters a student has with the intervention experience. Intensity has similarities with repeated opportunities, but is focused more globally on session frequency. Intensity is increasingly recognized as a critical element in effective intervention (Gillam, 1999; Gillam et al., 2001; Torgesen et al., 2001; Torgesen et al., 2005). Discrete skill interventions that produce ecologically significant improvements in reading or oral language have been shown to occur with two or more hours of daily individual instruction for two or more months.

In contextualized skill intervention, time in the activity is expected to be distributed over the day rather than presented in massed-practice, scripted events (Cole, 1995). Intervention objectives are expected to be taught both in the language-intervention session and at other times in the day by teachers and aides. In preschool activity-based intervention, the expectation is that careful planning of opportunities in a team approach allows an objective to be addressed repeatedly across contexts throughout the day (Pretti-Frontczak & Bricker, 2004). This approach may be effective, but only works if there is true collaboration in both assessment and intervention.

In school situations, language or literacy objectives may be addressed throughout the day, because language is a part of almost every interaction (Ukrainetz & Fresquez, 2003). However, it should not be assumed that effective individualized mediation is occurring in the classroom simply because literate language instruction is occurring. As another caution, the presence of a one-to-one aide assisting the student in the classroom is not typically a therapeutic interaction. Without intentional and strategic mediation that is intended to lead over time to greater independence (i.e., decreased dependence upon the aide's help), one-to-one aide support should not be counted as part of an intense intervention.

The SLP's ability to provide intense intervention is determined by the service delivery structure. School settings typically use 60 minutes of intervention per week, often in a group situation with students of diverse needs. Special events such as field trips, programs, and achievement testing cut into scheduled time. Some students may receive less than 60 minutes, even to the point of receiving only consultation services. Intensity can be augmented by additional classroom programming or resource room services, but unless repeated opportunities with explicit support are programmed, little improvement beyond that achieved in daily life will be expected. SLPs must work towards caseload sizes and school cultures that allow intensive service delivery. They must also explore redefining eligibility standards; reducing the range of their responsibilities; reducing nontherapeutic activities; increasing collaboration with resource and classroom teachers; and providing cycles of short-term, intensive intervention.

Systematic Support

Systematic learning support is critical. Naturalistic intervention has sometimes been criticized for its lack of systematic support, but scaffolding can be systematically provided. Scaffolding can be both preplanned and dynamically responsive to the moment. Tallies can be kept on numbers of opportunities, high versus low responsibility moves, number of prompts, and types of prompts. Students' increasing independence and use of modeled actions and words can be used as evidence of skill transfer. See the earlier material for a detailed consideration of scaffolding.

Explicit Skill Focus

An explicit skill focus involves directly targeting a skill for both SLP and student. Explicitness may be the most challenging aspect of contextualized skill intervention. The SLP must remember to explicitly target the operations (skills and processes) desired for independent, fluent task performance. Purposeful activities are rich contexts for enacting myriad skills and processes. Clearly defined, explicit skill foci take instruction beyond simply being a language enrichment activity to being therapeutic. An explicit focus both allows for and is revealed by the repeated opportunities and systematic scaffolding that highlights for the student when the target is used. In addition, the opening and closing of an intervention session indicates the skill focus: *We will be learning about counting sounds in words... What did we learn about today? Counting sounds. Yes, we read a book and played a game today to learn to count sounds.*

Explicitness is simple to achieve in discrete skill instruction. The controlled contexts, scripted elicitations and responses, and single skill focus lead unavoidably to explicitness. In purposeful contexts, explicitness involves a skill focus, clear and systematic preplanned instructional cues, along with the opportunity for open-ended responding and instructional feedback (Berninger et al., 2003).

To achieve explicitness within purposeful contexts, the SLP selects one or two objectives for that activity. The activity will involve much more than the one or two behaviors or strategies targeted, but the others will not receive the therapeutic focus. School-age students should be aware themselves of the behaviors and strategies being addressed. For example, students are told that, while they are creating their butterfly report, for the next 20 minutes, they will be focusing on improving two areas: (1) using specific vocabulary, and (2) producing at least three sentences that have two verbs in them. With a specific focus, the SLP can support students' internalization of the behaviors and strategies, ultimately leading to automatization as skills and processes. In this example, the SLP might remind students to use a strategy for generating vocabulary or write two-verb sentences on the board as students produce them. To allow the students to achieve an understandable butterfly report, the SLP will assist nontargeted behaviors. The SLP may spell words for a student, help find keys on the keyboard, and provide an outline for the text organization. Observations of performance will be informally noted, but the purpose in those nontargeted areas will be supporting students' participation in a meaningful activity rather than developing those specific behaviors.

Conclusion

Contextualized skill intervention involves providing a therapeutic focus within a purposeful and meaningful activity. Contextualized skill intervention is challenging to carry out. It requires methodologies that recognize the inseparability of skills and contexts such as activity analysis. An activity analysis reveals five components: motive, goals, conditions, conscious actions, and unconscious operations. It leads to intervention objectives and guides intervention planning. Purposeful activities are selected as intervention contexts. Within the activity, both positive and negative student motivations are recognized. The goal of the activity and the facilitating and constraining environmental conditions dictate what actions (conscious behaviors and strategies) and operations (unconscious skills and processes) need to be employed. Intervention involves targeting one or two components, and assisting the student to achieve the rest to allow participation in the purposeful activity.

Intervention must facilitate the transfer and internalization of the clinician's skills to the student. This internalization is the learning process that results in developmental changes. Supported behaviors and strategies become increasingly independent until they develop into unconscious skills, freeing up the student's attention for more learning. Internalization is facilitated through intentional, systematic scaffolding on the part of the SLP. Scaffolding can take many structural and interactive forms. It must be applied within the student's zone of proximal development, providing optimal challenge and growth. Scaffolding is part of the quality indicators of effective therapy: repeated opportunities, intensity, systematic (scaffolded) support, and explicit focus (RISE).

References

Bates, E. (1976). *Language in context: The acquisition of pragmatics.* New York: Academic Press.

Bates, E., & MacWhinney, B. (1987). Competition, variation, and language learning. In B. MacWhinney (Ed.), *Mechanisms of language acquisition* (pp. 157–193). Mahwah, NJ: Erlbaum.

Berninger, V. W., Vermeulen, K., Abbott, R. D., McCutchen, D., Cotton, S., Cude, J., et al. (2003). Comparison of three approaches to supplementary reading instruction for low-achieving second-grade readers. *Language, Speech, and Hearing Services in Schools, 34,* 101–116.

Bricker, D., Pretti-Frontczak, K., & McComas, N. (1998). *An activity-based approach to early intervention* (2nd ed.). Baltimore: Brookes.

Brown, J. S., Collins, A., & Duguid, P. (1989). Situated cognition and the culture of learning. *Educational Researcher, 17*(1), 32–42.

Bruner, J. (1983). *Child's talk: Learning to use language.* New York: Norton.

Camarata, S. M., Nelson, K. E., & Camarata, M. N. (1994). Comparison of conversational-recasting and imitative procedures for training grammatical structures in children with specific language impairment. *Journal of Speech and Hearing Research, 37,* 1414–1423.

Cole, K. N. (1995). Curriculum models and language facilitation in the preschool years. In M. E. Fey, J. Windsor, & S. F. Warren (Eds.), *Language intervention: Preschool through the elementary years* (pp. 39–62). Baltimore: Brookes.

Cole, M. (1981). Preface. In J. V. Wertsch (Ed.), *The concept of activity in Soviet psychology* (pp. vii–x). New York: M. E. Sharpe.

Duncan, P. W. (2003, November). *What is the evidence for rehabilitation? How do we translate evidence into practice?* Presentation at the 13th Annual National Institute on Deafness and Other Communication Disorders (NIDCD)-Sponsored Research Symposium: Outcomes Research and Evidence-Based Practice, Chicago, IL.

Ehren, B. J. (2000). Maintaining a therapeutic focus and sharing responsibility for student success: Keys to in-classroom speech-language services. *Language, Speech, and Hearing Services in Schools, 31,* 219–229.

Englert, C. S. (1990). Unraveling the mysteries of writing through strategy instruction. In T. E. Scruggs & B. Y. L. Wong (Eds.), *Intervention research in learning disabilities* (pp. 186–223). New York: Springer-Verlag.

Englert, C. S. (1992). Writing instruction from a sociocultural perspective: The holistic, dialogic, and social enterprise of writing. *Journal of Learning Disabilities, 25*(3), 153–172.

Englert, C. S., Berry, R., & Dunsmore, K. (2001). A case study of the apprenticeship process: Another perspective on the apprentice and the scaffolding metaphor. *Journal of Learning Disabilities, 34,* 152–171.

Feuerstein, R. (1980). *Instrumental enrichment.* Baltimore: University Park Press.

Fey, M. E. (1986). *Language intervention with young children.* Boston: College-Hill.

Fey, M. E., Cleave, P. L., Long, S. H., & Hughes, D. L. (1993). Two approaches to the facilitation of grammar in children with language impairment: An experimental evaluation. *Journal of Speech and Hearing Research, 36,* 141–157.

Gillam, R. B. (1999). Computer-assisted language intervention using Fast ForWord. *Language, Speech, and Hearing Services in Schools, 30,* 363–370.

Gillam, R. B., Loeb, D. F., & Friel-Patti, S. (2001). Looking back: A summary of five exploratory studies of Fast ForWord. *American Journal of Speech-Language Pathology, 10,* 269–273.

Gillam, R. B., & Pearson, N. (2004). *Test of Narrative Language.* Austin, TX: Pro-Ed.

Girolametto, L., Pearce, P. S., & Weitzman, E. (1996). Interactive focused stimulation for toddlers with expressive vocabulary delays. *Journal of Speech and Hearing Research, 39,* 1263–1273.

Greenfield, P. M. (1984). A theory of the teacher in the learning activities of everyday life. In B. Rogoff & J. Lave (Eds.), *Everyday cognition: Its development in social context* (pp. 117–138). Cambridge, MA: Harvard University Press.

Harris-Schmidt, G., & McNamee, G. D. (1986). Children as authors and actors: Literacy development through 'basic activities.' *Child Language Teaching and Therapy, 2,* 63–73.

Isaacson, S. L. (1992). Volleyball and other analogies: A response to Englert. *Journal of Learning Disabilities, 25,* 173–177.

Johnston, J. (1985). Fit, focus, and functionality: An essay on early language intervention. *Child Language Teaching and Therapy, 1,* 125–134.

Kaiser, A. P., Yoder, P. J., & Keetz, A. (1992). Evaluating milieu teaching. In S. F. Warren & J. Reichel (Eds.), *Communication and language intervention series: Vol. 1. Causes and effects in communication and language intervention* (pp. 9–47). Baltimore: Brookes.

Kratcoski, A. M. (1998). Guidelines for using portfolios in assessment and evaluation. *Language, Speech, and Hearing Services in Schools, 29,* 3–10.

Larson, V. L., & McKinley, N. L. (2003). *Communication solutions for older students: Assessment and intervention strategies.* Greenville, SC: Thinking Publications.

Leontiev, A. N. (1981). The problem of activity in psychology. In J. V. Wertsch (Ed.), *The concept of activity in Soviet psychology* (pp. 37–71). New York: M. E. Sharpe.

Lidz, C. S. (1991). *Practitioner's guide to dynamic assessment.* New York: Guilford.

Lidz, C. S., & Peña, E. D. (1996). Dynamic assessment: The model, its relevance as a non-biased approach, and its application to Latino American preschool children. *Language, Speech, and Hearing Services in Schools, 27*(4), 367–372.

Manolson, A. (1983). *It takes two to talk—A Hanen early language parent guide book.* Toronto: Hanen Early Language Resource Centre.

Maslow, A. (1970). *Motivation and personality* (2nd ed.). New York: Harper and Row.

Merritt, D. D., & Culatta, B. (1998). *Language intervention in the classroom.* San Diego, CA: Singular.

Nelson, K. E. (1986). *Event knowledge, structure, and function in development.* Mahwah, NJ: Erlbaum.

Nelson, K. E., Camarata, S. M., Welsh, J., Butkovsky, L. & Camarata, M. N. (1996). Effects of imitative and conversational recasting treatment on the acquisition of grammar in children with specific language impairment and younger language-normal children. *Journal of Speech and Hearing Research, 39,* 850–859.

Nelson, N. W. (1989). Curriculum-based language assessment and intervention. *Language, Speech, and Hearing Services in Schools, 20,* 170–184.

Nelson, N. W. (1995). Scaffolding in the secondary schools: A tool for curriculum-based language intervention. In D. F. Tibbits (Ed.), *Language intervention beyond the primary grades* (pp. 375–420). Austin, TX: Pro-Ed.

Ninio, A., & Snow, C. (1996). *Pragmatic development.* Boulder, CO: Westview Press.

No Child Left Behind Act of 2001, 20 U.S.C. § 6311 *et seq.* (2002).

O'Shaughnessy, T. E., & Swanson, H. L. (2000). A comparison of two reading interventions for children with reading disabilities. *Journal of Learning Disabilities, 33,* 257–277.

Palincsar, A. S. (1986). The role of dialogue in providing scaffolded instruction. *Educational Psychologist, 21,* 73–98.

Palincsar, A. S. (1998). Keeping the metaphor of scaffolding fresh—A response to C. Addison Stone's "The metaphor of scaffolding: Its utility for the field of learning disabilities." *Journal of Learning Disabilities, 31,* 370–373.

Palincsar, A. S., & Brown, A. L. (1984). Reciprocal teaching of comprehension-fostering and comprehension-monitoring activities. *Cognition and Instruction, 1,* 117–175.

Peña, E. (1993). *Dynamic assessment: A nonbiased approach for assessing the language of young children.* Unpublished doctoral dissertation, Temple University, Philadelphia, PA.

Peña, E., Quinn, R., & Iglesias, A. (1992). The application of dynamic methods to language assessment: A nonbiased procedure. *The Journal of Special Education, 26,* 269–280.

Pretti-Frontczak, K., & Bricker, D. (2004). *An activity-based approach to early intervention* (3rd ed.). Baltimore: Brookes.

Rice, M. L. (1995). The rationale and operating principles for a language-focused curriculum for preschool children. In M. L. Rice & K. A. Wilcox (Eds.), *Building a language-focused curriculum for the preschool classroom: Vol. 1. A foundation for lifelong communication* (pp. 27–38). Baltimore: Brookes.

Rogoff, B. (1984). Introduction: Thinking and learning in social context. In B. Rogoff & J. Lave (Eds.), *Everyday cognition: Its development in social context* (pp. 1–8). Cambridge, MA: Harvard University Press.

Rogoff, B. (1990). *Apprenticeship in thinking: Cognitive development in social context.* New York: Oxford University Press.

Rogoff, B., & Gardner, W. (1984). Adult guidance of cognitive development. In B. Rogoff & J. Lave (Eds.), *Everyday cognition: Its development in social context* (pp. 95–116). Cambridge, MA: Harvard University Press.

Schneider, P., & Watkins, R. V. (1996). Applying Vygotskian developmental theory to language intervention. *Language, Speech, and Hearing Services in Schools, 27,* 157–170.

Scribner, S. (1984). Studying working intelligence. In B. Rogoff & J. Lave (Eds.), *Everyday cognition: Its development in social context* (pp. 9–40). Cambridge, MA: Harvard University Press.

Stone, C. A. (1998). The metaphor of scaffolding: Its utility for the field of learning disabilities. *Journal of Learning Disabilities, 31,* 344–364.

Strong, C. A., & North, K. H. (1996). *The magic of stories: Literature-based language intervention.* Greenville, SC: Super Duper Publications.

Tharp, R. G., & Gallimore, R. (1988). *Rousing minds to life: Teaching, learning, and schooling in social context.* New York: Cambridge University Press.

Torgesen, J. K., Alexander, A. W., Wagner, R. K., Rashotte, C. A., Voeller, K. K. S., & Conway, T. (2001). Intensive remedial instruction for children with severe reading disabilities: Immediate and long-term outcomes from two instructional approaches. *Journal of Learning Disabilities, 34,* 33–58.

Torgesen, J. K., Al Otaiba, S., & Grek, M. L. (2005). Assessment and instruction for phonemic awareness and word recognition skills. In H. W. Catts & A. G. Kamhi (Eds.), *Language and reading disabilities* (pp. 127–156). Boston: Allyn and Bacon.

Ukrainetz, T. A. (1998). Beyond Vygotsky: What Soviet activity theory offers naturalistic language intervention. *Journal of Speech-Language Pathology and Audiology, 22,* 122–133.

Ukrainetz, T. A. (2005). What to work on how?: An examination of the practice of school-age language intervention. *Contemporary Issues in Communication Sciences and Disorders, 32,* 108–119.

Ukrainetz, T. A., & Fresquez, E. F. (2003). What isn't language? A qualitative study of the role of the school speech-language pathologist. *Language, Speech, and Hearing Services in Schools, 34*, 284–298.

Ukrainetz, T. A., Harpell, S., Walsh, C., & Coyle, C. (2000). A preliminary investigation of dynamic assessment with Native American kindergartners. *Language, Speech, and Hearing Services in Schools, 31*, 142–153.

Vygotsky, L. (1978). *Mind in society: The development of higher psychological processes.* Cambridge, MA: Harvard University Press.

Wertsch, J. V. (1981). *The concept of activity in Soviet psychology.* New York: M.E. Sharpe.

Wertsch, J. V. (1984). The zone of proximal development: Some conceptual issues. In B. Rogoff & J. V. Wertsch (Eds.), *Children's learning in the "zone of proximal development"* (pp. 7–18). San Francisco: Jossey-Bass.

Wertsch, J. V., & Hickmann, M. (1987). Problem solving in social interaction: A micro-genetic analysis. In M. Hickmann (Ed.), *Social and functional approaches to language and thought* (pp. 251–266). New York: Academic Press.

Westby, C. (1997). There's more to passing than knowing the answers. *Language, Speech, and Hearing Services in Schools, 28*, 274–287.

Whitmire, K. (2002). The evolution of school-based speech-language services. *Communication Disorders Quarterly, 23*, 68–76.

Wood, D., Bruner, J. S., & Ross, G. (1976). The role of tutoring in problem solving. *Journal of Child Psychology and Psychiatry, 17*, 89–100.

Wyoming Department of Education. (2003). *Wyoming content and performance standards.* Author.

Yoder, P. J., Kaiser, A. P., Alpert, C., & Fischer, R. (1993). Following the child's lead when teaching nouns to preschoolers with mental retardation. *Journal of Speech and Hearing Research, 36*, 158–167.

Zinchenko, V. P., & Davydov, V. V. (1985). Foreword. In J. V. Wertsch (Ed.), *Vygotsky and the social formation of mind* (pp. vii–xi). Boston: Harvard University Press.

Chapter 2

Language Intervention through Literature-Based Units

Ronald B. Gillam and Teresa A. Ukrainetz

Introduction

This chapter describes a method of organizing contextualized skill language intervention in which intervention activities are organized around book reading and book discussion contexts. The procedures described are designed to be used with school-age students who have unusual difficulty learning and using language. This difficulty, which is referred to by a variety of terms including *language disorder, language-learning disability, specific-language impairment,* and *language-learning impairment,* often leads to serious social, academic, and vocational ramifications (Aram & Hall, 1989; Johnson et al., 1999; Snowling & Hulme, 1989; Stothard, Snowling, Bishop, Chipchase, & Kaplan, 1998). Our primary goal with literature-based language intervention is not to teach these students to read. Rather, our goal is to improve the many aspects of language (vocabulary knowledge, grammatical acceptability, grammatical complexity, pragmatic awareness, phonological awareness, conversation, and narration) that influence the ability to participate in, and profit from, instruction in general education classrooms in both oral and print modalities.

The first two sections of this chapter discuss the foundations and attributes of providing intervention organized within a literature-based unit. Then, the chapter presents the general sequence of activities in literature-based language intervention and an example of a unit based on a selection of children's literature.

Foundations for Literature-Based Language Intervention

Our approach to literature-based language intervention was initially influenced by the work of Carol Strong and Kelly Hoggan (Hoggan & Strong, 1994; Strong & Hoggan North, 1996), Lynn Rhodes and Curt Dudley-Marling (1988), and Jan Norris (Norris, 1989; Norris & Hoffman, 1993). Prior to this time, language remediation had often been delivered as discrete skill instruction with picture cards and games. Contrived paragraph-length passages from workbooks were the longest connected texts that were typically employed. However, these authors promoted the idea that language intervention could also occur within authentic literature contexts and meaningful activities. They provided ways of embedding language skills within thematic units and children's literature units. We have continued to develop these basic ideas—sometimes combining old and new—as we investigate ways of being therapeutic in functional contexts. The ideas we present in this chapter and elsewhere in this book are based on both our research and our clinical experiences.

The Need for Literature and Skills

One early study we conducted in this area was important in developing our thoughts on attending to skills within literature contexts (Gillam, McFadden, & van Kleeck, 1995). In this study, we evaluated the effects that literature-based intervention and skills-based intervention had on the development of narration. The sample size was small, but our findings were revealing. Eight students with language impairments between the ages of 9 and 12 years *(M =* 10;10) participated in the study. Four students had received all of their special education assistance in a combined speech-language/learning disabilities class-room that provided literature-based instruction in oral and written language for a period of two years. The focus in this classroom was on reading books and then using them to create and publish personal stories. The four other students in our study had received pull-out skills-based intervention from speech-language pathologists (SLPs) and learning disabilities specialists for an equivalent period. Their focus was on discrete skill drills that targeted vocabulary and sentence construction. The students in the two groups performed at similar levels on a variety of language, intelligence, reading, and writing tests.

After the second year of intervention, we compared the students' spoken and written narratives. One of the most interesting findings of this study was that there were clear differences in the relationships between language form and language content in the students' spoken and written narratives. The spoken and written narratives produced by the students who received skills-based instruction earned higher scores on measures of language form (mean length of utterance, percent of grammatically acceptable utterances, and number of conjunctions). The spoken narratives produced by students in the literature-based intervention group earned higher scores on measures of language content (propositions per utterance, number of episodes, and percent of embedded episodes) and on holistic judgments of story quality. There were no consistent differences in measures of language content for the students' written narratives.

These results were somewhat problematic for proponents of both skills-based and literature-based approaches to narrative intervention. The finding that the spoken narratives of students in the skills-based group received lower scores on the content measures than the narratives produced by students from the literature-based group suggests that an educational emphasis on subskills related to written language form may not be sufficient in and of itself to aid in developing narrative skills. Traditional didactic instruction that focuses on written language form seems to have very little to offer students in the way of helping create richer narratives in spoken or written modes. If the skills-based teachers had focused on language content to a greater extent, their students might have produced better-organized and more interesting stories.

The spoken and written narratives produced by students in the literature-based intervention group did not compare well with those of students in the skills-based group on language form measures of sentence length, grammatical acceptability, and use of conjunctions. In addition, there was a greater dissociation between spoken and written language forms for the students who received literature-based instruction. Clearly, students who received literature-based language intervention would have benefited from a greater instructional emphasis on language form.

We found that students' stories provide an interesting, meaningful, and linguistically complete means for demonstrating ways that concepts, vocabulary, and sentences weave together to create coherent, cohesive, and informative texts. Intervention that targets language comprehension and production in the context of listening to, reading, and talking about stories enhances the development of interpersonal communication and cognitive/academic communication in students with language impairments. The results of our first study revealed limitations in the way we were conducting literature-based intervention. Therefore, in our current approach we incorporate aspects of both the literature-based and skills-based approaches that were used in our preliminary study. The intervention activities in this revised approach are all related to the form and content of particular children's books (hence, the name literature-based), but we now include subactivities that encourage learners to focus on specific aspects of language form in pragmatically relevant ways. We also intentionally embed explicit attention to particular skills, with repeated opportunities for learning and systematic learning support.

Language and Language Disorders

Like the Committee on Language of the American Speech-Language-Hearing Association (ASHA, 1983), we view language as a dynamic system that involves the ability to integrate knowledge of phonology, morphology, syntax, semantics, and pragmatics to create sentences within conversational, narrative, and expository discourse contexts. Students with language impairments learn language more slowly than their typically developing peers for a variety of reasons, including slower information processing, inefficient attention, imprecise perception, and/or ineffective working memory functions (Gillam, Hoffman, Marler, & Wynn-Dancy, 2002). These problems result in less distinct mental representations of the language input these students receive. As a result, language learning requires more mental energy for students with language impairments, and their language usage is more variable. We expect deficits in multiple domains of language and we expect these domains to dynamically interact: when one domain is stressed, another will suffer. For example, a student with weak syntax will have difficulty with fluency and vocabulary choice while struggling to construct a complex sentence. As a result, we try to be aware of performance and demands across domains even when we are focusing on one area.

Literate Language

Language form and content can be placed on a continuum of formality. An oral conversation among friends about ongoing events would be at the informal end of the continuum. A written essay intended for an unfamiliar audience about the nature of the universe would be at the formal end of the continuum. Students must learn to deal with and acquire versions of the formal or literate end of the language continuum to participate more fully in classroom communication contexts and to acquire needed academic content and skills.

Literate language tends to be decontextualized, more abstract, and more formal than conversational language. It is also language that is more carefully crafted through repeated revisions, with attention to rhetoric as well as content. Literate language has many features with which students must become familiar. It is fluent and well-planned, with a minimum of fillers *(you know)* and vague words *(the thing there)*. Vocabulary choices within literate language tend to include diverse, abstract, multisyllabic, and sophisticated words (Nippold, 1998). The syntax of literate language is strikingly different from that of informal conversations (Scott, 1988), as illustrated by two versions of a story in Table 2.1 on page 64. Some examples of literate lexicon and syntax are:

- **Sentence conjoining** with conjunctions and adverbials, such as *however, consequently, as a result, nevertheless*

- **Sentence embedding,** especially objective relative clauses, such as *I want the book that is new.*

- **Elaborated noun phrases,** especially with postmodification, such as *The tall man with the great booming voice took control of the rowdy crowd.*

- **Expanded verb phrases** expressing subtleties of tense or aspect, such as *I would have preferred that he had left immediately.*

Table 2.1

Comparison of Conversational and Literate Storytelling

Conversational Language	Literate Language
Goldilocks walked down the road and she saw the bear's house.	A little girl named Goldilocks was walking down the road when she saw the house where the three bears lived.
She knocked on the door. Nobody answered, so she looked in.	After knocking loudly on the door a few times, she opened it up very quietly and peeked in.
She saw some bowls of soup on the table so she sat down to eat.	As she stepped into the kitchen, she noticed three hot steaming bowls of soup on the table. She was very hungry, so she went for the biggest bowl that belonged to the papa bear.

- **Mental and linguistic verbs,** such as *wonder, ponder, discuss, clarify*

- **Adverbs, adverbial phrases, and adverbial clauses,** particularly fronted forms, such as *Quickly and silently, he dropped into the tunnel.*

Attributes of Literature-Based Language Intervention

Functional Activities

In literature-based language intervention, the aim is to teach students the literate language required for the classroom. This intervention approach is based on narrative and book discussion. Narrative is the chosen discourse form for several reasons.

Narrative is the earliest emerging monologic discourse form; it is the first language form that requires the speaker to produce an extended monologue rather than engage in an interactive dialogue. Language can occur in oral or literate styles (see Table 2.2). Narrative shares elements of both styles and can thus serve as a bridge from the oral, face-to-face language of the home to the logical, scientific thought presented in the decontextualized and abstract language of school (Bruner, 1986; Westby, 1985). The monologic nature of narrative demands that the narrator consider audience perspective without the ongoing feedback of conversation. Narrative involves more distancing and generalizing from reality than conversational language, while retaining the familiarity of event-retelling content. Learning to write and to think involves moving from the on-line commentary of dramatic play; to the after-the-event narrative; and then to the generalization, inference, and objectivity of the scientific report (Moffett, 1968). We focus on that middle point of the discourse spectrum, listening to and telling stories.

We work on telling stories within a book discussion format. Book discussions are purposeful communication events that require literate language. They are also prevalent in classrooms. To make our intervention as functional and relevant to classroom communication as possible, we decided to create focused language-learning activities that occur as clinician and students read and discuss children's literature. In contrast to the classroom, we focus on individual

Table 2.2

Features of Oral and Literate Styles of Language

Oral Style	Literate Style
Dialogic	Monologic
Known Audience	Presumed Audience
Casual	Formal
Gestures and Intonation	Punctuation
Exophoric	Endophoric
Implicit	Explicit
Contextualized	Decontextualized
Episodic and Specific	Generalized and Abstract

students' needs in a primarily oral context. We systematically target specific language skills such as vocabulary development or sentence complexity, scaffolded in repeated opportunities through planned oral interactions. But, like the classroom, we embed those skills within interesting literature-based activities that have value for their own sake and that require the integration of multiple language skills.

Thematic Unity

Our literature-based intervention approach thematically links a series of activities occurring across multiple sessions to an initial storybook and a final story creation. The number of activities and sessions may vary—and there will be a variety of skills addressed—but there is some conceptual or purposeful link among a set of activities. For example, the series of activities we present in the example later in the chapter (see pages 71–91) are united through each being related to an aspect of the *Mushroom in the Rain* story (Ginsburg, 1974). Rather than each session existing as an isolated event, a series of sessions is united by a theme or purpose. Table 2.3 describes how this organization provides benefits related to planning time, structure, coherence, extended learning, and activity mix.

Whole-Part-Whole

A whole-part-whole structure works well for the therapeutic setting. Beginning with the whole provides the larger, meaningful, and rich context from which to draw other activities. The whole involves a complete written or oral discourse unit. In our version of literature-based intervention, we start with sharing a piece of children's literature and we end by returning to the book to build a parallel story. We provide some prestory warm-up activities, but the book is a focal point. It serves as a model and source early on, and as a culminating integration of skills at the end.

After the initial whole activity, any number of focused skill activities can occur. We usually engage students in two or three different or repeated activities related to each goal. For the sake of simplicity and length, we limited the number of example activities for each of the language targets. Specific activities are selected that provide repeated opportunities to work on specific objectives. We also select activities with an eye toward their contribution to the larger unit purpose. Students could compose a story, identify

Table 2.3   **Benefits of Thematic Intervention Units**

Benefit	Explanation
Saves Planning Time	It is easier to plan a single unit than a dozen separate activities. The structure of a unit—particularly a unit that is leading up to a culminating product—makes activity selection easier. Once there is a unit structure that works, skills, content, activities, and difficulty levels can be easily modified.
Provides Structure	The unit provides predictability for the student as well as the clinician. Complex activities can have elements of the familiar, providing contextual—and even scripted—supports for a student's learning.
Builds Coherence	Learning is facilitated when an item to be learned fits into a larger, meaningful whole. Ten thematically—or semantically—linked words will be learned more easily, with greater depth of meaning, than 10 assorted words.
Allows for Extended Learning	A larger purposeful whole can be erected over multiple short sessions, which allows for activities that cannot fit within a single session, such as composing a written narrative or reading a chapter book.
Provides Activity Mix	In addition to purposeful activities where multiple skills are integrated, purposeful activities with single foci and even discrete skill activities can be employed, while retaining the coherence of the whole.

expanded noun phrases in a magazine article, or select words from a student's New Word Book (i.e., personal dictionary) to use in a story. The advantage of brief focused skill activities, even if somewhat contrived, is that they provide the opportunity for massed practice without the distraction or complication of the larger context. Like basketball players doing dribbling drills and wind sprints between practice games, this focused time to develop skills is a small, but important aspect of intervention units (Isaacson, 1992).

Therapeutic Interactions

Many of the activities that we discuss in this chapter are similar to the kinds of literacy activities that occur routinely in regular classrooms. That adds to the functionality of our approach. But, our intervention activities differ from everyday classroom experiences because they employ the therapeutic principles outlined in Chapter 1. We believe that *how* language intervention is carried out is just as important as *what* is done. To be therapeutic, our language intervention experiences are designed to elicit and support specific language targets; to provide multiple opportunities for repetition and variation of the targets; to provide guided transfer or scaffolding that fosters independence; and to promote the metacognitive awareness needed to automatize strategies and behaviors into skills and processes. We try to ensure that the RISE elements (repeated opportunities, intensively delivered, with systematic support on explicit skill targets) are consistently provided.

There are many ways of scaffolding learning in purposeful contexts. Box 2.1 presents literature-based examples of facilitations. *Linguistic facilitations* are adult responses that are contingent—or directly related—to the content or form of the student's prior utterance. *Response facilitations* provide support or structure to encourage student responses. *Regulatory facilitations* raise students' awareness of the targeted language skill as the purpose for completing the activity. Regulatory facilitations are oriented toward helping students know what is important in the activity, to make links from old to new learning, to inhibit impulsive responding, to evaluate their own performance, and to apply the new learning in other situations. We recommend that 40 to 60 percent of the utterances directed to students employ facilitation devices.

Intervention Intensity

We believe that one of the primary problems with the way language intervention is currently conducted in schools is that it is not intensive enough. Most students receive services from school SLPs twice each week for 30-minute sessions. The sessions are often conducted in groups that may be as large as six to eight students. Learning requires many repeated opportunities, both within an activity and across activities. For students with language-learning impairments, learning is particularly inefficient and effortful. These students require more time on task and more learning support than that provided in the regular classroom. When intervention occurs for so little time in a week and attention must be distributed over many students, it is doubtful that gains can be made relative to those obtained in the regular classroom without special support.

Facilitation Devices Embedded
Box 2.1
in Oral Interactions around Storybooks

Linguistic Facilitations

1. **Syntactic Expansion**—A contingent verbal response that makes the student's utterance grammatical.

   Student: That bird gonna ask him come in.
   Adult: Yes, the bird is gonna ask him to come in.

2. **Semantic Expansion**—A contingent verbal response that adds new, relevant information to the student's utterance (also called an *extension*).

   Student: Then him fell all over that.
   Adult: Yea, the kangaroo fell into the bear's swimming pool.

3. **Recast**—A contingent verbal response that retains the semantic information from the student's previous utterance but alters the syntactic structure.

   Student: That board picture was from Jason.
   Adult: Yea, Jason drew that picture on the board.

4. **Prompt**—A comment or question that induces the student to complete a thought or to change an ungrammatical utterance.

   Student: Hims going to run back home.
   Adult: Who's going to run back home?
   Student: He's going to run back home.

5. **Elaboration Question**—A question that induces the student to expand on what he or she has said.

   Student: He was scared of that dinosaur.
   Adult: Why was he scared?
   Student: He thought the dinosaur might chase him and bite him.

6. **Vertical Structure**—The clinician asks a question to obtain additional information; the student answers it; then the clinician puts the original utterance and the response to the question together to form a more complex utterance.

   Student: That moose holding up a hammer.
   Adult: What would happen if he dropped it now?

Continued on next page

Box 2.1—*Continued*

Student: It would hit his toe.

Adult: If the moose dropped the hammer, it would hit his toe.

Response Facilitations

1. **Model**—The clinician models the target word or form.

    Adult: Little Grunt is very sad because he doesn't think he'll ever see his dinosaur again.

2. **Question to Elicit a New Utterance**—The clinician asks a question or makes a statement designed to elicit the target structure.

    Adult: [points to a picture] Tell me how each person in the Grunt family feels about what the chief said and why each person feels that way.

3. **Prompt**—The clinician pauses, repeats the student's utterance, or provides a partial response to encourage the student to use the target structure.

    Adult: Little Grunt is very sad....

Regulatory Facilitations

1. **State the Goal or Target**—The clinician tells the student what they will be working on.

    Adult: We're going to look at the book again, and we're going to focus on talking about how the characters feel about what happens.

2. **Compare or Contrast**—The clinician highlights the similarities or differences between related words or grammatical structures.

    Adult: Little Grunt is sad about having to tell his dinosaur to go away. But Chief Rockhead Grunt is happy that the dinosaur is leaving because he was too big to live in the cave.

3. **Informative Feedback**—The clinician tells the student whether something he said was right or wrong and explains why.

    Student: Everyone was happy that the dinosaur left.

    Adult: Not Little Grunt. Little Grunt was sad when the dinosaur left because the dinosaur was his pet.

Recent intervention research with students who have learning disabilities has shown that to be effective, intervention needs to be intensive. For example, Torgesen (2001) found that students with severe learning disabilities who received hour-long individual intervention twice each day for eight weeks moved into the average range for reading accuracy and comprehension, with smaller gains in reading rate. To make this kind of academically significant change in language, we recommend providing literature-based language intervention to small groups (two to four students) in daily sessions that are at least one hour in length. Using block-scheduling practices, daily sessions can be arranged to last for four- to eight-week cycles. In this way, there is much greater learning continuity, motivation is kept high, reasonable numbers of students are supported, and students' classroom schedules are disrupted for shorter periods of time.

A Literature-Based Language Intervention Unit

The basic sequence in our current iteration of literature-based language intervention is set out in Box 2.2 on page 72. It moves from prestory knowledge activation, to shared reading of the story, to post-story comprehension and focused skill activities, then finally returns to create a parallel story that integrates the skills introduced previously. Storybooks, language skill targets, and focused activities vary within this framework. Almost any language objective can be taught within literature-based language intervention. In the section that follows, we discuss each step in the process with an example activity and clinician-student interaction. The activities are based on the children's book, *Mushroom in the Rain* (Ginsburg, 1974).

Our approach to literature-based intervention has evolved considerably over the past 10 years. What hasn't changed about our approach is our focus on real talk about meaningful texts, but we now put greater emphasis on therapeutic interactions within well-specified, explicit, and carefully designed activities that target specific content-form interactions. We select a unifying theme for each unit that arises out of the piece of literature chosen. By having a single theme across multiple activities, we provide repeated opportunities for learning concepts and vocabulary. This results in continuity of learning and depth of understanding. In addition, we provide purposeful activities to open and close each literature-based unit. This allows the opportunity to orchestrate all the objectives addressed in an integrated manner. Finally, we work directly

Sequence of Literature-Based Language Intervention Activities

Box 2.2

A. Prestory Knowledge Activation

1. Graphic Organizer

2. Prestory Discussion

   a) Use linguistic facilitations (e.g., semantic expansion) to make the student's language more complete and complex.

   b) Discuss the pictures on every page, using questions to help guide the student through the main story line.

B. Shared Reading of the Entire Story

Read the book aloud, stopping occasionally to comment or discuss concepts, sentence structures, or plot elements.

C. Post-Story Comprehension Discussion

Use general comprehension and story grammar questions.

1. Who are the most important characters in this story?
2. What do we know about them?
3. Describe what they look like, their personalities, their values, etc.
4. How do we know that?
5. What did (name of main character) do?
6. Why did he/she do that?
7. What happened after he/she (name the main activity)?
8. What was the main problem in the story?
9. How was the problem solved?
10. What is the main point of this story?

D. Focused Skill Activities

1. Semantic Activities

   a) Select vocabulary from the story and/or related vocabulary.

   b) Make a New Word Book that lists words from the story.

   c) Define and discuss the words in student-friendly language.

   d) Create a wall chart and encourage use of the target words in other activities.

Box 2.2—*Continued*

2. Syntax Activities

    a) Select a sentence pattern that is repeated throughout the book.

    b) Read the sentences with the student.

    c) Place the noun and verb phrases onto sentence strips that students can manipulate.

    d) Have students draw pictographs to represent the sentences.

    e) Match the sentence strips to the sentences.

    f) Retell the story with an added focus on using the target sentence pattern.

3. Narrative Activities

    a) Retell through pictography.

    b) Create a retold book.

    c) Create a parallel story.

4. Pragmatics Activities

    a) Select a pragmatic ability represented within the story (e.g., politeness, requesting, topic shifting, restating, justifying).

    b) Discuss how the characters used language to handle a situation in the story.

    c) Create parallel situations.

    d) Discuss how language could be used in these situations.

    e) Act out the situations.

    f) Apply one of the created situations and the pragmatic usage in the parallel stories.

E. Book as Model for Parallel Story

1. Discuss the original graphic organizer and revise it if necessary.

2. Review the vocabulary in the student's New Word Book.

    a) Find the target vocabulary in the original book.

    b) Read the sentences containing the target vocabulary.

    c) Create new parallel sentences containing the vocabulary.

3. Review the retold story book.

4. Create another parallel story or revise the earlier ones.

5. Share the parallel stories and review the target skills learned.

and explicitly on intervention objectives: telling the students what they are learning, encouraging reflections on their own learning, providing repeated opportunities for learning and practice, and systematically moving the student toward greater independence in both the skills required and the activities in which they occur. The remainder of this chapter provides a detailed example of intervention activities and the clinician's scaffolding talk (i.e., facilitations) within those activities.

Book Selection

This approach to intervention is organized around children's literature. The SLP selects a book that is to be read aloud, discussed, and built upon. Many children's books are suitable for language intervention because they are rich in language, but some provide more repeated opportunities or clearer models for skills than others. Clinicians should look for books that have multiple demonstrations of vocabulary, sentence structures, and/or text structures that are appropriate language targets for the students with whom they work. We advise clinicians to select books that can be read aloud in 10 minutes or less. The text can be simplified or shortened, but the changes should be documented so that the same structures and vocabulary are presented during repeated readings.

Mushroom in the Rain is a story about an ant who seeks shelter from a driving rainstorm. He sees a mushroom in a clearing, and he squeezes under it. As the rain continues, a butterfly, a mouse, a bird, and a rabbit ask if they can come in under the mushroom with the ant. At first, the ant tells each animal there is no more room. After they ask a second time, the ant agrees to let each one come in to escape the rain. When the rain stops, the ant wonders how they could all fit under the mushroom when there was barely enough room for him in the beginning. A frog asks the ant, "Don't you know what happens to a mushroom when it rains?" The ant thinks about it for a while, and then concludes that mushrooms grow in the rain.

This story is composed of a series of coordinated episodes in which animals seek shelter during a rainstorm. All but one of the episodes contains the same initiating event (getting wet in the rain), attempt (requesting to come in under the mushroom), complication (the ant tells them there is not enough room), secondary attempt (requesting that the animals that are already under the mushroom squeeze together), and consequence (the request is granted). There is one episode in which the animals hide a rabbit that is being chased by a fox. This book is particularly good for teaching students about basic episodes with the pattern of same initiating event, similar attempts, and similar consequences. It can also be used to show how to embed multiple associated episodes within a story. Each episode provides opportunities for the knowledge and skills we address: relative size of forest animals and plants (knowledge), objective relative clauses (syntax), inferential comprehension (text comprehension), "wet" words and similes (vocabulary), clausal complements through dialogue (syntax), character motivations (narrative), and social access (pragmatics).

Prestory Knowledge Activation

Graphic Organizers

Students with language impairments often have difficulty comprehending stories that they read or that are read to them (Bishop, 1997; Bishop & Adams, 1992; Boudreau & Hedberg, 1999; Ellis Weismer, 1985; Evans, 2002; Montgomery, 2002; Paul & Cohen, 1985). Discussing information related to the story helps to activate students' existing knowledge on the topic so new information can be incorporated into an existing schema. A number of studies have shown that creating and discussing visual and spatial displays that represent key concepts, text content, and/or text structure is effective in improving reading comprehension in students with learning disabilities (Kim, Vaughn, Wanzek, & Wei, 2004).

We employ *graphic organizers* in a variety of formats to provide students with a visual representation of the relationships between key ideas in a story and to highlight important vocabulary (for example, see Bos & Anders, 1990, 1992). Before reading the book, the clinician and students work together on the first day of intervention to create a *semantic map,* which is a type of graphic organizer that represents the relationships between concepts and vocabulary that are critical for understanding the story. The semantic map, along with the story questions and picture descriptions that follow its development, are intended to activate students' prior knowledge and start them thinking about what will occur. Particular concepts or vocabulary words may be introduced at this point. Those words will be emphasized repeatedly throughout the story reading and subsequent activities.

The semantic map shown in Figure 2.1 on page 76 introduces important concepts for understanding *Mushroom in the Rain.* To comprehend this story, students need to understand the spatial relationships between the size of a plant and the size of animals that seek shelter under it. The clinician begins by telling students that they will be reading a book about animals in a forest. Then the word *forest* is written where all can see it. The SLP can ask students what they might find in a forest. When students suggest that forests contain plants and animals, the clinician says something like, "Yes, forests have plants and animals. Plants can be big or small, and animals can be big or small." The clinician then writes the words *big* and *small* on the semantic map and asks, "Can you think of a big plant that lives in the forest?" The relative size of the plant that the student named is discussed and written on the board. Then the clinician asks questions to elicit other examples of big and little plants and animals.

We have found that semantic maps provide a good context for working on complex sentence structure. The map in Figure 2.1 is also useful for demonstrating and eliciting objective relative clauses. As students suggest words to add to the organizer, the clinician demonstrates a sentence structure that expresses the relationships. For example, the relative clause in "Mushrooms are small plants that live in the forest" expresses the critical relationships between the concepts in the *Mushroom in the Rain* organizer. The following clinical sample demonstrates how this process worked with a student named Chris.

Figure 2.1   **Semantic Map for *Mushroom in the Rain***

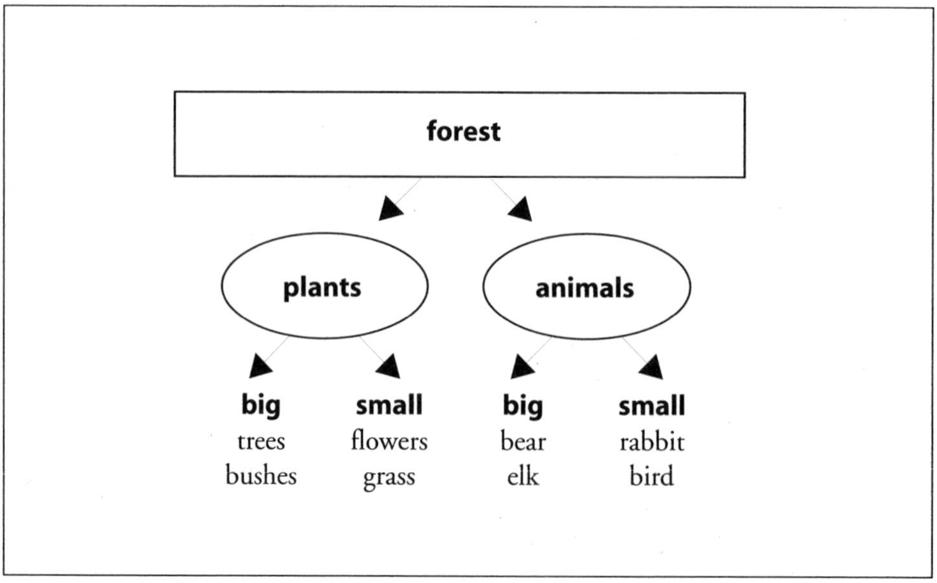

SLP: Can you think of a big plant that lives in the forest?

Chris: A tree?

SLP: [writes *tree* on a dry-erase board under **plants/big**] Yes, a **tree** is a **big plant** that lives in the **forest**. [said while pointing to each of the bold words on the dry-erase board] Can you think of a small plant that lives in the forest?

Chris: Well, grass is pretty small.

SLP: [writes *grass* under **plants/small**] Yes, **grass** is a **small plant** that lives in the **forest**. What are we saying about trees?

Chris: Trees are big. They're plants. And they live in the forest.

SLP: Yes, **trees** are **big plants** that live in the **forest.** [recast of the student's utterance into an objective relative clause while pointing to the words written on the semantic map] Look how we made those sentences. [reread each sentence and underline the two descriptive elements] We told two things—size and place—about each plant in one sentence. We will practice making more sentences like that later on.

After the clinicians and students work together to complete the semantic map, clinicians ask the students to review the concepts again. Students talk through the vocabulary that they have added to the organizer, and clinicians respond to their utterances using contingent facilitative devices. The semantic map provides visual support for representing the relationships between concepts, for demonstrating a target sentence structure, and for repeatedly eliciting the target sentence structure from students. Chris was producing simple sentences and some coordinating conjunctions at the beginning of the graphic organizer activity. By the end of the activity, he was producing objective relative clauses that were consistent with the clinician's models. This is a good example of embedding a form goal within a functional activity that was designed to promote story comprehension. For enduring learning to occur, this will have to be followed up by additional opportunities in other activities to create relative clauses for describing.

Prestory Discussion

After creating the graphic organizer, the clinician asks students questions that are designed to tie the concepts in the graphic organizer directly to the story. In the case of *Mushroom in the Rain,* the semantic map addressed forest animals and their relative sizes. So the prestory questions can follow up on that, as in the following:

1. *Could a bear go under a tree to get out of the rain?*
2. *Could a bear go under a flower to get out of the rain?*
3. *Could a rabbit go under a flower to get out of the rain?*
4. *What animal could go under a flower to get out of the rain?*

The questions lead to further discussion about relative sizes of animals and where certain animals could go to escape the rain. The discussion can also stimulate general knowledge, as in the following example, which ends by bringing the conversation back to animals hiding under mushrooms:

1. *How does rain help plants?*

2. *Have you ever eaten a mushroom?*

3. *What do mushrooms look like?*

4. *Can you think of any animals that might be able to crawl in under a mushroom?*

As part of the prestory discussion, the clinician and students step away from the printed text and create their own oral descriptions to match the illustrations in a book. This can occur for the entire story as a creative retelling or it can be limited to a few pictures. This is an excellent communicative context for facilitating language development through the use of linguistic facilitations from Box 2.1. In the following example, the clinician focuses on relative clauses again. You'll see that the clinician uses a facilitation device after every student utterance, and that most of the facilitation devices highlight relative clauses. Notice also that the student's utterances get longer and he reaches the point at which he is producing his own relative clauses.

SLP: Now we're going to look at the pictures and talk about them. [shows the first picture] What's happening here? *(question to elicit a new utterance)*

Student: A ant is crawling under the mushroom.

SLP: Where is the mushroom? *(first part of a vertical structure)*

Student: Out in the clearing.

SLP: Yes, the ant is crawling under the mushroom that is out in the clearing. *(completion of the vertical structure)* Tell me about this picture. *(prompt)*

Student: The ant's looking out from under the mushroom.

SLP:	The ant's looking out from under the mushroom that is in the clearing. *(syntactic and semantic expansion)* Tell me about the butterfly.
Student:	The butterfly is talking to the ant that's under there.
SLP:	The butterfly is talking to the ant that is under the mushroom. *(semantic expansion)*
Student:	Then that ant that's under there lets the butterfly in.
SLP:	I'll bet the butterfly thanked the ant that was under the mushroom. *(model)*

Shared Reading and Post-Story Comprehension Discussion

The next step in the sequence is reading the book. This is the heart of the intervention and should be engaging and meaningful to the students. We encourage clinicians to pause occasionally while reading aloud to check for comprehension and to talk about the book's content. Students' individual interests and spontaneous comments are linked back to the book with brief comments and explanations (e.g., student: *I have mushrooms in my yard!* SLP: *Yes, mushrooms grow in yards and forests when it rains. Sometimes they can appear overnight).* There is no single skill focus at this point; so as long as the clinician maintains the story flow, brief comments can go in many directions.

After reading the book, the clinician guides a discussion by asking a series of comprehension questions. The questions may relate to literal and inferential comprehension, or they may focus on story grammar components such as setting, problem, internal response, attempt, and resolution. As in all our activities, clinicians should respond to approximately half of the students' utterances with the facilitation devices detailed earlier. The clinician and students may return to the book to reread sections or seek answers. The focus is not on testing the students or obtaining a precise number of correct answers. Rather, the clinician focuses on helping the students understand the story and concepts presented.

Students may not know the answer to some of the clinician's questions. When this happens, the clinician should scaffold the student's answer with questions that become more specific when the student has difficulty answering them, and with increased use of prompts and cues. The following interaction between Chris and his clinician demonstrates a clinician scaffolding to help Chris with an inference. The clinician opened by talking about how people or animals get along, sometimes helping and sometimes hurting each other. The clinician then asks an inferential question about the ant's personality that Chris answers incorrectly. Chris says the ant in the story is mean, but the ant is really quite nice because he lets the other animals come in under the mushroom with him. The discourse sample shows how the clinician provides various levels of support to lead Chris to an accurate answer. Notice that the clinician's questions narrow as Chris continues to answer them incorrectly. Also, notice how the clinician uses the pictures in the book to support the student's answers to the questions. At the same time, the clinician uses linguistic facilitations to foster the development of more complex form-content interactions.

SLP: Tell me what we know about the ant. *(prompt)*

Chris: The ant was soaking wet.

SLP: Yes sir, we know the ant was wet. *(recast of Chris' simple sentence into a clausal complement)* What else do we know about the ant? *(broad question)*

Chris: [hesitates]

SLP: Think about how the ant treated the other animals. *(prompt)*

Chris: Mad. Mean?

SLP: Was he mean? How was he mean? *(narrower question)*

Chris: Cause just a little space for him, so um…

SLP: There was just a little space for the ant under the mushroom, so … *(semantic and syntactic expansion plus a prompt)*

Chris: [no response]

SLP: Does he share his space with any of the other animals? *(narrows the focus with an elaboration question)*

Chris: No.

SLP: He didn't? [pointing to the picture] It looks to me like all the animals are in under the mushroom. *(narrows the focus)*

Chris: But they're not, he didn't, not all of them are there.

SLP: They're not? Let's see. [turns back to the beginning of the book] Look, first the ant is in under the mushroom all by himself. Then what happens? *(broadens the focus with an elaboration question)*

Chris: A butterfly came.

SLP: A butterfly came in. *(syntactic expansion)* Remember he said, "Cousin ant, I am so wet I cannot fly. Please move over so that I can come in." What happened then? *(elaboration question)*

Chris: They, the ant pushed him in there.

SLP: The ant moved over and made room for the butterfly. *(semantic and syntactic expansion)*

Chris: [turns the page] Then the mouse…[hesitates]

SLP: Did they make room for the mouse? *(elaboration question)*

Chris: Yes, and the bird, too. You said they had all of them in there, but we're missing one.

SLP: Which one?

Chris: [turns the page] The rabbit.

SLP: Did they make room for the rabbit?

Chris: [turns the page and looks at the picture] Yes.

SLP: You've just said that the ant made room for the butterfly, the bird, the mouse, and the rabbit. Do you still think the ant was mean? *(narrow elaboration question)*

Chris: No, he was pretty nice.

SLP: How do you know that? *(beginning of vertical structure)*

Chris: 'Cause he made room for all of them.

SLP: I agree. We know the ant was pretty nice because he made room under the mushroom for all the other animals. *(end of vertical structure)*

Focused Skill Activities

Following the book-reading and book-discussion phases of literature-based language intervention, the clinician presents a variety of thematically related activities within each of three intervention domains: semantics, syntax, and narration. Within each of these domains, the specific skills addressed will depend on the needs of the students involved. If the instruction occurs in groups, scaffolding support and performance expectations should be individualized to each student as much as possible. A key element is that school-age students should know what they are learning beyond the activity in which it is embedded. When asked what they are doing with the SLP, the answer should not be "reading a book," or "drawing pictures." Rather, students should be able to provide answers such as, "telling what happened in order," "stopping to plan before I talk," "using complete sentences," or "using more describing words."

Semantic Activities

The focused skill phase of the literature-based language intervention cycle begins with a semantic activity in which students add vocabulary to their New Word Book (i.e., personal dictionary). Each student has a book of new words they collect from the stories. When we're working with a group of students, all the students in the group have the same target words. We try to target 8 to 12 words that are important for understanding the story, that appear on multiple pages, and that we have not heard the students say. Using practices that have been shown to be effective in vocabulary intervention research (Beck, McKeown, & Kucan, 2003; Coyne, Simmons, Kame'enui, & Stoolmiller, 2004; Jitendra, Edwards, Sacks, & Jacobson, 2004), clinicians and students discuss the meanings of the target words from the story, write the words in their vocabulary books, and create sentences like the ones in the book in which the words occur. During discussions, we also add target words to a wall chart for quick, ongoing reference.

Additional vocabulary activities teach students to think about words and their relationships. Depending on the students' level of ability, we engage them in word-learning tasks that relate to definitions, associations/categorizations, synonyms/antonyms, semantic absurdities, and multiple meanings. For example, in *Mushroom in the Rain,* we will often work on an activity that concerns different ways of saying the same thing. In the book, the author uses such expressions as "drenched to the bone," and "my wings are dripping" to explain that the animals are wet. The clinician makes a list of expressions for saying that you are cold, tired, thirsty, or hungry based on the students' experiences or on examples from other stories that we provide. Then the clinician creates mini-episodes, like the ones in *Mushroom in the Rain,* in which students practice using the expressions from the brainstorming activity. Clinicians are encouraged to use a high percentage of semantic expansions in their responses to students' utterances.

Syntax Activities

After working on an activity that focuses on vocabulary development, the next step is a syntax activity that targets complex sentences. Keeping with the literature-based context, a sentence pattern is selected that is repeated throughout the book. The object relative clause structure could be repeated here for additional learning opportunities. For another possibility, we often talk about character dialogue, which overlaps with the social cooperation examined in the earlier inferential comprehension section and the upcoming pragmatics section. Character dialogue is usually expressed with a clausal complement. In a clausal complement, the object of the verb takes the form of an entire clause. In the sentence, *The ant said, "But there is no room here"* the clause *but there is no room here* complements the main verb, *said.*

The clinician puts a few examples of character dialogue on an overhead or a dry-erase board, and reviews the examples with the students. Then each student is asked to create some dialogue that is consistent with the dialogue in the story. For example, the clinician might ask, *Can you think of something that the mouse said? Remember to start with, "The mouse said..."*. The clinician works through the characters in the book, creating sentences that each one may have said and using a facilitation device from Box 2.1 on page 69 for each student utterance.

Next, we talk about how characters might ask questions, changing the initial verb from *said* or *told* to *asked* or *begged.* The clinician might say something like, *Sometimes characters ask questions. The narrator might say, "The butterfly asked, Can I come in under the mushroom with you?"* Then, we make up questions that each of the characters might ask. Again, the clinician uses facilitation devices to help shape complete and complex utterances that the SLP has written down.

The next step in the syntax activity is to write the sentences onto sentence strips that students can manipulate. We also ask students to draw quick pictographs (see the next section) that represent the sentences. We usually use 3 × 5 inch index cards for this. There are a variety of language intervention activities that make use of the sentence strips and the accompanying pictographs. For example, the clinician can cut the sentence strips into clauses *(The butterfly said, the ant said, the mouse said),* then show the main clause and the accompanying pictograph. The clinician asks the student to say the entire sentence, including the main clause and the clausal complement. The clinician should use expansions, vertical structures, and other facilitation devices in response to at least 50 percent of the students' utterances. In a group variant of this activity, every student gets a sentence strip. When we show a pictograph, the students all say the sentence that goes with it. The two students holding the main clause and the clausal complement put them on the table. Then everyone "reads" the sentence.

Any game that clinicians can think of that elicits clausal complements from students will work. The specific activity is not nearly as important as the level of engagement from the students and the clinician's use of facilitative devices in response to at least half of the students' utterances. In subsequent activities, further opportunities for learning are provided when the clinician calls students' attention to the target sentence structure (clausal complements for character dialogue in this case) while retelling the story or creating a parallel story.

Narrative Activities

Next, the students retell the story. Students with language impairments often have difficulties retelling stories (Botting, Faragher, Simkin, Knox, & Conti-Ramsden, 2001; Fazio, Naremore, & Connell, 1996; Gillam & Carlile, 1997; Schneider, 1996; Wright & Newhoff, 2001). For story retelling, we use a modification of the pictography approach presented in Ukrainetz (1998) and summarized in Chapter 5 of this book. Narration is a complex activity, with many potential areas for breakdown. The focus of this narrative activity should be on a particular aspect of narration, such as sequencing events, providing complete episodes, or detailing attempts to solve a problem. In this example, the clinician facilitations focus on character motivations within episodes.

We begin by printing out blank handouts with six small boxes on each page. (These can be made from a Microsoft PowerPoint® template or with the Microsoft Word® textbox tool.) The boxes limit the size of the pictographs. The clinician and the student each take a handout with six blank boxes. They discuss what content needs to be illustrated in each pictograph and how it can be illustrated quickly. The clinician models the first few pictographs, and the student follows. After each picture is finished, the clinician models how to narrate that picture, and the student follows. The student should accept greater amounts of responsibility for the pictographs as the activity progresses, until he or she is modeling the pictograph and the narration for the clinician. Figure 2.2 on page 87 shows the pictography used during the following example of a retelling activity.

SLP: Now we're going to make our own *Mushroom in the Rain* book. We're going to draw some pictures to help us remember the story. This sheet of paper has blank boxes in it, and we'll draw our pictures in these boxes. We're going to draw FAST pictures. They won't be fancy. They're just there to help us remember the story. How are we going to draw our pictures?

Student:	Really fast?
SLP:	Yes, we're going to draw our pictures as fast as we can. Let's start. What's the first thing that happens in this story?
Student:	The ant is getting wet.
SLP:	So let's draw an ant real fast in this first box. Watch me. [clinician draws an ant] Is that a good picture of an ant?
Student:	No.
SLP:	But I drew it real fast and I can remember it's an ant. Now you draw an ant like mine, real fast.
Student:	[draws an ant but starts to fill in details]
SLP:	Oh wait, are we making fancy pictures?
Student:	No.
SLP:	Right. The pictures only have to be good enough so that we remember what they're about. We're drawing them as fast as we can. How did the ant get wet?
Student:	In the rain.
SLP:	The ant got wet because it was raining. I'm going to draw rain real fast. [clinician draws a series of straight lines] Okay, you do that even faster than I did it.
Student:	[draws the rain very quickly]
SLP:	Great! Now, what did the ant do?
Student:	He got under a mushroom.
SLP:	Why? *(beginning of a vertical structure)*
Student:	'Cause he was wet.
SLP:	Yes, the ant got under a mushroom because he was wet. *(completion of the vertical structure)* So, what do we need to draw next?
Student:	A mushroom.
SLP:	Right. Watch me draw a mushroom super fast. [draws a mushroom] Now you do it.
Student:	[draws the mushroom just as fast as the clinician]

SLP: Okay, let's practice talking about our pictures. Here's mine. An ant is out in the rain and he's really wet. He wants to get out of the rain. He sees a mushroom, so he squeezes in under it. *(model)* Now you tell me about your picture.

Student: A ant is in the rain. He's wet so he get in under the mushroom.

SLP: He's wet so he gets in under the mushroom. *(syntactic expansion)* Okay, let's go on. What happens next in the story?

Student: A butterfly comes up.

SLP: What's the butterfly say?

Student: Ant, I want to come in there 'cause I'm wet.

SLP: Exactly! He asks, "Cousin ant, can I come under the mushroom to get out of the rain?" *(recast)* What does the ant say?

Student: "No, you can't." Then he says, "Yes, you can."

SLP: Right again. The ant says, "There isn't enough room under here." Then the butterfly asks again, and the ant says, "Okay." What should we draw to help you remember that?

Student: A butterfly and a mushroom.

SLP: We can draw a butterfly and a mushroom. What can we draw to help you remember that the butterfly is wet?

Student: Some rain stuff. And we can put the ant in there, too.

SLP: Okay, let's do that. I'll go first. You count to see how long it takes me. [draws the picture as the student counts to 12] Now, I'll count while you draw. Try to get your picture done even faster than I did. Remember, we only want to make pictures good enough for us to help us remember the story.

Seven or eight pictographs are usually sufficient to provide reasonable support for retelling most stories. The clinician and student practice talking about each picture after they draw it. After all the pictures are drawn, the clinician retells the entire story to the student. Then, the student retells the story to the clinician. This activity usually takes about 20 minutes to complete. There are many opportunities for the clinician to use facilitative utterances, and it provides the student with repeated practice in retelling the story.

Pictographic Plan for Retelling

Figure 2.2
Mushroom in the Rain

Between sessions, we cut up the pictographs. At the beginning of the next session, we give the cut out pictographs to the student. The student orders them, then retells the story again. The clinician uses facilitation devices to shape the completeness and complexity of the student's story, again with the skill focus on specifying character motivations for behaviors.

Pragmatics Activities

We believe that all students can benefit from activities that focus on language use in literate language contexts. Social language occurs during group activities and models of how to interact can be found in storybooks.

The clinician begins by discussing with the students how the characters in the target book used language to handle a particular situation in the story. For example, the characters in *Mushroom in the Rain* are persistent in asking the ant to let them in under the mushroom, even after the ant tells them there is no more room. After their first request for shelter is rejected, the butterfly, the mouse, and the bird politely say something like, "Please, move over just a little." Their second request meets with success. The clinician role-plays the situations from the book, with students acting out the roles of the ant, the butterfly, the mouse, the bird, and the rabbit. Previous intervention discussions about cooperation during the clausal complement activity that targeted inferential comprehension and dialogue elements provide foundations for this pragmatics activity.

Next, the clinician and students discuss situations in which it is and is not appropriate to ask for something even after someone says, "No." Requesting is contrasted with demanding. Examples of situations in which persistence is appropriate include asking a friend to let you join a game, asking for assistance from a parent or friend, or asking a sibling to let you borrow something. For those situations in which we determine it is appropriate to be persistent, we discuss the best way to request something a second time. Then, we role-play those situations.

Book as a Model for Parallel Story

The clinician rereads the target book at least one more time. Students also listen to a clinician-made audiotape of the book at home or during a book-reading center time in their classrooms. The story retelling activity is repeated several times at the beginning of the next three or four sessions. As the students' retellings become more complete, the clinician uses the semantic map and students' New Word Books to facilitate the inclusion of target vocabulary and sentence patterns in their story. Once students are reasonably proficient at retelling the story, the clinician asks them to take their pictographs home so that they can practice telling the story to their parents. Before doing this, the SLP assures that parents know what the pictographs are and what purpose they were designed to serve.

Finally, the clinician works with students to create what we refer to as a *parallel story*. The clinician takes critical plot elements, vocabulary, and sentence patterns from the target book and applies them to a story that the students create. Students are asked to think of characters different from the ones in the target book and a different (but similar) set of circumstances. For example, in *Mushroom in the Rain,* an ant tries to find shelter from the rain. The clinician begins the parallel book discussion by asking students about other kinds of bad weather from which some animals might want to find shelter. Invariably, the answer is snow. Then the clinician asks students to think of some animals that might be out in the snow and where they might go for shelter. A graphic organizer like the one in Table 2.4 can represent the story line. The clinician and students work their way through the creation of a shared parallel story (or one per student) with the clinician's ample use of facilitation devices. The clinician prompts students to create episodes that are like those in *Mushroom in the Rain.* The skills addressed in earlier sessions are integrated in this parallel story creation and performance. An example of the clinical dialogue for composing the story follows.

SLP: You've said you want to have a caterpillar, a skunk, an eagle, a deer, and a bear in your story. You said they're going to try to fit into a cave. How should the story start?

Student: There's a caterpillar in the snow. He's cold.

Table 2.4   **Graphic Organizer for Parallel Story Problems**

Character	Problem Statement
Caterpillar	I need to get warm.
Skunk	I'm too cold to stink.
Eagle	My wings are frozen so I can't fly.
Deer	The bear is chasing me.
Bear	Have you seen a deer around here?

SLP: Okay. [long pause, expectantly waiting]

Student: And he's looking at a place for getting dry.

SLP: The caterpillar is looking for a place to get dry. *(syntactic expansion)* What happens next? *(elaboration question)*

Student: He sees a cave and go over there.

SLP: He sees a cave and he crawls over to it. *(syntactic expansion)* You used the word *and* to put two sentences together. *(statement of target, informative feedback)*

Student: And him get all warm in there.

SLP: And he's nice and warm in the cave. *(syntactic and semantic expansion)* What other animal comes along?

Student: The skunk.

SLP: Tell me what happens with the skunk. Remember the chart we made up.

Student: That skunk's cold so he goes up at the cave to ask the um caterpillar. He says, "Hey caterpillar, can I came in out from being cold in the snow? It's too cold to be stinking you out."

SLP: Yeah, the skunk asks if he can come in to the cave and he tells the caterpillar that he's too cold to stink up the cave. *(recast)* What happens next?

Student: The eagle comes.

SLP: Wait, what does the caterpillar say to the skunk? And, remember how the animals in *Mushroom in the Rain* ask twice?

Student: Oh yea. That caterpillar tell the skunk, "Nope, you can't come in here." Then the skunk say, "But please let me in 'cause I'm freezing out here." The caterpillar say, "Okay."

SLP: Excellent! First the caterpillar told the skunk, "You can't come in here." Then the skunk asked nicely, "Can I please come in because I'm freezing out in the snow?" The caterpillar felt bad for him so he said, "Okay, you can come in with me." *(textual recast that focused on clarifying semantic and syntactic relationships)* Very nice! What's the next animal that comes along?

The clinician and the student continue this type of exchange until the parallel story is completed. The clinician writes the student's parallel story with repaired grammar and specific referents where needed. When the story is finished, the clinician reads it back to the student slowly, asking clarification questions to fill in missing or incomplete information. Then, the clinician types the story and gives it to the student to take home. A journal of all the retold and parallel stories can be kept. These stories can be brought out and read aloud every two weeks or so. Students should "hear" their narrative voice at the same time that they are working on new stories.

Conclusion

Literature-based language intervention embeds therapeutic interactions within functional communication contexts that are centered around reading and discussing children's literature. Language abilities within the multiple domains of syntax, semantics, narration, and pragmatics are organized into a whole-part-whole plan that moves from reading a story aloud through a series of focused skill activities, then returning to the story to create their own parallel version of the story that incorporates as many of the targeted language skills as possible. The emphasis is on provision of repeated opportunities for learning and systematic support of explicit skills throughout the activities, both in terms of how activities are set up and how the clinician interactively scaffolds the talk. As demonstrated in the example of a literature-based language intervention unit, multiple skills across domains can be targeted with this approach.

References

American Speech-Language-Hearing Association. (1983). A definition of language. *Asha, 24*(6), 44.

Aram, D. M., & Hall, N. E. (1989). Longitudinal follow-up of children with preschool communication disorders: Treatment implications. *School Psychology Review, 18,* 487–501.

Beck, I. L., McKeown, M. G., & Kucan, L. (2003). Taking delight in words: Using oral language to build young children's vocabularies. *American Educator, 27,* 36–46.

Bishop, D. V. M. (1997). *Uncommon understanding: Development and disorders of language comprehension in children.* Hove, UK: Taylor & Francis.

Bishop, D. V. M., & Adams, C. (1992). Comprehension problems in children with specific language impairment: Literal and inferential meaning. *Journal of Speech and Hearing Research, 35,* 119–129.

Bos, C. S., & Anders, P. L. (1990). Effects of interactive vocabulary instruction on the vocabulary learning and reading comprehension of junior-high learning disabled students. *Learning Disability Quarterly, 13,* 31–42.

Bos, C. S., & Anders, P. L. (1992). Using interactive teaching and learning strategies to promote text comprehension and content learning for students with learning disabilities. *International Journal of Disability, Development, and Education, 39,* 225–238.

Botting, N., Faragher, B., Simkin, Z., Knox, E., & Conti-Ramsden, G. (2001). Predicting pathways of specific language impairment: What differentiates good and poor outcome? *Journal of Child Psychology and Psychiatry, 42,* 1013–1020.

Boudreau, D. M., & Hedberg, N. L. (1999). A comparison of early literacy skills in children with specific language impairment and their typically developing peers. *American Journal of Speech-Language Pathology, 8,* 249–260.

Bruner, J. (1986). *Actual minds, possible worlds.* Cambridge, MA: Harvard University Press.

Coyne, M. D., Simmons, D. C., Kame'enui, E. J., & Stoolmiller, M. (2004). Teaching vocabulary during shared storybook readings: An examination of differential effects. *Exceptionality, 12,* 145–163.

Ellis Weismer, S. (1985). Constructive comprehension abilities exhibited by language-disordered children. *Journal of Speech and Hearing Research, 28,* 175–184.

Evans, J. L. (2002). Variability in comprehension strategy use in children with SLI: A dynamical systems account. *International Journal of Language and Communication Disorders, 37,* 95–116.

Fazio, B. B., Naremore, R. C., & Connell, P. J. (1996). Tracking children from poverty at risk for specific language impairment: A 3-year longitudinal study. *Journal of Speech and Hearing Research, 39,* 611–624.

Gillam, R. B., & Carlile, R. M. (1997). Oral reading and story retelling of students with specific language impairment. *Language, Speech, and Hearing Services in Schools, 28,* 30–42.

Gillam, R. B., Hoffman, L. M., Marler, J. A., & Wynn-Dancy, M. (2002). Sensitivity to increased task demands: Contributions from data-driven and conceptually driven information processing deficits. *Topics in Language Disorders, 22*(3), 30–48.

Gillam, R. B., McFadden, T. U., & van Kleeck, A. (1995). Improving the narrative abilities of children with language disorders: Whole language and language skills approaches. In M. Fey, J. Windsor, & J. Reichle (Eds.), *Communication intervention for school-age children* (pp. 145–182). Baltimore: Brookes.

Ginsburg, M. (1974). *Mushroom in the rain.* New York: Macmillan.

Hoggan, K. C., & Strong, C. J. (1994). The magic of once upon a time: Narrative teaching strategies. *Language, Speech, and Hearing Services in Schools, 25,* 76–89.

Isaacson, S. L. (1992). Volleyball and other analogies: A response to Englert. *Journal of Learning Disabilities, 25,* 173–177.

Jitendra, A. K., Edwards, L. L., Sacks, G., & Jacobson, L. A. (2004). What research says about vocabulary instruction for students with learning disabilities. *Exceptional Children, 70,* 299–323.

Johnson, C. J., Beitchman, J. H., Young, A., Escobar, M., Atkinson, L., Wilson, B., et al. (1999). Fourteen-year follow-up of children with and without speech/language impairments: Speech/language stability and outcomes. *Journal of Speech, Language, and Hearing Research, 42,* 744–760.

Kim, A. H., Vaughn, S., Wanzek, J., & Wei, S. (2004). Graphic organizers and their effects on the reading comprehension of students with LD: A synthesis of research. *Journal of Learning Disabilities, 37,* 105–118.

Moffett, J. (1968). *Teaching the universe of discourse.* New York: Houghton-Mifflin.

Montgomery, J. W. (2002). Understanding the language difficulties of children with specific language impairments: Does verbal working memory matter? *American Journal of Speech-Language Pathology, 11,* 77–91.

Nippold, M. A. (1998). *Later language development.* Austin, TX: Pro-Ed.

Norris, J. A. (1989). Providing language remediation in the classroom: An integrated language-to-reading intervention method. *Language, Speech, and Hearing Services in Schools, 20,* 205–218.

Norris, J. A., & Hoffman, P. (1993). *Whole language intervention for school-age children.* San Diego, CA: Singular.

Paul, R., & Cohen, D. J. (1985). Outcomes of severe disorders of language acquisition. *Annual Progress in Child Psychiatry and Child Development,* 413–429.

Rhodes, L. K., & Dudley-Marling, C. (1988). *Readers and writers with a difference: A holistic approach to teaching learning disabled and remedial students.* Portsmouth, NH: Heinemann.

Schneider, P. (1996). Effects of pictures versus orally presented stories on story retellings by children with language impairment. *American Journal of Speech-Language Pathology, 5,* 86–96.

Scott, C. M. (1988). Spoken and written syntax. In M. A. Nippold (Ed.), *Later language development* (pp. 49–96). Austin, TX: Pro-Ed.

Snowling, M., & Hulme, C. (1989). A longitudinal case study of developmental phonological dyslexia. *Cognitive Neuropsychology, 6,* 379–401.

Stothard, S. E., Snowling, M. J., Bishop, D. V. M., Chipchase, B. B., & Kaplan, C. A. (1998). Language-impaired preschoolers: A follow-up into adolescence. *Journal of Speech, Language, and Hearing Research, 41,* 407–418.

Strong, C. J., & Hoggan North, K. C. (1996). *The magic of stories: Literature-based language intervention.* Greenville, SC: Super Duper Publications.

Torgesen, J. K. (2001). Intensive remedial instruction for children with severe reading disabilities: Immediate and long-term outcomes from two instructional approaches. *Journal of Learning Disabilities, 34,* 33–59.

Ukrainetz, T. A. (1998). Stickwriting stories: A quick and easy narrative representation strategy. *Language, Speech, and Hearing Services in Schools, 29,* 197–206.

Westby, C. E. (1985). Learning to talk—Talking to learn: Oral-literate language differences. In C. S. Simon (Ed.), *Communication skills and classroom success: Therapy methodologies for language-learning disabled students* (pp. 181–213). San Diego, CA: College-Hill Press.

Wright, H. H., & Newhoff, M. (2001). Narration abilities of children with language-learning disabilities in response to oral and written stimuli. *American Journal of Speech-Language Pathology, 10,* 432–441.

<table>
<tr><td>Chapter 3</td><td>

Finding the Words: Vocabulary Development for Young Authors

</td></tr>
</table>

Nickola Wolf Nelson and Adelia M. Van Meter

Introduction

I need how long bats live.

Thus said third grader, James, as he headed out of the classroom toward the library. James had just finished reading his animal report aloud from the author's chair and taking questions from his peers, one of whom asked the question about how long bats live. James was not so enthusiastic about writing his words and ideas when we first met him midway through his second-grade year. His teacher was worried about his emotional and academic health and suspected that he might have learning disabilities. James actively avoided writing and had difficulty communicating orally. How did James, by the middle of his third-grade year, become not only aware, but also enthusiastic about the need for words? That question is the main focus of this chapter.

To preview the answer—words provided the symbols James needed for communicating about ideas; an appreciative audience provided the motivation; and explicit scaffolding about spoken and written word forms helped him develop the tools. So, this chapter is about words, the concepts they represent, and the forms they take. It is also about how students learn words by needing them, and how they use word-knowledge to learn other things—particularly, to read and write. Further, it is about how learning to read and write can help students learn words. Explanations of such reciprocal relationships, and the scaffolding to encourage them, provide the framework for describing how to embed intervention for vocabulary learning within other curriculum-based, contextualized, language-learning experiences.

Vocabulary Instruction for All and Intervention for Students with Special Needs

The approach promoted in this chapter capitalizes on the natural processes and strategies people use to learn words, whether or not they have disabilities. It adds elements of vocabulary *instruction,* which is a feature of the general education curriculum for all students, and vocabulary *intervention,* which is individually tailored for those with special needs. In some aspects, instruction and intervention are indistinguishable.

General education vocabulary instruction often focuses on "reading vocabulary," based on the expectation that students do better at comprehending texts they read if they know the words. Research indeed has shown that readers' knowledge of words is one of the most powerful predictors of reading comprehension (Anderson & Freebody, 1981). Students who read extensively also have many more opportunities than nonreading peers to learn new words and concepts (Cunningham & Stanovich, 1998). As students read more, they know more, and the expanded knowledge base helps them tackle ever more advanced texts and read them with comprehension. This "rich get richer" phenomenon has been dubbed, biblically, "the Matthew effect" (Stanovich, 1986). Literacy learning and educational success are also compromised when school-age children and adolescents must compensate for reduced experience with the vocabulary of schooling because they are growing up in homes affected by poverty (Hall, Nagy, & Linn, 1984; Hart & Risley, 1995), where a language other than the English of schooling is spoken (Carlo et al., 2004; White, Graves, & Slater, 1990), or when their capacity to benefit and to participate from vocabulary learning experiences is limited by disability.

Communicators need a large and varied vocabulary to be successful in any curriculum-based activity—whether, for example, listening to the teacher and following directions; trying to convince peers to join in a game; reading a story and comprehending its figurative meanings; writing a story about something scary or humorous; going online to find Internet-based information to use in a report; understanding story problems in math; or reading a science or social studies textbook. An individual's vocabulary also must be conventional enough and produced clearly enough (through articulation while speaking, and spelling while writing) to communicate adequately with others. As vocabulary grows, the richness of associations (phonological, orthographic, semantic, syntactic) within a person's inner lexicon grows as well. Rich associations help students cast an even wider net for noticing new words, detecting their features, trying them out, and weaving them into increasingly complex conceptual networks.

The need for vocabulary instruction is clear, but what qualifies as good instruction, and how does intervention differ from instruction? What are the implications for designing service delivery models? Those are the questions addressed in this section of the chapter.

Quality Vocabulary Instruction

Carr and Wixon (1986) provide four guidelines for evaluating vocabulary instruction programs. They indicate that effective instruction should be designed to help students: (1) relate new vocabulary to background knowledge,

(2) develop elaborated word knowledge, (3) become active participants in learning new vocabulary, and (4) develop strategies for acquiring new vocabulary independently.

Nagy (1988) summarized available research on effective vocabulary instruction as supporting three principles: integration, repetition, and meaningful use. The *integration principle* involves integrating the meanings of targeted words with other knowledge. Consistent with schema theory, Nagy noted that knowledge is not structured as lists of independent facts, but as sets of relationships, and new information is understood by relating it to what one already knows. The suggestion for implementing this principle is to use clustering and thematic relations among new and old vocabulary to establish depth of understanding. Nagy described the *repetition principle* as providing repetitive and in-depth experiences with new words as a means of bringing them to an automatic level so they can be immediately available for decoding, speaking, or writing. The suggestion for implementing this principle is to find a way to use the new words meaningfully at least five times each within a week because repetition is important to establish learning. Nagy explained application of the *meaningful use principle* as providing multiple encounters in activities that support students to process words meaningfully (i.e., to make inferences based on their meanings) in tasks that involve normal speaking, reading, and writing. In this case, the suggestion for implementation is to use repetitions in contexts of actual communicative use, not workbook exercises requiring students to copy definitions and make up decontextualized sentences with the words.

Other researchers have come up with similar recommendations for vocabulary instruction, which are summarized in Box 3.1. Stahl (2004a) summarized features of vocabulary instructional programs for students with learning disabilities. The themes of his summary were similar to those suggested for general education by Carr and Wixon (1986), and Nagy (1988). That is, Stahl's summary indicated that vocabulary instruction should: (1) be interactive, (2) teach words in clusters or themes rather than in isolation, (3) involve students with learning disabilities in group work with their peers, and (4) be engaging, if not outright fun!

The National Reading Panel (2000) reported evidence of beneficial results with vocabulary instruction. They identified five main methods for teaching vocabulary that contributed to effective instruction. These were: (1) *explicit instruction,* in which students are given definitions or other attributes of words to be learned; (2) *implicit instruction,* in which students are exposed to words orally or in extensive reading experiences; (3) *multimedia methods,* in which

Box 3.1   **Recommendations for Vocabulary Instruction**

Do:	**Don't:**
• Integrate the new word's meaning with other word meanings.	• Teach words in isolation.
• Provide repeated opportunities.	• Develop vocabulary lists by their presence in a story.
• Provide meaningful use opportunities.	• Have students copy definitions.
• Teach meaning through use in context.	• Rely on dictionary definitions to provide meaning.
• Employ peer models.	• Preteach unfamiliar words out of context.
• Use multimedia methods.	• Forget to relate the words to the lives of your students.
• Have fun with words.	• Make word learning tedious.
• Provide both explicit and implicit instruction.	
• Aim for fluent, automatic understanding and use.	
• Teach students to be better, more independent word learners.	

Sources: Carr & Wixon (1986); McKenna (2004); Nagy (1988); National Reading Panel (2000); Stahl (2004a)

instruction goes beyond text to include other media such as graphic representations, hypertext, or American Sign Language; (4) *capacity methods* in which practice is used to increase capacity and make reading automatic; and (5) *association methods,* in which learners are encouraged to draw connections between what they know and words they do not know.

Extending beyond lists of *dos* for vocabulary instruction, McKenna (2004) offered a series of *don'ts,* including: (1) don't require students to copy definitions because copying does not ensure engagement; (2) don't rely on definitions alone because definitions are difficult to understand without contextual examples and most words have more than one definition; (3) don't preteach all the unfamiliar words in a story because it is possible to comprehend fiction reasonably well even when one does not know 15 percent of the words, and also because the words will be learned better through the meaningful context of the book; (4) don't base general vocabulary instruction on the words in a story because appearance in the same story does not ensure that words are related in meaning and amenable to clustering; and (5) don't forget to link new words to the lives of your students because associations with existing world knowledge make word learning meaningful.

Finally, it is important to remember that there are far too many words to teach, either explicitly or implicitly. Students need to become better and more independent word learners. They need to learn how to recognize when they don't know a word or when they need a word. For reading, the students need to know how to figure out the meaning from context or morphological analysis. For writing, they need to know how to reflect on their own knowledge to seek the words that will express the desired meanings. Finally, students need to know how to use tools, such as thesauri and dictionaries, to further comprehension and expression goals.

Language Intervention

As Ukrainetz pointed out in the first chapter to this book, the basic principles of language acquisition apply to language instruction and intervention, but some distinctions apply as well. The first distinction facing an intervention team might involve overcoming avoidance. Avoidance strategies are particularly well-developed among students with special needs when they have experienced school failure. Students avoid work they perceive as difficult by getting drinks, making trips to the bathroom, sharpening pencils, and even instigating trouble so as to be removed from the room. Students who avoid also may claim to have no original ideas to communicate. To reduce or eliminate avoidance strategies requires a combination of patience, supportive scaffolding for generating ideas and the means to communicate them (sometimes involving dictation or a shared pencil at first), and experiences with an appreciative audience of teachers and peers (Nelson, Bahr, & Van Meter, 2004).

A further distinction between instruction and intervention is in the nature of the targets. Instruction tends to target academic reading vocabulary; whereas intervention may need to target basic vocabulary typically learned at younger ages, and therefore, taken for granted (e.g., *center, top, front, back, before, after, while, during, each, both).* The problem is compounded when students and teachers attribute comprehension and learning problems to general intellectual weakness, attention problems, or obstinacy, rather than recognize vocabulary and other language deficits. In fact, students may not actually *lack* basic vocabulary, but rather have word meanings encoded only partially or with slightly erroneous semantic features. Thus individualized assessment and intervention must aim at identifying sources of specific vocabulary misconceptions or missing elements.

For example, one student correctly read the words in the math story problem, "There are seven bike racks. If each bike rack has eight bikes, how many bikes in all?" (Nelson, 1998, p. 421) When asked to draw the problem, the student correctly represented the racks with seven horizontal lines, but then drew a vertical line representing only one bike on each rack. Dynamic assessment and intervention scaffolding involved framing the phrase, "*each* bike rack has eight bikes*," and focusing the student on the meaning of *each,* with feedback (including visual supports of gesturing and drawing) to help the student form a more accurate representation of the meaning of *each.* Then practice opportunities were provided to fully internalize the understanding. Finally, the enlarged concept was assessed to check its stability.

This example also illustrates another distinction between vocabulary instruction and intervention—a methodological one. That is, students with special language-learning needs often require more explicit, intensive, individualized scaffolding and repeated opportunities to encode words in their mental lexicons on multiple levels (semantically, phonologically, orthographically) in order to develop deep associations and automaticity; whereas students with typical development may be able to acquire such concepts and forms more quickly and incidentally in the context of whole-group instruction.

Service Delivery Options

Language instruction and intervention can be delivered in inclusive classroom settings, but also separately. When language intervention occurs in pull-out sessions, word learning must still be embedded in the language and textual materials of the general education curriculum. That is, intervention can be embedded and curriculum-based, even when not classroom-based.

Language Intervention in Pull-Out Settings
Pull-out sessions offer some advantages over fully embedded classroom interventions. For example, more quiet and controlled pull-out settings make it possible to provide individual scaffolding apart from the pressing demands of

many students completing complex assignments. In special education settings, speech-language pathologists (SLPs) and special educators have opportunities to control the learning activities and pace, to provide more opportunities for repetition, and more opportunities for students to participate actively in small group discussions.

Pull-out sessions also present particular perils, however. One has to remember, for example, that when students are pulled out during the school day, not only are they going *to* something, but also *from* something. When students are pulled out, they miss classroom instruction and work time as well as opportunities to interact meaningfully with peers and general education teachers, whom most regard as their *real* teacher (Nelson, 1998). Also, when students are pulled out, classroom teachers have less access to consulting support regarding the nature of language-learning difficulties and less opportunity to develop awareness and ownership for important roles they can play in promoting spoken and written language development for all their students. Another danger of pull-out intervention is that students with special needs might be taking baby steps while classmates are taking giant steps toward language and academic proficiency.

If one is aware of these perils, however, plans can be made to minimize their effects and increase the relevance of pull-out service delivery. In particular, it is important to be guided by the goal to keep students in the content and pace of the general education curriculum, if possible, or to help students take increasingly larger steps toward it, if the gap is too large. Gaining access to textbooks, assignments, and other classroom activities can occur through consultative interactions with students' teachers in which information is shared in both directions. Brief phone conversations, mailbox notes, or email exchanges with classroom teachers make it possible to bring general education curricular materials into pull-out sessions and to use them to provide the vocabulary content and context for intervention.

The authors of this chapter have applied the principles of curriculum-based language assessment and intervention (Nelson, 1989, 1995, 1998) in a variety of service delivery contexts, including after-school "homework labs" for middle and junior high school students, as well as more traditional individual and small group sessions in our university clinic. The common denominator has been to provide interventions grounded in authentic activities of the students' own general education curriculum, and to augment it with special projects that yield communication products, which students work on over time individually and in small groups. For example, middle school students in homework labs have written and produced skits, videotaping them or acting them live for an appreciative audience of parents and peers. Students in other homework labs have written articles and published a newsletter, or written stories and read them aloud at publishing parties, also to an appreciative audience of parents and peers. For two years we worked in an after-school program in a local elementary school's media center, which was dubbed CREW lab (for Computers, Research, Exploring, and Writing). In these experiences, students selected topics, did research in books and online, and wrote reports on related topics, such as constellations, planets, and outer space, which they read for an audience of parents and peers at publishing parties.

Each of these pull-out style programs had a slightly different organizational framework, but all comprised three main components: (1) group minilessons were used to briefly introduce a topic that could be discussed actively by the whole group, (2) opportunities were provided to develop the topic and practice skills as the students worked on products that they would later share with an appreciative audience, and (3) contextualized assessments identified individualized intervention targets involving discourse-, sentence-, and word-level language abilities that instructors scaffolded toward independent use during whole-group and individual activities.

Language Intervention in an Inclusive Writing Lab

Recognizing the limitations of pull-out approaches, we have spent the last decade or so collaborating with teachers across elementary grades in classrooms to develop the *writing lab approach to language instruction and intervention.* We have described this work in a book of that name (Nelson, et al., 2004) and in several other articles and chapters (Nelson & Van Meter, in press; Nelson, Van Meter, Chamberlain, & Bahr, 2001).

The writing lab approach provides an ideal context for embedding language intervention in classroom instruction. In writing labs, therapeutic interactions occur in the context of meaningful, curriculum-based, small group, and individual activities. These are activities in which whole classes of students learn writing processes, produce meaningful products, and share them with an authentic audience of peers, teachers, and parents. Although writing processes are used as the instructional context, any language intervention goal or objective (spoken or written) can be addressed in writing lab activities, including learning new vocabulary.

One reason that the writing lab context is ideal for embedded intervention is that everyone benefits. The teacher has an extra pair of hands for helping students with a difficult task, and students have added supports for developing fluency in written language. Another reason that teachers are willing to collaborate in a writing lab approach is that writing process activities (often called "writers' workshops") already are a feature of many general education classrooms (e.g., Atwell, 1987, 1990; Calkins, 1986, 1990, 1994; Graves, 1983, 1991, 1994). This means that the intervention is not a dreaded "add-on" to an already overloaded curriculum. Teachers also are motivated to devote class time to teaching writing processes because, in many states, written language samples are a part of high-stakes testing. It helps that any part of the curriculum, not just language arts, can be addressed through research and writing activities. This means that collaborative activities can be scheduled at any mutually agreeable time of day (e.g., during science or social studies, as well as during language arts), with relatively minor rearrangement to academic schedules.

Within the *writing lab approach,* the instructor—SLP, special educator, general education teacher, parent, or a team of all of the above—arranges conditions so that students have time and scaffolding supports to generate texts (e.g., biographical sketches, personal narratives, stories, reports) through their own writing (or with dictation or a "shared pencil," if necessary) to convey their ideas using interesting words, clear sentences, and well-organized discourse structures. Ideally, some of the writing takes place on computers, using the technological scaffolds that many students' writing programs have to offer (Nelson, et al., 2004). At multiple points toward completion, students read their works in progress to peers and adults in small group or "author chair" interactions. Audience members, or peer and teacher editors, provide feedback about what they liked, what they want to know more about, and specific suggestions about how to make the work even better.

Writers' workshops also have advantages in that they provide opportunities for a variety of oral and written communication interactions, both formal and informal. Group mini-lessons are used to introduce topics and provide opportunities for explicit instruction and group discussion, followed by repetitive practice opportunities using new vocabulary and skills. A special service provider, such as an SLP, can provide scaffolded support without disrupting the flow of the rest of the class, by pulling up a chair. The SLP can guide a student with special needs to replace common words with more interesting words and to provide explicit instruction for recognizing word chunks that can be used for spelling and reading without disrupting the flow of the rest of the class. Students can talk to each other about their work in editing pairs or small author groups. During such interactions, SLPs can scaffold typically developing peers to interact positively with students with special needs, such as modeling how to request clarification when necessary and how to encourage elaboration without taking away ownership.

In writers' workshops, students can be taught to use technological supports, including writing software that translates their spoken ideas into writing or makes revision easier, and the Internet to research topics of interest. Instructors can assist students to understand the vocabulary and concepts that they are reading, take notes using the new vocabulary, and then insert the words into a written report. The ideal writing lab is one in which students are working actively to achieve personal goals for communicating original ideas or reporting new information through writing, and all have a genuine interest in what others have to say.

Theories of Vocabulary Learning: Implications for Intervention

It is remarkable that teachers actively teach only about 200 new curricular words per year, but students learn closer to 3,000 new words per year (Miller & Gildea, 1987). In order to reach this number, students must be learning most words through incidental experiences. How do students (or adults, for that matter) learn words? And how many can one person know? No matter how large a person's vocabulary, there is always room for more. There is no known upper capacity to the number of words a person can know. New words can be generated at any time through compounding and other derivational processes, which make immediate sense to other speakers of the same language. These elements make vocabulary development unique among language acquisition systems. No one has provided an adequate account of word learning or word capacity, but we do know that they are functions of the language propensities of the human brain.

What It Means to "Know" a Word

On the surface, most mature language users have a concept of what it means to "know" a word and to "have" it in their vocabulary, but the concept is a little shakier when examined closely. At the most basic level, most would agree that for a word to be considered to be "in" a person's vocabulary, a word must: (1) hold meaning for the person; (2) be recognized as a real word (i.e., one with meaning) when it is heard in speech or read from print (or even presented in sign language); (3) be available for selection from some inner lexicon when appropriate to fill a particular communicative purpose; and (4) be possible to produce with recognizable spoken phonology or written orthography (or manual sign).

With regard to literate language learning, students may already have some words in their oral vocabularies, and only need to learn to decode them. Other words represent new labels for familiar concepts. Still others represent new concepts that must be learned (Nagy, 1988). Although people can have words in their vocabulary that they do not know how to spell or read, literate language users have strategies for transferring spoken words into print and vice versa.

It also is possible to "know" a word, but to have cataloged a meaning for it that is incomplete or even slightly erroneous. Partial word knowledge, as we shall see, is viewed as a stage of normal development of word meanings (Shore & Durso, 1990), but it is a particular risk for students with language-learning difficulties.

Word Learning Robustness and Fragility

Words are both a robust and a fragile component of human communication. The robustness of word learning is supported by evidence on the size and speed of vocabulary acquisition in normal development. Beginning at about 10 months through the entire process of normal aging, humans soak up tens of new words per day, hundreds per week, and thousands per year (Anglin, 1993). By the time students graduate from high school, it is estimated that they know about 40,000 words; twice that if proper nouns and idiomatic phrases are added to the list; and three or four times more if all the morphological variants of word roots (e.g., *write, wrote, written, writing, writer, rewrite, unwritten)* are added (Miller & Gildea, 1987; Nagy & Herman, 1987).

It also can be said, however, that words are particularly fragile components within language knowledge systems. The fragility of words has been experienced by almost all typical language users in the sensation of being unable to find a known word that is on the tip of the tongue but elusive at the moment of need. The harder one tries to remember, the more the word seems unavailable. To some extent, word-finding problems plague everyone. This is particularly the case when the elusive word is a proper noun for which no synonym will adequately do, such as a name. After the person relaxes, the name might pop into mind, even in the middle of the night, suggesting subconscious processing. Many students also report such word-finding difficulties while taking a fill-in-the-blank test. Some have strategies for dealing with the problem, such as leaving the item blank and returning to it later, visualizing the specific position of the word on a page in a textbook or set of notes, or using a self-cuing or word-association technique to retrieve the missing vocabulary or phrase. Others have no strategies, but might learn them through intervention.

For most communicators, word-finding problems are merely a temporary nuisance. For students and adults with language disorders, word-finding problems interfere with primary communicative and academic functions. People with specific word-finding impairments may have extensive vocabularies, yet experience information-processing glitches that interfere with their word retrieval (German, 1983). Generally speaking, however, the more words one knows, and the richer the associations of meaning among words and their concepts, the more quickly one can find the perfectly tuned meaning for a particular moment of communication (Kail & Leonard, 1986). Word retrieval is a complex cognitive behavior, however, which is thought to entail multiple steps (Levelt, Roelofs, & Meyer, 1999) and a combination of semantic, syntactic, phonological, and motor processes. Any of these processes and skills may be subject to inefficiencies (Lahey & Edwards, 1996), especially in a system under stress.

Fast Mapping and the Vocabulary Sponge

A fully developed word-learning theory must account for how, when a student or adult hears a new word and attends to it within a running stream of speech (even peripherally), the brain begins to perform parallel tasks of analyzing and storing word form and meaning. *Form* for lexical items involves the phonological system: retrieving the phonemes and combinations that represent a word. If the word is printed, retrieval of the form would involve the graphemic and possibly phonemic representations, since automatic print recognition skips the phonemic step (Apel & Swank, 1999). *Meaning* involves the concepts that are verbally and imaginably encoded. Past theories (e.g., Miller & Gildea, 1987) emphasized "mastering the mechanics of uttering and recognizing a word and mastering the concept that it expresses [as] separate learning processes" (p. 94). Recent theories, however, have emphasized connections between form and meaning in word learning.

Word forms are mapped by pattern detecting. Pattern detectors recognize the phonotactic shape of a word and salient phonemes. Concurrently, word meanings are mapped by categorizing and sorting the features of a word to arrive at a unified meaning. These two mapping systems must be associated (e.g., /kæt/ = small furry animal often contrasted with the other common pet, dog) if words are to be completely understood and available for fluent, productive use. Form and meaning processes must be associated for learners to be able to distinguish words newly encountered in speech or reading as known, novel, or nonsense words. The reciprocal nature of learning both form and meaning also is supported by evidence that novel words are easier to reproduce if they incorporate frequently heard phonotactic patterns (e.g., CVC words like /kæt/ are easier than VCC words like /æsk/), but that students with larger vocabularies, who may be more accustomed to linking new forms and meanings, do better with novel words even if the words have low-frequency sound patterns (Edwards, Beckman, & Munson, 2004).

How must word-learning processes work? First, the auditory-perceptual (or visual-perceptual) system must provide enough data for the brain to represent the word's spoken (i.e., phonemic), signed (i.e., gestural), or written (i.e., orthographic) form for comparison with other words in the lexicon, so it can be analyzed as a new or known word. Secondly (actually, more likely in simultaneous-parallel fashion), the brain must compare and rapidly map the word's fit within an existing semantic category (e.g., as a color word, animal name, or action word), associating and contrasting it with other words and concepts that have similar or distinctive semantic features.

This process is sometimes called *fast mapping* (Carey, 1978) because it seems to represent the ability to map, almost automatically, the meaning of a word in the brain by connecting it to other knowledge. In a classic study of fast mapping, Carey and Bartlett (1978) worked with a group of three-year-olds in a context that included a blue cafeteria tray (known word and concept) and an olive-colored one (known concept but unknown word). The researchers requested each child to, "Hand me the chromium tray. Not the blue one, the chromium one." When a child paused and pointed to the olive tray and asked, "This one?" the researcher would say, "Yes, that one, thank you." When asked to name the colors a week later, although they did not remember the word *chromium,* the children now knew that the color was not brown or green. The researchers concluded that a single exposure to a word was sufficient to begin a reorganization of a child's lexicon for color words.

In earlier writing, Nelson (2002) likened the natural process of vocabulary learning as a "vocabulary sponge" to emphasize the manner in which typically developing individuals seem to be able to soak up words without effort, merely by exposure to new words in contexts that make their meaning clear. It is a process that seems to come as a preprogrammed function of language learning, and it is only when something interferes with the reception, perception, and active processes of meaning making, that vocabulary learning is impaired. The intervention process must be designed not only to provide specialized supports where necessary, but also to reactivate the natural and joyful processes of learning new words.

First Words and the Vocabulary Spurt

Two major milestones of language development are first words, which appear around the first birthday, and the vocabulary spurt that occurs later that year. Consistent with evidence relating form and meaning in word learning, Edwards, Fourakis, Beckman, and Fox (1999) pointed out that these milestones are not as sudden or distinct as they may seem. Rather, they build on earlier experiences with acoustic-analytical perceptual features of the speech infants hear and motor-kinesthetic phonetic features of the babbling infants produce.

To pick the word *dog* out of an acoustic string of mother's speech as the same word a preschool-age sibling pronounces *dah,* an infant/toddler's brain must be able both to segment the word out of the ongoing speech stream and cope with the contextual variability (Beckman & Edwards, 2000) associated with different voices, clarity, positions in sentences, and phonetic and morphological variants (e.g., *See dah; Look at those dogs; Where's the doggie? That dog is so big; Did you notice how fat the dog is getting?).* From experiencing these varied, embedded productions, the infant/toddler must recognize recurring patterns (i.e., word forms) and associate them with a growing concept of dogness. The process seems even more remarkable when one considers the different sizes, shapes, colors, and even behaviors that different breeds of dog can demonstrate. Yet, somehow, a child who experiences multiple exemplars of the category *dog* develops a concept of what a dog is, discriminates it from other closely related concepts, such as cat or horse, abstracts the reliable phonological features of the spoken word that remain constant across varied phonetic productions, and encodes the sound and meaning to be recognizable or retrievable in the future.

Solidifying Word Knowledge across Levels and Modalities

Although a single episodic encounter with a new word can initiate the mapping process, word learning is not complete with the first experience of a word.

Learners are able to recognize phonological forms of words for some time before they can retrieve forms with a map of articulatory features for production (Beckman & Edwards, 2000). Knowledge about a word that has been experienced and can be used in absence of awareness of "knowing" the word is considered *implicit*. Conscious word knowledge, on the other hand, is associated with *explicit* memories of the word and what it means (Schacter, 1987). However, word knowledge is not an all-or-none phenomenon. Shore and Durso (1990) identified three levels of word knowledge as being: *unknown,* in which a person knows nothing about a word; *known,* in which a person's knowledge of a word is complete; and *frontier,* which falls somewhere in between.

At the same time that the acoustic-articulatory patterns of new words are being detected and mapped in the brain, semantic mapping processes must be occurring as well. Miller and Gildea (1987) reported that such processes involve a rapid initial stage, in which new words are detected and assigned to a broad semantic category; a slower intermediate stage, in which the words are categorized at more refined levels, but only partially understood; and a final stage, in which words are fully classified and the features and privileges of use are distinguished. Supporting this multiple stage process, with an intermediate stage of partial word knowledge, Shore and Durso (1990) found that language learners have "quite a bit of information about the constraints of words, even words they denied were part of their language" (p. 317).

Word and Language Fundamentals

Effective scaffolding of word learning during intervention requires appreciation of the complexities of semantic relationships and the multiple aspects of words. It also requires an appreciation for how words fit into sentence- and discourse-level structures. With such background knowledge, intervention teams are better prepared to assess a student's current word knowledge and word-learning strategies in order to scaffold them effectively. Consistent with the scaffolding metaphor, a building materials metaphor illuminates the roles and relationships among language structures in contributing to meaningful vocabulary use and communication.

Words, Sentences, and Discourse as the Building Materials of Meaning

Words are the bricks of effective communication. They can stand alone as meaningful units. Each word consists of at least one morpheme, which is defined as the smallest meaningful unit of language. *Free* morphemes can stand alone, but many words also include *bound* morphemes, which are added to word roots to derive slightly different meanings. Thus, they are called *derivational* morphemes. Derivational morphemes may be prefixes (e.g., *re-, un-, bi-)* or suffixes (e.g., *-able, -tion, -ology)*. Other bound morphemes *inflect* words to make them fit properly within a grammatical structure. *Inflectional* morphemes (e.g., *-ing -ed, -s, -es)* indicate verb tense, plurality, possession, and subject-verb agreement. They form a closed, relatively small set of suffixes in English.

If words are the bricks of language (with shaping through morphological variation), syntax is the mortar. Syntactic structures (phrases, clauses, and sentences) clarify meanings and relationships among words. A word by itself can be *defined,* but its meaning is not *confined* until it becomes part of a phrase or sentence. For example, depending on the context, a simple word like *bat* can refer to a small flying mammal, a baseball bat, or a slab of cotton for stuffing a quilt. It also can refer to such actions as batting in a baseball game or shooing away an insect. The meaning of the word becomes clear (i.e., confined) when it appears in a particular semantic-syntactic context.

Within the bricks and mortar construction metaphor, discourse is the completed building. Like a fully constructed building, discourse situates constructed meanings in a broader context. Communication partners (speakers and listeners, authors and readers) collaborate on building whole discourse units (e.g., stories, conversations, informational reports) according to shared schematic blueprints. They also tinker with schematic designs based on their cultural and educational experiences, variations in particular situations, and intentions to achieve particular desired effects. Speakers and authors use their knowledge of culture and pragmatics to create nuances in meaning (e.g., sarcasm, irony, indirect requests), using linguistic (i.e., word and syntax choices) and paralinguistic (e.g., intonation patterns) variations to do so. Discourse structures not only provide the added cues to enable the interpretation of non-literal meanings; they also provide the networks for showing the relatedness among a group of words and concepts.

Words refer to concepts (i.e., meanings), which may be roughly divided into two types—content and function. Content words may have either concrete referents (e.g., *dog, table, Parthenon, run)* or abstract ones (e.g., *pretty, thought, very, contemplate)*. Function words or grammatical morphemes (e.g., *is, than, because, for)* all refer, in a relatively abstract manner, to relationships among concepts represented by content words. As a result, in the bricks and mortar metaphor, function words are contrasted with content words by being more closely related to mortar than bricks (thus the term *morphosyntax,* which comprises both grammatical morphemes and word order).

Metalinguistic versus Pragmatic Uses of Words

It is easier to use language in pragmatic ways to communicate about needs, wants, and ideas than to use language in metalinguistic ways to communicate about language itself. Talking with words is easier than talking about words—this distinction is important when deciding how to teach vocabulary to students. Students are more likely to learn the meanings of words in interactive communicative contexts such as asking for the *delicious* cookie and discovering the outcome than in structured metalinguistic ones, such as writing a definition for *delicious.*

In fact, the frequently used pedagogical tool of having students look up words in a dictionary and abstract their meaning has limited value. Definitions can be hard to understand (Scott & Nagy, 1997), particularly for students with learning disabilities (Stahl, 2004b). Miller and Gildea (1987) described strategies that most students use when they have encountered the words only in dictionary definitions and then attempt to employ them in sentences as: (1) find a familiar concept in the definition, (2) compose a sentence embodying that concept, and (3) substitute the new word. They illustrated the limitations of this strategy with an example in which a student used the definition of *meticulous* as "very careful or too particular about small details." The student abstracted the concept of "very careful," which resulted in the sentence, "I was meticulous about falling off the cliff" (p. 99).

Although metalinguistic knowledge should be activated with forethought, it can be used effectively in concert with interactive, meaningful activities, to support vocabulary learning in a number of ways. For example, identifying overused words in a student's written composition, then having the student generate words in that category or synonyms for that word, then returning to improve the composition, provide a series of tasks that move from pragmatic to metalinguistic and back to pragmatic use. The same sequence could be used for instructional scaffolds that lead students to focus directly on the inflectional and derivational morphological components of words, such as practicing the use of *-ly* to turn adjectives into adverbs.

Research on morphological learning (Carlisle, 1996) has shown that students without learning disabilities can use inflectional morphological markers in written compositions by second grade; by third grade, students with learning disabilities also can use inflectional morphology accurately. By fourth grade, both groups begin to recognize derivational morphological elements and incorporate them in complex words. It is at about this point that students may benefit from explicit instruction regarding influences of Latin, Greek, and other foreign languages on English word spelling and pronunciation. Such instruction can help them acquire vocabulary with metalinguistic word analysis, decoding, spelling, and memory strategies (Adams & Henry, 1997).

Assessing Vocabulary Size, Word Knowledge, and Strategies

For diagnostic and research purposes, a number of formal vocabulary tests are available to gauge whether the size of an individual student's receptive or expressive vocabulary is commensurate with that of same-age peers. The Peabody Picture Vocabulary Test–III (Dunn & Dunn, 1997) has long been a mainstay of formal language assessments. The Expressive One-Word Picture Vocabulary Test (Brownell, 2000) also may be used as part of a battery for diagnosing language impairment or measuring vocabulary for research or clinical purposes. Any prechosen list of words, however, runs the risk of cultural-linguistic bias. Students learn the words of the speech communities that are meaningful for them. Standardized tests are not particularly useful for instructional or intervention purposes, in any case, other than to identify vocabulary as an area of concern. It is both unethical and bad psychometric practice to directly teach students words they miss on a formal vocabulary test.

So how should a core set of vocabulary be selected, and how should vocabulary-learning strategies be assessed to guide intervention? The answer to the question about vocabulary selection comes from the literature on best educational practices and normal development. Both sources indicate that vocabulary should be chosen, not from a particular list, but from conceptually related content that holds meaning for an individual or learning community (such as a classroom) at a particular point in time. This would include the specialized vocabulary that accompanies units of instruction in language arts, science, social studies, and mathematics, and also basic vocabulary (including function words and directional terms) that students with learning disabilities may have represented only partially in their mental lexicons.

One way to assess an individual student's vocabulary knowledge is to assess word-level language skills within samples of reading and writing (Nelson & Van Meter, 2002). Both quantitative and qualitative measures can be taken. For example, in the area of reading, word recognition knowledge can be assessed by computing the percentage of words in a particular passage that a student reads fluently and with apparent recognition as being "real words." Although this is a flawed measure, when a student pronounces words with the wrong vowel or syllable stress or produces them as nonsense words, it can generally be assumed that he or she has not recognized them as real words. If it appears the student decoded most of the word, but still had trouble recognizing it, then incomplete word knowledge should be suspected. In this case, the examiner can probe further by returning to the passage and asking students to: (1) provide a definition, (2) paraphrase the sentence that used the word, or (3) select the best meaning from an array of multiple choices. Table 3.1 provides methods for informally assessing vocabulary.

Assessment can go beyond current word understanding to examine a student's ability to learn words. Dynamic assessment, in a test-teach-test format, can get beyond experiential limits to reveal a student's learning potential (Lidz & Peña, 1996; Ukrainetz, Harpell, Walsh, & Coyle, 2000). For example, after the test of word knowledge described above, the SLP can briefly teach the student to use a particular word-learning principle, such as getting clues from context or thinking about words that sound similar. The SLP notes how much and what kind of help was needed for the student to achieve the task. Then the SLP and student return to the unknown words and the student is evaluated for use and success of those strategies. Assessment that gives the SLP a sense of how much help is needed and how much learning results, is helpful in determining individual learning needs and planning intervention.

In writing samples, a quantitative measure can be taken of the number of different words the student uses (Nelson & Van Meter, 2002), supplemented by qualitative information in terms of particularly interesting or unusual words the student writes spontaneously. The computation of number of different words may be done by hand if the sample is short, but transcribing samples for analysis with computer software, such as the Systematic Analysis of Language Transcripts (SALT; Miller & Iglesias, 2004), greatly facilitates counting of the number of different words and other analyses for longer samples. It also provides an age-reference comparison for conversation and narrative samples. Dynamic assessment related to breadth of vocabulary knowledge in written language samples consists of the SLP indicating a desire to know more about a character, setting, or event, and observing the resources the student can draw on to retrieve more interesting and descriptive words. Often the best way to scaffold this is to comment on a particularly unusual and well-chosen word, telling the student how the word made one feel a certain way, or how it drew a clear mental picture.

Informal Assessment Methods for Vocabulary Knowledge and Strategies

Table 3.1

Aspect	Methods
Vocabulary Knowledge Assessment	• When reading text, identify words sounded out dysfluently or without recognition. • Check understanding with definitions, sentence paraphrases, or multiple-choice recognition.
Vocabulary Use Assessment	• Calculate number of different words used. • Note interesting or unusual words. • Request more information and note the variety of words used in the response.
Word Decoding Strategies	• Have student slowly sound out the word when reading, and note how syllables and phonemes are managed. • Draw attention to the orthographic representation and ask about spelling patterns. • Ask about how the word could be chunked to determine morphological awareness.
Vocabulary Comprehension Strategies	• When reading text, stop the student periodically and ask about contextual cues to word meaning. • Observe whether the student is understanding words by making connections with prior story events, the story line, ideas beyond the text, or the author's writing style. • Note if deficits in word decoding are affecting word comprehension.

Dynamic assessment of the student's knowledge of word forms (phonological make-up and orthographic spelling patterns) starts with indication of a desire to understand exactly what the student wrote or said. The examiner might ask for clarification of a particular word by asking the student to reread the sentence, or might pause at the word while reading aloud. Once identified, the examiner helps the student pronounce the word slowly, with heightened attention to how the word sounds and feels, taking it a sound or syllable at a time, and figuring out the orthographic combinations of letters to represent those sounds, syllables, and morphemes. If the word has derivational prefixes or suffixes, or inflectional suffixes, the examiner might pose a question first to see if the student has encoded more information about word "chunks" than was displayed spontaneously.

After this initial assessment, dynamic assessment can continue to be used to check the stability of the strategies introduced or the concepts acquired, and how much more instruction is needed to fully internalize the learning. When assessment that combines teaching with testing is used, students become aware of how they can develop into better and more independent learners. Most students respond by becoming more alert to opportunities to use words they already know and to detect new and interesting words in their environment.

In this way, dynamic assessment techniques are also embedded within contextualized intervention activities. These are similar to the facilitative or scaffolding moves that parents use when they interact with their children in everyday communication experiences. That is, when a child uses a word in a way that indicates that the meaning of the word is not completely mapped, or mapped in a way that is not quite accurate, the parent asks questions or makes comments that help the child map the meaning and its phonological structure more accurately, such as differentiating the pronunciation and meaning of such similar words as *anecdote* and *antidote.*

Harmon (2000) offered an outline for assessing word learning strategies during reading among adolescents. Her list could be used as a guide to dynamic assessment and objectives for intervention for younger students as well. First, the examiner observes the *use of contextual cues* and whether the student examines: (1) local context (before or after the word, or elsewhere in the sentence containing the word), (2) distant contexts, or (3) other locations. Second, the examiner observes whether the student *makes connections* that refer to: (1) immediate story events, (2) knowledge of the story line, (3) ideas beyond the text, (4) language structures, or (5) the author's style of writing. Third, the examiner observes *word-level strategies* for: (1) sounding out, (2) structural analysis, and (3) word appearance. Other observations address whether the student uses a dictionary or other outside sources, relies on syntax, focuses on relevant information, or determines plausible word meanings in other ways. All of these strategies are important components of becoming a successful word learner.

Embedded Vocabulary Instruction and Intervention

In this section, we explain a model of curriculum-based vocabulary instruction and intervention, integrating the four elements of the RISE mnemonic (see Chapter 1) as including repeated, intensive, systematically supported, explicit components in purposeful activities. Instruction should use the following strategies that build students' motivation to develop deep meanings and a rich vocabulary:

- Establish a culture involving *purposeful* encounters with vocabulary where students need words for communicating with an audience of adults and peers interested in their ideas.

- Highlight the importance of shared word knowledge and the pleasure of words with precise meanings, so that students develop a *motivational* framework in which words are valued.

- Provide activities that involve *repeated* needs for particular vocabulary items so that the word understanding and use will become internalized and automatic.

- Provide *intense* encounters with words and word-learning strategies by engaging in frequent sessions of individualized learning support.

- Provide intentional, goal-directed systematic support through *scaffolding* so that students recognize new words, build strategies for forming rich reciprocal associations between the *meanings* of words and their spoken and written *forms,* and move these strategies into automatic word-learning processes that occur within meaningful communicative activities.

- Make instruction *explicit* so that both the SLP and students focus on word learning despite the distractions of the many other components of meaningful communicative activities.

The keys to the intervention approach are three-fold. Students first must experience the *need* for a variety of interesting words for communicating in meaningful ways. Second, the best way to trigger this need is to engage them actively in *meaningful interactions* about interesting topics, starting with an audience of adults and peers who are clearly *interested* in what the students have to say. Third, once the natural processes are evoked by enhancing alertness to new words and their meanings, intervention can focus repeatedly, intensively, supportively, and explicitly on problems with the forms or meanings of words and strategies for decoding and comprehending them while reading.

To explain this approach, we draw on experiences with the writing lab approach and other intervention activities of our own, our graduate students, and the parents and teachers with whom we have worked, as well as on research-based literature on vocabulary development.

Establish a Culture That Values New and Interesting Words

One of the ways that communicative partners convey that they are listening and interested in what each other is saying is to use the other's concepts and terms in reply. James, who was introduced at the beginning of this chapter, responded to his audience's genuine interest in his work by immediately seeking to respond to a relevant question. His willingness and ability to do so reflect a gradual change in James as a communicator. Important to this change was an awareness of and belonging to a learning community that valued his ideas and supported the development of language forms needed to convey these ideas. This was in contrast to his familiar learning environment where participation was expected only when ideas were clearly formulated. Scaffolding questions and comments were used to guide James to identify and articulate what he knew and to articulate what he needed help with, while keeping a consistent focus on shared meanings, providing regular feedback on the impact of this shared meaning, and explicitly teaching new skills and strategies.

Act as an Authentic Audience
Vocabulary development can be infused into group and individual interactions across the various learning activities of the writing lab approach. Critical to building young authors' desire to choose new and interesting words is providing them with an authentic audience who will reflect on the impact of their words. Teachers and SLPs model how to express appreciation for specific features, such as interesting words. Parents and grandparents pick up on these cues at publishing parties and provide a naturally powerful audience. Peers,

especially high-prestige peers, can stimulate essential motivation to communicate with clarity and interest.

Author chair is one learning context that gives students an opportunity to reflect on their own work—in progress or published—and the work of others. Author chair involves students having a discussion about a particular student's work. Each student takes a turn having the composition examined by peers (Nelson et al., 2004). In this context, instructors may support thinking about words and more sophisticated figurative language by drawing attention to key vocabulary. For example, a teacher might comment on a student's word choice, "Wow, when you used the word *whispered,* it helped me picture how she was talking" or invite others to comment on vocabulary, "Did any of the words in Tommy's story catch your interest?"

In one third-grade classroom, the teacher delivered a lively lesson on colorful language and asked her students to create pictures with their words. During author chair, one of her students, Spencer, a boy identified with special education needs and delayed in literacy development, described a watermelon as "like a big beach ball" (Nelson et al., 2004, p. 343). The teacher excitedly pointed out that Spencer had used figurative language and granted him high praise. In a later writing activity, he described emotions as "my temperature rised." Clearly recognizing the impact his words would have on his audience, Spencer declared, "You're going to love this," before showcasing his story to his teacher. Spencer's example inspired his own writing, but also that of his peers. Students quickly rallied with their own figurative language examples, expanding the classroom list of interesting descriptions and creating an atmosphere of learners who were sensitive to both language and perspective.

An important element of this process is to view the first step in scaffolding as helping students to see and celebrate what they do know, rather than to point out what they do not know. Some students are more fragile or shy than others, but we have not found a single student among the hundreds we have worked with who did not begin to respond to the positive rewards of an audience of adults and peers interested in their ideas and the powerful words with which they communicated those ideas.

Focus on Vocabulary across Learning Contexts

Within lessons and individual scaffolding, opportunities for vocabulary teaching regularly arise. Sometimes the lessons are carefully crafted to include elements of reflective thinking about key vocabulary items and processes for understanding and using these new concepts. This instruction works best when focused on concepts rather than labels. One can do this by evoking a mental schema for related concepts before mentioning the word itself. Nagy (1988) provided an example:

> A teacher asked, "Have you ever had the feeling that something was going to go wrong or that something bad was going to happen? Not that you had any good reason to think that—just a sort of feeling. Has anyone ever had such a feeling? Did anything bad actually happen?" The teacher might extend the discussion for a minute or so before introducing the actual term, "Well, that sort of feeling is called a *premonition.*" (p. 21)

Following the demonstration of concept generation, intervention takes place through discovery supported by scaffolding. Students are interactively scaffolded into generating concepts and then finding words to fit those concepts. This approach of finding words to fit concepts can accompany the methods already discussed for teaching word meaning, morphological parts, word pronunciation, and spelling strategies.

At other times, vocabulary development may not be the primary goal of a lesson, but will present itself in teachable moments. In one fourth-grade writing lab session, for example, the teacher had students prepare to write a biography about a famous person by reading a text about Henry Ford. The goals for students were to demonstrate comprehension by paraphrasing and taking notes. The following example shows how, after reading a paragraph about Ford's early invention of a quadricycle, the instructional dialogue focused on word meanings and important concepts.

T: What's important there?

S1: [with specific language impairment] He had a business. Yeah, sort of he was working for someone but then...[trailed off]

S2: [with word-writing difficulties] Several years later he had went, I forget what it was called, his wife [looking back to text projected on screen], yeah, he moved back to Detroit, but there's something more important...[trailed off]

T: [highlights word *quadricycle* in projected text] What about this right here? Let's read this word together.

Class: [led by teacher in choral response] Quad-ri-cy-cle.

S2: That's important.

T: Why? Why do you think it's important?

S3:   [average student] That was his first vehicle he made.

SLP: [sitting on the sidelines] Ms. J, do your students know what quad might mean in the word quadricycle?

Class: [several students start to talk about a math concept]

T: We've seen quad before in the word quadrangle in math, haven't we?

The teacher scaffolded word knowledge and a process for analyzing morphemes as a strategy for figuring out new words, guiding her students to apply what they knew about words and word parts to new situations. The SLP, collaborating with the teacher, modeled assessment of student understanding and supported construction of new meaning at the word level, after which the class returned to a discourse-level focus on important facts to incorporate into their notes.

Establish the Importance of Shared Word Knowledge

The writing lab approach offers many opportunities to teach the vocabulary of the instructional process in a repetitive and recursive manner. Within the activities of the writing lab, opportunities for guiding students to higher levels of vocabulary learning and use include individual and group mini-lessons, individual scaffolding, author group sharing, and peer and instructor conferencing. The varied writing genres and curriculum contexts of the writing lab approach also generate opportunities for developing basic, as well as content-specific, vocabulary. Important to success in school and other endeavors is an understanding of vocabulary that describes processes and tools that are integral to shared routines, such as in the following examples:

- Vocabulary related to the recursive stages of the writing process to promote increased reflection on their work using the stages of the writing process (e.g., *planning, organizing, drafting, revising,* and *editing)*

- Computer-related terminology so that students can ask questions more specifically and teach their peers with greater ease (e.g., *keyboard, cursor, caps lock, enter, word wrap, paragraph, period, shift)*

- Content words that help students organize and realize curricular and genre-specific writing tasks (e.g., *justice, injustice, unfair, common good, individual rights)*

Mini-lessons, brief lessons embedded within a larger purposeful activity, are often used to introduce new vocabulary for describing processes and routines. Calibrating word use across contexts, students, and teachers makes it possible to increase repetition and reduce confusion for students in the early stages of learning processes and routines. For example, educators often describe the stages of the writing process in different ways. One teacher may refer to the initial stage as *prewriting,* while another calls it *planning and organizing.* Students benefit when teachers collaborate on terminology that will be used in connection to familiar routines. Ideally, these terms will be recorded in the district's standards and curricula for uniform use across teachers and grade levels. Gradually, instructional terminology is internalized by students and becomes a part of self-directed routines and a foundation for further word learning.

One method to support learning terminology is to design mini-lessons that begin with a demonstration of communication breakdown or awkwardness due to nonspecific word choices. For example, a teacher might instruct students to follow directions in the computer lab without specific vocabulary, such as, "I could say move that blinking thing that looks like a capital I by pushing down the button on the little thing that moves that sits next to the board with the ABCs on it." Students, engaged and amused, then help to construct directions using more specific word choices, such as, "move the *cursor* by clicking on your *mouse,* which is next to the *keyboard.*" The new terminology can be discussed further for richer understanding. Structural scaffolding that aids recall and strengthens learning can be provided, including mnemonic cues or print supports, such as word walls, print labels, and mini-lesson notes.

Instructors tuned in to students' language often find they can interpret messages which are far less transparent to an unfamiliar audience. Individual scaffolding can draw a student's attention to a part of a message that is clear, but express uncertainty about a part that is not, thereby creating an opportunity for students to revise with more specific word choices, such as, " I know I'm supposed to move something, but I didn't hear a specific word that tells me what to move." Additional scaffolding questions might focus and guide students more directly and provide explicit teaching as needed, such as, "Did you know this thing has a name? Do you think you might already know it? It's called a *mouse.* Why do you think it is called that? What can you do to remember that?" In the process, the student learns new words as well as the value of shared word knowledge and logical strategies for storing new words in long-term memory.

Use Curricular Vocabulary to Develop Conceptual Networks

Reading and writing expository text is one of the curricular goals of elementary and secondary education. Embedded in these activities is new vocabulary that forms the framework for understanding a topic. In one third-grade science activity, students were required to write animal reports. In this case, classroom mini-lessons addressed reading strategies for getting information from expository text, how to take notes, and how to use graphic organizers to plan and draft. To develop ownership, each student selected his or her own animal, becoming the animal's class expert and champion. Important curriculum vocabulary embedded in the lesson included: *mammal, food source, migrate,* and *hazards.* Each primary vocabulary word led to new words. For example, *food source* led to words for both general and specific food types; *migration* led to discussion about different places around the world; *hazards* led to the need for words such as *habitat, endangered, enemies, predator,* and *environment.*

Intervention for James, the student introduced at the beginning of this chapter, involved repetition and use of new vocabulary in inclusive and pull-out settings. In particular, James needed support in reading decoding and text comprehension, as well as support in putting his ideas into words and linking them logically. A planning guide helped James to direct his research to specific content, giving him repeated opportunities to consider the content vocabulary. Scaffolding that asked him questions about the relationship between ideas helped him to formulate sentences and link information logically, such as, "I'm confused; now why does this animal migrate?" "Oh, when does that happen?" "What will your reader need to know about how it gets there?"

James required more time to complete the reading research and writing project than his peers, but scaffolding enabled him to produce a report on bats with simple sentences, causal links, and curriculum vocabulary. He happily found illustrations for his report and independently rehearsed reading it, negotiating with his SLP, "OK, you read it first; then, I'll read it second." After author chair, in response to a question asked by a peer, James headed to Internet resources, directing his own research efforts with self-talk, "I need how long bats live."

We observed this need for words in another third-grade writing project where students developed personal businesses as part of a social studies lesson (Nelson, 2002). The students needed to learn curriculum vocabulary related to three types of resources: *natural, capital,* and *human.* The new words represented difficult concepts, so concept maps were introduced to teach features, definitions, and applications of the new terms. With support of individualized scaffolding, vocabulary concepts were extended and deepened by encouraging students to visualize what they would experience walking into their business, such as, "When I walk into your store, what will I see, hear, and smell?" "What people (I mean *human resources)* will I see?" "What will they be doing?" This led to the generation of concepts for roles, machines, and materials students were aware of but had no single word to describe, for example, the person who makes the food at a restaurant (*chef*), the machine where you pay *(cash register),* the person who takes your money *(cashier).*

In addition to opportunities to teach students new words desired and needed for projects, individual scaffolding also framed morphologic and orthographic cues supplied by words such as *cash register* and *cashier.* Superordinate and subordinate categorical associations could be scaffolded as students considered what types of people and roles might be considered *human resources* and what materials might be considered *natural resources.* One group of students with scaffolding support engaged in a discussion of what could be called a *building* and concluded that a *house, factory,* and *store* in a *mall* were all different *buildings* and that these were types of *capital resources.*

Promote Incidental Learning Possibilities

New words present themselves in every context of the writing lab. Sometimes there is a difficult word written in the activity instructions or readings; sometimes new words or idiomatic expressions present themselves in author chair; and sometimes new words appear in conversations. In one classroom, a teacher addressing two students in conflict, reflected on one student's accusation and stated, "That's like the pot calling the kettle black." The student, unsure of the meaning, paused briefly, then asked for interpretation. Together the students and teacher interpreted the figurative language and decided they did not agree 100 percent that it was appropriate to the situation at hand.

Opportunities also arise to help students extend and deepen their meanings by helping them form associations across contexts. For example, when the fourth-grade students were learning about Henry Ford and considering the meaning of the word *assembly line,* their teacher reminded them of how, earlier in the school year, the class had formed an assembly line for making peanut butter sandwiches. These students were also assisted to understand the concept by a photograph on the web page that enabled them to visualize the term's meaning in more than one way to better abstract its distinctive semantic features.

Brainstorm New Words and Set Goals for Use

Some students, while motivated to use new words, may lack vocabulary diversity and flexibility. These students may benefit from lessons that teach new vocabulary explicitly and brainstorm word relationships. All stages of the writing process approach offer opportunities to focus young authors on the task of relating information in a clear and interesting fashion. Instructor scaffolds might help students to set personal goals for: (1) using at least one descriptive word in each sentence, (2) identifying ordinary words and finding better alternatives, and (3) using at least five interesting words per day.

One example of vocabulary instruction might start with the teacher putting a word or phrase representing a basic theme on the board, such as *fear*. At that point, the class might participate in a group or individual brainstorm, writing down any words they think of that relate to this theme. Next, the students could group the words into categories (e.g., *emotions/reactions, people/creatures, opposite words, places, other words*) and receive scaffolding to help them apply appropriate labels for the categories. The teacher then might scaffold the students in new directions, such as to think of words that tell a person is *not afraid*. In encouraging the discussion, teachers can ask students to relate stories about fearful or frightening experiences they have had, thus facilitating assessment and activating appropriate background knowledge for individual students (Nagy, 1988). Such activities set the stage for enriching subsequent reading, talking, and writing experiences in the classroom.

A brainstorming activity to support expression is illustrated in the work of a fourth-grade teacher who routinely selected examples of "over-used words" (e.g., *said, went, good, pretty*) and brainstormed with students a list of more descriptive alternative words. In whole class and small group work, students developed semantic webs from team brainstorms, literature resources, and references, such as the thesaurus. The teacher then guided her students to compare and contrast the different ideas conveyed by the words on their maps, considering how different choices might alter meaning and reader interest. To conclude the lesson, this teacher challenged her students to revise their own written work, replacing "retired" words with new and more specific words from their semantic maps ("wow" words). A classroom semantic map posted as a classroom writing support also served as a resource for lesson repetition. At the end of the lesson, students shared their revisions in the context of their sentences from their stories. This lesson guided students to:

- Look for targeted words in their stories, "Do you notice any over-used words in your story?"

- Describe how a person said something or how he went, "Can you describe how he said it?" "How did he go?" "What did it look like?"

- Use class resources (brainstorming maps and lists, author notebook, thesaurus), "Where can you look for help?"

- Reflect on alternate word choices, "Say it with your new word and see how it sounds." "Do you want to think of other words or put that one in your story?"

- For students who used simple word choices because spelling new words is too risky, scaffolding began with assurance that picking the best word is valuable to communication and that spelling can be a joint activity.

Another example of this brainstorming and personal goal-setting came from Brett, a sixth-grade student participating in an after-school language lab, who showed difficulty with social-pragmatic skills and written expression. He spoke in short sentences with simple word choices, reluctantly approached writing tasks, and needed much scaffolding to participate in one-on-one and small group interactions. In collaboration with Brett's teacher, the narrative genre was chosen to support his ability to relate stories. In planning sessions, he decided to write a story about a favorite topic, baseball. Together with his SLP, he planned each of the components of this story, beginning with a list of eight characters. When Brett was prompted to add some description for each character, he wrote an age next to each. He was scaffolded again to provide more information about his characters, "Now that I know your characters' names and ages, I'm wondering if you can tell me something about your characters that will help me picture them or know them better." Brett then extended his descriptions to include: "Not so smart but a good hitter," "Handsome," "Tall and a little fat," and "The best, the captain."

After drafting his story, Brett read it aloud to his SLP. Following his sentence, "The team was winning," Brett's SLP scaffolded, "Oh wow, how did the team feel then? I wonder what that felt like." Pausing for several minutes, Brett added, "So they were stunned and speechless." To promote more independence, his SLP commented on how this part made the story even more interesting; then asked him how many more emotions he could add to his story. Enjoying the enthusiastic response his descriptions had already elicited, he independently wrote, "They were bummed because they lost their game."

Scaffold Word-Learning Skills and Basic Vocabulary Knowledge

As discussed earlier, students with language-learning difficulties sometimes struggle with basic vocabulary, leaving gaps in their comprehension of school language. Some students have particular difficulty with function words that establish relationships within sentences, or words that convey spatial and directional relationships.

Susan, a seventh-grade girl identified with language difficulties, was reported by her teacher to be doing well in math calculations, but struggling with story problems. Probing Susan's understanding of a homework problem that asked students to calculate distance from the center of a pond, her SLP had Susan read a story aloud. Susan read without difficulty. Her SLP then asked her to draw a picture that represented the question. Susan drew the pond. When asked what she needed to do next, she stated, "Mark the center." But instead of placing her pencil in the center of the drawing, she placed it in the middle of the top of the box in which the pond was drawn. This led to a discussion about the word *center* and an objective aimed at assessing and teaching this and other basic relational vocabulary in the context of story problems, using drawing as a tool to assess the student's current meanings and to expand them as necessary.

Model Self-Talk about Word Meaning and Forms

Metalinguistic knowledge can be used effectively to support vocabulary learning in a number of ways. Generating words in a category or finding synonyms for an overused word in a written composition are examples of tasks that require metalinguistic knowledge and processing. Metalinguistic understandings also are central to discussions of relationships among word meanings using graphic organizers to compare and contrast, categorize, and illustrate shades of meaning along a continuum. Metalinguistic awareness also may be used to help students learn about inflectional and derivational morphology "chunks" and how they relate to the spoken (phonological) and written (orthographic) structures of words, their prefixes, and their suffixes (Blachowicz & Fisher, 2004).

Self-talk that draws attention to and reflects on the characteristics of words provides a model of how to think about words. These metalinguistic strategies support students in developing a process for exploring words. To make the process repetitive and explicit, students can be taught to ask and respond to a specific set of queries designed for the class and individualized based on student need. For example, students might be taught to assess their own word knowledge with questions such as, "Is there a word I'm not sure of?" and "Do I know the meaning of this word?" They also might be instructed to guide themselves through the process of constructing meaning using self-talk questions such as, "What parts of this word do I recognize?" and "Should I look it up or ask someone for help?" Scaffolding first promotes responses to and integration of information gathered from these questions, then proceeds to teach students to bring their own "word detective" strategies online independently, thereby becoming actively engaged in processing new vocabulary.

Provide Print and Technological Supports

Print and technological supports give students tools to become more independent learners. One type of support—graphic organizers—help students to visualize word relationships. Venn diagrams, word lines, two-column charts, and semantic maps of word associations or word features are all types of graphic organizers (McKenna, 2004). Figures 3.2–3.6 display examples. Synonym webs are similar to semantic webs, except semantic webs include all types of related concepts, whereas a synonym web includes only words that are synonyms (Blachowicz & Fisher, 2004). Once completed, graphic organizers serve as a resource and can be posted in classrooms or copied into an author notebook.

Author notebooks are learning tools that evolve as students become more actively engaged in language activities. We have used writing notebooks (also called *authors' journals*) as a place to keep mini-lesson handouts, individualized scaffolding self-talk strategies, a personal dictionary, and other resource materials.

Figure 3.2   **Venn Diagram**

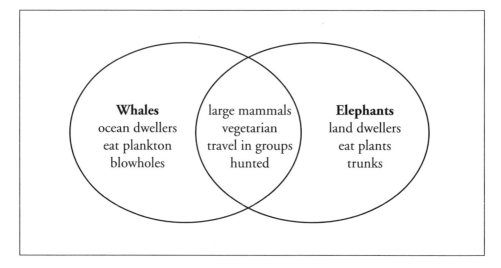

Figure 3.3

Word Line

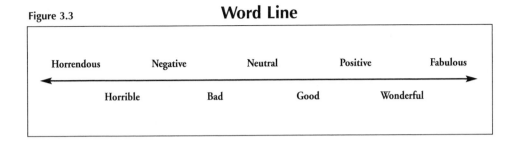

Horrendous   Negative   Neutral   Positive   Fabulous

Horrible   Bad   Good   Wonderful

Figure 3.4

Two-Column Chart

Tired Words	Wow Words
good	mouth-watering
pretty	glowing with health
happy	joyful
make	create
fast	at the speed of sound
nicely	respectfully

Figure 3.5

Semantic Map

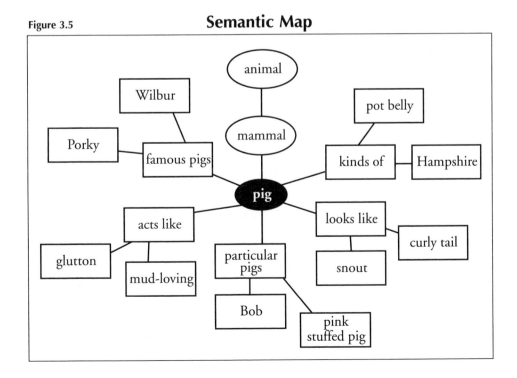

Figure 3.6   **Synonym Web**

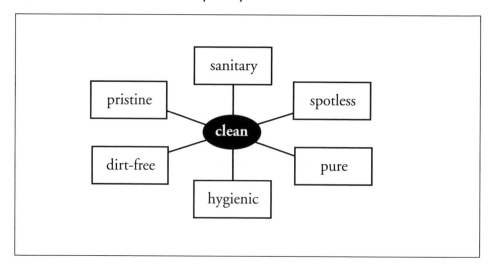

Vocabulary supports also come in the form of word walls, classroom charts, and diagrams that make available commonly used words, morphemes, and orthographic patterns. Word walls are large spans of wall space dedicated to words sorted by spelling patterns (e.g., *-ion* words). As new words are encountered, students add them to the appropriate group on the wall.

Computer software features can be used at every stage of the writing process. They provide motivating and useful tools for students as young as first grade. Computer software features make revising easier and take the sting out of scaffolding spelling. Software features can provide the following support:

- Support word generation and fluency (e.g., word prediction, word banks, speech recognition; Raskind & Higgins, 1999)

- Give feedback on spelling accuracy (e.g., spell-checkers and speech synthesis)

- Offer alternate spellings (spell-checkers)

- Reference a word meaning (dictionaries) or synonym (thesaurus)

As with other support tools, students need repeated and guided experience to use the computer tools independently. While sitting at a computer terminal side-by-side with students and focusing on their language, educators can read students' work aloud, take the audience perspective, trip over errors as they occur, appreciate the content, and wonder aloud about additional details. An alternative to the reader tripping over errors is for the student to have the computer read his or her work using the speech synthesis feature. Often students notice the mismatch between their intended words and the computer's pronunciation, or a missing word. This electronic feedback leads students to revise syntax, punctuation, words, and spellings as needed.

Connect Word Meaning and Printed Form

To become literate, students must make associations between the phonological and orthographic patterns of words (i.e., spoken and written forms) as well as between word forms and meanings. This process is facilitated in the preschool years for students who have *phonological awareness* abilities for rhyming and playing with syllable patterns in books and oral activities. By the time they are in kindergarten, students are expected to be able to demonstrate *phonemic awareness* by recognizing individual sounds in spoken words and telling what sound, for example, a word starts or ends with. They also begin to acquire *phonics skills* for associating sounds with print symbols. Knowledge of letter and sound associations is followed by knowledge of connections among orthographic patterns, syllables (also called word families), and morphemes. Eventually, most students develop fluency for reading and spelling a large corpus of words automatically. Current evidence suggests that learning across language levels and modalities (listening, speaking, reading, spelling) does not occur in just one direction, but reciprocally and recursively (Ehri, 2000).

Apply Word Decoding Strategies

To help students with the acquisition, use, and monitoring of effective word identification strategies, Lovett et al. (1994) designed a word identification strategy training (WIST) program. It utilizes four decoding strategies to help students with dyslexia use what they already know to: (1) identify words by analogy, (2) attempt variable vowel pronunciations, (3) seek the part of the word that they know, and (4) "peel off" prefixes and suffixes in multisyllabic words. When reading, students must first be able to decode words if they are to have access to meaning, and this involves shifting to a metalinguistic attitude if they come to a word that they do not know. At such a point, the reader must make a decision whether to try other decoding strategies until a known word pops out, to treat the item as a new vocabulary word, or simply to continue reading (whether or not the text makes sense without the word in question). Lovett et al. investigated the impact of these strategies with a group of 7 to 13 year-olds with learning disabilities. They found significant post-test gains in word reading and transfer for students who learned decoding strategies relative to a control group who had received only their accustomed classroom instruction. They also observed that students taught with this strategy-based method demonstrated greater metacognitive control over their own decoding processes.

Shondra was a student who learned to connect meaning and form through self-talk. She was a seventh-grade student who participated in an after-school writing and homework lab. One day, Shondra brought in a school assignment to read a book and write a book report. During planning for her book report, her SLP noticed that Shondra had difficulty reporting main ideas and ordering ideas sequentially. A return to reading some passages from the book showed that Shondra had difficulty reading many of the multisyllabic words aloud and tended to ignore unknown words or produce substitutions that were nonwords or best guesses based on context. She did not stop to work through words strategically or return to words later. When asked about words with which she had previously demonstrated difficulty, Shondra made educated guesses based on context, but shared that there were a lot of words she did not know. Her primary strategy for reading comprehension was to make sense of text as best as she could by relying on words she knew and ignoring those she did not. Shondra also revealed a personal goal of reading faster, which had been negatively influencing her motivation to spend time figuring out difficult words. When her SLP modeled reading of some of the words, Shondra reluctantly repeated multisyllabic words and demonstrated difficulty with sequencing sounds in syllable-by-syllable production. Goals were established for Shondra to independently identify unknown words in her reading, to use self-talk question-guides to figure out meaning, and to use syllable-by-syllable articulation strategies to improve speech production. Her self-talk questions and instructions (listed in Table 3.2) were printed on a sheet and Shondra was guided through them until she could use the process independently.

As Shondra moved from a get-it-done-fast approach to a reading approach that reflected on meaning, she stopped more frequently to check for meaning and ask for help. In one session, during a reading activity, she identified the word *inexplicable* as unknown. With support, she constructed meaning from its root and bound morphemes, and practiced its pronunciation. It was a word that caught her interest and triggered her imagination. To aid recall and use, she wrote the word in her author's notebook, followed by an original and personally relevant sentence, "I had an inexplicable feeling of happiness when I got a horse." On the way out of the clinic she used the word, eliciting a surprised and

Table 3.2

Sample Self-Talk Strategies to Improve Word Comprehension and Word Decoding

Level of Question	Strategy
1. **What can I ask myself when I don't know how to read a word?**	• Do I know this word? • What are the parts I recognize? • Does it look like another word I already know?
2. **What can I do to say this word?**	• Look at the word parts or syllables. • Say each syllable. • Practice the syllables and see if it sounds right.
3. **What can I do to figure out the meaning of this word?**	• Read the whole sentence and see what it tells me about the word. • Look for parts of the word that are similar to words I already know. • Read beyond the sentence and make sure that my ideas about the word still make sense. • Ask someone if my ideas about the word's meaning are on the right track. • Try out the new word when I write or talk about what I've been reading.

appreciative look from her mother. A week later, the word showed up in her book report, then later in a personal narrative.

Although Shondra continued to approach new words with some caution and awkwardness, each session she found words that she embraced (e.g., *exaggerating, stark, aimlessly,* and *scowled),* and then employed across oral and written contexts. This intervention resulted not simply in new vocabulary acquired, but a new attitude toward noticing and figuring out words she formerly believed were inaccessible, and new strategies that Shondra applied to understanding new words as she encountered them. Increased independence and flexibility in using these strategies was expected to develop across contexts as she experienced further opportunities to apply her strategies.

Integrate Connections among Sounds, Letters, and Words

Encoding words in print (i.e., spelling) emphasizes the integration of sound-level and word-level language skills and builds reciprocal skills for written and spoken word knowledge. Effective scaffolding for spelling varies with the developmental level of students. Research supports early intervention for at-risk spellers, starting with teaching the alphabetic principle (i.e., that phonemes are represented by graphemes). This helps students make connections between sound and letter, the whole word, and onset-rime feedback (Berninger, 2000). Students who are beginning to develop phonemic awareness and to connect sound-symbol associations can be guided to spell words represented in their oral vocabularies by saying words slowly, with heightened attention to how the words sound and feel, reproducing them one sound or syllable at a time, and figuring out the orthographic combinations of letters to represent those sounds, syllables, and morphemes.

The following example from a dialogue between A'leyah, an emotionally fragile first-grader identified as being at-risk for learning difficulties, and her SLP, illustrates this scaffolding process. The scaffolding language of the clinician helped A'leyah to apply her emerging knowledge of the alphabetic principle, while providing enough support to keep her from becoming discouraged by the process.

SLP: Why are you upset?

A: I can't spell sponge.

SLP: Say the word and tell me the sounds you hear.

A: [writes S-U-G]

SLP: You wrote sug. It has some of the sponge sounds, but some are missing. Say the word again and see if you feel any other sounds in your mouth.

A: I feel a /p/ [inserts p]. Now I feel a /dʒ/.

SLP: You're very close. This is the dictionary spelling of sponge [writes].

A: The "g" and the "j" make the same sound!

SLP: You're exactly right, but in this case you need the letter "g." I guess you'll have to remember that. Do you want to put it in your personal dictionary?

Support Growing Knowledge of Morphemes and Patterns

As students begin to acquire and apply sound-symbol knowledge, educators can assist them to make more connections between words and orthographic patterns. Scaffolding at this level focuses students to attend to patterns of spelling represented in:

- Root morphemes and derivational prefixes and suffixes (e.g., *repeat, repetition*)

- Inflectional bound morphemes (e.g., *walk, walked*)

- Orthographic patterns (e.g., *-ight* word family, silent *-e* rule)

Scaffolding at this level guides students to integrate sound-by-sound spelling strategies with information they have learned about how orthographic patterns (i.e., word parts) relate to word meaning. For example, students relying on sound cues alone may confuse words such as *in* and *and*. Scaffolding first acknowledges what the student has mastered, such as, "You are really listening to how words sound when we talk. When I say, 'me and my mom,' the *and* sounds like *in.*" Many students will discover the difference between these words with this level of feedback and eagerly make a change. For others, scaffolding continues by more explicitly demonstrating meaning differences, as for example, "What does *in* mean?" "What does *and* mean?" "Which one do you want in your sentence?" "Do you know how it is spelled?"

If the word has inflectional suffixes, the SLP might pose a question first to see if the student has more information encoded than was displayed spontaneously. For example, if the student spelled *walked* as *wokt,* the SLP might first observe, "You are hearing the /t/ sound that comes at the end of the word *walked* when we say it, but you know what? There is a chunk that we use when we write about things that happened in the past. Do you know that chunk?" If this appears to be a new concept, an individual mini-lesson can be developed to teach this concept. Often a student's written work will offer other opportunities to apply the new spelling strategy. The student is guided to look for more examples and to revise spelling as supports are gradually withdrawn. If other examples are not present, an individual mini-lesson might provide some direct practice with repeated experiences.

Develop Spelling Supports Collaboratively

Together, students and educators should develop spelling resources to add learning and independence. Personal dictionaries can be arranged alphabetically, but also by meaning categories, and to emphasize morpheme or orthographic pattern lesson supports. For example, one student who had difficulty with encoding and decoding *wh* question words developed a page that listed each *wh* question word with an example: *who, what, where, when, why.* When he felt some confusion about which word to use, he could refer to the page to help him make decisions about spelling. Pages can be developed for morphological patterns, word families, or self-talk guides like Shondra's in Table 3.2 on page 133 that would include such examples as: "Do I know any word parts?" "Do I know any words like this one?" "Is there any part of the word that I know?"

Writing Lab Evidence for Promoting Vocabulary Learning

What evidence is there to support the effectiveness of contextualized vocabulary intervention? We have reported data from a feasibility study conducted in three third-grade classrooms in which gains by students with disabilities were compared with gains by typically learning classmates (Nelson et al., 2004; Nelson & Van Meter, in press).

The golden goal of special education is "catching up," but it is one that is rarely accomplished. We reasoned, therefore, that if we could show gains by students with special needs that equaled or surpassed those made by peers, we would be able to conclude at least preliminary support for use of an inclusive, collaborative, computer-supported writing lab approach to language instruction and intervention.

The study extended across one school year and involved 32 typically developing students and 9 students with special needs. Each student produced written story probes at the beginning (September 3) and end (May 4) of the school year. Diagnoses for the special needs group included speech-language impairment, learning disability, emotional impairment, and autism spectrum disorder. The special needs students participated in all classroom-based writing lab activities with peers three days per week for one hour each. Written story probes and classroom observations were used to set goals collaboratively for all students at discourse-, sentence-, and word-levels, and for writing processes and social interaction. Stories for students with special needs, however, were analyzed more completely, using goals and benchmarks coordinated with goals and objectives in the students' individualized education programs (IEPs). SLPs provided extra scaffolding to help students with special needs achieve their goals, including supports for vocabulary development and word-form knowledge related to speaking, reading, and spelling, as described in this chapter.

Results for discourse measures (story scores and total words), sentence measures (measures of syntax and sentence combining), and word measures indicated gains for the students with special needs that were comparable to or better than those of their typically developing peers (Nelson & Van Meter, in press). The word-level measure that best captured vocabulary growth was a diversity measure calculated with the SALT software program (Miller & Iglesias, 2004) as the number of different words (NDW) included in each sample.

The mean (and standard deviation) for NDW produced by the students with special needs in their September baseline probe was 13.8 *(SD = 6.4)*. By May, those students produced a mean of 54.7 *(SD = 40.1)* different words in their probes. This yielded a significant mean gain of 40.88 *(SD = 35.6)* and an effect size, which is a quantitative estimate of practical significance, of 1.15. This was more than one standard deviation of gain and considered a large effect size. Meanwhile, the students in the typical development group started with a mean NDW of 27.7 *(SD = 10.7)* and advanced to a mean of 62.4 different words *(SD = 32.7)*. This gain also was significant and resulted in an effect size of 1.01, which was almost one standard deviation of gain. Although both groups showed high variability for the NDW measure, this was taken into account and there were still significant and large group differences. Thus, we concluded that the effect size for the gains by students with special needs compared with that made by peers with typical development. Our findings provided preliminary support for use of an inclusive, collaborative, computer-supported writing lab approach to promote vocabulary development. Such an approach may help students with language disorders close the written expressive vocabulary gap.

The results for word spelling gains, measured as percent of words spelled correctly, were less encouraging. In fact, spelling percentage was the only measure in which students with special needs did not equal the growth made by peers. The students with special needs made a nonsignificant change in percent of words spelled correctly from 79.8 percent *(SD = 13.53)* to 82.7 percent *(SD = 13.02),* for a small effect size of .19. Typical group students made significant gains from 79.0 percent *(SD = 18.6)* to 85.8 percent *(SD = 9.5)* words spelled correctly, for a modest effect size of .37. These findings are consistent with Berninger's (1999) observation that spelling ability is particularly difficult to modify. Interpretations should be tempered, however, by recognizing that the percentages are computed on a much larger group of different words at the end of the school year than at the beginning.

As a formative evaluation index, we took spelling results as evidence that we needed to focus more explicitly on spelling knowledge and strategies within writing lab activities. In a subsequent study (Ansell, Nelson, Van Meter, & Clark, 2004), we compared qualitative changes in spelling abilities and percent correct measures for two groups of students. One group received writing lab instruction and intervention from mid-second through third grade, and a comparison group of students received writing lab instruction and intervention during the last half of second grade only. In that research, the intervention group students (which included those with both typical development and special needs) made significant gains in the use of increasingly mature spelling strategies, as well as percent correct; whereas control group students (also including those with typical development and special needs) did not achieve significant growth in any of the measures.

Conclusion

The literature on vocabulary learning, as well as our clinical experience, points to the importance of supportive language-learning environments in which new vocabulary learning is embedded in meaningful, thematic-based discussions, where students experience the communicative power of words to evoke images and affect their audience in meaningful ways. We have emphasized techniques and service delivery models, including the writing lab approach, in which students participate in active learning experiences, with extended work on meaningful projects and an expectation of sharing products with an appreciative audience. The value of such projects is in their ability to lead students to become aware of and to need words to achieve their own communicative and learning goals.

Scaffolding techniques have been described for starting with what students know and framing and focusing them on previously missed cues about words' meanings and forms so they can make connections with prior knowledge through repeated practice. We also have emphasized that complete word learning involves not only mapping meanings onto concepts and into semantic networks, but also the development of fluent automatic skills and conscious self-directed strategies for word identification (in reading), accurate pronunciation (in speaking), and strategic spelling (in writing). Finally, we have shared stories about the joy of discovering a new word or strategy that works in embedded intervention. Our hope is that readers will take these ideas and develop them further, having fun with language and the creativity of language learners. It is by stimulating the expression of original ideas in words that vocabulary learning can be activated best.

Acknowledgments

The funded projects reported in this chapter were co-directed by Dr. Christine Bahr, our longtime colleague and coauthor. This work was supported by the U.S. Department of Education Office of Special Education Programs research grants H180G20005 and H324R980120. Engagement of graduate students in the activities also was supported by training grants H029B10245, H029B40183, and H325H010023. We are grateful to the teachers, administrators, parents, our graduate students, and particularly the students, who agreed to collaborate with us in this work and to grant their permission to share the results of our joint efforts. In particular, this chapter includes contributions of teacher discourse by fourth-grade teacher Katherine A. Jackson, and clinician discourse by graduate students Blessing Bamiro, Katie Brinks, Ella Lutzska, Elizabeth McKinley, Andrea Postma, Claudia Suero, and Rebecca Williams.

References

Adams, M. J., & Henry, M. K. (1997). Myths and realities about words and literacy. *School Psychology Review, 26,* 425–436.

Anderson, R. C., & Freebody, P. (1981). Vocabulary knowledge. In J. Guthrie (Ed.), *Comprehension and teaching: Research reviews* (pp. 77–117). Newark, DE: International Reading Association.

Anglin, J. M. (1993). Vocabulary development: A morphological analysis. *Monographs of the Society for Research in Child Development, 58*(10, Serial No. 238).

Ansell, P., Nelson, N. W., Van Meter, A. M., & Clark, M. J. (2004, November). *Measuring spelling growth over time in elementary writing samples.* Poster session presented at the annual convention of the American Speech-Language-Hearing Association, Philadephia, PA.

Apel, K., & Swank, L. K. (1999). Second chances: Improving decoding skills in the older student. *Language, Speech, and Hearing Services in Schools, 30,* 231–242.

Atwell, N. (1987). *In the middle: Writing, reading, and learning with adolescents.* Portsmouth, NH: Heinemann.

Atwell, N. (Ed.). (1990). *Coming to know: Writing to learn in the intermediate grades.* Portsmouth, NH: Heinemann.

Beckman, M., & Edwards, J. (2000). The ontogeny of phonological categories and the primacy of lexical learning in linguistic development. *Child Development, 71,* 240–249.

Berninger, V. W. (1999). Coordinating transcription and text generation in working memory during composing: Automatic and constructive processes. *Learning Disability Quarterly, 22,* 99–112.

Berninger, V. W. (2000). Development of language by hand and its connections with language by ear, mouth, and eye. *Topics in Language Disorders, 20*(4), 65–84.

Blachowicz, L. Z., & Fisher, P. (2004). Building vocabulary in remedial settings: Focus on word relatedness. *Perspectives: Newsletter of the International Dyslexia Association, 30*(1), 24–31.

Brownell, R. (2000). *Expressive One-Word Picture Vocabulary Test–2000 Edition (EOWPVT–2000).* Eagan, MN: Pearson Assessments.

Calkins, L. (1986). *The art of teaching writing.* Portsmouth, NH: Heinemann.

Calkins, L. (1990). *Living between the lines.* Portsmouth, NH: Heinemann.

Calkins, L. (1994). *The art of teaching writing* (2nd ed.). Portsmouth, NH: Heinemann.

Carey, S. (1978). The child as word learner. In M. Halle, J. Bresnan, & G. Miller (Eds.), *Linguistic theory and psychological reality.* Cambridge, MA: MIT Press.

Carey, S., & Bartlett, E. (1978). Acquiring a single new word. *Papers and Reports in Child Language Development, 15,* 17–29.

Carlisle, J. F. (1996). An exploratory study of morphological errors in children's written stories. *Reading and Writing: An Interdisciplinary Journal, 8,* 61–72.

Carlo, M. S., August, D., McLaughlin, B., Snow, C. E., Dressler, C., Lippman, D. N., et al., (2004). Closing the gap: Addressing the vocabulary needs of English-language learners in bilingual and mainstream classrooms. *Reading Research Quarterly, 39,* 188–215.

Carr, E., & Wixon, K. K. (1986). Guidelines for evaluating vocabulary instruction. *Journal of Reading, 29,* 588–595.

Cunningham, A. E., & Stanovich, K. E. (1998). What reading does for the mind. *American Educator, 22,* 8–15.

Dunn, L. M., & Dunn, L. M. (1997). *Peabody Picture Vocabulary Test–III (PPVT–III;* 3rd ed.). Circle Pines, MN: American Guidance Service.

Edwards, J., Beckman, M. S., & Munson, B. (2004). The interaction between vocabulary size and phonotactic probability effects on children's production accuracy and fluency in nonword repetition. *Journal of Speech, Language, and Hearing Research, 47,* 421–436.

Edwards, J., Fourakis, M., Beckman, M. E., & Fox, R. A. (1999). Characterizing knowledge deficits in phonological disorders. *Journal of Speech, Language, and Hearing Research, 42,* 169–186.

Ehri, L. C. (2000). Learning to read and learning to spell: Two sides of a coin. *Topics in Language Disorders, 20*(3), 19–36.

German, D. J. (1983). I know it but I can't think of it: Word retrieval difficulties. *Academic Therapy, 18,* 539–545.

Graves, D. H. (1983). *Writing: Teachers and children at work.* Portsmouth, NH: Heinemann.

Graves, D. H. (1991). *Build a literate classroom.* Portsmouth, NH: Heinemann.

Graves, D. H. (1994). *A fresh look at writing.* Portsmouth, NH: Heinemann.

Hall, W. S., Nagy, W. E., & Linn, R. (1984). *Spoken words: Effects of situation and social group on oral word usage and frequency.* Mahwah, NJ: Erlbaum.

Harmon, J. M. (2000). Assessing and supporting independent word learning strategies of middle school students. *Journal of Adolescent & Adult Literacy, 43,* 518–527.

Hart, B., & Risley, T. (1995). *Meaningful differences in the everyday experience of young American children.* Baltimore: Brookes.

Kail, R., & Leonard, L. B. (1986). Word-finding abilities in language impaired children. *ASHA Monographs, 25.*

Lahey, M., & Edwards, J. (1996). Why do children with specific language impairment name pictures more slowly than their peers? *Journal of Speech and Hearing Research, 39,* 1081–1098.

Levelt, W. J. M., Roelofs, A., & Meyer, A. S. (1999). A theory of lexical access in speech production. *Behavioral and Brain Sciences, 22,* 1–75.

Lidz, C. S., & Peña, E. D. (1996). Dynamic assessment: The model, its relevance as a non-biased approach, and its application to Latino American preschool children. *Language, Speech, and Hearing Services in Schools, 27,* 367–372.

Lovett, M. W., Borden, S. L., DeLuca, T., Lacerenza, L., Benson, N. J., Brackstone, D. (1994). Treating the core deficits of developmental dyslexia: Evidence of transfer of learning after phonologically and strategy-based reading training programs. *Developmental Psychology, 30,* 805–822.

McKenna, M. C. (2004). Teaching vocabulary to struggling older readers. *Perspectives: Newsletter of the International Dyslexia Association, 30*(1), 13–16.

Miller, J. S., & Iglesias, A. (2004). Systematic Analysis of Language Transcripts (SALT; Version 8). [Computer software] Madison, WI: Language Analysis Lab, Waisman Center, University of Wisconsin–Madison.

Miller, G., & Gildea, P. (1987). How children learn words. *Scientific American, 257*(3), 94–99.

Nagy, W. E. (1988). *Teaching vocabulary to improve reading comprehension.* Urbana, IL: National Council of Teachers of English; and Newark, DE: International Reading Association.

Nagy, W. E., & Herman, P. A. (1987). Breadth and depth of vocabulary knowledge: Implications for acquisition and instruction. In M. G. McKeown & M. E. Curtis (Eds.), *The nature of vocabulary acquisition* (pp. 19–35). Mahwah, NJ: Erlbaum.

National Reading Panel. (2000). *Report of the National Reading Panel: Teaching children to read.* Washington, DC: National Academy Press.

Nelson, N. W. (1989). Curriculum-based language assessment and intervention. *Language, Speech, and Hearing Services in Schools, 20,* 174–184.

Nelson, N. W. (1995). Scaffolding in the secondary school. In H. Winnitz (Series Ed.) & D. Tibbits (Vol. Ed.), *Language intervention: Beyond the primary grades* (pp. 375–419). Austin, TX: Pro-Ed.

Nelson, N. W. (1998). *Childhood language disorders in context: Infancy through adolescence* (2nd ed.). Boston: Allyn and Bacon.

Nelson, N. W. (2002). Activating the vocabulary sponge: What happens when young authors need words to tell their stories. *Perspectives on Language, Learning, and Education, 9*(3), 18–24.

Nelson, N. W., Bahr, C. M., & Van Meter, A. M. (2004). *The writing lab approach to language instruction and intervention.* Baltimore: Brookes.

Nelson, N. W., & Van Meter, A. M. (2002). Assessing curriculum-based reading and writing samples. *Topics in Language Disorders, 22*(2), 35–59.

Nelson, N. W., & Van Meter, A. M. (in press). The writing lab approach for building language, literature, and communication abilities. In R. McCauley & M. Fey (Eds.), *Treatment of language disorders in children: Conventional and controversial interventions.* Baltimore: Brookes.

Nelson, N. W., Van Meter, A. M., Chamberlain, D., & Bahr, C. M. (2001). The speech-language pathologist's role in a writing lab approach. *Seminars in Speech and Language, 22,* 209–220.

Raskind, M. H., & Higgins, E. L. (1999). Speaking to read: The effects of speech recognition technology on the reading and spelling performance of children with learning disabilities. *Annals of Dyslexia, 49,* 251–281.

Schacter, D. (1987). Implicit memory: History and current status. *Journal of Experimental Psychology: Learning, Memory, and Cognition, 13,* 501–518.

Scott, J. A., & Nagy, W. E. (1997). Understanding the definitions of unfamiliar verbs. *Reading Research Quarterly, 32,* 184–200.

Shore, W. J., & Durso, F. T. (1990). Partial knowledge in vocabulary acquisition: General constraints and specific detail. *Journal of Educational Psychology, 82,* 315–318.

Stahl, S. A. (2004a). Vocabulary and the child with learning disabilities. *Perspectives: Newsletter of the International Dyslexia Association, 30*(1), 1–4.

Stahl, S. A. (2004b). Scaly? Audacious? Debris? Salubrious? Vocabulary learning and the child with learning disabilities. *Perspectives: Newsletter of the International Dyslexia Association, 30*(1), 5–12.

Stanovich, K. E. (1986). Matthew effects in reading: Some consequences of individual differences in the acquisition of literacy. *Reading Research Quarterly, 21,* 360–407.

Ukrainetz, T. A., Harpell, S., Walsh, C., & Coyle, C. (2000). A preliminary investigation of dynamic assessment with Native American kindergartners. *Language, Speech, and Hearing Services in Schools, 31,* 142–153.

White, T. G., Graves, M. F., & Slater, W. H. (1990). Growth of reading vocabulary in diverse elementary schools: Decoding and word meaning. *Journal of Educational Psychology, 82,* 281–290.

Chapter 4

Grammar: How Can I Say That Better?

Sarita L. Eisenberg

Introduction

An important focus for language intervention with school-age students who have language impairments is to address deficits in the grammatical system. Grammatical deficits limit a student's ability to express meaning, encode a variety of messages, and effectively participate in discourse (Donahue, 1987; Leonard & Fey, 1991; Mentis, 1994). The importance of making grammatical skills a focus of intervention is supported by research that shows the persistence of grammatical deficits beyond the preschool years (Stothard, Snowling, Bishop, Chipchase, & Kaplan, 1998) and the impact of grammatical deficits on academic success and literacy (Catts & Kamhi, 1999; Scarborough, 2001; Snowling, Bishop, & Stothard, 2000; Stothard, et al.). Many students exhibiting poor reading and writing skills demonstrate grammatical deficits, even if they have not been diagnosed as having a language disorder (Catts, Fey, Zhang, & Tombin, 1999; Juel, 1988).

The Nature of Grammatical Deficits in School-Age Students

Grammatical Development in the School Years

The typical plan for targeting grammar in preschool children is to follow a developmental template for introducing new structures into conversation in a particular order and at particular ages or developmental levels (see for instance, Miller, 1981). However, this type of developmental progression for grammar is not available for school-age students. There are several reasons for this.

First, the typical oral conversational format (e.g., Evans & Craig, 1992; Hadley, 1998) is not amenable to sampling the range of grammatical forms important to academic discourse. For instance, the passive form (e.g., The speeding train had been hijacked by the terrorists), which occurs frequently in expository writing, is less likely to be observed in conversational speech (Biber, 1988). Forms produced within narrative and expository genres as well as the written modality must, therefore, also be considered (Scott, 1988; Scott & Stokes, 1995). The differences between genres or modalities may mask any subtle developmental changes within a genre or modality. For example, while there is an increase in noun phrase complexity during the elementary and middle school years (Eisenberg, Ukrainetz, Justice, Gillam, & Kaderavek, 2004; O'Donnell, Griffen, & Norris, 1967), more elaborate noun phrase structures are seen in the writing of 9 year-olds than in the speech of 12 year-olds (Perera, 1986). Even within a single genre, sampling differences can affect the presence of expanded noun phrases (Eisenberg et al., 2004).

Second, the later-developing forms are often infrequent or involve combinations of earlier-learned forms. Examples of this include verb forms with both the perfect and progressive (e.g., had been thinking) and noun phrases with both adjective phrases and relative clauses (e.g., the deceptively slender contender who had defeated the champion). This necessitates a fine-grained analysis of the structures produced in multiple and varied samples. Third, many syntactic structures serve discourse as well as grammatical purposes. For example, the conjunction *and,* in addition to its additive meaning between clauses, is used by school-age students to maintain the main flow of a story line, separating it from subsidiary events (Peterson & McCabe, 1991).

Finally, students may vary more within an age group than between adjacent age groups (see Loban, 1976; Scott, 1988). Scott notes that even the target "adult" level of competence varies considerably if one considers "realistic" versus "ideal" standards of performance. Educated adults display a wide range of syntactic sophistication, in both academic writing and oral conversation. As a result of these discourse, modality, and experiential effects, a strictly developmental view of grammatical sophistication provides limited guidance for assessment and intervention.

Determining Targets for Grammatical Intervention

Two areas of investigation reveal the grammatical structures that are likely to require intervention. One area includes studies that have directly investigated grammatical deficits in school-age students with language impairments. These studies show an overall immaturity in grammatical structure with less elaboration and fewer complex forms than age peers (Fletcher, 1991; Simms & Crump, 1983; Thordardottir & Weismer, 2001a). In addition to immaturity, there is a low but significant frequency of grammatical errors (Bishop, 1994; Ingham, Fletcher, Schletter, & Sinka, 1998; King & Fletcher, 1993), particularly in written text (Gillam & Johnston, 1992; Scott & Windsor, 2000; Windsor, Scott, & Street, 2000).

The other area includes studies that have documented aspects of grammatical development that typically are later acquired and may occur only in writing. These later-developing structures may be completely lacking or less frequently used by students with language impairments. For instance, Loban

(1976) reported that students in a low language-proficiency group produced fewer propositions per C-unit at the end of high school than did a high language-proficiency group in first, second, and third grades. (A *C-unit* is a main clause with all attached subordinate clauses and nonclausal phrases. It includes elliptical utterances such as "Me too.") Paul (2001) suggests "preventive intervention" to target these literate language structures. Box 4.1 on page 150 lists problematic and later-developing grammatical structures that could be targets for intervention, and Box 4.2 on page 152 provides definitions of conjunction types.

Students with language impairments show a limited variety of verb forms. The persistence of deficits with grammatical morphemes, particularly those that mark verb tense, into the school years has been well-documented. Students with language impairments may show inconsistent usage of bound grammatical morphemes such as the past tense *-ed* or third person singular *-s* (Bishop, 1994; King & Fletcher, 1993; Windsor et al., 2000), and show limited ability to generalize morphemes to new word roots (Bellaire, Plante, & Swisher, 1994). Students with language impairments show limited use of the copula, auxiliaries, and modals, as well as aspectual verb forms such as the perfect (e.g., *had driven),* progressive (e.g., *was driving),* and passive (e.g., *was driven by)* that involve verb suffixes and auxiliaries (Fletcher, 1991; King & Fletcher). For instance, King and Fletcher reported errors with the passive verb form, such as, "The cow can milk by it" (instead of "The cow can be milked by it"). More elaborate forms that combine these basic verb forms (e.g., "The girl may have been seen as she left work") are later developing and are also likely to be problematic (Nippold, 1998).

Other aspects of grammar related to verbs also present problems for school-age students with language impairments. Students with language impairments produce fewer verb arguments (Ingham et al., 1998; King, 2000; King & Fletcher, 1993; Rice & Bode, 1993; Thordardottir & Weismer, 2001b). Omissions of required arguments may result in ungrammatical utterances. Students omit direct objects, for example, "I told Ø already," "There is something white but I can't find Ø," "You can take Ø over there" (King & Fletcher), "When he went home he had Ø at the nighttime" (Scott, Windsor, & Gray, 2002). They also omit locative elements, for instance, "Put the chair Ø," or "I can't fit him Ø" (King & Fletcher). Omissions of this sort can seriously reduce the understandability of a student's utterances. Consider a student in Ingham et al. who produced the sentence "The little boy blow a gate" to describe a picture in which a boy was blowing bubbles towards a gate, giving a misleading idea about what was being blown. Students with language

Box 4.1   **Later-Developing Grammatical Structures**

Noun phrase expansion

- Adjective phrase with two or more adjectives (the *three main* parts)
- Adjective phrase with adverbs (the *extremely* cold conditions)
- Post-noun modifying prepositional phrase (the details *of the plan*)
- Post-noun modifying relative clause (Thomas Edison, *who invented the light bulb)*
- Post-noun modifying nonfinite clause (the best way *to study)*
- Post-noun modifying appositive (Gonaïves, *the country's third-largest city)*
- Post-noun elaboration (Other countries *such as Italy and France)*

Verb form expansion

- Perfect aspect (The enemy *had reached* the outskirts of the town.)
- Passive voice (The evidence *was found* after a long search.)
- Combination of modals and auxiliaries (The company *could have been spending less.)*

Predicate expansion

- Combination of two-object noun phrases (The architect showed *the town council the plans for the new building.)*
- Combination of object-noun phrase and prepositional object (The assistant leaked *the scandal to the press.)*
- Combination of object-noun phrase and locative (The attorney placed the *confidential papers in a locked cabinet.)*

Conjunctions

- Coordinating conjunction (She had missed breakfast *but it was still too early for lunch.)*
- Subordinating conjunction (The storm destroyed many homes *even though its intensity had lessened.)*
- Correlative conjunction (Elevated blood sugar increases the risk of heart disease *not only in people with diabetes but also in those with high-normal readings.)*

Box 4.1—*Continued*

Complement clauses (nominal constructions)

- Infinitive clause (The general decided *to invade* before dawn.)

- Tensed verb clause (The woman realized *that she had seen the stranger before.)*

- *Wh* clause (They didn't know *when the attack would start.)*

- Participial clause (The bank recently began *charging* for money machine withdrawal.)

Adverbial constructions

- Adverbs (I can't, *unfortunately,* get you more paper.)

- Adverbial clause with a subordinating conjunction (The space capsule crashed *when its parachutes failed to open.)*

- Adverbial clause with an infinitive verb form (He saved up his money *[in order] to buy a new computer.)*

Other complex sentence constructions

- Subject complement clause *(Patients taking the new medications* had not been told the risks.)

- Subject relative clause *(The students who had taken the review course* scored higher on the exam.)

- Preposed subordinate clause *(As the dust cloud drew closer,* the man could see that there were four horsemen riding towards him.)

- Cleft construction *(It was yesterday that* she came home from the hospital.)

- Extraposition construction *(It would be sensible* to leave early.)

- Sentences with three or more clauses *(Because the state has underfinanced its public schools, some schools have been forced to cut programs.)*

Sources: Nippold (1998); Weaver (1996)

impairments also produce fewer optional verb arguments. For instance, the participants in a study by King produced sentences such as "Some dogs bite" or "It's running," which, although not ungrammatical, contained limited information since they did not include objects and locatives. Thordardottir and Weismer (2001b) reported less use particularly for the later-developing argument types of source (e.g., He started out by throwing bricks at them from the roof) and beneficiary (e.g., Should I tell you about the traps?).

Box 4.2   # Definitions of Conjunction Types

Coordinating

Join two independent clauses *(and, but, for, nor, or, so, yet)*

Subordinating

Introduce a dependent clause *(after, although, as, as if, because, before, even if, even though, if, since, so [that], unless, until, when, whenever, wherever, whereas, while)*

Correlative

Signal a symmetrical relation *(Both...and, either...or, neither...nor, not only...but also.)*

Grammar also involves rearrangement of the basic declarative sentence to form different sentence types such as negatives and questions, and combinations of simple, single clause sentences into complex utterances with two or more clauses. Students with language impairments produce fewer questions and a more limited range of questions, both in the range of *wh* words used and in the range of auxiliary and modal elements. School-age students with language impairments produce fewer complex sentences and have more difficulty producing these forms, as demonstrated by maze behaviors and the large amount of ungrammaticality for these sentences (Fletcher 1991; Gillam & Johnston, 1992). Later-developing complex forms that are likely to be problematic include adverbial connectives used for syntactic conjunction and for discourse cohesion (Greenhalgh & Strong, 2001; Scott & Klutsenbacker, as cited in Scott, 1995), left-branching structures (such as preposed adverbial clauses, center-embedded relative clauses, and clauses used as subjects), combinations of clause types within one sentence, and word order variations such as passives and cleft sentences (Scott & Stokes, 1995).

One other aspect of grammar involves phrasal expansions. Noun phrases can include one or more adjectives and these adjectives can themselves be modified by adverbs. Noun phrases can also be followed by phrasal and clausal modifiers. Students with language impairments show limited production of noun phrase expansions (Fletcher, 1991; Greenhalgh & Strong, 2001). Complex noun phrases involving more than two modifiers, modification of adjectives by adverbs, and postnoun modification are all later developments likely to be problematic for students with language impairments (Scott & Stokes, 1995).

Although school-age students with language impairments may be totally lacking in some grammatical structures, many structures may be known but used less frequently, with reduced productivity, less fluency, and less flexibility (Fletcher, 1991). A known structure may not be extended to all applicable cases. For instance, the passive verb form may be produced only with some verbs, or relative clauses may be produced in object position but not in subject position. There may also be pragmatic limitations on usage. The specific grammatical form is partly determined by discourse needs and presuppositional inferences. Students with language impairments might not be able to adapt sentence forms to meet these demands but instead, may limit use of sentence forms to single discourse contexts. For instance, questions might be used to seek information, but might not be used to seek clarification or to be more polite to an authority figure. The third-person morpheme might be used for talking about a scripted event, but might not be used in expository writing.

Grammatical limitations are particularly apparent in written discourse and, for some students with language impairments, may only be seen in writing. In a study by Windsor et al. (2000) comparing oral and written text for narrative and exposition, omissions of the regular past tense *-ed* only appeared in the written language samples. Whereas students with typical language show more sophisticated language in their writing than in their spoken discourse, Gillam and Johnston (1992) found the reverse for students with language impairments. School-age students with language impairments might continue to use spoken language forms in their writing and might not develop the more literate forms specific to written discourse (Scott, 2002).

Finally, selection of grammatical targets takes into account discourse demands and curricular expectations. If the student is expected to produce narratives, descriptions, and procedures, then the grammar required to compose these genres should be considered. Guidelines for selecting grammatical targets based on discourse considerations can be found in Leonard and Fey (1991), and Mentis (1994). In addition, the SLP should examine the curriculum to determine language structures that the student needs in order to successfully complete class assignments and participate in the classroom (Nelson, 2002). The teacher can be asked to identify average students, whose classroom participation and work products can be used as a basis for comparison to the student's performance. This is important so that targets can be prioritized in a way that matches discourse demands and teacher expectations.

Intervention Studies

Instructional approaches for targeting grammar fall on a continuum of natural-ness (Fey, 1986). At one end are the more natural enrichment approaches and at the other end are discrete skill approaches. Enrichment approaches assume that language development will occur naturally when authentic opportunities are provided. Discrete skill approaches provide direct lessons on specific aspects of language in isolation from their usage in context.

There have been few studies investigating the efficacy of either of these approaches on grammatical development and usage by school-age students with language impairments. Studies of enrichment approaches have looked mostly at the impact of intervention on overall reading and writing perform-ance, or on language objectives for content, organization, or quantity of output. Studies of discrete skill approaches have looked mostly at usage of grammatical structures within the specific intervention context. What evi-dence exists suggests that teaching discrete skills may not be sufficient for improving grammatical usage outside of the intervention setting. There is, therefore, little or no empirical information on whether oral or written grammar improves for students with language impairments within either of these approaches.

Most of the evidence for efficacy comes from clinical interventions for pre-school children with language impairments and from classroom instruction for students with typical language in general education or English as a second lan-guage (ESL) classes. The preschool intervention studies provide evidence that intervention approaches that employ naturalistic contexts and follow child interests may be more effective in achieving spontaneous usage of language tar-gets than structured drill approaches (see Leonard, 1998, for a review). However, intervention for school-age students differs from intervention for preschool children in some important ways and so it is not clear to what extent we can generalize efficacy results from younger children to beyond age six. For school-age students with language impairments, it is not sufficient to target grammar within conversation. Since use of grammatical structures becomes increasingly context-dependent (Nippold, 1993; Scott, 1995), it is necessary to target structures within the specific contexts that call for those structures. Grammar must also be targeted within monologic discourse and for written language as well as for conversational discourse. The different nature of these activities may require different types of instruction.

Discrete Skill Approaches

Discrete skill approaches provide instruction on grammatical forms separate from usage of those forms in discourse, either oral or written. While some massed practice can be helpful (Paul, 2001; Wallach & Butler, 1994; Wiig & Semel, 1980; see also Chapters 1 and 2), the use of discrete skill instruction as the sole intervention approach, without embedding use of newly acquired structures in meaningful activities, is not recommended. Discrete skill procedures that provide concentrated practice opportunities without using structures within meaningful discourse contexts can be grouped into the categories of grammar analysis, modeling, imitation drills, error detection, and sentence combining.

Grammar Analysis

In grammar analysis, students are taught labels for grammatical constituents and analyze isolated sentences for those constituents. Killgallon (1998) referred to this as "sentence dissection" and reported that it did not result in improved sentences in student writing. Weaver (1996) reviewed a large number of studies on the efficacy of explicitly teaching grammar analysis within general education classes. Students showed little generalization of grammatical structures to contexts of use. Furthermore, they demonstrated low performance even on classroom examinations that tested their sentence analysis skills. Weaver's conclusion was that the study of grammar—that is, labeling constituents and analyzing sentences—is a difficult activity even for typically achieving older students and, whether used alone or in combination with other instructional methods, does not contribute to functional usage of grammar in language expression, to reading skills, or to actual writing.

This lack of efficacy has significant implications for language intervention. Grammar analysis continues to be one of the predominant approaches used by speech-language pathologists (SLPs) for school-age students with language impairments. For example, Gerber (1993) recommended having a student circle or underline specific grammatical forms such as conjunctions or pronoun referents in lists of sentences. Gerber also suggested having students break up complex sentences into component clauses. The results reported by Weaver (1996) suggest that such formal instruction in grammar analysis is not helpful and takes time away from other procedures that may be beneficial.

Modeling

In modeling approaches, students are exposed to the target form within a text or list of sentences. Teachers have used modeling in general education classrooms, including the presentation of model compositions that exemplify the characteristics of good writing (Hillocks, 1987). Teachers have also presented isolated sentences taken from published sources to provide models of literate language forms not found in their students' writing (Killgallon, 1998).

Modeling has been shown to facilitate production of grammatical forms by preschool students with language impairments within the intervention context (see Fey & Proctor-Williams, 2000 for a review). Models may be presented in a list of sentences before requiring the student to attempt the form (e.g., Leonard, 1975), a procedure that Fey and Proctor-Williams called *observational modeling*. Models may also be alternated with production attempts by the student (e.g., Connell, 1987), called *imitative modeling* by Fey and Proctor-Williams. Connell compared a modeling condition, in which the student was not allowed to produce the target, to an imitation condition, in which the student attempted the target immediately after each model. In both conditions, the target emerged in production after one session, but there was a higher proportion of usage with untrained exemplars following the intervention that included production. Ellis Weismer and Murray-Branch (1989) compared a condition of modeling without production to a condition providing intermittent opportunities for production of the target. Again, students showed improvement in both conditions but there was more consistent usage in the condition that included production opportunities. These results suggest that modeling combined with imitated productions may be beneficial for development of grammar, although the next section suggests that these improvements may not generalize well.

Imitation Drills

In an imitation approach, students are prompted to repeat an utterance and are then reinforced for correct production. Elley (1991) reviewed studies of ESL instruction that compared an imitation approach to an indirect program that included sustained silent reading, shared book experiences (discussion and activities related to the books), and/or experience-based approaches (reading material that the student had previously dictated). Students in the indirect approach did better than students in the imitation condition not only on their overall reading, listening, and writing but also on tests of the grammatical structures that had been explicitly taught in the direct instruction programs.

In intervention studies for preschool children with language impairments, imitation drills have been shown to be successful in facilitating correct production of grammatical targets, although this effect was limited to production of the same type of utterances in response to the same verbal prompts (see Fey & Proctor-Williams, 2000 for a review). As pointed out by Fey and Proctor-Williams, most imitation interventions involve having the child hear and produce only the target form. Connell (1982) has suggested an alternative imitation approach, in which children imitate both the target and a contrasting form that is semantically and/or grammatically related to the target. Using this approach, Connell (1986) did find generalization of grammatical targets to spontaneous usage during a play period that immediately followed a contrastive imitation activity. Imitation drills also typically have the child repeat the exact model. Another option is partial imitation, which retains the structure of the model while changing the content (Ellis Weismer & Murray-Branch, 1989; Killgallon, 1998). These studies suggest that imitation drills incorporating grammatical contrasts and partial imitations can lead to generalization beyond the immediate intervention setting. These results also suggest that the most effective timing of the imitation drill is immediately prior to an activity that involves contextual use of the same structure.

Error Detection

As part of language intervention, Wiig and Semel (1980) suggested having students make grammaticality judgments, judging individual sentences as "right" or "wrong," or signaling when they hear an ungrammatical sentence in a list of sentences or a paragraph. Gerber (1993) suggested practice exercises in detecting and correcting errors, using sentences taken from student writing. McQuade (1980), however, reported on the lack of success of a classroom approach based on error detection. The class first studied parts of speech and basic sentence structure (i.e., grammar analysis) and then applied this to the task of looking for errors in a list of sentences written specifically for that purpose. McQuade found a decrease in the total number of errors in student writing. However, a closer look showed that this decrease was only for mechanical errors such as capitalization. Most importantly, the quality of writing did not improve and may actually have become worse since students "awkwardly and...self-consciously constructed sentences to honor correctness above all virtues, including sense" (p. 29) and the students did not incorporate this instruction into their editing.

Structured practice in catching errors on isolated sentences does not, therefore, appear to lead to improvements in grammatical usage or even to improvements in editing. Even practice with error detection on larger passages may not be helpful if it is done outside of a context that makes the editing meaningful.

Sentence Combining

In sentence combining, students are presented with two or more sentences and required to create a single, longer sentence. Combining can either be cued or open (Strong, 1986). Cued combining indicates (e.g., by underlining) the constituent in one sentence that is to be inserted into another sentence and provides additional words, such as conjunctions, to achieve particular forms of combining. In open combining, students can experiment with different ways to combine the sentences. A related procedure involves sentence expanding, having students build sentences of increasing length and complexity by adding to a kernel sentence (Gould, 2001). Both sentence combining and sentence expanding are used by SLPs in language intervention (Gerber, 1993; Paul, 2001). Gerber and Paul also suggest another alternative, paraphrasing. In this procedure, the SLP models pairs of contrasting sentences that have the same content but differ in some aspect of form. The student is then given another sentence in one of the two forms (typically the less elaborate of the two forms) and is asked to change that sentence into the modeled contrasting sentence form.

The efficacy of sentence combining in increasing grammatical complexity has been well-documented for general education students (see Strong, 1986; and Weaver, 1996, for reviews). O'Hare (1973) investigated the efficacy of explicit practice in sentence combining without any prior study of grammar analysis and without having students learn grammatical terminology. He reported that the group who participated in sentence combining exercises showed more improvement in writing than did a control group, who spent more time in a regular language arts curriculum. O'Hare reported improvement in overall writing quality as well as in "syntactic maturity," based on the range of sentence types used.

Of particular importance for language intervention is the conclusion by Weaver (1996) that this procedure works particularly well for remedial or at-risk students. This is supported by a study of college students by Smith and Hull (1985), which reported both a structure-specific effect for the trained target forms and an overall increase in syntactic complexity. However, only the students with an initially low usage-frequency for the target forms showed improvement after the sentence combining program. Students with an initially high usage-frequency actually showed a decrease in usage of the targeted forms after the program of sentence combining.

Evaluating Discrete Skill Approaches

In sum, some discrete skill approaches that target production of grammatical forms may be beneficial in achieving production of grammatical forms. Potentially beneficial approaches include imitation involving contrasting sentences and content alterations, modeling combined with production, and sentence combining. However, not all discrete approaches are useful. Grammar analysis and error detection for isolated sentences do not seem to be beneficial.

In addition, discrete skill approaches, although useful, cannot do the whole job and should not be used alone. Studies of both preschool language intervention and classroom instruction have found limited generalization of discrete skill instruction to contexts other than the practice drill context itself. This result is expected in a framework that suggests that skills are learned and deployed within purposeful activities (see Chapter 1). Intervention should, therefore, embed discrete skill exercises within a larger context of meaningful communication.

Another consideration is the time spent on discrete skill instruction. Most of the programs using discrete skill teaching methods involve prolonged periods of such instruction. Killgallon (1998), for instance, has developed a curriculum for classroom instruction that uses presentation of model sentences from published texts and production activities that include imitation and sentence combining. In language intervention, many SLPs provide large amounts of discrete skill instruction on grammatical targets (hence the large number of published materials for this type of instruction). Strong (1986) suggested that it may not actually be necessary to spend a lot of time on these activities. Instead, Strong advocated for classroom teachers to engage in sentence combining two to three times per week for short periods of time while monitoring student writing for problem sentences and transferring this practice back into actual writing. The Smith and Hull (1985) study of writing instruction for college students supports Strong's idea. These authors found that a week of sentence combining paired with directions to use the longer sentences in their writing was comparable to an entire semester of practice in sentence combining. This suggests that discrete skill instruction, when it is provided, should occur in brief sessions followed by instruction that applies the lesson in meaningful writing or speaking activities.

Enrichment through the Writing Process Approach

Enrichment approaches seek to provide learning opportunities within authentic reading and writing activities. This may be particularly important for students with language impairments who may be placed in separate classrooms that emphasize basic skills and restrict the time available for reading and writing (Christenson, Thurlow, & Ysseldyke, 1989; Graham & Harris, 2002; McGill-Frazen & Allington, 1991). The underlying philosophy of enrichment approaches is constructivism. Constructivism views the student as an active learner involved in constructing his or her own knowledge. The adult functions as a facilitator who guides the student through the discovery process (Graham & Harris, 1997) by providing task organization and interactive scaffolding.

Process-oriented classrooms provide extended opportunities for writing. Students choose their own topics and they write for a real purpose and to a real audience. Writing is preceded by brainstorming; proceeds through the stages of drafting, revision, and editing; and is followed by sharing (Gould, 2001). As characterized by Graham and Harris (1997), "children have meaningful things to say and the teacher's job is to help them learn how to say it" (p. 242). Instruction within a process approach is motivated by teacher observation of student writing difficulty rather than reflecting a preplanned series of steps (Brinkley, 1998). Within a writing process classroom, instruction takes place during individual writing conferences, mini-lessons, modeling, peer collaborations, and classroom dialogue (Gould; Graham & Harris). Nelson, Van Meter, Chamberlain, and Bahr (2001) list these same strategies in their writing lab approach to written language intervention, as well as instructional scaffolding to help students identify and repair communicative breakdowns (see also Chapter 3).

Process-oriented learning experiences utilize *teachable moments*, the teaching of specific skills when and if needed (Graham & Harris, 1997; Nelson, 1995). This approach to learning was articulated by Backus and

Beasley (1951; as cited in Newman, Creaghead, & Secord, 1985) as a process that moves from the whole to the parts and back to the whole. Spiegel (as cited in Graham & Harris), however, has criticized reliance on teachable moments as leading to haphazard and incomplete instruction. In a study of an ESL classroom, Reyes (as cited in Graham & Harris) reported that a process approach to writing did not increase student usage of conventional forms (such as punctuation and capitalization) in their writing. Graham and Miller (1979) reported less gain in spelling by a group of poor readers and spellers in a process-oriented classroom than in a condition which included direct spelling instruction as well as frequent reading and writing. In a study by Gillam, McFadden, and van Kleeck (1995; described more fully in Chapter 2), students with language impairments who experienced a more process-oriented learning experience composed oral narratives with lower form scores than students who experienced a more discrete-skill approach (but showed better content and overall quality). Based on their review of such studies, Graham and Harris (1997) advocate the need to systematically teach both spelling and grammar. However, there are several possible reasons other than the process-oriented approach for the limited learning of what Graham and Harris (1997) call basic skills. One issue is the amount of time actually devoted to basic skills. For instance, Graham (1992) found that process-oriented teaching in classrooms focused mostly on discourse level skills, such as content and organization, with little attention given to skills such as grammar or handwriting.

Another issue is the stage in the writing process at which grammar is usually addressed. Grammar is typically worked on during the editing stage (e.g., Montgomery & Kahn, 2003; Nelson et al., 2001; Wong, 2000). Montgomery and Kahn suggest that "the editing process is an ideal point at which to teach language structure to students who want to learn, because it pertains to their stories" (p. 148). However, writing more than one draft is initially a struggle, even for typically achieving high school students (Callies, 1998). Students may resist revision aimed at correcting and modifying grammar, particularly if this occurs after previous revisions for content and organization. Such late-stage revision suggests to students that grammar is only a formality, rather than an important part of how meaning is expressed. Furthermore, attending to grammar only during editing may provide assistance for the current project rather than serving as a means for learning and practicing grammatical forms that can then be internalized and used more independently in subsequent writing.

The experience of Eva, an eighth-grade girl with a written language impairment, illustrates how late-stage grammatical editing can be a problem.

On her first draft of a book report, Eva had written three paragraphs, each consisting of three sentences. The speech-language pathologist (SLP) worked with her on revising her report to add content, with a focus on story grammar elements. After two cycles of revision, Eva had increased the quantity of writing to two pages and had increased the number and length of paragraphs. Her final report adequately covered the story events and provided characters and setting information. However, her report demonstrated repetitive clause structure, numerous run-on sentences connected with *and,* tense shifting between past and present, a lack of descriptive elaboration, and frequent ambiguity due to overuse of pronouns. These difficulties were presented as subsidiary editing issues, rather than as integral parts of writing that affected meaning. Not surprisingly, Eva resisted going back to her work with the SLP to do this final editing.

It may also be the case, as suggested by Freedman (1993; cited in Graham & Harris, 1997), that instruction at teachable moments may not occur frequently enough or be explicit enough for students with special needs. Whereas students with typical language can learn new forms from minimal exposure within larger contexts, students with language impairments may not benefit from such incidental or "rare event learning" (Graham & Miller, 1979; Nelson, 1988). Instead, they may need more concentrated exposure and practice opportunities in order to learn new grammatical forms (Fey & Proctor-Williams, 2000; Johnston, 1985; Nelson, Welsh, Camarata, Butkovsky, Camarata, 1995). A process-oriented approach may not, therefore, by itself provide a sufficient density of exposure and practice for learning and mastery of grammatical forms.

It seems that neither discrete-teaching nor enrichment-learning environments are sufficient for the student with a language impairment to develop and use grammatical forms. The isolated skill focus of discrete approaches directly teaches grammatical forms but does not ensure that students can transfer those forms into their conversation or writing. The holistic focus of enrichment approaches provides the meaningful context for using grammatical forms, but does not provide the explicit guidance needed for school-age students with special needs to acquire strategies and skills. SLPs will therefore need to incorporate features of both approaches to teach production of specific grammatical forms and foster use of those forms in speaking and writing. In other words, SLPs should provide repeated opportunities for intense, systematically supported, explicit skill instruction within purposeful contexts.

A Framework for Targeting Grammar

Intervention for grammatical targets should include both direct teaching and opportunities to engage in meaningful activities for oral and written language. Intervention, whether in a separate room or in the classroom, should occur mostly within activities that come from the classroom curriculum, using the texts and assignments designated by the student's teacher. The SLP can also work with the classroom teacher to develop alternative assignments that would target specific grammatical forms.

Intervention for grammatical targets should incorporate meaningful production of those targets. Although grammar has traditionally been considered a lower-level aspect of discourse, this view needs to be changed. Grammar exists to code meaning. Meaning cannot be targeted independently from the grammatical forms used to express that meaning. Consider, for instance, the following complex sentence with two embedded clauses: *Jerry told me that he is going home now.* A student lacking knowledge of such structures and limited to simple sentences is likely to encode only one of the ideas expressed in the more complex sentence and produce only the following simple sentence: *Jerry is going home now.* Alternatively, a student might produce a series of simple sentences that separately code each of the ideas, but without conveying the relationships among them: *Jerry is going home now. He told me.* Targeting grammar, then, should occur as a first-order goal rather than occurring after content has been covered.

Explicit instruction for grammatical forms occurs during mini-lessons and micro-lessons. *Mini-lessons* are brief explanations (5 to 10 minutes) of how to do something (Atwell, 1987) and are used prior to an activity to highlight one or more grammatical forms that will be used within that activity. Note that the author uses the term somewhat differently than has been suggested for classroom teachers. Mini-lessons in classrooms involve teacher explanation and demonstration with little or no interaction with the students and with no practice exercises (Weaver, 1996). In mini-lessons for language intervention, the student learns by doing, with opportunities not only for hearing but for practicing the target. The term mini-lesson is used here to distinguish this method from the prolonged practice in isolation that typically occurs in pull-out language intervention. Mini-lessons for language intervention are interactive lessons that may include brief, focused skill drills engaged in prior to scaffolded use of a structure within a meaningful activity.

Micro-lessons are provided in a whole-part-whole paradigm within a single activity (Backus & Beasley, 1951). Micro-lessons involve interruption of an activity as problems arise in using specific aspects of grammar. Micro-lessons are very brief explanation and practice, taking no more than a few minutes before returning to the activity (Brinkley, 1998). To introduce micro-lessons within an activity, the SLP might say something like, "That was a hard sentence for you to write/say. Let's practice that kind of sentence."

Based on the prior literature review, instruction that involves extended practice in identifying and labeling grammatical constituents and in analyzing isolated sentences for errors should not be used. This does not exclude the use of grammatical terminology. There are some grammatical terms that the student needs to know because these are essential components of a language arts curriculum and because these terms are needed to comment on grammar during composing and revising of written work (Weaver, 1996). Students need to be able to recognize word categories such as nouns and verbs. They also need to distinguish between the subject and predicate. Rather than asking students to complete traditional grammar exercises, such as circling all the nouns, these concepts can be incorporated into comments about grammar during meaningful activities. More complex forms can also be labeled as they become relevant, but the emphasis should be on teaching through example and meaning, not formal definitions (Weaver). We must keep the goal in mind that "it's not important that they learn the grammatical terms...only that they use varied sentence structure" (Rowe, 1998, p. 107). For example, a mini-lesson to highlight relative clauses could be introduced by saying,

> *This new type of sentence has a relative clause in it: 'The cup that is green is my favorite.' This part that starts with 'that' is the relative clause and it gives extra information about this noun, the cup. Let's practice making up relative clause sentences and then we can try them out in your paper.*

Grammar must be targeted systematically. Within any activity, no more than three new or emerging targets should be addressed. The SLP can continue to support previously targeted forms by commenting on them when they are used by the student and by providing scaffolding when they are not used. The SLP should keep a list of grammatical targets for each student, which includes previous as well as current targets. It is also helpful to list structures that have been identified as future targets. This helps the SLP to modulate current expectations for the student's performance so that too much is not expected, keeping in mind that "the goal for students is to steadily increase their skills, not necessarily to produce a flawless product" (Gould, 2001, p. 194). In addition, the expected performance of the student should not be achievement of structures in isolated sentences (e.g., John will produce expanded noun phrases), but rather integrated use within meaningful discourse (e.g., John will write a description that appropriately employs expanded noun phrases, subject-verb agreement, and compound sentences).

Mini-Lesson Procedures

Mini-lessons present examples of grammatical forms and include brief massed practice opportunities for production of those forms prior to an activity incorporating embedded skills instruction. The purpose of the mini-lessons is to familiarize the student with grammatical forms that will be useful and appropriate to the subsequent activity. Mini-lessons can also help the student achieve fluency in generating grammatical forms that have been previously targeted but are still not readily generated by the student. This section describes five methods for teaching school-age students syntax targets during mini-lessons: *observational modeling, content alterations, contrastive modeling and imitation, sentence expanding,* and *sentence combining.* These methods are described separately but, in actual practice, will often be used together. A modification for school-age students is the addition of simple metalinguistic comments that address the forms being used and the meanings conveyed by those forms.

Observational Modeling

In observational modeling, a series of sentences containing a target form are presented to the student. Fey and Proctor-Williams (2000) suggest presenting between 10 and 20 model sentences that describe pictures so that the student can see the form-meaning relationship. In their approach, the student listens to the entire set of models before any production attempts are elicited. The student is then asked to produce the same sentence form to describe either the same set of pictures or a different set of pictures. The student is given feedback about linguistic accuracy. An example of observational modeling for relative clauses is presented in Table 4.1 on page 166.

As an alternative, the student could be presented with short cohesive texts that include a high density of the target form. Short books and poems work well for this. Ratner, Parker, and Gardner (1993) provide a list of books for younger students grouped according to grammatical form. Note that to

Table 4.1

Observational Modeling Procedure
for Teaching Relative Clauses

Step	Example Script
Step 1 SLP models sentences with relative clauses, pointing to the people in the picture.	SLP: (Picture 1) Here's a boy who is wearing a raincoat. And here's another boy who is wearing a sweatshirt. This girl knows the boy who is wearing the sweatshirt. She doesn't know the boy who is wearing the raincoat. (Picture 2) Now I see some children who are hungry. And here are some other children who are thirsty. The teacher's giving bread to the children who are hungry. She's giving juice to the children who are thirsty.
Step 2 Student produces delayed imitation of sentences with relative clauses.	SLP: Tell me about this picture. Student: These ones are wearing coats. And these other ones are wearing sweatshirts. SLP: These children will be the warmest. They're the ones who are wearing coats. Who will be the warmest? Student: The boys what are wearing the coats. SLP: Listen to how I say it. Who will be warmest? The boys who are wearing sweatshirts or the boys who are wearing coats? Student: The boys who are wearing coats. SLP: Yes, the boys who are wearing coats will be the warmest.

Source: Fey & Proctor-Williams (2000)

achieve a sufficient density of models, it is often necessary to modify the text. As in the observational modeling procedure above, the student can be asked to produce the same sentence form by retelling the story or by talking about a new set of pictures. Another possibility is to incorporate observational modeling into joint book reading (Kirchner, 1991; Ratner et al.). In this procedure, a book is read several times so that the student can become familiar with it. The book is read again, with pauses added at various points so that the student can participate in the book reading and produce the target form.

Content Alterations

A different procedure is to alternate between the SLP's models and the student's productions and to have the student produce sentences that replicate the structure of the modeled sentence with different content (Killgallon, 1998). As for observational modeling, the modeled sentences should describe pictures so that the student can see the connection between form and meaning. Books can be used here as well, with the adult and student taking turns reading the text or describing the pictures. Box 4.3 presents an example of content alteration for a perfect verb form.

Box 4.3

Content Alteration Procedure for a Perfect Verb Form

Context	Example Script
A sequence of two pictures: 1. A boy running and a girl riding a bike 2. Both students at home with the boy looking out of breath and the girl not looking out of breath	SLP: The boy and the girl are late going home. Look, the boy is really out of breath. He had run so fast. The girl isn't so tired. Why not? Student: She rided her bike. SLP: The boy is really out of breath. He *had run* home. He *had not ridden* his bike. And the girl? Student: She had ridden her bike.

Contrastive Modeling and Imitation

Contrastive modeling and imitation (Connell, 1982) exposes the student to the target form and to another form that is semantically and/or grammatically related to the target. The contrasting sentences differ in some aspect of grammar that results in a meaning difference. Providing this contrast makes the target form more salient and helps the student to figure out the meaning of the new form. Depending on the type of structure being targeted, the contrast may be limited to a discrete part of the sentences (e.g., *The boy should wear long pants* versus *The boy should be wearing shorts to school* to target combinations of an auxiliary and modal) or may involve rearrangement of the entire sentence (e.g., *The battle was over late in the day* versus *It was late in the day before the battle was over* to target cleft constructions). This latter example could be regarded as a paraphrase rather than a true contrast. However, the shift in focus engendered by the change in form does create a subtle shift in the meaning being conveyed.

Cleave and Fey (1997) suggest presenting 10 models of the target followed by 10 models of the contrasting form. After hearing the models, the student is required to imitate the two forms in alternation, one after the other. Another format would be to present alternating models of the target and contrast, and then ask the student to produce just the target.

In the Cleave and Fey (1997) formulation, all the models and student productions describe pictures so that there is a relationship between form and meaning. However, the sentences themselves are isolated from each other so the activity is rather contrived and artificial. An alternative is to link the sentence into a larger meaningful unit, which makes it easier to discuss the meaning being imparted by the target structure. Table 4.2 demonstrates an example in which all the sentences lead to a fanciful image of breakfast across time and for different students. A metalinguistic comment introduces the discussion, to focus the student's attention on the target structures. The exchange ends with a nontechnical comment about the contrastive meanings achieved by the two structures.

Sentence Expanding

Sentence expanding starts with one simple sentence, called a *kernel sentence.* Students build sentences of increasing length and complexity by adding to the kernel sentence (Gould, 2001; Killgallon, 1998). Students are prompted to expand on the kernel in several ways: by providing a model and then having the student suggest other possibilities, by asking the student a *wh* question, or

Contrastive Imitation Introduced by Metalinguistic Comments

Table 4.2

Steps	Example Script
Skill Target	SLP: Listen, I'm going to say sentences about what happened in the past, two different ways. One way, "ate," shows it just happened once. The other way, "had eaten," shows it happened a lot.
Simple Past Models	SLP: First listen to these. • This morning, John ate yogurt for breakfast. • Yesterday, John ate bananas for breakfast. • Last week, John ate eggs for breakfast. • Two weeks ago, John ate cereal for breakfast. • At Christmas, John ate a candy cane for breakfast. John **ate** each kind of food only once.
Past Perfect Models	SLP: Now, listen to these. • Bill had eaten yogurt for breakfast every day for the last week. • Sally had eaten bananas for breakfast every day for the last two weeks. • Bill had eaten eggs for breakfast every day for the last month. • Janelle had eaten cereal for breakfast every day for the last six months. • Sari had eaten candy canes for breakfast every day for the last year! These children **had eaten** the same thing over and over again!

Continued on next page

Table 4.2—*Continued*

Steps	Example Script
Student-Imitated Productions	SLP: Say this: This morning, John **ate** yogurt for breakfast. Student: This morning, John ate yogurt for breakfast. SLP: Yes, John ate yogurt just this morning. Maybe he'll eat some again tomorrow. SLP: Kari, now say this: Bill **had eaten** yogurt for breakfast every day last week. Student: Bill had eaten yogurt for breakfast every day last week. SLP: Yes, Bill **had eaten** yogurt so many times, he's really sick of it now!

by suggesting the content to be added. Box 4.4 provides an example, based on a discussion of *Ordinary People* (Guest, 1982). Alternatively, the student could be presented with an incorrect constituent expansion and then be prompted to correct it (Grauberg, 1988).

Sentence Combining

In sentence combining, students are presented with two or more simpler sentences and asked to combine them into one longer sentence (Strong, 1986; Wiig & Semel, 1980). Combining can be either cued or open. Cued combining aims to establish prespecified sentence forms, whereas open combining allows students to experiment with different ways to combine sentences. Strong describes four types of cues that can be given, listed in Box 4.5 on page 172. Ordering the sentences to be combined cues students to the order they should use in the new sentence. Underlining cues students to the constituents to be embedded at another place within the new sentence. Striking out words cues students to what should be deleted from the existing sentence to form part of the new sentence. Providing additional words and morphemes, capitalized and within parentheses, cues students to details needed for completing the final sentence. Students learn the cues through demonstrations and while participating in sentence combining exercises rather than by having them directly explained.

Example Sentence Expansion for Preposed Adverbial (Subordinate) Clause

Box 4.4

Starting sentence:	**"He can feel the eyes on him."**
SLP:	Where was he when he felt this?
Student:	He was standing in an aisle in a library.
SLP:	Let's put that at the start of the sentence. Start by saying where he was.
Student:	Where he was…
SLP:	He was standing in an aisle at the library. Start with "when" and give the location.
Student:	*When he was standing in an aisle in a library,* he felt the eyes on him.

Source: Killgallon (1998)

Examples of sentence combining for various structures are provided in Box 4.6 on page 173, with target sentences drawn from an authentic reading source. Sentence combining is useful for targeting complex sentences (Scott, 1995; Strong, 1986; Westby & Clauser, 1999). Complement clauses, for instance, can be targeted using SOMETHING as a placeholder for the complement clause. To target relative clauses, as suggested by Gerber (1993), the constituent to be embedded after the noun is cued by underlining it and the relative pronoun to be added is also cued. Sentence combining can also be used to target phrasal elaborations. In targeting adverb use, as suggested by Westby and Clauser, underlining cues the adverb embedding and the adverb morpheme is also cued. Strong and Strong (1999) provide an example of a systematic method of approaching this.

Sentences can be taken from published sources such as newspapers or literature. Sentences can also be taken from classroom texts. Gould (2001) suggests taking sentences from student writing and having them experiment with different combinations. Students can decide which option is best and why, including the option not to combine if that better represents the intended

Box 4.5
**Sentence Combining Procedure
for a Sentence Taken from the *New York Times***

Strong's cues

- Order of sentences
- Underlines
- Strike-outs
- Additions

Simple sentences using cues to prompt sentence combining

In ~~some~~ people the disease is ignored. (EVEN)

~~Some people~~ have the most severe and frequent symptoms. (WHO)

Doctors don't pick up on the signs. (BECAUSE)

Target complex sentence created from cues

"Even in people who have the most severe and frequent symptoms, the disease is ignored because doctors don't pick up on the signs" (p. F10).

Sources: O'Connor (2004); Strong (1986)

meaning. Using the students' own writing for the sentence sources is the most meaningful context and would be expected to be the most likely to result in students applying sentence combining in their own subsequent compositions. Regardless of the source of sentences for this exercise, students will need subsequent micro-lessons during writing to combine their own sentences into more sophisticated constructions.

Embedding Grammar Instruction into Meaningful Activities

Students benefit from learning about word categories and sentence structure, and there are ways to work on this in a meaningful way without using grammar analysis. A fill-in procedure can be used to work on word classes. Excerpts from children's literature that employ a particular structure repetitively or ready-made

Sentence Combining Examples for
Box 4.6 ## Target Sentences Taken from the *New York Times*

Cuing sentences:	Some experts say SOMETHING. The problem stems from preschool itself. (THAT)
Tensed complement sentence:	"Some experts say that the problem stems from preschool itself" (p. 1).
Cuing sentences:	Some experts wonder SOMETHING. Standards are too high. (WHETHER)
Wh complement sentence:	"Some experts wonder whether standards are too high" (p. 4).
Cuing sentences:	Proponents of education equity are critical of government programs like Head Start. ~~Head Start programs~~ are less academic and more focused on emotional and behavior issues. (WHICH)
Nonrestrictive relative clause sentence:	"Proponents of education equity are critical of government programs like Head Start, which are less academic and more focused on emotional and behavior issues" (p. 4).
Cuing sentences:	Disruptive students can destroy the classroom experience for others. ~~The disruption is~~ certain. (-LY)
Adverb embedding sentence:	"Certainly, disruptive students can destroy the classroom experience for others" (p. 4).

Source: Steinhauer (2005)

materials, such as the commercially available *Mad Libs* (Penguin Books, 2005), can be used. The SLP presents the story with crucial words missing. Students are asked to supply a particular type of word or phrase. For example, emotion adverbs (e.g., sadly, angrily, curiously, excitedly) can be used to describe how the monkey and the keeper acted in *Curious George* (Rey, 1952). The activity can be made easier by initially limiting the missing elements to a single word type and gradually incorporating additional word categories, one at a time. A similar activity involves a substitution game in which the student suggests changes to words or phrases in a story (Gould, 2001). Temple and Gillett (1984) suggest having students construct sentences in which a single word category is repeated and which ends with a contradictory instance (e.g., *The bird sailed, swooped, swayed, and soared but never stopped)* to target verbs.

Word classes can also be worked on in a meaningful way within poetry. Gould (2001) suggests an *insert-a-word* procedure for adding descriptive elements to students' sentences. Students first brainstorm kernel sentences that follow a modeled form and then combine those sentences to create a poem. The poem is then expanded by adding a designated word or phrase type to each sentence. The following poem, for example, is made up of subject-verb kernel sentences that students generated from a list of rhyming words.

Cars beep.
Deer leap.
Chicks cheep.

The kernel sentences of the poem can be expanded to add word categories such as adjectives *(Fluffy chicks cheep)* or adverbs *(Cars loudly beep)*.

Peterson (1998) suggests using a graphic organizer for constructing what she calls *adjective/verb poems*. An example is shown in Figure 4.1. Students create the graphic organizer during prewriting. They choose a topic (e.g., *Dad)* and write that topic in a circle at the center of a page. Next, they think of words that describe that topic and place these words in circles connected by spokes around the topic (e.g., *helpful, smart)*. The students then think of action words to go along with their adjectives (e.g., *coaches, solves problems)* and add them in an outer ring of circles to the cluster. Using different shapes or colors, as shown in the example, can help to separate the different word categories. Finally, the student creates sentences, such as "Helpful dads coach softball," (by taking one word from each level of the organizer) and puts these sentences together to form a poem.

Adjective/Verb Poems through a Graphic Organizer

Figure 4.1

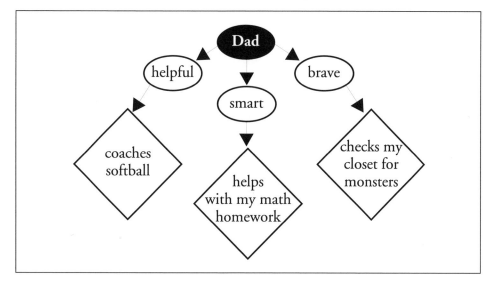

Poetry activities can also be structured so that the student has to follow instructions about the form of each line. Gould (2001) gives an example of an 11-word, 5-line poem adapted from the cinquain form, made up of a noun (line 1), two adjectives describing that noun (line 2), three *-ing* verbs describing the noun (line 3), a 4-word descriptive phrase about the noun (line 4), and a second noun related to the first noun (line 5). An example of using a cinquain poem to identify and employ nouns, adjectives, and verbs is shown in Box 4.7 on page 176. Within each of these fill-in and poetry activities, the student would hear grammatical terms such as *noun, adjective,* and *verb* but would always learn these concepts in an incidental, functional manner.

Scaffolding and Micro-Lessons during Writing

There are a variety of successful strategies for targeting conversational language in preschool students (see Fey, 1986; and Fey & Proctor-Williams, 2000, for reviews). Interactive scaffolding, described by Ukrainetz in Chapter 1, can be used to develop grammatical forms in school-age students during writing activities such as personal experience letters, letters for persuasion, fictional stories, journalistic reporting, explanations, and poems. Scaffolding can be provided immediately after the student produces a sentence that provides a

Box 4.7

Meaningful Grammar
Practice Using a Cinquain

Line 1: One word, the title (a noun)

Line 2: Two words, each describing the title (adjectives)

Line 3: Three words, each expressing an action (verbs)

Line 4: Four words, expressing a feeling (start with an adjective)

Line 5: One word, a synonym for the title (a noun)

Flame

Hot, bright

Burning, raging, spreading

Warm on my face

Fire

---

context for using a specific target form. Alternatively, the SLP can wait until the student has written an entire paragraph and then review that paragraph with the student, selecting a sentence that provides a context for using the target and scaffolding support for modifying that sentence to include the target. Models presented during scaffolding can be written down for the student as well as spoken. If a computer is being used, the student can try out different options. The student can then choose among the alternatives, including the choice not to make any change.

The following descriptions of interactive scaffolds are arranged from most to least supportive: expansions and extensions, vertical structuring, paraphrasing, multiple-choice modeling, partial modeling, and prompting. These scaffolds are intended to be used interactively within the context of a writing activity. Each of the scaffolding strategies is described separately, but different scaffolds can be used during a single activity to promote a particular grammatical structure. They can also be combined with self-regulatory scaffolds, such as reminding the student about the target form or prompting the student to explain how the target structure helps express a particular meaning.

Scaffolding may target structures that were introduced in a mini-lesson just prior to an embedded skills activity, as well as structures that were targeted in other sessions. Scaffolding should function not only to offer assistance to the student at a moment of difficulty, but also to promote acquisition of the target. If needed, the embedded skills activity can be briefly interrupted so that additional scaffolding can be provided in micro-lessons. These micro-lessons provide a quick review and practice for difficult structures. It is important that these interruptions be kept brief, one to two minutes at most, and the activity quickly resumed. If additional practice is needed for a structure, the SLP can include that structure in another mini-lesson before an activity in which the structure will be used.

Expansions and Extensions

Expansions and extensions provide consequent modeling after a student's sentence. Expansions involve repeating the student's sentence and adding any grammatical elements that have been omitted. Examples of expansions that add bound morphemes, grammatical words, and phrases to the student's sentence are shown in Table 4.3 on page 178. Extensions also repeat the student's sentence but add new information to an otherwise correct sentence or in addition to the expansion. Extensions can add words, phrases, or even clauses. The expansion or extension can be said out loud, with the student writing down the change. The expansion or extension can also be accompanied with an explanation about what is being added.

Vertical Structuring

Another strategy that follows a student sentence is vertical structuring (Schwartz, Chapman, Prelock, Terrell, & Rowan, 1985). The SLP follows up on the student's utterance by soliciting additional information. This can be done by asking one or more *wh* questions that indicate the specific type of information to be provided by the student (e.g., "Who wanted it?") or through mands (i.e., a directive that requests information, such as, "Tell me who wanted it"). After the student's response, the SLP can model the target form by saying or writing an utterance that combines the student's original content with the new content provided in response to the SLP's queries, as shown in Box 4.8 on page 179. Alternatively, following the student's response, the clinician can start the target sentence and prompt the student to complete it with the new content, as shown in Box 4.9 on page 179.

Table 4.3

Examples of Expansions and Extensions during Writing Activities

Element	Example Script
Bound Morphemes	Student sentence: You pour the acid slow into the beaker. Adult expansion: You pour the acid *slowly* into the beaker.
Words	Student sentence: Reptiles called cold-blooded animals. Adult expansion: Reptiles *are* called cold-blooded animals.
Phrases	Student sentence: The boy found under the chair. Adult expansion: Hm, this doesn't say what the boy found. The boy found *the missing ball* under the chair.
Words	Student sentence: The sun keeps reptiles warm. Adult extension: The sun keeps *cold-blooded* reptiles warm.
Phrases	Student sentence: The girl drove home. Adult extension: Let's add how she drove home. The girl drove home *in her new car.*
Clauses	Student sentence: Spain gave Florida to the United States. Adult extension: Let's add why Spain did that. Spain gave Florida to the United States *to avoid war.*

The first three rows are grouped under **Expansions**; the last three rows are grouped under **Extensions**.

Example of Vertical Structuring for a Subject Relative Clause

Box 4.8

Student is shown a picture of children at a zoo.

SLP: Tell me about the children in this picture.

Student: This boy sees the lion.

SLP: Uh-huh. Tell me something else about him.

Student: He's wearing a baseball cap.

SLP: Yeah, the boy *who is wearing a cap* sees the lion. And what about this other boy?

Source: Paul (2001)

Example of Vertical Structuring and Prompting for a Nonrestrictive Relative Clause

Box 4.9

SLP: So tell me some things about Zeus.

Student: He was the king of all the other gods.

SLP: And what else?

Student: He always had a thunderbolt.

SLP: OK, so we have two things to say about Zeus. One, he was the king of all the other gods. Two, he had this thunderbolt. How about using the word *who* to combine those ideas? Zeus, who was...

Student: He was the king of all the other gods.

SLP: Zeus, who was...

Student: The king of all the other gods?

SLP: Yes, Zeus, who was the king of all the other gods, always had...You try it.

Student: Zeus, who was the king of all the other gods, always had a thunderbolt.

Source: Paul (2001)

Vertical structuring works well for any structure that adds information to a sentence. This includes adding an adjective, prepositional phrase, or relative clause to a noun phrase. It also includes adding a coordinate or subordinate clause to a simple sentence. During initial writing, the SLP can use vertical structuring after the student has written a sentence, or can first suggest a sentence based on the prewriting information and follow up on that sentence with the vertical structuring. Additional help can be given through prompts following the question or mand. The student can be given options for constituent elaboration or the SLP can provide an incorrect answer for the student to correct (Grauberg, 1988). Vertical structuring works particularly well after a mini-lesson in which the student has practiced sentence expansion.

Paraphrasing

This scaffold involves repeating the student's sentence and then providing a model that retains the content of the student's sentence but changes the form (Connell, 1982, 1986). The student can then be asked to choose between the two contrasting sentences—the original sentence and the paraphrase. This strategy is particularly suited for targeting different conjunctions for a student who over-uses *and* (e.g., student sentence: I went to the store and I went to the park and I went home; paraphrase: I went to the store before I went to the park and then I went home). It can also be used for targeting sentence forms that involve rearrangement of the basic active, declarative sentence into other patterns such as cleft constructions or passive sentences (e.g., student sentence: The police attacked the demonstrators with tear gas; paraphrases: The demonstrators were attacked by the police with tear gas; Tear gas was used by the police to attack the demonstrators). The SLP can introduce the contrasting sentence by saying, "What if you say it this way instead? How would this change the meaning?" As illustrated above, the SLP can present more than one paraphrase option. The paraphrase strategy is particularly effective when contrastive imitation has been used during the mini-lesson that precedes the writing session and uses the same types of sentence pairs.

Multiple-Choice Modeling

Options for elaborating on sentences can be provided by giving the student choices. Choices can be provided in the form of a multiple-choice question. For instance, in response to the student's utterance, "This boy sees the lion," the SLP could model a choice of two relative clauses, "Which boy sees the lion, the boy who is wearing a cap or the boy who is wearing the red shirt?" An alternative is to ask the student questions such as, "Which one is right?" and then present two or three sentences with the same form but differing content. The student thus hears several models of the target and selects one based on accuracy of the content. Like vertical structuring, this strategy is good for targets that involve adding constituents to the student's sentence and would work well after a mini-lesson in which the student has practiced sentence combining or sentence expansion.

Partial Modeling

Support can be decreased by reducing the exactness of the model while still demonstrating the target form. The SLP makes a suggestion that the student use a particular form, saying for instance, "How about this type of sentence?" then models a sentence that uses the target form. The SLP then prompts the student to try using the same form in a new sentence, as shown in Box 4.10. The sentence can be written down and the student can construct his sentence underneath, matching each constituent of the model sentence. A partial model can also be presented by producing the target form with inaccurate content. The student would then use the modeled sentence form with different content as a correction of the model.

Prompting

The scaffold that provides the least support is the prompt. The SLP asks questions to prompt the student to add constituents or rearrange the sentence,

Box 4.10	### Example of Partial Modeling for a Tensed Verb Complement Clause

SLP:	So tell me about muscles.
Student:	Muscles are part of the body and they make you move.
SLP:	What about writing that with a relative clause sentence like this one? Cereal is a kind of food that you eat for breakfast.
Student:	Muscles are a part of the body that make you move.

without providing a model. The student can be asked, "Remember about using more description. Can you add anything here?" to prompt noun phrase elaboration. Nelson et al. (2001, p. 215) suggest the prompt, "Remember your goal to start sentences in interesting ways. What's another way besides *and then*" to prompt use of sentence-initial subordinate clauses. For a less interactive scaffold, symbols can be written into a piece of work to prompt additions or rearrangements of constituents. This is easy to do if using a computer, either immediately after a sentence is written or in reviewing parts of the written piece. For handwritten pieces, the student should skip lines when writing to leave room for additions and changes. The student can refer to a key that explains the symbols and then make his or her own corrections. This structural scaffold assumes the student has an emerging mastery and requires only reminders to understand and enact the changes.

Addressing Grammar throughout the Composing Process

The preceding section described the interactive scaffolds that can be employed during a writing activity. Attention now turns to the composing process and ways to teach grammar at each stage of this process. The composing process typically begins with a prewriting activity to generate content. The initial draft is then written, followed by rewriting and then editing. Content and organization are addressed during the initial drafting and revision stages. Elaboration of grammatical forms and correction of grammatical errors are usually targeted during the editing stage of the writing process (Montgomery & Kahn, 2003; Nelson et al., 2001; Sturm & Koppenhaver, 2003; Wong, 2000). This typical organization of the writing process addresses the complexity of composition, but ignores the importance of grammar in establishing the initial meaning to be conveyed.

Targeting Grammar during the Drafting Stage

Grammar can be worked on during collaborative writing of initial drafts. In fact, for some students, it is essential to work on form while the meaning is being encoded in a first draft. Even typically achieving students find it difficult to write more than one draft (Callies, 1998). Students find self-evaluation difficult and this is particularly true for students with weaker discourse skills (Kaderavek, Gillam, Ukrainetz, Justice, & Eisenberg, in press). Once they put ideas into words on paper, it is difficult for these students to think of another way to state the ideas. Students may also be less aware of grammatical errors or ambiguities than of missing or inaccurate content, so it is difficult for them to identify sentences that need editing for grammar. Many students—even those who are typically developing—may not be able to make grammatical changes during revision or editing, particularly changes that modify simpler grammatical forms into more complex and elaborated sentences rather than catching errors (Rowe, 1998). Students may resist further revision to correct and improve grammar after they have already revised their writing content and organization. These problems are circumvented by targeting grammar as it encodes meaning during the initial draft and then revising grammar while adding to and modifying content. To target grammatical forms during initial drafts, prewriting must be used to identify the content to be included and to group the information to be included in each paragraph. Then guidance is needed in developing key words and phrases into suitable sentences. Brief mini-lessons can be used in the prewriting and drafting stages to introduce the new grammatical forms that will be integrated into the writing assignment.

Revising and Editing

Students with typical development need instruction in revision and editing (Rosen, 1998; Rowe, 1998; Weaver, 1996). We can, therefore, expect that students with language impairments will need explicit instruction on the process of revising and editing their writing, in addition to lessons focusing on specific grammatical forms. The focus of these lessons should be on making choices to convey meaning rather than on correcting mistakes (Brinkley, 1988). These lessons teach strategies, such as making multiple passes through a writing draft to check on various aspects of grammar (e.g., checking for missing sentence constituents, looking for places where ideas could be combined into longer sentences, and checking for omitted word endings).

The SLP should model the revision and editing process. This introduces the student to specific editing strategies, but also demonstrates that these steps are a natural part of the writing process. Students initially do better in modifying others' writing rather than their own writing, so it can be helpful to have students first practice with peer writing samples (Brinkley, 1988; Rosen, 1998; Scott, as cited in Paul 2001). Just as we gradually introduce grammatical targets during drafting, we must be selective during the revision and editing process. It is important to limit the extent of revision and editing regarding the number and range of changes. Rosen suggests selecting a few problems and then showing "benign neglect" for everything else.

Revision and editing strategies can be set up as questions, such as, "Have I connected the ideas?" (Paul, 2001) or as question-answer pairs as shown in Box 4.11. Once a strategy has been presented and practiced in an authentic activity, it can be added to an editing checklist to which the student can refer.

Box 4.11   **Question-Answer Pairs for Revision and Editing**

- **Does your piece have complete sentences?**
  Add words or rewrite each complete sentence so it will be complete.

- **Does your piece make sense?**
  Rewrite any sentences you want to make clearer.

- **Does your piece show connections between ideas?**
  Combine sentences so ideas will be connected.

Source: Brinkley (1998)

Targeting Grammar in Reading and Conversation

Using Published Texts to Target Grammar

The model of intervention advocated here focuses on production. That does not mean that comprehension is ignored. Rather, since grammatical forms are only worked on in contexts that tie them to meaning, comprehension and production develop together. Reading activities can be used in a way that allows opportunities for production while incorporating comprehension. Class reading assignments in textbooks and literature can be used for working on grammatical forms. Books and poems can also be chosen that exemplify particular grammatical patterns. Descriptive passages from a chapter book can illustrate how expanded noun phrases are employed to provide detailed imagery. Instructions from computer manuals can be used to illustrate imperative sentence structure. Seeing how actual authors compose sentences to achieve particular meanings and purposes provides the students with a larger direction for their structured and embedded grammatical intervention activities.

Joint Book Reading

In joint book reading, a book or passage is read aloud to the student several times, using prosody to segment and highlight the target patterns. Once the student is familiar with the text, the SLP inserts pauses during the reading to give the student opportunities to produce the target form in the memorized text (Kirchner, 1991; Ratner et al., 1993). Joint book reading is often used as a strategy for preliterate students, but it can also be used with older students to introduce new grammatical forms. Joint book reading can be used as a mini-lesson prior to writing activities. The story or poem used for joint book reading can serve as a model for the students to subsequently write their own stories or poems using the same form.

The joint reading procedure is most appropriate for brief texts with repetitive patterns, including poetry, since it involves multiple readings of the same text. Tompkins and Webeler (1983) have organized books according to their structural characteristics. Two of their categories are particularly good for targeting specific grammatical structures: books with repetitive language patterns in which a certain phrase or sentence is repeated at various points throughout the story (e.g., *Brown Bear, Brown Bear, What Do You See?* [Martin, 1967]) and books in which a word, phrase, or sentence is added to a repeating sequence in succeeding episodes (e.g., *The Very Hungry Caterpillar* [Carle, 1969]). Ratner et al. (1993) also provide a list of books, grouped by grammatical form.

An alternative read-aloud procedure is an adaptation of Interactive Language Development Teaching (Lee, Koenigsknecht, & Mulhern, 1974). This procedure can be implemented with texts of any length, either on the first or in subsequent readings of a text. It can be used to work on a single form or on several forms concurrently. The SLP reads aloud while the student listens and follows along in the text or the SLP follows along with the student as they listen together to a recording of the book. The reading is interrupted whenever instances of a target form have been read. At that point, the student is asked a question that prompts an imitation of that sentence. During the read-aloud activity, the SLP makes reflective comments that help the student to recognize the constituents of the sentence and how they are combined. A break-down procedure can be used for this. As shown in Box 4.12 on page 186, the SLP first reads a sentence, then separates out clauses and phrases, and lastly says the whole sentence again.

Box 4.12

Example of a Break-Down Procedure for Extraposition

SLP reads from a newspaper article: It would be a huge upset for Stepping Out to win both the Preakness and the Derby.

SLP recaps the sentence (after first checking that the student understands the word "upset" and knows what the Preakness and Derby are): So this horse, Stepping Out, maybe will win these races. But no one really expects him to, right? People don't expect that, so it would be an upset.

SLP restarts the sentence: It would be a huge upset for what?

Student: If he won the race.

SLP repeats the sentence: Yeah, it would be a huge upset for Stepping Out to win both of the races.

Source: Fey (1986)

Conversational Activities

In much of school-based remediation, reading and writing will be the major activities for language intervention. This reflects the difficulty that students with language impairments have with written language. However, some students may also need to work on grammar in conversational discourse. This intervention should also be situated in meaningful activities, although it may not be possible to implement grammatical instruction procedures in naturally occurring discourse contexts. As an alternative, group situations can be set up in which the students select and discuss topics that are relevant and interesting.

As described for writing intervention, mini-lessons that focus on particular forms can precede the discussion and then scaffolding can be provided during the discussion for these same forms. Most of the scaffolding strategies discussed above were originally developed for conversationally based intervention and so the SLP can use those same methods—such as *vertical structuring, expansion,* or *prompting*—to scaffold each student's participation in the discussion.

Conclusion

This chapter has set out a contextualized skills approach towards grammatical intervention for school-age students with language impairments. This approach situates grammatical intervention within meaningful reading, writing, and speaking activities that provide repeated opportunities to learn and use grammatical forms to express meaning and participate in discourse. The approach incorporates some discrete skill instruction, but always in a way that helps students to apply the discrete skills to authentic activities involving reading, writing, and speaking. This authenticity is crucial. Students must have a reason for doing the things that lead them to learn and use grammar so that they can read, write, and speak better. However, the setting is less crucial. This hybrid instruction can take place in the classroom but can also be provided in pull-out sessions, with individual students as well as with groups.

For many SLPs, contextualized skill instruction will be a big change. However, this approach actually uses many of the same procedures as the more traditional isolated skill intervention but packages them somewhat differently. Rather than concentrating on discrete skill training as an end in itself, this chapter incorporates the use of massed practice (i.e., contrived opportunities to get students started on particular targets) by presenting mini-lessons before activities. More scaffolded types of help are provided when students experience difficulties during writing or speaking. There will be some instructional procedures that must be retired (such as having students memorize parts of speech), but many other options remain, such as imitation (contrastive and content alteration), modeling (with production), and sentence formation procedures (combining, paraphrasing, and expanding). In addition, there are some types of interactive scaffolding that have traditionally been used for preschool students (such as modeling, vertical structuring, expansion, and extension) that can also be used with school-age students.

Finally, the view advocated in this chapter may require a change in thinking about working on grammar. Focusing on the meanings encoded by grammatical structures is one essential change. Another is focusing on the ability to access and use a variety of grammatical forms. There are certainly other aspects of language that will be difficult for students with language impairments and these must be targeted. However, facility with grammar is necessary to express meaning and to participate in discourse. Grammatical intervention must be included in intervention along with vocabulary, discourse, and pragmatic intervention objectives.

References

Atwell, N. (1987). *In the middle: Writing, reading, and learning with adolescents.* Portsmouth, NH: Heinemann.

Backus, O., & Beasley, J. (1951). *Speech therapy with children.* Boston: Houghton-Mifflin.

Bellaire, S., Plante, E., & Swisher, L. (1994). Bound morpheme skills in the oral language of school-age, language-impaired children. *Journal of Communication Disorders, 27,* 265–279.

Biber, D. (1988). *Variation across speech and writing.* Cambridge, MA: Cambridge University Press.

Bishop, D. V. M. (1994). Grammatical errors in specific language impairment: Competence or performance limitations. *Applied Psycholinguistics, 15,* 507–550.

Brinkley, E. (1998). Learning to use grammar with precision through editing conferences. In C. Weaver (Ed.), *Lessons to share: On teaching grammar in context* (pp. 120–136). Portsmouth, NH: Heinemann.

Callies, R. (1998). When grammar matters. In C. Weaver (Ed.), *Lessons to share: On teaching grammar in context* (pp. 110–119). Portsmouth, NH: Heinemann.

Carle, E. (1969). *The very hungry caterpillar.* New York: Penguin Books.

Catts, H. W., Fey, M. E., Zhang, X., & Tombin, B. (1999). Language basis of reading and reading disabilities: Evidence from a longitudinal investigation. *Scientific Studies of Reading, 3,* 331–361.

Catts, H. W., & Kamhi, A. G. (1999). *Language and reading disabilities.* Boston: Allyn and Bacon.

Christenson, S., Thurlow, M. L., & Ysseldyke, J. E. (1989). Written language instruction for children with mild handicaps: Is there enough quantity to ensure quality? *Learning Disabilities Quarterly, 12,* 219–229.

Cleave, P. L., & Fey, M. E. (1997). Two approaches to the facilitation of grammar in children with language impairments: Rationale and description. *American Journal of Speech-Language Pathology, 6*(1), 22–32.

Connell, P. J. (1982). On training grammatical rules. *Language, Speech, and Hearing Services in Schools, 13,* 231–248.

Connell, P. J. (1986). Teaching subjecthood to language-disordered children. *Journal of Speech and Hearing Research, 29,* 481–492.

Connell, P. J. (1987). An effect of modeling and imitation teaching procedures on children with and without specific language impairment. *Journal of Speech and Hearing Research, 30,* 105–113.

Donahue, M. (1987). Interactions between linguistic and pragmatic development in learning-disabled children: Three views of the state of the union. In S. Rosenberg (Ed.), *Advances in applied psycholinguistics. Volume 1: Disorders of first language development* (pp. 126–179). New York: Cambridge University Press.

Eisenberg, S., Ukrainetz, T., Justice, L., Gillam, R., & Kaderavek, J. (2004, June). *Noun phrase elaboration in children's stories.* Poster session presented at the annual Symposium on Research in Child Language Disorders, Madison, WI.

Elley, W. B. (1991). Acquiring literacy in a second language: The effect of book-based programs. *Language Learning, 41,* 375–411.

Ellis Weismer, S., & Murray-Branch, J. (1989). Modeling versus modeling plus evoked production training: A comparison of two language intervention methods. *Journal of Speech and Hearing Disorders, 54,* 269–281.

Evans, J., & Craig, H. (1992). Language sample collection and analysis: Interview compared to free play assessment contexts. *Journal of Speech and Hearing Research, 35,* 343–353.

Fey, M. E. (1986). *Language intervention with young children.* Boston: Allyn and Bacon.

Fey, M. E., & Proctor-Williams, K. (2000). Recasting, elicited imitation and modeling in grammar intervention for children with specific language impairments. In D. V. M. Bishop & L. Leonard (Eds.), *Speech and language impairments in children: Causes, characteristics, intervention, and outcome* (pp. 177–194). East Sussex, UK: Psychology Press.

Fletcher, P. (1991). Evidence from syntax for language impairment. In J. Miller (Ed.), *Research on child language disorder: A decade of progress* (pp. 169–187). Austin, TX: Pro-Ed.

Gerber, A. (1993). *Language-related learning disabilities: Their nature and treatment.* Baltimore: Brookes.

Gillam, R., & Johnston, J. (1992). Spoken and written relationships in language/learning impaired and normally achieving school-age children. *Journal of Speech and Hearing Research, 35,* 1303–1315.

Gillam, R. B., McFadden, T. U., & van Kleeck, A. (1995). Improving the narrative abilities of children with language disorders: Whole language and language skills approaches. In M. Fey, J. Windsor, & J. Reichle (Eds.), *Communication intervention for school-age children* (pp. 145–182). Baltimore: Brookes.

Gould, B. W. (2001). Curricular strategies for written expression. In A. M. Bain, L. L. Bailet, & L. C. Moats (Eds.), *Written language disorders: Theory into practice* (2nd ed.; pp. 185–220). Austin, TX: Pro-Ed.

Graham, S. (1992). Issues in handwriting instruction. *Focus on Exceptional Children, 25*(2),1–14.

Graham, S., & Harris, K. R. (1997). Whole language and process writing: Does one approach fit all? In J. W. Lloyd, E. J. Kame'enui, & D. Chard (Eds.), *Issues in educating students with disabilities* (pp. 239–260). Mahwah, NJ: Erlbaum.

Graham, S., & Harris, K. R. (2002). The road less traveled: Prevention and intervention in written language. In K. G. Butler & E. R. Silliman (Eds.), *Speaking, reading and writing in children with language learning disabilities* (pp. 199–218). Mahwah, NJ: Erlbaum.

Graham, S., & Miller, S. (1979). Spelling research and practice. *Focus on Exceptional Children, 12,* 1–16.

Grauberg, E. (1988). 'Writing frames' for children with expressive language problems. *Child Language Teaching and Therapy, 4,* 125–141.

Greenhalgh, K. S., & Strong, C. J. (2001). Literate language features in spoken narratives of children with typical language and children with language impairments. *Language, Speech, and Hearing Services in Schools, 32,* 114–125.

Guest, J. (1982). *Ordinary people.* New York: Penguin.

Hadley, P. (1998). Language sampling protocols for eliciting text-level discourse. *Language, Speech, and Hearing Services in Schools, 29,* 132–147.

Hillocks, G. (1987). Synthesis of research on teaching writing. *Educational Leadership, 44,* 71–80.

Ingham, R., Fletcher, P., Schletter, C., & Sinka, I. (1998). Resultative VPs and specific language impairment. *Language Acquisition, 7,* 87–111.

Johnston, J. R. (1985). Fit, focus and functionality: An essay on early language intervention. *Child Language Teaching and Therapy, 1,* 125–134.

Juel, C. (1988). Learning to read and write: A longitudinal study of 54 children from first through fourth grades. *Journal of Educational Psychology, 80,* 437–447.

Kaderavek, J. N., Gillam, R. B., Ukrainetz, T. A., Justice, L. M., & Eisenberg, S. L. (in press). School-age children's self-assessment of oral narrative production. *Communication Disorders Quarterly.*

Killgallon, D. (1998). Sentence composing: Notes on a new rhetoric. In C. Weaver (Ed.), *Lessons to share: On teaching grammar in context* (pp. 169–183). Portsmouth, NH: Heinemann.

King, G. (2000). Verb complementation in language impaired school age children. In M. Aldridge (Ed.), *Child Language* (pp. 84–91). Clevedon, UK: Multilingual Matters.

King, G., & Fletcher, P. (1993). Grammatical problems in school-age children with specific language impairment. *Clinical Linguistics and Phonetics, 7,* 339–352.

Kirchner, D. M. (1991). Reciprocal book reading: A discourse-based intervention strategy for the child with atypical language development. In T. M. Gallagher (Ed.), *Pragmatics of language: Clinical practice issues* (pp. 307–332). San Diego, CA: Singular.

Lee, L. L., Koenigsknecht, R. A., & Mulhern, S. T. (1974). *Interactive language development teaching.* Evanston, IL: Northwestern University Press.

Leonard, L. B. (1975). Modeling as a clinical procedure in language training. *Language, Speech, and Hearing Services in Schools, 6,* 72–85.

Leonard, L. B. (1998). *Children with specific language impairment.* Cambridge, MA: MIT Press.

Leonard, L. B., & Fey, M. E. (1991). Facilitating grammatical development: The contribution of pragmatics. In T. M. Gallagher (Ed.), *Pragmatics of language: Clinical practice issues* (pp. 333–355). San Diego, CA: Singular.

Loban, W. D. (1976). *Language development: Kindergarten through grade twelve* (Research Report No. 18). Urbana, IL: National Council of Teachers of English.

Martin, B., Jr. (1967). *Brown bear, brown bear, what do you see?* New York: Harcourt Brace.

McGill-Frazen, A., & Allington, R. L. (1991). Every child's right: Literacy. *The Reading Teacher, 45,* 86–90.

McQuade, F. (1980). Examining a grammar course: The rationale and the result. *English Journal, 69,* 26–30.

Mentis, M. (1994). Topic management in discourse: Assessment and intervention. *Topics in Language Disorders, 14,* 29–54.

Miller, J. F. (1981). *Assessing language production in children.* Baltimore: University Park Press.

Montgomery, J. K., & Kahn, N. L. (2003). You are going to be an author: Adolescent narratives as intervention. *Communication Disorders Quarterly, 24,* 143–152.

Nelson, K. E. (1988). Towards a differentiated account of literacy development and ASL in deaf children. *Topics in Language Disorders, 18,* 73–88.

Nelson, K. E., Welsh, J., Camarata, S. M., Butkovsky, L., & Camarata, M. (1995). Available input for language-impaired children and younger children of matched language levels. *First Language, 15,* 1–17.

Nelson, N. W. (1995). Scaffolding in the secondary school: A tool for curriculum-based intervention. In D. F. Tibbits (Ed.), *Language intervention: Beyond the primary grades* (pp. 375–419). Austin, TX: Pro-Ed.

Nelson, N. W. (2002). Assessing curriculum-based reading and writing samples. *Topics in Language Disorders, 22,* 35–59.

Nelson, N. W., Van Meter, A. M., Chamberlain, D., & Bahr, C. M. (2001). The speech-language pathologist's role in a writing lab approach. *Seminars in Speech and Language, 22,* 209–219.

Newman, P. W., Creaghead, N. A., & Secord, W. A. (Eds.). (1985). *Assessment and remediation of articulatory and phonological disorders.* Columbus, OH: Merrill.

Nippold, M. A. (1993). Developmental markers in adolescent language: Syntax, semantics, and pragmatics. *Language, Speech, and Hearing Services in Schools, 24,* 21–28.

Nippold, M. A. (1998). *Later language development.* Austin, TX: Pro-Ed.

O'Connor, A. (2004, May 25). Restless legs: Uncomfortable and overlooked. *The New York Times,* p. F10.

O'Donnell, R. C., Griffen, W. J., & Norris, R. D. (1967). *Syntax of kindergarten and elementary school children: A transformational analysis.* (Research Report No. 8). Urbana, IL: National Council of Teachers of English.

O'Hare, F. (1973). *Sentence combining: Improving student writing without formal instruction.* (Research Report No. 15.) Urbana, IL: National Council of Teachers of English.

Paul, R. (2001). *Language disorders from infancy through adolescence* (2nd ed.). St. Louis, MO: Mosby.

Penguin Books. (2005). *Mad libs.* New York: Author.

Perera, K. (1986). Language acquisition and writing. In P. Fletcher & M. Garman (Eds.), *Language acquisition* (2nd ed.; pp. 494–518). Cambridge, UK: Cambridge University Press.

Peterson, C., & McCabe, A. (1991). Linking children's connective use and narrative macrostructure. In A. McCabe, & C. Peterson (Eds.), *Developing narrative structure* (pp. 29–54). Mahwah, NJ: Earlbaum.

Peterson, S. (1998). Teaching writing and grammar in context. In C. Weaver (Ed.), *Lessons to share: On teaching grammar in context* (pp. 67–94). Portsmouth, NH: Heinemann.

Ratner, N. B., Parker, B., & Gardner, P. (1993). Joint book reading as a language scaffolding activity for communicatively impaired children. *Seminars in Speech and Language, 14,* 296–313.

Rey, H. A. (1952). *Curious George rides a bike.* New York: Houghton Mifflin.

Rice, M. L., & Bode, J. V. (1993). GAPS in the verb lexicons of children with specific language impairment. *First Language, 13,* 113–131.

Rosen, L. M. (1998). Developing correctness in student writing: Alternatives to the error hunt. In C. Weaver (Ed.), *Lessons to share: On teaching grammar in context* (pp. 137–154). Portsmouth, NH: Heinemann.

Rowe, S. (1998). Using mini-lessons to promote student revision. In C. Weaver (Ed.), *Lessons to share: On teaching grammar in context* (pp. 100–109). Portsmouth, NH: Heinemann.

Scarborough, H. S. (2001). Connecting early language and literacy to later reading (dis)abilities: Theory and practice. In S. Neuman & D. Dickinson (Eds.), *Handbook for research in early literacy* (pp. 97–110). New York: Guilford Press.

Schwartz, R. G., Chapman, K., Prelock, P. A., Terrell, B. Y., & Rowan, L. E. (1985). Facilitation of early syntax through discourse structure. *Journal of Child Language, 12,* 13–25.

Scott, C. M. (1988). Spoken and written syntax. In M. A. Nippold (Ed.), *Later language development* (pp. 49–96). Austin, TX: Pro-Ed.

Scott, C. M. (1995). A discourse approach to syntax teaching. In D. F. Tibbits (Ed.), *Language intervention: Beyond the primary grades* (pp. 435–463). Austin, TX: Pro-Ed.

Scott, C. M. (2002). A fork in the road less traveled: Writing intervention based on language profile. In K. G. Butler & E. R. Silliman (Eds.), *Speaking, reading and writing in children with language learning disabilities* (pp. 219–237). Mahwah, NJ: Erlbaum.

Scott, C. M., & Stokes, S. L. (1995). Measures of syntax in school-age children and adolescents. *Language, Speech, and Hearing Services in Schools, 26,* 309–319.

Scott, C. M., & Windsor, J. (2000). General language performance measures in spoken and written narrative and expository discourse of school-age children with language learning disabilities. *Journal of Speech, Language, and Hearing Research, 43,* 324–399.

Scott, C. M., & Windsor, J., & Gray, T. (2002, November). *A typology of grammatical error in older children with language learning disorders.* Paper presented at the American Speech-Language-Hearing Association Convention, Atlanta, GA.

Simms, R., & Crump, W. (1983). Syntactic development in the language of learning disabled and normal students at the intermediate and secondary level. *Learning Disability Quarterly, 6,* 155–165.

Smith, H. L., & Hull, G. A. (1985). Differential effects of sentence combining on college students who use particular structures with high and low frequencies. In D. A. Daiker, A. Kerek, & Morenberg, M. (Eds.), *Sentence combining: A rhetorical perspective* (pp. 17–32). Carbondale, Il: Southern Illinois University Press.

Snowling, M., Bishop, D. V. M., & Stothard, S. E. (2000). Is preschool language impairment a risk factor for dyslexia in adolescence? *Journal of Child Psychology and Psychiatry and Allied Disciplines, 41,* 587–600.

Steinhauer, J. (2005, May 22), Maybe preschool is the problem, *The New York Times,* pp. 1, 4.

Stothard, S. E., Snowling, M., Bishop, D. V. M., Chipchase, B. B., & Kaplan, C. A. (1998). Language-impaired preschoolers: A follow-up into adolescence. *Journal of Speech, Language, and Hearing Research, 41,* 407–418.

Strong, W. (1986). *Creative approaches to sentence combining.* Urbana, IL: ERIC Clearinghouse on Reading and Composition Skills and the National Conference on Research in English.

Strong, C. J., & Strong, W. (1999). *Strong rythms and rhymes: Language and literacy development through sentence combining.* Greenville, SC: Super Duper Publications.

Sturm, J., & Koppenhaver, D. A. (2003). Supporting writing development in adolescents with developmental disabilities. *Topics in Language Disorders, 20,* 73–92.

Temple, C., & Gillett, J. W. (1984). *Language arts: Learning processes and teaching practices.* Austin, TX: Pro-Ed.

Thordardottir, E. T., & Weismer, S. E. (2001a). High frequency verb diversity in the spontaneous speech of school-age children with specific language impairment. *International Journal of Language and Communication Disorders, 36,* 221–244.

Thordardottir, E. T., & Weismer, S. E. (2001b). Verb argument structure weakness in specific language impairment in relation to age and utterance length. *Clinical Linguistics and Phonetics, 16,* 233–250.

Tompkins, G. E., & Webeler, M. (1983). What will happen next? Using predictable books with young children. *The Reading Teacher, 36,* 489–502.

Wallach, G. P., & Butler, K. G. (1994). *Language learning disabilities in school-age children and adolescents.* New York: Merrill.

Weaver, C. (1996). *Teaching grammar in context.* Portsmouth, NH: Boynton/Cook Publishers.

Westby, C. E., & Clauser, P. S. (1999). The right stuff for writing: Assessing and facilitating written language. In H. W. Catts & A. G. Kamhi (Eds.), *Language and Reading Disabilities* (pp. 259–324). Boston: Allyn and Bacon.

Wiig, E. H., & Semel E. M. (1980). *Language assessment and intervention for the learning disabled.* Columbus, OH: Merrill.

Windsor, J., Scott, C. M., & Street, C. K. (2000). Verb and noun morphology in the spoken and written language of children with language learning disabilities. *Journal of Speech, Language, and Hearing Research, 43,* 1322–1336.

Wong, B. Y. L. (2000). Writing strategy instruction for expository essays for adolescents with and without learning disabilities. *Topics in Language Disorders, 20,* 29–44.

Chapter 5

Teaching Narrative Structure: Coherence, Cohesion, and Captivation

Teresa A. Ukrainetz

Introduction

Language is used in organized units called *discourse*. The type of discourse to be addressed in this chapter is narrative. *Narrative* is the verbal recapitulation of past experiences (Labov, 1972) or the telling of "what happened" (Moffett, 1968, p. 121). The experiences reported may be real, imaginary, or somewhere in between.

Narrative is a complex but familiar discourse structure. Narrative can be employed in many ways within language intervention: as a direct goal of instruction, as a context for the development of general language and literacy skills, and as a familiar vehicle for the transmission of knowledge. In Chapter 2, narrative was presented as a context of intervention for semantic, syntactic, and pragmatic objectives (as well as narrative itself).

Intervention with narrative structure is presented from the contextualized skill perspective presented in Chapter 1. Explicit skills are systematically scaffolded in repeated opportunities within purposeful activities through students' literature and created stories. Interactive scaffolding occurs through the speech-language pathologist's (SLP's) talk during modeling, analysis, composition, revision, and story sharing. Pictography, a temporally ordered, quick-sketch method, is presented as a particularly useful structural scaffold for quick and easy visual representation of stories, supporting narrative recall and organization.

Intervention for the youngest children deals with extending young children's turns and gradually reducing scaffolding. Children move from a supportive, conversational context for storytelling into the more literate style of telling the story alone, as a monologue. For older students, three narrative structure analyses are presented: episodic structure (i.e., story grammar), cohesion, and story art. Instruction for all three approaches follows a general pattern of using children's literature as a model and source of inspiration, identifying target structures, then following story creation with a focus on the target structures.

The Narrative Genre

Narratives, or stories, are integral parts of our social interactions and our ways of conceptualizing the world. By having at its core the telling of experience (Deese, 1983), narrative encompasses much of our daily discourse. Narratives are used to report on, evaluate, and regulate activities, as well as to provide an implicit common organization of experience (McCabe, 1991) and feeling of emotional involvement and solidarity (Polanyi, 1989). Narrative is compelling because it provides an account not only of what happens to people, the "landscape of action" (Bruner, 1986, p. 99), but what those involved in the action (and those telling it) know, think, or feel—the "landscape of consciousness" (p. 99).

Community is established and students are socialized through the daily flow of narratives. Narratives maintain the social history and historical knowledge base of the community (Bauman, 1986). Narrative discourse occurs in all societies, with variation that reflects the culture of its tellers (Au, 1980; Gee, 1989; Heath, 1983; Michaels, 1991; Minami, 2002), but also with certain universal characteristics (Deese, 1983; Mandler, Scribner, Cole, & DeForest, 1980). Topic-centered, chronological, and decontextualized recounts are most typical, but other narrative structures exist, such as the topic-associated, poetic, and contextualized style of some African Americans (Gee; Labov, 1972; Michaels) or the short, minimalist, and implicit style of some Japanese Americans (Minami).

The narrative is the earliest emerging monologic discourse form. It has aspects of both oral and literate styles of language, so can be an effective context in which to learn language skills and acquire knowledge (Westby, 1985). Not only do we talk in stories, but we think in them. Bruner (1986) describes the episodic organization of mind as a narrative mode of thought, predominant in young children, but basic to all human experience. Narrative organization may arise out of children's earliest concepts: generalized scripts reflecting the daily life events through which world knowledge is experienced (Nelson, 1991; Nelson, Engel, & Kyratzis, 1985). Decontextualization and abstraction of events gradually occur, but the primacy of the activity schema as an organizing framework continues. This means that children (and adults) often learn a concept as part of a meaningful event, and may continue to remember the concept as part of a generalized version of that event.

Narrative Structure Analyses

The structure of narrative discourse cannot be captured by any single analysis. Four ways of analyzing narratives are presented: (1) degree of independence, (2) story grammar, (3) cohesion, and (4) story art. Ways of analyzing and then facilitating each of these are presented.

Degree of Independence

The first approach to understanding narrative performance is considering the narrative as a single extended turn, and examining how children move toward a single-speaker telling or monologue. In Western culture, young children do not typically tell stories independently. They are surrounded by the children and adults who support their tellings. Stories are social co-constructions rather than independent performances. For a literate style of narrative performance, children must learn to move toward being the single teller of a tale. Thus, young children's storytelling can be examined for the degree and nature of prompting required, in addition to the more conventional independent performance sampling and analysis.

For young children, imaginative narrative and dramatic play are inter-twined. Children tell their own stories and co-construct stories within the play context (Galda & Pellegrini, 1988; Sachs, Goldman, & Chaillé, 1985). Wolf and Hicks (1989) report that children move among the perspectives of narrator (telling the story), stage-manager (discussing interpretations and directing actions), and actors (providing the dialogue of the story characters). Children learn to weave imaginative narratives around their own life, toys, storybook, and television experiences. Together, they plot narratives that will be enacted in their play. Paley (1990) captured many illuminating verbal interactions among young students in her kindergarten classes. An example of kindergartners' ability to co-construct a narrative is presented in Box 5.1. This group of students was playing at a sand table and discussing how to imaginatively (and therapeutically) deal with a problematic peer. They were able to create a single narrative by combining individual contributions into a greater whole.

Children also tell their stories, typically recounting recently experienced events, in the company of supportive, familiar adults who work towards max-imizing the student's narrative performance. Parents initially scaffold these re-ports during conversation with prompting and questions, gradually reducing support as students gain competence in oral reporting (e.g., Eisenberg, 1985; McCabe & Peterson, 1991). During shared storybook reading, parents also scaffold children into greater participation (Snow, 1983; Sulzby & Teale, 1990; van Kleeck & Woude, 2003; see Chapter 9). The parental questions and comments that occur during story reading support increasingly extended turns, moving the child from a single-utterance contribution to several utter-ances within a turn, eventually leading to independent telling of a tale. The adults' turns also introduce the child to the categories of information that eventually are needed in his or her own imaginative narratives (e.g., event elab-orations and character motivations, such as, "Then the frog jumped away, didn't he? Why do you think he did that?"). Arising out of the repeated read-ings of favorite books in early parent-child book reading, very young children will re-enact or pretend to read familiar stories before they can read conventionally (Sulzby, 1985; Sulzby & Zecker, 1991).

Co-Constructed Narrative
Box 5.1   **from a Group of Kindergartners**

Arlene:	In five minutes, this tissue turns to magic. I wetted it. Is five minutes over yet?
Alex:	First we buried something in the sand and then it's all buried and that magic is helping us make it magical. The kind me and Simon made? First we buried something in the sand and then it's all buried and that magic is helping us make it magical.
Arlene:	To blast people?
Alex:	To blast Jason. To the sky. Because he keeps fighting us, even just me in the story room.
Arlene:	Tissue in the sand. He'll be blasted?
Alex:	To a million pieces.
Arlene:	The whole world forever.
Alex:	Let's lift up the whole sand. Help me. Superman can carry the whole school up and we'll all fall in the river.
Arlene:	But not us, right? But everyone else. But not our mom and dad. Only Jason?
Alex:	And Joseph. And Petey. Not Simon. Blast them to pieces in the helicopter. Put them here. This is the helicopter.
Arlene:	They'll blast to French fries and we'll eat them up. Not Samantha and Katie.
Alex:	I can't wait to do this. First we explode Jason.
Arlene:	Then we fix him up, right? Then he's our baby. Our new baby.
Alex:	Yeah, and I'm the superdad and you're the supermom.

The need for conversational support of narrative is determined by examining the frequency and nature of prompting. Ninio and Snow (1996) suggest three types of adult support: conversational, historical, and psychological. *Conversational support* involves help in selecting the incident, organizing the telling, providing needed details, and elaborating on the details. *Historical support* involves helping the child sort out what happened in the original event and which aspects of the event should be recounted for the story. Historical support is commonly needed, particularly when the original event was a long and busy one. The third type, *psychological support,* helps in telling a good story. A narrator is often not trying to report information (e.g., about scary dogs) so much as trying to have the listener understand his emotions (e.g., fear and courage). An adult may help show or even determine the child's emotional perspective. Box 5.2 presents an example that shows scaffolded support from all three directions. The child had been asked to recount a scary incident. The mother helped the child initiate the story and clarified various referents. She did most of the talking. But in the final turn, the child came out with a story segment of her own, related to the conversation but not directly contingent upon the mother's prompting. A contrasting example in Box 5.3 shows how scaffolding can be limited to only a few prompts. In this case, the mother assisted only in providing perspective on the event by explaining why it was funny.

The need for interactive support to manage monologic text is most relevant for preschool children. Elementary-age students are expected to tell

Box 5.2   Maternal Scaffolding of a Scary Event Story

Mom:	Have you been scared?
Child:	Mmhm.
Mom:	By whom?
Child:	By Matthew's dog.
Mom:	Oh Matthew [laughs]. Yeah, yeah. Little dog but small dog, but she didn't really know the dog. So yeah.
Child:	But I wasn't scared of the white dog that died.
Mom:	Yeah, yeah, the other one.

Box 5.2—*Continued*

Child:	Matthew had another dog and he was white. And he died.
Interviewer:	Oh.
Mom:	Yeah. But then uh…they…bought another one. That's the family…where I used to work.
Child:	And now he's black.
Mom:	The dog? Yeah. The little dog. Because they had a white one. He died, but then, she grew up with that dog.
Interviewer:	Oh.
Mom:	And then, uh, I mean, not grew up but…she was used to. But I used to work for them.
Child:	You know. One day uh Matthew told me, "Caroline, that's so big you're six," and I said, "No I'm five." Then um…then Matthew goes, "My um…Beverly, Beverly, she's six." She said, "No Matthew, she's still five!"

From *Pragmatic Development* (p. 181), by A. Ninio and C. E. Snow, 1996, Boulder, CO: Westview. © 1996 by Westview Press. Reprinted with permission.

Psychological Scaffolding
Box 5.3 of a Funny Event Story

Child:	I saw something funny [one day]…yesterday when we were coming home? A truck with a board on the back? Carrying a tow truck? And a tow truck carrying a car.
Mom:	A tow truck, carrying a tow truck, carrying a car. And we thought that was really funny!
Child:	[laughs]
Mom:	[laughs] Huh? Because you usually just see a tow truck on (with) a car.

From *Pragmatic Development* (p. 184–185), by A. Ninio and C. E. Snow, 1996, Boulder, CO: Westview. © 1996 by Westview Press. Reprinted with permission.

narratives independently. However, assistance through interactive scaffolding is provided during the learning process. The SLP will give considerable assistance at early points in acquiring a narrative skill. The desired endpoint is independent production, but achieving that involves conscious strategic support and transfer of skills from adult to child.

Story Grammar Analysis

Story grammar analysis deals with episodic structure: how propositions (idea units, or, for simplicity, utterances) are related to form goal-directed, problem-solution units that describe a protagonist's motivations and goals, the efforts to achieve the goals, and the outcomes of such efforts. Story grammar originated as a description of the mental schema used for encoding, representing, and retrieving events (Mandler & Johnson, 1977; Stein & Glenn, 1979). Story grammar can be broadly divided into the pre-episodic narratives of young children and the episodic narratives of school-age students.

Pre-Episodic Organization

The narratives of preschoolers are not typically organized into episodes. There are three types of pre-episodic sequences:

- Descriptive sequences
- Action sequences
- Reaction sequences

The least sophisticated narrative is the *descriptive sequence* (Applebee, 1978; Peterson & McCabe, 1983; Sutton-Smith, 1986), which is a thematically united, or verse-united, collection of labels or statements about actions ("He is running") and states ("He is hungry"). A test of a descriptive sequence is that the statements can be reordered without significantly changing the text meaning. An illustration of a descriptive sequence is presented in the first of five stories in Box 5.4. These stories were created by second graders based on the cover and title of Mercer Mayer frog books in a study examining the effects of three types of narrative planning (McFadden, 1998). The first frog story, *A Boy, a Dog, a Frog and a Friend,* provides an example of a descriptive sequence. In that story, the boy, the dog, and the frog could have caught the fish in any order.

The *action sequence* is the next level of narrative complexity, but still pre-episodic. Action sequences show temporal relations between propositions

Box 5.4

Second-Grader Stories Based on the Covers of Mercer Mayer Frog Books

1. *A Boy, a Dog, a Frog and a Friend* (1971)—Descriptive Sequence

One day a boy and a dog and a frog and a friend were fishing. The boy caught one fish. The dog caught two. And the frog caught none.

2. *One Frog Too Many* (1975)—Action sequence

Once there was a boy. He loved to play in the pond right across from his house. One day he was playing in the pond. And he found a frog. And he took it home and put it in his room and went to eat dinner. He went back to his room. And there were frogs jumping everywhere. And he kept all the frogs.

3. *Frog, Where Are You?* (1969) Version A—Complete episode

Once there was a boy, a dog, and a frog. Once the frog left. And he went into the forest. And the boy kept looking for him. And then finally the frog came out. And they all went home.

4. *Frog, Where Are You?* Version B—Complex episode

A boy had a frog. The frog jumped off. He went into some trees. In a minute he was no longer in sight. The boy called and called for him. And then he saw that his frog had took a scary path. So he decided to take the scary path. So he took the scary path. And it was very, very creepy. Then he saw something jumping. He grabbed it. And it was his frog.

5. *Frog, Where Are You?* Version C—Complex episode

There was a boy. And he had a frog. Then he lost his frog. He looked downstairs. But he was not there. So he looked in his room. The window was opened. So he went outside. He did not find him. So he looked by a pond. Then he heard a sound. So he went to a hollow log. He found two frogs.

(Peterson & McCabe, 1983; Stein & Glenn, 1979). This chronology is demonstrated in the second frog story in Box 5.4 with the boy finding a frog, taking it home, the frog multiplying, and the boy keeping all the frogs. The statements could not be reordered without changing the meaning of the story. However, the propositions are not causally related to each other.

Causal relations appear with the highest level of pre-episodic sequence, called a *reactive sequence* (Peterson & McCabe, 1983; Stein & Glenn, 1979). Reactive sequences occur when the causality is automatic; there is no agent seeking to resolve the complication. For example, the statements, "The rock crushed the frog" and "So the frog died" are causally linked; the frog's death was caused by the rock. However, there is no goal-directed attempt to resolve the complication, which is the essential element of an episode. Peterson and McCabe suggested that children's frequent use of reactive sequences in personal narratives of frightening events was possibly due to their participation in events beyond their control, such as being in a car that almost crashed.

Episodic Structure

Episodic organization is the central aspect of story grammar analysis. The first judgment in analyzing a story is deciding whether or not the story is episodic. If there is some evidence of a disequilibrium or complication that a character is seeking to resolve, then the story is episodic. If not, then the story fits one of the sequences described above. Once the initial determination of episodic structure is made, the variety of elements present and the type of episode formed are determined. A *complete episode* consists of three parts: a complication, some evidence of goal-directedness (such as an internal response or an attempt), plus a consequence. Other types of episodes have fewer or additional elements compared to a complete episode. Table 5.1 summarizes the elements that comprise episodes and Table 5.2 on page 206 shows the types of episodes that can be formed from these elements.

The story grammar elements are illustrated in the the third and fourth stories in Box 5.4 on page 203. The third story contains a setting statement and a complete episode consisting of a complication, an attempt, and a consequence. The fourth story contains a setting statement and a complex episode consisting of a complication, three attempts, a plan, a reaction, and a consequence. Stories can contain multiple complications, such as both losing one's frog and getting lost searching for the frog.

Interactive episodes involve two characters operating in goal-directed ways. This author limits interactive episodes to those in which the character attempts to resolve complications in opposing ways (i.e., good guy–bad guy). Interactive episodes are complicated, because one character's resolution to the complication is the other character's problem.

Not all statements in a story have an episodic role. Statements that have no causal relation to preceding or following statements can only be considered

Table 5.1   **Elements of Episodic Structure**

Episodic Element	Description
Setting	Characters, surroundings, and habitual states and actions
Complication	Event that initiates agent state or action
Motivating State	Feeling or cognition resulting from the complication and leading to an attempt; also called internal response
Attempts	Actions resulting from motivating state and leading to consequence
Consequence	Outcome of successful or unsuccessful attempts
Reaction	Feeling or cognition resulting from prior condition but not motivating further plans or attempts

Source: Peterson & McCabe (1983)

states or actions that add descriptive elements or move the action along. For example, in the fourth story in Box 5.4 (see page 203), the statement "In a minute, he was no longer in sight" elaborates on how fast the frog disappeared, which adds quality to the narrative, but is not a story grammar element.

Classifying a statement as a particular episodic element requires analysis of the role of the statement in the narrative. Statements cannot be evaluated in isolation. In the fourth frog story of Box 5.4 on page 203, "very, very creepy" is a reaction, because it results from the prior statements, but it does not lead to any subsequent statements. In another story, "very, very creepy" could be a motivating state to seek another route or it could be a setting statement about the forest. In the second story, *One Frog Too Many,* the boy's frog turns into "frogs jumping everywhere." While this might be of concern to the unstated mother, it was not a concern for the boy. Thus, there is no complication in this story, and the story is not considered episodic. For a statement to be considered a complication, it must result in a feeling, a plan, an attempt, or a consequence.

Table 5.2   **Story Grammar Episode Types**

Structure	Description
Incomplete Episode	Complication + motivating state or attempt
Abbreviated Episode	Complication + consequence
Complete Episode	Complication + motivating state or attempt + consequence
Complex Episode	Multiple attempts to resolve a complication or multiple complete episodes
Interactive Episode	Two or more characters with opposing complications and consequences

Source: Peterson & McCabe (1983)

An event without such evidence cannot be called a complication. As a result, the second story has a series of states and actions, but it is only an action sequence.

Story grammar analysis can be difficult when students lack explicitness. In the fifth frog story of Box 5.4 (see page 203), *Frog, Where Are You?* an explicit statement that one of the two frogs the boy had found was his pet frog would more clearly show the resolution of the complication. As it is, we guess that this finding resolves the complication. In a story about an ant attack, *The Revenge* (see Box 5.5), the attack is implied as a complication for the people by the clearly undesirable consequences affecting protectors (parents, teachers, and doctors) and the detailed description of the attack and its results, but the lack of explicit evidence such as a motivating state (being upset) or a plan (trying to kill the ants) makes this story only an abbreviated episode.

Written Class Assignment Story from a Second-Grader

Box 5.5

The Revenge

One day the ants had to wear dresses. But they didn't wear it. They wanted revenge anyway. They bit Miss Mackie. They bit Sidney. They bit Doug. They bit Harry. And they bit Mrs. Foxworth. And they almost died. And almost the whole school got it. The school doctor almost got sick. Their moms and dads almost got sick from their kids. The whole school got sick. They almost died because the whole school was sick. Everyone threw up because they were so sick.

NOTE: Spelling corrected

Finally, utterances can sometimes be viewed in more than one way, especially where there are two agents operating in the story. In *The Revenge,* the ant attack is both an attempt by the ants to redress the insult and an unresolved complication for the people. This dual perspective is an interactive episode that engages logical reasoning to sort out.

Development

Descriptive sequences and action sequences are typical of preschooler productions (Applebee, 1978; Botvin & Sutton-Smith, 1977; Peterson & McCabe, 1983). Stories containing causal relations and problems with efforts at resolution emerge around kindergarten and are clearly established by 8 years of age (Botvin & Sutton-Smith; Peterson & McCabe). Elements that continue to develop in frequency and variety after 8 years of age are internal responses, attempts, and consequences (Peterson & McCabe). The frequency with which complete and embedded episodes occur in stories and personal narratives continues to increase through the age of 14 (Roth & Spekman, 1986).

One difficulty in specifying a developmental order is that elicitation context can affect the story produced. A second grader can produce both a descriptive sequence in response to an unappealing picture and a complete episode in response to an intriguing story starter. For example, for 6 to 10 year-old students, Schneider (1996) found that picture sequences resulted in the least story grammar information and the greatest extraneous information, but the most fluent productions. Stories retold without pictures resulted in the most accurately reproduced narratives. Merritt and Liles (1989) reported that stories generated through a simple request to tell a story were longer, but episodically less well-formed, than stories generated in response to a picture.

In addition, modality can affect complexity. Written narratives lag in comparison to spoken language (Freedman, 1987). Freedman reported that only half of the 5th grade students in his study achieved the level of plot development that all of the 7 year-olds in the Botvin and Sutton-Smith (1977) study had achieved orally. The development of written narration continues throughout the school years, with the percentage of stories that include at least one episode increasing through the 12th grade.

Cohesion of the Tale

Cohesion is the method by which one sentence is related to another through sentence structure and word choice (Halliday & Hasan, 1976). Cohesion unites sentences into a text. Cohesion is not specific to narrative, but rather is present in all discourse. It starts with the earliest conversations and develops throughout the school years.

Cohesion can be *exophoric,* meaning the referent is outside the text (e.g., "Put that here") or *endophoric,* with the meaning fully retrievable from inside the text (e.g., "Put the box on the table beside the door"). Cohesive devices include conjunctive cohesion, pronominal reference, lexical and structural parallelism, and ellipsis.

Conjunctive Cohesion

Conjunctive cohesion involves conjunctions and adverbials. According to Halliday and Hasan (1976), they can be additive *(and),* adversative *(but),* temporal *(finally),* causative *(therefore),* or continuative *(anyway).* The fifth frog story in Box 5.4 on page 207 demonstrates multiple *so* conjunctions and *The Revenge,* in Box 5.5 on page 211, provides *but* and *because.* These words link subsequent actions with prior actions in causal and adversative relationships.

Connectives at the discourse level are the same connectives that occur at the syntactic level, but they link meaning across, rather than within, sentences. This cross-sentence link is not a clear distinction in practice, particularly when compound utterances are divided for T-units ("She wants a dog. And I want a cat").

T-units or *C-units* are grammatically based ways of dividing discourse into sentences. A terminal- or T-unit consists of one independent clause and any dependent constituents, including clauses and phrases (Hunt, 1965). Clauses connected by a coordinating conjunction (e.g., *and, but, or*) are divided into separate T-units when the subject is repeated (e.g., "Sam went to the store/And he bought an apple"). Communication- or C-units (Loban, 1976) have the same rules, but were developed for oral discourse and include elliptical utterances (e.g., "Me too"). Both are particularly helpful for language that lacks pauses in oral delivery or punctuation in print delivery.

Conjunctive cohesion can be considered basic or sophisticated (Ukrainetz, 2001). Basic cohesion (e.g., *or, but, because*) will be the most common level addressed for students with language impairments. However, middle school students who show control of these basic connectives but are still underperforming compared to their peers may benefit from increasing the sophistication of their cohesion. For these students, appropriate use of adverbials (e.g., *although, instead, however, consequently, nevertheless*) can be introduced. Teaching the meaning and use of these words will be more challenging, but will clearly increase the sophistication of the student's work.

Pronominal Reference

Pronominal reference involves the relations between pronouns and their referents (e.g., *girl–she, report–it*). An *anaphoric referent* (e.g., *Sally*) precedes the pronoun (e.g., *her*), such as in the sentence "Sally reached for her coat." Less typically used cataphoric reference employs the referent following the pronoun, as in the sentence "Her name was Sally."

Pronominal reference falls within a larger grouping called reference cohesion, along with articles *(a, the)*, and demonstratives *(this, that)*. Of all the types of cohesion, pronominal reference is likely the most easily identified and taught. In addition, pronominal reference is a frequent form within the character actions and intentions focus of narrative (Bruner, 1986).

Cohesive usage of pronouns differs distinctly from syntactic usage. In syntactic usage, correctness of the pronoun can be clearly established, regardless of appropriateness or clarity (e.g., the referent is a girl and the word will be used in the subject position, so *she* is the correct pronoun choice). In contrast, for cohesive usage, judgments are made about relative appropriateness and clarity of pronoun choice (e.g., can it easily be determined to whom *she* refers?). Cohesive use of a pronoun must always have a retrievable reference. In the frog stories in Box 5.4 on page 203, *boy/he* and *frog/it* are used appropriately. In *The Revenge* story presented in Box 5.5 on page 207, *they* is confusingly applied because there are groups of both ants and people.

There are distinctly different standards for pronominal reference in informal oral and formal written contexts. In oral language, reference cohesion can be exophoric (e.g., pointing to the person). Cohesion can also be vague. It is not uncommon for competent adults in conversation to say, "She talked to her about the girl," or to use the pronoun *it* with several possible referents present. Oral contexts often involve common background knowledge of the participants, paralinguistic cues, and the acceptance of greater ambiguity, which allow a wider latitude in pronoun use. In written language, pronominal reference must be endophoric (i.e., retrievable from within the text and usually preceding the pronoun). There are no rules on how many times a pronoun can be used before the referent should be repeated, but the guideline is to judge when a reasonable audience would become confused based on the context of expression (e.g., oral or written, informal or formal, familiar or absent audience).

Lexical and Structural Parallelism

Lexical parallelism involves repeating a word, such as the repeated use of *frog* in the frog stories. This is the simplest way to cohere sentences and occurs in most narratives. Parallelism can also involve substituting synonyms. Lexical substitution involves the provision of related words *(frog–toad, frog–amphibian)*, which none of the Box 5.4 samples (see page 203) contained. Students do not typically provide substitutions spontaneously (Crowhurst, 1987) and need explicit guidance and an adequate vocabulary to do so.

Parallel structures involve repeating a syntactic structure. The same words can be used or the similarity can derive from the syntactic form, such as the verb tense or the predicate structure. *The Revenge* story in Box 5.5 on page 207 displays strong parallelism. The repeated statements of "They bit X and almost + verb" provide unity to the story and help spoken language flow. In poems, parallel structures provide repeated opportunities to practice a particular syntactic structure in a short, authentic discourse unit. The poem in Box 5.6 demonstrates the cohesion of using a parallel structure.

Substitution and parallel structures add more to narrative quality than to clarity. Frogs can be described using only the label *frog,* and be understood. If *amphibians, creatures,* and *pets* are substituted, the report provides more shades of meaning and is more interesting. Parallel structures can be effective narrative (or poetic) art, but may also be considered monotonous or unsophisticated.

Box 5.6

Poem Demonstrating Cohesion through Repeated Parallel Structure

If I Were a Bug

If I were a butterfly, I would flutter in the air.
If I were a caterpillar, I would crawl in the leaves.
If I were a spider, I would spin a sticky web.
If I were a bumblee, I would hum in the flowers.
If I were a fly, I would buzz in your ear.
Bzzz, bzzz, bzzz.

Ellipsis

Finally, ellipsis, or zero substitution, involves the omission of an item retrievable from elsewhere in the text (e.g.,"May I go to the store? You may"). Ellipsis results in incomplete sentences, which are fully appropriate and desirable; continual use of complete sentences would result in a stilted and redundant manner of communication. Ellipsis can be seen in the first story in Box 5.4 on page 203, in which the boy caught one fish and the dog caught two (fish). Appropriate ellipsis depends on context. Ellipsis occurs more frequently in conversation than in narrative. Informal narratives for a familiar audience involve more ellipsis than formal narratives. Written narratives are likely to involve more expansion and explicitness. There are typically few examples of ellipsis in student stories (Crowhurst, 1987). Instruction would focus on when and how to omit or include parts of sentences.

Development

Developmentally, students move from exophoric to endophoric reference (Crowhurst, 1991; Pellegrini, Galda, & Rubin, 1984). The development of discourse cohesion parallels the order of logical relations found in sentence development, moving from additive, to temporal, to causal logical relations. By eight years of age, students can generally provide clear and cohesive narratives (Pellegrini et al., 1984), but sophistication in the use of cohesion continues to develop through adolescence (Bennett-Kastor, 1984; Crowhurst; Klecan-Aker & Hedrick, 1985; Liles, 1985). Changes involve increases in the frequency and variety of forms and the distance between cohesive ties as well as further reductions in ambiguity. Cohesion continues to be a challenge into the college years (Crowhurst, 1987; Neuner, 1987) because of the high standards for clear endophoric reference within formal written language.

Story Art

Analyses of degree of independence, story grammar, and cohesion focus on the transmission of information within narrative. However, skillful narrators care about more than making sense; they strive to achieve feelings such as humor, suspense, mystery, and emotional involvement (Kernan, 1977; McFadden & Gillam, 1996). Story art focuses on what makes a story special, sophisticated, or appealing (Ukrainetz, Justice, et al., in press). The examination of this expressive function is story art analysis. Story art analysis is directed at distinguishing casual or minimal expression ("I was scared") from elaborated or artful expression of perspective ("Terrified, I shook like a leaf"). It also examines how the narrator uses these artful expressions to build the story toward its climax.

Story Art Analysis

Story art analysis is based on high point analysis. High point analysis was originally developed to examine how narrator perspective is transmitted to an audience and how the emotional high point or climax is achieved for personal narratives (Kernan, 1977; Labov, 1972; Labov & Waletsky, 1967; Peterson & McCabe, 1983). The version presented here considers these factors, but more in terms of how a narrative is crafted as an artful performance.

High point analysis captures the difference between an informational narrative versus a narrative where the event and the story matter. Peterson and McCabe (1983) illustrate this difference with two students' stories about bee stings. One eight-year-old girl provided a factual recount of the event. After being stung, she said she, "just went in the house and had to have something on it" (p. 30). In contrast, a five-year-old girl described her response to the bee sting as, "I screamed and I screamed and I cried and I cried" (p. 30). She then detailed how three adults had to carry her into the house to recover. The second story has a clear climactic moment with considerable evaluative language that displays the narrator's view of the event.

In high point analysis, a fully formed narrative has six components: opening appendage, orientation, complicating action, evaluation, resolution, and closing appendage (Labov, 1972; Peterson & McCabe, 1983). Complicating actions and resolutions form the informational body of the story. They overlap with the complications and consequences of story grammar, so are not a focus of this analysis. Table 5.3 presents three of the

Table 5.3   **Story Art Elements**

Category	Element	Example
Appendage	Introducer	*Once there was*
	Abstract	*This story is about a very bad day.* *The Lost Frog*
	Theme	*This was turning out to be a bad day.*
	Coda	*To this day, he always remembers to tell the boy when he leaves for an adventure.*
	Ender	*The end.*
Orientation	Character names	*Joe, Froggie*
	Character relations and roles	*the mother, his pet, the teacher*
	Ongoing external conditions	*It rained all day long.* *He was left all alone.*
	Personality attributes	*He loved adventure.* *He was always late.*
Evaluation	Modifiers	*quickly, so, almost, consequently*
	Phrases and expressions	*woke up on the wrong side of the bed, rather a lot, as fast as he could*
	Repetition	*very very fast, he looked and looked and looked*
	Direct dialogue	*He thought, "I am so in trouble!"* *He yelled, "I've been looking everywhere for you!"*
	Internal state words	*decided, thought, concluded, discouraged, angry, tired*

Sources: Labov (1972); Peterson & McCabe (1983); Ukrainetz, Justice, et al. (in press)

components that can be examined for artful aspects: appendages, orientations, and evaluations. *Appendages* are statements that introduce, comment on, and conclude the story. They include: (1) *abstracts,* which suggest what the story will be about; (2) *themes,* which are restatements of the main idea during the story; and (3) *codas,* which provide a lesson learned or bring the listener back to the present. *Orientations* provide background information on the habitual actions and nature of the characters or on external conditions. They are generally clustered at the beginning of the narrative. Successful orientations invite the listener to care about the characters and understand their critical characteristics. *Evaluations* are a large category of verbal and nonverbal elements that contribute to the art of story and the effective transmittal of listener perspective. While evaluations can appear anywhere in the narrative, they are generally concentrated after the complication, stopping the action to build interest and suspense towards an emotional high point (Labov; Peterson & McCabe). There can be many evaluations of many types in a narrative.

Story art analysis focuses on the elements that provide expressive elaboration, resulting in a more literary, creative, or sophisticated story. For example, "The end" is more literary than "That's all," "He stared back silently like a cat" is more creative than "He didn't answer," and "A mere slip of a girl" is more sophisticated than "a little girl." Story art analysis examines whether story grammar or cohesion elements go beyond the minimum. For example, basic setting information of character, place, and time is not considered particularly artful. Of more interest are character names, relations, and personality features. A connective such as *consequently* is more sophisticated than *because.* Complications may be present, but it is the placement of evaluative elements in a concentration around the complication that makes the moment climactic in a story. Thus, story art adds a dimension to episodic and cohesive analyses, showing how students go beyond reporting information to make their stories special.

Not all stories show clear climactic moments. Stories that would be considered description sequences or chronological sequences do not have climaxes. The student may build toward a climax, but end the story there, leaving the audience hanging. Preferably, the narrator will resolve the story with a satisfying ending that may include a coda about the lesson learned.

Looking for Story Art

The stories in Box 5.4 on page 203 can be examined for narrative art. None of the frog stories provide elaborated appendages or orientations. The narrators do not forewarn us about the point of the story or tell us the moral of the story.

They also give little orientation information. However, there are some story art elements.

The first two stories have no high points; they simply describe and list events. In the first story, the appendage "One day…" cued the listener that the narrator intended this to be a story, despite its lack of evaluative elements and a high point. In the second story, the orientation is better developed compared to the other stories, with a statement about the boy's love of playing in the pond.

The third story is short but shows clear story art. A lengthy search for the frog is implied with two well-chosen evaluations: *kept looking* and *finally.* In this story, the complication is developed with three lines that contain details about where the frog went and how fast he disappeared. The high point is the search. To transmit the atmosphere surrounding the boy's determined and frightening search, the narrator uses descriptive words *(creepy, scary, grab),* repeated words *(called and called; very, very),* and parallel structures *(taking a scary path).* The search is minimally resolved by finding the frog, but there is a lack of denouement. A more effective story would elaborate on how the boy felt, how he and the frog made it back home, and what the boy learned from this event. In contrast to the third story, the fifth frog story is longer and has more sophisticated story grammar structure, but is less artful. The search could be called the high point because it is an extended search. However, there is no heart to this story. It reads like a factual reporting of the search, rather than a desperate seeking for a beloved pet.

Another example of concentrations of evaluations is found in *The Revenge* in Box 5.5 on page 207. The high point is a combination of the attack and the effects of the attack. The repetition of the biting statements prolong this action-building part of the story. The effects are emphasized by listing everyone who got sick or almost sick, even people of power and responsibility, such as the doctor and parents. This artful use of evaluations brings the audience to the high point with everyone almost dying.

Development

Story art shows some developmental progression. For personal narratives, Peterson and McCabe (1983) found that preschoolers tend to produce confused or chronological plot patterns. Five-year-olds favored ending at the high point. This pattern dropped in frequency but continued to be a noticeable pattern to nine years of age. By seven years of age, half of the students in Peterson and McCabe's study could tell personal narratives with the components of a classic plot. Students as young as three could provide orienting information, but the detail, variety, and tailoring to audience needs developed to the oldest age sampled, nine years. Likewise, appendages and evaluations were present from the earliest ages, but increased in frequency and variety to at least nine years of age (Peterson & McCabe; Umiker-Sebeok, 1979). Sophistication in personal storytelling continues to develop into adolescence and adulthood (Kernan, 1977; Labov, 1972).

Picture-based fictional narratives are a more common elicitation context in school. For picture sequence narratives from the Test of Narrative Language (Gillam & Pearson, 2004), Ukrainetz, Justice, et al. (in press) examined the use of appendages, orientations, and evaluations in almost 300 students, 5 to 12 years of age. Appendage use was lowest in both presence and frequency, and did not change with age. Orientations showed small increases with age. Evaluations were most frequent and showed the greatest age changes. The largest changes in presence and frequency were observed between 5 and 9 years of age.

Story art is more of a holistic evaluation than a discrete item judgment. Box 5.7 on page 217 provides an example of a "typical" narrative for each of 3 age groups for picture-based narratives. These narratives demonstrate the mean length and percent of appendages, orientations, and evaluations for each of 5–6 years, 7–9 years, and 10–12 years. In sum, the picture-based imaginative narratives of younger students tend to be of static images, chronological progressions without a story sense, or progressions with evaluative elements dispersed throughout. The appendages and orientations tend to be minimal. Students over 7 years of age commonly had stories with high points, but satisfactory resolutions were infrequent. Interesting word choices and character dialogue were frequently present. Sometimes, these students provided story titles, abstracts, and codas.

It should be noted that story art can sometimes occur in unexpected ways. For example, stories are usually told in past tense. Present tense or tense mixing is typically an indicator of linguistic immaturity or discourse control difficulties. In addition, long or complex sentences are often assumed to be better. However present tense and short, active sentences can be used strategically to amplify exciting parts of the story, as demonstrated in this excerpt from an 11 year-old's narrative:

> One beautiful foggy Tuesday morning, Michael and Sonia, they were brother and sister. So they woke up. And they decided to go for a walk. Since it was summer they loved the nice breeze and the weather. So they decided to go out to a

Box 5.7

Narratives Illustrating Expressive Elaboration from Three Age Groups

5–6 Years

Once there was a little boy. He was sleeping in his bed. And he went to go eat his breakfast and accidentally took the string out of his shoe and accidentally broke. And then he tried to go to school with the bus. But the bus leaved already. And he had to walk to school. And then the teacher said he was late.

7–9 Years

One morning Bob woke up. And it was twenty after seven. And he was running late for school. And he started pouring a bowl of cereal. And he wasn't paying attention. And he spilled some milk. So he started to clean it up. And then he said I just can't have breakfast this morning. And he went and got dressed. He accidentally tore his shoelace. So he got some tape and taped it. When he got his backpack and ran to the school bus stop he missed the school bus. So he had to run all the way to school. Her teacher got mad at him because he was late. She was wondering if he would come. The end.

10–12 Years

One morning a kid woke up. And his name was Todd. He got up and he looked at his clock and it turned out he was almost late for school. And so he got out of bed. And got dressed hurriedly. And he went into the kitchen. This is where he poured his favorite cereal was out. So he had to do his least favorite which is crunchymunchys. And while he was looking at the clock worrying about time he poured milk all over his cereal. After he got dressed he started to tie his shoe. And the shoelace snapped. After a long time of trying to repair the shoelace he decided to give up. He put on his backpack ran outside and discovered his school bus had raced ahead of him. After a long and treacherous time of walking to school the teacher said he was late. And he had to spend the recess inside.

forest just to watch and sit down and talk and enjoy the weather. And then they **hear** some noises. They **hear** people talking. They **hear** things moving. So they **go** out. And they **go** behind a bush. And they **look**. And they **can't believe** their eyes… (Ukrainetz, Eisenberg, Justice, & Kaderavek, in press)

Appealing stories, which can be created in many ways, can occur at any age. In general, there is a gradually increasing sense of story and expressive sophistication, which may peak at about 10 years of age for picture-based narratives, but continue to develop for personal anecdotes outside of a school context. Attention will now turn to assisting students in developing more complex narrative structure from story art and other perspectives.

Books and Notations for Improving Narrative Structure

Two foundational tools are provided here for teaching narrative structure. The first tool is children's literature. It is used as a model, a context, and a source of inspiration for the lessons to follow. The other tool is pictography, a way of temporarily representing chronological story events for recall, revision, and retelling.

Narrative Structure through Children's Literature

Story structure and other language skills are readily and enjoyably taught through children's literature (Strong & Hoggan North, 1996; Ukrainetz & Trujillo, 1999; van Dongen & Westby, 1986). Reading and guided discussion of storybooks with follow-up activities leads to better story retelling, emergent reading, book concepts, and story comprehension (Morrow, O'Connor, & Smith 1990). Storybooks abound that exemplify types of story grammar structure, from action sequences to complex episodes. Stories often contain multiple examples of the story grammar structure, allowing repeated opportunities for discussion and analysis. Cohesion is present in all stories. Some are good examples of particular cohesive devices. Children's literature is worthwhile just for the pleasure of story. Across words and pictures, in myriad ways, good books exemplify the ways of story art.

Books should be selected for the combination of the narrative structure to be taught and the appeal of the story. There is no need to select literature based on reading level when it will be shared orally. Reading aloud allows young students to enjoy books beyond their independent reading level. Conversely, illustrated books with a minimum of text can be used for complex and sophisticated narrative structure intervention with older students.

A description of books that employ repeated examples of particular episodic structures, narrative art, and cohesion follows. The books are ordered from simplest to most sophisticated story grammar structure. The simplest levels can be used as starting points for the students to increase the story grammar complexity of the tale told by adding a complication, an attempt, or a resolution. A bibliography of children's books cited in this chapter is provided as an Appendix (see page 246).

Thematic Sequence

Two classic, patterned storybooks that exemplify thematic or descriptive sequences are *Goodnight Moon* (Brown, 1975) and *Brown Bear, Brown Bear, What Do You See?* (Carle, 1995). The first story consists of a series of good night wishes to items in the room and in the sky. The thematic unity occurs through the repetitive goodnight wishes and the verse element. *Brown Bear, Brown Bear, What Do You See?* involves one animal seeing the next animal, until the animals see the teacher who sees the students, who see the animals, and the circle is completed. Its melodic line, patterned sentences, simple observations, bold illustrations, and circular thematic line are entrancing. Cohesion is present in both these stories primarily in terms of parallel structures and lexical repetition.

These two stories are clearly not episodic narratives. They do not even fit the definition of a narrative and would not be used as a model of narrative structure. However, they reflect how young children tell their earliest stories and they evidence narrative art. The patterning and verse allow young children to manage extended story turns.

Action Sequence

All by Myself (Mayer, 1983) details the independent accomplishments of a little furry fellow. The actions are organized from getting up in the morning through going to bed at night. The chronological format, without complications or causal relations, represents an action sequence. Adding cohesive temporal connectors would make this more clearly an action sequence. Cohesion is contributed mainly through the parallel structure of "I can." This would be a good model for the first step in narrative structure development. Generating temporal connectors to improve the story could be the next step in refining action sequence and cohesion structure.

The Berenstain Bears Go to School (Berenstain & Berenstain, 1978) has a more developed story structure. It is still basically an action sequence, recounting the steps prior to and during Sister Bear's first day of kindergarten. However, it has more description, feelings, and thoughts than *All by Myself*. There are even moments of abbreviated episodic structure (complication plus resolution) such as when Sister Bear comforts her nervous seatmate on the school bus. This story would be a step up from *All by Myself*, while still presenting a series of primarily temporally linked actions.

Incomplete Episode

Alexander and the Terrible, Horrible, No Good, Very Bad Day (Viorst, 1972) details the trials and tribulations of one very bad day. This story is basically a repeated reactive sequence in which bad things keep happening without character control, but some episodic relations are apparent. Alexander has reactions (leading nowhere), internal motivations (leading to protests), and some futile attempts to solve the problems that are bigger than the six-year-old. A next step might be problem solving better solutions to his situation, moving the incomplete to complete episodes.

In terms of narrative art, *Alexander* uses many evaluative techniques, but no climactic high point. The long, compound sentences emphasize the number of bad things that happen within one breath. Short, parallel sentences, with Alexander's lot last also emphasize his plight. The refrain "terrible, horrible, no good, very bad" day and thoughts of Australia unite the story. The seemingly mundane events are those that matter very much to a child.

Complete Episode

Gregory, the Terrible Eater (Sharmat, 1980) presents two linked complete episodes. Gregory the goat prefers foods his parents consider unhealthy (complication). The worried parents take him to the doctor who says to introduce healthy foods gradually (motivating state). The parents do so (attempt). Gregory learns to enjoy the supposed healthy goat diet of cans, tires, and glass (consequence). But he starts to eat too much (next complication). His parents worry about his overconsumption (motivating state). They fill his room with items from the dump and let him eat to his heart's content (attempt). Gregory gets ill. When he recovers, he still wants goat food, but in reasonable amounts (consequence).

This book's appeal comes from the reversal of the notions of edibility and healthy food, placed in the familiar issue of parents frustrated with a picky eater. The densely packed lists of "healthy" and "bad" foods shows the narrator's focus on edibility and eating consequences. The juxtaposition of *picky* and *terrible* versus *I want what I like, good* versus *revolting, goat* versus *pig,* emphasizes the issue.

Mushroom in the Rain (Ginsburg, 1974) provides multiple complete episodes. An ant takes shelter under a mushroom. Then a series of creatures seek to hide under a mushroom. This demonstrates an attempt to resolve complications, with a repeated, simple-episode pattern. In addition to structure, synonyms for *wet,* conditional verbs, and peer interactions are possible targets for intervention. This book can also provide a lesson in reference cohesion. The many characters necessitate clear pronoun reference. How does one select *he* or *she* and who is referred to by *they?* A lesson is demonstrated later in this chapter. Other lessons based on this story were presented in Chapter 2.

Multiple Attempts

Mercer Mayer wordless picture books are ideal for language intervention. The small, detailed, black-and-white drawings make the stories suitable for older students. *Frog Goes to Dinner* (Mayer, 1974) is an example of repeated attempts to solve a problem, with hilarious consequences. In addition to narrative structure, this particular book presents many vocabulary opportunities dealing with instruments, food, clothing, and facial expressions.

Frog, Where Are You? (Mayer, 1969) has probably been studied more than any other children's story. Berman and Slobin (1994) and Berman (2004) are two volumes almost entirely dedicated to cross-linguistic narrative studies of this book. *Frog Where Are You?* is a single episode with multiple attempts to solve the problem of the frog's disappearance and entertaining outcomes of each attempt. Narrative art options are open with these wordless books. A simple story opener or an abstract and detailed orientation can be taught. A few internal state words or many feeling and cognition words can be modeled. An example is presented later in this chapter.

The Legend of the Lady Slipper (Lunge-Larsen & Preus, 1999), a storybook retelling of an Ojibwe tale, is another example of multiple complications with multiple attempts to resolve. However, its main strength is in the story art. The story, along with its multiple layers of climax, imagery, and word choice, is detailed in a story art lesson later in this chapter.

Multiple Complications

Sheep in a Jeep (Shaw, 1986) is a popular verse story that details the misadventures of six sheep in a jeep. The sheep have three accidents with the jeep, each of which necessitates multiple attempts to solve the problem. The story is sparse, so the complication and attempts are easy to identify. This structure can be charted. This could be a model for a parallel humorous story on other critters dealing with troubles with motor-powered vehicles, or without the verse element. In addition, the rhyme and alliteration provide a context for teaching phonemic awareness (see Chapter 10).

A Promise Is a Promise (Munsch & Kusugak, 1988) is an entrancing story about a Canadian Inuit girl's promises to her mother and sea monsters called Qualupilluit. Allusha's attempts to extricate herself from her promise to the Qualupilluit and from the subsidiary complications that arise provide multiple episodes with multiple attempts to solve problems. A story grammar lesson is presented on *A Promise Is a Promise* later in this chapter. Contrary to Western style, as the problem develops, the dialogue diminishes, with the characters doing more thinking and acting than talking. In addition, the solution comes from the family, rather from an individual heroic figure. This story tells universal tales about boogeymen, promises, and the wisdom of parents.

Alternate Episodic Structure

Not all good stories follow episodic structure. Western stories are typically *topic-centered,* with a chronologically ordered flow of events. In an alternate structure, called *topic-associated,* one topic generates another. An element in one topic will stimulate a memory of another topic. This storytelling is often co-constructed, without a clear narrator and audience (e.g, "Do you remember when...?" "Yeah, I remember that day..."). While this organization of storytelling has been associated with African-American storytelling (e.g., Michaels, 1991), it also can occur in informal conversational storytelling among participants familiar with the event (Westby, 1985).

Tell Me a Story, Mama (Johnson, 1989) is an example of topic-associated story structure. In this lovely story, a young girl and her mother move through reminiscences of the mother's childhood. They have a common understanding of the events and characters and need only refer to them briefly to stimulate a flood of memories. They share in the telling, strengthening their bonds of family history and emotional closeness. This alternate structure is not used in literate discourse in the school years, and so would not be a target for intervention. However, it can be appreciated as an alternate way of storytelling suitable for informal contexts.

Pictography: A Narrative Representation Tool

Stories are long and multifaceted, and the spoken word is a transitory event. The SLP needs a way of representing stories with structural support that aids memory, reflection, revision, and sharing.

An obvious method of representation is writing. Unfortunately, writing is painfully slow for many students with language-learning disabilities. Text production fully occupies their mental resources and they may be challenged to even read their own work. Revision, if it occurs at all, deals with only the mechanics of writing (Butler-Nalin, 1984; Flower & Hayes, 1980). Story content and organization are forgotten. The dynamic and pleasurable interchange of narrative creation grinds to a halt under the demand to write.

Drawing is an alternative to writing. In the early grades, drawing is often recommended as a prewriting strategy. It stimulates story ideas and provides visual reminders of story details (Calkins, 1986; Myers, 1983). However, beyond the first grade, drawing has limited utility within the composition process. Static, detailed images do not lend themselves to temporal or causal organization. As well, the aesthetic involvement distracts the author from the task of narrative composition.

An alternative to drawing and writing is a notation that employs aspects of both. *Pictography*, or picture writing, does not represent words directly. Rather, it represents ideas and events that can also be carried in language (Gelb, 1952). Such a representation system requires only a handful of scenes to represent a narrative. Pictography is composed of simple, schematic sketches, organized in a left-to-right, chronologically based layout. Figure 5.1 on page 224 illustrates a pictographic representation. Pictography combines the ease of simple drawings with some of the representational ability of writing. Pictography falls within the general domain of graphic organizers, which present information in words, phrases, or occasionally pictures, using schematic networks that emphasize the relationship among concepts (Pehrsson & Denner, 1988). Pictography differs from other graphic organizers in that the representation is primarily pictorial, and the focus is on representing the chronology of events rather than concept analysis.

Pictography provides memory and organizational support for stories, allowing recall and discussion of oral narratives and early drafts of written narratives or procedural exposition. As a low-technology tool that students can use independently, pictography has applications both as a structural support for language development and as an ongoing compensatory strategy within the classroom (McFadden, 1998; Ukrainetz, 1998).

Figure 5.1   Clinician's Pictographic Planning—Scary Visitor

From "Stickwriting Stories: A Quick and Easy Narrative Representation Strategy," by T. A. Ukrainetz, 1998, *Language, Speech, and Hearing Services in Schools, 29,* p. 199. © 1998 by the American Speech-Language-Hearing Association. Adapted with permission.

Facilitating Sequence and Content

Pictography has powerful effects on temporal organization and quality of discourse. The multiple scenes and arrows clearly suggest movement through time. Students who employ primarily description sequences move into action sequences with the aid of pictography (McFadden, 1998; Ukrainetz, 1998). Pictography, lacking the complications of print, also allows greater attention to idea production. Students' stories are longer, better quality, and are drafted faster. This advantage is most apparent for students with the greatest difficulty writing.

Teaching Pictography

Pictography, or picture writing, is easily taught to students, who often call it "stickwriting," reflecting the stick figure people inhabiting the pictures. Pictography can consist of as few as three scenes (beginning, middle, and end), or as many as a dozen. The pictography is organized left-to-right and top-to-bottom, to make it similar to writing. Movement through time is represented with arrows between each action scene. Complex episodic structure can be graphically represented as shown in Figure 5.2. This story, about the solution to an overturned truck, emphasizes the multiple attempts to solve and the outcomes of each.

Figure 5.2 ## Clinician's Pictographic Planning—Truck

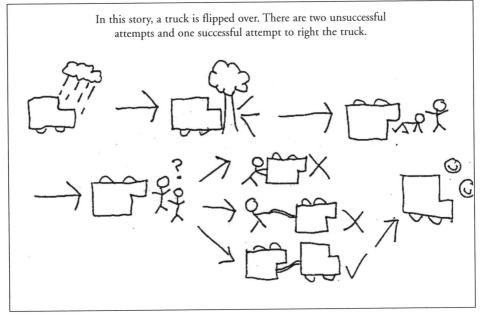

In this story, a truck is flipped over. There are two unsuccessful attempts and one successful attempt to right the truck.

From "Stickwriting Stories: A Quick and Easy Narrative Representation Strategy," by T. A. Ukrainetz, 1998, *Language, Speech, and Hearing Services in Schools, 29*, p. 205. © 1998 by the American Speech-Language-Hearing Association. Reprinted with permission.

Students learn the physical form of pictography without difficulty. For example, a second grader provided the pictography in Figure 5.3 on page 226 in his second encounter with this representational form. Within as little as a single teaching session, students from first to seventh grade can accomplish the schematic sketches and graphic organization. To keep the focus on the story rather than the drawing, the sketches must be "quick and easy" and "just enough to remember."

Pictography is presented to students via modeling. The SLP demonstrates the story's pictographic creation, not just the finished product. The SLP thinks aloud throughout the process, demonstrating how to select key ideas, make simple sketches, and organize the content. Box 5.8 on page 227 illustrates this process. The students then retell the story from the pictography.

A small next step has the students take dictation. The SLP tells a short story and the students use pictography to represent it. The SLP talks them through their sketching, commenting on their selection of key notations, using the quick and easy rule, and organizing left-to-right with arrows. After this step, students move into using pictography for their own ideas. The SLP again

Figure 5.3   ## Second Grader's Pictography

From "Stickwriting Stories: A Quick and Easy Narrative Representation Strategy," by T.A. Ukrainetz, 1998, *Language, Speech, and Hearing Services in Schools, 29,* p. 200. © 1998 by the American Speech-Language-Hearing Association. Reprinted with permission.

talks them through the story and the sketching. The emphasis is always on "quick and easy." Writing is not allowed unless it is produced quickly and easily. This rule has some related benefits, which will be discussed later.

Applications

Narrative structure and pictographic representation go hand in hand. Although students have story ideas, they need help sequencing and chunking the ideas in manageable pieces, both for the story and for the visual representation. As the student learns to represent narratives with pictography, chronological order and sequence also emerge.

After the pictographic draft, the story is discussed. The parts can be coded as setting, complication, attempt, and consequence. As students compose or revise their stories, they are guided into using motivating states, plans, attempts, or consequences. Depending on the language objectives, the lesson's focus may be on retelling the story coherently and sequentially, using a particular story structure, or revision and extension. Particular words, events, details, or sequences that would improve the story can be added.

Pictography is applicable to the classroom composition process. Within the composition process, substantive revision is particularly challenging for students with writing difficulties. Pictography supports revision. It is best

Box 5.8 Teaching Pictography through Modeling the Process for the *Scary Visitor* Story

I am going to make up a story about kids who get tricked. I'll start over here, in the top-left corner. I'll go to the right, like writing. The story is going to be about a girl, Teresa, and her brother, Paul. *Once, there were two children, named Teresa and Paul. They stayed home one Saturday morning to watch cartoons.* I'll draw two stick people. No faces, that takes too long. Quick and easy, that's the rule. I will just put a roof shape over their heads to show the house. That isn't a very good house, is it? But it is good enough to remember. There is a sun to show daytime. And here is a quicky television. A figure with a circle inside. Good enough. *Then.* See, I put an arrow to the right to show where to go for the next part of the story. *Then the children heard a knock at the door.* See the lines? That means a loud sound. *They looked through the window and saw something furry. Teresa thought it might be a bear! They were scared, so they hid behind the chair. Someone knocked again, louder. Teresa locked the door.* See that X? That means lock the door. *Then a voice said, "Hey kids, it's Mom!"* I put "Mom" in a balloon like in the comics. Just one word, that's quick and easy, and enough to remember. Now another arrow. *It was just their mother. She had groceries in both hands, so she couldn't open the door. She was all fuzzy because she just got a perm.* See, I made her hair really big and gave her groceries in both hands. *They helped her carry the groceries in and laughed about how silly they had been. The end.* I put a period for the end. Kind of like writing.

suited to organizational revision, where episodic elements are added or parts are rearranged. They can be inserted or the pictography can easily be redone. Some word level revision can also occur. Nouns, pronouns, verbs, adjectives, and adverbs can be noted at points in the story. So long as the need is limited to a few words, they can be combined with pictography.

A classroom teacher had her third- and fourth-grade students use pictography in composing imaginative narratives (Ukrainetz, 1998). The students were asked to imagine and write a story about a day in the life of a dinosaur. The teacher discussed story possibilities, then modeled drafting a story using pictography on chart paper. The teacher's story was long, with 15 action scenes. The students then did their own pictography and followed it with written composition. The teacher reported that the pictography procured such sufficiently good written results that she considered it a first draft, rather than a prewriting draft.

Pictography works well in cooperative groups. One student can devote full attention to the story generation while another student scribes pictographically. Pictography can also assist listening comprehension. While students are listening to a story, the SLP periodically stops reading and asks them to sketch the part of the story they have heard. Students attend better and recall more details this way than by simply listening to the story.

Older and Younger Students

Pictography is challenging for kindergartners and preschoolers, who have difficulty producing these schematic images. Stickwriting and artistic drawing look much the same at this age, and mental resources are fully occupied producing the simplest images. However, young students can tell stories from adult pictography. Paley's (1990) kindergartners dramatized stories that they had previously composed via dictation. Instead of dictation, which the students cannot read themselves, adult-composed pictography can be used to support their tellings. Charting out a cooperatively created story or a previously read storybook allows for a visual guide that can be used for story retelling or dramatic reenactments.

A benefit for older elementary students is improvement of note taking. Students' prior lessons in spelling, grammar, and presentation interfere with note taking, which involves writing only significant words and phrases while maintaining online comprehension of the content read or heard. Students tend to write full sentences with correct spelling even when explicitly directed to generate only key words (Bereiter & Scardamalia, 1982). With pictography, the SLP already models key words and strategic punctuation such as "Help!" in a speech bubble. This model can be moved intentionally into a written rather than pictorial display. Older students may spontaneously take writing further (Ukrainetz, 1998). They start to "sneak in" written words. They must select words they can write fast enough to keep within the "quick and easy" rule and they tend to select words that they could have pictorially represented, predisposing without direct instruction toward selection of key words. Figure 5.4 on page 232 shows the spontaneous key-word planning composed by three older elementary students with learning disabilities.

Figure 5.4   **Key Word Planning in Place of Pictography**

This story of an overturned truck and a lost child is by older elementary students and contains an embedded episode.

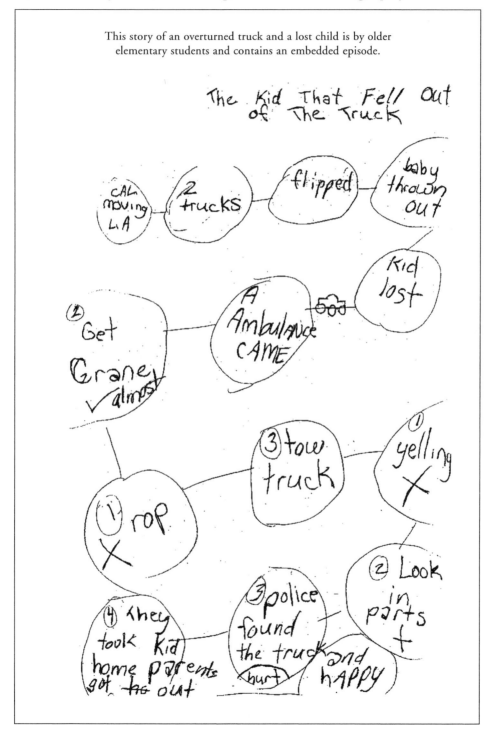

Moving Young Children into Independent Storytelling

Intervention with preschoolers involves moving children toward independent, monologic discourse. Children may retell personal events or familiar stories. Stories are co-constructed by the SLP and children telling the story. The aim is to prompt the child into progressively longer turn sequences until the story is clearly owned and shaped by the child.

In teaching about narratives, the SLP's knowledge of the narrative's source event aids in interactive scaffolding, such as prompting the child, modeling story parts, and taking a supportive turn in the storytelling. Familiarity with preschool activities, contact with the home, and knowing the child as an individual all allow awareness of life experiences upon which personal narratives are based. Familiarity with recurring or recent storybooks, television shows, and movies lead to supportive retellings of imaginary narratives. Sharing a storybook several times before retelling, reenacting, or creating parallel stories provides a mutually familiar event structure. Repeated readings also promote more child talk, more spontaneous commenting, changing talk focus, and increased quality of thought (Martinez & Roser, 1985).

In addition to mutual event familiarity, an underlying interest in the child's telling and a willingness to let the child do the talking are necessary parts of moving the young child into greater independence. Trousdale (1990) read and retold stories to a child until they became familiar and the child started participating in the retelling. Trousdale described how the child, Tim, modified the *Jack and the Beanstalk* retelling by adding 10 dollars to the beans exchanged for the cow, thus eliminating the mother's punishment of Jack. Tim later added Superman and a magic zapping power to the story to help Jack. Tim was able to move back and forth between the roles of listener and teller during the co-narrated story. For another story, *The Bremen Town Musicians,* Tim listened several times to an audiorecording. He then spontaneously provided a 15-minute complete retelling of the story—a significant accomplishment for a six-year-old.

After several readings, children can often independently pretend-read entire stories with eyes on the print and appropriate story intonation (Sulzby, 1985; Sulzby & Zecker, 1991). Story retelling and dramatic reenactments with SLP guidance allow the child to manage longer and more coherent pieces of text (Culatta, 1994; Morrow, 1985; 1986; Paley, 1990). Owens and Robinson (1997) suggest using group chanting of repetitive patterns as a way of responding that provides structural support for retelling segments of stories without calling notice to one particular child. Kirchner (1991) provides a structured sequence of prompting, called *reciprocal reading*. Reciprocal reading involves reading a book aloud several times, then pausing at moments for a cloze response on a desired segment of text. With repetitions, the cloze response involves progressively longer segments of text. Once the text is well-practiced, roles are reversed, and the child prompts the SLP to respond. Finally, the child can retell the story in its entirety.

As previously suggested, preschoolers' storytelling can be supported through pictography. For young children, the SLP sketches out the main or salient story events in chronological order. The children retell the story from these sketches. After the SLP has modeled drawing the story, for the next retelling, the children assist in drawing individual scenes. The SLP prompts for the event recount before they draw and again afterward (e.g., *Your turn. What happened next in the story... That's right, the mouse asked the ant to let him under the mushroom. OK, you draw the mushroom and the mouse... Good work, now tell me again what happened*). The focus is on the children telling the main events of the story in order. In addition, character feelings, causal relations, and sentence structures can be emphasized (e.g., *Why did the mouse want to get under the mushroom? Because he was wet? Say the whole sentence so we understand. The mouse wanted to get under the mushroom because he was wet*).

These recurring readings and retellings allow both a mutually familiar event structure and repeated opportunities for learning. Guided storybook reading and retellings form the foundation for moving into activities involving parallel stories that reflect the storybook theme or children's own stories (Paley, 1990; Trousdale, 1990). For young children, these can be enacted through dramatic play or as monologues with visual props such as felt boards, toys, and pictures. While temporal ordering and story art are introduced, the primary focus for these activities is a movement toward independent telling and basic event ordering, rather than improvement in specific episodic, cohesive, or artful structures.

Teaching Story Grammar

Story grammar is a common target of instruction in the elementary grades. While terminology may vary, students are often familiar with settings, characters, problems, feelings, and solutions. First graders are beginning to formulate episodes to tell their stories and older elementary students are exploring the complexities of motivating conditions, multiple attempts, multiple episodes, and multiple agents operating in support or in conflict.

Story Grammar Cues

Students can be taught to use more complex story grammar organization in their narratives. Graves and Montague (1991) provided upper-elementary and junior high students with story grammar cue cards during planning time to remind them of basic episodic elements to include in their narrative compositions: setting, character, problem, plan, and ending. The students checked off story parts as they incorporated the parts into their stories. This procedural facilitation served to help students self-monitor and resulted in longer and qualitatively better stories. The story grammar checkoff proved to be more helpful than planning time alone or planning time combined with a simple review of story grammar elements. Students with learning disabilities were able to dictate or write narratives that were similar in quality to those of typically achieving students when they were given planning time and procedural facilitation.

Graham and Harris (1999) suggest teaching the mnemonic SPACE for *setting, problem, action, consequences,* and *emotions.* Along with the task-specific mnemonic, Graham and Harris teach general self-regulation procedures dealing with defining the task, planning, self-evaluation, self-reinforcement, and coping. They emphasize teacher modeling of self-talk and composition. Students develop background knowledge, discuss strategy goals, have the strategy modeled, memorize the mnemonic, and practice the strategy with guidance. Through this process during repeated composition opportunities, students are scaffolded into independence and increased levels of narrative performance.

A Story Grammar Lesson

Explicit attention to story grammar structures improves students' narrative performance (e.g., Morrow, 1986). Facilitation of specific narrative structures involves a focused skill plan. The following is a several-session guideline for teaching multiple attempts to solve a problem. The author has used versions of this in pull-out, self-contained, and inclusive settings. A key to providing intervention in larger group settings is to minimize whole group instruction and maximize interactions with individual students through co-teaching and cooperative group arrangements.

Analyzing Multiple Attempts

The process starts with students brainstorming the parts of a story they know, to determine initial knowledge of story grammar terminology. The SLP prompts by asking what is needed at the beginning of a story, what is needed in the middle, and what is needed at the end. As the students offer words, the SLP introduces the terminology for each element and enters the word in the left-most column of a blank story grammar chart. (A completed story grammar chart for this lesson is shown in Table 5.4 on page 234.)

The story to be shared is then introduced by showing the cover and reading the title of the book. A favorite storybook for this lesson is *A Promise Is a Promise.* The students guess what the story might be about, with the SLP filling in students' key words for each of the story grammar elements in the Prediction column of the chart.

After students predict the story, the SLP begins reading. The story is halted after each episode. The complication, internal responses, attempts to solve, and consequence are discussed and charted in the Episode columns. Sometimes components must be inferred because they are not stated explicitly (e.g., *Allusha was probably scared when the Quallupilluit dragged her under the sea ice*). Predictions are compared to actual happenings. Incidental comments on vocabulary, illustrations, and life in the north may occur.

After reading the storybook, the episodes are reanalyzed with attention focused on the multiple attempts to solve each problem. Each student pictographically charts out an episode with its multiple attempts. The students then cooperatively retell the entire story by narrating individual pictographically represented episodes.

Creating Multiple Attempts

Students then move into creating their own stories. The SLP guides the students into a theme of bad promises from *A Promise Is a Promise* (but the students sometimes insist on boogeymen stories). They each pictographically chart their stories. They start with the setting components of who, when, and where in the first scene, then sketch the actions leading to a complication. Three attempts to solve each complication, with the results of each attempt, are charted out in a fan. The successful attempt leads to the final consequence and story resolution. Students narrate their stories from their pictography.

To provide another opportunity to internalize this structure, students can take turns playing reporter. They interview and audiotape each other regarding each adventure, with attention to the attempts made and their consequences.

Story Grammar Prediction and Charting
for *A Promise Is a Promise*

Table 5.4

Element	Prediction	Episode #1	Episode #2	Episode #3	Episode #4
Setting					
Characters	Student, Monster	Girl (Allusha), Quallupilluit, family			
Place	Alaska	Canadian North			
Time	Winter	Spring			
Complication	Monster attacks.	A not allowed to fish on the sea ice.	Q drag A under the sea ice.	A falls in snow, wet and freezing.	A's promise to the Q
Motivating State					
Feeling	Scared	Probably mad	Probably scared	Dad was probably worried	Dumb move
Plan	Thinks of running	No plan	No plan	No plan	Mom and Dad think and think
Attempt 1	Offers a fish	Lies and goes anyway	Tells Q she didn't insult	Puts A to bed	Mom begs and pleads
Attempt 2	Screams	Calls out insults to Q	Tells Q they are lovely	Parents cuddle A	Mom tricks Q with candy, bread, and dancing
Attempt 3	Hits the monster, lies, and goes anyway		Promises Q her siblings	A. drinks 10 cups of sweet hot tea	
Consequence	Gets away	Starts all the troubles in the story	Q let her go	A recovers	A fulfills her promise safely
Reaction		Scared to go near the sea ice	Probably relieved about being free	Probably relieved	Family happy but A still nervous

The recordings are played and the students identify and discuss the attempts and alternatives.

Motivating States and Reactions

Students often fail to employ the feeling words involved in character descriptions, motivating states, and reactions. Montague and Graves (1992) describe an instructional study that explicitly taught this aspect of narrative text. They started with general story grammar instruction, then focused for three sessions on character development. This started with a discussion on the importance of characters to a story; their identities, attributes, and motivations; and the problems they encounter. The instructor and students then read a story and underlined words that described the characters and their actions, ideas, and emotions. The second day's lesson involved writing a group story using the story grammar cue cards. The focus was on the affective qualities of the characters. The teacher recorded ideas on chart paper. Then the students dictated the story, which was written on chart paper and audiorecorded. The instructor then composed a modified version of the story with all words reflecting character cognition and emotion deleted. The students evaluated and compared the two stories.

The feeling word lesson by Montague and Graves (1992) provides a good example of how to teach a particular aspect of narrative structure. This instruction went beyond "inserting feeling words" to thinking about feelings and cognitions that were appropriate to a character and related well to the story. A refinement in this instruction would be to focus more on the functional role of the targeted story grammar element. A feeling word such as *sad* can be an enduring character attribute, a motivating state leading to action, or a reaction at the end of the story. Students learn why to use *sad* at different points in a story.

Teaching One Kind of Cohesion

Cohesion involves the appropriate selection of words and phrases to unify text. It overlaps with syntax (conjunction, parallel structures, pronouns) and vocabulary (lexical substitution). It could also involve word finding, if the student is saying pronouns (e.g., *it*) and proforms (e.g., *something*) excessively due to an inability to find the reference word. Despite these overlaps, the essential element of cohesion is reference—not whether the correct pronoun was used but whether the pronoun clearly referred to a prior or upcoming entity.

Storybooks with multiple characters provide repeated opportunities for confusing and clear pronoun reference. The book *Mushroom in the Rain* is suited to this because of the many characters with indeterminate genders. After an initial reading, a second reading and discussion focuses on how to refer to the various agents in the story. Box 5.9 provides a sample dialogue that highlights cohesion use. This discussion is followed up with an analysis of an SLP-created parallel short story with confusing reference, or blanks for the reference elements. Box 5.10 provides an example. It concerns an owl, a woodpecker, a termite, and two boys. As the students read along in the story with the SLP, they circle the pronouns and their referents. They discuss how the pronoun reference is confusing and how to improve it. They then cooperatively fix the story.

Sample Dialogue Highlighting Cohesion
Box 5.9   Use for *Mushroom in the Rain*

One day an ant was caught in the rain. "Where can I hide?" he wondered. He saw a tiny mushroom peeking out of the ground in a clearing, and he hid under it. He sat there, waiting for the rain to stop. But the rain came down harder and harder. We just read about an ant. Here the author says "ant" to let us know who the first character is. Then the author uses the pronoun "he." How many times does the author use "he"? Is four times okay? Does this confuse the reader? Why is this okay?

Then the butterfly joins him. *The butterfly says, "I am so wet I cannot fly"* and the ant says, *"How can I let you in? There is barely room enough for one."* Who is "I?" Is "I" the butterfly or the ant? Does that depend on who talks?

A mouse ran up. Now a mouse appears. Is this mouse a boy or a girl? Could we say "he" or "she?" The author just says "mouse" again and doesn't use a pronoun again. Why is that is a good strategy? He does it for the sparrow too.

They moved over, and there was room enough for the sparrow. Now the animals are described as "they." Who are "they?" How do we know?

"Have you seen the rabbit? Which way did he go?" Who is "he?" "He" refers back to the rabbit. How do we know? *The fox turned up his nose, flicked his tail, and ran off.* "His nose" is whose nose? That is the fox. We go back to the first name in the sentence and that is who the pronoun refers to…

Excerpts from *Mushroom in the Rain*, by M. Ginsburg, 1974, New York: Aladdin. © 1974 by Mirra Ginsburg. Reprinted with permission.

Box 5.10

**Sample Short Story Illustrating
Confusing Pronoun Reference**

There once was an owl who tried to make a home in a hole in a tree. It couldn't fit. It was too big. So it asked it to make the hole bigger. It tried, but it couldn't. So it asked it to help. It tried to help, but it was in a hurry. It needed a hole to lay its eggs. Then they came along. It asked them to help. He stood on his shoulders. He reached up high with his pocket knife. He dug out more space in the hole. He peered in and thought that was a comfy, safe spot for his new friend. They found there was enough space for all of them, so they decided to try to live together. They thanked them and moved into their new home, just in time for it to lay its eggs. The end.

This process can be done several times with other SLP-created short stories. An important part of narrative intervention is lots of stories that demonstrate and allow practice with desired structures. Starting with real literature, then providing SLP-created stories, followed by students' own productions, is the best way to create a critical mass of opportunities for learning to cohere utterances into stories.

Making Stories Artful

The Pleasure of a Good Book

Story art instruction starts with children's literature. It begins with simple, common book concept comments, such as pointing out the title, how the story grabs your interest from the beginning, and how the illustrations add to the story. Then read through the story and pause to point out features such as word choice, word repetitions, parallel structures, sentence structure, dialogue, and even punctuation choices. High point structure is most easily illustrated with suspenseful stories. In suspenseful stories, there is a buildup to the climax, then a resolution that brings together the story elements. There are usually a lot of descriptive words. Story voice intonation and exclamatory dialogue add tension.

Many suspenseful children's tales have a humorous air to them, presumably to lower the fear factor. The fairy tale *The Three Little Pigs* could qualify as a suspenseful story, as the pigs' houses are successively destroyed and the wolf attempts to gain entry into the final house, but the refrain "not by the hair on my chinny chin chin" reduces the tension.

The Legend of the Lady Slipper, a storybook retelling of an Ojibwe tale, presents a young girl's harrowing trip to a distant village in the winter to obtain medicines for her people. The tension builds as she encounters one challenge after another. She becomes colder, weaker, and sicker. Will she make it back to her village with the healing herbs?

This story starts with an abstract that is an opening metaphor for the heroine. The Foreword describes the Lady Slipper flower and informs the reader that this story will explain how such a delicate flower came to grow in such rugged country. The story begins with orientation information that includes how the girl's brother was her favorite family member. This sets up her strong, brave brother as the girl's model. The story uses similes, such as the description of her brother: "He was as strong as a bear, as fast as a rabbit, and as smart as a fox." Nature is both harsh and supportive; the elements hiss, sting, and tug, but still encourage her to be strong and quick. Even as the snow buries her, it whispers, "be wise." Descriptive words emphasize the suffering, such as *bare, cold, swollen,* and *bleeding;* and the relief, such as, *glowing, soft, thick,* and *warm.* The girl eventually triumphs in returning with the healing herbs. The story ends with a coda that underlines the memorability of the girl's heroism. In the spring, Lady Slipper flowers bloom wherever her bleeding feet touched the ground, commemorating her heroic journey.

This story has sufficient story art to serve as a model at multiple levels. First, the overall high point structure can be demonstrated. Then the appendages and orientations can be discussed. The third focus can be the evaluation elements, especially the animal similes.

Creating Artful Stories

After enjoying and reflecting on the story art of a piece of literature, students move into composing their own artful stories. If the lesson focus is story art, then episodic structure and cohesion should be supported, but are not the explicit focus. By starting with a picture sequence of a story or using stories created in an earlier lesson, the referential information and organization is supplied, and the focus can be on adding artful elements.

The wordless picture book *Frog, Where Are You?* can be used to provide a structural scaffold upon which to base an artful elaboration. The story is pictographically sketched in advance. The pictography provides the event progression, while the visual details in the pictures provide ideas and inspiration for the story art. Words and phrases are written into each pictographic scene by the SLP and students as the artful revisions and additions are made. The story opening alone has multiple artful possibilities: a title, an introducer, an abstract, literary word choices, external and internal orienting conditions. Some of these foreshadow the direction or even the end of the story, so the full plot line needs to be familiar to the students. The beginning might look like: *Curiosity Almost Killed the Frog. Once there was a boy who truly loved his little frog. His frog was a curious fellow and the boy feared that someday this curiosity would get the frog in trouble.*

Tension is built through the search by making the boy progressively more concerned and frustrated. Expanded phrases such as "even more worried," or "thought he would never find his frog," show the buildup better than just *worried.* Metaphors are added to the boy's misadventures; instead of being knocked over a cliff by a deer, he is "tossed in the air like a rag." After finding the frog and expressing his relief, a coda in the form of a moral to the tale can be expressed, such as *Both the boy and his frog learned that curiosity is OK, but tell your friends where you are going.* With this, voila, an artful story with high point structure has been devised.

After building the revised and expanded story, the story is told and retold, with oral expression. Story art is essentially meant to be enjoyed, by both narrator and audience, so this lesson should be fun. Such a piece of composing demands oral sharing or publication. Storytelling needs listeners and written stories need readers. Students who enjoy the composing process recognize the importance of a formal endpoint with an audience (Hubbard, 1985). Give students opportunities to share their creations with an audience.

The possibilities of story art are so diverse that it is difficult to capture them all in a single lesson. SLPs who enjoy using literature and storytelling during intervention will provide incidental exposure during other explicit narrative objectives. Story art is modeled every time a good story is shared and people talk about why they liked the book. But some explicit attention with repeated opportunities for learning is needed to produce consistent improvements in students' story art. Brief explicit attention to particular devices, even within a lesson focused on another objective, will reap later rewards. As students develop a shared history of stories, they will refer back to prior tales to glean ideas and inspirations: "Remember in *A Promise Is a Promise* when Allusha said the Quallupilluit smelled like a dead whale in August? The monster in my story smells like the gym clothes in my locker!"

Conclusion

Stories occupy much of our daily discourse, at home and at school. Stories are important as both direct targets of instruction and as contexts for teaching language, literacy, and concepts. This chapter focused on direct instruction in narrative, with an emphasis on structure.

Children's literature provides a wonderful context and model for narrative structure intervention. Story retelling and reenactments provide familiar scripts to support a movement toward greater stretches of monologicity. Episodic structures, cohesion, and story art can easily be found in storybooks.

As students move into telling their own stories, they need a way to represent their creations. Pictography—a series of schematic sketches—is a simple and effective way of representing narratives that provides memory and organizational support. Pictography facilitates temporal organization, story content, and complex episodic structure.

Four ways of examining narrative structure were considered. The first was consideration of the degree of interactive support needed for a preschooler to tell a story. Children must learn to tell stories monologically, without support from familiar adults or peers. The second approach to narrative structure was the commonly used story grammar or episodic analysis. Story grammar deals with an agent's goal-directed attempts to resolve a complication. Young children are guided from pre-episodic sequences to episodic structure, and school-age students are supported into more elaborated episodic structure. Cohesion was the third approach. Cohesion unites sentences into discourse units. Pronominal reference, one cohesive device, was focused on as a way of adding clarity to a narrative. Finally, expressive elaboration or story art is a critical element of narrative. This analysis considers how factors such as story openings, character background, climactic organization, and word choice contribute to the appeal of a narrative.

Narrative is a significant discourse structure and enjoyable to teach. Each analysis presented contributes a different aspect to the coherence, cohesion, and the captivating nature of a good story. Selecting a few intervention objectives from these analyses and providing an explicit skill focus for each, over repeated opportunities with systematic scaffolding, will result in improvements in narrative competence.

References

Au, K. H. (1980). Participation structures in a reading lesson with Hawaiian children: Analysis of a culturally appropriate instructional event. *Anthropology & Education Quarterly, 11*(2), 91–115.

Applebee, A. (1978). *The child's concept of story: Ages two to seventeen.* Chicago: The University of Chicago Press.

Bauman, R. (1986). *Story, performance, and event: Contextual studies of oral narrative.* Cambridge, UK: Cambridge University Press.

Bennett-Kastor, T. L. (1984). Cohesion and predication in child narrative. *Journal of Child Language, 13,* 353–370.

Bereiter, C., & Scardamalia, M. (1982). From conversation to composition: The role of instruction in a developmental process. In R. Glaser (Ed.), *Advances in instructional psychology: Vol. 2* (pp. 1–64). Mahwah, NJ: Erlbaum.

Berman, R. A. (2004). The role of context in developing narrative abilities. In S. Stromqvist & L. Verhoven (Eds.), *Relating events in narrative (Vol. 2): Typological and contextual perspectives* (pp. 261–280). Mahwah, NJ: Erlbaum.

Berman, R. A., & Slobin, D. I. (1994). *Relating events in narrative: A crosslinguistic developmental study.* Mahwah, NJ: Erlbaum.

Botvin, G. J., & Sutton-Smith, B. (1977). The development of structural complexity in children's fantasy narratives. *Developmental Psychology, 13,* 377–388.

Bruner, J. (1986). *Actual minds, possible worlds.* Cambridge, MA: Harvard University Press.

Butler-Nalin, K. (1984). Revising patterns in students' writing. In A. Applebee (Ed.), *Contexts for learning to write: Studies of secondary school instruction* (pp. 121–134). Norwood, NJ: Ablex.

Calkins, L. M. (1986). *The art of teaching writing.* Portsmouth, NH: Heinemann.

Crowhurst, M. (1987). Cohesion in argument and narration at three grade levels. *Research in the Teaching of English, 21,* 185–201.

Crowhurst, M. (1991). Interrelationships between reading and writing persuasive discourse. *Research in the Teaching of English, 25,* 314–338.

Culatta, B. (1994). Representational play and story enactments: Formats for language intervention. In J. F. Duchan, L. E. Hewitt, & R. M. Sonnenmeier (Eds.), *Pragmatics: From theory to practice* (pp. 105–119). Englewood Cliffs, NJ: Prentice-Hall.

Deese, J. (1983). Foreword. In C. Peterson & A. McCabe, *Developmental psycholinguistics: Three ways of looking at a child's narrative* (pp. xiii–xxxi). New York: Plenum Press.

Eisenberg, A. R. (1985). Learning to describe past experiences in conversation. *Discourse Processes, 8,* 177–204.

Flower, L. S., & Hayes, J. R. (1980). The dynamics of composing: Making plans and juggling constraints. In L. W. Gregg & E. R. Steinberg (Eds.), *Cognitive processes in writing* (pp. 31–50). Mahwah, NJ: Erlbaum.

Freedman, A. (1987). Development in story writing. *Applied Psycholinguistics, 8,* 153–170.

Galda, L., & Pellegrini, A. D. (1988). Children's use of narrative language in peer interaction. In B. A. Rafoth & D. L. Rubin (Eds.), *The social construction of written communication* (pp. 175–194). Norwood, NJ: Ablex.

Gee, J. P. (1989). Two styles of narrative construction and their linguistic and educational implications. *Discourse Processes, 12,* 287–307.

Gelb, I. J. (1952). *A study of writing.* Chicago: University of Chicago Press.

Gillam, R. B., & Pearson, N. (2004). *Test of Narrative Language.* Austin, TX: Pro-Ed.

Graham, S., & Harris, K. R. (1999). Assessment and intervention in overcoming writing difficulties: An illustration from the self-regulated strategy development model. *Language, Speech, and Hearing Services in Schools, 30,* 255–264.

Graves, A., & Montague, M. (1991). Using story grammar cueing to improve the writing of students with learning disabilities. *Learning Disabilities Research and Practice, 6,* 246–250.

Halliday, M. A. K., & Hasan, R. (1976). *Cohesion in English.* London: Longman.

Heath, S. B. (1983). *Ways with words: Language, life, and work in communities and classrooms.* Cambridge, UK: Cambridge University Press.

Hubbard, R. (1985). Second graders answer the question "Why publish?" *Reading Teacher, 38,* 658–662.

Hunt, K. W. (1965). *Grammatical structures written at three grade levels.* Urbana, IL: National Council of Teachers of English.

Kernan, K. (1977). Semantic and expressive elaborations in children's narratives. In S. Ervin-Tripp & C. Mitchell-Kernan (Eds.), *Child discourse* (pp. 91–102). New York: Academic Press.

Kirchner, D. M. (1991). Reciprocal book reading: A discourse-based intervention strategy for the child with atypical language development. In T. M. Gallagher (Ed.), *Pragmatics of language: Clinical practice issues* (pp. 307–332). San Diego, CA: Singular.

Klecan-Aker, J. S., & Hedrick, D. L. (1985). A study of the syntactic language skills of normal middle school children. *Language, Speech, and Hearing Services in Schools, 16,* 2–7.

Labov, W. (1972). *Language in the inner city.* Philadelphia, PA: University of Pennsylvania Press.

Labov, W., & Waletsky, J. (1967). Narrative analysis. In J. Helm (Ed.), *Essays on the verbal and visual arts* (pp. 12–44). Seattle, WA: University of Washington Press.

Liles, B. Z. (1985). Cohesion in the narratives of normal and language disordered children. *Journal of Speech and Hearing Research, 28,* 123–133.

Loban W. (1976). *Language development: Kindergarten through grade twelve.* Urbana, IL: National Council of Teachers of English.

Mandler, J. M., & Johnson, N. S. (1977). Remembrance of things parsed: Story structure and recall. *Cognitive Psychology, 9,* 111–151.

Mandler, J. M., Scribner, S., Cole, M., & DeForest, M. (1980). Cross-cultural invariance in story recall. *Child Development, 51,* 19–26.

Martinez, M., & Roser, N. (1985). Read it again: The value of repeated readings during storytime. *Reading Teacher, 38,* 782–786.

McCabe, A. (1991). Preface: Structure as a way of understanding. In A. McCabe & C. Peterson (Eds.), *Developing narrative structure* (pp. ix–xvii). Mahwah, NJ: Erlbaum.

McCabe, A., & Peterson, C. (1991). Getting the story: A longitudinal study of parental styles in eliciting narratives and developing narrative skill. In A. McCabe & C. Peterson (Eds.), *Developing narrative structure* (pp. 217–254). Mahwah, NJ: Erlbaum.

McFadden, T. U. (1998). The immediate effects of pictographic representation on children's narratives. *Child Language Learning and Teaching, 14,* 51–67.

McFadden, T. U., & Gillam, R. (1996). An examination of the quality of narratives produced by children with language disorders. *Language, Speech, and Hearing Services in Schools, 27,* 48–57.

Merritt, D. D., & Liles, B. Z. (1989). Story grammar ability in children with and without language disorder: Story generation, story retelling, and story comprehension. *Journal of Speech and Hearing Research, 30,* 539–552.

Michaels, S. (1991). The dismantling of narrative. In A. McCabe & C. Peterson (Eds.), *Developing narrative structure* (pp. 303–352). Mahwah, NJ: Erlbaum.

Minami, M. (2002). *Culture-specific language styles: The development of oral narrative and literacy.* Tonawanda, NY: Multilingual Matters.

Moffett, J. (1968). *Teaching the universe of discourse.* New York: Houghton Mifflin.

Montague, M., & Graves, A. (1992). Teaching narrative composition to students with learning disabilities. In M. Pressley, K. R. Harris, & J. T. Guthrie (Eds.), *Promoting academic competence and literacy in schools* (pp. 261–277). San Diego, CA: Academic Press.

Morrow, L. M. (1985). Reading and retelling stories: Strategies for emergent readers. *The Reading Teacher, 38,* 871–875.

Morrow, L. M. (1986). Effects of structural guidance in story retelling on children's dictation of original stories. *Journal of Reading Behavior, 18*(2), 135–152.

Morrow, L. M., O'Connor, E. M., & Smith, J. K. (1990). Effects of a story reading program on the literacy development of at-risk kindergarten children. *Journal of Reading Behavior, 22,* 255–272.

Myers, C. (1983). Drawing as prewriting in preschool. In M. Myers & J. Gray (Eds.), *Theory and practice in the teaching of composition* (pp. 75–85). Urbana, IL: National Council of Teachers of English.

Nelson, K. (1991). Event knowledge and the development of language functions. In J. Miller (Ed.), *Research on child language disorders: A decade of progress* (pp. 105–124). Austin, TX: Pro-Ed.

Nelson, K., Engel, S., & Kyratzis, A. (1985). The evolution of meaning in context. *Journal of Pragmatics, 9,* 453–474.

Neuner, J. L. (1987). Cohesive ties and chains in good and poor freshman essays. *Research in the Teaching of English, 21,* 92–105.

Ninio, A., & Snow, C. E. (1996). *Pragmatic development.* Boulder, CO: Westview.

Owens, R. E., & Robinson, L. A. (1997). Once upon a time: Use of children's literature in the preschool classroom. *Topics in Language Disorders, 17*(2), 19–48.

Paley, V. G. (1990). *The boy who would be a helicopter: The uses of storytelling in the classroom.* Cambridge, MA: Harvard University Press.

Pehrsson, R. S., & Denner, P. R. (1988). Semantic organizers: Implications for reading and writing. *Topics in Language Disorders, 8*(3), 24–37.

Pellegrini, A., Galda, L., & Rubin, D. (1984). Context in text: The development of oral and written language in two genres. *Child Development, 55,* 1549–1555.

Peterson, C., & McCabe, A. (1983). *Developmental psycholinguistics: Three ways of looking at a child's narrative.* New York: Plenum.

Polanyi, L. (1989). *Telling the American story: A structural and cultural analysis of conversational storytelling.* Cambridge, MA: MIT Press.

Roth, F. P., & Spekman, N. J. (1986). Narrative discourse: Spontaneously generated stories of learning-disabled and normally achieving students. *Journal of Speech and Hearing Disorders, 51,* 8–23.

Sachs, J., Goldman, J., & Chaillé, C. (1985). Narratives in preschoolers' sociodramatic play: The role of knowledge and communicative competence. In L. Galda & A. D. Pellegrini (Eds.), *Play, language, and stories: The development of children's literate behavior* (pp. 45–61). Norwood, NJ: Ablex.

Schneider, P. (1996). Effects of pictures versus orally presented stories on story retellings by children with language impairments. *American Journal of Speech-Language Pathology, 5,* 86–95.

Snow, C. E. (1983). Literacy and language: Relationships during the preschool years. *Harvard Educational Review, 53,* 165–189.

Stein, N. L., & Glenn, C. G. (1979). An analysis of story comprehension in elementary school children. In R. Freedle (Ed.), *New directions in discourse processing: Vol. 2* (pp. 53–120). Norwood, NJ: Ablex.

Strong, C. J. A., & Hoggan North, K. (1996). *The magic of stories: Literature-based language intervention.* Greenville, SC: Super Duper Publications.

Sulzby, E. (1985). Kindergartners as writers and readers. In M. Farr (Ed.), *Advances in writing research: Vol. 1, Children's early writing development* (pp. 127–199). Norwood, NJ: Ablex.

Sulzby, E., & Teale, W. (1990). Emergent literacy. In P. D. Pearson (Ed.), *Handbook of reading research: Vol. 2* (pp. 727–757). New York: Longman.

Sulzby, E., & Zecker, L. B. (1991). The oral monologue as a form of emergent reading. In A. McCabe & C. Peterson (Eds.), *Developing narrative structure* (pp. 175–214). Mahwah, NJ: Erlbaum.

Sutton-Smith, B. (1986). The development of fictional narrative performances. *Topics in Language Disorders, 7*(1), 1–10.

Trousdale, A. M. (1990). Interactive storytelling: Scaffolding children's early narratives. *Language Arts, 67,* 164–173.

Ukrainetz, T. A. (1998). Stickwriting stories: A quick and easy narrative representation strategy. *Language, Speech, and Hearing Services in Schools, 29,* 197–206.

Ukrainetz, T. A. (2001). Narrative assessment: Coherence, cohesion, and captivation. *Perspectives on Language, Learning, and Education, 8*(2), 11–15.

Ukrainetz, T. A., Eisenberg, S. L., Justice, L. M., & Kaderavek, J. N. (in press). *The uses of present tense in children's picture-based narratives.* Manuscript submitted for publication.

Ukrainetz, T. A., Justice, L. M., Kaderavek, J. N., Eisenberg, S. L., Gillam, R. B., & Harm, H. M. (in press). The development of expressive elaboration in fictional narratives. *Journal of Speech, Language, and Hearing Research.*

Ukrainetz, T. A., & Trujillo, A. (1999). "You know, I just don't know what else you'd do?" Five SLPs' perspectives on children's literature in speech-language intervention. *Contemporary Issues in Communication Sciences and Disorders, 26,* 35–48.

Umiker-Sebeok, D. J. (1979). Preschool children's intraconversational narratives. *Journal of Child Language, 6,* 91–109.

van Dongen, R., & Westby, C. E. (1986). Building the narrative mode of thought through children's literature. *Topics in Language Disorders, 7*(1), 70–83.

van Kleeck, A., & Woude, J. V. (2003). Booksharing with preschoolers with language delays. In A. van Kleeck, S. A. Stahl, & E. B. Bauer (Eds.), *On reading books to children: Parents and teachers* (pp. 58–94). Mahwah, NJ: Erlbaum.

Westby, C. E. (1985). Learning to talk–talking to learn: Oral-literate language differences. In C. S. Simon (Ed.), *Communication skills and classroom success: Therapy methodologies for language-learning disabled students* (pp. 181–213). Boston: College-Hill Press.

Wolf, D. P., & Hicks, D. (1989). The voices within narratives: The development of intertextuality in young children's stories. *Discourse Processes, 12,* 329–351.

Appendix: Bibliography of Children's Books

Berenstain, S., & Berenstain, J. (1978). *The Berenstain bears go to school.* New York: Random House.

Brown, M. W. (1975). *Goodnight moon.* New York: HarperTrophy.

Carle, E. (1995). *Brown bear, brown bear, what do you see?* New York: Henry Holt.

Galdone, Paul. (1984). *The three little pigs.* Boston: Houghton Mifflin.

Ginsburg, M. (1974). *Mushroom in the rain.* New York: Aladdin.

Johnson, A. (1989). *Tell me a story, Mama.* New York: Orchard Books.

Kellogg, S. (1997). *Jack and the beanstalk.* New York: Harper Trophy.

Lunge-Larsen, L., & Preus, M. (1999). *The legend of the lady slipper.* Boston: Houghton Mifflin.

Mayer, M. (1969). *Frog, where are you?* New York: Dial Books.

Mayer, M. (1974). *Frog goes to dinner.* New York: Dial Books.

Mayer, M. (1983). *All by myself.* New York: Golden Book.

Mayer, M., & Mayer, M. (1971). *A boy, a dog, a frog and a friend.* New York: Dial Books.

Mayer, M., & Mayer, M. (1975). *One frog too many.* New York: Dial Books.

Munsch, R., & Kusugak, M. (1988). *A promise is a promise.* Toronto: Annick.

Orgel, D. (2004). *The Bremen town musicians: And other animal tales from Grimm.* Brookfield, CT: Roaring Brook Press.

Sharmat, M. (1980). *Gregory, the terrible eater.* New York: Scholastic.

Shaw, N. (1986). *Sheep in a jeep.* Boston: Houghton Mifflin.

Viorst, J. (1972). *Alexander and the terrible, horrible, no good, very bad day.* New York: Aladdin.

Chapter 6

The Many Ways of Exposition: A Focus on Discourse Structure

Teresa A. Ukrainetz

Introduction

To successfully negotiate a social and academic world, students must be able to describe, explain, analyze, and persuade. These communicative acts fall within a heterogeneous collection of discourse structures, loosely grouped under the label exposition. This is the discourse most commonly addressed in the academic context beyond the early grades. Book reviews, science displays, speeches, opinion essays, advertisements, and history reports are all examples of this diverse discourse category. In this chapter, expository structure is addressed in terms of the macrostructure (i.e., overall discourse organization) and the microstructure (i.e., words that signal the larger organization), with a focus on written production. Chapter 12 deals with expository text comprehension, which is the accompanying ability to comprehend, analyze, and synthesize what is heard or read, so these two chapters form a complementary whole. Both chapters espouse intervention in expository discourse through repeated opportunities to intensely and supportively address explicit skills (RISE) within purposeful activities.

Explaining Exposition

Defining Exposition

Exposition is used primarily for informative purposes (Black, 1985). It expresses logical and scientific thought, and is developed and elaborated through schooling experiences (Bruner, 1986; Scollon & Scollon, 1981). Expository discourse is the predominant school discourse in the upper-elementary grades and beyond. Students compose expositions of many forms and lengths across diverse subject areas. They must understand expositions in the form of lectures, textbooks, and reference books. Exposition is sometimes difficult to recognize because of its many varieties. Some features common to many types of exposition will be considered.

Exposition is abstract, with a greater mental distance between the speaker and the event than that occurring for narrative (Moffett, 1968). Moffett suggests a continuum of discourse abstraction across genres. Table 6.1 summarizes the continuum. This continuum is exemplified by a person sitting in a cafeteria, observing and mentally recording the unfolding events; then moving into retelling the events later to a friend; then analyzing why Americans tend to behave in such a way; finally synthesizing this example with others into an anthropological explanation of how people interact publicly. Expository

Table 6.1

Continuum of Discourse Abstraction across Genres

Distance from Speaker	Discourse Genre	Type of Activity
What is happening	Drama	Verbally encoding an observed event
What happened	Narrative	Reporting a past specific event
What happens	Exposition	Generalizing about typical events
What may happen	Logical argumentation	Theorizing about possible events

Source: Moffett (1968)

structure comprises Moffett's latter two levels of discourse abstraction, but this chapter focuses on generalized exposition rather than the highest level of theory construction.

The abstraction of exposition occurs through its generalizing stance. In exposition, the stated material is considered to transcend specific events (Bruner, 1986; Moffett, 1968). It is not considered to be situated in a single time or place. For example, procedural exposition involves events in a temporal sequence (e.g., first combine flour and salt, then add milk, finally blend together), but the first element can potentially occur for any of us at any time. The present or infinitive verb tenses favored in exposition are related to this position outside the experienced time line (Fleischman, 1991; Longacre, 1983).

The continuum of discourse abstraction is reflected in the developmental progression of discourse. Learning to write and to think involves moving from the online commentary of dramatic play to the after-the-fact report of the narrative to the generalization and inference of the scientific report. Students gradually move from personal and culturally specific uses to the more formal, and decontextualized genre found in literature and science (Freedle & Hale, 1979; Moffett, 1968). Mastery of description, exposition, and argument in writing is achieved later than control of the more familiar form of narration

(Bereiter, 1980; Perera, 1984). Elementary school-age students produce shorter expository than narrative texts, with less semantic well-formedness and weaker cohesion (Crowhurst, 1987; Hidi & Hildyard, 1983; Pellegrini, Galda, & Rubin, 1984).

Students may use narrative as a familiar frame during the process of learning exposition, mixing anecdotes and story-structured material into expository assignments (Applebee, 1984; Perera, 1984). Applebee suggests that, "though these stretches of narrative are often inappropriate to the analytic task, they help the writer maintain fluency and coherence in an otherwise very difficult situation" (p. 185). Teachers may inadvertently encourage such discourse mixing by teaching generalized information through the familiar discourse structure of stories. Students read a story about a child planting a seed and caring for it to learn about how a plant grows from a seed, rather than reading a generalized, expository account. While this genre mixing may be a helpful way of introducing exposition, it may also confuse students about genre distinctions and prolong mixing even in simple compositions where clear genres should be demonstrated.

Exposition is a difficult discourse form for several reasons. It often involves knowledge transmission, which means readers are taking in new information as well as dealing with unfamiliar organizational structures. It involves generalizing and theorizing. There is no basic organization such as episodic structure. Forms are suited to purposes and contexts, of which there are many. Exposition does not have the social closeness of conversation, nor the magic of a good story. Finally, exposition also often involves writing, which is very difficult for many students, and this writing is of the hard kind, involving revision and editing for rhetorical and informational effectiveness.

Types of Exposition

There are many expository genres and many different ways of dividing up the expository pie. Moffett (1968) separates logical argumentation from exposition and suggests that description is not a true genre. Longacre (1983) suggests that all discourse genres can be placed along multiple axes. Two of these axes relevant to this discussion are temporal succession and agent orientation. As illustrated in Figure 6.1, narrative has both temporal succession and agent orientation. It is the telling of a story that has already happened. Procedural discourse has temporal succession, but no attention to the agent. It describes the sequence involved in completing a task, but is not concerned with who

Figure 6.1   Discourse Genres Plotted per Degree of Agent Orientation and Temporal Succession

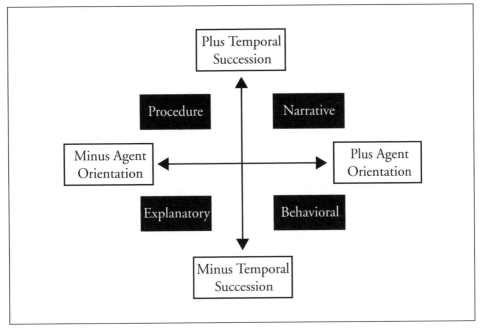

Source: Longacre (1983)

performs the task. Behavioral discourse, a category that includes sermons and political speeches, has agency (e.g., what one ought to do, what the candidate will do) but not temporal succession. It addresses the actions a person will or should take, but does not set forth specific procedures. Finally, explanatory discourse (e.g., how gravity works, Napoleon's psychological profile) has neither temporal succession nor agency. It develops information about concepts or ideas for the sake of better understanding, but is not concerned with specific actions or actors.

Other authors do not provide an overarching conceptual organization, instead simply listing types of exposition. For example, Stewart (1985) lists the following types: description, comparison-contrast, sequence, and enumeration. Westby (2005) adds to this list cause-effect and problem-solution. Table 6.2 on page 252 sets out the list that will be referred to in this chapter. This selection reflects a broad conception of exposition as non-narrative, monologic, generalizing, logical discourse intended primarily to transmit information.

Table 6.2   **Expository Discourse Genres**

Genre	Example
Description	Describe the sweater you liked.
Enumeration	List the items that were stolen.
Procedure	Tell how to operate your stereo system.
Explanation	Explain how fish breathe.
Comparison/Contrast	Compare basketball to life.
Persuasion	Take a position on forest management and justify it.

Each genre of exposition has some characteristic organizational features (summarized in Table 6.3), but format is loosely specified and subject to topic, purpose, and audience. For example, the degree of detail in procedures is dependent on audience prior knowledge (e.g., knowing what *creaming* and *rubbing* mean in baking), and the logic or transparency of the steps and sequence (e.g., the milk carton must be opened before it can be poured, so carton opening may not be specified). In the genre of persuasion, promoting a position is most effective if the audience is open to argument and emotional bids are matched to audience susceptibilities. Determining the structural demands of an exposition involves determining a daily-life example and then judging what organization and content occurs for that example.

Within one type of exposition, structure and content varies with the specific purpose of the author. For example, at its most basic, the genre of description consists of features detailing a concept with some organizational structure. It involves evocative nouns and verbs, expanded noun phrases, and adverbial phrases. It is usually considered to be a visual description, but could be a description of odors, sounds, or emotions. But a description can have diverse manifestations. Table 6.4 on page 254 presents types of descriptive discourse with structure and content varying with purpose.

The first passage is an excerpt taken from a sample presented in a handbook intended to help teachers of grades three to five prepare students for the

Table 6.3

Expository Genres, Organizational Structures, and Examples

Expository Genre	General Structure	Daily-Life Examples
Description	• Topic plus sufficient detail to create an image • Details are presented in organized manner	1. Classified ad 2. Eye-witness account 3. Passage in a novel
Enumeration	• Categories, subcategories, members • Spatial arrangement shows relationships • Presented in words and phrases	1. Nutrition label 2. Table of contents 3. Family genealogy
Procedure	• Materials, time required, and sequenced steps	1. Manual 2. Recipe 3. Driving directions
Explanation	• Purpose, rationale, question, method, findings, analysis • Diagrams may illustrate logical or causal relationships	1. Internet health article 2. Nature magazine article 3. Investigative news report
Comparison/ Contrast	• List of similarities and differences • Compare/contrast features are presented in an organized manner	1. Consumer report 2. Product guidance in a catalog 3. Job candidate selection report
Persuasion	• Thesis plus argument then conclude with thesis restatement • Arguments are point plus elaboration of reasons and rebuttal	1. Editorial 2. Customer complaint letter 3. Official position statement

Table 6.4   **Examples of Types of Descriptive Discourse**

Type of Description	Example
Description for Essay Portion of a State Achievement Test	...The raft that the dog and cat are on is made of eight boards nailed together and laid across three round logs. All the boards are almost exactly as long as the others and most of them look about as wide as the others except the one on the left side and it looks a little bit wider. You can see the circles in the ends of the logs... (Texas Education Agency, 1991, p. 90)
Classified Advertisement	Log raft, 6 x 8 ft., treated fir and brass nails, 8 ft. pole included, excellent condition, used once, $50.
Commercial Advertisement	This is a beautiful raft. It is big enough for you and your friends. It is well-constructed with close fitting logs and nails every 6 inches. The water-resistant treated fir and brass nails mean that the raft will last for years. A sturdy 8 foot oak pole is included. The raft is in excellent condition. The owner is willing to let this beauty go for only $50.
Eye-Witness Account	It was a rough log raft, just big enough to hold the two passengers. It looked like a Latino boy, about 12 years old. He had a dark-colored cap on and was in shorts and a T-shirt. He had a small, black-and-white dog with him. I could see a pole lying on the raft, but at that time, they were just sitting, not poling it down the river. They waved at me and looked fine. However, they didn't have any gear with them and it was late afternoon. It started to get cold and windy just after that, so I hope they were okay.

state-wide achievement examinations (Texas Education Agency, 1991). The picture used for this passage was of a cat and a dog, dressed in clothes, and on a raft. The dog was poling and the cat was fishing. A sea monster was showing his head out of the water behind the raft. All the animals were smiling. The instructions were to, "Look at the picture and write a composition for your teacher in which you describe what you see." The scoring rubric consisted of a specific, well-elaborated description with a consistent organizational structure, and consistent control of written language. The excerpt shows a detailed focus on describing the logs. The full sample was long, with the degree of detail varying across the items described. The sample achieved the highest holistic score possible.

This arbitrary description, without purpose or audience, diverges considerably from those occurring for functional reasons in daily life. Three other examples are provided in Table 6.4: a classified ad, a commercial ad, and an eye-witness account. The classified ad is a brief listing of the critical features of the raft, attending to the dual purpose of keeping the ad cost low while providing sufficient information to the consumer. The order of listing is a standard order for classified ads. The commercial advertisement is less concerned with cost and more concerned with presenting an appealing image. The eye-witness account focuses on the identity and condition of a student on the raft, with the raft itself of minor significance. Each of these descriptions are shaped by what the writers or speakers considered important to achieve their purpose.

Signaling Devices within the Text

Expository structure consists of both macro-level discourse organization and micro-level structures called signaling devices. Signaling devices lend both cohesion (i.e., unified text) and coherence (i.e., making sense) to exposition. They are insertions that indicate the central content or direction of a section of text and how this section relates to prior and upcoming sections. Signaling devices include overviews, summaries, headings, and key words. These devices are particularly important for expository text, with its loosely specified and varied organizational structures. The longer a piece of text, the more important are these devices in aiding both the writer to organize and develop the composition, and the reader to understand and recall it (Lorch & Lorch, 1996).

Overviews precede long expositions. In textbooks, they are typically titled Preface, Foreword, or Introduction. An abstract of a research report is an overview. An overview for a shorter piece may simply be the introductory paragraph. Overviews are short summaries of the purpose and content of the upcoming material. Concluding summaries briefly review the material discussed, highlight the main concepts, and end with the take-away message. Both overviews and summaries are important parts of expositions, whether delivered orally or in print.

Headings and subheadings that reflect the main idea over a span of several paragraphs are easily recognized signaling devices. For example, science reports have standard headings, such as Method, Participants, and Results. Topical subheadings may further subdivide each section. Headings and subheadings are easily inserted in a text to aid in organization and meaning. They can be collected to provide an overview enumeration at the beginning of a book or chapter in the form of a table of contents.

Key words are less obvious than headings because they are embedded within the ongoing text. Key words also provide direction and content of prior and upcoming material. They signal transitions from one part of the text to another. Table 6.5 presents examples of negotiation markers (i.e., signaling words) for elements of persuasive discourse. These words signal not only sections of the persuasive composition, such as premise and arguments, but can also indicate how an audience ought to respond or how committed the speaker is to the position (Golder & Coirier, 1994), as in "Surely, it must be clear from the evidence that my position is the correct one."

In summary, there are a variety of expositional forms, each of which has loosely specified characteristic features. Across expositional genres, there are

Table 6.5   **Signaling Words for Persuasive Discourse**

Function	Words
Premise	*I propose that, my position is*
Argument	*The first reason, in addition*
Counterargument	*even if, however*
Obligation and Judgment	*one should, it is good that*
Degree of Certainty	*maybe, surely*
Endorsement and Accountability	*in my opinion, the evidence indicates*
Wrap-Up	*in conclusion, in summary*

Source: Golder & Coirier (1994)

typically signaling devices consisting of overviews, summaries, headings, and key words that help organize text for both the composer and the audience. Specific content and form of each type of exposition depend on the needs of the audience and purpose of the speaker. The process of creating an expository work is further complicated by the challenge of written composition, considered next.

Written Composition

Formal academic writing has very different demands than oral expression. The speech-language pathologist (SLP) must be aware of these demands in order to plan both how to teach a particular intervention objective and how to compensate for the many other skills and processes involved.

Written and oral language are the same, but different. Ideas are formulated and communicated in both modalities. However, the process of formulation takes on distinct dimensions in the written modality (Bereiter & Scardamalia, 1982). Writing involves much more than putting oral ideas down with graphic representation, spelling, and punctuation. Writing demands a particular grammar, lexicon, and discourse structure (Kamhi & Catts, 2005; Scott, 1995, 2005). More importantly, it is composed without the support of a conversational partner. In oral discourse, a partner provides myriad cues, often unintentionally, that guide and shape discourse:

> [C]ues to proceed, cues to stop, cues to elaborate, cues to shift topic, and a great variety of cues that stir memory. They serve as text grammarians for one another, raising questions when some needed element of a discourse has been omitted…"But you still haven't told me where the money's going to come from." They serve as auxiliary memory aids, helping each other stay on topic, keep a goal in mind, or recall a previous remark. (Bereiter & Scardamalia, 1982, pp. 1–2)

The demands of written expression can make writing hard and writers struggle. Bereiter and Scardamalia (1987) term this hard way of writing *knowledge-transforming* writing. In this type of writing, the writer reflects on the work and revises at multiple levels, striving to improve both the craft and the clarity of the message. The writer may strive to adhere to standard American English, formal academic requirements, and discipline-specific demands. The writer may engage in predicting the knowledge and presuppositions that readers will bring to the task. Knowledge-transforming composition is a lengthy process, involving multiple, overlapping, recursive stages (Flower & Hayes, 1980). Writers engage in planning, drafting, revising, and editing as they take their initial ideas to a final, polished form. This way of writing is not a series of tidy sequential steps, but a juggling of demands and constraints on attention (Flower & Hayes). To accomplish this type of writing, many of the parts of the writing process, such as spelling and sentence structure, must be highly automatized and well enough coordinated to permit efficient time sharing among the aspects that require conscious attention, such as how to construct a comprehensive and detailed argument but at the same time, how not to be wordy or tedious about it (Bereiter, 1980).

This kind of writing stands in contrast to the easy kind: *knowledge-telling* writing (Bereiter & Scardamalia, 1987). Knowledge-telling writing is enjoyable for people of many literacy levels. It involves writing like one talks, using one's natural linguistic endowments and basic word-encoding skills. Although it is a monologic text, it is close to the informal, interactive language typical of oral contexts. Social emails, an immensely popular form of written communication, provide good examples of knowledge-telling writing. They are composed in the same way as one speaks, executed in a single draft, may contain spelling errors and oral-style syntax, and have insertions such as happy faces to approximate some paralinguistic cues.

Knowledge-transforming writing is promoted in schools—appropriately so for the goal of advancing academic expression. Knowledge-telling writing is typically present only with the youngest grades and in activities outside of school. First graders may be allowed to write as they talk because their mental energy is directed primarily at getting words on paper. They also have difficulty regarding their composition as an object of study, the metalinguistic aspect of the task. However, as early as first or second grade, students are expected to begin to engage in the writing process. They are instructed, albeit at a superficial level, to reflect on and revise their written products. Even seven-year-olds can embark on the careful reflection and multiple revisions of composing, entering into the process of learning to make writing difficult (Graves, 1975). Teachers aim at making students aware of the multiple dimensions of quality, such as ideas and content, organization, voice, and word choice (Spandel & Stiggins, 1990), and guide them in attending to all these aspects.

This knowledge-transforming writing is very difficult for young and unskilled writers whose writing skills are not automatic and integrated. Without carefully structured scaffolds and compensations, such students will not be able to attend to the multiple processes targeted in intervention, such as idea generation, sentence choice, and textual organization. Instead, they will remain bound up in issues of spelling, word choice, and grammar (Butler-Nalin, 1984; MacArthur, 2000). This difficulty with written text production is evident when comparing the greater sophistication of orally dictated stories to less well-developed written stories. This disparity lasts until the later elementary years, when text production becomes more automatized (MacArthur).

Students can be directed by the teacher to attend to expository organization. However, they still must learn to think on their own about the composition as an object of analysis. Across several studies, Bereiter and Scardamalia (1987) describe how adolescents and students were able to respond to planning prompts related to purpose and audience. The planning notes composed by the adolescents were key words and phrases, which were expanded into sentences and unified text. Their think-aloud protocols contained numerous idea units. In contrast, the 10-year-olds were unable to respond to the planning prompts. Their notes were complete sentences that were replicated and linked in text, and they had only half the number of idea units in their think-aloud protocols. The older students were capable of more mature planning, that "consist[ed] of thinking about the composition rather than planning that consist[ed] of mentally rehearsing or creating the composition" (Bereiter & Scardamalia, p. 210).

Although older students can respond to planning prompts like those of Bereiter and Scardamalia (1987), their independent writing often primarily involves correction to grammar and punctuation (Butler-Nalin, 1984; Hayes & Flower, 1987). One of the difficulties students have in revision may be related to the absence of a standard of comparison. Students are not often exposed to quality exposition (Kirby, Liner, & Vinz, 1988), and even when they read reasonable pieces, attention may be directed primarily at learning content, rather than at how the piece is composed (Taylor, 1984). A study examining elementary student judgments of writing quality showed that students move from affective responses (e.g., *I didn't like it*) to more objective responses (e.g., *This part was confusing*) from fourth to sixth grade. They also moved from single to multiple evaluation criteria, including text-based criteria (McCormick, Busching, & Potter, 1992). However, there was considerable variation in the results, with many students struggling to specify any criteria, others repeating favored parts of the text, and still others providing only personal associations. According to McCormick et al., even high-achieving students lacked a uniform template applied across composition samples. Instead, they seemed to construct a standard based on each piece they read, without reference to other pieces.

Considering the challenges facing the typically achieving student, it is surprising that students with learning disabilities succeed at all. Scott (2005) summarizes the research on the many difficulties these students show in composing expository discourse. Their products are lower for a variety of measures: length in words and sentences, fewer cohesive ties, fewer logical adverbial sentences, overuse of *and,* and less-developed text structures that included redundancies and abrupt terminations. They have difficulty with all parts of the writing process, deal only with surface features in their revision, have little sense of the whole in terms of expository structure, and deliver composition in a knowledge-telling format.

Written composition is a challenging process, particularly when students are writing in a knowledge-transforming way, with attention to the clarity and appeal of their message to an audience. When students are also dealing with the knowledge transmission demands and unfamiliar format of expository text, the result can be overwhelming, especially for students with language impairments.

Development in Exposition

Exposition is considered to be primarily a written academic discourse category best suited to the later elementary years and beyond (Burkhalter, 1995). However, young students do engage in exposition, albeit orally. With peers and parents, students argue, expound, explain, inform, describe, and persuade. A major difference with this nonschool exposition is that it occurs as a motivated event embedded in supportive conversation.

A sample of explanatory exposition from a group of kindergartners is presented in Box 6.1. In this unusual kindergarten room, the teacher, Vivian Paley, asked the students to explain to her their reasoning on human growth. One student, Rose, told the class she was much taller on her birthday and every student in the class agreed. In this sample, the position is given by the students, along with an illustration to help the teacher understand. The students then provide supporting evidence and a physiological explanation. Eddie even asks the teacher for a better explanation, which she doesn't provide, lending implicit support to their argument. This sample shows that extended and contingent reasoning with appropriate expository structure on a topic is possible for a group of young students.

Kindergartners' Explanatory Exposition about Growing Taller

Box 6.1

Teacher:	Do you mean taller since yesterday?
Rose:	Because I'm six.
Wally:	Yesterday she was five. She is taller today.
Lisa:	On that very day when it's your birthday, you're bigger. If I was four and on one day I got to be five, I'd be much bigger.
Teacher:	Then would you have to wait until your sixth birthday to grow some more?
Eddie:	Otherwise, how would you grow bigger?…
Teacher:	Then must you get new clothes?
Eddie:	Sure, everything was too small on my birthday.
Lisa:	When you start running, it makes you have more energy. It makes you stronger and bigger every day. But on your birthday is when you grow inches.
Teacher:	Fred, you're the only other student here who is six, so we'll ask you. We didn't see you on your birthday because it was during vacation. Did you feel taller on that day?
Fred:	I really was taller. My bed was too short. I'm getting a new bed.

From *Wally's Stories* (p. 114–115), by V. G. Paley, 1981, Cambridge, MA: Harvard University Press. © 1981 by the Presidents and Fellows of Harvard College. Reprinted with permission.

Development of persuasion in conversation involves moving from considerable interactional support toward greater spans of monologicity. Interactional support is provided for conversational contingency, historical details, and interpretive stances to the talk (Ninio & Snow, 1996). It also involves a movement from considering self to considering others (Axia, 1996). Axia studied four- to eight-year-old Italian children negotiating with caregivers over a toy purchase. The results showed a shift from efforts to control the adult at four years of age to considering the adult objections at six years. By eight years of age, the children made efforts to overcome potential conflict and orient the exchange towards cooperation. They attempted to consider the adult point of view.

Young children are aware that there is an expository genre that contrasts with the narrative genre. Kindergarten students pretend to read information books differently from their pretend reading of storybooks (Pappas, 1991). First graders specify that nonfiction books provide information, help people, and teach people (Duthie, 1994).

Chapman (1995) examined how students come to create written discourse genres in a first-grade classroom. She observed that the students were not simply passive recipients of instruction, but actively created their own understandings from their social and physical environment. They could not yet write conventionally, but they combined pictures with emergent writing to create a discourse whole. The students' print and picture combinations could be recognized as narration about past events, conversation (e.g., "I love you," ballooned out of a character's mouth), and exposition. For expository discourse, the students described, listed, and explained through print and picture.

There is clearly growth in expository performance over ages from preschooler into the later school years. The vocabulary and syntactic building blocks of exposition grow in sophistication and complexity throughout the school years. Managing abstract concepts and taking an impersonal stance develop in the later elementary years and beyond. The ability to organize exposition into recognizable genres with signaling markers appropriate to the task improves with age and experience. An example of structural development is presented in a study of written persuasion by Golder and Coirier (1994). These investigators found that students showed age-based increase in use of persuasive signal words like *however, one should, surely, in my opinion* from 10 to 16 years of age. They also improved the maintenance of thematic continuity, and improved in recognition of invalid inferences and argument statements. The main age improvement occurred between the 10 to 11 year-olds and the older students. This finding is consistent with Bereiter and Scardamalia's (1987) finding of a split between 10 year-olds and adolescents in the ability to treat text as an object of analysis and to systematically plan a larger whole.

Despite some developmental change between later childhood and adolescence, performance in exposition is more a function of learning experiences and composing context than age. Developmental stages for writing from the early grades to high school have been outlined (e.g., Bereiter, 1980; Scott, 2005). However, such stage depictions do not reflect the individual variation encountered across students. They are less useful than considering why a student is writing, whether the writing is knowledge-telling or knowledge-transforming, and what abilities and experiences the student brings to the task (Bereiter & Scardamalia, 1987; Moffett, 1968). Even elementary-age students can achieve quality written exposition. Moffett observed this degree of variability for students from 4th to 12th grade:

> The development of writing is unbelievably relative, to the point that pupil capacity seems to vary as much horizontally throughout a population of one grade as it does vertically through the grades...the past conditioning of the students (and of the teachers) accounts for more variation than anything else...At every turn of the road we ran into the disconcerting fact that what a student could write seemed to depend more on his out-of-school language environment and previous school training than on his age. (pp. 54–55)

Moffett (1968) takes a positive stance toward this variation, emphasizing that, given experience with high-quality exposition in activities that engage student motivation and purpose, teachers can guide students of a wide age-range to accomplish sophisticated written exposition. Intervention with expository text must consider how to support students with language impairments in the complex process of expository composition. Attention now turns to aiding students to become better explainers and persuaders.

Guiding Students into Better Exposition

Supporting Early Expository Conversations

Interventions for preschoolers involve a conversational approach, without explicit attention to structure. The focus is on supporting the student to explain the claim, based on his own knowledge and belief structures. The student is scaffolded into generating supporting details, relating them to the topic, and extending from the details to additional details or a conclusion. For a procedural exposition, the focus may be on eliciting steps in order as well as increasing the number of steps or details in the student's turn. The SLP provides comments to link, extend, and clarify discourse meaning. The clinician models how to explain or describe an event, but independent monologic performance would not be expected from the student. Cooperative explanations from several peers can be encouraged. Intervention objectives involve improving the logical links, sequencing, or span of the conversational turn, rather than increasing the complexity of the discourse structure.

Picture representations, created by the clinician or the students, are recommended to support emergent exposition. Clinician writing from student dictation can accompany the picture. Exposition can also be represented in the student's own print, as emergent writing (letter strings or semiphonetic spellings). As Chapman (1995) showed, meaning can be derived from the student's pictorial creation in combination with the written message. In this way, the picture is a structural scaffold to create a complete discourse whole.

Emergent writing alone can also be used as a temporary mnemonic. For example, this author composed a grocery list with a five-year-old that consisted of an enumeration represented by the first letters of food items. Peas and pumpkins were distinguished by a small and a large "p" respectively. This child was able to use the list to guide the subsequent shopping trip although he could not recall the items the next day.

Students should be introduced to exposition early on, because it is a useful and recurring discourse form. However, the context is primarily oral in a supportive conversational context, without explicit attention to structure. Emergent writing can be introduced. The aim of intervention is to increase the student's production of increasingly longer spans of monologic oral discourse and to increase the proportion of a message represented by conventional print.

Teaching Expository Structure

Instruction in expository structure is not a new concept. Teachers have long provided general compositional guidance on essay and paragraph structure, and there is evidence that explicit attention to discourse structure aids student comprehension and production of exposition (Crowhurst, 1991; Taylor & Beach, 1984). Moffett's 1968 work, *Teaching the Universe of Discourse,* provides still-relevant guidance on teaching drama, narrative, exposition, and the grammar needed for each.

Within the general education sphere, the emphasis is on teaching expository writing to students of a range of ages and abilities, using published works as models, in a motivating and dynamic manner (e.g., Graves, 1989; Kirby et al., 1988; Moffett, 1968). Authors emphasize engagement with the topic and a focus on the quality of ideas over the structure of the exposition. Kirby et al. caution that teachers talk too much about structure before students have a subject they understand well enough to write about. They suggest that "students hear talk on thesis statements, topic sentences, outlines, 500 words, and five paragraphs, but they hear little talk about collecting, percolating, generating information" (p. 203). These authors contend that teachers should avoid simplifying the process by reducing it to a formula because they argue it leads to poor writing and poor thinking. They provide limited formal instruction in their classroom, instead providing and discussing examples of good writing, providing writing ideas, and stimulating good thinking. They provide guidance based on the needs of the students who are engaged in self-paced writing assignments. Learning to write may involve acquiring a new, formal register. Acquiring the tone of this register requires substantial communicative interaction, which includes having a purpose that requires the targeted genre, reading many published works in that genre, and having guidance from peers and teachers on how better to achieve the purpose within the genre (Moffett, 1968).

There is considerable evidence that students in the general education classroom improve expository structure with instruction. Guiding students to examine published models, having peer models demonstrate particular points, guiding students in each part of a composition, demonstrating and encouraging self-regulatory talk (e.g., "First, I need to state my purpose"), and providing genre-specific schematics are all important components of instruction (e.g., Bereiter & Scardamalia, 1982, 1987; Burkhalter, 1995; Charney & Carlson, 1995; Crowhurst 1991; Smagorinsky, 1991; Taylor & Beach, 1984).

Crowhurst (1991) studied sixth-grade students' development of persuasive writing by teaching a schematic model of persuasive structure, combined with practice in reading or writing persuasive texts. The first session consisted of presenting the schematic and examining a teacher model for the persuasive elements. Students then participated in one of these experimental conditions for nine subsequent sessions. The writing condition involved recalling the structural elements, brainstorming pro and con reasons for the topic of the day, writing in support of or against the position, then peer editing, and final revising. The reading condition involved guided reading of a succession of teacher-created persuasive texts. The control condition consisted of writing book reports. Crowhurst reported higher writing quality; organization; number of conclusions and text markers; and reason elaboration for both the writing and the reading conditions compared to the control condition.

Bereiter and Scardamalia (1987) reported on a variety of investigations of writing prompts that aid students across genres. These include increasing length by prompting with *say more* and using noncontent priming, such as *I think..., The main point..., For example..., Even though...*; improving lexical diversity by listing relevant words in advance; and promoting attention to the whole text by providing the final sentence. For example, students were taught to list all the relevant single words they could think of that might be used in their compositions. The students who were taught to use the word-listing strategy wrote essays twice as long and used three times as many uncommon words. In another example, students were sensitized to communication difficulties arising from incomplete or vague procedural exposition by having them view a video of a person incompetently carrying out a task. The students' subsequent expositions reflected attention to the potential difficulties of the task. These researchers caution that, while students can be taught the strategies, the ongoing challenge is to move students into initiating and maintaining these strategies independently. Students need repeated opportunities with systematic scaffolding to move from teacher-guided strategies to self-initiated strategies to automatic skills that can be deployed without conscious attention.

Expository Intervention Research

Education research on the nature of expository composition by students with learning disabilities and how to facilitate learning for these students began in the 1980s (Newcomer & Barenbaum, 1991). The instructional approach is distinguished from that occurring in general classrooms by the context—small groups in self-contained classrooms. There is also a greater focus on formal instruction, with greater attention to skills than to content and engagement. There is greater attention to providing support in smaller task increments or through greater teacher participation. This instructional situation is similar to what an SLP might offer in language intervention. Controlled studies have demonstrated the success of this supportive, explicit instruction (e.g., Sexton, Harris, & Graham, 1998; Wong, Butler, Ficzere, & Kuperis, 1996, 1997).

Graham, Harris, and Troia (2000) provide excellent guidance and empirical evidence on teaching self-regulatory processes and genre-specific structures to students with learning disabilities. Their approach, called Self-Regulated Strategy Development (SRSD) is emerging in the speech-language pathology literature (e.g., Graham & Harris, 1999; Scott, 2005; Wong, 2000). This approach sets the instructional guidance out in six steps:

1. Develop background knowledge.
2. Discuss the strategy goals and significance.
3. Model the strategy.
4. Have student memorize the strategy.
5. Support strategy practice.
6. Have student engage in independent performance.

Graham and Harris (1999) describe teaching specific expository genres. The authors detail how to set up a structure and an outline. They emphasize mnemonic tools for remembering discourse structure, for example, the DARE acronym to represent persuasive essay structure:

Determine your premise.

Assemble reasons to support your premise.

Reject arguments for the other side.

End with a conclusion.

Englert (1990, 1992) emphasizes the sociocultural context of the classroom and how learning occurs through the internalization of social models and interactions. Englert and colleagues also provide mnemonics such as POWER (Plan, Organize, Write, Edit, Rewrite/Revise) and task-specific "think-sheets" that each ask for reflection on questions such as, "Who am I writing for?" "Why am I writing?" "What do I know?" However, the emphasis is on individual engagement within the writing process, teacher "think-alouds," and purposeful composition with scaffolded assistance. Chapter 13 sets out an adaptation of POWER, called EmPOWER, that focuses on acquiring better self-regulatory and planning behavior.

Englert (1992) describes how teachers can model the composing process. Englert demonstrates how teacher talk often consists of giving directions or asking students knowledge-testing questions, rather than providing talk that shows the thinking and understandings needed to compose. When a teacher talks her way through a composing task by modeling statements such as, "I wonder if the reader understands what I said here," "I need to move this part up here," "I think I need another step here," students can learn what they should be thinking and saying to themselves as they compose. Students gradually internalize this model of competence from the teacher to use in their own composing (Vygotsky, 1978).

Word processors can provide significant structural support for text production, content generation, editing, and revision. The ease of modifying text increases the likelihood of substantive revision. MacArthur (2000) described the many technologies potentially useful for students with writing difficulties, but warns that only limited investigation of efficacy has been completed. MacArthur also cautions that technology alone will not produce significant changes, it is a tool that needs to be combined with good teaching. MacArthur and Graham (1987) examined the effect of computer processing compared to handwriting and dictation on the performance of students with learning disabilities who had substantial experience using word processing. The investigators found that students showed slower composition and no overall improvement on computer production compared to handwritten production. More revisions were made on the first draft for the computer and on the second for the handwritten product, but the overall quality was similar. For younger typically achieving students, dictated work (where there were no text production issues) was faster and of higher quality, with fewer grammatical errors.

Wong and colleagues have also empirically investigated instruction in expository structure for students with learning disabilities in several studies (Wong, 2000; Wong et al., 1996, 1997). The instruction provided by Wong and colleagues was a combination of SRSD, word processors, teacher modeling, and peer collaboration. The instruction involved both genre-specific guidance and self-regulatory guidance. Results of comparison/contrast and opinion essay instruction showed higher quality student writing, lending support for this multifaceted approach.

Contextualized Instruction in Exposition

The literature on teaching expository structure shows that general and special education students can improve expository structure with instruction. Much of this work can be borrowed directly for language intervention purposes. It fits well within contextualized skill instruction, described in Chapter 1, which involves amplifying discourse structure and explicitly supporting student internalization of clinician models and guidance through repeated opportunities and systematic scaffolding. For intervention from such a perspective, the following general considerations are discussed:

- Oral and written modalities
- Communicative function
- Knowing your topic
- Therapeutic focus
- Individualizing class assignments
- Using authentic texts

Oral and Written Modalities

Exposition is typically taught as a written product. SLPs may choose to work only with written composition, but that is neither necessary nor recommended. Formal oral productions can be functionally equivalent to written productions, allowing skill transfer. Print can be a tool to aid oral organization and production and, conversely, oral commentary can aid print content and production. The primary goal is expository structure, regardless of modality.

Oral compositions can be produced more quickly than written compositions, without the distraction of spelling, written grammar, and punctuation issues. This is a benefit within the time constraints of intervention sessions. There are a variety of representations available to aid in oral revision, including tape-recording, student dictation, collaborative writing, note taking, and sketching. Some of these involve student writing, but they do not require the student to write large amounts of text independently. Oral production is also better suited to a knowledge-telling delivery, where the focus is more on communication than skilled crafting of the message. The final product can be entirely oral, such as a speech. Or it can be oral with print used as a representational tool, such as a speech accompanied by PowerPoint slides. Finally, exposition can be specifically a written product, in which the student engages in the writing process and attends to the conventions and demands of the formal written context, but is achieved through considerable oral discussion. In writing composition situations, the clinician must take care to compensate for the many aspects of composition beyond expository structure. The student cannot learn how to design a comparison/contrast essay while struggling with idea generation or spelling.

Communicative Function

Exposition should be composed with a clear purpose in mind. Students need a reason to describe, explain, enumerate, or persuade. As previously described, description varies considerably with purpose. Moffett (1968) suggests having students write the same topic for different purposes, to explore how words, grammar, and discourse change with purpose. Students can write a description of what they are wearing as if they are (1) describing to a friend the desirable (or ugly) item seen in a store, (2) composing a classified ad to sell worn clothing, (3) identifying the clothing of a possible participant in a crime, or (4) describing a lost piece of clothing.

Expository structure and signaling devices can be taught toward a basic and functional end in which writing is a tool (knowledge-telling), or toward a more literary and sophisticated end in which writing is a rhetorical act (knowledge-transforming). Young students may not have the mental processing space or metalinguistic abilities to extensively consider and revise their work. For older students who have developed a dislike and avoidance of writing, the primary need may be to change the attitude toward both exposition and writing. Once students recognize that both can be successful, useful, and enjoyable, the clinician can move toward the more difficult metalinguistic parts of the composing process. For some students, including those with developmental disabilities or those who have had little academic success and whose schooling years are almost over, the focus should be on motivation to write and basic success in communication (Sturm & Koppenhaver, 2000). It may be better to maximize knowledge-telling across genres and modalities, rather than persisting in trying to improve the quality of written expression. Adults who can communicate functionally in a range of discourse texts (e.g., filling in application forms, completing repair checklists, writing customer complaint letters), albeit with organizational and mechanical errors, are better off than those who believe they cannot write at all.

For example, consider a 19 year-old man in a residential educational setting. This individual is deaf and communicates via American Sign Language (ASL). His writing shows basic word-coding abilities and word order that reflects ASL. He hopes to enter the local automotive training program after leaving the residential school. For such a student, a beneficial activity might be procedural exposition through creation of a mini-manual on hot rod modification. The skills addressed could be English morphosyntax and procedural structure. The aim in this case would be to create comprehensible, purposeful communication in a recognizable discourse form, without a lengthy revision process or high standards of rhetorical competence.

It is important that the communicative function of the task be in the foreground and not overwhelmed by structural scaffolds. Use of mnemonic devices such as DARE help organize discourse. However, the student must select the appropriate mnemonic, remember the letters, the words they represent (e.g., D stands for Determine your premise), and what the words mean in relation to the discourse structure (e.g., *determine means, premise means…*). A graduate student, Anna, used the DARE method with Nick, an adolescent with learning disability. While Nick could follow Anna's use of DARE, Anna reported repeated difficulty with him memorizing and independently generating the meaning of the DARE elements. Thus, while mnemonics can be helpful, they should not be the focus of instruction. Students need to reflect on the purposes and likely parts of an exposition, to determine the best way to achieve the goal, and to actually use the appropriate strategy independently. Repeatedly taking the student through a reflective process on a genre, which leads up to the mnemonic, may help the student manage multiple genres. Discussing the genre purpose and ways it occurs in daily life (e.g., persuasion in advertising) helps the student understand the many ways of achieving the goal (e.g., sometimes an appeal to emotion is more effective persuasion than reasoned argumentation). In addition, having a firm grasp on the content matter, both in terms of individual propositions and content schema, will help the student develop a composition. If the student can ask himself or herself about likely purpose and parts, and can reflect easily on the content, he is likely to generate a reasonable expository structure.

Knowing Your Topic

Exposition is a challenging discourse form to teach. However, if it is taught within a contextualized skill perspective, it can be interesting and motivating for students. Three important aspects are teaching structure as part of a purposeful activity, having the students invested in the topic, and composing with the intention to share the product with an audience. A single topic is addressed to promote deeper understanding. Kirby et al. (1988) warn about the superficial engagement that occurs if students are directed to choose their topic from a list of composition topics that have no connection to students' interests.

Exposition is content as well as form, so the student should have some understanding of the topic upon which he is about to expound. Westby (2005) describes how expository text is a combination of individual propositions, content schema, and textual organization. The content schema is a superordinate organization of content facts into broader concepts. For example, a persuasive essay on the merits of dog ownership compared to cat ownership requires that the student know about cats, dogs, pets, suburban family habits, and how these intersect. Expository instruction may involve content exposure and idea discussion as well as teaching expository structure. If the topic parallels class activities, then the required content exposure time during intervention sessions can be minimized. If the topic is not class-related, some time will need to be spent on engaging the students in the content. Situating the structure lesson within a larger thematic unit is the most efficient use of intervention time, because content is gained through the thematically related activities that address several objectives. Units can be used with students of mixed ages and abilities, with differing objectives highlighted for each student or group.

To continue the example with the graduate student Anna and her client Nick, Anna noted how Nick's motivation and behavior improved when she switched from lessons that used a series of unconnected practice topics to a topic actually being addressed in his classroom. Nick's eighth-grade class was researching and developing a position statement on climbing a Wyoming rock formation, Devil's Tower, that is also a Native American spiritual location. The project encompassed several weeks of independent, challenging work for small cooperative learning groups. Anna used this class assignment to provide a series of lessons related to this purposeful context. When she integrated her instruction in persuasive organization, the DARE mnemonic, and signaling devices into this motivating context, Nick's interest and participation increased.

Therapeutic Focus

Within the lengthy and multidimensional process of composing exposition, it is imperative that clinicians keep a therapeutic focus. Working with the student on a history report can easily degenerate into assisting the student to complete the project and receive an acceptable grade. The SLP should not simply provide curriculum assistance. Instead, the SLP should focus on teaching a few specific strategies within a purposeful context that can be internalized, automated as skills, and applied independently across the curriculum.

Being therapeutic involves explicit instruction in strategies and skills. Purposeful and engaging contexts are not sufficient to result in greater change than would occur in daily-life contexts. Embedding skill instruction in purposeful contexts allows for both skill and activity. However, the cost of being therapeutic is that the integrity of the event will suffer to some degree (it will be *naturalistic,* not *natural).* The attention devoted to making real change in one aspect of exposition may affect the full authenticity of the event and may temporarily affect performance negatively in other areas. When focusing on expository structure, student ideas may lack depth or creativity, or student spelling and punctuation may suffer. The clinician will have to provide compensations for skills not being taught at the time, such as providing the correct spelling for a word. Such a therapeutic focus with compensations for nontargeted skills will result in better internalization of the targeted structural knowledge. Content and mechanics await another intervention session in which they can be the focus. In the classroom, this differential attention occurs through multiple drafts. In contrast, the focus of intervention may stay on expository structure, with the other aspects compensated, without moving through the multiple draft process with its changing focus.

It is possible to focus explicitly on structure in contrived activities and still remain within a broader contextualized intervention perspective. Englert's (1992) approach to instruction, with its emphasis on engagement and purposeful composition, has been criticized for its lack of attention to component skills (Isaacson, 1992). Isaacson recommended that while the completeness of the composition task is important, so also is providing contrived, discrete-skill tasks on occasion to practice components of the composition process. So long as these discrete-skill tasks are short diversions from the large, complete composition process, they do not distract from students' understanding of the whole.

Anna's work on the DARE mnemonic with Nick provided a clear theraputic focus, in contrast to the type of feedback provided by Nick's resource teacher. Anna spent many sessions teaching Nick the DARE structure and applying it to a variety of writing scenarios. Early on, Anna kept the focus on structure by writing to the student's dictation, which is shown in Box 6.2 on page 274. Anna then had Nick turn his notes into a written composition on the computer. The DARE notes provided the discourse structure, a lexicon, spelling, and possible sentences. From these notes, Nick typed two reasons supporting his argument and one reason against it, organized into two paragraphs. His composition can be viewed in Box 6.3 on page 275. Following this, to solidify the student's awareness of persuasive structure, Anna identified his arguments in his text with color-coding and discussed them further. Anna addressed only one other area: spelling. She had Nick correct his spelling with her assistance. Although spelling was not a direct teaching objective in this activity, this was part of the larger self-regulatory goal of reflective reading and self-correction.

In this series of tasks, Anna taught two objectives: persuasive discourse structure (DARE) and key word signaling devices (*I believe, there is evidence, first, in addition, in conclusion*). Other areas of weakness that were not the instructional focus were accepted (e.g., no demands to expand length), corrected without instruction (e.g., spelling corrections with a brief comment), or compensated (e.g., writing to student dictation).

When Nick's resource teacher taught exposition, she used several one-paragraph historical biographies. Each paragraph was presented on a single sheet below a scanned photo of the historical personage. These biographies were excellent contexts for expository intervention: they were whole units, short, with repeated opportunities for teaching descriptive structure. However, the teacher chose to comment on problems in multiple areas of composition, including cohesion, capitalization, grammatical morphology, punctuation, sentence structure, sequencing, and coherence (see Box 6.4 on page 276). Not all errors were noted, such as the incorrect choice of *there* for *their*, the absence of periods, and the grammatical difficulties of "The north ask he to..." sentence.

Use of the DARE Mnemonic and Carrier Phrase to Develop Position Statement

Box 6.2

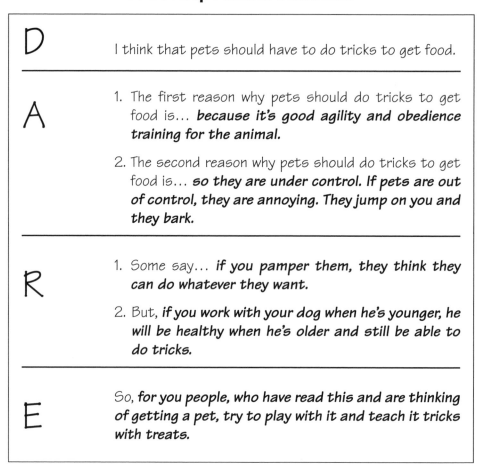

D   I think that pets should have to do tricks to get food.

A
1. The first reason why pets should do tricks to get food is... **because it's good agility and obedience training for the animal.**

2. The second reason why pets should do tricks to get food is... **so they are under control. If pets are out of control, they are annoying. They jump on you and they bark.**

R
1. Some say... **if you pamper them, they think they can do whatever they want.**

2. But, **if you work with your dog when he's younger, he will be healthy when he's older and still be able to do tricks.**

E   **So, for you people, who have read this and are thinking of getting a pet, try to play with it and teach it tricks with treats.**

Graduate students are likely familiar with this array of commenting in their diagnostic reports and thesis drafts. There is a lot of feedback provided and able students can wend their way through it. However, it is not therapeutic because it does not provide an explicit skill focus, systematic scaffolding, nor sufficient learning opportunities. While this type of support may lead to an acceptable rewrite and a passing grade on the assignment, it is unlikely to result in improvement in the student's own abilities. Students may appear to be performing at grade level, but they have not truly achieved the goal of the No Child Left Behind Act (2002) because they have not become better learners who can maintain this performance without ongoing supplementary support.

Box 6.3	**Written Persuasive Composition Based on Schematic Structure and Dictation Notes**

Why pets should do tricks to get food.

I think that pets should do tricks to get food. One of the many ~~resons~~ reasons is ~~whaen~~ when they get older they are ~~weker~~ weaker then they were. If you make them do ~~triks~~ tricks they will be ten times more ~~hrlthly~~ healthy. Also when they are ~~yonger~~ younger you should make them work ~~hader~~ harder for there food because when they are in ~~obdince~~ obedience class they will ~~lisen~~ listen to you ~~beter~~ better then if you just gave them food.

Some people think that there pets should not have to ~~make them~~ do tricks to get food also they just want to love there pet so they can play with them and have not to work. But most people think that there pet should work for food because if they don't they will be spoiled and just get food and not work for it, and once you aren't ~~spileing~~ spoiling your pet as much they will be very mean and not like what took place there.

In ~~Coution~~ conclusion if you are thinking about getting a dog try and teach it tricks and ~~yonshing~~ useing dog ~~trites teart~~ treat and loveing your pet.

Individualizing Class Assignments

Classroom projects present purposeful, complex activities within which to embed intervention objectives. However, the classroom schedule and specifics constrain intervention possibilities. Assisting in completing the project may take predominance over teaching students skills to allow for future greater independence. Even a resource classroom can be a heterogeneous and fragmented setting that hosts multigrade students with diverse needs. Sometimes the emphasis even here is on doing what needs to be done to get an assignment accomplished or a test passed. In contrast, the services provided by the SLP allow for individualization with a focus on strategies and skills. The intervention should be functionally linked to the classroom curriculum, and in the case of the resource room, may even occur in the room. However, the clinician needs to deliver intervention in a manner that allows repeated opportunities for systematic support of explicit skills.

Multiple Areas of Correction with No Explicit Skill Focus

Box 6.4

Who?

He was born in 1807. He graduated from west point in

1829. He became the superintendent for a academy in 1852

it was a military academy. In 1857 the death of his father in

this is not a complete

law he ask for a series of leaves to settle the estate. The north

sentence. What happened first? This

ask he to still be there general he said no this was in 1861. doesn't

make

Early in 1862 he was recalled to Richmond and made an   sense.

advisor to the president. He gradually became "Uncle

Robert" and " Marse Robert". *How? Why are*

you including this information?

Anna took the classroom unit on the Devil's Tower position statement and modified it to fit Nick's current level of performance. The teacher had assigned Nick to do the graphic support for the class project, because all the other aspects of the task required more intensive instruction than she was able to provide in the whole-class setting. Instead of limiting Nick to artwork and assisting him inclusively, Anna developed a miniature version of the classroom assignment in a pull-out setting. She worked with Nick on developing his own position statement based on the class discussions and materials. Anna used the DARE structure to lay out the reasons and help Nick compose a persuasive paragraph from this argument schematic.

An example from another SLP illustrated how to keep the student's work parallel to classroom expectations, but still allow individualization (Ukrainetz, in press). This author observed a fifth-grade class where the SLP, Chris, worked individually in the classroom when the students were working independently and in pull-out at other times. As the class researched and composed science reports, one student was exhibiting particular difficulties organizing information. Sara had a deep and enduring interest in sharks, and knew a tremendous amount about them. However, Sara displayed indications of Asperger syndrome and had great difficulty selecting and organizing facts.

For Sara's library research project, her fifth-grade teachers provided structural support through a clearly delineated process. Students had to write note facts on strips of paper color-coded for source (e.g., encyclopedia, online, science text), with source references and relevant page numbers. The note facts were then physically sorted by category, such as habitat, appearance, and type. Then, the note facts had to be translated into paragraphs, with all the details kept within a category. The teachers provided a handout that described how to build a report. It listed an introductory paragraph, body paragraphs, and a concluding paragraph. The introductory paragraph told the reader what would be discussed, started with a topic sentence, and ended with a concluding sentence. The body paragraphs each started with a topic sentence, had at least three supporting details related to the topic sentence, and had a minimum of four sentences. The concluding paragraph listed what topics were discussed and reported a generalization or something the author had learned about the topic. Students were reminded to not use the personal pronouns *you* or *I*. They were told to use a serious tone, no slang, and their best vocabulary. They were told to go back to their resources and get more information if they did not have enough when they started to write. Finally, they were told to be prepared to do several rewrites on their papers.

This was an excellent initial support structure. Chris then provided the interactive support. She focused on teaching text organization and assisted completion in the other areas. The clinician did the writing and Sara told her which note facts she wanted within each paragraph, using the strategy of matching detail to main idea. Chris guided the student in selecting from her categorized note facts and adding details within the topic of the paragraph. This project allowed for repeated opportunities to internalize categorization and organization strategies, developing the student's independent skills in these aspects of the activity. Taking student dictation compensated for the non-targeted writing difficulties and allowed completion of a purposeful project within a reasonable time frame.

Using Authentic Texts

The previous section outlined general guidelines on contextualized intervention for expository structure. This section provides additional specific examples, including the steps to teaching enumeration and description in a visitor brochure.

Expository discourse structure has general features, but specific organization and details depend on context and purpose. Earlier in this chapter, the descriptive discourse genre was demonstrated in four different examples: an essay in a standardized achievement exam, a classified advertisement, a commercial advertisement, and an eye-witness report. Intervention could target one of these types of descriptive discourse, with explicit attention to the structure of the text and repeated opportunities to compose descriptions orally or in writing. Another way to approach descriptive discourse would be to move among these four types, encouraging style flexibility. This provides an interesting reason for repeated opportunities around the same description topic. In addition, students will demonstrate a robust competence in descriptive discourse if they can maintain the core aspect of descriptive discourse (i.e., a mental image) while adjusting their language to match purpose and audience.

Short authentic texts that demonstrate a particular discourse structure, such as those found in nature books or children's magazines, provide valuable models and ideas for activities. For example, the book *202 Oozing, Bubbling, Dripping, and Bouncing Experiments* (VanCleave, 1996) provides many examples of short scientific discourse. The experiments are procedural discourse and the results are very short explanatory discourse. While the goal of each activity is to demonstrate a scientific principle, the intervention objective is not to learn science, but to teach students procedural structure and content. Each experiment states a purpose, materials, four to eight sequenced steps, and expected results.

The SLP can direct the students to attend to how each experiment is structured, requesting similarities and differences. When a common structure is discerned by the students, the attention turns to producing such a structure. Students can compose their own experimental procedures or they can simply develop oral fluency in delivering procedures. Students can verbally direct each other and the clinician through the procedures (like the traditional barrier games often used in intervention, but in a more authentic activity). The experiments can be used to teach: (1) staying on a single topic; (2) providing the three main components of purpose, materials, and steps; (3) using the signaling devices of subtitles and key words; (4) providing steps in order using specific vocabulary; or (5) answering a *why* question with two to three complete sentences containing relevant, understandable information.

An Enumeration and Description Lesson
A Visitor Brochure

This section illustrates teaching expository structure through the purposeful context of a visitor brochure, in this example, for a zoo. Authentic contexts often involve more than one genre and this is no exception. The two genres illustrated are enumeration and description. A visitor brochure is a purposeful discourse form that occurs in daily life. It is also a simple form with a minimum of text. Using a simple but realistic form such as a brochure provides a structural scaffold that gives a manageable composing task while engaging the student in a meaningful activity.

The zoo brochure occurs during a thematic unit on zoos (see Chapter 2 for more on intervention units). Multiple objectives in addition to expository structure are addressed within the unit. By the point of brochure construction, the prior zoo activities will have contributed toward zoo content knowledge. Even though the first step involves developing engagement and content, engagement does not occur at a single point, but throughout the thematic unit with each meaningful activity and with recognition of the skill accomplishments.

The zoo brochure intervention activity involves an explicit skill focus, repeated opportunities, and systematic support through scaffolding. A brochure provides a context for purposeful description and enumeration because elements are selected and organized for the goal of attracting and informing potential zoo visitors. There are three explicit intervention objectives in this activity: enumerative structure, description structure, and structural cohesion. The activity invokes many other linguistic and academic skills such as vocabulary, categories, and spelling, but the clinician assists and compensates for these other areas. The brochure provides repeated opportunities for multiple description paragraphs and enumerative lists. Each student can compose a complete brochure or several students can engage in repeated opportunities through composing several pieces with the best selected to be combined into the larger product. The task is meaningful but simple, providing structural scaffolding. The clinician interactively scaffolds the students by showing models, discussing possibilities, and having the students talk aloud about the explicit objectives through the composing process. The fourth critical intervention component—intensity—depends on having only a few students in a group, focusing on a select number of skills, and having the students engage in the skills frequently.

The Instructional Sequence

The basic sequence of instruction for expository structure is presented in Table 6.6. The zoo brochure is a logical and engaging extension of a piece of literature about zoos. It could be part of a larger zoo or exotic animal unit that targets other intervention objectives or an interesting story or nature book could simply be initially shared.

After sharing the piece of literature and introducing the idea of creating a brochure that makes people want to visit a zoo, the students brainstorm on what they think goes into a visitor brochure. They consider purpose, audience, and known information. Notes are made in a discovery draft. This is an idea-generating draft. It focuses on student thinking more than on the formal textual composition.

To organize the expository structure for the brochure, students examine models of the target structures. Several visitor brochures from other tourist sites are shared and discussed. Brochures from past student projects provide very helpful models, even if the quality is not ideal (Charney & Carlson, 1995). The content and layouts of the models are noted. Items the students like and don't like are also noted. Discussion results are recorded by students dictating to the SLP. The clinician writes the notes, modeling and explicitly commenting on the use of key words and grouped items, rather than full sentences. An outline of the brochure is then developed. (Box 6.5 on page 282 provides an example.) The brochure topics might consist of: title, catchy slogan, animals, habitats, other attractions, and access details. The information is presented in short paragraphs and bulleted lists. Illustrations of exotic or cute animals, happy families, and warm weather can be added.

The SLP leads the students in discussing and determining what they know and what else they need to find out to fill in the outline. For example, they each may consider they know enough about their favorite animals for a short descriptive paragraph, but they aren't sure of what habitat categories (wetland, desert, cave, etc.) they need to list. The clinician should not spend a lot of time

Basic Sequence of Contextualized Skill Instruction for Expository Structure

Table 6.6

Stage of Creation	Steps to Get There
1. Setting the Scene	a. Present topic, purpose, and expository genre. b. Develop student engagement. c. Determine content, known and not known. d. Present content necessary for the topic.
2. Content Generation	a. Brainstorm what is needed and why. b. Jot down in a discovery draft. c. Focus on content, not form.
3. Expository Structure	a. Show models of structure. b. Lay out needed macro- and microstructure. c. Organize into text structure outline. d. Consider communication effectiveness and revise.
4. Structure into Text	a. Start with headings. b. Expand schematic into text. c. Add other signaling devices. d. Identify structures in the text. e. Collate and illustrate.
5. Share and Reflect	a. Share through presentation or publication. b. Discuss what has been learned.

on this aspect, but missing facts could be obtained quickly from an encyclopedia or the Internet.

Then, focus turns to each description and enumeration. Enumeration is the easiest to compose, because it is more like an outline than connected text. It is simply a heading plus listing of topically unified items. Enumeration is ideal for students with limited writing competence. A byproduct of enumeration is instruction in note taking—how to compose a record of the critical concepts

Box 6.5   **Outline of Visitor Information for Imaginary Zoo**

Zoo name and locations	**Description** of the zoo	**List** of animals	**Description** of guided activities	**Description** of favorite animal #2	**List** of access info
Slogan name and locations	**List** of attractions	**Description** of habitats	**Description** of favorite animal #1	**Description** of favorite animal #3	**Location** map and driving instructions

using key words and short phrases. Enumeration provides an excellent opportunity to teach the cohesive device of parallel structures. Lists can be simply noun series with matching number structure (bears, wolves, snakes, raccoons, lizards, etc.) or they can be more elaborate predicate structures with repeated verb or adverb opportunities (bears woofing, wolves growling, snakes hissing, etc.). Students practice fixing a poorly presented list, then move to generating their own lists, as shown in Box 6.6).

The genre of description is more difficult to lay out. The topic is followed by a series of details, like enumeration, but the details are more varied. They need to be organized categorically and expanded into sentences. The order and selection of details depends on the task purpose. For example, the favorite animal descriptions would highlight appealing features of the animals and invoke visitor curiosity. An example is provided in Box 6.7. An approach might be to not name the animal, leaving the visitor to guess its identity and thus be more intrigued by what is in the zoo.

The individual samples are then selected and collated for the brochure. The six-column layout presented allows for legal-dimension paper to be folded into six narrow pages or letter-dimension paper to be folded into three double-sided pages. If the work is typed on a word processor, it can be put

Enumeration Schematic with Two Contrasting Examples

Box 6.6

Schematic	Poor Enumeration	Good Enumeration
Header:	Animals:	You will see:
• Item	• An otter	• Otters swimming
• Item	• Bears sunning	• Bears sunning
• Item	• Lizards	• Lizards creeping
• Item	• Some raccoons	• Raccoons wrestling
	• The wolf	• Wolves howling

Schematic for Describing Favorite Animals in a Visitor Brochure with Two Contrasting Descriptions

Box 6.7

Schematic	Poor Description	Good Description
Paragraph describing: • Physical • Movement • Preferred activity • Preferred food • Special characteristic	*Otters are furry and fast. They are slower than greyhounds and smaller too. They eat stuff from the sea. The fur is brown. They float. They eat. They swim. They are fast. They like the water.*	*I am a small, furry, brown beast. I am slinky and speedy. I love swimming in cold water and sliding down mud banks. My favorite food is abalones. I eat them off my tummy while I float on my back. Come visit me!*

into a presentation software to create a brochure layout. The old-fashioned method of cutting and taping selections onto a page, adding illustrations, and photocopying also works well.

Finally, the composition should be shared—the brochure will fall short of a purposeful activity if no one sees it but the participants. Publication refers to a formal print-sharing endpoint, and presentation refers to a formal oral-sharing endpoint. In this case, a multipage illustrated visitor brochure has been published. The sharing can occur with other students in the group, with parents, with teachers, or with students from other groups or classrooms. Brochures can be posted in the speech-language room or school hallway with a description of the purpose of the activity and what students learned from it. Blank paper can be posted beside the brochure inviting positive and constructive comments.

This activity addressed expository structure. If it is part of a thematic unit, other zoo activities may address other intervention objectives, such as developing narrative or syntactic structures. New vocabulary is presented repeatedly across the varied activities, providing coherence and depth of word learning without directly targeting vocabulary acquisition. Strategies for learning the meaning of new words, such as using context and dictionaries, are also introduced incidentally across the varied activities within the thematic zoo unit.

Conclusion

Exposition is a discourse form highly valued in school. The term exposition refers to a collection of discourse structures united by a generalizing stance and an intention to inform. There are a variety of expository genres, with loosely specified organizational structures, such as description, enumeration, explanation, procedure, comparison/contrast, and persuasion. The specifics of each expository genre vary with the particular purpose of the presenter. Signaling devices guide the audience to the organization of a particular piece of exposition. They consist of overviews, summaries, headings, and key words.

Exposition is typically considered to be an activity of later elementary and beyond. However, young students can produce oral expository discourse. They can explain, describe, and persuade. Their productions will be more dialogic than monologic. Development in preschool through first grade involves increasing independence and extended spans of discourse. Older students must learn to manage the composing process for written exposition. Middle schoolers are better at this abstract and objective discourse form than elementary students, but even later elementary-age students can show impressive written expositions.

Instruction in expository structure involves teaching within purposeful activities. Both genre-specific and general regulatory knowledge need to be taught. Intervention involves oral and written modalities, an emphasis on communicative function, a clear therapeutic focus, purposeful discourse activities, and individualization within purposeful expository activities related to classroom activities or a thematic unit. Students experience and analyze models, generate ideas, plan discourse structure, and move from notes to oral presentation or written text with systematic support from the SLP. Opportunities to publish and present the work provide a motivating and purposeful endpoint.

Exposition is a frequent activity in school and in life. Students need to be able to inform, explain, and persuade across subject areas. Teaching expository structure allows students success in this important discourse form, which is used commonly in adult vocational, professional, and personal tasks.

References

Applebee, A. (1984). *Contexts for learning to write: Studies of secondary school instruction.* Norwood, NJ: Ablex.

Axia, G. (1996). How to persuade mum to buy a toy. *First Language, 16,* 301–317.

Bereiter, C. (1980). Development in writing. In L. W. Gregg & E. R. Steinberg (Eds.), *Cognitive processes in writing* (pp. 73–93). Mahwah, NJ: Erlbaum.

Bereiter, C., & Scardamalia, M. (1982). From conversation to composition: The role of instruction in a developmental process. In R. Glaser (Ed.), *Advances in instructional psychology, Vol. 2* (pp. 1–64). Mahwah, NJ: Erlbaum.

Bereiter, C., & Scardamalia, M. (1987). *The psychology of written composition.* Mahwah, NJ: Erlbaum.

Black, J. B. (1985). An exposition on understanding expository text. In B. K. Britton & J. B. Black (Eds.), *Understanding expository text* (pp. 249–267). Mahwah, NJ: Erlbaum.

Bruner, J. (1986). *Actual minds, possible worlds.* Cambridge, MA: Harvard University Press.

Burkhalter, N. (1995). A Vygotsky-based curriculum for teaching persuasive writing in the elementary grades. *Language Arts, 72,* 192–199.

Butler-Nalin, K. (1984). Revising patterns in students' writing. In A. Applebee (Ed.), *Contexts for learning to write: Studies of secondary school instruction* (pp. 121–132). Norwood, NJ: Ablex.

Chapman, M. (1995). The sociolinguistic construction of written genres in the first grade. *Research in the Teaching of English, 29,* 164–192.

Charney, D. H., & Carlson, R. A. (1995). Learning to write in a genre: What student writers take from model texts. *Research in the Teaching of English, 29,* 88–123.

Crowhurst, M. (1987). Cohesion in argument and narration at three grade levels. *Research in the Teaching of English, 21,* 185–201.

Crowhurst, M. (1991). Interrelationships between reading and writing persuasive discourse. *Research in the Teaching of English, 25,* 314–338.

Duthie, C. (1994). Nonfiction: A genre study for the primary classroom. *Language Arts, 71,* 588–595.

Englert, C. S. (1990). Unraveling the mysteries of writing through strategy instruction. In T. E. Scruggs & B. Y. L. Wong (Eds.), *Intervention research in learning disabilities* (pp. 187–223). New York: Springer-Verlag.

Englert, C. S. (1992). Writing instruction from a sociocultural perspective: The holistic, dialogic, and social enterprise of writing. *Journal of Learning Disabilities, 25,* 153–172.

Fleischman, S. (1991). Discourse as space/discourse as time: Reflections on the metalanguage of spoken and written discourse. *Journal of Pragmatics, 16,* 291–306.

Flower, L. S., & Hayes, J. R. (1980). The dynamics of composing: Making plans and juggling constraints. In L. W. Gregg & E. R. Steinberg (Eds.), *Cognitive processes in writing* (pp. 31–50). Mahwah, NJ: Erlbaum.

Freedle, R., & Hale, G. (1979). Acquisition of new comprehension schemata for expository prose by transfer of a narrative schema. In R. O. Freedle (Ed.), *New directions in discourse processing* (pp. 121–135). Norwood, NJ: Ablex.

Golder, C., & Coirier, P. (1994). Argumentative text writing: Developmental trends. *Discourse Processes, 18,* 187–210.

Graham, S., & Harris, K. R. (1999). Assessment and intervention in overcoming writing difficulties: An illustration from the self-regulated strategy development model. *Language, Speech, and Hearing Services in Schools, 30,* 255–264.

Graham, S., Harris, K. R., & Troia, G. (2000). Self-regulated strategy development revisited: Teaching writing strategies to struggling writers. *Topics in Language Disorders, 20*(4), 1–14.

Graves, D. (1975). An examination of the writing processes of seven year old children. *Research in the Teaching of English, 9,* 227–241.

Graves, D. (1989). *Investigate nonfiction.* Portsmouth, NH: Heinemann.

Hayes, J., & Flower, L. (1987). On the structure of the writing process. *Topics in Language Disorders, 7,* 19–30.

Hidi, S., & Hildyard, A. (1983). The comparison of oral and written productions in two discourse types. *Discourse Processes, 6,* 91–105.

Isaacson, S. L. (1992). Volleyball and other analogies: A response to Englert. *Journal of Learning Disabilities, 25,* 173–177.

Kamhi, A. G., & Catts, H. W. (2005). Language and reading: Convergences and divergences. In H. W. Catts & A. G. Kamhi (Eds.), *Language and reading disabilities* (2nd ed., pp. 1–25). Boston: Pearson.

Kirby, D., Liner, T., & Vinz, R. (1988). *Inside out: Developmental strategies for teaching writing* (2nd ed.). Portsmouth, NH: Boynton/Cook.

Longacre, R. E. (1983). *The grammar of discourse.* New York: Plenum.

Lorch, R. F., & Lorch, E. P. (1996). Effects of organizational signals on free recall of expository text. *Journal of Educational Psychology, 88,* 34–48.

MacArthur, C. A. (2000). New tools for writing: Assistive technology for students with writing difficulties. *Topics in Language Disorders, 20*(4), 85–100.

MacArthur, C. A., & Graham, S. (1987). Learning disabled students composing under three methods of text production: Handwriting, word processing, and dictation. *Journal of Special Education, 21,* 22–42.

McCormick, C. B., Busching, B. A., & Potter, E. F. (1992). Children's knowledge about writing: The development and use of evaluative criteria. In M. Pressley, K. R. Harris, & J. T. Guthrie (Eds.), *Promoting academic competence and literacy in schools* (pp. 311–336). San Diego, CA: Academic Press.

Moffett, J. (1968). *Teaching the universe of discourse.* New York: Houghton-Mifflin.

Newcomer, P. L., & Barenbaum, E. M. (1991). The written composing ability of children with learning disabilities. A review of the literature from 1980 to 1990. *Journal of Learning Disabilities, 24,* 578–593.

Ninio, A., & Snow, C. E. (1996). *Pragmatic development.* Boulder, CO: Westview.

No Child Left Behind Act of 2001, 20 U.S.C., § 6311 *et seq.* (2002).

Paley, V. G. (1981). *Wally's stories.* Cambridge, MA: Harvard University Press.

Pappas, C. (1991). Young children's strategies in learning the "book language" of information books. *Discourse Processes, 14,* 203–225.

Pellegrini, A., Galda, L., & Rubin, D. (1984). Context in text: The development of oral and written language in two genres. *Child Development, 55,* 1549–1555.

Perera, K. (1984). Language acquisition and writing. In P. Fletcher & M. Garman (Eds.), *Language acquisition* (pp. 494–521). Cambridge, MA: Cambridge University Press.

Scollon, R., & Scollon, S. B. K. (1981). *Narrative, literacy, and face in interethnic communication.* Norwood, NJ: Ablex.

Scott, C. (1995). A discourse approach to syntax teaching. In D. F. Tibbits (Ed.), *Language intervention beyond the primary grades* (pp. 435–464). Austin, TX: Pro-Ed.

Scott, C. (2005). Learning to write. In A. G. Kamhi & H. W. Catts (Eds.), *Reading disabilities: A developmental language perspective* (pp. 224–258). Boston: College-Hill.

Sexton, M., Harris, K. R., & Graham, S. (1998). Self-regulated strategy development and the writing process: Effects on essay writing and attributions. *Exceptional Children, 64,* 295–311.

Smagorinsky, P. (1991). The writer's knowledge and the writing process: A protocol analysis. *Research in the Teaching of English, 25,* 339–364.

Spandel, V., & Stiggins, R. (1990). *Creating writers: Linking assessment and writing instruction.* New York: Longman.

Stewart, S. R. (1985). Development of written language proficiency: Methods for teaching text structure. In C. S. Simon (Ed.), *Communication skills and classroom success* (pp. 341–361). San Diego, CA: College-Hill.

Sturm, J., & Koppenhaver, D. (2000). Supporting writing development in adolescents with developmental disabilities. *Topics in Language Disorders, 20*(2), 73–92.

Taylor, K. K. (1984). Teaching summarization skills. *Journal of Reading, 27,* 389–393.

Taylor, B. M., & Beach, R. W. (1984). The effects of text structure instruction on middle-grade students' comprehension and production of expository text. *Reading Research Quarterly, 19,* 134–146.

Texas Education Agency. (1991). *TAAS and the writing process: A composition handbook, grades 3 through 5.* Author.

Ukrainetz, T. A. (in press). What to work on how: An examination of the practice of school-age language intervention. *Contemporary Issues in Communication Sciences and Disorders.*

VanCleave, J. (1996). *202 oozing, bubbling, dripping, and bouncing experiments.* New York: Wiley.

Vygotsky, L. S. (1978). *Mind in society.* Boston: Harvard University Press.

Westby, C. E. (2005). Assessing and facilitating text comprehension problems. In H. W. Catts & A. G. Kamhi (Eds.), *Language and reading disabilities* (pp. 157–232). Boston: College-Hill.

Wong, B. Y. L. (2000). Writing strategies instruction for expository essays for adolescents with and without learning disabilities. *Topics in Language Disorders, 20*(4), 29–44.

Wong, B. Y. L., Butler, D. L., Ficzere, S. A., & Kuperis, S. (1996). Teaching low achievers and students with learning disabilities to plan, write, and revise opinion essays. *Journal of Learning Disabilities, 29,* 197–212.

Wong, B. Y. L., Butler, D. L., Ficzere, S. A., & Kuperis, S. (1997). Teaching adolescents with learning disabilities and low achievers to plan, write, and revise compare-and-contrast essays. *Learning Disabilities Research & Practice, 12,* 2–15.

Chapter 7

Improving Peer Interaction and Learning in Cooperative Learning Groups

Bonnie Brinton and Martin Fujiki

Max and the Group

Troy, Kevin, and Max are all first graders in a middle-class neighborhood school (Brinton, Fujiki, Montague, & Hanton, 2000). Troy and Kevin are typically developing, but Max has a language impairment. The three boys are working at a table making a periscope out of a cardboard box. Materials have been provided; each boy has been assigned a specific role. Troy checks the time allotted to the project, Kevin makes sure everyone participates, and Max manages the materials. All the boys have been urged to work together. Troy and Kevin are cutting holes, decorating the box, and discussing how much time they have left. Max is standing in close proximity, watching. He picks up the box to look at it and puts it back down. After a few minutes, he takes a pink piece of paper, moves away from Troy and Kevin, and announces, "I'm gonna make me a toothbrush." Troy and Kevin continue their activity and periodically dart glances at Max. Subsequently, they announce to a nearby teacher, "He's making him a toothbrush." When the teacher does not respond, Troy and Kevin continue to assemble the periscope. Max keeps working alone. At one point, he holds up his pink paper toward Kevin and Troy and sings, "La la la la la" several times. Kevin directs Max back to the joint project, asking for materials, "You do the markers, Max." Max disregards the directive and continues to work alone. Troy asks Max for paper. Max ignores Troy's repeated requests. Max approaches Troy and says, "I need the scissors for a minute." Troy does not relinquish the scissors he is holding, and Max repeats, "I need the scissors," several times. Max grabs the scissors that Troy is holding and the two boys scuffle as both tug on the scissors. Kevin intercedes, "Guys, break it up, break it up, break it up!" Max moves to the other end of the table with the scissors and cuts paper for his toothbrush. Troy and Kevin are now a dyad working together to build a periscope. Max is working in isolation.

Learning Together

Collaborative learning tasks, such as the one assigned to Max, Troy, and Kevin, have received considerable attention as a means to include students with disabilities in classroom activities. These tasks are usually based on cooperative learning models that seek to enhance the learning of students with a variety of abilities and perspectives by "teaching students to work and learn together" (Putnam, 1998, p. 13). The idea that students with developmental differences could benefit from interacting with their peers is intuitive. Parents who have concerns about their students' development may seek structured preschool settings as their first line of defense against the specter of disability. This is especially true for parents of students with disorders that may not be obvious in infancy, such as language impairments. Most speech-language pathologists (SLPs) have seen the following scenario many times: Timmy Edwards is slow to begin talking, but Mr. and Mrs. Edwards reason that Timmy has little need to talk because his older brother "talks for him." At three years, Timmy still produces mostly one- or two-word sentences, however, and he tends to play alone rather than seek out the neighborhood children. Mr. and Mrs. Edwards become concerned about Timmy and enroll him in a preschool to stimulate his language development. Rather than alleviating Timmy's difficulty, however, the group context highlights his differences. He tends to play beside the other children rather than with them, he wanders off at group story time, and his language shows little change. Mr. and Mrs. Edwards conclude that Timmy cannot take full advantage of the group-learning context, and on the advice of his preschool teachers, seek further diagnostics and intervention.

In cases like Timmy's, the intuitive notion that students with language impairments should be learning with and from their peers is sometimes suppressed as they are pulled out of their classes for special services. Individualized learning models may be adopted that emphasize the interaction between the student and the clinician, but not the interaction among students. This is understandable considering that students with language impairments need highly individualized programs of intervention. The necessity of individualized intervention programs, however, is sometimes misconstrued as a need for solitary learning contexts. Nevertheless, as Max's interaction with Troy and Kevin illustrates, it can be difficult to involve students with language impairments in cooperative groups. Max never really becomes part of his group, despite the fact that the project is designed to foster collaboration. He does not seem interested in working with Kevin and Troy, and he lacks strategies to participate in the joint work. Troy and Kevin's requests to complete his assigned role have little effect on Max, and he is soon excluded from his peers' activity.

Even though students with language impairments may typically experience little success working in groups, a cooperative learning model still holds promise for them. Consider Max as an example. He has no reciprocal friends in his first-grade class, and his academic achievement is depressed in comparison with his peers. Working in cooperative groups might foster Max's peer acceptance and enhance his academic and cognitive growth (see Johnson & Johnson, 1999; and Slavin, 1995, for review). Max may benefit from the good language models that typical peers can provide. In addition, group work may provide Max with valuable opportunities to utilize and practice not only language but also social skills in a supportive setting. Group activities can immerse Max in the work of the class and scaffold his contribution to the society of the classroom.

The catch, of course, is making groups work for students like Max. As emphasized earlier, students with language impairments form a heterogeneous population and each student needs an individualized intervention program. Most, if not all, of these students also require individual attention and considerable one-on-one interaction with teachers and special service providers. In addition, students with language impairments rarely thrive in a group context without extra support. In Max's case, for example, the structure designed to foster cooperative learning is clearly inadequate to assure his participation, and the triad quickly dissolves into a dyad and a solo.

Despite their potential, cooperative models will be of little use for students with language impairments if they are allowed to become one more context for their exclusion (Brinton, Fujiki, & Higbee, 1998; Brinton, Fujiki, & McKee, 1998; Brinton et al., 2000). The purpose of this chapter is to consider the nature of cooperative groups and to describe ways to foster the meaningful inclusion of students with language impairments within those groups.

The Nature of Cooperative Groups

Group Interactions

The nature of cooperative groups is best understood within the wider context of possible group interactions. "For any task, humans can organize their efforts in three ways: competitively, individualistically, or cooperatively" (Johnson & Johnson, 1999, p. 2). In classroom and other intervention contexts, therapeutic tasks may be structured to include one or more of these organizational methods depending on what is to be accomplished. In competitive contexts, success can only be realized at the expense of others. If one student wins, others must lose. Competitive models of interaction abound in western society. (The competition relished in athletic events is exceeded in entertainment venues where cooperation is valued primarily as a temporary tool to be used to further one's success. One wonders if students will come to their intervention groups prepared to vote a member out!) By the time most students come to school, they are well-versed in competitive practices, and they gradually learn to gauge their value in comparison to their peers (Harter, 1999). Although educators may be committed to the success of each student, many employ competitive tasks that encourage students to enjoy the failure of others (Slavin, 1995). For students with disabilities, competitive contexts can be particularly discouraging. Competition is motivating only if one perceives some chance of winning. Competitive experiences often teach students with language impairments that they are bound to lose. In the words of a 17 year-old boy with a language impairment, "It's like they're driving sports cars and I'm on a bike with training wheels." As Slavin notes, "For most low achievers, a competitive situation is a poor motivator; for some it is almost constant psychological torture" (p. 3).

In contrast, individualistic teaching models stress, "working by oneself to ensure one's own learning meets a preset criterion independently from the efforts of other students" (Johnson & Johnson, 1999, p. 7). That is, students work alone on tasks, and their performance is evaluated individually as well. This model might seem ideal for students with language impairments in that they could work on tasks geared to their needs at their own pace. Only certain tasks can be accomplished in isolation, however, and individualized efforts can be lonely. Individualized work does not draw on an exchange of ideas, it does not place a student within an interactive learning environment, and it offers little opportunity to practice expressive language skills in communicative contexts. In fact, if all teaching methods are individualized, a student need not come to a school at all.

In cooperative models, students are grouped so that the success of the group depends on the success of each student. Group members may be diverse in terms of background and ability, but each is expected to bring something to the task. There are several types of cooperative groups. Johnson, Johnson, and Smith (1998) explain that successful cooperative teams share the following characteristics:

- Cooperative teams foster interdependence among group members who understand that they succeed or fail together. This intertwined relationship is mediated by individual accountability. "Assessing the quantity and quality of each member's contributions" (p. 1:38) ensures that each member of the group has meaningful input.

- Cooperative group members work together to promote each member's productivity. "Members explain, discuss, and teach what they know to teammates" (p. 1:38).

- Cooperative groups also focus on the group process per se as they take "time to discuss how well they are achieving their goals and maintaining effective working relationships among members" (p. 1:38).

- Social skills are imperative in building cooperative teams: "groups cannot function effectively if members do not have and use the needed social skills" (p. 1:38), including decision-making, trust-building, communication, and conflict management.

In summary, cooperative groups are structured in such a way that group members share a common goal and succeed or fail together. Each member is accountable for making a significant contribution to the group work. Task completion is interactive as group members share and discuss ways to proceed and solve problems. The focus of work extends beyond the task itself to the group process that guides the work. This level of cooperation requires both communication and social skill.

Cooperative Groups in Classrooms

Many teachers place students in work groups for various activities. Not all of these groups involve organizational strategies that are associated with cooperative learning, however. There are many types of cooperative structures described in the literature (e.g., Johnson & Johnson, 1999; Johnson et al., 1998; Mandel, 2003; Putnam, 1998; Slavin, 1995) that may be employed within classrooms for various purposes. Some teachers use cooperative learning structures fairly consistently, and others employ these strategies for specific tasks or units of study.

Successful groups require a classroom where students have a cooperative mindset, and each class member's contributions are considered valid. The classroom atmosphere may differ from more traditional environments. For example, a physical layout that permits group members to cluster together is important. A relaxed turn-taking structure permits group members to discuss and collaborate together with spontaneity. Several groups may be involved in different activities at any one time. As a result, cooperative classrooms may appear busy, even chaotic, to the uninitiated observer. What is important, however, is that each class member is familiar and comfortable with the structure and goals of the classroom as well as the smaller groups to which he or she belongs.

When employing cooperative groups, teachers typically choose task objectives that align with academic goals. They structure these groups by determining the educational objectives for the group work, the group size and makeup, and the cooperative framework (or rules) the group will use. It is the group's job to discover knowledge as they seek solutions to problems and answers to questions together. Johnson and Johnson (1999) describe the role of the teacher as a "guide on the side" (p. 18) who facilitates and monitors the group process and progress. As indicated earlier, the cooperative aspect of these groups holds promise as a context for typically developing students to provide scaffolding for the contributions of students with language impairments as they work together to achieve a common goal. In addition, the positive affiliation with a group could provide a social oasis for lonely students with language impairments and might help these students find a place within social groups that are formed at free time and on playgrounds (Fujiki, Brinton, Isaacson, & Summers, 2001; Fujiki, Brinton, & Todd, 1996).

Barriers to Cooperative Work

As Max, Kevin, and Troy illustrate, groups are not always cooperative. Max's behavior effectively torpedoes any three-way collaboration. Max demonstrates a number of barriers to group work that are associated with language impairments. Several of these barriers are discussed below. Because the communication and academic problems of students with language impairments are well recognized, we briefly mention each, and spend more time on issues that may be less familiar to some readers.

Poor Language and Academic Skills

Obviously, Max's language skill is limited. As Johnson and Johnson (1999) emphasize, communication skill is essential to the group process. Even though Max talks readily to Troy and Kevin, his communication skill is undermined by his language problems. Students with language impairments can be expected to have various degrees of difficulty expressing their thoughts and ideas and understanding their peers' language in group interactions. When the group process is effective, a rapid verbal exchange may ensue as students excitedly share their ideas and pose possible solutions to problems. Students with language impairments may have difficulty keeping up with the linguistic demands of the situation.

In addition to oral language difficulties, students with language impairments frequently have academic problems as well. These students may struggle with literacy, and other content areas may also be weak. A disparity of academic levels among group members may lead to the exclusion of less capable students, as "students who are perceived to be less skillful are ignored by other group members" (Slavin, 1995, p. 19).

Inappropriate Social Goals

In many cases, language and academic difficulties are not the only barriers to inclusion in groups. Lack of social competence may be just as devastating (Brinton & Fujiki, 2004). On a very basic level, some students with language impairments may not have social goals that are conducive to group work. For example, Max does not buy into the group process and is not particularly motivated to work as part of a group. He asks to be allowed to work alone. This is somewhat puzzling considering that Max seems eager to interact with his peers at free time. The reticence that is prevalent in students with language impairments is characterized by approach-avoidance feelings where students are both eager and wary about interacting with peers (Fujiki, Brinton, Morgan, & Hart, 1999; Fujiki et al., 2001; Hart, Fujiki, Brinton, & Hart, 2004). It may be the case that many students with language impairments have little positive experience interacting with peers, and do not anticipate much success in group work. In this regard, it has been proposed that these students may consciously avoid contexts, such as group interactions, where their impaired language skills will put them at risk for failure (Redmond & Rice, 1998). Some students with language impairments may seek out adults rather than initiate interaction with their peers (Rice, Sell, & Hadley, 1991).

Adopting social goals that are contrary to group collaboration may have deeper roots than just past experience, however. For example, recent work has indicated that students with language impairments may have difficulty with some aspects of regulating emotion. That is, they may be unable to "gear themselves up" to interact with others and may lack affect and empathy. They may also fail to respond to the positive overtures of others (Fujiki, Brinton, & Clarke, 2002). Poor emotional regulation plays as large a role as does language impairment in explaining reticence, a significant social difficulty in students with language impairments (Fujiki, Spackman, Brinton, & Hall, 2004).

Poor Social Skills

Even if students with language impairments have positive social goals, they may lack the social skills required to interact successfully. For example, like many students with language impairments, Max does not readily join in group work or play (Brinton, Fujiki, Spencer, & Robinson, 1997; Craig & Washington, 1993). He wanders from group to group at recess, sometimes watching others play and sometimes trying to engage his peers. Max has difficulty gaining access to group activities, and as a result, he spends much of his free time alone (Fujiki et al., 2001).

Students with language impairments may have many issues with social skills beyond gaining access to groups. Johnson et al. (1998) underscore the importance of interpersonal skills: "groups cannot function effectively if members do not have and use the needed social skills" (p. 1:38). Many students with language impairments contribute little to group work, tending to watch others or leave the group altogether (Brinton, Fujiki, & Higbee, 1998). They are frequently withdrawn, and may be unable to gear up to interact with peers (Fujiki, Brinton, Morgan et al., 1999; Fujiki et al., 2004; Hart et al., 2004). Students with language impairments may also have difficulty negotiating with peers (Brinton, Fujiki, & McKee, 1998), resolving conflicts (Stevens & Bliss, 1995), and making joint decisions (Grove, Conti-Ramsden, & Donlan, 1993). These are all social skills that are essential for successful group interaction.

Poor Social Acceptance

The success of cooperative groups depends, to a large extent, on mutual respect among group members. Each group member's contribution must be considered as valid, and each member's success must be important to the group (Slavin, 1995). Students with language impairments have several potential strikes against them in the social world of the classroom, including low academic status, weak social skills, and a combination of other factors. Students with language impairments may be poorly accepted or even actively rejected, and they may have few or no friends (Asher & Gazelle, 1999; Fujiki, Brinton, Hart, & Fitzgerald, 1999; Gertner, Rice, & Hadley, 1994). Typically developing students may not view classmates with language impairments as valuable group members.

Summary of Barriers to Cooperation

Cooperative work settings may be most difficult for the students who need them the most. The deck seems stacked against students with language impairments due to their impaired language, depressed academic achievement, solitary social goals, poor social skills, and limited social acceptance and friendships. "Simply placing students together in social contexts will not ensure that they will interact" (Nelson, 1998, p. 170). Research has demonstrated that placing a student with a language impairment into a group will most likely lead to that student's exclusion (Brinton et al., 1997). Careful scaffolding is necessary to help students with language impairments take advantage of cooperative groups.

Breaking Down the Barriers

Educational teams can help students with language impairments to find a place within group interactions. Since students with language impairments form a heterogeneous population, efforts must be geared to the needs of each student. Some students with language impairments will do well in groups with little support, but others may require considerable support to be successful (Brinton et al., 2000). There are many points where educational teams may intervene to enable a student with a language impairment to get around barriers to inclusion. We have labeled several target areas including language comprehension and production, social goals, and specific social skills. Each of these areas is elaborated upon below. In addition, there are a number of ways that educational teams can manipulate the group structure to enhance the participation of students with language impairments.

Some of the intervention targets and procedures that we suggest require that a student work individually or in a small group with an SLP or other professional. The irony of needing to work individually in order to learn to work in a group is not lost on us! It is our experience, however, that supporting the real inclusion of a student with a language impairment in a group may require a variety of service delivery methods, a great deal of patience, and considerable time and perseverance. Evidence from a meta-analysis of social skills programs indicates that less successful programs do not spend enough time or provide the comprehensive array of methods required (Gresham, Sugai, & Horner, 2001). There are no easy solutions.

Language Comprehension and Production

As indicated earlier, communication skills are critical to successful group interaction. The effects of language impairments are pervasive and persistent, and will almost assuredly undermine communication when a student is placed in a group setting. Each student with a language impairment will need intervention aimed at facilitating language expression and/or comprehension on a general level. In addition, there are several areas of language that may be targeted specifically to help a student work in a group.

First, students with language impairments may benefit from a more intense "preparatory set" than most typically developing students require. For example, a student with a language impairment may benefit from knowing the objective of the group task, the makeup of the group, the time allowed for the work, his or her role in the work, and the expected product of the group before general instructions are provided for the group. Understanding the structure of the group may provide a framework in which students with language impairments can interpret the language of their peers. Some students with language impairments experience anxiety as they approach group work, which may have a negative impact on their ability to communicate effectively. Knowing about the task and demands ahead of time may ease the anxiety and free up cognitive resources to focus on language comprehension and production.

Students with language impairments will likely miss some of the content of group talk as members discuss how to approach the task. Thus, these students may benefit from a few strategies or clues about how to approach the task the group will be working on ahead of time. Some notion about possible steps to accomplish the task may support comprehension of peers' comments. Students with language impairments may also benefit from some practice formulating their ideas about a project and asking and responding to questions that might emerge from the group.

When cooperative groups are assigned specific tasks, there may be new lexical items introduced in conjunction with an academic unit. Typically developing group members may pick up these new words quickly, but students with language impairments may need much more exposure before they become familiar with the vocabulary items. Intervention procedures designed to teach new vocabulary words may support both comprehension and production in group work. It is especially important to help students with language impairments understand the appropriate use of new words in the context of the academic content area and the assigned task.

In summary, a language impairment is likely to hinder a student's participation in groups. Students with language impairments may have trouble keeping pace with the rapid exchange of ideas among group members and may struggle to formulate and express their own thoughts. Careful preparation in a few areas may reduce the language demands and facilitate the ability of a student with a language impairment to contribute to the group. These areas include the structure of the group, the nature of the task, and the vocabulary needed to talk about the task.

Social Motivation: It's Fun to Work with Other Kids

In any interactional context, in addition to the stated goal of the activity, students have social motivations (see Chapter 1 for a discussion of underlying motivations, activity goals, and intervention objectives). These motivations vary from situation to situation depending on a number of factors. For example, when playing games with peers, students may have goals ranging from dominating, to winning, to improving skills, to forming relationships, to avoiding humiliation (Taylor & Asher, 1984). Ideally, students working in groups should have personal social motivations that foster cooperation. These motivations might include mastering subject matter, solving problems, forming and maintaining relationships, and sharing with others. Having a friend is a concrete attainment that is motivating for many. Friendship is both compelling and encompassing enough that most learning situations can be tied to that one motivating factor. It is particularly important that students with language impairments have social motivations that include interacting positively with others. Students who have social motivations of avoiding interaction are not likely to respond well even to the most expertly executed efforts to include them in groups. They need intervention aimed at directing their social needs more positively.

Although positive social motivation may be a desired outcome, it is not advisable to target individual social objectives explicitly (Taylor & Asher, 1984). It will do little good to attempt to foist social objectives on another individual. (We are reminded of an instance in our youth when a frustrated mother dropped her petulant adolescent and his friend off at an amusement park with the injunction, "Have fun or I'll kill you!"). It is feasible, however, to present possibilities implicitly and suggest ideas that may lead students to rethink their social goals. For example, Max wants to work alone if possible. When he plays games, he wants to win. He is determined to be first when taking turns in an activity; first in line to go to class, first in line for lunch, first in line to get a drink. Still, he appears interested in other students and seems to want to be accepted. His teacher and SLP look for moments to help him see that cooperating with his peers in groups can be satisfying. Max's clinician tells stories and directs role-plays where a solitary student joins in a group. She notes, "The boy wants to join the group. It's fun to play with other people." When Max avoids his peers, his clinician structures his entry into the group and adds, "It's fun to work with other people." When Max plays a game with classmates, his clinician helps him reflect on his participation, notes any cooperative behavior, and compliments him saying, "You played with Tom and Mary. It looked like fun." A moment often comes when Max cannot be first in line. His clinician introduces a concept new to Max, "What if you *let* Lucy be first in line this one time? That would make her happy. How would you feel?" Gradually, Max comes to view interaction differently. Interacting positively in games becomes important to him, and his day is not ruined if he's not first in line. These changes do not occur in isolation, however. They are associated with Max's improving social skills and the resulting success in group work.

Social Skills

Even if students with language impairments have basic social goals in harmony with positive peer interactions, they also need adequate social skills to work cooperatively in groups. In fact, social skills are probably as important as linguistic skills in facilitating group interaction. A few years ago, we evaluated a group of students with language impairments. We considered their language skills and then we obtained social profiles on each student using the Teacher Behavioral Rating Scale (TBRS; Hart & Robinson, 1996). This scale consists of two questionnaires containing 161 items focusing on several behavioral subtypes. We then placed each student in carefully structured cooperative groups with two other typically developing students. We found that their social profiles, more than their language levels, predicted their behavior in the group context. Students whose social behavior reflected withdrawn, reticent profiles tended to be inactive in the group; students whose profiles suggested reactive or relational aggression tended to disrupt the group work. In contrast, students with stronger social skills functioned quite well in the group context, despite their impaired language skills (Brinton et al., 2000).

The results of this study supported the idea that, "cooperative group social skills instruction should be the backbone of cooperative learning experiences" (Prater, Bruhl, & Serna, 1998, p. 170). We can identify some specific social behaviors critical to group inclusion that may be problematic for students with language impairments. These behaviors include entering group interaction, responding to the bids and actions of others through validating comments, and staying with the play (work). These are certainly not the only behaviors that are important to group interaction, but they are basic, they are valued by peers (Goldstein & Morgan, 2002), and they lend themselves well to intervention procedures, even for young students.

Gaining Access to Social Activities

Getting into the Group

Picture yourself walking into an evening reception following a professional meeting. You are alone, but you see several groups of people chatting and laughing together. You are there to network, therefore, your task is to select a group to join and to become part of the conversation within that group. You look around the room, deciding which group to join. If you don't know which group to join immediately, you may get something to eat or drink while you stall for time. Perhaps you see someone you know in one of the groups, or someone you would like to meet. Maybe you overhear a snippet of conversation that sounds interesting to you. You select a group. You walk over to that group. You may hover a bit. You may watch and listen for a moment, waiting for a pause. Perhaps you greet the group members or introduce yourself to members you do not know. Most likely, you already know at least some of the group members, so you listen to the conversation to determine the topic and flow. You wait for an opportunity to add something new about the topic, agree with a previous comment, or ask a related question. Other group members acknowledge your comment, respond to your question, or invite your input. You attend to the conversation, respond to the input of others, and ask more questions. Other group members respond to you as well. You're in!

Most of the time the group access process is quick and smooth. Other times it is more challenging. In the previous scenario, if one does not move fairly quickly toward a group, one can be left alone holding a canapé and feeling rather awkward. The process described is similar for a student joining a group of students at work or play. Students approach a group, see what is going on, and join in. The ability to gain access to a group is important in social development (Black & Hazen, 1990; Corsaro, 1979, 1981; Dodge, Schlundt, Schocken, & Delugach, 1983; Hazen & Black, 1989; Putallaz & Gottman, 1981). Typically developing students usually gain access to groups easily and quickly. Students with language impairments, on the other hand, find this task very difficult. They may avoid groups altogether, or they may hover and watch without joining in (Brinton et al., 1997; Craig & Washington, 1993). In fact, students with language impairments may not join in groups even when invited to do so (Brinton et al.).

A Procedure for Facilitating Group Access

Students with language impairments may not understand what is required to join in ongoing group activity. They may need exposure to, and practice with, the steps involved. We have experimented with the following procedure to facilitate entry into play or work groups for elementary school students with language impairments. We usually work with a group of three students in these tasks.

1. *Introduce the social objective.* The clinician explains that sometimes people are doing things together and you want to join in. She emphasizes that it

is fun to play or work with other people and discusses how to choose a group by noticing what other students are doing or talking about.

2. *Walk.* The clinician manipulates toys to demonstrate that you can't play with people if you're not close to them. The students act out trying to determine what other students are doing when they are across the room from them. They walk closer to each other and try it again with more success. (Some students may need help determining just how close they should stand or sit near other students.) The clinician writes the word *walk* on a 5 × 7 inch card and draws a stick figure walking above it. The students manipulate toys and act out approaching groups in a number of different scenarios.

3. *Watch.* The clinician explains that after you walk near a group, you need to watch what is going on (this may be a difficult concept for students who are impulsive or disruptive). The clinician demonstrates using toys and acting out the scenario. She helps the students act out noticing a group at play or work, walking toward the group, and watching what the group is doing in a variety of different contexts. The clinician writes *watch* on a 5 × 7 inch card and draws two eyes above the word. The clinician uses the cards to cue the students as they act out walking near a group and watching what the group is doing.

4. *Talk.* The clinician emphasizes the strategy of joining the ongoing play or work by contributing something that supports the activity. This may not prove to be an easy task, and the clinician needs to present many different strategies, highlighting verbal contributions. Some of these include making a positive comment about what others are doing (e.g., "You're building a good tower"), offering a suggestion (e.g., "You could use a stick to dig"), asking a question (e.g., "Where's the door to the house?"), and helping (e.g., placing a block on the building the group is working on). The clinician writes *talk* on a 5 × 7 inch card, and draws a picture of stick figures talking together above the word. The clinician uses the cards to cue walking toward the group, watching, and joining in the activity. The talk step requires repeated exposure and experience.

5. *Try again.* The clinician stresses the idea that one's first bid may not be accepted by the group, and one should expect to keep trying. The students practice these steps using toys to act out scenarios and also acting out scenarios themselves. The clinician asks two students to coach a third using the cards as the third student tries to join them in play or work. The clinician also acts out joining the group.

6. *Reflect.* After such a scenario has been acted out, the clinician recaps what has happened and discusses what works. After the students know the steps well, the clinician may illustrate how important the steps are by purposely violating the steps and then inviting the students to correct her. For example, the three students sit at a table putting a puzzle together. The clinician stands in the corner and says, "That looks like fun. I want to do puzzles with them." The students call to her, "Walk!" When she approaches the table, she disrupts the activity by grabbing materials. The students correct her, saying, "No! Watch us!" She watches for a minute when one student prompts her, "Now say something nice!" After a number of trials, the clinician removes the cards and simply reminds the students of the steps verbally. In subsequent activities, the clinician's prompts are limited to encouraging students to join a group, "Go work with the group at the green table. You know what to do."

What to Expect

Based on our experience, we expect students with language impairments to learn to verbalize and act out the steps for gaining access to groups within about six weeks (four 15-minute sessions a week targeting access and other social-language goals). In other words, they will learn *what* to do relatively quickly. Learning *when* to do it and *how* to adjust it for different situations will require more time and effort. Prompts and encouragement in real work and play settings can be helpful (e.g., in class, "Look, those kids are playing a game. You go play with them. Remember the steps to join in"). In subsequent activities, the clinician may call attention to the entry strategies by reinforcing their use. For example, if the clinician observes a student joining a playgroup at recess, she may later note:

> I noticed that Tim and Mary and Jose were playing four square at recess. I noticed that you went to play with them. You walked over to them. You watched them play for a minute, and then you asked for a turn. You played with them till the bell rang. You did a great job. It looked like fun.

When a student successfully joins a group task in the classroom, the clinician may also draw the student's attention to successful entry:

> I saw that your group was working on the math quiz when you got here today. I noticed that you walked to your group, and you sat down with them. You looked at what they were doing, and you gave an idea about the problem. You did a good job working with your group.

Responding to Others

Validating Comments

When interacting in a group, it is extremely important to be responsive to other group members. That is, it is important to respond to others' questions and bids, to acknowledge their contributions and periodically offer support and approval. Validating comments are one mechanism whereby group members can positively respond to others. The most obvious type of validating comment is a personal compliment ("You're smart"). For the purposes of our work, we use a much broader definition for validating comments, however. In essence, we consider any comment that acknowledges the attributes, actions, or feelings of others in a positive way to be validating. These comments include compliments on actions ("Good job," "Nice catch," "You're going to win"), offers of encouragement ("You almost made it," "You'll get it next time," "You can do it"), sympathy or consolation ("Oh, that happens to me too," "Too bad, but it'll be okay," "Don't feel bad"), neutral or positive comments on actions ("You got two of them done," "You're drawing a circle," "You chose a red one"), offers to help ("I'll get you a pencil," "I'll color that for you," "Do you need this eraser?"), and social acknowledgments ("Thank you," "You're welcome," "Sorry").

Well-accepted (popular) students tend to produce validating comments in interactions with peers, but many students with language impairments may have difficulty doing so. It may be that they are not attending to their peers closely enough to notice their actions and attributes. It may be that their communication systems are already taxed in peer discourse and they do not concentrate on "nonessentials." It is most likely, however, that a dearth of validating comments reflects a nonresponsive interactional pattern often observed in these students. Peers value positive feedback, and facilitating the production of validating comments is a way to increase a student's connection with others in the group. The process a student goes through in making a validating comment may be at least as important as the comment itself. The student must tune into the behavior of other group members and adjust his or her contribution accordingly. This is essential to cooperation and acceptance within a group.

A Procedure for Facilitating Validating Comments

Many students with language impairments need encouragement to produce validating comments, since they are not accustomed to doing so. Some intervention programs emphasize these kinds of behaviors, especially personal compliments.

We are a little wary of teaching personal compliments because the application of these comments can be quite complex. (Misapplied personal compliments can go awry and do more harm than good. Consider the student at a bus stop who says, "I like your shirt" to every person she sees.) Since traditional compliments (e.g., "Your hair looks good") may not be critically important in the context of cooperative groups, we concentrate on comments that describe, applaud, or encourage the actions of others. The following steps, which overlap in terms of time, are helpful:

1. *Define.* The clinician helps students understand the nature of validating comments and defines them as *saying something nice* within a specific context. She directly discusses the various types of comments and when they may be used within a scenario she acts out with toys. More importantly, she indirectly identifies and highlights validating comments within ongoing activities.

2. *Notice.* The clinician engages the students in activities and games that require them to observe the actions of others. Initially, these games may be simple, such as watching a student draw cards with different shapes and putting thumbs up whenever the red circle appears.

3. *Say something nice.* The clinician sets up group activities and games. She stresses saying something nice about the contributions of others. Activities include board games where students comment on the turns of others ("Good move," "You got a two," "Almost," "Maybe next time") and work projects such as making a group collage ("You're using pink," "Good coloring," "You need this glitter?"). The clinician may need to prompt and reinforce students initially to help them to recognize what a validating comment is and to encourage their production of validating comments. The clinician's prompts are gradually reduced and eventually replaced by occasional passing comments such as, "That was a nice thing to say."

4. *Emotion understanding.* The clinician stresses recognizing and anticipating the emotional reactions of others to validating comments. She emphasizes how validating comments make others feel (happy, encouraged, better). These attempts to sensitize students to the emotions of others are embedded within cooperative activities.

What to Expect

Again, based on our experience, we expect some students with language impairments to increase their production of validating comments within six weeks of intervention, at least in structured cooperative settings. Generalization beyond structured groups will require ongoing effort. We have also come to expect these procedures to increase the cooperative participation of students with language impairments within groups as they become better attuned to their peers' contributions. Ongoing emphasis on the importance of each individual's contribution to the group's success should reinforce validating comments. In addition, we have also noticed that as students produce more validating comments, they become more sensitive to, and more eager to, receive them from others.

Sustained Cooperation

Staying with the Play

Students with language impairments who successfully gain access to groups may not understand that they need to remain with the group for a period of time (Brinton et al., 1997). For example, students with language impairments may wander from group to group at recess or free time without staying with the group long enough to become fully integrated (Fujiki et al., 2001). Students who are assigned to cooperative work groups may withdraw from the group interaction as well. For example, Max moved away from the group to work on a project of his own. Even students who stay within the group physically may withdraw from the interaction to the extent that they are not really part of the group at all (Brinton et al., 1997). It may be the case that students with language impairments become overwhelmed in groups and retreat from group interaction because it is just too difficult for them. It is also possible that they have had so little positive experience within groups that they do not understand the cooperative nature of group work. In any event, for students with language impairments to take advantage of collaborative contexts, they need to learn to stay with the interaction, even when it becomes challenging.

A Procedure for Staying with the Play

Procedures designed to help students with language impairments stick with group interactions are embedded into other procedures and activities. In other words, staying with the play or work becomes a component of other group tasks. The following activities may be useful:

1. *Stay.* The clinician may add a step to the procedures described above to enhance access. The four steps then become *walk, watch, talk,* and *stay.* The terms *work* or *play* may be more suitable for older students. This

introduces the idea that there is an expectation that group members will stay together until the completion of an activity or assignment.

2. *Cooperate.* A student's withdrawal from a group is often precipitated by a lack of participation and collaboration with other group members. Activities designed to help students with language impairments cooperate with their peers increase the chance that they will stay with the group work. To stress cooperation through the conclusion of an activity, the clinician may adapt procedures described by Oden and Asher (1977) using simple commercial games. Commercial games can be useful because the duration of the group task is delineated. That is, it is clear when the game is over and when it is not. Using the game context, the clinician employs an instruct, practice, and review format. Initially, the clinician lets the student with a language impairment play a game with two typically developing peers. Then, the clinician meets with the student with a language impairment to learn strategies to "make the game more fun." These strategies include observing the turn structure of the game, managing the game materials appropriately, and assisting others as needed. The student with a language impairment then plays a game with two different peers without the clinician's input.

3. *Reflect.* Subsequently, the clinician and the student review the game (which may be videotaped) and note instances where the student cooperated and how the cooperation made the game more fun. The clinician highlights the fact that all players cooperate until the game is completed. The instruction component is phased out as the student plays more adeptly with peers. (Other social-language skills such as making validating comments can also be included in this format.)

What to Expect

We have observed that students tend to stay with the play longer as they become integrated into that play. They rarely leave formal game situations once they understand the cooperative nature of the activity. For some students, it may take some time and effort to get to that point, particularly if students do not understand the basics of turn exchange or cannot tolerate losing a game. We have also found that students tend to stay with less structured play (free time, recess) groups longer if they can negotiate a role within that play. They may need occasional reminders to stay with a group or to employ specific prosocial behaviors that support cooperative play.

Structuring Groups

Cooperative groups rarely just happen by themselves. Rather, they are usually structured in a way to foster collaboration and joint endeavor. There is extensive literature explaining various ways to organize cooperative groups for various purposes and for different ages of students. This literature details methods to establish the basic elements of cooperative groups described by Johnson et al. (1998), including positive interdependence, individual accountability, face-to-face interaction among group members, interpersonal skills, and group processing. In addition to the valuable ideas available in this literature, we would like to highlight some considerations for putting together groups that include students with language impairments.

Positive Interdependence

Johnson et al. (1998) note the importance of assigning groups a clear, measurable task. It is particularly important that students with language impairments understand what the group is supposed to accomplish. Comprehension checks may be necessary to assure that a language impairment has not blocked their understanding of the group goal. The types of projects selected are also important. Projects should be compelling enough to engage students with language impairments who are wary of groups. In addition, Goldstein and Morgan (2002) note that novel and exciting projects can "increase the rewards and minimize the cost" (p. 20) for typical students who interact with students with disabilities. It is also helpful to begin cooperative groups with projects that are not only interesting, but also fairly intuitive. In other words, the project needs to appear doable, even to the least skilled member of the group. As Max's group demonstrated, a novel, doable project is not, in and of itself, sufficient to include students with language impairments. It is, however, an important step in encouraging positive interdependence.

Another way to encourage positive interdependence is to assign each member of a group a role that is important to the project completion. Roles should be interdependent (Johnson & Johnson, 1999) in that each member's work should depend, to some extent, on their peers' fulfilling their roles. Role assignment alone may not influence the participation of students with language impairments, however (Brinton et al., 2000). Remember that Max did not effectively carry out his role of materials manager when he worked with Kevin and Troy. Students with language impairments may need extra support to understand not only the nature of their roles, but also the importance of their roles. They must recognize the fact that others depend on their taking responsibility for their assignments. It is particularly important for these students to rotate through a series of roles, lest they become rigidly identified with a role or come to view themselves as limited to a specific role.

It may also be helpful to prepare the group members who work with students with language impairments to accommodate each member's needs within the group. For example, students with language impairments may need extra time to respond to questions or help formulating written comments. It may be helpful to coach peers who collaborate with students with language impairments. The most helpful peers are those who can facilitate each member's participation without taking over the task.

Individual Accountability

Each member of a cooperative group must feel that his or her contribution matters. Building individual accountability for each student's work into the group process highlights the idea that each student's participation is valued. Johnson and Johnson (1999) describe a number of ways to establish individual accountability including keeping the size of the group small and assessing each student's contribution individually. We have found that groups of three students are manageable and not as susceptible to splitting into smaller groups. Mandel (2003) notes, however, that three-person groups can be problematic because they may result in a two-versus-one situation in decision making. Here again, it may be important to help typically developing peers understand the importance of considering each member's opinions in order to arrive at a consensus.

With regard to assessing each student's work, this needs to be done carefully to avoid highlighting the differences in students' abilities and accomplishments. Different assessment measures may be needed for different students in the group, and students with language impairments may require individually tailored evaluations of their work. It may not be wise to assess contributions in a way that results are in any way transparent to the group as a whole. In other words, when skill levels are variable, it may be best for the evaluation criteria and results to be kept between the teacher and each student.

Face-to-Face Interaction

"Group members need to do real work together" (Johnson et al., 1998, p. 5:16). That is, they need to have meaningful discussions and action on joint endeavors. For students with language impairments, small groups are the most conducive to their involvement in the work. The composition of the group is also important. The level of participation of students with language impairments is highly dependent on the people with whom they work (Brinton et al. 2000). Some typically developing peers are more accepting than others. Some students will invite a student with a language impairment to participate and scaffold that student's contribution. In contrast, other students may be impatient and quick to ridicule or exclude. Goldstein and Morgan (2002) note that students are more likely to work cooperatively with friends, and by the same token, working cooperatively fosters friendship formation.

Students with language impairments, then, could be expected to collaborate more readily with their friends. But there's the rub; students with language impairments may not have any reciprocal friends within their classes (Fujiki, Brinton, Morgan, et al., 1999). The next best choice may be to group students with language impairments with peers who accept them as playmates. It may be helpful for teachers to conduct peer acceptance and friendship measures on the class as a whole, using methods such as those employed by Fujiki, Brinton, Morgan, et al., or Gertner, et al. (1994). In these measures, students might rate how well they like to interact with every other student in the class as well as list their three best friends in the class. These measures can be performed in a way that the results are not evident to the class (Kaczmarek, 2002). If a student cannot be grouped with friends, she can at least be grouped with peers who report that they like to play with her. Such peers are most likely to provide support and encouragement.

Another consideration in fostering interaction is proximity. We routinely place students with language impairments between their peers in group tasks. The students may move around, but they tend to gravitate back to their assigned seats, and it is some advantage to be placed in the middle of the action. Some students with language impairments may have difficulty understanding how close they should sit or stand to another student. For example, we worked with one first grader who tended to place herself so close to her peers that they felt uncomfortable. It was helpful for her to have a concrete notion of how close was too close. Her teacher specified an appropriate distance between the girl and her peers and then helped her monitor this space in classroom activities.

Group Processing

Group processing refers to the time groups spend considering the process itself (Johnson et al., 1998). This is the recap or debriefing aspect of group work. Group processing demands a type of "meta-group" skill, an ability to step outside of the group interaction and reflect upon it. Students with language impairments might need extra support with this task. We have found that when we address issues of group processing with groups including students with language impairments, typical group members tend to be the ones reflecting on the level and quality of collaboration. In fact, students with language impairments may respond "Yes" to questions such as, "Did everyone work on the project?" when they have done little but sit and watch.

Students with language impairments may be better equipped to engage in group processing if they have a good understanding of the group goal and the nature of the group process. As indicated earlier, this warrants special attention and may be part of a preparatory set for participating in cooperative groups. In preparing these students to work in groups, and in helping groups reflect on the group process following tasks, it is important to stress the positive behaviors that contribute to group work. It is helpful to call a student's attention to the behaviors that he or she displays that further group process. When we review videotapes of group work with students with language impairments, we concentrate on things the students did well, and draw their attention to the reactions of other group members to these positive behaviors.

Summary

The inclusion of students with language impairments into cooperative groups can be supported by organizing the structure of the group in a way to preserve the basic elements of cooperative work. Keeping groups relatively small and placing students with language impairments with peers who like to play with them fosters positive interdependence and promotes face-to-face interaction. Assigning novel, compelling tasks that are easily understood also fosters collaboration between students of differing ability levels. Managing the seating and proximity of group members helps to place the student with a language impairment in the midst of the interaction. Making sure that students with language impairments understand the nature and importance of their specific roles in the interaction enhances their appreciation of their individual accountability in group tasks. Working individually with a student who has a language impairment to highlight that student's positive contributions to the group process helps the student determine what behaviors work best. It is important to remember that the most carefully structured group may not result in a positive experience unless the student has the communication and social skills to be a contributing member. It is essential, therefore, to combine careful structuring of groups with intervention designed to support language and establish specific social-language behaviors that are important for group work.

What about Max?

The periscope-building task that Max, Kevin, and Troy work on incorporates several of the defining characteristics of cooperative learning teams as described by Johnson et al. (1998). Positive interdependence is encouraged by instigating a group goal in which the boys seem interested. Each boy is assigned a specific role. The boys are placed at a table in close proximity to each other with Max seated between Troy and Kevin. Individual accountability is built in, to some extent, when the instructor indicates she would determine each student's participation at the conclusion of the task. When the group has finished work, the instructor leads the group in a discussion of how well the group process works. Nevertheless, the structure of the group is not adequate to support Max's becoming an integral part of the group. Additional groups in which Max is included, with different partners, yield a similar pattern of interaction. It seems clear that Max is not prepared to take advantage of the benefits of working in cooperative groups.

Max is enrolled in an intervention program along with two first-grade girls, Annie and Mindy, who also have language impairments. The program lasts about 10 weeks, and each student is seen four times a week for about 15 minutes. In two of these sessions, Max, Annie, and Mindy work together. In one session, Max works with two typically developing boys from his class. These typical boys are randomly selected from a group, including most of the boys in the three first-grade classes in the school, whose parents have granted permission for their participation in the intervention. During this session, the clinician typically sets up a work activity or game and then lets the group manage the interaction without her input. In the final session of the week, Max works with the clinician one on one. Max's intervention targets include gaining access to ongoing peer interactions, making validating comments in group work and play, and staying with the work or play. His clinician looks for opportunities to guide Max's social goals toward cooperative interaction with others. She often reminds him, "It's fun to play (work) with other kids."

In the first session of the week, Max, Annie, and Mindy work on gaining access to a group. Although he has difficulty initially, Max learns about the steps to gain access and can verbalize these steps, with and then without, the use of the cards, within several weeks. The three students act out the steps with toys and in role-plays.

Although Max seems to want to interact with other students at recess, he tends to withdraw from the other members of a group. He works on making validating comments within the context of commercial games and in art projects. This is difficult for him at first. The clinician must sit at his shoulder and whisper prompts for him to repeat. Gradually, he begins to produce these comments on his own.

When Max first begins to play games in a group, he concentrates on winning and seems unaware of the needs of others. We consider it a breakthrough when Max is playing a game with Annie and Mindy one day and he makes a good move. He pauses, looks expectantly at them, and says, "You're supposed to say something nice!" Evidently, Max is beginning to understand the importance of group members' supporting each other in collaborative endeavors. His interactions with the peers in his third session of the week begin to improve. The day following the peer session, he views the video of the group with the clinician. She highlights his cooperative behaviors and encourages him to continue to do those things to "make the game (work) more fun." As Max works with different classmates in his peer sessions, it becomes clear that some students interact better with him than others. As might be expected, if peers are impatient and abrasive, Max does not do well in the group.

As indicated earlier, it is important to Max to be first in line, no matter what the context. As he becomes more responsive to other students in a group (e.g., watches what they are doing before he enters, makes validating comments about their actions), his clinician addresses his need to be first. She helps him choose to allow another student to be first. It's hard at first, but Max makes progress. Perhaps his "first obsession" reflects his feeling powerless in groups. As he feels more involved, he may find he has a place with his peers, even if it isn't at the head of a line.

At the end of ten weeks, Max's social profile is assessed as he works with three different cooperative groups in a structure similar to that described for his initial interaction with Troy and Kevin. Max's validating comments increase both in number and in type during intervention. Max works cooperatively the majority of the time in all three groups. He does not withdraw from the groups, and he acts much like his peers. No "scissor fight" incidents occur. A sociometric profile shows a very slight improvement at the end of ten weeks as compared to pretreatment. An additional measure documents decreased loneliness at school. Before intervention, no student named Max as a friend in a friendship measure. After ten weeks, one student names him as a friend.

Max seems better prepared to participate in cooperative groups following a relatively brief period of indirectly addressing his social goals while directly targeting specific social and social-language skills. Max's social functioning in his school classroom seems to be headed in a positive direction. The intervention program seems worth the time and clinical resources. Max's intervention program has just begun, however. If he is to take advantage of the benefits of cooperative learning contexts, he will most likely require support for his social-language skills over an extended period of time, perhaps through high school (Brinton & Fujiki, 2004; Brinton, Robinson, & Fujiki, 2004). We learn from his case that facilitating the inclusion of students with language impairments in cooperative group structures requires planning, effort, and time.

Conclusion

Collaborative learning contexts can provide a powerful means to integrate students with language impairments within the social and academic fabric of the classroom. The notion that students with language impairments should be learning with and from their typically developing peers is intuitive. In practice, however, students with language impairments often experience difficulty working in groups. Their impaired language ability and limited social competence combine to undermine their involvement in group activities. It is possible, however, to structure cooperative groups to support the successful inclusion of students with language impairments. In addition, specific intervention methods and techniques may help students with language impairments develop the positive social goals and behaviors that make successful group participation possible. Facilitating the inclusion of students with language impairments in peer groups is a long-term process that requires careful planning and commitment on the part of educational teams.

Acknowledgments

We would like to acknowledge the support of the David O. McKay School of Education for much of the research that is cited in our chapter. We would also like to recognize our colleagues who have been involved in many of these studies: Craig Hart, Marriage, Family, and Human Development, Brigham Young University; and Matthew Spackman, Department of Psychology, Brigham Young University. We are also indebted to our students, who have assisted in the work cited: Jill Allen, Shelley Jones Burton, JoLyn Carter, Diane Clarke, April Fitzgerald, Andrea Hall Comeau, Julie Hanton, Kerstine Hart,

Lisa Higbee, Ted Isaacson, Shane James, Lara McKee, Elizabeth Montague Skinner, Donna Nelson, Janet Pearson, Lee Robinson, Julie Campbell Spencer, Connie Summers, Cindy Todd, and Valyne Anderson. Special thanks to our colleagues in the schools who made it possible to conduct the studies reported: Rebecca Garda and Janet Howe from Jordan School District, Sandy, Utah; and Ginger Pierce from Alpine School District, American Fork, Utah.

References

Asher, S. R., & Gazelle, H. (1999). Loneliness, peer relations, and language disorders. *Topics in Language Disorders, 19*(2), 16–33.

Black, B., & Hazen, N. L. (1990). Social status and patterns of communication in acquainted and unacquainted preschool children. *Developmental Psychology, 26,* 379–387.

Brinton, B., & Fujiki, M. (2004). Social and affective factors in children with language impairment: Implications for literacy learning. In C. A. Stone, E. R. Silliman, B. J. Ehren, & K. Apel (Eds.), *Handbook of language and literacy development and disorders* (pp. 130–153). New York: Guilford.

Brinton, B., Fujiki, M., & Higbee, L. (1998). Participation in cooperative learning activities by children with specific language impairment. *Journal of Speech, Language, and Hearing Research, 41,* 1193–1206.

Brinton, B., Fujiki, M., & McKee, L. (1998). The negotiation skills of children with specific language impairment. *Journal of Speech, Language, and Hearing Research, 41,* 927–940.

Brinton, B., Fujiki, M., Montague, E. C., & Hanton, J. L. (2000). Children with language impairment in cooperative work groups: A pilot study. *Language, Speech, and Hearing Services in Schools, 31,* 252–264.

Brinton, B., Fujiki, M., Spencer, J. C., & Robinson, L. A. (1997). The ability of children with specific language impairment to access and participate in an ongoing interaction. *Journal of Speech, Language, and Hearing Research, 40,* 1011–1025.

Brinton, B., Robinson, L. A., & Fujiki, M. (2004). Description of a program for social language intervention: If you can have a conversation, you can have a relationship. *Language, Speech, and Hearing Services in Schools, 35,* 283–290.

Corsaro, W. A. (1979). We're friends, right? Children's use of access rituals in a nursery school. *Language and Society, 8,* 315–336.

Corsaro, W. A. (1981). Friendship in the nursery school: Social organization in a peer environment. In S. R. Asher & J. M. Gottman (Eds.), *The development of children's friendships* (pp. 207–241). Cambridge, MA: Cambridge University Press.

Craig, H. K., & Washington, J. A. (1993). The access behaviors of children with specific language impairment. *Journal of Speech and Hearing Research, 36,* 322–336.

Dodge, K. A., Schlundt, D. C., Schocken, I., & Delugach, J. D. (1983). Social competence and children's sociometric status: The role of peer group entry strategies. *Merrill-Palmer Quarterly, 29,* 309–336.

Fujiki, M., Brinton, B., & Clarke, D. (2002). Emotion regulation in children with specific language impairment. *Language, Speech, and Hearing Services in Schools, 33,* 102–111.

Fujiki, M., Brinton, B., Hart, C. H., & Fitzgerald, A. (1999). Peer acceptance and friendship in children with specific language impairment. *Topics in Language Disorders, 19*(2), 34–48.

Fujiki, M., Brinton, B., Isaacson, T., & Summers, C. (2001). Social behaviors of children with language impairment on the playground: A pilot study. *Language, Speech, and Hearing Services in Schools, 32,* 101–113.

Fujiki, M., Brinton, B., Morgan, M., & Hart, C. (1999). Withdrawn and sociable behavior of children with specific language impairment. *Language, Speech, and Hearing Services in Schools, 30,* 183–195.

Fujiki, M., Brinton, B., & Todd, C. M. (1996). Social skills of children with specific language impairment. *Language, Speech, and Hearing Services in Schools, 27,* 195–202.

Fujiki, M., Spackman, M. P., Brinton, B., & Hall, A. (2004). The relationship of language and emotion regulation skills to reticence in children with specific language impairment. *Journal of Speech, Language, and Hearing Research, 47,* 637–646.

Gertner, B. L., Rice, M. L., & Hadley, P. A. (1994). Influence of communicative competence on peer preferences in a preschool classroom. *Journal of Speech and Hearing Research, 37,* 913–923.

Goldstein, H., & Morgan, L. (2002). Social interaction and models of friendship development. In H. Goldstein, L. A. Kaczmarek, & K. M. English (Eds.), *Promoting social communication: Children with developmental disabilities from birth to adolescence* (pp. 5–25). Baltimore: Brookes.

Gresham, F. M., Sugai, G., & Horner, R. H. (2001). Meta-analysis of social skill program outcomes. *Exceptional Children, 67,* 331–344.

Grove, J., Conti-Ramsden, G., & Donlan, C. (1993). Conversational interaction and decision-making in children with specific language impairment. *European Journal of Disorders of Communication, 28,* 141–152.

Hart, K. I., Fujiki, M., Brinton, B., & Hart, C. H. (2004). The relationship between social behavior and severity of language impairment. *Journal of Speech, Language, and Hearing Research, 47,* 647–662.

Hart, C. H., & Robinson, C. C. (1996). *Teacher Behavioral Rating Scale (TBRS).* Unpublished teacher questionnaire, Brigham Young University, Provo, UT.

Harter, S. (1999). *The construction of the self.* New York: Guilford Press.

Hazen, N. L., & Black, B. (1989). Preschool peer communication skills: The role of social status and interaction context. *Child Development, 60,* 867–876.

Johnson, D. W., & Johnson, R. T. (1999). *Learning together and alone: Cooperative, competitive, and individualistic learning* (5th ed.). Needham Heights, MA: Allyn and Bacon.

Johnson, D. W., Johnson, R. T., & Smith, K. A. (1998). *Active learning: Cooperating in the college classroom.* Edina, MN: Interaction Book Company.

Kaczmarek, L. A. (2002). Assessment of social-communicative competence. In H. Goldstein, L. A. Kaczmarek, & K. M. English (Eds.), *Promoting social communication: Children with developmental disabilities from birth to adolescence* (pp. 55–115). Baltimore, MD: Brookes.

Mandel, S. M. (2003). *Cooperative work groups preparing students for the real world.* Thousand Oaks, CA: Corwin Press.

Nelson, N. W. (1998). *Childhood language disorders in context: Infancy through adolescence* (2nd ed.). Boston: Allyn and Bacon.

Oden, S., & Asher, S. R. (1977). Coaching children in social skills for friendship making. *Child Development, 48,* 495–506.

Prater, M. A., Bruhl, S., & Serna, L. A. (1998). Acquiring social skills through cooperative learning and teacher-directed instruction. *Remedial and Special Education, 19*(3), 160–172.

Putallaz, M., & Gottman, J. M. (1981). An interaction model of children's entry into peer groups. *Child Development, 52,* 986–994.

Putnam, J. W. (1998). The movement toward teaching and learning in inclusive classrooms. In J. W. Putnam (Ed.), *Cooperative learning and strategies for inclusion* (2nd ed., pp. 1–16). Baltimore: Brookes.

Redmond, S. M., & Rice, M. L. (1998). The socioemotional behaviors of children with SLI: Social adaptation or social deviance? *Journal of Speech, Language, and Hearing Research, 41,* 688–700.

Rice, M. L., Sell, M. A., & Hadley, P. A. (1991). Social interactions of speech-and-language-impaired children. *Journal of Speech, Language, and Hearing Research, 34,* 1299–1307.

Slavin, R. E. (1995). *Cooperative learning* (2nd ed.). Boston: Allyn and Bacon.

Stevens, L. J., & Bliss, L. S. (1995). Conflict resolution abilities of children with specific language impairment and children with normal language. *Journal of Speech and Hearing Research, 38,* 599–611.

Taylor, A. R., & Asher, S. R. (1984). Children's goals in social competence: Individual differences in a game playing context. In T. Field, J. L. Roopnarine, & M. Segal (Eds.), *Friendship in normal and handicapped children* (pp. 53–78). Norwood, NJ: Ablex.

Chapter 8

There's More to Passing Than Knowing the Answers: Learning to Do School

Carol Westby

Introduction

When one thinks of students performing successfully in school, one generally thinks about students learning academic subject matter—doing reading and math at appropriate grade levels and moving along in the scope and sequence charts of the curriculum. Certain skills and knowledge are expected at different grade levels. Students in first grade learn sound-letter relationships and basic addition and subtraction facts; third graders read relatively fluently, produce coherent stories, and learn multiplication; fifth graders use reading to access science and social studies content, write expository paragraphs, and master division and fractions.

Students are generally referred for special services when they are not successfully acquiring the skills of the curriculum. Traditional testing may indicate if the student is significantly below expectations and qualifies for services, but it provides little information about how a student functions in the classroom. Federal mandates require that students with special needs have access to the general education curriculum, and this involves students doing more than simply sitting in the room completing assignments. Students must be able to interact with teachers and other students to achieve their educational goals and objectives. Even smaller, segregated settings involve social interactions that students may have difficulty negotiating, which can lead to negative impacts on academic learning. Some students who may perform adequately on norm-referenced tests of discrete skills and knowledge still may not function adequately in the classroom. Difficulties managing the social interactions of the classroom will impede both social development and academic learning. Teachers and speech-language pathologists (SLPs) need to understand the reasons why students are having difficulties achieving both academic and social competence.

What will it take for all students to acquire academic and social competence? To be successful, students must learn how to "do school," which involves more than acquiring the academic content curriculum. They must learn how to negotiate the multiple official and unofficial curricula of the classroom, which involve dealing with teachers, peers, and materials. Many aspects of doing school are implicit. For culturally/linguistically diverse students and students with learning disabilities, the implicitness of how to do school presents a roadblock to their acquiring the academic content of school (Delpit, 1988).

This chapter describes the components of learning to do school: the components of classroom scripts; the influence of disabilities and culture on doing school; and how the scripts for doing school change across the grades, particularly with respect to expectations for increasing self-regulation. Suggestions are given for collaborative strategies teachers and SLPs can use in classrooms to facilitate the ability of students with language impairments to be successful in doing school.

Learning to Do School

In the 1970s and 1980s, a number of researchers began to explore what was involved in doing school (Cahir & Kivac, 1981a, 1981b; Cazden, 1988; Eder, 1982; Green & Harker, 1988; Green & Wallet, 1981; McCollum, 1989; Mehan, 1979; Peterson & Wilkinson, 1984; Philips, 1983; Wilcox, 1982). They documented the structure of traditional lessons, the types of language used by teachers and students, and variations in teaching strategies with differing ability groups and differing socioeconomic and cultural/linguistic groups. More recently, researchers have been interested in exploring just how learning takes place within classrooms; how teachers scaffold interactions to facilitate students' mastery of content, how students with disabilities participate in classroom lessons, and how the values of a culture influence how lessons are taught (Cazden, 2001; Marton & Tsui, 2004; National Center for Education Statistics, 1996; Stigler & Hiebert, 1999).

Learning to do school requires that students master several curricula (Nelson, 1989):

1. The *official* curriculum is the outline of material that is to be learned at each grade level (i.e., the reading, math, writing, science, and social studies skills and knowledge that students are expected to master).

2. The *cultural* curriculum is the world knowledge that students must acquire if they are to become literate, educated members of their societies. This may include Hirsch's (2002) idea of cultural literacy (i.e., what one needs to know about history, literature, science, and religion to understand what one reads), but it also includes knowledge for functioning in daily experiences such as scripts for using fast-food restaurants, navigating buses and carpools, or engaging in holiday events.

3. The *de facto* curriculum is the academic knowledge required as a result of textbook choices made by the school or the materials the teacher uses to conduct lessons.

4. The *school* or *classroom* curriculum is the set of implicit and explicit rules that students must acquire to act appropriately in particular

classrooms, such as the length and detail expected in answers to teacher's questions.

5. The *hidden* curriculum is the set of expectations instructors have for determining who are considered the good or problem students in their classrooms, such as considering messy work a sign of a student not caring.

6. The *underground* curriculum consists of the rules for social interaction that determine peer attitudes and acceptance, such as considering students who show eagerness to learn as wanting to be "teacher's pets."

The first three of Nelson's curricula involve primarily academic-knowledge content; the second three involve primarily social-knowledge content. The curricula of schools can be defined as the things to be learned (academic knowledge) and the ways of learning (social knowledge; Cook-Gumperz & Gumperz, 1982). Much of this learning occurs in what are called *lessons*. Lessons can be defined as the products of interactions among teachers and students with texts and materials (Green, Weade, & Graham, 1988). Lesson formats or scripts vary from *ritualistic* to *flexible*. Ritualistic scripts are highly routinized, with little variation (e.g., drills). Flexible scripts allow for variations and rarities, such as discussing a specific problem or interacting with a classroom visitor (Erickson & Shultz, 1981; Gumperz, 1981; McDermott, 1978). For students' answers to be considered correct, the answers must be acceptable in both academic content and social form (Mehan, 1979). To understand what students must know to give correct answers, Creaghead (1992a) outlines how teachers must consider the following:

- The classroom scripts (what students must know about how to act in the classroom)

- The teacher's cues for defining and activating these scripts (how students know how to act in this classroom)

- The student's knowledge of the script and awareness of the teacher's cues (what students know about the scripts for this classroom—which cues the student notices and which ones he or she misses, what the student knows about the significance of these cues)

When a teacher refers a student who is not doing well in classroom activities, the SLP should consider the match between the student and classroom. This involves understanding the teacher, the classroom, and the identified student. For example, does the student (and his or her peers) know and respond to scripts and cues, such as the following:

- What you are supposed to do when you come into class in the morning

- What you have to do to get a turn in science class (math class, reading class)

- How you know if you have given a correct answer/an incorrect answer

- What the teacher says when the lesson is finished

- When you are allowed to talk in class

- What you are supposed to do if you need help

- What you are supposed to do when announcements come on the P.A. system

Teachers often do not make these scripts explicit and may not be fully aware of their own expectations of students. Students are expected to observe the social interactions and draw conclusions about the expectations. Students from culturally/linguistically diverse backgrounds may misinterpret the scripts because they have different expectations for what is to happen in school. For example, Native American students may expect to collaborate on a task, but their teacher might view this collaboration as cheating. Many students with language impairments find it difficult to integrate the multiple pieces of information necessary for interpreting classroom scripts. They must consider factors such as the situation or environment, the task, the content of the task, the persons involved, and the roles of the persons involved. Students with semantic-pragmatic disorders and Asperger syndrome experience particular difficulty in integrating all components of scripts. Many students with specific language impairments also exhibit deficits in social skills that limit their ability to participate fully in group activities (Brinton & Fujiki, 2004; Fujiki, Brinton, Robinson, & Watson, 1997). This becomes particularly problematic in science, where a great deal of content is often learned within the context of small-group activities that require students to negotiate roles and cooperate in integrating information.

As illustrated in Figure 8.1 on page 324, teachers and students draw simultaneously on two sets of procedural knowledge during lessons: (1) knowledge of the academic task structure, and (2) knowledge of the social participation structures (Erickson, 1982). Both areas are influenced by a variety of intrapersonal and interpersonal factors (Green et al., 1988). Teachers present academic

Figure 8.1   **Components of Lessons**

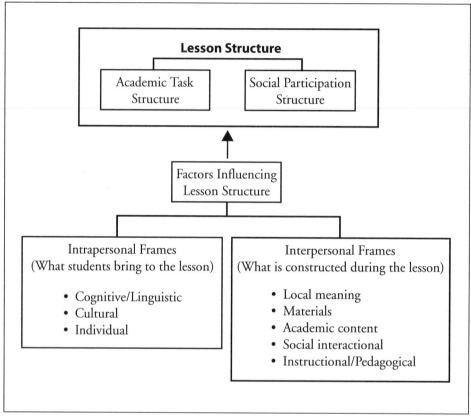

Source: Erickson (1982), Green et al. (1988)

content and simultaneously signal how the lesson is to be accomplished. Table 8.1 shows how teachers indicate to students the required sequence of the lesson, the steps and strategies for completing a task, the information content of the steps, and the physical materials. Along with these four aspects of the academic structure, teachers also direct students in the four components of social participation dealing with gatekeeping, turn allocation, timing, and simultaneity of actions.

In teaching and learning lessons, teachers and students construct both the academic and social scripts. The way teachers guide the construction of the social script influences what students can access in lessons and what they view as important to know and do. Teachers monitor what information is presented, signal how students are to participate, monitor the students' understanding of

Academic Structure and Social Participation
for Lessons from Different Subjects

Table 8.1

Academic Structure	
Type	**Example**
Sequence of the Lesson	**Math lesson** 1. Teacher models how to do a math problem. 2. Students work with manipulatives in small groups to complete several problems. 3. Students then complete a set of problems individually. 4. Students exchange papers to correct.
Steps and Strategies for Completing a Task	**Timeline of U.S. history, 1600 to present** 1. Students are assigned to centuries. 2. A computer timeline program is used to discover important events within each century. 3. Students select events to summarize and decide who will summarize each event. 4. Events are organized along a timeline.
Information Content of the Various Sequential Steps	**Science experiment with three components, each with different information** • Procedures: describe the steps in the experiment. • Results: describe observations. • Conclusion: explain the results.
Materials Used to Present and Complete Lessons	**Math lesson** Manipulatives such as Cuisenaire® Rods for understanding base numbers or plastic fraction pies

Continued on next page

Table 8.1—*Continued*

Social Participation	
Type	**Example**
Gatekeeping: Access of People and Other Information Sources during Lessons	Teachers, not students, may allocate communication rights.
Allocation of Communicative Rights and Obligations among the Various Partners	Who can talk, when, where, in what ways, with whom, for what purposes.
Sequencing and Timing of Interaction	Students answer in turn, wait to be called on, or answer as a group.
Simultaneous Actions of all Persons Engaged in Interaction during Lesson	In science class, each student in a group has a particular responsibility and the teacher circulates through the room observing and offering suggestions.

the academic content, and adjust the lesson content and social participation rules to ensure that students are acquiring the lesson content. Teachers must monitor both the group and individual students. Students with language impairments should be carefully monitored so they receive instruction that ensures they are meeting the goals and objectives of their individualized education programs (IEPs). General education teachers, however, tend to treat students with language impairments like all other students (McIntosh, Vaughn, Schumm, Haager, & Lee, 1993). Although this may suggest students are being accepted and treated fairly, it also indicates that they are not receiving the necessary differentiated instruction to meet their needs (Fletcher, Boss, & Johnson, 1999; Schumm, Moody, & Vaughn, 2000).

For students to participate in lessons, they must monitor and interpret the verbal and nonverbal actions of the teacher and other students while they monitor and interpret the content of the lesson. They must recognize the requirements for participation in the lessons as they evolve over time, as well as the requirements for their participation at any given point in the lesson. For students in both general education and special education classrooms, the more they participate during instruction, the greater their academic growth (Greenwood, Abbott, & Tapia, 2003). The degree to which teachers and students establish and maintain shared understanding of both the content and form of the social and academic scripts of the lesson is the degree to which the lesson will develop smoothly.

Observing Students in Classrooms

If lessons are to develop smoothly, teachers must understand what students bring to lessons and what lessons require. This necessitates an evaluation of students' strengths and needs and an analysis of lesson content and structure.

SLPs typically employ inside-out approaches to assessment: documenting students' cognitive and linguistic processing abilities and disabilities and the cultural values and beliefs they bring to the classroom. Inside-out assessment can make use of norm-referenced assessment tools, language sampling, and interviewing of students and their families. There is considerable developmental data available that can be used to determine the students' current developmental language levels in phonology, syntax, semantics, and discourse organization.

Teachers must also know how students use their language skills within the classroom context to further their learning. Consequently, assessment should also include an outside-in approach: noting the academic demands of the classroom and the characteristics of classroom social and academic scripts and other environmental influences on learning (Nelson, 1992). Although there is considerable information regarding students' development of language skills, there is less information available on how students acquire the knowledge and skills of classroom scripts and how environmental scripts and expectations may change over time. What might be adequate language skills at one grade level or in one lesson context may not be sufficient in another lesson context. For example, Nelson (1984) noted that between first and sixth grade, teachers' speech rates and mean length of utterance increased. SLPs are somewhat aware of how language skills link to the academic content at particular grade levels, but they are less likely to be aware of how expectations for participation and access of this information changes across grades—information which is essential for the outside-in aspect of student evaluation.

An outside-in evaluation for students should employ a multiple-lens approach (Silliman & Wilkinson, 1991). Such an approach considers (1) the overall context of the lesson, (2) the structure or organization of the lesson, (3) the interactional patterns used to get the lessons done, and (4) communication breakdowns experienced by individuals. Wide-angle and regular-lens views provide information about the context and overall structure of the classroom and classroom lesson—the lesson macrostructure. The wide-angle lens view considers the backgrounds of the persons involved and the context in which the lesson takes place, such as who is teaching, who is assisting, size of the room, adequacy of space, noise level, and the number of students in the room. The regular-lens view considers the structure of the activity—the components of the lesson and their sequence, how the teacher introduces the lesson, and what tasks the students are required to do in the lesson.

The information gained through the wide-angle and regular-lenses is necessary for interpreting the interaction patterns observed through the close-up lens. These patterns involve teachers and students in a given activity at a specific point in time. They include the ways students are invited to participate, the degree of complexity or abstraction of the questions teachers ask, how students respond to questions with varying levels of language complexity, and how teachers react to student responses. Using a micro close-up lens, the observer notes the types of social or academic breakdowns a student exhibits and the possible basis for those breakdowns in light of the information gathered through the other lenses. The appendix on page 384 provides a listing of teacher and student behaviors that can be observed through the close-up lens view. (NOTE: This list can be used as an observational checklist or can be used to code specific behaviors from videotaped lessons using the Computerized Language Analysis program [MacWhinney, 2000] or the Systematic Analysis of Language Transcripts [Miller & Iglesias, 2004]).

By documenting these behaviors, SLPs and teachers can obtain a good understanding of the classroom academic and social scripts, and students' mastery of the scripts. To participate in lessons, students must, of course, comprehend the content of the lesson. But in addition, they must understand how they are expected to take turns, the types of responses they are expected to give, whether or not their responses have been judged correct or incorrect, and how to make use of the teachers' attempts to scaffold their performance.

Classroom Turn Taking

Turn-Taking Strategies

A primary goal of education is for students to learn the content necessary to achieve identified standards and benchmarks. If students are to learn academic content, they must be able to access it, and accessing content is dependent on their ability to participate in the social processes of learning. For example, students must know the ways to take turns in class discussions, and they must be able to recognize whether their contributions are appropriate and correct. Teachers and SLPs employ a variety of turn-taking strategies as they lead activities (Cahir & Kivac, 1981b). No one method is ideal. Different methods serve different purposes, including the following:

- *Automatic turn taking.* The order of responses is determined by the teacher or the situation. The teacher may go around the circle or up and down the rows; or students may be called on based on content groupings (e.g., "We'll begin with the group that did the timeline for the sixteenth century, then the group that did the timeline for the seventeenth century, and then the twentieth century group"). Automatic turn taking allows the teacher to focus on the lesson content, rather than on organizing turns. A possible problem with automatic turn taking is that while some students are waiting for their turn, they are rehearsing their responses and do not attend to what others are saying.

- *Lottery nomination.* The order of responses can be determined randomly by teachers drawing names from a cup. This ensures all students have an equal number of turns and that students cannot predict when they will be called upon.

- *Individual nomination.* The teacher calls each student by name to respond. This allows the teacher to bring any student into the lesson at any time. Teachers may call on a student because they expect that student to have the answer; or they may call on a student to engage him or her in the activity when they think the student's attention is drifting. Individual nomination can be intimidating to the shy student or the student who does not have an answer readily available. Students from collective or more group-oriented cultures may experience discomfort when nominated because it separates them from the group and requires that they "show off" knowledge.

- *Invitation to bid.* The teacher asks a question and students who want to answer (and have an answer) are to raise their hands. Young students or students with language-learning difficulties sometimes get caught up in the excitement of bidding and do not know what to say. Teachers tend to use invitations to bid to allow as many students to be involved as want to participate. Students who self-select to participate' are more likely to have something to say than students who are nominated. A major difficulty with this strategy is that generally the same few students consistently bid, and often the students who are the quickest to bid give the answers. Students who do not feel competent and confident or students from collective, group-oriented cultures are unlikely to bid.

- *Invitations to reply.* The teacher asks questions to the group as a whole, and students are free to call out answers. This system is less intimidating to many students. Students who are uncertain of answers may shadow what others are saying, that is, they give the response after they hear what others have said and thus give the appearance of fully participating. Furthermore, in group responses, no student is singled out and perceived as "showing off" or trying to look better than others. This approach may be particularly beneficial for students from collective, group-oriented cultures.

Because active participation in lessons promotes academic achievement, it is important that the teacher or SLP ensure that all students have opportunities to participate in lessons. Ideally, one would use a variety of turn-taking strategies depending on the content of the lessons and the types of students in the class. When teachers understand the abilities of their students, they can effectively use even individual nomination with students with disabilities in a general education classroom. They can ask questions that they know students should be able to answer or questions that they can assist the students in answering.

Cultural Variation

Turn-taking strategies vary across cultures. An observer who is not aware of these variations may misjudge the teacher's goals in a lesson, the students' responses, or the effectiveness of the turn taking for a particular group. For example, McCollum (1989), investigating turn-taking patterns in classrooms led by an Anglo teacher and a Puerto Rican teacher, noted that the Anglo teacher used individual nomination to initiate 62 percent of turns and invitation to reply to initiate 24 percent of turns. In contrast, the Puerto Rican teacher used individual nomination for only 34 percent of turns and invitation to reply for 62 percent of turns. Westby, Dezale, Fradd, and Lee (1999) observed a similar pattern of initiations in fourth-grade science classes taught by Hispanic teachers in Miami. The majority of the teachers' initiations involved invitation to reply, with some invitations to bid. The Hispanic teachers also nominated groups of students seated at tables, but rarely nominated individual students. This invitation-to-reply strategy resulted in louder classrooms and students talking over one another. The teachers had to listen carefully to the various responses in attempting to formulate their feedback. Persons not familiar with this teaching style who have watched videotapes of these lessons reported feeling that the classrooms are chaotic or that students are not behaving appropriately.

Individual nomination and invitation to bid are also seldom used in classrooms of Native American students (Crago, Eriks-Brophy, Pesco, & McAlpine, 1997; Erickson & Mohatt, 1982; Philips, 1983). Philips observed that teachers of Warm Springs Indian students used choral responding (a variation of invitation to respond) and some automatic turn taking. She noted that when mainstream teachers used invitation to bid with Native students, many students never attempted to gain the floor. Crago and colleagues reported similar observations of Inuit students. When Inuit students failed to respond when called on by non-Inuit teachers, they were judged as being disrespectful or uncooperative. In contrast, Inuit teachers used group nomination and informed Crago and colleagues that calling on the group as a whole emphasized the important cultural value of group participation.

Students socialized to function in classrooms with one particular type of turn taking may exhibit confusion when they must function in classrooms with a different turn-taking style. Students with language impairments tend to have difficulty in identifying expected classroom scripts, and consequently may have particular difficulty if they have several teachers or must move between classrooms (as expected in middle and high school). Students used to invitation-to-reply turn taking may be perceived as unruly or as lacking understanding if they call out answers rather than waiting to be nominated. Students who are uncomfortable with invitation to bid or individual nomination may be perceived as unknowing or as uncooperative.

Teachers and SLPs must realize that there are many possible reasons for students not to participate in turn taking, such as:

- They may not understand the content of the lesson sufficiently to be able to respond.

- They may not recognize the rules for turn taking.

- They may not feel comfortable with the turn-taking strategies being used.

- They may not be interested or motivated enough to respond.

- They may not be able to process information and formulate a response quickly enough to respond.

- They may simply prefer to listen.

Active participation in lessons improves students' academic performance (Greenwood et al., 2003). Consequently, whether or not a student who does not participate in turn taking has any learning difficulties, teachers should attempt to determine why the student is not participating and make adjustments so he or she will be more likely to participate.

Evaluation or Feedback Strategies

Many of the interactions between teachers and students involve *initiation-response-evaluation (IRE)* or *initiation-response-feedback (IRF)* (Mehan, 1979; Wells & Chang-Wells, 1992). That is, the teacher initiates an interaction with a question or comment, students give a response, and the teacher then either evaluates the response or gives the students some type of feedback on their response. For example, when reading the book, *The Three Little Hawaiian Pigs and the Magic Shark* (Lowell, 1992), a teacher asked:

Teacher:	What did the shark pretend to be? (I)
Student:	A shave ice salesman. (R)
Teacher:	You're right! He pretended to sell shave ice. (E)

Teachers evaluate in *overt* and *covert* ways (Cahir & Kivac, 1981a). Teachers occasionally use overt evaluations like, "That's very good!" or "That's not right," but their evaluations are frequently not so direct. Teachers more often use covert evaluations, such as:

Teacher:	What's the fourth letter of the alphabet, Mark?
Mark:	D.
Teacher:	What's the second letter of the alphabet, Joe?
Joe:	B.

Both Mark and Joe are required to recognize that because the teacher asked Joe a different question than Mark, the teacher had judged Mark's response as correct. In contrast, note the following interaction:

Teacher: What is 4 times 4, Billy?
Billy: 12.
Teacher: What is 4 times 4, John?
John: 16.

Billy and John now must realize that, because the teacher asked John the same question she had asked Billy, Billy's answer was incorrect. Teachers rarely explain these covert evaluations. Consequently, students with learning disabilities frequently assume that their answers have been correct.

When observing teacher responses or feedback to students, attempt to determine if the students recognize whether their answers are being judged as correct or incorrect. One of the most common covert evaluations used by the Hispanic teachers in a science project conducted in Miami schools was statement repetition, that is, the teachers repeated what a student said, sometimes when it was correct and sometimes when it was incorrect (Westby et al., 1999). In this way the teachers made students feel their contributions were heard and valued, even when they were not accurate in terms of science knowledge. These restatements, however, gave no clue as to the correctness of the students' responses. Graduate students who assisted in coding this classroom data reported difficulty coding the correctness of students' responses because the graduate students themselves did not know the answers to the science questions, and from the teachers' responses, they could not determine if the teachers were judging the students' answers as correct or incorrect.

Teachers may do more than evaluate students' responses; they may provide additional feedback by expanding on the information, as a teacher did when discussing the story, *Esperanza Rising* (Ryan, 2000):

Teacher: What did Esperanza's mother decide to do after the hacienda burned?

Student: To run away so Tio Luis wouldn't hurt them.

Teacher: Yes, and they had to do it secretly at night, hiding in the false bottom on a wagon so that Tio Luis did not know they were fleeing.

Revoicing (or *reconceptualization*) is a potentially more beneficial response of teachers to students' responses than evaluation or simple feedback (Cazden, 2001;

O'Connor & Michaels, 1996). Revoicing goes beyond the concept of expansion of information. When revoicing, the adult listens carefully to the student, then reframes the student's response into a more formal academic style. The adult carries out revoicing in a specialized manner. The adult begins the response with "so" and the student's name, thus crediting the information to the student. The adult then foregrounds some aspect of what the student has said using a more academic language style. The structure of this revoicing allows the student the option to agree or disagree with what the adult will say, for example:

Teacher: Why did the soda can we put in the freezer split?

Miguel: 'Cause like the water got really cold. It turned to ice and ice is bigger than water. So, like all the ice couldn't fit in the can.

Teacher: So, Miguel, you're explaining that the low temperature in the freezer caused the water to freeze and turn to ice. Water expands when it freezes, so the can split.

Revoicing accepts the ideas the student is attempting to express (positioning the students in participant roles of predictors, hypothesizers, and theorizers), and models academic discourse. Revoicing is a relatively rare form of teacher feedback, but one that is especially beneficial in assisting students in acquiring academic discourse. Such a strategy is essential for students with language-learning disabilities and students from culturally/linguistically diverse backgrounds.

Teacher Initiations

In all activities, teachers or SLPs initiate communication with students. Observation of classroom interactions should document the type of teacher initiations and the levels of abstraction of these initiations. The observer should note the relationship between the initiation types—including functions and levels of abstraction—and the correctness or appropriateness of student responses.

Initiation Types and Functions

When teachers engage in teaching activities with students, they employ several types of initiation acts:

- They give directions for what to do and how to do it.

- They give information about topics or how to do something.

- They ask several types of questions:

  Product   *What is the capital of New Mexico?*

  Choice   *Was the Declaration of Independence signed in New York or Philadelphia?*

  Process   *Explain to Devon how to solve this faction problem.*

  Metaprocess   *Why do you think the Anasazi Indians left Chaco Canyon?*

In addition to these academic initiation acts, teachers may also initiate communication for a variety of social reasons.

In mainstream classrooms, teachers are typically communication gatekeepers, determining who can talk, when they can talk, and what they can talk about. The gatekeeping strategies may vary based on teachers' personal styles or preferences or their cultural expectations for educational interactions. In their gatekeeping role, mainstream teachers initiate the vast majority of the turns or communicative interactions. For example, McCollum (1989) reported that in the classroom taught by an Anglo teacher, 91 percent of communicative sequences were initiated by the teacher. In contrast, in a Puerto Rican teacher's classroom, the teacher initiated 62 percent of the sequences and the students initiated 38 percent. The two teachers managed student initiations in markedly different ways. The Anglo teacher ignored 44 percent of the students' initiations, acknowledged but did not extend 27 percent of students' initiations, and in 7 percent of the instances sanctioned the initiation, indicating it was an inappropriate interruption. In contrast, the Puerto Rican teacher incorporated 33 percent of student initiations into the lesson, acknowledged 44 percent, and never sanctioned any student initiation. The students in these two classrooms were learning markedly different ways to do school.

When observing teacher-student interactions in classrooms, SLPs should note the degree to which both teachers and students initiate, and what teachers do when students initiate. In some cases, one might want teachers to permit more initiations from students, but the quality of the initiations should be considered—are the initiations related or tangential to the topic under discussion? Eder (1982) observed that teachers acknowledged more initiations from students in lower than in higher reading groups. (Teachers reportedly did this to encourage students' participation.) Many of the comments of students in the low reading group, however, were not directly related to the reading lesson. As a consequence, students in the low reading group learned a different script for reading. By the end of the year, they were talking more, but their comments were no more related to the lessons. Consequently, they did not develop an understanding of the type of discussion characteristic of higher reading groups. Without this understanding they would have difficulty moving out of the low reading group.

Levels of Abstraction

It is particularly useful to evaluate the relationship between the level of abstraction (or complexity) of a teacher's questions and the quality (or correctness) of a student's response. An understanding of this relationship is critical for developing strategies that will facilitate a student's ability to be successful in a class. A variety of systems for judging levels of language abstraction are available. Bloom's taxonomy (1956) is probably the most familiar. Table 8.2 shows examples of questions from the six Bloom levels from a fifth-grade ecology unit and a language arts lesson on the novel, *Holes* (Sachar, 1998). (NOTE: In *Holes*, Sachar describes the experiences of Stanley Yelnats and other boys at Camp Green Lake, a juvenile detention facility in a dry lake bed in west Texas. Stanley, who lives under an old family curse, has been unjustly convicted of stealing a pair of shoes. At Camp Green Lake, Stanley and the boys spend their days digging holes in the sun; avoiding rattlesnakes and deadly spotted lizards; and dealing with the warden, who is seeking something in the holes. Gradually friendships and loyalty develop among the boys.)

Blank, Rose, and Berlin (1978) also provided a system for evaluating what they term *perceptual-language distance,* which refers to how close or how far removed language is from the material being discussed. Looking at a lion in a zoo and asking, "What's that?" involves a one-to-one correspondence between what the students see and what they say. In contrast, answering the question, "How are a lion and a monkey alike?" requires the student to think of a verbal response that is appropriate to the two, but not immediately evident in either. Table 8.3 on page 338 presents definitions for each of the Blank language levels (Blank et al., 1978) and examples based on the book, *Ghost Wings* (Joose, 2001).

The observer should note the levels of questions teachers ask and the levels of questions students answer accurately. Are teachers asking questions at all levels of abstraction, or are they asking questions only at lower levels? The author and colleagues (Westby, 1997; Westby et al., 1999) observed that in several classrooms, students appeared to have trained teachers to ask only low-level questions. When teachers asked higher level questions, students either did not respond or responded incorrectly. When this occurred, teachers generally responded by asking a lower-level question rather than by assisting the student to answer the more abstract question. For effective instruction, teachers should provide scaffolding that enables students to respond to more abstract language.

Table 8.2   ## Examples of Applying Bloom's Taxonomy

Level	Types of Questions	Science Example	Literature Example
Recall (remember or recognize)	What were you told is an example of ____? Identify the following.	Label the parts of a terrarium.	Who were the main characters in *Holes?*
Comprehension (understand)	What is the main idea of ___? How would you summarize___? What facts or ideas show ___?	Describe the procedures you used to put your terrarium together.	What were the boys' lives at Camp Green Lake like?
Application (make a connection)	What examples can you find to ___? How would you show understanding of ___?	Put worms and a variety of "garbage" into your terrarium. Record your observations over a week. Explain what you saw happen.	What did Stanley and Zero do for one another that showed they were friends?
Analysis (take apart)	How would you classify ___? What conclusions can you draw___? Why do you think___?	Compare and contrast the lives of plants and animals in an aquarium and in a terrarium.	Why do you think the warden is having the boys dig holes in the dry lake bed? What clues are there in the story to support your hypothesis?
Synthesis (create something new)	What would happen if___? Suppose you could ___? What would you do?	Based on what we have learned about ecological systems, develop a plan for what the city of Albuquerque could do to preserve the Bosque (the wooded area near the river).	What might have happened if Stanley had not carried Zero up the mountain?
Evaluation (give a reasoned opinion)	What is your opinion of ___? Why was it better than ___? What judgment would you make about___?	A housing developer wants to buy a large section of the Bosque and build expensive homes there. Write a letter to the editor of the Albuquerque Journal about your opinion of this idea.	Do you think that a family can be cursed? Why might someone think they have been cursed?

Source: Bloom (1956)

Table 8.3

An Application of Blank's
Levels of Language Abstraction

Level	Description	Example
I: **Matching** **Perception**	Reporting and responding to perceptually obvious material in the environment	• Point to a monarch butterfly. • What do you see on Grandma's ofrenda?
II: **Selective** **Analysis of** **Perception**	Reporting and responding to perceptual information that is less salient	• What is a metate used for? • What colors are monarch butterflies?
III: **Reordering** **Perception**	Using language to restructure perceptual information and inhibit predisposing responses for completing the task	• What is a migration? • What would the girl not put on the ofrenda?
IV: **Reasoning** **About** **Perception**	Using language to predict, explain, theorize, and reason about relationships	• Why are scientists tagging butterflies? • Why did the girl tremble when she was in bed?

Source: Blank, Rose, & Berlin (1978)

Scaffolding Strategies

If students are to engage in language at increasing levels of abstraction, they require systematic scaffolding that guides them in gaining new knowledge and skills (Vygotsky, 1962). Teachers must select scaffolding strategies appropriate for the student's zone of proximal development, that is, the range within which a student can perform a task with assistance but not independently. Students must be able to recognize that scaffolds are meant to be temporarily supportive and they must understand how they are to participate in them.

A scaffold may be a static, structural support or an interactive, dynamic support (Silliman & Wilkinson, 1994; see also Chapter 1). In a static, structural scaffold, such as in traditional lectures, the teacher gives students information at a preplanned level of complexity that the teacher believes is matched to student ability. If the student does not know the answer, the teacher simply supplies it and moves on. In contrast, with dynamic, interactive scaffolding, the teacher assesses student understanding and modifies instruction based on student responses during the course of the lesson. There is active, purposeful participation by teachers and students in this teaching/learning process in both a teacher-directed and an among-student manner.

Scaffolding may be used to facilitate students' success by encouraging them to clarify what they mean or by minimizing potential breakdowns. The teacher provides cues or simplifies the task in some way (Blank et al., 1978). For example, a teacher may ask the student for clarification of something that the student has said that was unclear to the teacher, or the teacher may focus a student's attention on elements of the message the student has not understood, or may assist the student in retrieving the correct word. The teacher may cue the student by using a cloze procedure (e.g., "We added heat to the water and it…" or "When tectonic plates move apart, we say they di…"). Table 8.4 on page 340 shows a number of strategies a teacher may use to simplify a task. Alternately, teachers can promote collaboration among students by asking or directing students to assist those who have difficulty or by highlighting the positive behavior of students with the intention that other students will emulate the behavior. Table 8.5 on page 342 presents ways of engaging peers in supporting each other. The types of scaffolding are built around four metacognitive strategies that are part of a larger method of teaching text comprehension called Reciprocal Teaching (Palincsar & Brown, 1984; see Chapter 11):

1. Summarizing the essential information to determine if comprehension has occurred

2. Generating questions to determine understanding of specific points

3. Clarifying ambiguous or inconsistent interpretations

4. Predicting what comes next based on current understanding

Students who are unfamiliar with interactive scaffolding from teachers or other students may perceive the attention as threatening or challenging, and may initially withdraw from the teacher's efforts to assist them. Repeated exposure to supportive interactions—and opportunities to support others as well as receive support—will accustom students to the process.

Table 8.4   Instructional Discourse Simplification Strategies

Strategy	Example
Delay	**Sample problem:** Teacher says, "Pick up the…" Student starts grabbing objects. **Simplification:** Teacher says, "Wait a minute. Listen to what I want you to pick up."
Focus for Attention	**Sample problem:** Teacher says, "Go to the science center and get three pipettes." Student goes to the center and reaches for the first thing she or he sees, which is a glass. **Simplification:** Teacher asks, "Do you remember what I asked you to bring?"
Repeat Demand	**Sample problem:** Teacher says, "To make your terrarium, cut off the top two inches of one large soda bottle and the bottom two inches from a second large soda bottle." Teacher sees that student is beginning to cut the top off a second bottle. **Simplification:** Teacher says, "No, remember, cut the top off one bottle and the bottom off another bottle."
Synchronous Rephrasing	**Sample problem:** Teacher says, "After you put the baking soda in, watch the liquid effervesce." Students look puzzled. **Simplification:** Teacher says, "I mean I want you to watch the gas bubbles coming out of the liquid."
Partial Completion	**Sample problem:** Teacher asks, "What is the concave or convex surface of a liquid called?" Student says, "I don't remember." **Simplification:** Teacher says, "It's a men…" (meniscus)

Table 8.4—*Continued*

Strategy	Example
Restructure to Highlight	**Sample problem:** Teacher asks, "Why do you think we couldn't get this sponge into the [too small] cup and we could fit the marble?" Student says, "Because it's a sponge." **Simplification:** Teacher says, "OK, I'll cut the sponge into two. Now it's still a sponge. Why does it go into the cup now?"
Offer Relevant Comparisons	**Sample problem:** Teacher asks, "Who signed the Emancipation Proclamation?" Students say nothing. **Simplification:** Teacher says, "Well, was it Martin Luther King, Jr. or Abraham Lincoln?"
Didactic Presentation of Information	**Sample problem:** Teacher says, "When you put the pennies in the cup of water, be sure to watch the meniscus." Student is watching the pennies pile up in the bottom of the cup. **Simplification:** Teacher says, "Remember, the meniscus is the curved surface of the water. Look at how the meniscus changes as you add pennies."
Relate Known to Unknown	**Sample problem:** Teacher asks, "What would I have to do to turn this oil into a solid?" Student says, "I don't know." **Simplification:** Teacher asks, "Well, do you remember what we did to turn water to ice? Ice is solid water."
Directed Attention	**Sample problem:** Teacher asks, "How is the ice different from the water?" Student says, "I don't know." **Simplification:** Teacher says, "Well, let's see. Turn over the cup of water and turn over the tray of ice."
Focus on Relevant Features	**Sample problem:** Teacher asks, "Why does the girl named America feel sad living in Chicago (based on book, *America* [Rodriguez, 1998])? Students say nothing. **Simplification:** "Let's look at what the story says about how her life in Chicago is different from her life in Mexico."

Scaffolding Student Understanding through Peer Support

Table 8.5

Type of Scaffolding	Example
Soliciting Specific Clarification	• What do we do when we don't understand? • If you don't understand how to make your grids, what can you do?
Soliciting Collaborative Assistance for Clarification	• Who can explain to Marcus how to make his terrarium? • Who can show Elysia how to make the origami crane?
Supporting Transfer of Strategy Selection to Others	• Nathan has it figured out. Nathan, tell Austin how to change Centigrade to Fahrenheit.
Checking Understanding	• What is this lesson about? • Show me how you know that. • What do you think went wrong (when student says the experiment didn't work out)?
Supporting Question Generation	• What did I ask? • Lauren, ask Ernesto for some ideas for your timeline.
Supporting Prediction	• Can someone predict what will happen when we do this? • What do you need to do?

Interviews

A single observation of a classroom can be misleading. Observations over time are required to understand what teachers are doing and how students are understanding. In addition, to achieve better understanding of teacher and student behaviors, observations should be supplemented by interviewing teachers regarding their lesson goals and students regarding their expectations.

Interviewing Teachers

A teacher can be interviewed about performance of specific students and how the teacher accommodates the student of concern. Ysseldyke and Christenson (1978) suggest asking teachers questions about the observed student, such as:

- To what extent was _____'s performance typical?

- How does your instructional goal for _____ differ from his or her classmates?

- What are your expectations for _____? (probe quality of work, classroom participation, task completion, neatness, if assistance is needed)

- How do you plan instruction for _____? (probe for strengths, weaknesses, skill level, emotional needs, interests)

- How do you determine _____'s appropriate instructional placement?

- Tell me about _____'s independent assignments. (probe for amount of practice, kind of tasks student can handle independently, success rate)

- How do you evaluate _____'s progress? (probe for record keeping, decisions about what to teach next, mastery criteria)

Student Interviews

Interviews of students should include questions about classroom scripts and how students understand what they are to do in lessons and with assignments. Questions may include:

- Tell me what you needed to do on these assignments. (show student recent assignments)

    What did your teacher want you to learn?

    What did your teacher tell you about why these assignments are important?

    What did you have to do?

    Show me how you did this assignment.

- What does your teacher expect you to do on an assignment if you are confused?

- What does your teacher tell you about:

  Completing your work? (What happens if your work is not done?)

  Getting the answers correct? (What happens if you make mistakes?)

  Having neat papers? (What happens if your work is messy?)

Changing Expectations in Classroom Scripts

Students with language impairments may appear to do reasonably well in the early grades, but they may begin to exhibit increasing difficulties as they move through the educational system, because both the academic and social curricula change. Consequently, the SLP should be alert to changing teacher and student expectations across the grades. Table 8.6 presents some of the varying classroom events at three grade levels (Creaghead, 1992b). A number of studies have explored the nature of traditional recitation scripts for lessons in which teachers ask questions, students respond, and teachers evaluate the response (Cahir & Kivac, 1981a, 1981b; Cazden, 2001; Mehan; 1979). Studies have not generally investigated how the nature of the teachers' and students' roles and interactions in lesson scripts change over time. The author and colleagues (Westby, 1997; Westby, Moore, Roman, 2002; Westby, Watson, & Murphy,

Table 8.6

Typical Classroom Events at Three Grade Levels

Events	Preschool	Primary Grade	Secondary Grade
	arriving	reading group	doing oral reports
	show and tell	recess	doing written reports
	snack time	lunch	test taking
	cleaning up	doing homework	following teacher lecture
	bathroom	workbooks	note taking
	story time	art	working with other students
	going home	riding bus	participating in discussions

Source: Creaghead (1992b)

1994) have explored the changing academic and social scripts in several elementary schools that serve culturally/linguistically diverse students and students with disabilities in inclusive settings. As students move through school, not only are they exposed to content of increasing complexity, but they are also expected to become more responsible for their own behavior and learning. This responsibility for managing one's own behavior is termed *self-regulation* or *self-determination*. Special educators are increasingly expressing concern about the need to promote self-regulation (or self-determination) in students with learning disabilities (Zimmerman & Schunk, 2001; also see Chapter 13 for a more in-depth discussion of self-regulation). If specific efforts are not made to facilitate self-determination in students with language impairments, they are likely to develop a pattern of learned helplessness, believing that their own effort is unnecessary or futile and that others will take care of the matter (Abramson, Seligman, & Teasdale, 1978).

The concept of independence/interdependence (Triandis, 1995) is sometimes associated with the idea of self-regulation or self-determination. All societies must strike a balance between independence (relying on and being responsible for oneself) and interdependence (relying on and being responsible primarily for others). Middle-class Western cultures emphasize independence, whereas many working-class and non-Western cultures emphasize interdependence. Middle-class families socialize their children toward independence through the use of language to develop self-regulation and intellectual curiosity. In contrast, many working-class and nonmainstream families socialize their children more toward interdependence and obedience by watching and following instructions (Brislin, 1993). Children of working-class families are more likely to expect authority figures to set and monitor external standards. Children of middle-class families are increasingly expected to set standards of behavior and goals themselves and to monitor their own behavior and progress toward goals (Hofstede, Pedersen, & Hofstede, 2002).

Typically developing children in mainstream culture develop through a series of stages that lead to independence and self-regulation (Diaz, Neal, & Amaya-Williams, 1990). Some approximate ages and examples are presented below:

- *Infancy.* Neurophysiological modulation—Infants modulate arousal states through organized patterns of behavior that include reflex actions (e.g., child grasps an item placed in the hand).

- *Toddlers.* Sensorimotor modulation—Children coordinate nonreflexive motor actions in response to environmental stimuli (e.g., child grasps a crayon and colors on the wall).

- *Early preschool.* Control—Children are able to begin, maintain, and stop actions in response to an adult's directions (e.g., adult tells the child to stop coloring on the wall and the child complies).

- *Late preschool.* Micro self-control—Children are able to comply with the adult's individual commands and directives when the adult is not present (e.g., child remembers having been told, "Use this paper here for your coloring," and complies).

- *Early elementary.* Macro self-control—Children are able to carry out routine sequences of commands and directives when the adult is not present (e.g., child follows through on teacher's class direction to "start working on your first drafts of your project while I set up tomorrow's science experiment").

- *Mid-elementary.* Self-regulation—Children are beginning to plan, guide, and monitor their behavior from within; they can be flexible in changing circumstances (e.g., child says to self, "We are supposed to be working on our first drafts, but I need some information, so I will ask to go to the library").

This development toward self-regulation depends both on children's developing cognitive abilities and on socialization through verbal scaffolding practices and expectations for self-regulation. Typically developing middle-class children will generally follow this pattern of self-regulatory development. Because of differences in socialization experiences in their homes and classrooms, many working-class and nonmainstream children may show a different or delayed route into self-control, and may, in fact, develop limited self-control and self-regulation. Children with language impairments and children with executive function deficits (e.g., attention-deficit/hyperactivity disorder, autism spectrum disorders, traumatic brain injury) typically exhibit delays and deficits in the development of self-regulation (Westby, 2004). Such children may expect adults to continue to exercise control over them.

Teachers need to be alert to students' self-regulation stage of development, and structure their interactions to meet students' expectation. Students from cultural groups that emphasize socialization toward interdependence, rather than toward independence and self-regulation, may have difficulty accessing learning in classrooms where teachers expect students to take charge of their own learning (Delpit, 1988; Reyes, 1991). Delpit reported the confusion of African-American students when teachers expected these students to participate in whole language and process approaches to literacy but did not give explicit instructions regarding how they were to do this:

> I thought she was just a fool who couldn't teach and didn't want to try...I didn't feel she was teaching us anything. She wanted us to correct each others' papers and we were there to learn from her. She didn't teach us anything, absolutely nothing. (p. 288)

Reyes (1991) reported similar confusion among sixth grade Hispanic students when teachers expected students to find their own books for book reports and to monitor and edit their own writing. Students generally failed to find any books, and over the course of the year, they exhibited few or no changes in their journal writing. Delpit (1988) and Reyes suggest that teachers need to begin where students are, and consequently provide more explicit, direct guidance in social and academic expectations and how to meet those expectations.

Wilcox (1982) noted, however, that when teachers of culturally different students stay at the level of instruction using explicit, external controls, their students will not develop the internalized self-regulatory abilities that are essential in many vocations. To help students respond to societal expectations for self-determination, teachers should gradually expect and foster increasing degrees of self-regulation from students. Wilcox observed that a first-grade teacher working with students from a low socioeconomic background used explicit, direct instructions to control the students' behaviors (e.g., from page 288, "You have an assignment. Sit down and get busy"). The students were not expected to exercise self-control. In contrast, a first-grade teacher of middle-class students relied on indirect statements and suggestions to encourage self-control and self-regulation (e.g., "You have 15 minutes. Use your time wisely"). Both of the teachers used management strategies that appeared effective for the students in their classes. Wilcox expressed concern, however, that the students from low socioeconomic backgrounds were being socialized to "stay in their place." She hypothesized that if these students were not encouraged to develop self-regulatory abilities, they would later be denied access to managerial and professional positions that require independent, self-directed achievement.

Classroom Scripts That Promote Student Success

Attention to the academic and social scripts of lessons can promote student success. This section describes the scripts of three classrooms at La Chamisa Elementary School, a school that served a population with multiple challenges. Students were from culturally/linguistically diverse backgrounds—50 percent Hispanic, 22 percent African American, 12 percent Asian American, 9 percent Native American, and 7 percent Euro-American. The La Chamisa community was both highly mobile and economically disadvantaged. Approximately 91 percent of the students met the qualifications for free and reduced lunch. The school had a history of extremely poor performance, with more than 80 percent of its fifth graders reading 2 or more years below grade level. A new principal, however, brought about major reform influencing the conduct of teaching in classrooms that resulted in significantly improved academic performance. All students with special needs were included in general education classes for at least a portion of the day. Three classrooms are described here to show some of the scripts teachers may implement to facilitate successful participation and academic success of students in their classrooms. The second grade had 15 students, half of whom were limited English proficient and receiving English for Second-Language Learners (ESL) services. The third grade had 22 students. Because the teacher had specialized training in working with emotionally disturbed/behaviorally disordered students, a number of students with behavioral difficulties were assigned to her room. The fifth grade had 32 students, 8 of whom had significant learning disabilities. In addition, over half of the students received ESL services.

The teachers recognized the need to socialize students to the school environment if they were to acquire the academic content. The teachers wanted the students to feel comfortable in school and feel good about themselves, but more importantly, they believed it was essential that the students eventually learn to manage their own actions and learning. They needed to develop self-control and then self-regulation of both the social and academic scripts of the classroom. Each classroom demonstrated different ways of scaffolding students into competence and one—the fifth grade—revealed how challenging it may be to meet the scaffolding needs of students with learning disabilities in the general education classroom.

Second Grade: Learning to Participate

Ms. Hartman, the second grade teacher, structured her lessons to encourage a positive, supportive dependence on the teacher and an interdependence among the students. Desks were grouped together in sets of four or five. Most activities were begun as whole group activities with Ms. Hartman at the front of the room and information written on the board. Ms. Hartman introduced lessons by describing what the class would be doing, then giving explicit step-by-step instructions using visual aids and demonstrations. As a group, she had the students work through some samples of the activity being taught. Generally, after initial instruction about what to do, students worked individually or in small groups, with Ms. Hartman moving among the groups and assisting as needed. Students could and did seek assistance from the teacher, but Ms. Hartman took the lead in monitoring the students' progress on the assignments and giving assistance when she felt the students needed help. The students were not expected to organize the activity, nor were they engaged in a single joint project. Rather, each student was doing his or her own work. They could assist one another with the assignment, they might simply talk with one another about what they were doing, or they might talk about mutual interests. As long as they were not talking loudly and were making progress on their assignments, they were allowed to work together. During these times, students were also free to move to other parts of the room, select workmates, and change partners. Students who were misbehaving were generally talked to individually. Students were not reprimanded for misbehavior from the front of the room or singled out in front of others for misbehavior. Later in the year, Ms. Hartman conducted discussions about behavior issues that arose and had the students discuss what was appropriate and inappropriate and how certain behaviors should be handled. Ms. Hartman was consistently soft-spoken. In fact, if noise level in the room increased, she sometimes spoke more softly so that students would have to reduce their noise to hear her. She also flicked the lights to indicate that the class had become too noisy and was to quiet down.

Ms. Hartman was aware that classroom expectations changed across the grades, and as the year progressed, she tried to prepare students for expectations in third grade by gradually modifying the classroom scripts. Table 8.7 on page 350 shows changes in the second-grade scripts from early to late in the year. As the year progressed, Ms. Hartman attempted to reduce the students' dependence on her and to increase their ability to function more independently. She also increased response structure. As the year progressed, Ms. Hartman moved from flexible participation to raising hands before offering an

Variations in Second-Grade Scripts from Beginning to End of Year

Table 8.7

Early in Year	Late in Year
Students are to raise hands to answer, but teacher will accept calling out	Teacher does not accept calling out
All activities preset and structured by teacher	Students vote on some tasks and games
Teacher puts notes on board for students to finish work	Fewer notes; students expected to know if they have completed their work
Teacher occasionally asks class to evaluate performance (thumbs up/down for right/wrong; What suggestions can you give?)	Increase in class evaluations
Teacher repeats rules/directions	Teacher gives rules/directions once (then says, "If you don't know, find out from someone else")
Teacher models for students how to do each activity; includes personal experiences	Less modeling of how to do tasks
Teacher approaches individual student and stops behavior with command/few words	Teacher conducts class discussions on behavior
Partners work together (groups of 4); class problem solves with teacher	Class works together as group to problem solve
Teacher guides students to answer questions; mostly teacher directed (if student didn't know, teacher led to answer, "so that means they were...")	Teacher gives clues/hints to students (discussing plant needs, "There's something everyone needs to live. It's all around us...air. Something in the air." Student responds, "Oxygen")
Teacher tells class when it's time for activity	Teacher sets play clock to cue students to start activity

answer, and eventually she did not accept calling out. Students quickly caught on to the need to raise their hands in lessons; however, additional time elapsed before they realized what they were to do when they raised their hands. When called on, they might not have a response, or they might provide comments that were unrelated to the lesson. Ms. Hartman reminded students that they must have an answer to the question if they raised their hands.

Early in the year, Ms. Hartman guided the students in answering questions. If students did not know an answer to a question, she led them into it by filling in a blank with a word she had recently used. For example, she held up a ruler and said, "A foot has 12 inches; a yardstick has 36 inches. There are 12 inches in a..." Later in the year she gave them less direct cues or hints. When talking about growing plants, she asked, "What do plants need to live?" When she received no response, she continued, "There's something everyone needs to live. It's all around us." A student responded, "Air." Ms. Hartman continued, "Something in the air," in search of the response, "Oxygen." As the year progressed, Ms Hartman modeled tasks less and used more verbal instructions. If students did not remember the instructions to a task, she began to encourage them to ask other students. She increasingly encouraged the development of metacognitive skills by asking students to evaluate lesson responses and their own performance. In group lessons, students were asked to signal agreement with responses by putting their thumbs up or thumbs down. To increase student self-awareness, just before each of the three grading periods, Ms. Hartman gave the students sheets with a listing of all the areas in which they would be graded and asked them to grade themselves. Grading was done using symbols or faces. A superman symbol meant the student was doing exceptionally well in the subject; a star meant the student was doing a good job; a smiling face indicated OK performance; a face with a curved (quizzical) mouth indicated that the student could do better and needed to try harder; a face with a frown indicated the student felt he or she did not understand the subject.

Lessons in Ms. Hartman's class flowed smoothly when she was present. However, several times during the year, when a substitute teacher was present, the students were uncertain of what they were to do and their behavior degenerated. The substitute teacher expected there were clear pre-established rules and that the students would follow them without specific reminders. The substitute teacher became frustrated and angry until the observing graduate student, who was familiar with the classroom scripts, restored order.

Ms. Hartman's direct control of the students' behavior and her careful scaffolding of how to participate in lessons through modeling, explicit instructions, and individualized support helped the students enjoy school, feel good about their abilities, and acquire many of the academic skills and behaviors expected of second graders. Ms. Hartman provided considerable interactive scaffolding in a fairly dynamic and changing environment. As desired, independence increased and support decreased over the course of the year. This approach was successful, but required a teacher familiar with that particular classroom—there were too many implicit interactive scaffolds for a teacher unfamiliar with the classroom. The next classroom provided a very different example of scaffolding support.

Third Grade: Developing Self-Control

The scripts of the third-grade class were markedly different from the second grade. The third grade did not have the intimate feel of the second-grade class in which the teacher frequently attended to misbehavior by talking quietly to students individually. Ms. Brennan, the teacher, explicitly explained the class rules at the beginning of the year and posted them on a bulletin board. Each rule was numbered. If a student violated a rule, Ms. Brennan called out the student's name and rule number, then the identified student was to mark his or her violation on a chart on the board. Behavioral violations resulted in loss of recess time. Once the students were aware of what was considered appropriate and inappropriate behaviors, they were expected to remember the rules and monitor their own behavior. Ms. Brennan did not discuss violation of the classroom rules with individual students unless a student repeatedly violated the rules. By requiring the students to remember the rules that went with each number, Ms. Brennan was expecting that the students would begin to internalize the rules.

The academic structure of lessons also differed markedly between second and third grades. Ms. Brennan conducted whole-group lessons for language arts, math, science, and social studies and had the students work on assignments independently at their desks. Students were assigned to one of three reading groups based on their reading levels, from a first-grade reading level to a third/fourth-grade reading level. Each group met for approximately 20 minutes each day with the teacher. All reading groups were teacher-directed and structured along traditional lines, with Ms. Brennan asking questions, students responding, and Ms. Brennan evaluating their responses. The groups varied in the amount of scaffolding and the level of the questions asked. The highest reading group discussed reasons for characters' behavior in stories and made inferences about what might happen in stories. Ms. Brennan asked many "why" questions to encourage reasoning, and she provided students with opportunities to justify their responses, as in this example:

Teacher:	Why does Prunella want to scare Lady?
Student 1:	So she can live in the castle.
Teacher:	That's exactly right. Did you predict who the ghost was?
Student 1:	Dotson, 'cause she sneezed every time she was there.
Teacher:	Okay, you thought it was Dotson because she sneezed every time. Any other reasons that you figured it out?
Student 2:	Jones.
Teacher:	Okay, what did Jones do?
Student 2:	Whenever the ghost was passing by, she grabbed the blanket.
Teacher:	We've got two ways you figured it out—because somebody grabbed the blanket every time and because Dotson sneezed every time. Any other ways you figured out who the ghost was?
Student 3:	And she left the window open.
Teacher:	Yeah, she left the window open to get in and out.

In the low reading group, Ms. Brennan focused on basic reading skills and asked questions that primarily required recall of information rather than inferencing and predicting. She often guided students to the answers, as in the following example:

Teacher:	Today we're going to talk about ABC order. What is ABC order? [pause, no response from students] When I put things in order like the…
Student 1:	Like there's no A, and you put B.
Teacher::	If there's no A, then I put B first; if there's no B, then I put C first. So I go just like the ABCs.
Teacher:	What letter do I look at?
Student 2:	The first letter.
Teacher:	I look at the first letter in what?
Student 2:	The first letter in the alphabet.
Teacher:	In the alphabet or the word?
Student 2:	In the word.

The structure and interactions of Ms. Brennan's reading groups were similar to those reported in the literature (Cazden, 2001; Collins, 1996; Eder, 1982). Typically, with groups of high readers, teachers focus on interpretation of the text and ask open-ended questions. In contrast, with groups of low readers, teachers ask closed questions and focus on specific skills such as identifying letters and decoding words. In the process of participating in a group of low readers, students learn interactional patterns that may inhibit their ability to function in higher reading groups.

When not participating in whole-class lessons or working in teacher-led reading groups, the students in Ms. Brennan's class were to work quietly by themselves on assignments. Unlike Ms. Hartman, who moved through the room checking on students' progress, Ms. Brennan sat at her desk in the front of the room. Students were to raise their hands if they had questions or had completed their work, and proceed to the desk when Ms. Brennan acknowledged them. This approach required that the students make judgments themselves about how well they understood the tasks they were working on and how well they were progressing on the assignments. Hence, Ms. Brennan expected the students to have metacognitive skills to monitor their own understanding and learning.

Also, unlike Ms. Hartman's class, where students were generally permitted to move around the room and talk to one another as long as they did so quietly, students in Ms. Brennan's class were seldom permitted to talk with one another. At the beginning of the year, Ms. Brennan seldom gave permission for the students to talk with one another or to work together. When questioned about this, she said that the students were not able to work effectively together—that the noise level increased, and that they would argue and not complete their work.

One might wonder why second-grade students appeared to be successful working together, while third-grade students were not. Part of the explanation may be related to the nature of the tasks. Students in second grade were more frequently engaged in drawing tasks or manipulative activities, whereas third-grade students were doing more decontextualized academic tasks requiring writing. The second-grade students could complete their tasks while talking about a variety of topics. In contrast, the third-grade tasks required more sustained attention. To work together effectively in third grade required that the students all be able to focus their attention on the same task for an extended period of time and that their comments all relate to the task. Working in third-grade groups required greater self-control than working in second-grade groups.

The attitude toward school work itself also changed. There was an emphasis on "doing your own work" and being responsible for the quality and quantity of the work. In second grade, letter grades were not given at report card time. Students were evaluated largely in terms of effort they appeared to put forth, and they were marked as performing satisfactorily, improving, or needing improvement. In third grade, however, specific letter and percentage grades were given for the students' work.

Ms. Brennan used explicit, highly structured academic and social scripts in her room. The structural scaffolds of the classroom enabled students to control their own behavior and learning. They were expected to remember the classroom rules and implement self-correction when their misbehavior was identified. They were expected to be able to complete academic assignments, determine if they understood the task, monitor their progress, and edit their work. To do this, students had to remember and implement the rules the teacher had given them. However, students who needed more graduated, systematic, and interactive support to achieve this level would be expected to struggle and might be considered "bad" students. They would need additional mediation to facilitate their understanding and compliance with expectations.

This classroom provided considerable structural scaffolding with its explicit rules and clear expectations. The next step in development of self-control is to generate novel and adaptive plans. These plans or strategies should be applicable to environments less structured than that of Ms. Brennan's, and with less interactive support than that of Ms. Hartman's.

Fifth Grade: Developing Self-Regulation

Ms. Silver, a fifth grade teacher, was aware of the need to prepare students for middle school, where they were expected to be self-regulated learners. Like Ms. Hartman and Ms. Brennan, Ms. Silver wanted students to meet expected competencies and have improved self-esteem and discipline. In addition, she wanted them to develop higher reasoning skills, know how to set priorities, make choices, and organize their work. She expected the students to be capable of self-control of their behavior and emerging self-regulation of their academic learning. Success in middle school demanded not only the required academic knowledge, but also self-regulation abilities. Students had to be able to get to the right classes with the right books and materials; they had to take notes, complete homework, and turn it in; they had to adjust quickly to multiple lesson scripts of multiple teachers; they had to be independently goal-directed in long-term projects, and they had to manage their own behavior between classes when teachers were not present.

Like the third-grade teacher, Ms. Silver expected students to be more responsible for their behavior. Rules, however, were not posted—students were simply to know what was appropriate and inappropriate behavior in the classroom. Ms. Silver assumed that by fifth grade the students knew the rules for classroom behavior and would follow them. Even when students violated the rules, she was seldom explicit and direct in her reprimands. She cued students with indirect comments such as, "I didn't know this was recess," if students were talking loudly about things not related to the lesson or, "There must be something wrong with my eyes," if she saw a student grabbing materials from another student.

A major difference between the third- and fifth-grade teachers was their expectations for students' responsibility in mastering academic content. In third grade, Ms. Brennan gave explicit instructions for how tasks were to be completed and would work through some examples in the large or small groups for each lesson. Students were then to continue with additional examples independently at their desks. In fifth grade, Ms. Silver demonstrated for only some of the lessons. Particularly in language arts and social studies, Ms. Silver was likely to give instructions for a general task to be completed, but the students had increased responsibilities for determining the specifics of the task and how they would carry it out. For example, students might be assigned to work together in social studies to find out the kinds of work people did in a particular region of the country, or they might be assigned in language arts to work on a play they would present to the class. The students might have to determine how they would organize their activity and how they would present their products. In some instances, they had to determine a topic for a project. The students were to work in groups on a single task. Unlike second and third grade, where students working in groups were assisting one another in completing their individual assignments, fifth-grade students were given some tasks in which they were to work as a group to achieve a single goal. These lesson scripts were less structured than the lesson scripts in third grade, and consequently required more self-regulation of learning by the students.

Because the inclusion of eight students with learning disabilities in science and social studies had been successful, these and a number of ESL students were included full time in Ms. Silver's classroom. Ms. Silver and Ms. Lester, a special education teacher, team taught the class with the help of an educational assistant. Despite the students' positive feelings about the placement, difficulties arose that resulted in termination of the full-day inclusion. Although Ms. Silver's lesson and discipline scripts worked for the majority of students in the classroom, they were not effective for the students with learning disabilities. Their language processing deficits seriously affected their success in language arts and math lessons. Although the language levels of the ESL students were similar to that of the special education students, the ESL students needed fewer examples and repetition to comprehend.

Behavioral problems were also an issue. Ms. Silver's and Ms. Lester's teaching and behavior management styles differed. The special education students appeared confused by these differences and were uncertain about who was in charge. They were less able to regulate their own behaviors and required more explicit and external controls. They began to pit the two teachers against each other. Inattention and behavioral problems escalated. The teachers tried to make clear each of their roles in the classroom by Ms. Silver presenting the academic content and Ms. Lester managing behavior. The teachers found, however, that they needed to devote considerable time orchestrating each day. This slowed the pace of instruction and risked not covering the required fifth-grade competencies for the general education students. At the same time, the students with learning disabilities were not receiving the level of intervention needed to progress. Ms. Silver and Ms. Lester terminated the full-inclusion program and returned to partial inclusion for multicultural education, social studies, and science classes.

The fifth-grade classroom, with its high expectations for self-regulation and academic performance, was appropriate for the general education and ESL students. However, there was little structural or interactive scaffolding for students having learning difficulties. For the students with special needs, even with the presence of a special education teacher and an aide, the gap between independent performance and assisted performance was too large, and negatively affected both groups of students. This classroom could be considered beyond the zone of proximal development for these students.

Supporting Students in Classrooms

Increasingly, school districts are requiring that SLPs tie goals and objectives for students on their caseloads to curricular standards and benchmarks, and many students with learning disabilities receive much of their academic learning in general education classrooms. As a consequence, SLPs are collaborating with classroom teachers and providing services within classrooms. Even if clinicians are providing remediation in pull-out sessions, they need to understand what the students' academic and social demands are and how the students are meeting these demands. To achieve this, SLPs must observe students within classroom environments.

The changing classroom lesson scripts may trigger inside-out changes in students' abilities that move them from the stage of being controlled by others, to self-control, to self-regulatory management. In doing so, students use language to develop metacognitive skills that make self-control and self-regulation possible. If students do not master both the changing academic content and the changing social scripts that require increasing responsibility for their own behavior and learning, they are likely to be seen as unmotivated or as having a behavioral or learning disability. Students with learning disabilities must be able to access the curriculum in their classrooms. If they are to do so, SLPs and other special educators need to collaborate with classroom teachers to modify classroom scripts to allow greater successful participation by students with disabilities and to facilitate students' development of the language and cognitive skills required by the curriculum.

Collaborating with Teachers

The foregoing classrooms demonstrate some of the ways teachers expect or promote behavior and learning. Students with language impairments need additional structural and interactive support to succeed in regular classrooms. Through classroom observation and interactions with the teacher and students, SLPs can discover how the classroom supports and hinders student performance. This opens avenues for modifying classroom organization and teacher-student interactions.

Being observed in one's classroom can be an intimidating experience for teachers. Over time and through positive collaborations, SLPs can develop mutual, respectful relationships with teachers. To establish an opportunity for open observation, the SLP needs to explain that he or she is observing students to gain an understanding of the classroom demands that should be targeted during intervention. The focus is on the students and how they are managing the classroom demands and acquiring the academic content. The SLP should observe activities in which students are successful as well as activities in which students are exhibiting difficulties to understand what is working or not working for a student and why. The information from the observation is linked with other available information on the student, and the SLP's perceptions are shared with the teacher. The teacher also shares her or his experiences with and goals for the student (see Interviews on pages 343–344). Together, the SLP and teacher determine the classroom style; the match with the student's strengths and weaknesses; methods or activities that could promote the student's participation in class; and how the modifications can be implemented. It is important that the SLP is not judgmental about the teacher's classroom approach, but instead seeks a way to optimize the match between the classroom and student.

Assessing Language and Literacy Skills for the Classroom

Pragmatic Language Skills

Classroom success requires that students master conversational and textual discourse. Most formal language assessments evaluate discrete components of language. Although students may have the semantic, morphologic, syntactic, and pragmatic skills measured on many language assessments, there is no guarantee that they will be able to employ these skills in comprehending and producing conversational and textual discourse in lessons. Consequently, SLPs should investigate the types of discourse that are required in the classroom.

Damico (1985) classified pragmatic difficulties exhibited by students under the Grician postulates of quantity, quality, relation, and manner. Table 8.8 on page 360 summarizes difficulties exhibited in conversations. Damico suggested collecting a conversational language sample and coding each utterance for difficulties in these features of discourse. He suggested that inappropriateness in 25 percent or more of utterances is of concern. Such difficulties are based on clinician judgment, so knowing a teacher and the classroom (e.g., what is implicitly understood by most of the students) is important. The clinician also needs an understanding of typical expectations for a particular grade (e.g., mazes containing restarts, reformulations, and repetitions occur in 17 to 32 percent of a 9 year-old's conversational utterances [Miller et al., 2005]). If utterances are determined to be inappropriate, consider the source of the difficulty; for example, an off-topic comment may indicate lack of attention, poor language comprehension, or poor pragmatics.

A conversational language assessment should involve more than one type of topic, discourse genre, or conversational setting. Damico (1985) recommends the standard 100-utterance sample length for a pragmatic analysis, but a student may only speak a few times an hour in a general classroom setting. By combining multiple settings, more utterances will be available and contextual variation will be included. For example, while working in a general education

Table 8.8   ## Pragmatic Difficulties in Conversation

Category	Features
Quantity	• Failure to provide significant information to listeners • Use of nonspecific vocabulary (e.g., use of vague words such as *thing, stuff*), or deitics (e.g., *this, that,* pronouns) where no antecedent or referent is available in the verbal or nonverbal context • Informational redundancy (student continues to stress a point or return to a topic that has been covered) • Need for repetition (student requires frequent repetition of information in order to participate in the conversation)
Quality	• Message inaccuracy, the information is incorrect
Relation	• Poor topic maintenance (student makes rapid and inappropriate changes in topic without providing transitional cues to the listener) • Inappropriate response • Failure to ask relevant questions (the student does not seek clarification of information that is unclear) • Situational inappropriateness (the contribution violates social conventions of politeness and appropriateness) • Inappropriate speech style (the speaker does not change the structural, lexical, or prosodic nature of utterances to accommodate different listeners
Manner	• Linguistic nonfluency • Revision • Delays before responding • Failure to structure discourse • Turn-taking difficulty • Gaze inefficiency • Inappropriate intonational contour

Source: Damico (1985)

classroom which included students with learning disabilities, the author observed that many of the students did not exhibit obvious difficulties when discussing familiar personal topics or when talking about stories or activities from language arts. In contrast, when discussing science activities in a conversational interview, many of the students exhibited markedly more difficulties. They were more disfluent and struggled to find the words to describe the activities (often reverting to vague words such as *thing* and *stuff*). Discussing science topics appeared to stress working memory. The students had to use unfamiliar vocabulary (e.g., *meniscus, water tension, tectonic plates, condensation*) to express unfamiliar concepts in unfamiliar discourse structures (e.g., explanations).

Syntactic Complexity

Written texts require the use and comprehension of more complex syntactic structures than oral conversational texts. The SLP should note the types of syntactic structures used in textbooks and trade books that students are reading and the types of syntactic structures used by students in their oral and written communication in the classroom. Reviewing the Newbery Award books is a good way to become familiar with the syntactic structure of quality children's literature. Pay special attention to participial phrases and dependent clauses, because these are associated with language development during the school years. Table 8.9 on page 362 presents text examples on both.

Making Inferences

Many classroom interactions, particularly in social studies and language arts, involve group reading and discussing of texts. Reading involves more than decoding. By mid-elementary school and beyond, students must be able to "read between the lines" and integrate information within the text and from past knowledge to make appropriate inferences. Questions at higher Bloom and Blank levels require making inferences. Students with language impairments exhibit difficulty making appropriate inferences, even when they are fluent decoders (Oakhill & Yuill, 1996). Consequently, they are likely to miss the main point of questions and provide tangential information. If this occurs frequently, teachers may call on them less frequently or may resort to asking them only low-level knowledge questions. Such students will require assistance in understanding when inferences are needed and how to make inferences. To provide appropriate scaffolding, teachers need to understand the nature of students' inferencing difficulties.

Informal reading inventories, such as the Qualitative Reading Inventory–III (Leslie & Caldwell, 2001) and the Reading Inventory for the Classroom (Cooter, Cooter, & Flynt, 2003) provide a way to assess students' inferencing skills. Both of these instruments provide several narrative and

Table 8.9

Examples of Literate Syntax
Appearing in Children's Literature

Participial Phrases	
Opener	*Rising with two pups held close to my chest,* I asked if I owned anything. (Wilson Rawls, *Where the Red Fern Grows,* 1961)
S–V Split	Sophie, *sitting on the big friendly giant's hand,* peeped out of the cave. (Roald Dahl, *The Big Friendly Giant,* 1982)
Closer	Albert was standing in the middle of the dock now, *wrapping the kitten in the edge of his shirt* (Patricia Giff, *Lily's Crossing,* 1997)
Dependent Adverb Clauses	
When Did It Happen? *(as, when, while, before, after, until)*	*When the class took their seats at the conclusion of the patriotic hymn,* Asher remained standing to make his public apology as was required. (Lois Lowry, *The Giver,* 1993)
Why Did It Happen? *(because, since)*	Release of new students was always sad, *because they hadn't had a chance to enjoy life within the community.* (Lois Lowry, *The Giver,* 1993)
Under What Conditions? *(if, although)*	Her voice softened *as she looked at the sleepy little dog.* (Mildred D. Taylor, *Song of the Trees,* 1975)
Who (with S–V split)	The twins, *who had finished their homework,* were allowed to watch half an hour of TV. (Madeleine L'Engle, *A Wrinkle in Time,* 1962)
Which	Dudley hitched up his trousers, *which were slipping down his fat bottom.* (J. K. Rowling, *Harry Potter and the Chamber of Secrets,* 1999)
Whose (with S–V split)	Little Jon, *whose eyes were quicker than most,* should have seen the hole, but all his attention was on the stars. (Alexander Key, *The Forgotten Door,* 1965)

expository passages at each grade level that a student can listen to or read. Students retell the passage and are asked both explicit (literal) and implicit (inferential) questions about the passages. Dewitz and Dewitz (2003) suggested a strategy for analyzing the nature of students' error responses to the questions. Errors can be coded as:

- Failure to link ideas across a passage (required for making relational inferences)

- Failure to make causal inferences

- Failure to properly parse or interpret syntax, resulting in incorrect interpretation of a sentence

- Excessive elaboration (i.e., overreliance on prior knowledge rather than using the information in the text)

- Failure to know a key vocabulary word

- No response, did not answer

Facilitating Classroom Language and Participation

A Classroom Example

By collaborating in classrooms, SLPs and teachers can facilitate students' development of the language skills necessary for participating effectively in lessons. An assessment this author conducted of Kevin, a fifth-grade boy with language/literacy disabilities, resulted in an ongoing collaboration with Ms. Kent, his classroom teacher. As Ms. Kent gained an understanding of Kevin's strengths and needs in her classroom, she began to realize that he was not unique, and that other students would benefit from modifications in her lessons. Mimbres, Ms. Kent's school, served a largely Hispanic population, most of whom qualified for free and reduced lunch. On the last statewide assessment, Mimbres scores were among the lowest three schools in a district of nearly 100,000 students. Ms. Kent's classroom had several students who received ESL services and several students who received speech-language services because of histories of language impairments. In addition, seven students with severe learning disabilities were included in her science and social studies lessons.

Ms. Kent had received a grant to develop her science lessons. Few students at Mimbres had received science lessons in their previous classes. They were all enthusiastic about the new experiences, participated actively in the experiments, and reported what they had seen and why it had happened. Because the students were actively involved, Ms. Kent was initially unaware of the degree to which many of her students experienced difficulty with extended scientific discourse. She employed an IRE or IRF format when leading the discussion with the 28 students in the science class. Participation in the discussions generally required short answers of only a few words. Because of her careful scaffolding and cuing, student responses were often judged as correct.

The author interviewed students individually after a science lesson on water tension, in which students were to discover how many pennies they could put into a full glass of pure water and a full glass of water with soap before the water spilled. Each student was asked to describe the steps in the experiment just completed, what they observed, and what happened. (NOTE: The glass with soap cannot hold as many pennies before the water spills, because soap breaks the surface tension of water.) The majority of the students' responses were disfluent and incomprehensible, as in the following example:

> I got the blue…I got, uh, two cups and two bowls and we put them in…we put them each in one bowl and then Ms. Kent put some water, some plain water into a cup and then we put, she filled it all the way to the top of the rim and then we were putting pennies in it until and we have to keep track of counting so we can see how many pennies would go in to see if it would fall over. Because it was too, it was too much weight for it, because if the pennies were going, it was light for it because it was just plain water but if you put the pennies in then it makes it too heavier cuz it goes all to the bottom.

Ms. Kent was surprised and distressed when she reviewed transcripts of the students' conversations. Based on the ways the students had answered her questions in the lessons, she had assumed that they had an understanding of the procedures and concepts being discussed. When they were required to produce extended discourse, however, students had difficulty clearly describing the procedures and what they observed, and no one produced a correct, coherent explanation. Review of their science notebooks also revealed that they produced similar sentences and made little use of connective words that defined temporal and causal relationships. They were not developing the literate syntactic styles expected of students at their grade level. Ms. Kent decided to do directive teaching of syntactic structures so that the students would have sentence frames to use to express their ideas. The school SLP and this author provided a variety of materials to assist her and gave suggestion for where to begin based on our analysis of the students' discourse and the syntactic patterns in the language arts and science curriculum materials.

Developing Advanced Syntax

Students who exhibit the use of vague vocabulary, repetitions, and poorly structured sentences need assistance in developing academic language structures. They need to develop a variety of more complex phrase and clause structures and to realize that syntax can be flexible (i.e., an idea can be presented in more than one form). Over the year, Ms. Kent explicitly taught adverbial clauses, adjectival clauses, and participial phrases. These structures were initially introduced in language arts lessons where students were familiar with the vocabulary and concepts and, therefore, could attend to the sentence structures. Students were taught that dependent clauses and participial phrases can appear in different positions in sentences—as openers to sentences, closers to sentences, or between the subject and verb of sentences. They discussed the functions of clauses and phrases. For example, adverbial clauses use cue words to tell why, when, where, how, under what conditions, or to what extent:

- Time: *after, as, as long as, as soon as, before, until, when, since, whenever, while*

- Place: *where, wherever*

- Condition: *even though, if, unless, whether*

- Cause: *as, because, since*

- Purpose: *so that, in order that*

- Concession: *though, although*

- Comparison: *than*

- Manner: *as, as if, as though*

The sequence of practice activities outlined by Killgallon and Killgallon (2000) was used with materials that students were reading and discussing. An example of the sequence based on patterns from the novel *Holes* (Sachar, 1998) is provided in Table 8.10 on page 366.

After students had experiences with this sequence of practice activities based on model sentences from a familiar book, they were given activities to use the structures more independently. For example, they were asked to write three sentences with adverbial *when* clauses that told what happened when Stanley found the metal tube in the hole he had dug. And they were told to use the clauses in different positions in the sentences. Possible examples could be:

Instructional Sequence for Teaching Adverbial Clauses and Participial Phrases

Table 8.10

Instructional Step	Examples from *Holes* (Sachar, 1998)
1. Identifying First, students underline adverbial clauses in sentences.	• <u>If you take a bad boy and make him dig a hole every day in the hot sun,</u> it will turn him into a good boy. • "Not every Stanley Yelnats has been a failure," Stanley's mother often pointed out, <u>whenever Stanley or his father became so discouraged that they actually started to believe in the curse.</u> • The bus ride became increasingly bumpy <u>because the road was no longer paved.</u>
2. Combining Next, students combine two sentences by making the underlined part of the second sentence an adverbial clause, adding the clause at the ^, then writing the new sentence.	• ^ they would go not only to Doc Hawthorn but also to Sam. They did this <u>whenever they were sick.</u> Whenever they were sick, they would go not only to Doc Hawthorn but also to Sam. • It took Sam a week to fix the roof ^ It took Sam that long <u>because he could only work in the afternoons, after school let out and before night classes began.</u> It took Sam a week to fix the roof because he could only work in the afternoons, after school let out and before night classes began.
3. Unscrambling Students unscramble a list of sentence parts. They write out the new sentence.	• because he wouldn't have time to rinse off the suds • which was just as well • he never managed to use his bar of soap He never managed to use his bar of soap, which was just as well, <u>because he wouldn't have time to rinse off the suds.</u>

Table 8.10—*Continued*

Instructional Step	Examples from *Holes* (Sachar, 1998)
4. Expanding Students create an adverbial clause to complete a sentence.	• If...you'll get the rest of the day off. • It (the pool table) was full of bumps and holes because...
5. Combining to Imitate Students are given several novel, related sentences and asked to combine the sentences using the model sentence as a pattern.	• Example from the book: As he dug his hole, Stanley thought about what it would be like if Derrick Dunne had to fight Armpit or Squid. • Novel sentences from 3 parts: 1. if Marci had to help Jon or Keishia 2. Jodie wondered what would happen 3. as she cooked dinner As she cooked dinner, Jodie wondered what would happen if Marci had to help Jon or Keishia.

- *When Stanley found the piece of metal in his hole*, X-Ray demanded that he give it to him.

- Stanley wondered, *when he found the piece of metal in his hole*, what the warden would do.

- Stanley thought he would get the day off *when he found the lipstick tube in his hole*.

As students developed competence in using these frames in language arts, Ms. Kent introduced them into the science lessons. For example, when discussing tectonic plates, she requested, "Give me a sentence about tectonic plates using an adverbial clause with *because*."

Ernest: Earthquakes occur because tectonic plates slide against each other.

Lori: Mountains develop because tectonic plates converge.

Ms. Kent responded, "OK, now someone say that using the adverbial clause as an opener."

Joshua said, "Because tectonic plates slide beside each other, earthquakes occur." Mica then complained, "It's not fair Ms. Kent. You're making us do English in science class!" This comment provided a good opportunity to bridge between English and science. Ms. Kent explained that sentence combining is not an arbitrary grammatical exercise, but that it helps express meaning, and adverbial clauses are particularly helpful in science to link causes and effects.

Promoting Discourse

Students cannot be expected to generate sentence patterns and discourse if they have not experienced the discourse in authentic contexts. Classrooms can present students with opportunities to engage in authentic extended discourse, but often the IRE nature of lessons does not offer them this opportunity. Ms. Kent became aware that her students needed opportunities to experience and engage in extended discourse on the science topics. However, with 28 students in the class (7 with identified learning disabilities), it was not possible to engage all students in lengthy discussions during each lesson period. Therefore, each day Ms. Kent gave a few students the opportunity to give extended answers. Over the course of a week, all students had opportunities to give extended responses. General education students were usually called on before the students with learning disabilities so the students with learning disabilities heard some examples before they were asked to contribute. To facilitate students developing the expected discourse patterns, this author demonstrated revoicing to Ms. Kent, who then incorporated this method into her lessons. Miguel's explanation of the water tension experiment was relatively easy for Ms. Kent to revoice:

Miguel:	The soap the chemicals in the soap they would like get in in the middle of the regular water and make it not hold together.
Teacher:	So Miguel, you're explaining that the soap molecules separated the water molecules and broke the water tension.

In contrast, it was more difficult to revoice Mica's explanation because Ms. Kent was not certain what Mica meant:

Mica:	Cuz, the soap holds down the pennies and the the bubbles from the pennies goes up and it floats and you put one more and it floats out.

Teacher: So Mica, you're suggesting that the soap bubbles cause the water to overflow the cup.

Ms. Kent required students to produce a written report for each experiment that they conducted. For the first experiment on each new science topic, Ms. Kent provided a model report that presented the procedures, described her observations and results, and explained the results. For the second experiment, Ms. Kent and the students jointly constructed the three components of the report. On an overhead transparency, Ms. Kent wrote the sentences offered by students. She reminded them that students in another fifth grade class would use this report to conduct their experiment, so the report needed to be explicit and not contain irrelevant information. Students talked about the clarity of what they were writing and made revisions. Students copied these jointly constructed reports into their journals. For the third and other experiments on a topic, the students were to write their reports independently in their journals. A graphic organizer (shown in Figure 8.2) was placed in their notebooks to remind them of the components of each report.

Figure 8.2   **Science Report Graphic Organizer**

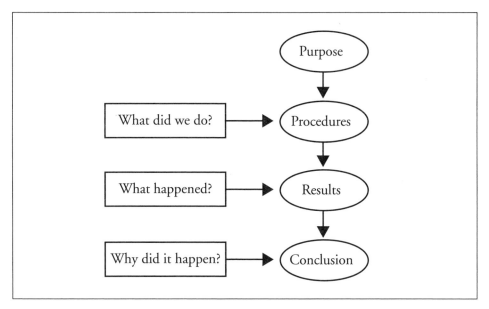

Learning to Inference

The majority of Ms. Kent's students were fluent decoders, but their reading scores were generally in the lowest quartile. In reviewing their responses on a reading assessment similar to the Qualitative Reading Inventory (Leslie & Caldwell, 2001), we noted that many students did not do well on questions that required inferencing. Inferencing is central to the comprehension process. It involves the process of generating assumptions, making predictions, and coming to conclusions based on the information provided in the text and illustrations. Students who have difficulty making appropriate inferences may lack the vocabulary or understanding of the texts' syntactic structure to make the necessary inferences. Or, they may make plausible, but incorrect, inferences because of underdeveloped reasoning abilities, lack of prior knowledge, or overreliance on prior knowledge. Students can benefit from explicit teaching about inferencing during their lessons.

There are two main types of inferences: causal and relational. Causal inferences require readers to infer the antecedent or consequence of an action. For example, in *Ghost Wings* (Joose, 2001), the little girl and her grandmother go to the Magic Circle, where the monarch butterflies are clinging to the trees. It was a cloudy day, and the butterflies were "still as stone." Students must realize that the clouds cause the day to be chilly, so the butterflies cannot move when they are cold.

Relational inferences require readers to make inferences across sentences. For example, when reading *The Stranger* (van Allsburg, 1986), students must pick up cues about who the stranger is. In this story, Farmer Bailey accidentally hits a man with his truck. He takes the stranger home with him. After checking the stranger, the doctor throws away the thermometer because the mercury is stuck at the bottom; when the stranger blows gently on his soup, the Baileys shiver; the summer continues for longer than usual and the leaves on the trees around the farm do not change color; the stranger never sweats, no matter how hard he works. When the stranger leaves the note, "See you next fall," readers need to infer that the stranger was Jack Frost.

Some students are not aware that they are expected to make inferences. They must recognize what information is explicitly stated in the text and what information they must bring from other experiences to the interpretation of the text. Students can develop their understanding of when inferencing is necessary as adults encourage them to reflect on relationships between questions that can be asked of texts and their answers. Table 8.11 shows the types of question-answer relationships and gives examples based on the book, *Harvesting Hope: The Story of Cesar Chavez* (Krull, 2003).

Table 8.11   **Question-Answer Relationships**

Type of Relation	Definition	Examples Based on *Harvesting Hope* (Krull, 2003)
Right There	The answer is explicitly stated in the text.	How old was Cesar when he moved to California?
Think and Search	The answer is in the text but the words in the question and the words in the text are not the same, or the answer is not in just one location.	What made farm work in California so miserable?
You and the Author	You must think about what you have learned from the text and use what you already know to answer the question.	Why do you think that Cesar Chavez used a nonviolent approach to achieve his goals?
On Your Own	The question is motivated by some information in the text, but the answer has to be generated from your prior knowledge.	In what other situations might it be best to use a nonviolent approach to bring about change?

Teachers can also assist students in making inferences by modeling how to reason, make assumptions, and come to conclusions. By using a *How do you know?* strategy, students can be helped to focus their attention on information that is explicitly stated in texts or shown in illustrations and to (1) make connections between explicit and implied information, and (2) examine their reasoning so they can justify their assumptions and conclusions (Richards & Anderson, 2003).

The teacher explains to students that there are two types of connections they must make when listening to or reading stories. The teacher then models how to make inferences by reading a book aloud, stopping at a place where an

Journal Entry Dealing with Inferential Comprehension of a Children's Book

Box 8.1

How Do I Know?

Book: *White Socks Only* by E. Coleman (1996)

Page and paragraph number/or situation: Water fountain with sign, "Whites Only." Little girl takes off her black shoes and steps up to the fountain in her white socks.

My inference: "Whites Only" doesn't mean white socks. It means only white people can drink from the fountain. White people will get mad when they see a Black girl drinking from the fountain.

How do I know? The story happened a long time ago. The person telling the story said she is telling a story about her grandmother. Before Martin Luther King, Jr., Black people couldn't eat or drink where white people did.

---

inference should be made, and asking a question that prompts students to infer important information. For example, when reading the book *America* (Rodriguez, 1998), about a Mixteco girl in Chicago, the teacher asks, "Does America feel happy to live in Chicago?" When the students respond, "No," the teacher confirms their answer and asks, "Does the author say that?" When the students reply, "No," the teacher asks them, "Then how do you know?" Then the clues that let them know she is unhappy are discussed. For example, the teacher might say that the girl thinks a lot about what she had done in her village in Mexico; she sits in the back of the room and doesn't talk, but she used to talk a lot; her father works in a factory and she rarely sees him because he works all night and sleeps all day.

Once students are familiar with the inferencing questioning strategy, teachers can shift the responsibility for identifying inferential connections to the students. The teacher can select paragraphs and ask students, "Can you think of any inferences you can make in this paragraph? Explain your thinking. How did you figure out the connections?" Students can also work individually or in groups to fill out inferencing journal charts on books they read. (Box 8.1 above provides an example of a journal entry.) The inferencing journal charts provide a way to document students' growth in making inferential connections, framing questions, reasoning, and sharing their thinking with peers.

Promoting Self-Regulation and Self-Determination

Many students in Ms. Kent's fifth-grade class exhibited a low self-esteem and sense of learned helplessness. While these students had made advances in their self-regulatory behavior (managing internal states and external behaviors to achieve specific tasks), they lacked a sense of self-determination (having confidence in one's ability to achieve important goals). With a grant from the local gas and electric company, Ms. Kent had been devoting additional attention to teaching science. She received an announcement from the National Atomic Museum regarding summer science camps and available scholarships. Eagerly, she described the opportunity to her students, explaining that with all their special science work that year, she had been assured that they could receive scholarships to attend—they simply had to write a paragraph on the topic, "Science Is Everywhere." The students looked at her and announced, "That's not for us; that's for smart kids." Initially shocked and disheartened by this response, Ms. Kent determined to change their attitudes.

Together, Ms. Kent and this author found a number of biographies that described well-known persons' early years, obstacles they experienced, and what they did to overcome the obstacles. From *What's the Matter with Albert: A Story of Albert Einstein* (Wishinsky, 2002), they learned about Einstein's temper, difficulty learning in school, and how he learned to work at what he loved. From *Thank You, Mr. Falker* (Polacco, 1998), they learned that the author had a reading disability as a student but overcame it with the help of her teacher, Mr. Falker, and went on to become a noted writer. From *A Picture Book of Thomas Alva Edison* (Adler, 1996), they learned that Edison's teacher didn't think he was smart enough to learn, but he became a famous inventor. From *Manya's Dream: A Story of Marie Curie* (Wishinsky, 2003), they learned that the famous scientist had not been permitted to speak her home language (Polish) in school and that, because she was a girl, she was not permitted to go to the university in Poland—she had to find a way to go to another country. From all of these books, they learned what the persons had done to succeed. Ms. Kent posted enlarged pictures with quotes from the books in prominent places in the room, such as:

> Anyone who has never made a mistake has never tried anything new. (Albert Einstein)

> We must believe that we are fitted for something and that this thing must be attained. (Marie Curie)

The objective of reading the books was to have students realize that well-known people had childhood experiences similar to theirs and to understand what these people had done to succeed. (NOTE: Eventually nine students wrote essays and received scholarships for science camp, including Mark, who had a reading disability.)

Teachers need to be consciously aware of the need for increasing self-regulation and self-determination during the school years. Although teachers will not be able to address within classrooms all the specific self-regulation skills students with language impairments and attentional deficits may need, there are some ways they can structure the environment and provide classwide interventions that will promote self-regulation (Dawson & Guare, 2004). By modifying the environment, teachers change conditions or situations external to the student to improve self-regulation or reduce the effects of weak self-regulatory skills. These changes may be specific to the student or may be classroomwide:

- **Changing the physical or social environment to reduce challenges.** Consider the teacher to whom the student is assigned. Students with self-regulatory deficits tend to do best with teachers who provide explicit structure and consistent routines. Consider where the student sits in the classroom—can the student easily see the board or charts that provide guidelines as to what to do?

- **Changing the nature of the task the student is to perform.** The teacher should provide a graduated task sequence beginning with the easier options below and moving to long tasks, few instructions, and open-ended responding:

  1. Making the task shorter
  2. Making the steps more explicit
  3. Making the task close-ended
  4. Providing scoring rubrics to define exactly what is to be included in class assignments

- **Changing the ways cues are provided.** Like tasks, prompts should become gradually less explicit and should turn the reminders back onto the students, such as, "What do you need to bring to writing group?"

1. Use verbal prompts or reminders. The teacher might say, "When you come to writing group, bring your notebook, pencil, and eraser."

2. Use visual cues. Classroom rules, steps in projects, or frameworks for writing can be posted in prominent places so they are readily visible. One can also attach sets of directions or graphic organizers on individual desks using wide transparent tape.

3. Use visual schedules. Create a schedule for a specific event or block of time.

4. Make lists of things to do and encourage students to make lists.

- **Providing classroom routines.** Regular routines help students internalize expectations. The teacher can employ beginning-of-the-day routines to accomplish tasks such as handing in homework, getting materials ready for the day, and making a schedule for the day. End-of-day routines can be done to make certain homework assignments are written in agenda books, make certain that students have what they need to take home, review assignments, and arrange the workspace so students can begin the next day smoothly.

- **Providing classroom rules.** Both Ms. Brennan at La Chamisa and Ms. Kent at Mimbres posted the class rules on large legible posters. The rules should be taught explicitly at the beginning of the year, using the following procedures:

  1. Tell the class the rule (e.g., "Ask before you borrow something").

  2. Practice the rule (e.g., "How can you ask politely for something? Jeremy, may I use your ruler?").

  3. Initially provide external rewards to students for following the rule (e.g., "Marcus, thank you for asking to use my tape").

  4. Cue the class to follow the rule (e.g., "We'll need to share materials in the science lesson. Be sure to ask before you borrow from someone").

  5. Fade the cue (e.g., "What's the rule when you need something?").

- **Providing organizational systems.** Teachers can develop systems that help students keep their materials and work organized.

1. Ms. Kent had an extensive library in her classroom. She organized the materials by genre (e.g., historical fiction, fantasy, realistic novels, biographies, science). Colored dots on the spines of books signaled categories of books. By consistently returning books to their correct location, students also began to recognize the various genres.

2. Provide separate bins for homework being turned in and for corrected homework. Always list homework or important information in the same place (e.g., upper-left corner of chalkboard).

3. A variety of organizational systems are available for students to use to keep track of schedules and assignments. Consider having the school adopt a gradewide or schoolwide system so that students who are in more than one classroom do not need to deal with multiple systems.

Structuring the classroom environment benefits all students, not just those with disabilities. Although initially setting up the systems and routines requires additional planning time, the organization results in more efficient use of lesson time.

Conclusion

IEPs for the majority of students with disabilities must facilitate students' access to the general education curriculum and their achievement of identified benchmarks and standards. SLPs and classroom teachers must work together to have a comprehensive understanding of students' strengths and needs and to develop interventions that not only enable academic success, but allow this learning to happen within regular classrooms. To accomplish this, educators must understand the multiple factors that support and compromise students' ability to perform in lessons. Therefore, they must consider what students bring to the classroom (inside-out evaluation) and they must reflect both on the lesson content and on the ways they construct and conduct the lessons (outside-in evaluation). Teachers and SLPs are more familiar with the cognitive and linguistic abilities students need to handle the academic content of classrooms than they are with the abilities students need for managing the social scripts that enable the students to access the academic content.

When observing what is happening in classroom interactions, Au (1993) suggested the importance of assuming that students' actions are inherently logical, even if that logic may be quite different from that of teachers, or from what is expected in mainstream education. The observer not only wants to identify behaviors, but also to explain why the behaviors are occurring. Teachers must be able to differentiate interactional classroom patterns that reflect language learning difficulties from those that reflect cultural differences. Teachers must have an understanding of the discourse and interactional styles of both the students' homes and communities, and of the academic disciplines that the students must master. Some aspects of home and community discourse styles are not compatible with the discourse styles of particular school disciplines. The trick is to determine what aspects of the home/community discourse style can be used to facilitate development of academic content, and what new types of discourse styles students need for mastering lesson content.

There is increasing interest in the United States in understanding how students perform in lessons and how to make lessons more effective for all students. Part of this interest is in response to the requirement of the No Child Left Behind Act (2002) for all students to show educational progress. Another impetus for this concern was the poor performance of U.S. students on the Third International Math and Science Study (TIMSS). In attempting to account for the better performance of Japanese students compared to U.S. students, researchers investigated how teaching differs between the U.S. and Japanese educational systems (Stigler & Hiebert, 1999). One factor was the number of topics covered in a subject area and the depth to which they were covered. Japanese teachers covered far fewer topics and explored each topic in greater depth. A second factor accounting for differences in structure and quality of lessons was the Japanese practice of lesson study. In lesson study, small, supportive groups of teachers observe one another conducting lessons and discuss the lesson goals and observations. By engaging in lesson study, teachers learn to see instruction through the eyes of their students. The ultimate goal of lesson study in Japan is student learning and development. Broad goals of lesson study (Lewis, 2002) are:

- To develop instruction that ensures students' basic academic abilities, fosters their individuality, and meets their individual needs

- For students to take pleasure in friendships and learning

- For instruction to be such that students learn eagerly

In lesson study, teachers observe more than the lessons themselves. They observe students' whole demeanor toward learning and toward one another. They gather evidence on students' learning, engagement, and treatment of one another, for example, how they work in small groups, the quality of their discussion within groups, and whether they show interest and motivation. Teachers scour the classroom for evidence of student learning and motivation. They look at everything from how students' thinking changed over a lesson to whether the quietest students spoke; and they gather information on their own actions, for example, the questions they ask students, how many students are called on, and how they evaluate or provide feedback on students' responses (Lewis, 2002). In the process, they are gathering evidence that they can use to foster both students' academic and social development.

The lesson study framework provides a ready mechanism for teachers and SLPs to collaborate. Ms. Kent at Mimbres had been participating in a lesson study group with other teachers at her school. As a result, she was comfortable having observers and discussing her lesson goals. The added collaboration of the school and consultant SLPs was readily incorporated into the process. SLPs bring valuable skills to the lesson study process. They are able to analyze the language of both the student and the curriculum, identify any mismatches, and suggest strategies to develop the language skills students need to succeed. Such input is especially critical for students with language impairments and students from culturally/linguistically diverse backgrounds. With federal education regulations requiring inclusion of the majority of students with disabilities in large-scale assessments and the mandate that all students make adequate yearly progress, principals and teachers are seeking additional classroom support. SLPs have a critical role to play in the education of students with limited language skills outside the traditional therapeutic interventions. Incorporating classroom consultation and collaboration within a lesson study framework can increase general education teachers' involvement in the process of educating students with disabilities and result in improved lessons for all students.

References

Abramson, L. V., Seligman, M. P., & Teasdale, J. D. (1978). Learned helplessness in humans: Critique and reformulation. *Journal of Abnormal Psychology,* 87, 49–74.

Adler, D. A. (1996). *A picture book of Thomas Alva Edison.* New York: Holiday House.

Au, K. H. (1993). *Literacy instruction in multicultural settings.* Orlando, FL: Harcourt Brace.

Blank, M., Rose, S. A., & Berlin, L. J. (1978). *The language of learning: The preschool years.* New York: Grune & Stratton.

Bloom, N. (1956). *Taxonomy of educational objectives: Handbook 1, cognitive domain.* New York: Longman.

Brinton, B., & Fujiki, M. (2004). Social and affective factors in children with language impairment. In C. A. Stone, E. R. Silliman, B. J. Ehren, & K. Apel, (Eds.), *Handbook of language and literacy* (pp. 130–153). New York: Guilford.

Brislin, R. (1993). *Understanding culture's influence on behavior.* Fort Worth, TX: Harcourt Brace.

Cahir, S., & Kivac, C. (1981a). *Teacher talk works.* Washington, DC: Center for Applied Linguistics.

Cahir, S., & Kivac, C. (1981b). *It's your turn.* Washington, DC: Center for Applied Linguistics.

Cazden, C. B. (1988). *Classroom discourse: The language of teaching and learning.* Portsmouth, NH: Heinemann.

Cazden, C. B. (2001). *Classroom discourse: The language of teaching and learning* (2nd ed.). Portsmouth, NH: Heinemann.

Coleman, E. (1996). *White socks only.* Morton Grove, IL: Albert Whitman.

Collins, J. P. (1996). Socialization to text: Structure and contradiction in schooled literacy. In M. Silverstein & G. Urban (Eds.), *National histories of discourse* (pp. 203–228). Chicago: University of Chicago Press.

Cook-Gumperz, J., & Gumperz, J. J. (1982). In L. C. Wilkinson (Ed.), *Communicating in the classroom* (pp. 13–24). New York: Academic Press.

Cooter, R. B., Cooter, R., & Flynt, E. S. (2003). *Flynt-Cooter Reading Inventory for the Classroom.* New York: Macmillan.

Crago, M., Eriks-Brophy, A., Pesco, D., & McAlpine, L. (1997). Culturally based miscommunication in classroom interaction. *Language, Speech, and Hearing Services in Schools, 28*(3), 245–254.

Creaghead, N. (1992a). Classroom interactional analysis/script analysis. In W. A. Secord & J. S. Damico (Eds.), *Best practices in school speech-language pathology* (pp. 65–72). Austin, TX: Psychological Corporation.

Creaghead, N. (1992b). *Classroom language intervention: Developing schema for school success.* Buffalo, NY: Educom Associates.

Dahl, R. (1982). *The big friendly giant.* New York: Puffin Books.

Damico, J. S. (1985). Clinical discourse analysis: A functional approach. In C. S. Simon (Ed.), *Communication skills and classroom success.* San Diego, CA: College-Hill.

Dawson, P., & Guare, R. (2004). *Executive skills in children and adolescents.* New York: Guilford.

Delpit, L. D. (1988). The silenced dialogue: Power and pedagogy in educating other people's children. *Harvard Educational Review, 58,* 280–298.

Diaz, R. M., Neal, C. J., & Amaya-Williams, M. (1990). The social origins of self-regulation. In L. C. Moll (Ed.), *Vygotsky and education: Instructional implications and applications of sociohistorical psychology* (pp. 127–154). New York: Cambridge University Press.

Dewitz, P., & Dewitz, P. K. (2003). They can read the words, but they can't understand: Refining comprehension assessment. *The Reading Teacher, 56*(5), 422–435.

Eder, D. (1982). Differences in communicative styles across ability groups. In L. C. Wilkinson (Ed.), *Communicating in the classroom* (pp. 245–264). New York: Academic Press.

Erickson, F. (1982). Classroom discourse as improvisation: Relationships between academic task structure and social participation structure in lessons. In L. C. Wilkinson (Ed.), *Communicating in the classroom* (pp. 153–181). New York: Academic Press.

Erickson, F., & Mohatt, G. (1982). Cultural organization of participation structures in two classrooms of Indian students. In G. Spindler (Ed.), *Doing the ethnography of schooling* (pp. 132–174). New York: Holt, Rinehart & Winston.

Erickson, F., & Shultz, J. (1981). When is a context: Some issues and methods in the analysis of social competence. In J. L. Green & C. Wallet (Eds.), *Ethnography and language in educational settings.* Norwood, NJ: Ablex.

Fletcher, T. V., Boss, C. S., & Johnson, L. M. (1999). Accommodating English language learners with language and learning disabilities in bilingual education classrooms. *Learning Disabilities Research & Practice, 14*(2), 80–91.

Fujiki, M., Brinton, B., Robinson, L., & Watson, V. (1997). The ability of children with specific language impairment to participate in group decision making. *Journal of Children's Communication Development, 18,* 1–10.

Giff, P. (1997). *Lily's crossing.* New York: Delacorte.

Green, J. L., & Harker, J. O. (Eds.). (1988). *Multiple perspective analyses of classroom discourse.* Norwood, NJ: Ablex.

Green, J., & Wallet, C. (1981). *Ethnography and language in educational settings.* Norwood, NJ: Ablex.

Green, J. L., Weade, R., Graham, K. (1988). In J. L. Green & J. P. Harker (Eds.), *Multiple perspective analyses of classroom discourse* (pp. 183–222). Norwood, NJ: Ablex.

Greenwood, C. R., Abbott, M., & Tapia, Y. (2003). Ecobehavioral strategies: Observing, measuring, and analyzing behavior and reading interventions. In S. Vaughn & K. Briggs (Eds.), *Reading in the classroom: Systems for the observation of teaching and learning* (pp. 53–82). Baltimore: Brookes.

Gumperz, J. J. (1981). Conversational inference and classroom learning. In J. Green & C. Wallet (Eds.), *Ethnography and language in educational settings* (pp. 3–23). Norwood, NJ: Ablex.

Hirsch, E. D. (2002). *The new dictionary of cultural literacy: What every American needs to know.* Boston: Houghton Mifflin.

Hofstede, G. J., Pedersen, P. B., & Hofstede, G. (2002). *Exploring culture.* Yarmouth, ME: Intercultural Press.

Joose, B. (2001). *Ghost wings.* San Francisco: Chronicle Books.

Key, A. (1965). *The forgotten door.* New York: Scholastic.

Killgallon, D., & Killgallon, J. (2000). *Sentence composing for elementary school.* Portsmouth, NH: Heinemann.

Krull, K. (2003). *Harvesting hope: The story of Cesar Chavez.* San Diego, CA: Harcourt.

L'Engle, M. (1962). *A wrinkle in time.* New York: Ariel.

Leslie, L., & Caldwell, J. (2001). *Qualitative Reading Inventory–3.* Longman: New York.

Lewis, C. (2002). Does lesson study have a future in the United States? *Nagoya Journal of Human Development, 1,* 1–23. Retrieved July 20, 2004, from http://www.teacherscollege.edu/lessonstudy/articles_papers.html

Lowell, S. (1992). *The three little javelinas.* Flagstaff, AZ: Northland Publishing.

Lowry, L. (1993). *The giver.* Boston: Houghton Mifflin.

MacWhinney, B. (2000). *The CHILDES project: Tools for analyzing talk.* Mahwah, NJ: Erlbaum.

Marton, F., & Tsui, A. B. M. (2004). *Classroom discourse and the space of learning.* Mahwah, NJ: Erlbaum.

McCollum, P. (1989). Turn-allocation in lessons with North American and Puerto Rican students: A comparative study. *Anthropology and Education Quarterly, 20,* 133–157.

McDermott, R. (1978). Relating and learning: An analysis of two classroom reading groups. In R. Shuy (Ed.), *Linguistics and reading.* Rawley, MA: Newbury House.

McIntosh, R., Vaughn, S., Schumm, J., Haager, D., & Lee, O. (1993). Observations of students with learning disabilities in general education classrooms. *Exceptional Children, 60*(3), 249–261.

Mehan, H. (1979). *Learning lessons: Social organization in the classroom.* Cambridge, MA: Harvard University Press.

Miller, J. S., & Iglesias, A. (2004). *Systematic analysis of language transcripts (Version 8).* Madison, WI: Language Analysis Lab, Waisman Center, University of Wisconsin–Madison.

Miller, J. F., Long, S., McKinley, N., Thormann, S., Jones, M. A., & Nockerts, A. (2005). *Language sample analysis II: The Wisconsin guide.* Madison, WI: Wisconsin Department of Public Instruction.

National Center for Education Statistics. (1996). *Pursuing excellence: Initial findings from the third international mathematics and science study.* Washington, DC: U.S. Government Printing Office.

Nelson, N. W. (1984). Beyond information processing: The language of teachers and textbooks. In G. P. Wallach & K. G. Butler (Eds.), *Language learning disabilities in school-age children* (pp. 154–178). Baltimore: Williams & Wilkins.

Nelson, N. W. (1989). Curriculum-based language assessment and intervention. *Language, Speech, and Hearing Services in Schools, 20,* 170–184.

Nelson, N. W. (1992). Targets of curriculum-based language assessment. In W. A. Secord & J. S. Damico (Eds.), *Best practices in school speech-language pathology* (pp. 73–85). Austin, TX: Psychological Corporation.

No Child Left Behind Act of 2001, 20 U.S.C. § 6311 *et seq.* (2002).

Oakhill, J., & Yuill, N. (1996). Higher order factors in comprehension disability: Processes and remediation. In C. Cornoldi & J. Oakhill (Eds.), *Reading comprehension difficulties: Processes and intervention* (pp. 69–92). Mahwah, NJ: Erlbaum.

O'Connor, M. C., & Michaels, S. (1996). Shifting participant frameworks: Orchestrating thinking practices in group discussion. In D. Hicks (Ed.), *Discourse, learning, and schooling* (pp. 63–103). New York: Cambridge University Press.

Palincsar, A. S., & Brown, A. L. (1984). Reciprocal teaching of comprehension fostering and monitoring activities. *Cognition and Instruction, 1,* 117–175.

Peterson, P. L., & Wilkinson, L. C. (1984). Instructional groups in the classroom: Organization and process. In P. L. Peterson, L. C. Wilkinson, & M. Hallihan (Eds.), *The social context of instruction* (pp. 3–12). New York: Academic Press.

Philips, S. (1983). *The invisible culture.* New York: Longman.

Polacco, P. (1998). *Thank you, Mr. Falker.* New York: Philomel.

Reyes, de la Luz. (1991). A process approach to literacy instruction for Spanish-speaking students: In search of a best fit. In E. H. Hiebert (Ed.), *Literacy for a diverse society* (pp. 157–171). Albany, NY: State University of New York at Albany.

Rawls, W. (1961). *Where the red fern grows.* Garden City, NY: Doubleday.

Richards, J. C., & Anderson, N. A. (2003). How do you know? A strategy to help emergent readers make inferences. *The Reading Teacher, 57*(3), 290–292.

Rodriguez, L. J. (1998). *America.* Willimantic, CT: Curbstone Press.

Rowling, J. K. (1999). *Harry Potter and the chamber of secrets.* New York: Arthur A. Levine.

Ryan, P. M. (2000). *Esperanza rising.* New York: Scholastic.

Sachar, L. (1998). *Holes.* New York: Random House.

Schumm, J. S., Moody, S. W., & Vaughn, S. R. (2000). Grouping for reading instruction: Does one size fit all? *Journal of Learning Disabilities, 33*(5), 477–488.

Silliman, E., & Wilkinson, L. C. (1991). *Communicating for learning: Classroom observation and collaboration.* Gaithersburg, MD: Aspen.

Silliman, E., & Wilkinson, L. C. (1994). Discourse scaffolds for classroom intervention. In G. P. Wallach & K. G. Butler (Eds.), *Language learning disabilities in school-age children and adolescents* (pp. 27–54). New York: Merrill.

Stigler, J. W., & Hiebert, J. (1999). *The teaching gap.* New York: The Free Press.

Taylor, M. (1975). *Song of the trees.* New York: Dial.

Triandis, H. C. (1995). *Individualism and collectivism.* Boulder, CO: Westview Press.

van Allsburg, C. (1986). *The stranger.* New York: Houghton Mifflin.

Vygotsky, L. S. (1962). *Thought and language.* Cambridge, MA: MIT Press.

Wells, G., & Chang-Wells, G. (1992). *Constructing knowledge together: Classrooms as centers of inquiry and literacy.* New York: Heinemann.

Westby, C. E. (1997). There's more to passing than knowing the answers. *Language, Speech, and Hearing Services in Schools, 28,* 274–287.

Westby, C. E. (2004). Executive functioning, metacognition, and self-regulation in reading. In A. Stone, E. Silliman, B. Ehren, & K. Apel (Eds.), *Handbook of language and literacy development and disorders* (pp. 398–428). New York: Guilford.

Westby, C. E., Dezale, J., Fradd, S. H., & Lee, O. (1999). Learning to do science: Influences of culture and language. *Communication Disorders Quarterly, 12*(1), 50–64.

Westby, C. E., Moore, C., & Roman, R. (2002). Reinventing the enemy's language: Developing narratives in Native American children. *Language and Linguistics, 13*(2), 235–269.

Westby, C. E., Watson, S., & Murphy, M. (1994). The vision of full inclusion: Don't exclude kids by including them. *Journal of Childhood Communication Disorders, 16,* 13–22.

Wilcox, K. (1982). Differential socialization in the classroom: Implications for equal opportunity. In G. Spindler (Ed.), *Doing the ethnography of schooling* (pp. 454–488). New York: Holt, Rinehart & Winston.

Wishinsky, F. (2002). *What's the matter with Albert? A story of Albert Einstein.* Toronto: Maple Tree Press.

Wishinsky, F. (2003). *Manya's dream: A story of Marie Curie.* Toronto: Maple Tree Press.

Ysseldyke, J. E., & Christenson, S. (1978). *The Instructional Environmental Scale.* Austin, TX: Pro-Ed.

Zimmerman, B. J., & Schunk, D. H. (Eds.). (2001). *Self-regulated learning and academic achievement: Theoretical perspectives.* Mahwah, NJ: Erlbaum.

Appendix: Close-Up Lens Observation of Teacher-Student Interactions

1. **Types of teacher initiation acts**

   a. Directive—*Please take out your reading books.*

   b. Information—*It's time for reading.*

   c. Question elicitation
      - Product—*What is 5 x 4?*
      - Choice—*Is California larger than Texas?*
      - Process—*How is butter made?*
      - Metaprocess—*Why do you think it is done that way?*

   d. Repetition—Teacher repeats a question twice before a response is given.

   e. Social initiations
      - Academic—Teacher refers to the lesson content but does not offer new information (e.g., encourages students to think back to other experiments they have completed).
      - Nonacademic—Teacher makes comments (some humorous) designed to create a positive learning atmosphere, conducive to student participation.
      - Structuring—Teacher makes comments designed to teach students the participatory structure of the activity, to inform students of expected behaviors (e.g., *I'll be coming around to your group and you better be ready.*)

2. **Levels of abstraction of teacher initiation (Bloom's taxonomy)**

   a. Knowledge—Student memorizes and repeats information presented; answers simple questions.

   b. Comprehension—Student demonstrates understanding by paraphrasing or stating it in another form.

   c. Application—Student uses information, rules, methods, or principles in new but similar situations.

   d. Analysis—Student identifies components, gives reasons, identifies problems.

   e. Synthesis—Student abstracts from prior knowledge to generate new solutions to problems.

f. Evaluation—Student compares alternatives, states opinions, justifies responses.

3. **Student response to teacher questions**

   a. Fully accurate—Content and terminology are correct.

   b. Partially correct—Content and use of terms are correct but not in style of subject matter discourse.

   c. Ambiguous—Content and use of subject matter terms are questionable/unclear.

   d. Incorrect—Content is clearly in error, important terms are absent or used incorrectly.

   e. Irrelevant—Response is off topic or unrelated to the preceding utterance.

   f. No response—Student does not provide an answer.

   g. Don't know—Student responds by stating, "I don't know."

4. **Types of turn taking**

   a. Individual nomination—Teacher calls on student by name.

   b. Invitation to bid—Teacher invites students to raise hands if they want to respond.

   c. Invitation to reply—Teacher invites students to call out a response.

   d. Automatic turn taking—Order of responses is determined by the teacher or situation.

   e. Group nomination—Teacher nominates groups of students to read according to seating.

5. **Teacher response to student response**

   a. Positive overt evaluation—*Very good, that's right.*

   b. Negative overt evaluation—*No, that's not it, you're wrong, try again.*

   c. Positive covert evaluation—When student gives correct response that the teacher accepts without clearly evaluating, teacher then asks a different question of another student.

   d. Negative covert evaluation—Teacher repeats the same question to the student who has responded or to another student indicating that the answer provided was not acceptable, without clear evaluation.

    e. Revoicing—Teacher restates student's contribution to make the statement more accurate by modeling the language style to be used in the response.

    f. Repetition—Teacher repeats the student's statement without making it more scientific. Each repetition is further classified to reflect the teacher's intended purpose (positive covert, negative covert, or ambiguous as identified by context).

6. **Teacher response to student initiations**

    a. Sanction—Teacher rejects student's initiation.

    b. Ignore—Teacher does not acknowledge student's initiation.

    c. Bound off—Teacher accepts student's initiation, but then drops the topic.

    d. Incorporated—Teacher incorporates student's initiation into the lesson.

    e. Acknowledgment—Teacher verbally gives permission for a student to speak, such as saying, "Yes" or "Go ahead" when a student raises a hand to ask a question.

7. **Language functions elicited from students**

    a. Self-maintaining—Personal needs such as requesting permission to use the restroom

    b. Directing—Monitoring one's own actions or the actions of others

    c. Reporting—Relating a sequence of events

    d. Predicting—Contemplating the future

    e. Reasoning—Use of logic, inference, or cause/effect

    f. Projecting—Insight into the motivation, thoughts, or feelings of others

8. **Teacher strategies for managing behavior**

    a. Direct explicit—*Sit down.*

    b. Direct inexplicit—*No, please excuse me.*

    c. Indirect explicit—*Would you sit down?*

    d. Indirect inexplicit—*Who's giving directions here?*

9. Teacher scaffolding

a. Direct static—Teacher provides content information *(The water evaporated and a cloud formed)*.

b. Direct dynamic—Teacher elicits a particular response:

- Cuing—Occurs when a cloze procedure is used or when the desired answer is pointed out through the way the question is phrased.

- Clarification—Occurs when teacher asks a student to repeat or restate to assure response was properly understood.

c. Reciprocal/dynamic—Focuses on communication and creation of collaborative dialogue:

- Soliciting specific clarification strategies—*What do we do if we don't understand?*

- Soliciting assistance for clarification—*Who can tell him what that line means?*

- Supporting transfer of strategy to others—*Aaron is using a good strategy. Tell Terry what you are doing.*

- Checking understanding—*What have we been talking about?*

- Supporting question generation—*But what is my question?*

- Supporting prediction—*What are you going to have to read?*

Chapter 9

Using Print Referencing to Promote Written Language Awareness

Laura M. Justice, Lori Skibbe, and Helen Ezell

Introduction

Emergent literacy is a term used to describe children's developing knowledge about print and sound in the years prior to receiving formal reading and writing instruction. In these years, coinciding generally with the toddler, preschool, and kindergarten years and well prior to formal literacy instruction, children begin to make sense of how print works and its functional value as a communication device. At the same time, children become increasingly sensitive to the segmental organization of oral language, particularly its phonological constituents including words, syllables, and phonemes. A broad range of achievements characterize the young children's developing knowledge about print and sound, and these earliest achievements in literacy help prepare the child for the eventual task of breaking the alphabetic code and becoming a conventional reader and writer. This is an important intervention focus for children with language impairments because they often lack timely development of emergent literacy skills, adding to their already considerable risk for later reading difficulties (Boudreau & Hedberg, 1999; Catts, Fey, Zhang, & Tomblin, 2001).

As a way to organize the many emergent literacy achievements that characterize young children's emergent reading and writing competencies, Justice and Ezell (2001) differentiated these achievements into two categories: *written language awareness* and *phonological awareness.* The former defines those achievements focused on making sense of print and orthography, whereas the latter defines those achievements concerning the sound structure of oral language. Both aspects of development contribute uniquely and importantly to children's emergent literacy achievements and to their progress towards conventional reading (see Storch & Whitehurst, 2002).

In this chapter, we focus specifically on therapeutic strategies and interventions that call children's attention to print features on the pages of books. These methods, called *print referencing,* raise children's written language awareness as they interact with adults during shared book reading.

The Importance of Written Language Awareness

Written language awareness has received relatively less attention than phonological awareness in the developmental and applied literature in recent years. However, some aspects of written language awareness (e.g., alphabet knowledge) are as important a predictor of later achievement as phonological awareness, as indicated by recent meta-analyses (e.g., Hammill, 2004). In addition, children benefit from a comprehensive, integrated approach that attends to the many components of literacy in a meaningful, contextualized way. *Written language awareness* refers to one's ability to understand how written language is organized, what it means, and how it is used. As children develop written language awareness, they come to realize that print is organized in highly specific ways, that written language reflects spoken language, and eventually come to understand how written language and oral language work together in the alphabetic principle (Justice & Ezell, 2002). Much written language awareness is accomplished within the emergent literacy period as children learn how to handle books, recognize their own and other names in print, and point to print when telling a memorized story from a book. Written language awareness will continue to develop in the school years as children are introduced to more advanced aspects of print, such as academic register, specialized terminology, and how to cite others' works in science papers. However, the focus in this chapter is upon the achievements in early childhood that are precursors to later conventional literacy achievements in reading, writing, and spelling (van Kleeck, 1998; Whitehurst & Lonigan, 2001).

Skilled Word Recognition

To better understand how early achievements in written language awareness fit into a broader picture of skilled reading, Adams' (1990) model of skilled word recognition is particularly useful. This model reflects the various competencies that are involved in the process of reading: orthographic processing, phonological processing, meaning processing, and context processing. This model represents fluent and skilled reading which is possible when children become able to integrate information from four separate processors (orthographic, phonological, meaning, context). In the emergent literacy period, these processors become increasingly sensitive to particular types of input. For instance, the orthographic processor becomes attuned to the specific features and distinctions of print units in the orthography of the child's written language.

During the emergent literacy period, the orthographic processor is the first processor to develop, triggered by children's experiences with and exposure to print within the environment, such as storybooks and signs. The orthographic processor processes spelled information, and it is reciprocally connected to both the phonological processor and the meaning processor in its applications to reading print. The orthographic processor becomes increasingly sensitive to the print conventions that comprise a child's use of writing. Meanwhile, the phonological processor is triggered through speech input, and helps to provide an "auditory image of any particular word, syllable, or phoneme" (Adams, 1990, p. 157). The meaning processor is used to provide meaning to print and to sound, and it is used as children ascribe meaning to the words they read. It is reciprocally related to the context processor, which helps children distinguish the meaning or use of a word based on its context, including the genre in which print appears and the child's greater knowledge of the text and its context. According to Adams, these four processes work together fluently and automatically for mature readers and writers, but in the earliest stages of development, children have difficulties integrating these processes. For example, children must use all four processors to decide whether to use the homophones *meet* or *meat* in a sentence, a task that would be highly challenging for beginning readers.

Although all four processors are viewed as being essential during fluent and skilled reading, orthographic processing is considered to be a vital foundational skill. As noted by van Kleeck (1998), "letter knowledge is the anchor for the entire reading system" (p. 36). Importantly, it is during the preschool years that the orthographic processing system begins to emerge and stabilize as children become familiar with the orthography of their printed language. This familiarity helps children enter beginning reading instruction with a maturing processing system that is geared to one's own orthography, to thereby merge this knowledge base with phonological, semantic, and contextual cues to arrive at skilled reading.

Written Language Awareness Achievements

Children's gains in written language during the emergent literacy period, which are considerable and diverse, are summarized in Table 9.1. These gains can be organized into four key areas, as described in Justice and Ezell (2001): print awareness, word awareness, graphic awareness, and metalinguistic awareness. These four areas of development comprise the broader construct of children's written language awareness.

Print awareness describes children's knowledge about print and book reading conventions, such as print directionality and the sequencing of book elements, such as that the front cover is followed by the title page in a storybook (Chaney, 1992; Mason, 1980). Children learn that books are held in a certain way, that print on a page flows from left to right, and that books are

Table 9.1

Preliterate Children's Achievements in Written Language Awareness

Type	Behaviors
Print	• Know that books are held in a certain way • Understand that books are read from front to back • Know that print runs from left to right • Identify the title of a book • Recognize environmental print • Point to print in a book if asked
Word	• Identify that letters are different from words • Understand that words are comprised of letters • Point to the space between two words • Recognize the relationship between printed words and spoken words
Graphic	• Recognize that letters have specific patterns • Name some or all letters of the alphabet • Know the name of the letters in their names • Print some letters
Metalinguistic	• Use metalinguistic vocabulary (e.g., *letter, read, write, word,* and *spell)* • Talk about print as an object of attention • Show interest in how print works • Understand that words are made up of letters

Sources: Adams (1990); Chaney (1992); Justice & Ezell (2001); Lomax & McGee (1987); Mason (1980); Treiman & Broderick (1998); van Kleeck (1998)

read from the front page to the back (van Kleeck, 1998). Also included in Justice and Ezell's (2001) description of print awareness is children's understanding of environmental print. *Environmental print* is print that is embedded within functional and situational contexts. These include signs in the environment, titles on storybooks, logos on clothing items, labels on boxes, and the like. Very early on, many children's literate tendencies are first revealed through their interest in situationally embedded environmental print. Children's ability to recognize such print is highly variable depending on the level of contextual support surrounding the print. Some literacy scholars theorize that this is the first stage of reading (e.g., Chall, 1983; Goodman, 1986), representing the first occurrence in which children begin to meaningfully engage with written language. However, the exact contribution of early interactions with environmental print to subsequent reading development has yet to be defined (Masonheimer, Drum, & Ehri, 1984).

Word awareness represents children's knowledge about the concept of word as it pertains to written language. Word awareness is a more narrow aspect of children's print awareness that describes the child's explicit awareness of words as units of print (Morris, Bloodgood, Lomax, & Perney, 2003). Children gradually acquire an understanding of words as orthographic units, becoming aware of words as different from letters and understanding that words are made up of letters (Justice & Ezell, 2001, 2002; Lomax & McGee, 1987). Several recent studies have shown that children's awareness of word units is a watershed event in beginning reading development. Clay (1991) explains that while learning to read, a child must learn to "break up his produced speech into word units; locate the visual patterns; move in the correct direction; and coordinate the timing of his pointing and looking within his uttering" (p. 162). Morris and colleagues have indicated that children's concept of word is a developmental skill that progresses over time as their conceptual knowledge of words as printed units matures. While the foundations of word awareness manifest in the preschool years, concept of word is elaborated with beginning reading instruction, representing an important developmental achievement that subsequently fosters critical achievements in phonemic awareness, word decoding, and spelling.

Graphic awareness describes children's knowledge of alphabet letters, to include initially an awareness of the distinctive features of letters and subsequently the knowledge of individual letter names (Lomax & McGee, 1987; Treiman & Broderick, 1998; Worden & Boettcher, 1990). A particularly important early achievement in this area is when children learn the letters in their own names. Children's own names appear to have a special status in alphabet learning, as children usually learn the letters in their own names prior to learning other letters. Treiman and Broderick refer to this as an "own-name advantage."

Metalinguistic awareness describes children's ability to attend to written language as an object of attention. As children develop an understanding of print concepts, concept of word, and the alphabet, these are coupled with an increasing disposition towards being able to talk and think about written language. Metalinguistic awareness is a particularly important early achievement in literacy, and represents a child's ability to engage with language at increasingly higher levels of abstraction. These engagements are supported through child-oriented activities such as reading picture books with family members or teachers, in which print is contextualized by illustrations and the story itself. Children's developing competencies in metalinguistic awareness are often signaled by their increased use of terminology that describes written language, such as *word, letter, read, write,* and *spell* (Justice & Ezell, 2001). These competencies can be revealed quite early when children are supported to engage with written language. For instance, the first author's daughter, at only 20 months of age, showed an emergent use (and understanding) of metalinguistic vocabulary by requesting of her mother, "I want to read the book."

Preschoolers' early achievements across these diverse areas of written language development are observed in a variety of incidental contexts, such as their participation in storybook reading interactions that include a print focus (e.g., Justice & Ezell, 2002) and in their use of dramatic play within the classroom. Concerning the former, research addressed later in this chapter has revealed that children's early written language concepts can be supported by helping children engage explicitly with print within the shared book reading context. Concerning the latter, if children are provided with literacy-enriched materials, they will utilize these props in their dramatic play. For instance, children will use mail and stamps to dramatize a post office in their play and will use a newspaper and checkbook when playing house (Schrader, 1990). Preschoolers will display fundamental knowledge of the many functions played by print within such play interactions, including getting and passing along information as well as daily activities such as paying bills, shopping, and cooking (Anderson & Stokes, 1984).

Early written language accomplishments are receiving increased attention given their influence upon setting the course for children becoming readers, even prior to their engagement in formal reading instruction (e.g., Storch & Whitehurst, 2002). Early accomplishments in written language during the preschool years help to prepare children for the challenges of beginning to read in kindergarten and first grade, and children who enter reading instruction with well-developed written language knowledge are more likely to succeed in reading relative to children without such knowledge. This point was supported by Lomax and McGee's (1987) investigation of various aspects of emergent literacy to children's development of word recognition skills. These researchers demonstrated that the developmental trajectory of children's word reading ability follows a course containing five different components: *concepts about print, graphic awareness, phonemic awareness, grapheme-phoneme correspondence knowledge,* and *word reading.* Lomax and McGee's concepts about print and graphic awareness comprise two of the four aspects of written language awareness development described by Justice and Ezell's (2001) depiction of early written language attainments. Importantly, however, Lomax and McGee examined the contributions of these early attainments to later, more sophisticated achievements in reading, such as knowledge of phonics (grapheme-phoneme correspondence knowledge) and decoding ability (word reading).

In Lomax and McGee's (1987) research on trajectories associated with reading development, they showed that children first learn concepts about print, referring specifically to knowledge about the general relation between print units and meaning, including directionality of print and recognition of print within the environment. This early awareness of print concepts in turn influences graphic awareness, namely children's awareness that letters and words have distinctive features. Children then acquire phonemic awareness, at which point they become able to segment and analyze words at the phonemic level and understand the similarities and differences between phonemic elements within words. This awareness, along with concepts about print, influences children's grapheme-phoneme correspondence, describing the ability to match letters with their corresponding sounds, and to use this knowledge in order to decode new words. Finally, children's grapheme-phoneme correspondence contributes to the development of word reading, namely children's ability to read isolated words. This model shows one path through which concepts about print directly influence children's later reading ability.

Influences on Early Written Language Awareness Achievements

Children's development of written language awareness is influenced by a variety of factors, including environmental and sociocultural factors, which are external to the child, and developmental influences, which are internal to the child. Several more salient influences are described in the subsequent sections.

Print Access

Although a variety of environmental factors may influence children's developmental competencies in written language awareness, one particularly critical factor is children's exposure to and access to print materials. Print access refers to the amount of print and literacy materials that children encounter in their everyday experiences at home and in the community. At home, children encounter print for many purposes associated with entertainment, religious, or other daily routines, such as meal preparation and event scheduling (Purcell-Gates, 1996). Access to print within the home environment is positively correlated with children's emergent literacy knowledge, particularly in the area of written language awareness (Leseman & de Jong, 1998; Purcell-Gates).

One home context that figures prominently in written language development is that of parent-child storybook reading. Children are repeatedly exposed to print during book reading interactions with their parents and other adults or siblings (Sulzby, 1985), making it a singularly important context for achieving a print foundation (Reese & Cox, 1999). In fact, shared book reading is considered to be one of the most important ways that parents can influence their children's early literacy skills (Neuman, 1999). Children's experience with alphabet books appears to support skills that are directly related to word recognition (Baker, Fernandez-Fein, Scher, & Williams, 1998), such as letter identification (Bus & van Ijzendoorn, 1988). However, books are not the only type of print artifact that children may be exposed to within the home. Other types of print artifacts may include newspapers, catalogs, calendars, cards or letters, and written lists. They are also exposed to print from less obvious sources, such as television, food labels, currency, clothing items, and wall plaques, to name a few (Leichter, 1984).

Access to print materials is influenced greatly by family resources. Family income level is an important factor that correlates positively with children's ability to learn important print awareness skills. A household income is often indicative of the types of resources available to children within that home. Chaney (1994) showed that household income was significantly correlated with preschool children's performance on print awareness tasks, such as letter knowledge and book-reading conventions. These findings were reinforced by Justice and Ezell (2001), who observed that children living in low-income homes show generally underdeveloped knowledge in many aspects of written language awareness, including concepts pertaining to the directionality of print, print function, and letter discrimination. One possible reason for these findings is that these children may have less exposure to experiences that foster early literacy skills. Adams (1990) estimates that middle-class children enter first grade having experienced approximately 1000 hours of shared storybook reading as compared to 25 hours for low-income children. Low-income children are also less likely to have access to a variety of high-quality books and are more likely to experience child care where basic needs are emphasized over educational ones (Neuman, 1999).

The importance of print experiences within other early childhood environments to complement those of the home has been well documented (Neuman, 1999). However, Neuman reports these care-giving environments can vary considerably in the attention placed on early written language achievements. Knowledgeable early childhood educators work to make print more salient to children by including a variety of print and literacy activities within the classroom environment, by putting those activities in close proximity to where children normally play, and by exposing children to literacy activities that are both culturally appropriate and relevant to children. The quality of the literate environment in the classroom and the number of literacy activities made available to children is closely related to the more global quality of the classroom environment (Dunn, Beach, & Kontos, 1994). When teachers place more emphasis on literacy activities within the classroom, they have classrooms with better language environments overall (Smith & Dickinson, 1994).

Sociocultural Influences

Sociocultural influences that relate to children's written language awareness achievements include community values and parental beliefs. Communities vary widely in their emphasis on early literacy practices and achievements, as described in Heath's (1994) seminal ethnographic research on literacy practices of two communities. Heath's ethnographic depiction of African-American and Caucasian working-class communities suggested that these two groups had distinct methods for socializing preschoolers' literacy skills. The literacy practices of Caucasian families were characterized by adults' intentional coaching of code-based literacy skills using storybooks and alphabet letters. The literacy practices of African-American families were characterized by more informal and implicit methods, such as listening to and participating in storytelling activities. In other words, homes varied considerably in the extent to which parents intentionally exposed their children to aspects of the code-based elements of written language. The way in which adults socialize their children to literacy and language contributes to the rate and type of literacy achievements made by young children.

Children's early written language achievements are also influenced by parents' understanding of the roles they play in shaping their children's overall literacy development, including the concept that children need to be exposed to literacy during everyday activities and that these activities should be child-centered in nature. Parental literacy beliefs represent a multidimensional construct that includes a variety of specific variables associated with how parents conceptualize their roles in their children's literacy development. DeBaryshe and Binder's (1994) Parent Reading Beliefs Inventory (PRBI) is one scale that measures parents' beliefs about their role in facilitating their children's early literacy, which captures the multidimensionality of parental literacy beliefs. The PRBI includes seven subscales: *affect* (e.g., "I find it boring or difficult to read to my child"), *participation* (e.g., "When we read, I want my child to help me tell the story"), *resources* (e.g., "I don't read to my child because there is no room and no quiet place in the house"), *efficacy* (e.g., "As a parent, I play an important role in my child's development"), *knowledge* (e.g., "Reading helps children learn about things they never see in real life"), *environment* (e.g., "Children inherit their language ability from their parents, it's in their genes"), and *reading instruction* (e.g., "My child is too young to learn about reading").

DeBaryshe and Binder (1994) determined that parents' beliefs about reading were significantly related to their reading practices with their children, including the quantity of books within the home and the quality of book-reading interactions between parents and child. Bennett, Weigel, and Martin (2002) found that parental beliefs about literacy correlated positively with the extent to which parents engaged their children in literacy activities within the home environment. Structural equation modeling showed not only that these two factors were related, but that they predicted children's emergent literacy performance over other family characteristics, such as family routines and parental attitudes and involvement with their children's school. While the quantity and quality of children's literacy practices within the home environment (e.g., the amount of time in which they are engaged in reading experiences) is clearly important to literacy development, Bennett and colleagues' work suggests that parental beliefs are also an important influence upon children's written language achievements.

How parents structure storybook reading experiences is an additional important aspect of environmental influences upon written language development. Some parents view reading time with their children as a time to intentionally instruct about how written language works and the role of print in storybook reading. Children are generally very responsive to parents who make print references during book reading sessions (Justice, Weber, Ezell, & Bakeman, 2002), suggesting that children have the skills that they need to engage in meaningful interactions about print and are willing to do so if prompted by a more knowledgeable adult. Parents who routinely engage in literacy activities with their children, such as reading aloud and telling stories, can make an important contribution to their children's literacy achievements (Bennett et al., 2002). Crain-Thoreson and Dale (1992) demonstrated that knowledge of print conventions for linguistically precocious children at four-and-a-half years of age was significantly predicted by both the amount of literacy instruction children were exposed to as well as the frequency with which parents engaged in storybook reading with their children.

Unfortunately, some parents may place a lower priority on literacy practices within the home. In one study, Marvin and Mirenda (1993) asked parents to rate their home literacy experiences and found that parents who have children with special needs and parents with lower incomes rated literacy experiences as less important than other activities, primarily those associated with spoken communication and self-help or daily living activities (e.g., feeding and dressing oneself). Children in these two groups were given less access to literacy-related materials relative to other children. Also, adults in these two groups did not hold high academic expectations for their children. As discussed earlier, such beliefs, while understandable in the face of other life challenges, can have a negative influence on the rate at which children achieve early written language knowledge. This finding emphasizes the importance of supporting such families in their literacy access and development.

Developmental Factors

Developmental factors, or children's own intrinsic interests and abilities, have been associated with children's written language awareness, particularly temperament and oral language ability. One of the most important early achievements in written language awareness is for children to demonstrate an interest in print. Children's print interest appears to lay an important foundation for children's later literacy achievements (Kaderavek & Sulzby, 1998). Children who are interested in print pay more attention to its role and its features, and come to learn print conventions, print functions, print forms, and print part-to-whole relationships more readily. Research has also shown that children who are interested in engaging in literacy activities appear to have more sophisticated letter-name and letter-sound knowledge than children without such interest (Frijters, Barron, & Brunello, 2000). Children's literacy interest may be related to their overall temperament. Children who display fewer negative emotions, have greater attention spans, and who have lower activity levels as rated by maternal report also display better written language skills relative to children with the opposite pattern of behaviors (Coplan, Barber, & Lagace-Seguin, 1999).

Oral language achievements are reciprocally linked to written language awareness achievements. Children with specific language impairments (SLI) are relatively more likely than other children to display low levels of interest in print (Kaderavek & Sulzby, 1998), which may diminish their print-related opportunities. Preschoolers with SLI also have more difficulties with print concepts compared to their typically developing peers (Boudreau & Hedberg, 1999; Catts et al., 2001). Children's early literacy skills seem to relate to their overall language development, which may explain why children with SLI often have particular problems with emergent literacy skills (Boudreau & Hedberg). Although it appears that children with SLI learn about print concepts in the same manner as their typically developing peers, children with SLI have a more difficult time understanding the symbolic significance of print and show delays in this achievement (Gillam & Johnston, 1985). These early deficits can impact children well into their school years, as they draw on their early written language knowledge base in more demanding literacy experiences. Early deficits in literacy development contribute to later problems with linguistic skills, especially for children who have not resolved their language problems by the time they reach five years of age (Snowling, Bishop, Chipchase, & Kaplan, 1998).

A wide variety of influences have been discussed that impact children's early written language achievements, including influences that are both external and internal to the child. Access to print materials, parental beliefs about literacy, and language difficulties are several such influences that affect whether children will enter formal reading instruction with adequate written language knowledge. The remainder of this chapter focuses on specific approaches to support these early achievements in order to help prepare children for reading later on.

Approaches to Supporting Early Written Language Achievements

When considering strategies to support young children's knowledge and interests about written language, it is important to frame practices using the best available evidence concerning preliteracy interventions. The current evidence suggests the importance of supporting children's achievements through a *balance* of both contextualized and decontextualized or discrete skill interventions (see Justice & Kaderavek, 2004). Contextualized interventions emphasize children's construction of meaning within functional, authentic, and child-oriented literacy contexts. For instance, to facilitate written language awareness, an interventionist might scaffold the child's "reading" of words on a menu during a dramatic play activity featuring a restaurant script. In contrast, discrete skill interventions emphasize children's learning of specific skills related to the alphabetic code in more controlled, contrived, and often trainer-oriented skill-based instruction. As an example, an interventionist might have an a priori list of words for a child to copy during a structured writing activity. When working with young children, a balance of interventions provides children with extensive and interdependent learning opportunities that facilitate both code-based and meaning-focused learning.

Contextualized and discrete skill interventions have often been represented as dichotomous and conflicting approaches, as exemplified in the historic "reading wars" (see Foorman, 1995). The term *reading wars* refers to a vigorous debate among reading researchers and practitioners that has lasted for more than 50 years concerning the most effective way to teach children to read. As Foorman details, at the heart of the matter is fierce advocacy for either a whole-language-oriented *meaning-focused* contextualized approach, or for a phonics-oriented *code-based* discrete skill approach (Foorman). In the simplest of terms, whole-language-oriented approaches emphasize teaching the whole word before its parts (i.e., sounds and letters), with instruction emphasizing children's construction of meaning by being engaged in authentic, functional contexts. Phonics-oriented or skills-emphasis approaches promote teaching the word parts before the word itself, with instruction often decontextualized and distanced from authentic applications.

The current best evidence on effective reading instruction for children emphasizes the dual importance of both meaningful contexts and an explicit focus on the alphabetic code. Effective interventions include direct and explicit teaching of code-based elements of literacy (e.g., sounds and symbols) with adequate attention to providing children with rich and meaningful opportunities to apply these skills to real literacy experiences (see National Reading Panel, 2000). Pressley (1998) describes this as *balanced teaching*, which ensures that children are immersed in meaning-making events and authentic literature, but that they are "armed with the skills necessary to attack the words in books"

(p. 270). In the field of reading instruction, balanced teaching refers to using an array of strategies to support children's reading achievements in both the comprehension of text and the code-based elements of reading. In elementary schools, this is often referred to as a balanced "literacy diet" in which blocks of time are allotted to various types of instruction that rotate across both meaning-focused and code-based instruction (see Walpole, Justice, & Invernizzi, 2004). With balanced teaching, educators explicitly focus on skills-based instruction, and support children as they apply these skills to authentic reading and writing activities (Pressley, 1998).

When considering interventions for preliterate children, providing balanced interventions is valuable. However, when working with children who are not yet receiving formal reading instruction, balanced teaching has a slightly different meaning than when it is applied to students in elementary classrooms. Balanced instruction for young students emphasizes the integration of both meaning and coding foci in a single session, to ensure that students develop the code-based knowledge they need to achieve literacy as well as the understanding of how to apply these codes to construct meaning from literacy texts.

For students with language impairments, both types of instruction may be provided within a single therapeutic activity as a contextualized skill intervention. A balanced preliteracy intervention allows students to engage in both part-to-whole learning as well as whole-to-part learning within a single instructional opportunity. Discrete skill interventions in which students are taught specific aspects of the alphabetic code without experiencing reading and writing in purposeful contexts may result in more efficient early gains relative to contextualized skill interventions (Justice, Chow, Capellini, Flanigan, & Colton, 2003). With discrete skill instruction, students' awareness of the individual segments develops more rapidly compared to implicit skill instruction delivered within authentic literacy events. However, with contextualized skill interventions that carefully and *explicitly* attend to specific skills while engaging students in real-life, functional, and authentic literacy activities, both explicit, systematic instruction and meaningful text interactions are provided. This promotes literacy interest as well as awareness of functional aspects of written language, such as how print serves as a vehicle for communication. While investigations of this balanced approach for emergent literacy are only recently developing (e.g., Justice & Ezell, 2002; Ukrainetz, Cooney, Dyer, Kysar, & Harris, 2000), we believe that speech-language pathologists (SLPs) can successfully address both skill and meaning within a single therapeutic interaction.

Specifically, these skill and meaning opportunities can be simultaneously addressed within a single activity through the use of storybooks. Adult-child storybook readings provide a contextualized event that is a familiar and engaging routine to many preschool children. From a contextualized perspective, children's engagement with the book as a whole is believed to enhance their construction of the parts, or the individual codes in literacy, such as letters and words. Through engagement at the meaning level, children begin to make sense of whole-to-part relationships transcending meaning to codes, and learn how literacy generally, and print specifically, is used for constructing meaning.

At the same time, the storybook reading context can be structured to explicitly target the child's development of specific code-based knowledge. Consistent with more decontextualized approaches, children's specific acquisitions can be targeted within discrete, deconstructed, adult-led activities that focus on specific code-based aspects of written language. Children's engagement with *parts* of the literacy code is used to enhance their construction of the whole, and the focus is on facilitating the child's understanding of part-to-whole relationships. For instance, as children are guided to focus on specific letters in storybooks, which reflect the code-based parts of the literacy code, they will then make sense of how these discrete units come together for the whole.

Contextualized Intervention Featuring Print Referencing

Simply engaging students in shared storybook readings without including an explicit focus on code-based elements reflects a contextualized approach to building early literacy skills, but it is not one that is likely to be therapeutic. In other words, while the simple act of reading storybooks with students can help them develop written language awareness, a therapeutic activity involves deliberately accentuating the role of print in the storybook reading event. The integration of code-based attention to the reading event increases the therapeutic effect of the activity (Justice & Ezell, 2000) and also reflects the clinician's awareness of the value of both naturalistic and discrete skill models of intervention. In this way, print referencing may be considered a hybrid approach in that it uses a contextualized framework to deliver specific therapeutic procedures (Fey, 1986). By capitalizing on the storybook reading context for students who are only just uncovering the symbolic properties of written language, the speech-language pathologist (SLP) grounds explicit attention to print within functional, meaningful, and authentic contexts. Print comprises a series of esoteric codes that, on their own, are meaningless and abstract. By embedding students' interactions with print in meaningful and engaging events, clinicians are better equipped to help students understand the functions and forms of print. Additionally, asking students to focus on written language as an object of their attention requires them to perform at a metalinguistic level, which requires greater cognitive demands than working at a non-metalinguistic level. Although even very young children may be able to be engaged at a metalinguistic level, the grounding of their interactions with print in authentic and contextualized contexts provides an important structural scaffold support to perform at metalinguistic levels. This is illustrated in the following transcript of a mother and her two-year-old son reading *Where's Spot?* (Hill, 2000):

Mother:	I don't think Spot is hiding in the piano. Do you? No! [points to the word *no,* presented as a speech bubble coming out of a penguin's mouth]
Son:	No! [points to word *no]*
Mother:	Wow! You read that word. What does it say? [points to the word *no]*
Son:	That says, "No!" [points to the word *no]*
Mother:	I am so impressed. Let's look at the letters in *no.* That's an "n." [points to the "n"]
Son:	That's an "n." [points to the "n"]
Mother:	Yep. And that's an "o." [points to the "o"]
Son:	And that's an "o." [points to the "o"]
Mother:	"n, o" spells *no.*
Son:	"n, o" spells *no.*
Mother:	No, Spot is definitely not in the piano.

This interaction clearly shows a child considering written language as an object of his attention, engaging in the book reading event at a metalinguistic level. Notably, the child is clearly engaged in the metalinguistic task, with mother and child alternating control of the interaction. By grounding this metalinguistic performance within a highly contextualized and engaging print environment, the storybook provides a natural scaffold supporting the child's performance. At the same time, the contextualized nature of the word *no* itself, in which it is presented in bold print within a speech bubble attached to a character, also provides a natural structural scaffold to help the child engage with the word itself. The mother uses the meaning-making context of the storybook as a springboard for a more decontextualized, code-based instructional sequence, where she talks specifically about the letters that make up the word *no*. This mother uses the contextualized framework of the storybook reading to describe whole-to-part relationships (e.g., her first two statements) and part-to-whole relationships (e.g., her last three statements) among various print units.

Description of Print Referencing

The example above of the mother reading with her son illustrates how deliberate verbal and nonverbal attention to print on the part of the adult can accentuate the role of print in the storybook and take the interaction to a metalinguistic level. *Print referencing* refers to interactive verbal and nonverbal cues provided by an adult to foster a child's active engagement with written language during storybook reading routines. Verbal cues include comments about print, questions about print, and requests about print. A *comment about print* is a nondirective, noneliciting model provided by the adult that focuses on some element of written language. For instance, an adult might comment, "This is where I start reading on this page." *Questions about print* and *requests about print* are, in contrast, more directive and evocative, and require the child to more explicitly engage with print to answer a question about print (e.g., the question, "What do you think this letter is?") or to interact with print in some way (e.g., the request, "Show me the word no"). Unlike comments about print, questions and requests about print serve as explicit turn-allocation devices. Accordingly, children are particularly more likely to respond to these types of print references relative to comments about print (Justice et al., 2002). Nonverbal cues include pointing to print and tracking the print, two types of cues which describe the adult's physical attention to print in storybooks. With *pointing to print,* the adult points out print that occurs within the storybook; with *tracking the print,* the adult tracks the narrative print by moving a finger beneath the text while reading.

In using these verbal and nonverbal techniques, adults deliberately recruit the child's attention to the print (i.e., the code) contained in storybooks. These cues often trigger a print-focused episode in which the child is recruited to participate in an adult-led decontextualized dialogue directed towards some aspect of print, such as a letter or a word. Without these adult behaviors designed to trigger print-focused dialogues, neither adults nor children are likely to view print as an interesting aspect of the storybook reading. Adults reading with young children are quite unlikely to point to or track the print while reading (Ezell & Justice, 2000) and they are even more unlikely to talk about the print in specific or even nonspecific ways (Ezell & Justice; Justice et al., 2002; also see Phillips & McNaughton, 1990; Yaden, Smolkin, & Conlon, 1989; Yaden, Smolkin, & MacGillivray, 1993). For the most part, when adults read with children, they tend not to depart from the text at high rates, focusing rather on reading the text and occasionally departing from the text to ask questions about pictures. At the same time, children tend not to view print as a particularly provocative element of storybooks; they rarely look at print (Justice & Lankford, 2003) and they only infrequently ask questions or make comments about print (Ezell & Justice; Yaden et al., 1993). These patterns are even evident when children are read storybooks in which print has a particularly salient quality, such as the *Spot* books (Hill, 2000) which feature large narrative text and print embedded within illustrations and under flaps (see Ezell & Justice). Yaden and colleagues' (1993) observations of children's behaviors during shared reading interactions led them to surmise that "the formal aspects of written letters and words, page formats, and even the conventional procedures for reading a book (e.g., left-to-right sequence) are of far less interest to the children than the meaning of the story" (p. 44).

Given the obvious lack of a print focus for both adults and children when sharing storybooks, *print referencing* is the term coined by Ezell and Justice (2000) to describe the strategic moves that can be introduced to adults (e.g., parents, clinicians, teachers) to promote the print focus of shared storybook reading. Print referencing is used to recruit children's attention towards the code-based elements of storybooks, and it is used most effectively when coupled with print-salient storybooks. *Print-salient storybooks* are a particular variety of storybook in which print is featured as a special characteristic. Smolkin, Conlon, and Yaden (1988) identified specific ways in which children's storybooks make print a salient characteristic, to include:

- Labeling elements of illustrations
- Placing environmental print within illustrations (e.g., signs, posters)
- Using speech balloons and sound bubbles
- Varying the style, color, size, and orientation of print

Print-salient storybooks transcend the particular genre of storybooks. Print-salient characteristics are seen in rhyming storybooks such as *Top Cat*

(Ehlert, 2001), in traditional narrative storybooks such as *Giggle, Giggle, Quack* (Cronin, 2002), in informational texts such as *1001 Things to Spot Long Ago* (Doherty, 1999), in lift-the-flap books such as *Spot Bakes a Cake* (Hill, 1994), in counting books such as *The Right Number of Elephants* (Sheppard, 1992), and—as would be expected—in alphabet books such as *Alphabet under Construction* (Fleming, 2002).

Intervention with Print Referencing

Consistent with other hybrid approaches, such as focused stimulation used for oral language interventions (e.g., Fey, Cleave, Long, & Hughes, 1993; Girolametto, Pearce, & Weitzman, 1996), print referencing is a hybrid therapeutic technique used in naturalistic contexts. As we have described, the meaningful and naturalistic context utilized is the shared storybook reading routine, which employs use of a print-salient storybook. The print-salient storybook, by featuring print as a specific characteristic of the storybook, helps to elicit the participants' focus on the code-based aspects of print within the more authentic and familiar routine. When providing interventions in context, a particular challenge to the clinician is going beyond enrichment to "be therapeutic within a complex, meaningful activity," as discussed in Chapter 1. The clinician is challenged to intensify the natural literacy supports provided to children through storybook reading interactions to accelerate the child's literacy learning. Like other hybrid approaches, key elements of the print referencing as a therapeutic approach include *purposeful contexts, naturalistic stimuli, scaffolds,* and *repeated opportunities.* In Chapter 1, Ukrainetz presented a useful description of these elements of therapeutic interventions delivered in context, to which readers are referred. Here we present a discussion of these elements as they apply specifically to print referencing.

Purposeful contexts

A purposeful context is one in which the event exists for a reason beyond intervention objectives. Contextualized literacy interventions emphasize the child's engagement and performance within an authentic event that has a purpose transcending that of the intervention. Three purposeful contexts commonly employed in literacy interventions for young children include dramatic play (Neuman & Roskos, 1993), classroom niches such as libraries and writing centers (Katims, 1991), and adult-child storybook reading (Justice & Ezell, 2000; Whitehurst et al., 1994). Print referencing uses the latter, employing adult-child shared storybook reading as the purposeful context in which the therapeutic activities are grounded. Obviously, storybooks have many clear purposes beyond that of targeted, specific literacy goals, the two most salient to children being to listen to a good story and to look at enticing illustrations.

When using storybook reading as a purposeful context for facilitating code-based literacy skills, such as the child's awareness of specific print concepts or knowledge of specific alphabet letters, it is important to link these code-based lessons to the larger purpose of the literacy event. The broader purpose of the activity—that is, to hear a good story (which emphasizes the meaning-making elements of the event)—should be explicitly linked to the code-based discrete instruction embedded within the purposeful event. The clinician does this, for instance, by noting the linkages between discrete elements of the code (letters, words, sentences) and the story itself. Studies of beginning readers have shown that helping children understand the broader purpose of code-based literacy activities strengthens the effectiveness of code-based instruction (Cunningham, 1990). The reason for placing interventions in purposeful contexts is to help children make part-to-whole and whole-to-part relationships, such as how words come together to make a story. Children are not likely, however, to make such connections on their own; thus, one of the clinician's responsibilities is to foster these connections for the child.

Here we present an illustration of a clinician supporting a child's awareness of the interactions between codes and meaning-making while reading Lois Ehlert's *Top Cat* (2001):

Clinician: Those words say Top Cat. [points to each word] Those were the words in the title. Two words: *Top, Cat.*

Child: T.

Clinician: Yes. That is a "T." Good job. The "t" is the first letter in *Top.*

Child: "T." And *Top.*

Clinician: Right, *Top Cat.* These words tell us about this cat. [points to cat] He is the top cat, he is the boss.

As seen in this transcript, the clinician uses the purposeful context to move deliberately from a whole-to-part focus (e.g., what the words say) to individual parts based on the child's comment (e.g., "T") and then back again to the whole. Working within a purposeful context such as storybook reading provides a natural support for engaging the child in both code-based and meaning-focused literacy learning opportunities.

Naturalistic Stimuli

A byproduct of working in contextualized formats is the clinician's commensurate loss of control over therapeutic stimuli, as stimuli used to target instruction arise naturally from the context and the discourse it provokes. In contrast, clinicians who work in decontextualized formats are able to carefully choose and control their stimuli. For instance, when targeting alphabet knowledge, a clinician might use alphabet cards and present these to the child in a select order and at a select pace. The clinician also might only work with a few select elicitation stimuli, focusing on the child's achievement of mastery with these targets before moving on to other targets. Using our alphabet example, the clinician might work with just a few letters—say, the first five letters of the alphabet, or the letters in the child's first name—and when the child has mastered these, will move on. Using this approach, the clinician exerts a great deal of control over the stimuli used for intervention.

When clinicians move into contextualized formats, as with print referencing in storybook reading, they lose much of this control and rely on stimuli that arise out of the purposeful context and the discourse contained within the context. These are referred to as naturalistic stimuli. Unlike controlled stimuli, where the flow and the difficulty level are highly limited, naturalistic stimuli vary considerably in the rate of presentation and the difficulty level. Often, these elicitation stimuli are selected by children rather than the clinician (as seen in the previous reading example), and the clinician capitalizes upon the child's interest as a "teachable moment" for addressing a particular therapeutic skill. A particularly important aspect of the naturalistic print referencing context, and which differentiates intervention from enrichment, is the *explicitness* of the print-focused interaction and the clinician's focus on several specific literacy goals or learning targets. The adult explicitly brings the code-based elements of literacy to an overt level, making the print elements of the text a salient aspect of the interaction.

An important point to make about using print referencing, as with other hybrid models, is that it provides a considerable amount of child-directed interaction. If the child chooses to focus on words as an object of attention, then words are the focus of the interaction; likewise, if the child chooses to focus on letters, then letters become the focus of the interaction. While child-directed interventions have clear value to children, clinicians must be skillful in their ability to seize teaching opportunities as they arise, and to present temptations that lead children to desired conversational topics without coercion.

When using print referencing, the clinician selects the storybook and finds repeated opportunities to attend to a specific skill, but makes few a priori decisions regarding therapeutic stimuli. That is, the particular written language stimuli that emerge within the therapeutic activity are not completely under the clinician's control. These emerge from the pages of the storybook during the flow of the interaction. Stimuli used to target specific skills may range considerably in difficulty and may even appear random. For instance, the clinician and child may discuss the letter "a" on one page of a storybook, and on the next page discuss the letter "w," to address a larger goal of teaching alphabet letters. Clearly, this sequence differs from the more controlled approach of moving sequentially through the alphabet (A, B, C...). Or, the clinician and child may talk about the concept of left-to-right directionality of print and the relationship between words and letters on the same page of a book, two written language concepts that vary considerably in difficulty (Lomax & McGee, 1987).

With print referencing, particular therapeutic targets or skills may transcend the entire range of written language units discussed earlier in this chapter, to include a focus on print concepts, alphabet knowledge, concept of word, or metalinguistic labels. Within each of these specific unit categories, targeted attention is focused on *interest* (viewing the unit as an object of attention), *function* (understanding the purpose served by the unit), *convention* (understanding the organizational scheme of the unit), *form* (learning the specific appearance and features of the unit), and *part-to-whole relationships* (learning how the unit interacts with other units). Within a particular intervention session, we suggest that specific attention focus on two or three skills to facilitate collection of data concerning the child's performance. However, while only several skills may be targeted in a single session, we do not advocate that these skills be addressed until mastery is achieved. Rather, the clinician can address several skills for a period of time and then address other skills in a cyclical fashion. Moreover, it is not necessary that the skills addressed in a single fashion be similar in difficulty; more difficult items can be addressed simultaneously to less difficult items. The clinician provides greater support for difficult items while allowing less support for items that are easier for the child.

This concept of addressing a wide range of skills that vary considerably in difficulty levels within a single therapeutic activity is different than more traditional trainer-oriented approaches that feature a vertical structure of controlled targets (see Fey, 1986). Unlike traditional trainer-oriented approaches, skills are addressed without explicit attention towards achieving mastery before moving on to more difficult targets. The assumption in such traditional approaches is that children's development proceeds in a linear fashion and that more difficult skills cannot be achieved until less difficult skills are mastered. Print referencing, as with other naturalistic paradigms, does not rely on this assumption of mastery and control. In contrast, such approaches recognize that children make advances in a wide range of areas, with differing degrees of support. Children actively contribute to their own development by indicating to the adult where their interest and thoughts are focused. The adult responds by systematically scaffolding the child's growing understanding. Learning across the range of skills involved in literacy contributes to an integrated and functional understanding of how reading and writing work. With print referencing during storybook reading, the focus is on facilitating the child's engagement with a variety of written language targets that vary in complexity. By addressing a wider variety of skill with commensurately less focus on mastery and control, the child is presumably able to achieve system-wide developmental change more rapidly than approaches that take a more narrowing focus and linear view of development.

The following transcript illustrates a clinician's targeting of three areas of written language skill—alphabet knowledge, concept of word, and print concepts—within a single interaction with a child while reading *Giggle, Giggle, Quack* (Cronin, 2002):

Clinician: Oh, look, the farmer left a note for Bob. The words on the note tell Bob what to do.

Child: Yeah, right there.

Clinician: Right, that's the note Bob is going to read.

Clinician: "Tuesday night is pizza night," it says.

Clinician: Pizza! The farmer says the animals want pizza. Can you find the word *pizza?*

Child: That one. [points to Tuesday]

Clinician: That says, "Tuesday." This word is pizza. It is just one word, but it has two "z"s in it. "z. z."

Child: "z. z." Pizza.

Clinician: Right. One word, pizza. Two "Z"s in pizza. I love pizza.

Child: I love pizza too.

Clinician:	The animals like pizza too, I think.
Clinician:	[reading] Giggle, giggle, cluck.
Clinician:	Three words. Giggle, giggle, cluck. Can you point to the words while I read? I'll help you.
Clinician:	[reading] Giggle, giggle, cluck. [helps child point to each one]
Child:	The animals are laughing.
Clinician:	The animals are laughing because...

In this transcript, the stimuli on this two-page spread are used to address the functionality of print ("The words on the note tell Bob what to do"), the names of specific alphabet letters ("z"), and concept of word ("Three words. Giggle, giggle, cluck. Can you point to the words as I read?"). The stimuli used to address these learning targets were not preselected by the clinician but, rather, emerged through the flow of interaction from the text and illustrations of the storybook. A variety of targets were addressed that ranged considerably in difficulty. The focus on print concepts required generally little support from the clinician, whereas the focus on concept of word, a relatively more complex and abstract concept, required more support (repetition, gesture).

Scaffolds

In contextualized paradigms, the child is engaged within complex and purposeful activities; at the same time, the clinician targets a range of skills that vary considerably in difficulty and are derived from the ongoing dynamic context, such as letters and words in storybooks. Essential to the child's ability to engage in whole, complex activities with a range of targets is the clinician's use of scaffolding. *Scaffolding* refers to the contextual and interactive scaffolds provided by a clinician to support the child's engagement in a task and employment of skills that surpass the child's independent level of performance. In more hierarchical clinician-level interventions, that clinician targets the child's skills at a level that is only *slightly* above the child's independent ability and works towards mastery at that level before moving on in task difficulty. In contextualized interventions, the clinician engages the child at levels that *far exceed* the independent level of performance, and this is facilitated by use of scaffolds that allow the child to work in whole and complex activities and to engage skills that far exceed what can be done independently. The clinician's goal is to focus child-adult interactions at a point that reflects the *cutting-edge* of the child's performance.

With print referencing, the clinician enables the child to engage with written language in the meaningful, functional context of storybook reading by using a variety of structural and interactive scaffolds that support the child's performance at the cutting-edge of knowledge. These scaffolds provide mediated supports to the child and allow the child to work within his or her zone of proximal development. The *zone of proximal development* is the area of learning potential for a child, representing the developmental zone between what a child can do independently and the maximum level a child can achieve when support is provided by another more knowledgeable partner. These concepts were originated by Lev Vygotsky (Cole, John-Steiner, Scribner, & Souberman, 1978) and are summarized by Justice and Ezell (1999) with a specific focus on their application to language and book-reading interventions.

Although young children possess considerable learning potential with respect to written language, their display and application of knowledge is best facilitated when their interactions with print are supported, or mediated, by a knowledgeable partner (e.g., an SLP). In the context of a clinician's expert scaffolding, children may become engaged with written language at levels that far exceed their independent performance. When children are engaged at these higher levels with support, their learning is accelerated beyond that which occurs if they are not so engaged. To illustrate, during typical storybook reading, children usually exhibit minimal interaction with print. They may, for instance, point out a familiar letter, such as the first letter in their names. Children's independent interactions with print reflect only about five percent of their time, as shown by studies of adult-child interactions during storybook reading (Ezell and Justice, 2000), preschoolers' vocalizations (Yaden et al., 1993), and children's eye-gaze fixations (Justice & Lankford, 2003). However, when adults introduce scaffolds to engage children at levels that surpass what children can do independently, children's interactions with print are accelerated about four- to five-fold (Ezell & Justice; Justice & Ezell, 2002), as are their developmental competencies concerning written language awareness.

Print referencing thus reflects the clinician's use of supports, or scaffolds, that allow children to participate in and learn about written language at levels that are developmentally ahead of their independent performance. Scaffolding precludes the need to address written language targets sequentially, as skills that differ in difficulty can be addressed within a single purposeful activity. More difficult tasks can be coupled with more extensive scaffolding, and easier tasks can be coupled with less intensive scaffolding. At any given time, a particular written language skill or concept is moving along the path from dependence to independence. A dependent skill requires adult mediation for realization of the skill, whereas an independent skill is possessed internally by the child. As children's knowledge of a particular written language concept moves from dependence towards independence, the adult gradually withdraws support. Low-level adult support may continue even when the child shows independence at a conscious level (e.g., "How do you make an 's'? Remember what you said yesterday, about how an 's' looks like a snake?"), until the skill is fully automatized and the child can independently deploy it across situations.

Ukrainetz describes the scaffolding process in detail in Chapter 1, and Gillam and Ukrainetz provide specific attention to clinicians' use of interactive scaffolds in Chapter 2. Interactive scaffolds (i.e., facilitation devices) are used by adults within interactive, dynamic exchanges to support learning. Box 2.2 on pages 72–73 identifies three types of interactive scaffolds: linguistic, response, and regulatory. *Linguistic scaffolds* provide contingent responses by clinicians that are derived from children's own utterances or their own activities. *Response scaffolds* are used to support and structure a child's responsiveness during activities. *Regulatory scaffolds* help children to evaluate their own performance in an activity and to consider the association between task goals and the overall activity.

Each of the three types of scaffold may be used with print referencing to support children's engagement with and knowledge about written language within the purposeful and complex storybook reading context, as shown in Table 9.2 on page 416. Linguistic scaffolds are the contingent responses provided by clinicians that are linked to children's own productions within the children's zone of proximal development. Linguistic scaffolding that is within the child's learning zone will aid the child's active acquisition of the language or literacy skill. Response scaffolds are used to structure children's engagement in metalinguistic print-focused discourse exchanges, and include modeling the response, questioning, repeating responses, pausing, and providing parts of responses. Regulatory scaffolds help children both learn in the current situation and become better learners in general. Regulatory scaffolds assist children to recognize the teaching objective, be aware of their own behavior and skill acquisition, and understand how the current situation and other situations are related.

When using print referencing, the clinician uses all these types of interactive scaffolding, along with the structural support of an interesting book with salient print representations to support the child's engagement and performance within the zone of proximal development. The scaffolds are used dynamically to provide differential levels of support that depend upon the child's

Facilitation Devices for Print Referencing within a Shared Storybook

Table 9.2

Facilitation		Example
Linguistic	**Model**	Child: I think it says . . . hmm. Clinician: It says, "No!" Child: It says, "No!"
	Repeat the Answer	Clinician: That's a "z." Child: Um. I forget. Clinician: It's a "z." Like in zoo. Child: It's a "z."
	Pause	Clinician: These are two words. Giggle. Giggle. [long pause] Child: Two words. Giggle. Giggle.
	Provide Part of the Answer	Clinician: These are two words. Giggle. [point to first word] Child: Giggle. [points to second word]
Response	**Expand the Response**	Child: That's an "n!" Clinician: Right! And it's the first letter in "No!"
	Focus on the Contrast	Clinician: That's a little word. Child: Little word. Clinician: And here's a big word. It's a long word. Child: Long word.
	Repeat the Response	Child: I'm gonna read this word. Clinician: You're gonna read this word.

Table 9.2—*Continued*

Move		Example	
Regulatory	**Provide the Task Goal**	Child:	That says, "Dear Zoo."
		Clinician:	Right. It's the name of the book. We're going to read all the words so we can find out what happens in this book.
	Provide Performance Feedback	Student:	That's an "o."
		Clinician:	Yes, you found the "o." That was really fast.
	Compare Tasks	Clinician:	Can you find the name of this book? You found it on the last book we read.
		Student:	Right there.
	Contrast Tasks	Clinician:	These two words are just the same: giggle, giggle.
		Student:	Two words.
		Clinician:	That's different than two letters being the same. Here are two letters just the same, "g" and "g." See?

knowledge of the task, familiarity with the stimuli, and complexity of the target. Along with the systematic scaffolding, SLPs should plan for repeated opportunities, intense scheduling, and explicit attention to written language awareness.

Repeated Opportunities

In contextualized interventions, clinicians do not engage children in mastery-focused massed learning trials as occurs in the more traditional discrete skill approaches. Nevertheless, repeated opportunities to practice and apply a given skill or concept are just as important in contextualized interventions as they are in more traditional approaches. Repeated opportunities to learn is a key characteristic of print referencing, and our studies have shown that repeating storybook readings featuring distributed practice in specific written language concepts is valuable for early literacy learning (e.g., Justice & Ezell, 2000, 2002). Print referencing builds on studies that have shown repeated storybook readings provide a valuable means for supporting early language achievements (e.g., Whitehurst et al., 1988). Repeated readings of the same storybook over time provide children with a natural learning support, as their acquisition of specific language concepts moves from an implicit generalized familiarity to a more explicit and abstract level of knowledge (Justice, Meier, & Walpole, 2004).

When implementing print referencing intervention, providing children with repeated opportunities to engage with the same written texts is an important therapeutic feature. Research on print referencing has suggested that repeated reading of storybooks four or more times provides a structural scaffold to support children's learning (e.g., Justice & Ezell, 2002). Children become familiar with the organization and content of specific texts, and this allows them to focus additional learning resources towards the task of learning about literacy. Within a given storybook reading, it is important to provide repeated exposure to print-focused learning episodes, to provide children with the opportunity to learn new concepts, and yet balance these opportunities with adequate attention to other aspects of the book-reading event, such as talking about the story events or discussing features of the illustrations. Embedding 9 or 10 print-referencing episodes within a single storybook is adequate for a therapeutic outcome (Justice & Ezell, 2000, 2002) when used repeatedly over time.

Research Support for Print Referencing

In the current context of evidence-based practice, clinicians must ensure that they ground their clinical decisions within the best available evidence concerning specific therapies. The following provides a brief overview of research examining the efficacy and effectiveness of print referencing as an emergent literacy enhancement strategy. This research has focused on the impact of this strategy on children's skills in a variety of areas under the written language awareness umbrella, including alphabet knowledge, print concepts, and concept of word. These studies have examined the print referencing technique in laboratory (Ezell & Justice, 1998, 2000), clinic (Ezell, Justice, & Parsons, 2000), preschool (Justice & Ezell, 2002) and home environments (Justice & Ezell, 2000; Justice et al., 2002). These studies have included children who are typically developing, children who are at risk for literacy difficulties due to the influence of poverty, and children with communication impairments. The following is a brief summary of four key findings from this corpus of work.

1. Adults reading with preschool children do not typically reference print.

2. Adults can be readily taught to incorporate print referencing into their reading interactions with young children.

3. When adults reference print, children do too; however, without adult guidance, children do not interact with print during book reading.

4. Children' participation in reading sessions that involve print referencing increases their emergent literacy skills in relatively short periods of time.

Adults and Print Referencing

A surprising early finding in research on print referencing was that adults reading with preschool children rarely referenced print, even when reading storybooks featuring print as a salient aspect of the book (e.g., large print, print embedded in pictures). This was true for speech-language pathology graduate students, for parents reading with typically developing preschoolers, and for parents reading with their preschoolers with communication impairments.

One study, for instance, examined SLP graduate students' verbal and non-verbal references to print when reading the storybook *Spot Bakes a Cake* (Hill, 1994) with 4 year-old children (Ezell & Justice, 2000). This book has multiple features encouraging adult use of print referencing, including 10 instances of print embedded within illustrations (e.g., a sign in a store that reads "chocolate" and a picture of a character holding a list of grocery items for purchase). Despite these features, the adults in this study rarely made verbal or nonverbal references to the print in the storybook. For instance, questioning about print occurred at a rate of .15 per minute, whereas pointing to print occurred at a rate of .71 per minute. Consequently, in a 5-minute reading session, the adults asked an average of .70 questions about print and pointed to print about 3.5 times. Findings of a limited print focus during adult-child storybook reading interactions suggested that valuable teaching and learning opportunities available within this context were being missed.

A positive finding in the print-referencing research was that adults could be easily instructed to use nonverbal and verbal references to print when reading with preschool children. In several studies, a seven-minute training videotape was used successfully to increase adults' use of print referencing. This seven-minute videotape provided an oral description of the five print referencing cues in addition to brief vignettes for visual depiction of the techniques. After viewing this videotape, adults have consistently been able to implement the full range of print referencing cues (e.g., Ezell & Justice, 2000).

The optimal type of training for print referencing appears to be video training in combination with modeling, discussion, and observation to ensure optimal use of these strategies by parents or other professionals. This multidimensional training combination was used in a clinic-based program in which parents of children with communication impairments received training in emergent literacy intervention using a variety of approaches over a four-week period (Ezell et al., 2000). In this program, print referencing cues were modeled live for parents following video training and discussion providing background information on emergent literacy development. Observation of parent implementation combined with coaching was used to enhance parents' implementation of these strategies with their children.

Children and Print Referencing

A recent study using eye-movement technology showed preschool children looking at storybooks rarely attend to print. In fact, according to this study, preschoolers spend only five percent of their time attending to print when looking at print-salient storybooks (Justice & Lankford, 2003). An earlier study examining the extent to which preschoolers talked about print when reading print-salient storybooks with adults found similar results. About four percent of children's utterances referenced some aspect of print (Ezell & Justice, 2000).

These low rates, however, are only true when children read books with adults who do not reference print. Ezell and Justice (2000) found when reading storybooks with adults who incorporated verbal and nonverbal print referencing, the proportion of children's utterances referencing print increased to about 25 percent.

This emerging research shows that if adults talk about print, children do too. This suggests that adult use of print referencing can dramatically shift the focus of storybook reading from a picture-focused event to a literacy-enhancing activity. If children are attending to print, with adult assistance, they can begin to make sense of it.

Print Referencing Accelerates Emergent Literacy Development

Several studies have shown that children's written language awareness is significantly increased by participating in reading sessions that include an explicit print focus. The first experiment involving print referencing examined effectiveness for 14 four-year-olds who were typically developing (Justice & Ezell, 2000). Parents of these children integrated verbal and nonverbal print references into 16 home reading sessions over a four-week period using a set of storybooks provided for this purpose. Compared to a control group of children whose parents read the same storybooks to them but did not use print referencing, these children made substantial gains in several key areas of written language awareness.

Similar results have also been obtained for children attending Head Start (Justice & Ezell, 2002). In this study, 15 children participated in 24 small-group reading sessions over an eight-week period in their Head Start center. Nine references to print were integrated into each reading session. As shown in Figure 9.1, compared to a control group who were read to using references to pictures instead, those in the experimental group made significant gains on tests of print recognition, alphabet knowledge, and words in print.

Post-Test Scores on Written Language Awareness Measures Following a Book-Reading Intervention in Head Start

 Figure 9.1

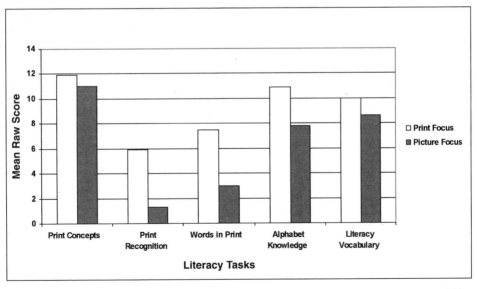

Print Focus = Children participated in 24 book-reading sessions featuring print referencing comments; Picture Focus = Children participated in 24 book-reading sessions featuring comments about pictures in the storybook

Source: Justice & Ezell (2002)

On the basis of these recent findings, print referencing may be viewed as an evidence-based practice (Lonigan, Elbert, & Johnson, 1998). *Evidence-based practice* refers to the use of intervention strategies or approaches for which there is adequate scientific evidence supporting their efficacy or effectiveness for a specific population. A task force of the American Psychological Association (APA; see Lonigan et al.) characterized childhood interventions as having probable efficacy when two or more well-conducted group-design studies have shown the intervention superior to no intervention or alternative intervention. Given the considerable adverse consequences associated with inadequate achievement of emergent literacy concepts and skills (see Snow, Burns, & Griffin, 1998; Stanovich, 2000), a clinician's selection of strategies for supporting literacy development in young children should be carefully grounded in scientific evidence. The tenets of evidence-based practice argue that the value of specific interventions can only be determined through scientific research, as it will be more efficient to employ proven strategies rather than relying on clinical impressions or a trial-and-error approach when addressing emergent literacy needs. Print referencing is a hybrid intervention approach used within contextualized frameworks to effectively support children's written language awareness achievements.

Conclusion

In this chapter, we presented background information concerning written language awareness achievements in young children. These accomplishments, in addition to phonological awareness, prepare children for the task of formal reading instruction and form a pivotal accomplishment in the path towards fluent, skilled reading. Print referencing is a particular type of contextualized intervention that is used to promote children's code-based knowledge within the context of whole, purposeful, and meaningful activities. Within the storybook context, adults interact deliberately with children in ways that bring print to an explicit level. This hybrid approach integrates purposeful contexts, naturalistic stimuli, scaffolds, and repeated opportunities to stimulate the child's developing written language competencies. By using these techniques, SLPs, teachers, and parents can help children develop critical early foundations of written language knowledge that will support their later and more formal achievements in reading and writing.

References

Adams, M. J. (1990). *Beginning to read: Thinking and learning about print.* Cambridge, MA: MIT Press.

Anderson, A., & Stokes, S. (1984). Social and institutional influences on the development and practice of literacy. In H. Goelman, A. Oberg, & F. Smith (Eds.), *Awakening to literacy* (pp. 24–37). Portsmouth, NH: Heinemann.

Baker, L., Fernandez-Fein, S., Scher, D., & Williams, H. (1998). Home experiences related to the development of word recognition. In J. L. Metsala & L. C. Ehri (Eds.), *Word recognition in beginning literacy* (pp. 263–288). Mahwah, NJ: Erlbaum.

Bennett, K. K., Weigel, D. J., & Martin, S. S. (2002). Children's acquisition of early literacy skills: Examining family contributions. *Early Childhood Research Quarterly, 17,* 295–317.

Boudreau, D. M., & Hedberg, N. L. (1999). A comparison of early literacy skills in children with specific language impairment and their typically developing peers. *American Journal of Speech-Language Pathology, 8,* 249–260.

Bus, A. J., & van Ijzendoorn, M. H. (1988). Mother-child interactions, attachment, and emergent literacy: A cross-sectional study. *Child Development, 59,* 1262–1272.

Catts, H. W., Fey, M. E., Zhang, X., & Tomblin, J. B. (2001). Estimating the risk of future reading difficulties in kindergarten children: A research-based model and its clinical implications. *Language, Speech, and Hearing Services in Schools, 32,* 38–50.

Chall, J. (1983). *Stages of reading development.* New York: McGraw-Hill.

Chaney, C. (1992). Language development, metalinguistic skills, and print awareness in 3-year-old children. *Applied Psycholinguistics, 13,* 485–514.

Chaney, C. (1994). Language development, metalinguistic awareness, and emergent literacy skills of 3-year-old children in relation to social class. *Applied Psycholinguistics, 15,* 371–394.

Clay, M. (1991). *Becoming literate: The construction of inner control.* Auckland, NZ: Heinemann.

Cole, A., John-Steiner, V., Scribner, S., & Souberman, E. (Eds.). (1978). *Mind in society.* Cambridge, MA: Harvard University Press.

Coplan, R. J., Barber, A. M., & Lagace-Seguin, D. G. (1999). The role of child temperament as a predictor of early literacy and numeracy skills in preschoolers. *Early Childhood Research Quarterly, 14,* 537–553.

Crain-Thoreson, C., & Dale, P. S. (1992). Do early talkers become early readers? Linguistic precocity, preschool language and emergent literacy. *Developmental Psychology, 28,* 421–429.

Cronin, D. (2002). *Giggle, giggle, quack.* New York: Simon and Schuster.

Cunningham, A. (1990). Explicit vs implicit instruction in phonemic awareness. *Journal of Experimental Child Psychology, 50,* 429–444.

DeBaryshe, B. D., & Binder, J. C. (1994). Development of an instrument for measuring parental beliefs about reading aloud to young children. *Perceptual and Motor Skills, 78,* 1303–1311.

Doherty, G. (1999). *1001 things to spot long ago.* London: Usborne.

Dunn, L., Beach, S. A., & Kontos, S. (1994). Quality of the literacy environment in day care and children's development. *Journal of Research in Childhood Education, 9,* 24–34.

Ehlert, L. (2001). *Top cat.* New York: Voyager Books.

Ezell, H. K., & Justice, L. M. (1998). A pilot investigation of parent questions about print and pictures to preschoolers with language delay. *Child Language Teaching and Therapy, 14,* 273–278.

Ezell, H. K., & Justice, L. M. (2000). Increasing the print focus of adult-child shared book reading through observational learning. *American Journal of Speech-Language Pathology, 9,* 36–47.

Ezell, H. K., Justice, L. M., & Parsons, D. (2000). Enhancing the emergent literacy skills of preschoolers with communication disorders: A pilot investigation. *Child Language Teaching and Therapy, 16,* 121–140.

Fey, M. (1986). *Language intervention with young children.* Boston: College Hill Press.

Fey, M. E., Cleave, P. L., Long, S. H., & Hughes, D. L. (1993). Two approaches to the facilitation of grammar in children with language impairment: An experimental evaluation. *Journal of Speech and Hearing Research, 36,* 141–157.

Fleming, D. (2002). *Alphabet under construction.* New York: Holt.

Foorman, B. R. (1995). Research on "The great debate:" Code-oriented versus whole-language approaches to reading instruction. *School Psychology Review, 24,* 376–392.

Frijters, J. C., Barron, R. W., & Brunello, M. (2000). Direct and mediated influences of home literacy and literacy interest on prereaders' oral vocabulary and early written language skill. *Journal of Educational Psychology, 92,* 466–477.

Gillam, R. B., & Johnston, J. R. (1985). Development of print awareness in language-disordered preschoolers. *Journal of Speech and Hearing Research, 28,* 521–526.

Girolametto, L., Pearce, P. S., & Weitzman, E. (1996). Interactive focused stimulation for toddlers with expressive vocabulary delays. *Journal of Speech and Hearing Research, 39,* 1274–1283.

Goodman, Y. M. (1986). Children coming to know literacy. In W. Teale & E. Sulzby (Eds.), *Emergent literacy* (pp. 1–14). Norwood, NJ: Ablex.

Hammill, D. D. (2004). What we know about correlates of reading. *Exceptional Children, 70,* 453–468.

Heath, S. B. (1994). What no bedtime story means: Narrative skills at home and school. In B. B. Schieffelin & E. Ochs (Eds.), *Language socialization across cultures* (pp. 97–124). Cambridge, UK: Cambridge University Press.

Hill, E. (1994). *Spot bakes a cake.* New York: Puffin Books.

Hill, E. (2000). *Where's Spot?* New York: Puffin Books.

Justice, L. M., Chow, S. M., Capellini, C., Flanigan, K., & Colton, S. (2003). Emergent literacy intervention for vulnerable preschoolers: Relative effects of two approaches. *American Journal of Speech-Language Pathology, 12,* 320–332.

Justice, L. M., & Ezell, H. K. (1999). Vygotskian theory and its application to assessment: An overview for speech-language pathologists. *Contemporary Issues in Communication Science and Disorders, 26,* 111–118.

Justice, L. M., & Ezell, H. K. (2000). Stimulating children's emergent literacy skills through home-based parent intervention. *American Journal of Speech-Language Pathology, 9,* 257–268.

Justice, L. M., & Ezell, H. K. (2001). Written language awareness in preschool children from low-income households: A descriptive analysis. *Communication Disorders Quarterly, 22,* 123–134.

Justice, L. M., & Ezell, H. K. (2002). Use of storybook reading to increase print awareness in at risk children. *American Journal of Speech-Language Pathology, 11,* 17–29.

Justice, L. M., & Kaderavek, J. N. (2004). Embedded-explicit emergent literacy intervention I: Background and description of approach. *Language, Speech, and Hearing Services in Schools, 35,* 201–212.

Justice, L. M., & Lankford, C. (2003). Preschool children's visual attention to print during storybook reading: Pilot findings. *Communication Disorders Quarterly, 24,* 11–21.

Justice, L. M., Meier, J., & Walpole, S. (2004). Learning new words from storybooks: An efficacy study with at-risk kindergartners. *Language, Speech, and Hearing Services in Schools, 36,* 17–32.

Justice, L. M., Weber, S., Ezell, H. K., & Bakeman, R. (2002). A sequential analysis of children's responsiveness to parental references to print during shared storybook reading. *American Journal of Speech-Language Pathology, 11,* 30–40.

Kaderavek, J. N., & Sulzby, E. (1998, November). *Low versus high orientation towards literacy in children.* Paper presented at the annual convention of the American Speech-Language-Hearing Association, San Antonio, TX.

Katims, D. S. (1991). Emergent literacy in early childhood special education: Curriculum and instruction. *Topics in Early Childhood Special Education, 11,* 69–84.

Leichter, H. (1984). Families as environments for literacy. In H. Goelman, A. Oberg, & F. Smith (Eds.), *Awakening to literacy* (pp. 38–50). Portsmouth, NH: Heinemann.

Leseman, P., & de Jong, P. F. (1998). Home literacy: Opportunity, instruction, cooperation and social-emotional quality predicting early reading achievement. *Reading Research Quarterly, 33,* 294–318.

Lomax, R. G., & McGee, L. M. (1987). Young children's concepts about print and reading: Toward a model of word reading acquisition. *Reading Research Quarterly, 22,* 237–256.

Lonigan, C., Elbert, J., & Johnson, S. (1998). Empirically supported interventions for children: An overview. *Journal of Clinical Child Psychology, 27,* 138–145.

Marvin, C. A., & Mirenda, P. (1993). Home literacy experiences of preschoolers enrolled in Head Start and special education programs. *Journal of Early Intervention, 17,* 351–367.

Mason, J. M. (1980). When do children begin to read? An exploration of four year old children's letter and word reading competencies. *Reading Research Quarterly, 2,* 203–227.

Masonheimer, P. E., Drum, P. A., & Ehri, L. C. (1984). Does environmental print identification lead children into word reading? *Journal of Reading Behavior, 16,* 257–271.

Morris, D., Bloodgood, J. W., Lomax, R. G., & Perney, J. (2003). Developmental steps in learning to read: A longitudinal study in kindergarten and first grade. *Reading Research Quarterly, 38,* 302–328.

National Reading Panel. (2000). *Report of the National Reading Panel: Teaching children to read.* Washington, DC: U.S. Department of Health and Human Services.

Neuman, S. B. (1999). Books make a difference: A study of access to literacy. *Reading Research Quarterly, 34,* 286–311.

Neuman, S. B., & Roskos, K. (1993). Access to print for children of poverty: Differential effects of adult mediation and literacy-enriched play settings on environmental and functional print tasks. *American Educational Research Journal, 30,* 95–122.

Phillips, G., & McNaughton, S. (1990). The practice of storybook reading to preschool children in mainstream New Zealand families. *Reading Research Quarterly, 25,* 197–212.

Pressley, M. (1998). *Reading instruction that works: The case for balanced instruction.* New York: Guilford Press.

Purcell-Gates, V. (1996). Stories, coupons, and the TV guide: Relationships between home literacy experiences and emergent literacy knowledge. *Reading Research Quarterly, 31,* 406–428.

Reese, E., & Cox, A. (1999). Quality of adult book reading affects children's emergent literacy. *Developmental Psychology, 35,* 20–28.

Schrader, C. T. (1990). Symbolic play as a curricular tool for early literacy development. *Early Childhood Research Quarterly, 5,* 79–103.

Sheppard, J. (1992). *The right number of elephants.* New York: HarperCollins.

Smith, M. W., & Dickinson, D. K. (1994). Describing oral language opportunities and environments in Head Start and other preschool classrooms. *Early Childhood Research Quarterly, 9,* 345–366.

Smolkin, L. B., Conlon, A., & Yaden, D. B. (1988). Print salient illustrations in children's picture books: The emergence of written language awareness. In J. E. Readance & R. S. Baldwin (Eds.), *Dialogues in literacy research. Thirty-seventh yearbook of the National Reading Conference* (pp. 59–68). Chicago: National Reading Conference.

Snow, C., Burns, M. S., & Griffin, P. (Eds.). (1998). *Preventing reading difficulties in young children.* Washington, DC: National Academy Press.

Snowling, M. J., Bishop, D. V. M., Chipchase, B. B., & Kaplan, C. A. (1998). Language impaired preschoolers: A follow-up into adolescence. *Journal of Speech, Language, and Hearing Research, 41,* 407–418.

Stanovich, K. E. (2000). *Progress in understanding reading.* New York: Guilford.

Storch, S. A., & Whitehurst, G. J. (2002). Oral language and code-related precursors to reading: Evidence from a longitudinal structural model. *Developmental Psychology, 38,* 934–947.

Sulzby, E. (1985). Children's emergent reading of favorite storybooks: A developmental study. *Reading Research Quarterly, 20,* 458–481.

Treiman, R., & Broderick, V. (1998). What's in a name: Children's knowledge about the letters in their own names. *Journal of Experimental and Child Psychology, 70,* 97–116.

Ukrainetz, T. A., Cooney, M. H., Dyer, S. K., Kysar, A. J., & Harris, T. J. (2000). An investigation into teaching phonemic awareness through shared reading and writing. *Early Childhood Research Quarterly, 15,* 331–355.

van Kleeck, A. (1998). Preliteracy domains and stages: Laying the foundations for beginning reading. *Journal of Children's Communication Development, 20,* 33–51.

Walpole, S., Justice, L. M., & Invernizzi, M. A. (2004). Case study of an exemplary elementary school: Research to practice through curricular reform. *Reading and Writing Quarterly, 20*(3), 261–283.

Whitehurst, G. J., Arnold, D. S., Epstein, J. N., Angell, A. L., Smith, M., & Fischel, J. E. (1994). A picture book reading intervention in day care and home for children from low-income families. *Developmental Psychology, 30,* 679–689.

Whitehurst, G. J., Falco, F. L., Lonigan, C. J., Fischel, J. E., DeBaryshe, B. D., Valdez-Menchaca, M. C., et al. (1988). Accelerating language development through picture book reading. *Developmental Psychology, 24,* 552–559.

Whitehurst, G., & Lonigan, C. (2001). Emergent literacy: Development from prereaders to readers. In S. B. Neuman & D. K. Dickinson (Eds.), *Handbook of early literacy research* (pp. 11–29). New York: Guilford.

Worden, P. E., & Boettcher, W. (1990). Young children's acquisition of alphabet knowledge. *Journal of Reading Behavior, 22,* 277–295.

Yaden, D. B., Smolkin, L. B., & Conlon, A. (1989). Preschoolers' questions about pictures, print conventions and story text during reading aloud at home. *Reading Research Quarterly, 24,* 188–214.

Yaden, D. B., Smolkin, L. B., & MacGillivray, L. (1993). A psychogenetic perspective on children's understanding about letter associations during alphabet book readings. *Journal of Reading Behavior, 25,* 43–68.

Chapter 10

Scaffolding Young Students into Phonemic Awareness

Teresa A. Ukrainetz

Introduction

Phonemic awareness is the understanding that words are composed of discrete sounds that are comparable and manipulable (e.g., *cat* has three sounds, /k/-/æ/-/t/). It is an oral language skill critical to learning to read and write. This chapter examines ways of teaching phonemic awareness to young students, with a particular focus on (1) instruction only at the phoneme level; and (2) instruction that is therapeutic but consistent with developmentally appropriate, emergent literacy instruction.

Phonemic Awareness Fundamentals

Phonemic and Phonological Awareness

Phonemic awareness is one of many kinds of metalinguistic knowledge that emerge in the preschool years. The awareness of the phoneme structure of words is critical to reading and writing in alphabetic print systems. Phonemic awareness allows students to understand the alphabetic principle, notice the regular ways that letters represent sounds in words, and generate possibilities for words in context that are only partially sounded out (Torgesen, Al Otaiba, & Grek, 2005). There are many ways of showing phonemic awareness, such as awareness that:

- /bæb/ differs by one sound from /mæd/
- /bæd/ is composed of three phonemes
- /b/ is first, /æ/ is middle, and /d/ is last
- /b/ and /æ/ and /d/ make /bæd/
- when /b/ is deleted, /æd/ is left
- add /s/ to /æd/ and you have /sæd/

Awareness of phonemes is part of a larger awareness of phonological structure that includes the larger segments of syllable (/bə/-/næ/-/nə/) and onset-rime (/b/-/æd/). Awareness of these larger segments arises earlier in the developmental sequence than does awareness of phonemes (e.g., Fox & Routh, 1975; Liberman, Shankweiler, Fischer, & Carter, 1974). Syllables and rhyme are often presented as building blocks for phonemic awareness. These skills are predictive of early word recognition and spelling, but are not directly related to these alphabetic skills (Hoien, Lundberg, Stanovich, & Bjaalid, 1995; Nation & Hulme, 1997; Storch & Whitehurst, 2002). Notably, despite conventional belief, this author has found no evidence that direct instruction in the phonological level of awareness is a necessary instructional precursor for teaching phonemic awareness. Instead, there is growing evidence that even young students can be taught at the phonemic level first without teaching awareness of larger sound segments (Gillon, 2000; Nuspl, 2005; Ukrainetz, Cooney, Dyer, Kysar, & Harris, 2000).

Other Types of Awareness

Phonological awareness curricula and assessment measures often include two other kinds of awareness—auditory and semantic (e.g., Adams, Foorman, Lundberg, & Beeler, 1998; Notari-Syverson, O'Connor, & Vadasy, 1998). *Auditory awareness* involves judgments about environmental sounds (e.g., a dog barking versus a bell ringing). Auditory awareness presumably promotes listening and attention to sound.

Semantic awareness involves dividing up compound words into root words (e.g., *hotdog* consists of two words, *hot* and *dog)* and dividing sentences into words. Dividing a sentence into words is more of a semantic than a sound-based act (Gillam & van Kleeck, 1998). Without understanding the words, it is only possible to divide a sentence into syllables, onset-rime, or phonemes. For example, it is impossible for persons who do not know French to count the number of words heard in a sentence, which would sound like a series of syllables, "Jevoudraisavoirdulait." Awareness of words in print and how they match up to spoken words is an important aspect of learning to read. Semantic awareness promotes treating language as an object of analysis and leads to deeper vocabulary knowledge. However, neither it nor auditory awareness is part of phonological awareness.

Development of Phonemic Awareness

Phonemic awareness develops through daily life activities, especially print-related experiences. Preschoolers' spontaneous verbal play with nonsense sound strings (e.g., Tri ya ya ya yangle) and word pronunciations (e.g., I want reanut rutter randwich, rease) provide early opportunities (van Kleeck & Bryant, as cited in van Kleeck & Schuele, 1987) to develop phonemic awareness. Phonemic awareness further develops as a result of learning to read and write, in both self-directed exploration (Richgels, 1995; Richgels, Poremba, & McGee, 1996) and formal sound-letter instruction (Dahl, Scharer, Lawson, & Grogan, 1999; Ehri & Wilce, 1986). As students learn that the word *cat* is represented by the letters "c-a-t," and that each letter represents a sound, they attend to the sounds and realize that the word contains three distinct sounds, /k/-/æ/-/t/, that match to the three letters.

Phonemic awareness in preschoolers develops from basic awareness of the first phoneme in words, to the last phoneme in words, and phoneme blending, and then, to segmentation of single-syllable words into phonemes. Phonemic-level awareness has generally been considered to develop in kindergarten and beyond (See Gillon, 2004). However, with literacy instruction moving downward in age (McGee, 2004), first-phoneme skills can be expected by the end of preschool. Kindergarten is when major changes can be observed in phoneme-level skills. As students gain experience with sounding out printed words in first and second grade, they become better at holding words in memory to blend, segment, delete, and substitute phonemes. Older students show sophisticated awareness that involves considerable spelling, auditory memory, and word retrieval demands, such as sounding out *decontextualize* or knowing that the word /wɛnzdai/ (Wednesday) is not written as it sounds.

Phonemic awareness develops *along with* rather than *before* experience in reading and writing. Phonemic awareness is a crucial component of the process of printed word recognition and word spelling. Students who have little awareness of the phonemic segments of language are likely to have difficulty learning the alphabetic principle and sound-letter correspondences of reading. In fact, phonemic awareness is one of the strongest kindergarten indicators for identifying the likelihood of a student later exhibiting a reading disability (Catts, Fey, Zhang, & Tomblin, 2001). Early difficulties with phonemic awareness lead to lags in the acquisition of word decoding, which impairs reading comprehension and reading fluency, resulting in long-lasting, pervasive reading difficulties (see Kamhi & Catts, 1999; Stanovich, 2000). By falling behind their peers in these early reading skills, these students are at risk of being trapped in the reciprocal causal relationship between reading success and language development, falling progressively farther behind their peers in both domains (Stanovich, 1986).

Phonological Processing

Phonemic awareness is one of three parts of phonological processing, which is a cognitive operation involving the storage, retrieval, and manipulation of speech sounds (Catts & Kamhi, 2005; Troia, 2004). The other two components are phonological code retrieval and phonological working memory.

Phonological code retrieval is more commonly known as word finding or lexical retrieval. Word finding involves retrieving and matching up the form and meaning of a word. A word-finding difficulty involves having a sense of the content or meaning for a word, but having difficulty retrieving the form or phonological pattern (McGregor & Leonard, 1995). In oral discourse, this may be evidenced as a high rate of pauses and mazes (i.e., repetitions, restarts, and reformulations) in discourse. It is often assessed by timing the rate of labeling a series of items (i.e., confrontational naming). Troia describes phonological working memory as the part of memory that involves temporarily holding the speech sound features of a word, so it can be analyzed or manipulated (Troia). Students who have low working memory capacity will have difficulty matching graphemes to phonemes (i.e., phonological recoding) and blending the phonemes into words, then holding that phonological representation in memory long enough to find its meaning.

Readers and writers need all the parts of phonological processing to rapidly and accurately access the word meanings encoded in the print they see (Wagner & Torgesen, 1987). Together, they form critical skills and processes that are at the core of most reading disabilities (see Catts & Kamhi, 2005; Stanovich, 2000). Phonological processing deficits present barriers to acquiring rapid and accurate word recognition, which then impairs text comprehension.

Interestingly, phonemic awareness may be one part of phonological processing that is directly accessible to instruction. The act of pulling a phonological representation from long-term memory and holding it in working memory to perform phonemic awareness tasks provides incidental intervention on the more difficult-to-teach areas of memory and retrieval (Gillam & van Kleeck,1998). A phonemic awareness intervention study for preschoolers with language impairments resulted in concomitant improvements in phonological processing, as measured by nonword repetition span performance (Gillam & van Kleeck, 1998). Thus, instruction in phonemic awareness may improve two other areas critical to reading and writing success.

Training Studies

Why Teach Phonemic Awareness?

The National Reading Panel (NRP; 2000) considers phonemic awareness one of five critical components of reading, along with word decoding, vocabulary, comprehension, and fluency. Phonemic awareness develops as students learn to read and spell, without direct instruction. Previous generations of adults read successfully despite absence of specific instruction in phonemic awareness. However, in nationwide efforts to start typically achieving students reading earlier and acquiring reading faster, there is evidence that additional direct, explicit instruction in phonemic awareness increases the rate and levels of reading acquisition. In addition, both younger students with specific language impairments and older students with specific reading disabilities frequently exhibit deficits in phonological processing (see Catts & Kamhi, 2005). Early preventive interventions directed at remediating these phonological processing deficits are critical for preventing and mitigating the severity of reading problems among students with specific language impairments. Direct intervention in phonemic awareness is needed to improve both the skill itself and its associated components of auditory memory and lexical code retrieval. As a consequence, there is a general consensus that direct phonemic awareness instruction is needed in addition to reading instruction (Ehri et al., 2001; Lyon, Alexander, & Yaffee, 1997; NRP).

Teaching Students

Numerous studies supported by the National Institutes of Health (Lyon et al., 1997) have shown the efficacy and effectiveness of phonemic awareness intervention. Research has shown positive effects of training in phonemic awareness on early reading development, including achievements in the alphabetic principle (the idea that letters represent sounds), isolated word reading, and spelling (e.g., Ball & Blachman, 1988, 1991; Byrne & Fielding-Barnsley, 1991; Lie, 1991; Sawyer, 1988). There are many research studies showing the effects of training in phonemic awareness. The NRP (2000; Ehri et al., 2001) reviewed available evidence from 52 controlled and well-described studies. The panel concluded that phonemic awareness can be taught in a variety of ways and that it leads to improved reading performance for typically developing students.

Studies examining phonological awareness instruction for prekindergarten and kindergarten generally include a mix of prephoneme and early phoneme activities (e.g., Hadley, Simmerman, Long, & Luna, 2000; Lundberg, Frost, & Peterson, 1988). Students are expected to count words, beat out syllables, rhyme, and identify first sounds. Generally, the more difficult tasks of phoneme segmentation and blending are taught in kindergarten and first grade (e.g., Ball & Blachman, 1988; Lie, 1991; Torgesen, Morgan, & Davis, 1992). Some commercial programs (e.g., Adams et al., 1998) control phonotactic shape (e.g., first CV with long vowels, then VC with long vowels, then VC with short vowels) and sound selection (e.g., continuants before stops). Tasks include identifying, counting, and comparing sounds in pictures, moving blocks to represent sounds, sound bingo, and matching sounds to letters. Print is added after practice at the phonemic level. Whereas research programs generally span less than six months, school instruction now occurs from prekindergarten to first grade.

Studies examining the combination of phonemic awareness training with print-related concepts (e.g., the alphabetic principle, sound-letter correspondence, or the purposes of breaking a word into its parts), have found that combinations are more successful than phonemic awareness instruction alone (Ball & Blachman, 1991; Bradley & Bryant, 1985). Cunningham (1990) coupled phonemic awareness training with discussions of why we think about the sounds in words, for kindergarten and first-grade students. This metalevel treatment group was directed to reflect upon phonemic awareness and its relation to reading, and provided opportunities for demonstration and practice. Measures of reading showed that first graders who had received the metalevel instruction surpassed the performance of students who had only received the phonemic awareness skills instruction.

For typically developing students, phonemic awareness instruction leads to improvement in phonemic awareness, along with improvement in early reading and writing. Training studies for young students with lower initial performance show more variability in results. Members of this lower ("at-risk") group present with a variety of characteristics: low initial phonemic awareness, low early literacy, parents with dyslexia, or developmental delay. Torgesen et al. (1992) reported that about one-third of their at-risk sample showed no measurable growth in phonological awareness following an eight-week training program. Lundberg (1988) also reported that gains were much smaller for the students in his sample from the lowest quartile of phonological awareness. By contrast, Schneider, Ennemoser, Roth, and Kuspert (1999) found that at-risk kindergartners gained as much as typically developing controls and more than the at-risk controls following a kindergarten phonological awareness program. This advantage over the untrained at-risk controls maintained into second grade.

Ukrainetz et al. (2000) addressed the effects of teaching first- and last-phoneme isolation, and phoneme segmentation and deletion. Skills were embedded within shared reading and writing activities for five- and six-year-old students of a range of abilities. The phonemic awareness tasks were presented concurrently in routine sound-talk episodes within a session, on word stimuli as they naturally occurred in the book reading. Other language and literacy areas were addressed incidentally. Thirty-six students were matched by ability level and then randomly assigned to treatment and control conditions. Instruction occurred in small groups three times per week for eight weeks. Results were examined for the group as a whole and for a lower achieving cluster. The students in the lower literacy group were identified by teacher concerns, lack of first-sound awareness, or knowledge of less than half the alphabet.

For Ukrainetz et al. (2000), in comparison to a control group, the students showed greater progress on three of the tasks: first-phoneme isolation, last-phoneme isolation, and phoneme segmentation. (Video analysis revealed that the instructors rarely addressed phoneme deletion, so the lack of gain was not surprising.) Additionally, parents of the treatment students reported greater incidence of interest in literacy activities following the intervention. Students with lower literacy abilities showed patterns of achievement similar to the full sample. These students were able to learn phonemic awareness within complex, meaningful text interactions. Although their absolute performance level was less than that of the higher achieving students, their performance showed a larger effect size (i.e., a measure of practical significance) and a tripling of pretest performance in only seven weeks.

Intervention for Students with Language Impairments

Notably few peer-reviewed studies have focused specifically on phonemic awareness intervention for students with specific language impairments, despite the likelihood of these students developing a reading disability. A handful of small-scale studies have explored the value of phonemic awareness intervention for this population and have obtained positive results.

Warrick, Rubin, and Rowe-Walsh (1993) found positive results in a training study with kindergarten students with speech-language impairments. An experimental group was taught syllable awareness, rhyming, and phoneme segmentation. The experimental group showed initial (and maintained significant) gains compared to the control group, and no significant differences from the typically developing group. In van Kleeck et al. (1998), examination of the effects of classroom rhyme and beginning sound instruction for preschoolers with speech-language impairments showed significant improvement compared to an older comparison group on beginning sound isolation, but not on rhyme. Laing and Espeland (2005) obtained significant improvement in phonological awareness for preschoolers with speech-language impairments who were taught rhyme identification/production and first-sound categorization.

Gillon (2000) taught students with speech-language impairments in awareness of syllables, rhymes, and phonemes. Targets were arranged horizontally, mixing phonological and phonemic levels. Phoneme-level tasks included different sound positions and segmentation. Results showed significant improvements in phonemic awareness and several reading measures compared to a control group, with performance similar to that of typically developing students of the same age.

A Contextualized Skill Framework for Phonemic Awareness Intervention

Instruction at the Phoneme Level

Formal instruction, and even intervention, in phonemic awareness, letter-sound knowledge, and print concepts are established practices in kindergarten and first grade. They are becoming more frequently recommended for preschoolers (e.g., Fey, Catts, & Larrivee, 1995). The most common approach has been to teach prephonemic skills (e.g. syllable and rhyme) through a vertical hierarchy of teaching objectives using contrived activities. Training in these prephonemic levels using this discrete skill approach can improve phonemic awareness. Lundberg et al. (1988) showed improvement in phonemic awareness for preschoolers with such a program.

Despite the prevalence of prephonemic instruction, there has been no evaluation of the benefit of presenting these levels in addition to phonemic levels, and some evidence that such instruction is contraindicated. Brady, Fowler, Stone, and Winbury (1994), in a study examining phonological awareness instruction with inner-city students, commented that having kindergartners segment sentences into words seemed to confuse students. Schneider, Kuspert, Roth, Vise, and Marx (1997) replicated the Lundberg et al. (1988) study with German kindergartners, but found superior effects on later reading and writing with a shortened rhyme instruction period and lengthened phoneme instruction. Van Kleeck and colleagues (1998) found no benefit of rhyme instruction: preschoolers who spent an entire semester learning rhyme acquired no better rhyming skills than students who merely participated in their regular instruction. Nuspl (2005) compared phoneme-only instruction to phoneme instruction preceded by syllable instruction for preschoolers. Nuspl found confusion at the transition between syllables and phonemes for the phoneme-plus-syllable condition, and no difference between the two conditions in final gain in phonemic awareness. Finally, from this author's experience, students who have an incipient sense of phonemes become confused when they are required to suppress this understanding and segment at the syllable level (e.g., when instructed to clap the syllables in single syllable words, they will attempt to clap for phonemes).

In conclusion, there is considerable evidence that even preschoolers can begin at the phonemic level of instruction. For example, the following controlled studies demonstrated that five-year-olds were able to learn some degree of phonemic awareness:

- In a variety of first-phoneme tasks (Byrne & Fielding-Barnsley, 1991)
- In phoneme isolation, blending, and segmentation tasks (Gillon, 2000; Nuspl, 2005)
- In phoneme isolation and segmentation tasks (Ukrainetz et al., 2000)
- In first-sound isolation (van Kleeck et al., 1998)

Contextualized Skill Instruction

Phonemic awareness can be taught in a contextualized skill manner, which is more consistent with developmentally appropriate, emergent-literacy instruction involving independent exploration, guided interactions, and minimal direct instruction (International Reading Association and National Association for the Education of Young Children, 1998; McGee & Purcell-Gates, 1997). A key feature of contextualized skill instruction is scaffolded support that enables a student to participate in and learn from developmentally advanced activities (Vygotsky, 1978). Preschoolers can only be expected to attain independent performance in simple phonemic awareness tasks such as first-phoneme isolation. However, with scaffolding, they can also show assisted performance in more difficult tasks, such as phoneme segmentation (Gillon, 2000; Nuspl, 2005; Ukrainetz et al., 2000). This early exposure and practice is expected to lead to faster gains in kindergarten, ultimately resulting in earlier mastery of phonemic awareness.

Contextualized skill instruction has been well developed for other language domains in the speech-language intervention literature (see Chapter 1 for more discussion). There is a large body of research showing that the acquisition of morphosyntactic forms can be accelerated through adult modeling, prompting, and expanding, (e.g., Camarata, Nelson, & Camarata, 1994; Fey, Cleave, Long, & Hughes, 1993; Girolametto, Pearce, & Weitzman, 1996; Nelson, Camarata, Welsh, Butkovsky, & Camarata, 1996). Conceptual and semantic attainments have been facilitated through mediated learning scaffolds that help the student self-reflect, organize, and intentionally learn (e.g.,

Feuerstein, 1980; Lidz & Peña, 1996). The premise here is that—similarly to other language domains—the extended assisted early practice in more difficult phonemic awareness tasks will increase the later rate of acquisition of these skills in kindergarten and first grade.

Phonemic awareness intervention is presented as three sets of activities: (1) song and word play, (2) single-skill contrived activities, and (3) interactions around printed text. Song and word play are activities in which students spontaneously engage. They are modified here to teach phonemic awareness. Single-skill contrived activities exist only for the skill being taught; they do not exist outside a lesson structure. Contrived activities are typically used in discrete skill instruction, but they are used here without the hierarchical organization and response shaping typical of discrete skill programs. Instead, scaffolding is used to support varying skill difficulty and individual student responses. In addition, single-skill activities are combined within sessions, so students experience more than one type of phonemic awareness at a time. Finally, interactions around printed text teach phonemic awareness through verse books and message writing. Instruction occurs through sound talk: (1) within the context of reading and writing authentic messages, (2) while targeting multiple skills, (3) across stimulus items of varying difficulty, and (4) within purposeful contexts where a variety of other language and literacy topics may be addressed.

In addition to the contextualized skill framework, Gillon (2004) provides important guiding principles consistent with the recommendations of this chapter:

- Phonological awareness intervention should be integrated with letter-sound knowledge training and should make explicit the links between speech and print.

- Phonological awareness intervention should focus on the development of skills at the phoneme level for school-age students.

- Instruction may involve a skill mastery approach or an integrated multiple skill approach.

- An individual or small group model of service delivery may be necessary for students with severe deficits.

- Flexibility in program implementation is required.

- Phonological awareness intervention is most effective after a period of general language instruction. (pp. 135–138)

The mix of name play, drill in contrived single-skill activities, and sound talk embedded in reading and writing is designed to maximize learning. The name play makes efficient use of transition times. The single-skill contrived activities provide massed practice opportunities for emerging skills and teach how to take tests. The contextualized skill activities provide meaningful print situations, aimed at internalizing a generalized and generative application of phonemic awareness in situations of use (Pretti-Frontczak & Bricker, 2004). All of these together result in integrated, flexible, print-based instruction at the phonemic level for individuals and small groups.

Maintaining a Therapeutic Focus

The use of complex activities such as sharing storybooks and writing messages for phonemic awareness instruction can easily result in a language-rich, but nontherapeutic situation (as discussed in Chapter 1). It is important that the key RISE elements of intervention (i.e., repeated practice opportunities, intense service delivery, systematic learning support, and explicit attention to target skills) occur regardless of intervention activity (Berninger et al., 2003; Gillam, Loeb, & Friel-Patti, 2001; Torgesen et al., 2005; Torgesen et al., 2001). Table 10.1 on page 452 summarizes RISE applied to phonemic awareness.

Repeated Opportunities

Repeated opportunities are easily set up within the contrived activities by controlling the number of picture cards or block manipulations. Ten first-phoneme matching trials (e.g., "What sound does this picture start with? And this picture? Do they match?") equals 20 repeated opportunities to isolate the first sound. Within book reading, a speech-language pathologist (SLP) must plan for first-phoneme isolation opportunities across the pages of the book. For example, in a 10-page book, each page could have 2 words identified for a sound-isolation trial to provide 20 opportunities.

Intensity

Intensity is a matter of service delivery structure, that is, individual or small group intervention delivered frequently and consistently on a limited number of skill foci. The required degree of intensity varies with the targeted skill (e.g., learning first-sound isolation requires less time than learning to read fluently). Evidence suggests 40–60 minutes a week for 8 to 10 weeks is sufficient to make considerable progress on phonemic awareness (Gillon, 2000; Ukrainetz et al., 2000).

RISE Elements of Intervention Applied to Phonemic Awareness within Verse Books

Table 10.1

RISE Element	Description
Repeated Opportunities	Two words per page for a 10-page book equals 20 trials
Intensity	Individual or small group structure, with 40–60 minutes per week solely on phonemic awareness for 8 to 10 weeks
Systematic Support	• Interactive response scaffolds (e.g., stress the target sound) • Interactive linguistic scaffolds (e.g., expand a partial into a full-word segmentation) • Interactive regulatory scaffolds (e.g., ask a student what is being learned in the activity) • Structural scaffolds (e.g., use of rhyming books to highlight form over content)
Explicit Skill Objective	Maintain a clear focus on phonemic awareness over other skill opportunities presented

Systematic Support

The student's learning is supported with scaffolding that enables the student to successfully respond and understand how to do better the next time. Instruction is interactively scaffolded in the following ways: (1) response prompts of repeating questions, slowing word enunciation, stressing sounds, giving physical cues, and requesting imitation; and (2) linguistic prompts of modeling, expanding, and recasting by giving the answer, segmenting more of the word than the student, and segmenting at the phonemic level given an onset-rime segmentation from the student. Additionally, regulatory scaffolding is provided by: identifying skill targets (e.g., "We are learning to say the sounds in words"), linking to the purpose of reading and writing (e.g., "Knowing the sounds in words helps you write words"), and commenting on performance and attention (e.g., "You hardly needed any help on first sounds today"). Finally, structural scaffolding occurs through simplifying the purposeful activity to highlight the intervention objective. For example, as will be explained in the talk around text activities, books that employ rhyme are used to foreground form over meaning.

Interactive scaffolding possibilities are preplanned, but enactment is dynamic and responsive to student needs. Scaffolding matches developmental order by varying with the difficulty of the task (e.g., first sound versus segmentation), word position (e.g., first versus middle), word shape (e.g., single versus multisyllabic), and phoneme (e.g., continuant consonant versus vowel). Progress toward independence is measured by tallying how many prompts are needed to enable the student to successfully respond and understand how to do better the next time. Assistance may range from a high degree (e.g., needing to hear stress on the target word in the prompt and hear other students' responses) to a mid-level (e.g., needing the word slowed down to count the segments) to a low-level (e.g., needing only repetition of the sentence containing the target word). Box 10.1 on page 444 demonstrates high and low levels of scaffolding for first-sound isolation and phoneme segmentation.

If the student can perform at 80 percent or better at a particular scaffolding level, a lower level of support can be given in the next session. If the student shows little progress, scaffolding may stay high throughout the intervention and the student may not achieve independence for that particular task. That may mean that a preschooler can identify first sounds fully independently and last sounds with medium support. The preschooler may require high support for phoneme segmentation and may use only onset-rime segmentation when she or he performs independently—which is still an impressive accomplishment for a preschooler and sets the foundation for further learning in kindergarten.

The aim of phonemic awareness instruction is not to teach a phoneme-by-phoneme or word-shape-by-word-shape skill, but rather to teach a robust, flexible awareness that there are phonemes that are separable and manipulable. This author's experience is that a task like phoneme isolation shows a bimodal performance, meaning either students understand the principle and can do phoneme isolation, or they do not understand and therefore cannot do the task. This is in contrast to alphabet names or grapheme-phoneme correspondence, which shows that students may understand there are letter names or sounds that go with letters, but must learn each pairing, resulting in a more incremental acquisition.

Levels of Scaffolding for Phonemic Awareness during Book Reading

Box 10.1

High Scaffolding

SLP: Okay, Amanda, here's another one for you. What's the first sound, Amanda, look at me. What's the first sound in *dare?*

Amanda: Don't you dare!

SLP: What's the first sound? Dare.

Amanda: /t-t-t-t/

SLP: Day–/d/

Amanda: day

Low Scaffolding

SLP: Here's a question for Henry. What's the first sound in *rest?*

Henry: /r-r/

SLP: /r-r-r/, good job!

Henry: It starts with the letter r.

SLP: It starts with an r!

Low Scaffolding, Simple Word

SLP: How many sounds are in the word *the?*

Jordan: Two.

SLP: Show me the sounds. There are two sounds. Tap my fingers and show me.

Jordan: /th-e/

SLP: Yes! /th-e/, /th-e/. Good job!

Low Scaffolding, Complex Word

SLP: What's the next word?

Jordan: Titanic.

SLP: Titanic! That has a lot of sounds in it. What do you think the first sound is?

Jordan: T-i-tan-i-c (sticks out five fingers as he says sounds).

SLP: Good!

Jordan: There's five sounds.

SLP: Okay, good.

Explicit Skill Targets

Finally, explicitness involves directly focusing on the skill in question for both teacher and student. Explicitness can be a challenging aspect of contextualized skill intervention. An explicit-skill focus involves identifying one or two targets for the activity. A purposeful activity, such as sharing books, involves much more than the one or two skills, but the nontargeted skills are achieved without the therapeutic focus. Here, phonemic awareness is the skill focus, while areas such as print concepts, literate vocabulary, spelling, and story structure are placed in the background.

Teaching Phonemic Awareness

Song and Name Play

The pleasure in song and name play can provide hidden lessons combined with a goofiness beloved by students. Combine the short activities with other longer phonemic awareness activities in a single session, or use them as transition activities to usefully occupy students standing in line or waiting for materials to be distributed.

Song

Songs naturally provide a focus on form at the early syllable and rhyme level, but can be modified to teach awareness at the phonemic level. Yopp (1992) describes modifications of preschool songs and games that allow a focus on a phonemic level of awareness. The activities involve incorporating sound matching, isolation, blending, addition or substitution, and segmentation.

Box 10.2 on page 446 presents two examples of song adaptations. A song sung to the melody of "Old MacDonald Had a Farm" targets phoneme isolation. The melody from "Twinkle, Twinkle, Little Star" is used to practice sound segmentation.

Name Play

Students enjoy name play activities, where they identify and count the sounds in their names. Use questions such as:

- What's the first sound in your name?
- Who has the same sound at the beginning?
- How many sounds in your first name?
- How many sounds in your last name?
- Who has the longest? The shortest?

Box 10.2 ## Song Adaptations for Phonemic Awareness

Sung to "Old MacDonald Had a Farm"

What's the sound that starts these words:

Turtle, time, and *teeth?*
[wait for a response]
/t/ is the sound that starts these words:
Turtle, time, and *teeth.*
With a /t/, /t/ here, and a /t/, /t/ there,
Here a /t/, there a /t/, everywhere a /t/, /t/.
/t/ is the sound that starts these words:
Turtle, time, and *teeth!*

What's the sound in the middle of these words:

Leaf and *deep* and *meat?*
[wait for a response]
/i/ is the sound in the middle of these words:
Leaf and *deep* and *meat.*
With an /i/, /i/ here, and an /i/, /i/ there,
Here an /i/, there an /i/, everywhere an /i/, /i/.
/i/ is the sound in the middle of these words:
Leaf and *deep* and *meat!*

Sung to "Twinkle, Twinkle, Little Star"

Listen, listen
To my word
Then tell me all the sounds you heard: R-a-ce [said slowly]
/r/ is one sound
/ei/ is two
/s/ is last in *race*
It's true.

Listen, listen
To my word
Then tell me all the sounds you heard: G-o [said slowly]
/g/ is one sound
/o/ is two
And that is all in *go*
It's true.

From "Developing Phonemic Awareness in Young Children," by H. K. Yopp, 1992, *The Reading Teacher, 45,* pp. 700, 702. © 1992 by the International Reading Association. Reprinted with permission.

Enhance names with appealing adjectives, such as *Terrific Teresa, Lovely Laura, Smart Sarita, Rocking Ron.* Sometimes a student will insist that he is *Burrito Ted,* and refuse to go along with the alliteration. In that case, pointing out the /b/ and /t/ difference is a lesson in itself.

Roll call is a perfect time for sound manipulation, with the "Sound for the Day." Call out each student's first name, with the first sound replaced by the sound of the day: "Teter" for Peter, "Tilly" for Billy, "Tara" for Sara. Students may take turns doing roll call, learning to manipulate, or recognize manipulations of names. Comment on names that do not change, such as "Terry? Oh, Terry's name doesn't change because it already starts with a /t/ sound."

Segment and count names, too. First, middle, and last names provide opportunities for everyone to have the "longest" name. Students enjoy routines and may turn the name play into an expected part of intervention. For example, Ukrainetz et al. (2000) described how the students spontaneously took an interest in the instructor's nametag, requesting her to read it and count the sounds in it during each session.

Games and Activities

Contrived activities are designed specifically to teach a skill. Identifying pictures from an array that start with a particular sound, circling the long words on a worksheet, and blending a word when the teacher pronounces the individual phonemes are all activities existing solely to teach the skill. Modify familiar games, such as I Spy or Bingo to practice phonemic awareness.

It is easy to control stimulus complexity in contrived activities, so phonotactic shape and phoneme contrasts can be limited if desired. Articulation picture cards provide multiple exemplars of particular phonemes. Phonological process cards control phonotactic shape. For instance, a "cluster reduction" card pack provides CCVC *(stick, slick)* and CVC *(sick, lick)* contrasts. Selections from either of these sources can be applied to these contrived activities. In addition, some phonotactic shapes and word possibilities are presented in Appendix A on page 466. In these contrived contexts, meaning is not essential, so nonsense words can also be used, providing strong control over word shape and phoneme composition (but are not usually picturable). Print can be present on the picture cards to provide exposure and incidental instruction in linking sounds to letters. However students may need reminders to focus on the sounds, not the letters. Some phoneme-level contrived activities are presented below.

Isolation and Matching

Concentration. Spread the cards face down on the table and have the students take turns choosing two cards. The students identify the picture, then isolate the phoneme. Then they draw a second card and do the same. The next step is determining if the isolated phonemes are the same or different. This same/different judgment on sounds (ignoring the pictures) is rather difficult initially and students will require practice to understand what is requested. If the cards match in first sound, the student keeps the pair. If the first sounds do not match, the pair is returned to the table. Having only two to four contrasting phonemes provides a number of opportunities to find matching sounds. The winner is the one with the most pairs.

Go Fish! Have one student ask another for a card beginning with the same sound as one in his or her hand of four cards. This is matching from an array, which is more difficult than judging a match from only two cards, such as in Concentration. The first step is isolating the sound, then asking another student for a card starting with that sound, then the other student must examine each of his or her cards to determine which start with that sound. This will require considerable interactive scaffolding initially. This game should not have more than six sound contrasts, and can be simplified (i.e., scaffolded) by providing fewer contrasts. Again, the winner is the one with the most pairs.

Blending

Food Bag. Display plastic food items that are labeled. Use known items with simple phonotactic structure (e.g., *bread* is simpler than *pineapple)*. Drop the food items into an opaque bag. Grasp one item in the bag, provide the segmented word (e.g., /b/-/r/-/ɛ/-/d/), and ask the students to guess the word from the parts. When a student says the word accurately, pull the item out of the bag.

Pick a Picture. Spread four pictures across the table. Tell students to guess the word from the parts you are saying. Say the word with each phoneme distinctly separate (e.g., /b/-/ʌ/-/n/). Use words with the same starting sounds and similar lengths (e.g., *bat, bun, back, ball)* to prevent guessing based only on the first sound or general length.

Segmenting

Catching and Cutting Phonemes. Spread paper fish with attached paper clips on the floor. Use a fishing rod made of a stick, string, and a strong magnet. The author prefers an extendable magnetic rod from the hardware store that is intended to retrieve tools dropped behind counters and large appliances. Have the students catch a fish with the magnet. Ask each student the picture label, then have them "cut the fish" by segmenting the word into phonemes. The students track who caught the "biggest" fish.

Fill-in-the-Blanks. Give the students a paper with four squares in a series. Tell students to listen to a word and place a chip in each square for each sound they hear. Demonstrate several words, one to four phonemes long, and have the students copy the segmentation and chip placement. Then you simply segment each word and have students place their chips independently. Give prompts as needed to assist the students into a correct segmentation. Students can then take turns segmenting words and see who has the longest word.

Deletion and Substitution

Chaining Card. This is challenging and not recommended for preschoolers, even with maximal scaffolding. Minimal pair articulation cards or rhyming cards are used for this activity. Show the students a card (e.g., *mat*) and ask what happens when /m/ is taken away. They will say, "The word changes to *at.*" Then ask what happens when the /m/ changes to a /b/? They will say, "It turns into a *bat.*" Show the bat card. Continue for each rhyming pair (e.g., "How about *sun?* If you take away the /s/, you get? Now add a /b/ and you get?").

The preceding are only a few possibilities for single-skill activities. Commercial curriculum guides such as *Phonemic Awareness for Young Children* (Adams et al., 1998), *Ladders to Literacy* (Notari-Syverson et al., 1998), *Phonological Awareness Success* (Walsh, 2002), *Sound Effects* (Spector, 1999), and *Road to the Code* (Blachman, Ball, Black, & Tangel, 2000) provide a variety of activity ideas at the phonemic level that can be used without committing to the entire sequenced program. Students can manage several phonemic awareness skills within one session, but until a routine is set up, they need to be reminded frequently which skill they are addressing, especially when moving from first to last sound. A consistent cue such as pointing to the front or back of a train picture can be a helpful reminder.

Phonemic Awareness through Shared Reading and Writing

In this third set of activities, phonemic awareness is taught within the contexts of use: reading and writing authentic texts. Learning is linked to the larger purposeful context. One skill can be addressed at a time, but routine sequences of events and differential scaffolding allow addressing multiple skills. Multiple skills at the phoneme level within a single activity allow:

- Matching to differing skill levels within a small group
- Exposure to skills that are beyond easy grasp
- Orchestration of component skills into a greater whole
- Flexibility in applying different skills as needed within a context

Verse Book Reading

The materials for shared reading activity are simply good books—books that are a pleasure to read and to look at. Any children's book can be used, but verse books with rhyme or alliteration provide a natural focus on sound while providing a meaningful literacy activity. Appendix B on page 477 provides a bibliography of verse books that this author has used successfully. Rhyme is used as an entry into phonemic awareness. Rhyme is a combination of a single phoneme or cluster with a larger segment (e.g., *r-an, m-an; h-appy, s-appy; sl-ip, d-ip),* called *onset* and *rime.* The onset-rime segmentation is an early way of becoming aware of phonemes (Gillam & van Kleeck, 1998). Starting with rhyme and moving to phonemes follows Adams' (1990) expectation that "exploitation of onsets and rimes could well provide the key to unlocking phonemic awareness" (p. 318).

In this approach to intervention, like the print referencing described in Chapter 9, the teaching occurs within actual situations of reading and writing, on words arising from the activity. Easier and more difficult tasks co-occur within the activity; for example, *cat* and *aristocrat* may be the rhyming pairs identified from the book and discussed. Structural scaffolds are provided with the verse books that are read and reread, and with predictable routines called sound talk episodes. Opportunities for use are not strictly controlled, but repeated opportunities are planned.

Other language and literacy topics are addressed incidentally. Topics include interesting vocabulary, personally relevant topics, arithmetic opportunities, and print concepts. For example, print concepts occur when the SLP and students identify the book title, author, and illustrator. In Ukrainetz et al. (2000), during a reading of *Drummer Hoff* (Emberly, 1967), one student suggested that she knew this was a "long part in the story" because there were so many words on that page. During another book reading, a student commented that he knew that a certain part of the story needed to be read loudly because there was an "explanation point" (i.e., exclamation point) in the writing. In this study, the students became excited over new storybooks and took great interest in the discussions around them. The students discussed vocabulary such as *aristocrat (Terrible Teresa;* Cuetara, 1997), *private, corporal,* and *general (Drummer Hoff);* and physically demonstrated the concept of *upside-down (Silly Sally;* Wood, 1992). The storybook *Is Your Mama a Llama?* (Guarino, 1989) sparked a lively conversation about llamas, leading the instructor to provide photos of her family's pet llamas in a subsequent session. Counting the sounds and comparing length provided mini-lessons in adding and subtracting. As is evident, this book-reading activity is rich in language and literacy possibilities. However, an explicit repeated focus on phonemic awareness is mandatory. Students should be told at the beginning of the session, reminded during the session, and asked at the end of the session what they are learning. The answer should be related to phonemic awareness, such as "first sounds" or "counting sounds," not "reading books" or "playing with picture cards."

The basic approach in this section is to perform multiple phonemic awareness tasks at intervals during the book reading, using words that arise in the text. Books can be read initially without discussion, then reread for sound talk. Alternately, sound talk may occur in the first reading, so long as the pleasure of reading is maintained. Rhyming verses provide natural stopping points that allow sound talk.

The tasks are organized initially with a predictable sequence called a *sound talk episode.* The sound talk episode consists of four parts: (1) identify the rhyming or alliterative words; (2) identify the first or last phonemes; (3) segment and count the sounds in the word; and (4) provide the phonemes of another rhyming or alliterative word to blend. The focus is on identifying the sounds in the words, not identifying which letters represent the sounds (although letter counting and letter-sound discussions often occur incidentally). The general sequence is illustrated in Box 10.3 on page 452 with a reading of *Terrible Teresa* (Cuetara, 1997). The sound episode sequence is used initially to provide a structural scaffold. As students become accustomed to the tasks, the questions can be asked out of order or selectively. The episode can vary in number of words discussed and skill questions asked, so long as there are repeated opportunities for each student to address each skill.

Writing to Dictation

Writing is another purposeful activity in which phonemic awareness can be taught. Writing is a powerful context for becoming aware of the phonemic construction of words. Writing a verse from a story just heard, generating a grocery

Box 10.3

Illustration of a Sound
Talk Episode on a Verse

SLP:	[reading] "The story of Fred. This is a boy named Fred. He hates to go to bed. He hides out in the shed, and stays awake instead."[1] Do you hear words that rhyme? [reads again, stressing rhyming words]
Sara:	Fred-bed. *(identify rhyming words)*
Deepa:	Shed.
SLP:	*(segmentation)* Yes, all those words rhyme, *Fred-bed-shed.* What's the first sound in *Fred?* [points to upper teeth touching lower lip]
Sara:	/f/ *(isolation)*
SLP:	And bed? /b/-/b/-/bɛd/
Deepa:	/b/
SLP:	Good job. Let's count the sounds in *Fred.* Put your fingers out for each sound. /f/-/r/-/ɛ/-/d/. *(segmentation)*
Students:	[raising a finger for each sound and saying along with the SLP] /f/-/r/-/ɛ/-/d/.
SLP:	How many sounds?
Students:	[count fingers] 4 sounds!
SLP:	How many in *bed?* /b-ɛ-d/.
Students:	[raising a finger for each sound and saying along with the SLP] /b/-/ɛ/-/d/.
SLP:	How many sounds?
Students:	3 sounds.
SLP:	Which one is longest?
Sara:	Fred.
SLP:	Yes, *Fred* has 4 sounds. Now I'm going to say a word for you to guess. It rhymes with Fred. /b-r-ɛ-d/. *(blending)*
Sara:	Bread?
SLP:	Yes, bread. *Bread* rhymes with *Fred* and *bed* and *shed.* [points to each picture]

1. Story from *Terrible Teresa and Other Very Short Stories* (pp. 4–5), by M. Cuetara, 1997, New York: Dutton Children's Books. © 1997 by Mittie Cuetara. Reprinted with permission.

list, writing a message to Dad, writing a story, or describing a picture are examples of authentic writing activities. Drawing a picture to write about in the session is not recommended, as too much time is spent drawing the picture and too little time writing. The verse or alliterative element is not as critical in the writing activity as in the reading. The act of writing itself demands consideration of the sound structure of words, even if invented or conventional spelling is not yet expected from the student.

In writing to dictation, a key element to this instruction is the SLP talking through the process (see Box 10.4 on page 454). As the clinician writes, he or she elicits isolation and segmentation of the phonemes in each word, and prediction of the number of letters required. The SLP is demonstrating how to think through phoneme isolation and segmentation for the purpose of writing. After writing, the SLP and students reread the sentences, identify component sounds, and count the number of sounds in those words.

Emergent Writing

In emergent writing, students use their own nonsense, invented, or conventional writing. They do not have to know conventional or even invented spelling. Depending on their level, they are learning that words are made up of sounds that are represented by letters, by particular letters, or by memorized letter combinations. The SLP again talks the student through the process. Every word does not have to be discussed exhaustively. The clinician may decide that two first-sound, two last-sound, and two sound-segmentation items are enough for this writing task.

A more structured way of teaching phonemic awareness through invented spelling is *kid writing* (McGee, personal communication, February 20, 2004). Kid writing is a spelling lesson that bridges students between self-directed invented spelling exploration and conventional writing. Students are directed to listen to the first and last sounds, then to use their best guesses for selecting letters to represent sounds. Box 10.5 on page 455 demonstrates how children's attention is focused on phonemic awareness while they direct the writing in a kid writing session.

The students will be concerned about spelling and letter formation issues, particularly if the classroom environment has allowed only copying and correct spelling. Having an alphabet strip available so the student can copy the letter alleviates letter formation concerns. Encouraging students to use their best guesses and to line up the number of letters with number of sounds is

Box 10.4

Example of Engaging Phonemic Awareness while Writing to Dictation

SLP:	Tell me what you want to say and I'll write it down.
John:	I went to the zoo today.
SLP:	I /w-ɛ-n-t/, what's the first sound I need?
John:	/w/
SLP:	Yes, /w/. /w-ɛ-n-t/. What's the last sound?
John:	/t/
SLP	Yes, /t/. Whew, four sounds in that word. That's lots to write. To, /t/-/u/. That's easy, /t-t-t/ and /u-u-u/, just 2 sounds. [writes them as says them] The zoo, /z/-/u/. [stretched out] What's the first sound I need?
John:	/u/
SLP:	Listen again, /zzz/-/u/.
John:	/z/
SLP:	Yes, /z/. I like /z/ words, zoo, zebra, zoom. Then the last sound?
John:	/u/
SLP:	You got it. /u/. Last word, *today*, /t/-/u/-/d/-/eɪ/. You count those sounds, fingers out.
John:	/t/-/u/-/deɪ/. 3.
SLP:	Hmm, let me check. /t/-/u/-/d/-/eɪ/. I count 4. /d-eɪ/ are 2 sounds—4 sounds, 4 letters. Hmm, it's written with 5 letters—oh well, sometimes spelling is strange. We wrote, "I went to the zoo today."

appropriate for emergent writers. Noting that a word has more letters than sounds can lead to the comment, "Oh well, spelling is funny sometimes, but usually it matches the sounds." For students who are using a lot of conventional spelling, "th," double "l" and silent "e" suggestions will likely occur. However, the discussions should be brief and not be bogged down in the complexities of spelling. The objective is not to hinder correct spelling, but to keep the focus on sound analysis, with spelling expectations matched to each student's individual level. Ukrainetz et al. (2000) detail the students' progress in

Box 10.5

Example of Engaging Phonemic Awareness in a "Kid Writing" Lesson

SLP:	What is the message we want to write for Valentine's Day?
Students:	I love Mama.
SLP:	[draws three lines on a strip of paper] I–love–Mama. [pointing to each line] Here are 3 spaces for those words. How should we write the first word, *I?* What sound do we hear?
Amari:	/aɪ/
SLP:	Yes, /aɪ/. That's all. That's a very short word, just one sound. What letter should we use, Amari?
Amari:	"A"
SLP:	"A" One sound, one letter. Next, I love, love. John, what is the first sound in *love?*
John	/l/
SLP:	/l/, yes. What letter should we use?
John:	"L"
SLP	"L" I will write that. Now listen for the last sound. What is the last sound in *love?*
Deepa:	/l/
SLP:	/l/ is the first sound. Let's listen again. /ʌv-v-v/.
John:	/v/
Deepa:	/v/
SLP:	/v/ What letter, Deepa?
Deepa:	I don't know.
SLP:	Use your best guess. This is kid writing. Kids can use their best guesses to write sounds if they don't know.
Deepa:	"B"
SLP:	I'll write that. Last word, I love you. You. What is the first sound?
Amari:	/j/, write a "u"
SLP:	You. /j/-/u/. There are 2 sounds. But we can write "u" for kid writing—1 letter, 2 sounds. Now it is your turn to write *I love you* on your cards. Use your best guesses for each word, first and last sounds.

comfort with spelling and composition:

> Initially, the children were hesitant to write. They protested that they did not know how to write and they repeatedly asked for correct word spellings. Gradually, the children began to believe they could write, and became comfortable guessing and helping each other with spelling. The children became familiar with concepts such as writing from left to right, leaving a space between words, putting a period at the end of a sentence, and starting a sentence with a capital. One student brought a letter to an instructional session that one of her classmates had written her. She requested the help of the group to write a letter in reply. The session was spent constructing a letter to her friend, engaging all children in the group in sound talk and writing. (p. 346)

Scaffolding Phonemic Awareness
The Very Start of Phonemic Awareness

Some preschoolers have difficulty achieving the simplest level of phonemic awarenes, which is first-sound isolation. The types of errors they show can reveal the depth of nonunderstanding. A student's error that involves providing a letter name rather than a phoneme is not a cause for concern. This error can easily be corrected with specific guidance to listen (point to the ear) for the sounds, not look (point to the eye) for the letters. Concerns arise, though, for students who persist in saying the whole word, related words, or a single sound perseveratively. These students do not understand the concept of listening for the first sound in a word and pronouncing only that sound (or, for stops, the consonant plus a schwa). In this author's experience with at-risk four-year-olds in Head Start, instruction to address such errors should not revert to pre-phonemic awareness activities, such as syllable clapping, or identifying bells and barks. Instead, additional scaffolds can be implemented at the phoneme level. A brief period of phoneme production practice will accustom the students to thinking about speech sounds. A few minutes can be spent stopping a word after the first sound and practicing saying the sound (e.g., "Listen to the first sound in *bat*. /b/-/b/-/b/. Look at my lips. Everyone say the /b/ sound"). The articulatory movements are noted and exaggerated. This is then contrasted with the /g/ from *ghost* or the /m/ from *man,* for which a brief practice period ensues.

Scaffolds during the lesson include directing the student to look at the SLP's lips (with finger cues such as an index finger over the lips for /ʃ/ or at the neck for /g/) and imitating the sounds. While this brief phoneme focus instruction is helpful, I do not recommend divorcing this instruction from first-sound isolation. Most students do not require (and young students will find it too abstract and structured) systematic teaching of the articulatory motions of all English phonemes accompanied by special vocabulary, such as that in the intervention program *Lindamood Phoneme Sequencing Program for Reading, Spelling, and Speech (LiPS;* Lindamood & Lindamood, 1998). Instead, simply providing focused attention on sounds at the beginning of the session and—based on their errors—periodically during the session, will orient even four-year-olds within one to two sessions.

The Adult Model

One feature of scaffolding that is particularly pertinent to instruction in phonemic awareness is the issue of the adult model. This author recommends that the adult always model the correct target, allowing the students to reach it to varying degrees. For example, segmentation is difficult and is acquired only gradually. Students may segment initially with onset-rime (e.g., *hunt* = /h/-/ʌnt/. They may skip less salient phonemes (*hunt* = /h/-/ʌ/-/t/). However, the SLP should consistently model accurate phoneme segmentation. The clinician will not demand correctness from the students, but instead can comment on the parts that were correct and provide the target to which the students aspire. Likewise, the students may use invented spelling and will be complimented on their good guesses, but the SLP should model conventional spelling in her or his own writing.

Phonemic awareness tasks are challenging for young students initially. They will require considerable demonstration, prompting, and feedback. The SLP uses a range of task difficulty within one activity and flexibly changes the degree of support, based on students' responses. As students begin to understand a concept, such as first-sound isolation, they become more independent and do not require demonstration and prompting. The length of time for this to occur varies among students.

Assisting Segmentation

Phoneme segmentation is a particularly difficult task. In contrast to the rhythmic divisions of syllable or onset-rime segmentation, it is awkward and jarring to stop at each individual phoneme. This level of segmentation is impossible for stops (a schwa vowel is appended); extends the continuants; and exaggerates liquids, glides, and vowels. However, it is the level required for an alphabetic writing system, so the SLP and students must persist in achieving mastery.

Segmentation can be assisted by the structural scaffold of having the students put their fists on the table and stick out a finger for each sound as the SLP or the students slowly say the word. The table and fist provide an anchor for limited motor coordination. The finger extensions form a portable, visual support that is not as distracting as colored tiles or paper drawings. Once the students are comfortable with finger extensions, the method can be used in impromptu practice activities, such as segmenting their names while they stand in line for a room change. The support withdrawal process for segmentation is as follows:

1. The students put fists on the table and imitate the SLP extending one finger for each sound as the clinician says each phoneme of the word.

2. The students say the word and extend fingers along with the SLP.

3. The SLP says the word without extending her fingers and the students both say the word and extend fingers.

4. The SLP only extends fingers while the students say the word and extend fingers.

5. The SLP says it is one of the students' turn to lead, and only mouths the sounds while the student says the word and everyone else extends fingers.

6. One student independently segments by saying the sounds and extending fingers.

Advanced Phonemic Awareness

This chapter has focused mainly on preschool to first grade students, teaching isolation, blending, and segmenting with phonotactically simple words or with expectations of partially correct performance for more difficult words. The goal is to achieve an awareness of the phonemic structure of words to build a foundation for phoneme-grapheme correspondences. Students must develop more than simple phonemic awareness skills. They need to apply skills with multisyllabic words, phoneme deletion and substitution, and sound segmentation while simultaneously dealing with graphemes—all of which places considerable demands on auditory memory, mental manipulation, and sound-letter knowledge.

These more difficult word reading tasks are reminders that there is not a simple causal relationship between phonemic awareness and word reading or spelling. Phonemic awareness helps reading and spelling. But the ability to read and spell words also helps phonemic awareness; one can segment a word phonemically more easily if the spelling is known. Spelling can even influence perception (Ehri & Wilce, 1986) in some cases, making the two line up better. For example, if students know that *butter* is written with a "t," they will override the heard production of a /d/-like phoneme and state that they hear a /t/, to everyone's satisfaction. This spelling/perception interaction can also serve as a warning against overtraining. Older students who are extensively drilled on listening for phonemic contrasts may get frustrated when their close listening is penalized for its resultant incorrect spelling (e.g., "budder" for *butter).*

Vowel distinctions are another challenging task. Vowels are less categorically perceived than consonants and vary with dialect, word context, and speed of articulation. In addition, vowel spelling rarely aligns with spoken vowels. Requiring extensive practice on distinguishing and spelling the carefully articulated vowels of the SLP is unlikely to be helpful for actual spelling situations. Focusing on building the store of visual-orthographic images would be more beneficial for improving spelling and word decoding (see Apel & Swank, 1999).

Later phonemic awareness skills should be integrated into direct reading and spelling instruction in second grade and beyond, using moments in sounding out printed words to reflect on the phonemic character of the spoken word and engaging in mini-drills on sounding out multisyllabic words. Often, for older students with reading disabilities, basic phonemic awareness and phoneme-grapheme correspondence is established, but the students lack conventional spelling knowledge (e.g., rules for use of a silent "e" or a "tion"). In addition, they have auditory memory and retrieval limitations that prevent accurate sounding out of longer words. These difficulties fall into the category of skills for decoding and encoding the printed word (commonly known as *word attack skills)* rather than phonemic awareness, per se.

This chapter does not address word attack skills. However, one comment may be helpful. For the older student and longer words, attention to larger chunks such as rime or syllable may be helpful. Syllable segmentation is easier than phoneme segmentation for sounding out longer words (e.g., *su-per-stitious).* There are often spelling patterns across rime units that can be pointed out (called analogy phonics by NRP, 2000). The alert reader will note the earlier recommendation against teaching phonological awareness with these larger units, but that was for younger students who primarily need the phoneme level of awareness. For older students who have the phonemic knowledge, syllable or rime attention can be helpful.

Repeated, intensive, supported, explicit word and text reading instruction will provide opportunities for improving both reading and the three underlying phonological processing domains of advanced phonemic awareness, auditory working memory, and rapid automatized phonological code retrieval. For older children, isolated phonemic awareness instruction is not recommended. Phonemic awareness should occur as part of reading and writing.

The popular program *LiPs* (Lindamood & Lindamood, 1998), which is now considered to be a phonemic awareness training program (and formerly a speech discrimination program) is much more than either. *LiPs* is a discrete skill intervention program with vertical structuring and systematic shaping procedures. *LiPs* provides an extensive focus on phoneme articulatory awareness, semiphonetic spelling, and single word decoding. *LiPs* is thus also a reading instruction program that stops before connected text. The activities provide a good workout in phonological memory and phonological code retrieval.

LiPs showed excellent results in teaching word decoding to older students with reading disabilities in a study by Torgesen and colleagues (2001). However, it is not alone in its success—other programs with the RISE quality indicators, particularly that of intensity, have also had excellent results. For example, in the same study, Torgesen and colleagues found success with a method called embedded phonics, which has a more incidental approach to phonics, lacks instruction on the articulatory process, has less attention to phonemic awareness, and provides more experience with reading connected text for meaning (NRP, 2000). The slight advantage found for *LiPs* in the study was attributed to better training of the instructors, resulting in better treatment fidelity for that condition.

So phonemic awareness instruction is important, but the question remains of how much explicit phonemic awareness instruction is necessary. What can be concluded with confidence is that integrated reading instruction, with attention to phonemic awareness, vocabulary, word attack, fluency, and comprehension can lead to impressive gains in reading competence even for older children with established reading disabilities (NRP, 2000; Torgesen, 2000).

Conclusion

This chapter presented methods of teaching phonemic awareness to preschool and early primary grade children. Phoneme-level scaffolded instruction in activities with varying degrees of contextualization were presented. Three sets of activities were detailed: song and name play; single-skill contrived activities;

and sound talk embedded in shared reading and writing. The activities were united by the intervention framework: teaching at the phonemic level only, teaching multiple phonemic awareness skills with some ahead of independent developmental level, with strategic support coming from structural and interactive scaffolding. All the activities provided intensive, repeated opportunities for explicit, supported learning.

References

Adams, M. J. (1990). *Beginning to read: Thinking and learning about print.* Cambridge, MA: MIT Press.

Adams, M. J., Foorman, B. R., Lundberg, I., & Beeler, T. (1998). *Phonemic awareness in young children: A classroom curriculum.* Baltimore: Brookes.

Apel, K., & Swank, L. K. (1999). Second chances: Improving decoding skills in the older student. *Language, Speech, and Hearing Services in Schools, 30,* 231–242.

Ball, E. W., & Blachman, B. A. (1988). Phoneme segmentation training: Effect on reading readiness. *Annals of Dyslexia, 38,* 208–225.

Ball, E. W., & Blachman, B. A. (1991). Does phoneme awareness training in kindergarten make a difference in early word recognition and developmental spelling? *Reading Research Quarterly, 26,* 49–66.

Berninger, V. W., Vermeulen, K., Abbott, R. D., McCutchen, D., Cotton, S., Cude, J., et al. (2003). Comparison of three approaches to supplementary reading instruction for low-achieving second-grade readers. *Language, Speech, and Hearing Services in Schools, 34,* 101–116.

Blachman, B. A., Ball, E. W., Black, R., & Tangel, D. M. (2000). *Road to the code: A phonological awareness program for young children.* Baltimore, MD: Brookes.

Bradley, L., & Bryant, P. (1985). *Rhyme and reason in reading and spelling.* Ann Arbor, MI: University of Michigan Press.

Brady, S., Fowler, A., Stone, B., & Winbury, N. (1994). Training phonological awareness: A study with inner-city kindergarten children. *Annals of Dyslexia, 44,* 26–59.

Byrne, B., & Fielding-Barnsley, R. (1991). Evaluation of a program to teach phonemic awareness to young children. *Journal of Educational Psychology, 83,* 451–455.

Camarata, S. M., Nelson, K. E., & Camarata, M. N. (1994). Comparison of conversational-recasting and imitative procedures for training grammatical structures in children with specific language impairment. *Journal of Speech and Hearing Research, 37,* 1414–1423.

Catts, H. W., Fey, M. E., Zhang, X., & Tomblin, J. B. (2001). Estimating the risk of future reading difficulties in kindergarten children: A research-based model and its clinical implications. *Language, Speech, and Hearing Services in Schools, 32,* 38–50.

Catts, H. W., & Kamhi, A. G. (2005). *Language and reading disabilities* (2nd ed.). Boston, MA: Allyn and Bacon.

Cunningham, A. (1990). Explicit vs. implicit instruction in phonological awareness. *Journal of Experimental Child Psychology, 50,* 429–444.

Dahl, K. L., Scharer, P. L., Lawson, L. L., & Grogan, P. R. (1999). Phonics instruction and student achievement in whole language first-grade classrooms. *Reading Research Quarterly, 34,* 312–341.

Ehri, L. C., Nunes, S. R., Willows, D. M., Schuster, B. V., Yaghoub-Zadeh, Z., & Shanahan, T. (2001). Phonemic awareness instruction helps children learn to read: Evidence from the National Reading Panel's meta-analysis. *Reading Research Quarterly, 36,* 250–287.

Ehri, L. C., & Wilce, L. S. (1986). The influence of spellings on speech. In D. B. Yaden & S. Templeton (Eds.), *Metalinguistic awareness and beginning literacy* (pp. 101–113). Portsmouth, NH: Heinemann.

Feuerstein, R. (1980). *Instrumental enrichment.* Baltimore: University Park Press.

Fey, M., Catts, H., & Larrivee, L. (1995). Preparing preschoolers for the academic and social challenges of school. In M. E. Fey, J. Windsor, & S. F. Warren (Eds.), *Language intervention: Preschool through the elementary years* (pp. 3–38). Baltimore: Brookes.

Fey, M. E., Cleave, P. L., Long, S. H., & Hughes, D. L. (1993). Two approaches to the facilitation of grammar in children with language impairment: An experimental evaluation. *Journal of Speech and Hearing Research, 36,* 141–157.

Fox, B., & Routh, D. K. (1975). Analyzing spoken language into words, syllables, and phonemes: A developmental study. *Journal of Psycholinguistic Research, 4*(4), 331–342.

Gillam, R. B., Loeb, D. F., & Friel-Patti, S. (2001). Looking back: A summary of five exploratory studies of Fast ForWord. *American Journal of Speech-Language Pathology, 10,* 269–273.

Gillam, R. B., & van Kleeck, A. (1998). Phonological awareness training and short-term working memory: Clinical implications. In R. B. Gillam (Ed.), *Memory and language impairments in children and adults* (pp. 83–96). Gaithersburg, MD: Aspen.

Gillon, G. T. (2000). The efficacy of phonological awareness intervention for children with spoken language impairment. *Language, Speech, and Hearing Services in Schools, 31,* 126–141.

Gillon, G. T. (2004). *Phonological awareness: From research to practice.* New York: Guilford.

Girolametto, L., Pearce. P. S., & Weitzman, E. (1996). Interactive focused stimulation for toddlers with expressive vocabulary delays. *Journal of Speech and Hearing Research, 39,* 1263–1273.

Hadley, P. A., Simmerman, A., Long, M., & Luna, M. (2000). Facilitating language development for inner-city children: Experimental evaluation of a collaborative, classroom-based intervention. *Language, Speech, and Hearing Services in Schools, 31,* 280–295.

Hoien, T., Lundberg, I., Stanovich, K. E., & Bjaalid, I. (1995). Components of phonological awareness. *Reading and Writing: An Interdisciplinary Journal, 7,* 171–188.

International Reading Association (IRA) and National Association for the Education of Young Children (NAEYC). (1998). Learning to read and write: Developmentally appropriate practices for young children. *Young Children, 53*(4), 30–46.

Kamhi, A. G., & Catts, H. W. (1999). Causes of reading disabilities. In H. W. Catts & A. G. Kamhi (Eds.), *Language and reading disabilities* (pp. 95–127). Boston: Allyn and Bacon.

Laing, S. P., & Espeland, W. (2005). Low intensity phonological awareness training in a preschool classroom for children with communication impairments. *Journal of Communication Disorders, 38,* 65–82.

Liberman, I. Y., Shankweiler, D., Fischer, F. W., & Carter, B. (1974). Explicit syllable and phoneme segmentation in the young child. *Journal of Experimental Child Psychology, 18,* 201–212.

Lidz, C. S., & Peña, E. D. (1996). Dynamic assessment: The model, its relevance as a non-biased approach, and its application to Latino American preschool children. *Language, Speech, and Hearing Services in Schools, 27*(4), 367–372.

Lie, A. (1991). Effects of a training program for stimulating skills in word analysis in first-grade children. *Reading Research Quarterly, 26*(3), 236–250.

Lindamood, P., & Lindamood, P. (1998). *The Lindamood Phoneme Sequencing Program for Reading, Spelling, and Speech* (3rd ed.). Austin, TX: Pro-Ed.

Lundberg, I. (1988). Preschool prevention of reading failure: Does training in phonological awareness work? In R. L. Masland & M. W. Masland (Eds.), *Prevention of reading failure* (pp. 163–176). Parkton, MD: York Press.

Lundberg, I., Frost, J., & Peterson, O. P. (1988). Effects of an extensive program for stimulating phonological awareness in preschool children. *Reading Research Quarterly, 23,* 263–284.

Lyon, G. R., Alexander, D., & Yaffee, S. (1997). Progress and promise in research in learning disabilities. *Learning Disabilities: A Multidisciplinary Journal, 8,* 1–6.

McFadden, T. U. (1998). Sounds and stories: Teaching phonemic awareness in print contexts. *American Journal of Speech-Language Pathology, 7,* 5–13.

McGee, L. M. (December, 2004). *The role of wisdom in evidence-based preschool literacy curriculum.* Presidential address to the National Reading Conference, San Antonio, TX.

McGee, L. M., & Purcell-Gates, V. (1997). "So what's going on in research on emergent literacy?" *Reading Research Quarterly, 32,* 310–318.

McGregor, K., & Leonard, L. (1995). Intervention for word-finding deficits in children. In M. E. Fey, J. Windsor, & S. F. Warren (Eds.), *Language intervention: Preschool through the elementary years* (pp. 85–106). Baltimore: Brookes.

Nation, K., & Hulme, C. (1997). Phonemic segmentation, not onset-rime segmentation, predicts early reading and spelling skills. *Reading Research Quarterly, 32,* 154–167.

National Reading Panel. (2000). *Teaching children to read: An evidence-based assessment of the scientific research literature on reading and its implications for reading instruction.* Washington, DC: National Institute for Child Health and Human Development. Retrieved November 30, 2003, from http://www.nichd.nih.gov/publications/nrp/findings.htm

Nelson, K. E., Camarata, S. M., Welsh, J., Butkovsky, L., & Camarata, M. N. (1996). Effects of imitative and conversational recasting treatment on the acquisition of grammar in children with specific language impairment and younger language-normal children. *Journal of Speech and Hearing Research, 39,* 850–859.

Notari-Syverson, A., O'Connor, R. E., & Vadasy, P. F. (1998). *Ladders to literacy.* Baltimore: Brookes.

Nuspl, J. (2005). *An investigation of teaching phonemic awareness to preschoolers with and without prior syllable instruction.* Unpublished master's thesis University of Wyoming, Laramie.

Pretti-Frontczak, K., & Bricker, D. (2004). *An activity-based approach to early intervention* (3rd ed.). Baltimore: Brookes.

Richgels, D. J. (1995). Invented spelling ability and printed word learning in kindergarten. *Reading Research Quarterly, 30,* 96–109.

Richgels, D. J., Poremba, K. J., & McGee, L. M. (1996). Kindergartners talk about print: Phonemic awareness in meaningful contexts. *The Reading Teacher, 49,* 632–642.

Sawyer, D. J. (1988). Studies of the effects of teaching auditory segmenting skills within the reading program. In R. Masland & M. Masland (Eds.), *Preschool prevention of reading failure* (pp. 121–142). Parkton, MD: York Press.

Schneider, W., Ennemoser, M., Roth, E., & Kuspert, P. (1999). Kindergarten prevention of dyslexia: Does training in phonological awareness work for everybody? *Journal of Learning Disabilities, 32,* 429–436.

Schneider, W., Kuspert, P., Roth, E., Vise, M., & Marx, H. (1997). Short- and long-term effects of training phonological awareness in kindergarten: Evidence from two German studies. *Journal of Experimental Child Psychology, 66,* 311–340.

Spector, C. (1999). *Sound effects: Activities for developing phonological awareness.* Greenville, SC: Super Duper Publications.

Stanovich, K. E. (1986). Matthew effects in reading: Some consequences of individual differences in the acquisition of literacy. *Reading Research Quarterly, 21,* 360–397.

Stanovich, K. E. (2000). *Progress in understanding reading: Scientific foundations and new frontiers.* New York: Guilford.

Storch, S. A., & Whitehurst, G. J. (2002). Oral language and code-related precursors to reading: Evidence from a longitudinal structural model. *Developmental Psychology, 38,* 934–947.

Torgesen, J. K. (2000). Individual differences in response to early interventions in reading: The lingering problem of treatment resisters. *Learning Disabilities Research & Practice, 15,* 55–64.

Torgesen, J. K., Alexander, A. W., Wagner, R. K., Rashotte, C. A., Voeller, K. K., & Conway, T. (2001). Intensive remedial instruction for children with severe reading disabilities. *Journal of Learning Disabilities, 34,* 33–58.

Torgesen, J. K., Al Otaiba, S., & Grek, M. L. (2005). Assessment and instruction for phonemic awareness and word recognition skills. In H. W. Catts & A. G. Kamhi (Eds.), *Language and reading disabilities* (pp.127–156). Boston: Allyn and Bacon.

Torgesen, J. K., Morgan, S. T., & Davis, C. (1992). Effects of two types of phonological awareness training on word learning in kindergarten children. *Journal of Educational Psychology, 84,* 364–370.

Troia, G. (2004). Phonological processing and its influence on literacy learning. In C. A. Stone, E. R. Silliman, B. J. Ehren, & K. Apel (Eds.), *Handbook of language and literacy* (pp. 271–301). New York: Guilford.

Ukrainetz, T. A., Cooney, M. H., Dyer, S. K., Kysar, A. J., & Harris, T. J. (2000). An investigation into teaching phonemic awareness through shared reading and writing. *Early Childhood Research Quarterly, 15,* 331–355.

van Kleeck, A., Gillam, R. B., & McFadden, T. U. (1998). A study of classroom-based phonological awareness training for preschoolers with speech and/or language disorders. *American Journal of Speech-Language Pathology, 7,* 65–76.

van Kleeck, A., & Schuele, M. (1987). Precursors to literacy: Normal development. *Topics in Language Disorders, 7,* 13–31.

Vygotsky, L. (1978). *Mind in society: The development of higher psychological processes.* Cambridge, MA: Harvard University Press.

Wagner, R. K., & Torgesen, J. K. (1987). The nature of phonological processing and its causal role in the acquisition of reading skills. *Psychological Bulletin, 101*(2), 192–212.

Walsh, S. (2002). *Phonological awareness success: A step-by-step activity guide.* Greenville, SC: Super Duper Publications.

Warrick, N., Rubin, H., & Rowe-Walsh, S. (1993). Phoneme awareness in language-delayed children: Comparative studies and intervention. *Annals of Dyslexia, 43,* 153–172.

Yopp, H. K. (1992). Developing phonemic awareness in young children. *The Reading Teacher, 45,* 696–707.

Appendix A:
Phonotactic Shapes and Word Possibilities

CV	VC	CVC	CCV	CCVC	CVCV
shoe	up	log	stew	clock	berry
boy	on	sad	slow	stop	sunny
say	egg	sun	play	click	pillow
moo	if	dog	glow	stick	happy
show	it	peach	blow	trout	kitty
dough	at	pen	blue	block	doggie
toe	oak	kite	stay	slick	baby
go	ill	kick	sly	stump	mommy
boy	eek	bed	glum	smear	minnow
no	ouch	moon	glue	smooth	coffee

Appendix B: Bibliography of Verse Books

Brown, M. W. (1982). *Goodnight moon.* New York: Harper Trophy.

Carlstrom, N. W. (1986). *Jesse Bear, what will you wear?* New York: Aladdin.

Cuetara, M. (1997). *Terrible Teresa and other very short stories.* New York: Dutton.

Emberly, B. (1967). *Drummer Hoff.* New York: Aladdin.

Guarino, D. (1989). *Is your mama a llama?* New York: Scholastic.

Hutchins, P. (1988). *Where's the baby?* New York: Greenwillow Books.

Numeroff, L. (1995). *Chimps don't wear glasses.* New York: Scholastic.

Shaw, N. (1986). *Sheep in a jeep.* Boston: Houghton Mifflin.

Teague, M. (1995). *How I spent my summer vacation.* New York: Crown.

Wolff, A. (1990). *Baby beluga.* New York: Crown.

Wood, A. (1992). *Silly Sally.* San Diego: Harcourt Brace.

Chapter 11

Promoting Reading Fluency and Motivation through Readers Theatre

Susan B. Leahy and Laura M. Justice

Introduction

Students who read well and who read often are relatively more likely than other students to be academically successful and to develop fluent automatic reading skills. Stanovich's (2000) recent review of decades of research on reading development asserts that students who are capable readers generally find the act of reading to be a rewarding experience. Consequently, these students are particularly likely to read widely and read often, a circumstance which enables them to become even better readers. Speech-language pathologists (SLPs) who target reading should provide therapeutic environments that not only develop fluent reading skills, but also spark students' desire and motivation to read.

The roles and responsibilities of SLPs concerning literacy development consist of prevention, assessment, and intervention in the diverse areas associated with literacy achievements. These include phonological and phonemic awareness; word recognition and decoding skills; comprehension; vocabulary; and fluency (American Speech-Language-Hearing Association, 2001). As Kamhi recently noted (2003), fluency has often been overlooked in instructional and remedial programs for students with language and literacy challenges. Although fluency can be increased by facilitating learners' skills in phonological awareness, decoding, comprehension, and vocabulary, more direct strategies for building fluency have been identified in the literature. For instance, the simplest strategy for building fluency is through rereading of text at one's independent reading level. Kamhi's overview of research on fluency noted that "rereading a text seven times is better than three times, which is better than one time" (p. 3). Through repeated readings of text that is at a level to slightly challenge students' skills, fluency fundamentals are improved, including rate, accuracy, and prosody.

In this chapter, we discuss repeated reading and other techniques for building fluency, all of which emphasize the contextualized skill approaches to building literacy performance. We focus on one method that targets both fluency and motivation, called *Readers Theatre*. Readers Theatre impacts the development of both the affective and skills-related domains of young readers, particularly in the area of fluency. Because fluency has received little attention to date in the speech-language literature, the first section of this chapter provides background information regarding fluency and motivation. The second part of the chapter describes general approaches to evaluating reading fluency and motivation. The third part describes several approaches to building fluency and motivation, with a focus on Readers Theatre as one example of a contextualized intervention that can promote fluency and motivation in young readers.

SLPs can readily integrate the approaches described here into direct service intervention for students who require assistance in developing reading fluency. With careful selection or adaptation of reading passages, Readers Theatre can be a motivating and meaningful context to practice and automatize particular vocabulary and grammar skills. Finally, such activities can be used as part of collaborative models of intervention in which SLPs are part of a team comprising classroom teachers, special educators, and reading specialists.

An Overview of Readers Theatre

Researchers have identified several key approaches for fostering students' motivation towards reading, all of which emphasize the importance of providing students with opportunities to interact socially with their peers about books and stories (Gambrell, 1996; Palmer, Codling, & Gambrell, 1994). One instructional strategy that is built on this premise of providing opportunities to develop reading skills while interacting socially with others is *Readers Theatre.* Readers Theatre refers to students' repeated reading of theatrical scripts at their reading level within social interactions with their peers. In a typical framework, students read these scripts several times over a week and then present the script to their peers. The repeated reading of scripts at a student's reading level is consistent with best practices in developing reading fluency: reading text at one's instructional reading level repeatedly over time is an evidence-based practice for building fluent and skilled reading (see National Reading Panel, 2000). The use of functional, meaningful scripts contextualizes the fluency-building intervention, with the theatrical scripts and engagement with peers as natural scaffolds for supporting fluency development. By embedding these repeated reading opportunities into social interactions with one's peers, Readers Theatre provides a rich, meaningful, and enjoyable approach for building students' motivation towards reading simultaneously. Readers Theatre is considered an "inherently meaningful, purposeful vehicle for repeated reading...[in] which effective performances are built upon positive social interactions focused on reading" (Worthy & Prater, 2002, p. 295).

Additionally, the Readers Theatre experience turns reading development into an overt language and communication building activity as students engage with one another for real, functional purposes. The repeated reading of scripts provides students the opportunity to repeatedly encounter and use particular vocabulary, syntax, and discourse structures, as well as public speaking elements of volume, fluency, eye contact, pacing, expression—all in the purposeful context of theater. One can surmise, for instance, that students' repeated exposure to new words over the week-long reading of a script, as with *straggling* and *pallor* in the adapted version of *Casey at the Bat* (Shepard, 2002), will help them develop and refine their vocabulary knowledge. Indeed, the repeated use of novel vocabulary words in authentic and functional contexts is considered one of the most effective ways to build struggling readers' vocabulary skills (Beck, McKeown, & Kucan, 2002; see also Chapter 3). Clinicians and teachers can realize greater potential of Readers Theatre beyond its impact on reading fluency and motivation by selecting scripts that target specific communicative or language skills or functions.

Recent studies have suggested the value of Readers Theatre for enhancing students' reading performance. For instance, Martinez, Roser, and Strecker (1998) implemented Readers Theatre with second-grade students and found significant pretest to post-test gains in students' oral reading fluency and reading levels after a 10-week period of daily lessons. An increase in students' comprehension of text, motivation, and confidence when reading was also demonstrated in this work. Other reports investigating the effects of Readers Theatre in general education classrooms have described similar outcomes (Forsythe, 1995; Liu, 2000; Millin & Rinehart, 1999; Rinehart, 1999, 2001; Worthy & Prater, 2002).

The use of Readers Theatre for students with language impairments concomitant with reading difficulties has yet to be explored in any literature of which we are aware. In fact, few studies have focused specifically on building reading fluency for this population, despite the integrative linkages between language impairment and reading disability (Catts, Fey, Zhang, & Tomblin, 2002) with more than half of kindergartners with language disabilities going on to exhibit reading difficulties that extend beyond word decoding in fourth grade. Although much literature has described difficulties in diverse areas of reading development for students with language impairment, including early print concepts and phonological awareness (Boudreau & Hedberg, 1999) and later achievements in phonemic awareness, grapheme-phoneme correspondence, word recognition, and text comprehension (e.g., Bishop & Adams, 1990), few studies have focused specifically on fluency. Fluency is an area of reading development that is usually the focus of instructional attention *after* students have begun to read; because students with language impairment exhibit significant difficulties in beginning to read (e.g., Catts et al., 2002), our attention as a discipline has primarily focused on assessment and intervention in developing foundational reading skills. Nevertheless, fluency is a critical skill in reading, and represents the student's achievement of automaticity in decoding texts at instructional and independent levels. Students who are fluent readers can focus their cognitive resources on reading for meaning, rather than the act of reading itself.

When considering how students build fluency in reading, their motivation to read is a clear influence. Motivation refers to students' affect and regard towards literacy-focused activities, particularly reading. The frequency with which students engage in reading makes a clear contribution to the achievement of fluent, skilled reading. Too often, students who are not motivated by reading stop reading; conversely, students who struggle with reading also stop reading. Educators and clinicians need to focus on building students' motivation towards reading to ensure that they do not stop reading, even when they are struggling with developing basic reading skills. So long as students are motivated to read, then attention can focus on other areas of need, such as text comprehension (described in Chapter 12) or self-regulatory behaviors (described in Chapter 13).

Reading Fluency and Reading Motivation

Reading Development

Reading development in the English alphabetic system follows a fairly invariant developmental pathway, although the time taken to achieve major milestones varies immensely across students as a function of developmental, dispositional, ecological, and instructional factors. (And indeed, some students "fall off" the developmental pathway before ever reaching its end [Spear-Swerling & Sternberg, 1994].) The reading development pathway proceeds through five general stages characterizing the emergent reader, the beginning reader, the transitional reader, the intermediate reader, and the advanced reader. For an excellent description of these stages, consult Bear, Invernizzi, Templeton, and Johnston (2004).

In the emergent and beginning reader stages, students become accustomed to the orthography and phonology of their language and the interconnections between the two, referred to as sound-symbol correspondence. The emergent stage involves the literacy knowledge acquired before the onset of formal instruction. Typically, these students have not yet figured out the alphabetic principle that allows students to read unfamiliar words. Instruction at this point is more informal, guiding the students' explorations of literacy (see Chapter 8). Beginning readers have become aware that letters represent sounds, know some of the sound-letter relations, and can sound out some simple printed words. Instruction and intervention at these stages focuses mostly on developing students' ability to decode words through application of sound-symbol correspondence. At the same time, instruction emphasizes learning the many systematic rules governing the English orthography, such as spelling of short vowel sounds (e.g., "i" for /ɪ/), spelling of long vowel sounds (e.g., "oo" for /u/), spelling of specific word families (e.g., "at," "ot," "it"), digraphs (e.g., "ch," "sh"), and consonant blend patterns (e.g., "st," "sp"). In addition, students are learning to confirm their decoding efforts by thinking about what the word means and whether it fits into the larger text meaning. By the end of the beginning stage, students are skilled in applying the alphabetic principle to decode a variety of words, and can read simple stories.

Transitional readers have a well-developed knowledge of the alphabetic system and are able to readily apply this knowledge to decode words. They may be learning to break up multisyllabic words into small pieces to sound out and to hold these pieces in memory long enough to blend them and retrieve the appropriate word meaning. Transitional readers are no longer reading in a word-by-word manner and are reading in phrases (Bear et al., 2004). Accordingly, transitional readers are beginning to read with more fluency and expression as decoding becomes more *automated.* Decoding becomes automated as students repeatedly experience words through reading and instruction. Letter-by-letter decoding and word-by-word reading is no longer required, as the processing of words becomes automatized either at the level of the whole word (a sight word) or at the level of the syllable as specific syllabic patterns are internalized by students. Transitional readers are able to read. Through the act of reading, word and syllable patterns become automatized through repeated exposure, which in turn builds reading fluency. Instruction at this stage focuses on building fluency of an increased variety of high-frequency words (e.g., *know, friend, went),* and instruction in orthographic patterns that build upon previous patterns learned (e.g., complex consonant clusters such as "shr" and "thr," or diphthongs such as "oi" and "oy").

The same process continues as students move into the later stages of reading development—the intermediate and advanced stages. At these stages, students are learning about and developing automatic sensitivities to more infrequent orthographic patterns, particularly those that occur at syllable junctures (e.g., *parade/parading, keep/keeper)* and those that relate to word derivations (e.g., *graph, graphic, photograph).* Intermediate readers could be considered to be reading to learn, instead of learning to read. Advanced readers can decode and understand specialized reading material, such as science and history. Intermediate and advanced readers have a huge store of visually recognized words that they can employ automatically, resulting in fast, fluent reading. While these readers primarily access words through automatic visual recognition, they may return to phonemically sounding out challenging or new words (Apel & Swank, 1999).

As students progress from emergent to advanced readers, their continual reading of texts that are at their level of development is the most important vehicle to improve their reading fluency and facilitate their move to the next stage of reading. Once students are able to read, their fluency in this act is strengthened through the act of reading, or the *practice effect*. However, not all reading materials are equal; to build fluency, students need to read materials that match their developmental level. This is a principle that will be revisited later in this chapter as we further explore Readers Theatre.

Explanations of Fluent Reading

We turn now to several theories proposed over the last several decades to explain the process of reading, particularly as it relates to the development of reading fluency. These include theories by Perfetti (1985), Rumelhart (1994), and Samuels (1994). Early reading researchers (LaBerge & Samuels, 1974) first introduced the argument that there is a trade-off between decoding and fluency, in which labored decoding takes up too much cognitive energy in comparison to automatic decoding. This principle is in essence that of *capacity and demand,* in which the slow decoders put most of their capacity towards decoding and thus cannot meet the demands of reading fluently. Readers who can decode well are able to read with great speed and accuracy—that is, with *fluency*—as their cognitive resources are freed from decoding and can focus on reading with expression and comprehension.

Mature and fluent readers have strong decoding skills. They do not have to labor over individual words the way a beginning or struggling reader does. One can therefore think of word recognition skill as a gatekeeper to successful reading and to reading with fluency and automaticity. Efficient word recognition is analogous to a secret password that allows readers accurate, quick word recognition skills to pass through the gates quickly. Those readers who struggle with word recognition can get through (or around) the gatekeeper, but it will take them longer. The effort expended to get through the gates leaves little energy to deal with the processes that lie beyond the gate, which include reading fluently and automatically, as well as comprehending what is read.

Readers who struggle to get past the "gatekeeper" may lack automaticity, according to Samuels' *automaticity theory* (Samuels, 1994). Automaticity is used to describe those processes that require little conscious attention. They occur "quickly and effortlessly, often beneath conscious awareness" (Walczyk, 2000, p. 557). In reading, processes are differentiated into automatic and control processes. If one wants to become a competent reader, word recognition is one process that needs to become automatic and to be relinquished from active control by the reader. Accurate word recognition must take place quickly, appearing almost effortless, for full fluency to occur (Nathan & Stanovich, 1991). If not, it is highly unlikely a student will ever become a truly fluent reader.

Perfetti's (1985) *verbal efficiency theory* provides a model of reading that highlights the importance of processing speed and its relationship to competent reading. Perfetti's model focuses on how lower level processes, such as phonological awareness and decoding, affect the ability of a student to comprehend, which is considered a higher level process. He explains how "efficient" processing enables the working memory to focus on understanding the text, not just decoding it. A beginning reader who reads word-by-word with little expression is still at a stage where the lower level processes take most of the cognitive resources from working memory.

While phonological awareness and decoding serve as vital processes for the development of fluency, it is important to recognize that students do not become fluent readers simply by learning how to decode words. Through repeated interactions with text, students expand their store of sight words, or words processed automatically without decoding (Ehri, 1991, 1997). Ehri considers sight word learning to be a connection-forming process. As students read, they make connection between graphemes in words and the phonological segments heard in the pronunciation of words, including phonemes. This process fosters interconnections among orthography, phonology, and meaning, and as these interconnections are fostered through experience, the student's processing of the written word becomes automatized. As students develop as readers, they begin to develop a large base of sight words which further enables them to read with efficiency.

Other researchers offer some other important points to consider when investigating the impact of oral reading fluency, particularly consideration of reading as an interactive process, as influenced by the work of Rumelhart

(1994). Rumelhart's theory of *parallel distributed processing* asserts that many types of information processing occur at once. He disputes the idea of a linear process of reading. Interactive processing means that understanding of information at one level often depends on concurrent understanding of information at a higher level. For instance, understanding the meaning of a sentence can have an impact on individual word recognition (e.g., deciding if a word is [rɛd] or [rid] in "I want to read this to you"). In an interactive model, multiple processes (e.g., phonological processing and orthographic processing) must work simultaneously and quickly. If not, cognitive resources will not be allocated to the most important goal of reading, which is comprehension.

Rumelhart's model (1994) delineates that the development of fluency requires more than efficient decoding skills. Several other important aspects of the reading process can help or hinder a student. For instance, a student that lacks experience with particular vocabulary (Beck et al., 2002) or background knowledge may have great trouble comprehending a school textbook, despite having competent decoding skills.

Finally, Stanovich (2000) presents an important theory of how the gap between skilled and poor readers becomes increasingly large, multifaceted, and difficult to remediate. Stanovich's theory is based on the earlier work of Walberg (Walberg, Strykowski, Rovai, & Hung, 1984) and Merton (1968). These researchers recognized that early achievement provides the reinforcement for subsequent academic effort. The *Matthew effect,* as presented by Stanovich, derives its name from the Gospel According to Matthew: "For unto every one that hath shall be given, and he shall have abundance; but from him that hath not shall be taken away even that which he hath" (Matthew 25:29). Or, in simpler words, the rich get richer and the poor get poorer.

Stanovich (2000) explains the application of this metaphor to reading by noting that from the earliest stages of reading development, young students with underdeveloped emergent literacy skills, particularly phonemic awareness, are slow to transition to beginning reading. These students are then unable to profit from the decoding lessons of kindergarten and first grade which require a threshold of reading development. They continue to struggle with perpetually *learning to read,* and cannot take advantage of the rich language presented in written text. In contrast, the students who enter school with good language and emergent literacy skills benefit from early reading instruction. They quickly move into *reading to learn* and begin to acquire literate vocabulary, grammar, and discourse structure (Scott, 1995). The students who can read fluently and have more sophisticated language (i.e., those who are "rich") will read *more* than those students who have reading difficulty and limited language (i.e., those who are "poor"). This difference can range from exposure to 16 words in a week of school for a less-skilled student to nearly 2000 words for a highly skilled student (Allington, 1984). In this way, the paths of better and weaker readers may permanently diverge.

These explanations of reading all emphasize that processing speed is a vital attribute for successful readers. Students (and adults) must be able to read quickly and thoughtfully. One easily measurable component of reading skill is oral reading fluency. Some researchers (Good & Kaminski, 2002; Shinn, 1989) consider oral reading fluency to be one of the most important and meaningful ways to measure a student's reading ability. They contend that the measurement of oral reading fluency gives educators and clinicians a quick and efficient way to monitor a student's reading progress. While their argument has merit, many SLPs still do not fully understand what oral reading fluency is and why it is so important to reading development.

Fluency Defined

The National Reading Panel's (NRP, 2000) report on successful strategies for reading instruction has increased attention to oral reading fluency as a crucial dimension of reading development and literacy achievement. The NRP report defines five areas of reading development as particularly critical: phonemic awareness, phonics knowledge, vocabulary, comprehension, and fluency. (A summary of this report can be downloaded at http://www.nichd.nih.gov/publications/nrp/smallbook.htm) This report highlights the importance of reading fluency as a distinct area of reading accomplishment.

The two words most commonly associated with fluency are rate and accuracy. Hasbrouck and Tindal (1992) state that the "combination of accuracy and rate is known as *oral reading fluency*…expressed as 'words correct per minute'" (p. 41). The NRP's report (2000) defines fluent readers as being "able to read orally with speed, accuracy, and proper expression" (p. 11). Other researchers define fluency in subtly different ways, such as reading "smoothly, easily, and readily, and having freedom from word identification problems" (Bear & Barone, 1998, p. 306); reading "quickly, effortlessly, and efficiently with good meaningful expression" (Rasinski, 2003, p. 26); with a fluent reader being "one whose decoding processes are automatic, requiring no conscious attention" (University of Oregon, n.d.). It is clear that rate, accuracy, and expression play major roles in reading fluency.

A student's reading fluency—strictly defined as rate and accuracy—varies across contexts. For instance, one might expect that a 10 year-old student's fluency would be compromised when reading a graduate textbook on language interventions. Likewise, this same student would likely show remarkable fluency if reading a toddler's board book. Barr, Blachowicz, and Wogman-Sadow (1995) emphasize the importance of considering fluency across various contexts by defining fluency as "reading unfamiliar as well as familiar selections with appropriate intonation, phrasing, and rate" (p. 36). To use a comparison that is familiar to SLPs, consider that the way in which context interacts with reading fluency is not unlike the way context interacts with oral fluency and dysfluency. For young students, their rate of dysfluency in speech increases in circumstances when the demand for speech exceeds their capacity for speech (Guitar, 1998). For instance, a young student might have a complex thought to communicate (e.g., "You sing the 'Eensy Weensy Spider' song and I'll sing the 'ABC' song") but not have the capacity to produce it in the way intended (e.g., "You, you, you, you sing the 'Eensy Weensy' song. I do, I do, I do 'ABC'"). Likewise, when a reader must contend with a text that exceeds his own reading capacity, the discrepancy between demand and capacity undermines the ability to read fluently.

The fact that fluency is not a constant should always be recognized. It is affected by a wide variety of factors, including the reader's prior knowledge, the type of text being read, and most importantly, the extent to which there is a discrepancy between the reader's capacity and the situational demands (Lipson & Lang, 1991).

Motivation Defined

Recently published volumes of scientifically based research (Adams, 1990; Barr, Kamil, Mosenthal, & Pearson, 1996; NRP, 2000; Ruddell, Ruddell, & Singer, 1994) provide well-grounded information on the important cognitive aspects of reading (Wigfield, 2000). However, a critical aspect of reading success that is too often overlooked is the key role that students' motivation towards the act of reading plays in their achievement as readers. Allington (1998) suggests that "if students only read when we are watching—when we coerce their involvement in reading—then students will not read enough to become proficient" (p. 107). The more students read, the better readers they become. The adage that "practice makes perfect" is one that clearly holds true with reading skills. Students who read often develop more rapidly as readers relative to those who read infrequently. Obviously, motivation towards reading is an important influence in guiding students towards texts as a leisure activity. Unfortunately, a recent study shows that voluntary reading declines as students move upward in grade (Worthy, Patterson, Salas, Prater, & Turner, 2002), and a recent national survey of students' attitudes toward reading (McKenna, Kear, & Ellsworth, 1995) indicates a steady decline in interest from first to sixth grade.

Reading habits get started early. Consider that students who experience reading success at an early age are far more likely to continue to engage in literacy experiences. Conversely, the students who struggle to read are far more likely to develop negative attitudes towards reading, particularly as they move through the upper-elementary grades (McKenna et al., 1995). Struggling readers realize they are not as capable as their peers and tend to avoid situations where they do not feel successful. On the other hand, students who perceive themselves as strong readers are more likely to continue to engage in reading and other literacy activities (Baker & Wigfield, 1999). A study by Nagy and Anderson (1984) estimated the difference in words read by the least motivated and highest motivated students in the middle grades to be 100,000 versus 1,000,000 words respectively. A particularly voracious reader may be exposed to as many as 50,000,000 words in a year. These differences reflect a variety of individual differences among students, but clearly represent a student's motivation and interest in reading.

Evaluating Fluency and Motivation

Evaluating Fluency

Oral reading fluency is a vital component of strong reading skills (NRP, 2000). Generally, reading *rate* (words per minute) and *accuracy* (number of errors) are used to measure fluency. One benefit for using rate and accuracy as indices of fluency is that it is relatively simple for teachers and clinicians to learn how to keep track of errors while using a stopwatch. Furthermore, calculating words per minute and the number of errors in a reading passage enables a teacher or clinician to use quantifiable information to determine how fluency is progressing. Researchers agree that using reading rate as a measure for fluency is a reasonable and useful tool (Nathan & Stanovich, 1991; Rasinski, 2000). While calculating errors and words per minute does not directly measure prosody—a key component of fluency—these techniques do enable clinicians to measure the other two important aspects of fluency relatively easily.

Even students who are in the same grade at school are likely to display diverse reading skills. Although some teachers differentiate instruction in reading by grouping students on the basis of reading level, referred to as *differentiated instruction,* many teachers do not use differentiated instruction and place all students in the classroom in the same level of text (e.g., second-grade materials for a second-grade classroom). Thus, even though a student is in second grade and is purported to be reading "second-grade materials" by the classroom teacher, this may not be the case. If one takes a close look at all the students in a particular classroom, they are likely to vary in their fluency (and other reading skills) dramatically. For instance, in one third-grade classroom, students' reading levels can range from first grade to well above third grade (Bear & Barone, 1998). If SLPs are requiring students to read in intervention, they need to be aware of each student's appropriate instructional reading level, regardless of grade level.

An important aspect of fluency assessment is identifying students' instructional, independent, and frustration reading levels. To improve decoding skills, students should be regularly reading texts that are at their *instructional reading level.* A student's instructional reading level is where he or she can read comfortably, but not to the point where it is too easy. The student should make no more than 8 errors for every 100 words read, be moderately fluent, and have good comprehension of what is being read (Bear & Barone, 1998). When reading at an instructional level, students need some support from an adult, but this support is not considerable.

When striving to build oral reading fluency, it is important that students have opportunities to read materials at their *independent reading level.* The independent level is the point at which students read with 98 to 100 percent accuracy, use good expression, and have excellent reading comprehension (Bear & Barone, 1998). At this level, students do not need any adult assistance with reading materials. When students read at their instructional or independent reading level, they do not experience any frustration. This is an important concept to understand, as reading frustration level texts (those that are too difficult) is not really useful for developing students' literacy skills.

The *frustration reading level* is the point at which students read with multiple errors (more than 10 per 100 words), have poor comprehension, and read with little or no expression (Bear & Barone, 1998). Students should never read material that is on their frustration level. Frustration level materials are too difficult to be beneficial. Students struggle to process the words in a frustration-level text. Because the bulk of their energy is directed at decoding words, little cognitive energy is left for comprehension (Nathan & Stanovich, 1991; Samuels, 1994; Singer, 1994). Unfortunately, students in the elementary grades are too often reading materials that are not well-matched to their needs. They are reading materials that are too difficult and they do not have adequate opportunities to build skills by reading both independent and instructional level texts.

To match students to the appropriate texts for developing reading skills, SLPs can utilize a variety of commercially available informal reading inventories to determine a student's independent, instructional, and frustrational reading levels. Table 11.1 provides one method to determine reading levels, based on accuracy in a 100-word reading passage. An instrument like the Qualitative Reading Inventory–3 (QRI–3; Leslie & Caldwell, 2001) provides leveled passages that begin at the preprimer reading level and continue up through a high school reading level. The QRI–3 and other similar assessment tools are designed to be given individually to students. The informal reading inventories provide clear directions for administration. To determine a reading level, the SLP presents a short passage to the student to read orally. As the student reads orally, the SLP takes a *running record* of the student's actual reading performance, which is an ongoing record of the student's reading performance while reading a particular text.

When conducting a running record, it is helpful for the SLP to have a copy of the passage that the student is reading. As the student reads orally, the SLP makes note of any substitutions, omissions, additions, or unknown words.

Table 11.1 **Reading Levels and Accuracy Percentages**

Reading Level	Word Reading Accuracy
Independent	98–100
Instructional	91–97
Frustration	< 90

NOTE: Number of words per 100 read aloud correctly
Source: Bear & Barone (1998)

After the student has completed the passage, the SLP can determine the reading accuracy by dividing the number of words read correctly by the total number of words in a passage. If the percentage of words read correctly below 90 percent, the passage is most likely on a frustration level for the student (Bear & Barone, 1998). If there are fewer than 10 errors per 100 words, then the text is at an instructional or independent level and can be used to support the student's reading development.

Clinicians might also consider the use of *curriculum-based measurement* (CBM; Shinn, 1989) to determine fluency. CBM originated in the special education field as a means to more effectively and efficiently identify students requiring reading support. In a CBM model, assessment is tied to a student's curricula, requires only a short amount of time to administer, and most importantly, is sensitive to student improvement. In reading assessment, the typical form of a curriculum-based measurement is similar to an informal reading inventory. Students read short passages (usually three) and are then assessed on accuracy, rate (reading speed), and reading comprehension (Idol, Nevin, Paolucci-Whitcomb, 1999). The Dynamic Indicators of Basic Early Literacy Skills (DIBELS; Good & Kaminski, 2003) is an example of a frequently used CBM reading assessment, which is available at no cost on the Internet (see http://dibels.uoregon.edu/).

The main advantage of CBM is that it is designed to be dynamic, in that it can measure and track changes in student performance over time (Good, Simmons, & Kame'enui, 2001). In addition, the tasks are designed to take only minimal time to administer. For example, with the oral reading fluency section of DIBELS, a student only reads a passage orally for one minute. The brevity of the assessment makes it relatively easy for an SLP to follow the progress of students. However, it is important for clinicians to realize that CBM is not designed to be a comprehensive diagnostic reading assessment tool. It is, however, an "efficient and parsimonious" (Good et al., p. 264) tool that gives clinicians important and quantifiable measurements.

When assessing oral reading fluency, it is vital that the student's oral reading is timed in order to determine a reading rate. The typical means for measuring oral reading fluency involves a passage with a known number of words, a stopwatch, and a pencil. As a student reads, the SLP uses a stopwatch to measure a one-minute time period. At the same time, the SLP also counts any errors the student makes. Divide total correct words by total words in one minute to determine the percentage of correct words. Report this percentage correct and the rate (number of correct words per minute).

The actual protocol an SLP should follow varies widely across measures. Some measures, such as DIBELS, recommend administering three different passages to determine an oral reading rate. The median rate of the three timed passages is used. The Qualitative Reading Inventory–3 (QRI–3; Leslie & Caldwell, 2001) measures both silent and oral rates, as well as narrative and expository passages. Like DIBELS and the QRI–3, the Gray Oral Reading Test–4 (GORT–4; Wiederholt & Bryant, 2001) consists of standardized passages that increase in difficulty. All three measures offer their own reading rate norms as well. In addition, various programs and researchers publish their own versions of reading rate norms. Tables 11.2 and 11.3 offer two examples of fluency standards currently in use.

Table 11.2

Hasbrouck and Tindal
Oral Reading Fluency Standards

Reading Level	Percentile	Words per Minute		
		Fall	**Winter**	**Spring**
Grade 2	75th	82	106	124
	50th	53	78	94
	25th	23	46	65
Grade 3	75th	107	123	142
	50th	79	93	114
	25th	65	70	87
Grade 4	75th	125	133	143
	50th	99	112	118
	25th	72	89	92
Grade 5	75th	126	143	151
	50th	105	118	128
	25th	77	93	100

From "Curriculum-Based Oral Reading Fluency Norms for Students in Grades 2 through 5," by J. E. Hasbrouck and G. Tindal, 1992, *Teaching Exceptional Children, 24,* p. 42. © 1992 by the International Reading Association. Adapted with permission.

Table 11.3

Leslie and Caldwell Oral Reading Fluency Standards

Reading Level	Words per Minute
Preprimer	13–35
Primer	28–68
1	31–87
2	52–102
3	85–139
4	78–124
6	113–165

From *Qualitative Reading Inventory–3* (p. 68), by L. Leslie and J. Caldwell, 2001, New York: Longman. © 2001 by Longman. Adapted with permission.

For clinicians who prefer to use a qualitative measurement tool, there exist other more holistic fluency rating scales. However, these may not exhibit the psychometric qualities of more objective quantitative indices, such as measuring accuracy and rate. Qualitative indices provide a general index for describing a student's pace, phrasing, and prosody when reading, including stress and intonation. For example, the Multidimensional Fluency Scale (Zutell & Rasinski, 1991) focuses on the qualitative aspects of oral reading fluency. The SLP uses a four-point rubric to measure expression and volume, phrasing, smoothness, and pace. After listening to a student read orally, the SLP rates the student on a four-point scale within each category. For example, for pace, a tester rates the student as being: (1) slow and laborious, (2) moderately slow, (3) uneven mixture of fast and slow reading, or (4) consistently conversational. Prosody is a vital component of reading fluency, but it is not easy to measure accurately. To make a reliable judgment on a student's level of prosody requires a great deal of knowledge about oral reading fluency on the part of the SLP. The more straightforward method of using reading rate and accuracy to measure oral reading fluency is simply more practical for the majority of clinicians.

Evaluating Motivation

When considering how to measure students' motivation towards reading, it is important to recognize the multifaceted nature of reading motivation (Baker & Wigfield, 1999). Educators and clinicians need to consider several different constructs, including intrinsic motivation, extrinsic motivation, and social motivation. *Intrinsic motivation* refers to the self-motivated reader who reads widely and frequently out of enjoyment or curiosity about a topic. *Extrinsic motivation* occurs when an outside influence, such as a reward or prize, causes a student to read. *Social motivation* refers to how students relate to others during literacy activities, or the social currency associated with reading. Wigfield (2000) suggests that some aspects of motivation are more helpful to learning than others. Students who are intrinsically motivated are often more committed to learning and will show a higher level of engagement in learning activities.

The idea that motivation is multifaceted is particularly important when considering assessment. Students may be highly motivated with certain tasks or subject areas that they find rewarding. Whereas a talented sprinter is motivated to improve his or her running form, an academically gifted student may be far more motivated to read than to run. Neither student should be unequivocally termed "motivated" or "unmotivated." Context also matters when assessing students' motivation. Baker and Wigfield (1999) point out that students should not be grouped as either high or low in motivation. Rather, they should be considered as having a variety of motivational characteristics. A student may be highly motivated to read a particular genre of books as a result of outside interests. In that instance, the student becomes an "idealized" reader (Winne, 1985). The *idealized reader* feels competent, and finds personal value and practical importance in reading (Gambrell, 1996). It is the combination of positive self-concept and a high task value that enables a student to feel motivated to read.

Recently, Gambrell (1996) designed the Motivation to Read Profile (MRP) as a means to assess specifically "students' self-concept as readers and the value they place on reading" (p. 519). The MRP is designed for use by classroom teachers and other professionals who work with students. It is a straightforward questionnaire that is used to monitor students' responses to specific reading programs or interventions. Gambrell and colleagues used the MRP with students as young as second grade. When using the MRP, students individually answer 20 questions regarding their reading attitude. The clinician reads each question orally to the student and marks the student's answer on a separate sheet of paper. For instance, students are asked: "Reading a book is something I like to do (a) never, (b) not very often, (c) sometimes, (d) often." Other questions may require more self-reflection on the part of the student. For example, students are asked: "When I am reading by myself, I understand (a) almost everything I read, (b) some of what I read, (c) almost none of what I read, (d) none of what I read." Clinicians can use a procedure such as the MRP to identify students' own attitudes and motivations towards reading. Studies have shown that attitudes change given particular interventions, and measures such as this are sensitive to documenting such change.

Methods for Building Fluency and Motivation

Building Fluency

Becoming a fluent reader is not a simple process. However, it is well within the grasp of SLPs to help develop oral reading fluency in the students with whom they work. Rasinski (2003) offers four general methods for promoting oral reading fluency in beginning through advanced readers, and emphasizes that these individual methods must be used in synergistic combination to maximize the likelihood of positive outcomes: (1) read aloud, (2) supported reading, (3) repeated reading, and (4) performance reading.

Read Aloud

One of the easiest and most valuable activities for developing oral reading fluency is a daily read-aloud session with the SLP. Because young students do not often read with prosody, they benefit greatly from hearing fluent, expressive reading from an adult (Rasinski, 2003). The SLP serves as a model of mature reading and should explicitly draw students' attention to the expressive elements of the reading.

Rasinski (2003) describes the importance of read-alouds for developing fluency within a broader theoretical framework titled *guided fluency instruction*. In this framework, fluency instruction is a dynamic process in which the clinician or educator and student are actively engaged in learning and teaching. Guided fluency instruction is grounded on the clinician and student's knowledge of what fluency is and what it looks like. At the start of instruction, the clinician models fluent reading while engaging the student in a metacognitive discussion and examination of what fluency looks like and how it is achieved. The use of metacognitive instruction for developing students' literacy skills has been supported in studies of word decoding and comprehension skills (e.g.,

Cunningham, 1990), although we are not aware of explicit empirical evidence supporting its use in fluency development. Nonetheless, from a theoretical standpoint, as Rasinski explains, demonstration of fluent reading through read-alouds is viewed as the foundation of fluency training by ensuring that the student and clinician have a shared understanding of what fluency looks like and how it is linked more broadly to the reading process.

Supported Reading

In supported reading activities, the clinician and the other students in a group provide oral support to the reader (Morris & Nelson, 1992). To provide oral support to a reader, they read along with the designated student. In doing so, the better reader can help to decode difficult words as well as provide an example of how fluent reading sounds. Morris and Nelson utilized small-group supported reading with a group of low-achieving second graders. They found that supported reading provided a model of fluent reading, provided a time for students to practice reading, and allowed for feedback from the teacher on the students' reading. They even noted positive attitudinal changes in some of the most reluctant readers.

Repeated Reading

Repeated reading provides a well-researched method for promoting oral reading fluency (Bowers, 1993; Dowhower, 1989; Herman, 1985; Homan, Klesius, & Hite, 1993; Koskinen & Blum, 1986; Samuels, 1979). In repeated reading, a student reads and rereads the same text multiple times. By rereading the text multiple times, the reading level of the text is transformed into an independent level, which is ideal for fluency work. In doing so, the student can focus energy on the prosodic features of the text. A research study by Herman found that repeated reading of text with intermediate-grade students over a three-month period resulted in significant increases in comprehension and a slight decrease in miscues, or word-reading errors. Homan et al. found transfer effects on both comprehension and fluency with sixth-grade students in a Chapter One program. Yaden (1988) found similar benefits with repeated read-alouds with young students. Generally speaking, the more often a student practices with a particular text, the more they develop their reading rates, accuracy, and prosody.

Performance Reading

Students also benefit from performance reading as an additional technique to develop fluency (Rasinski, 2003). In performance reading, students utilize repeated reading strategies, but with the additional goal of performing the text for an audience. Performance reading is particularly beneficial because "it requires students to use repeated reading in preparation for their performances, and to read for meaning and understanding before and during their performances" (Rasinski, p. 102). Readers Theatre, discussed in greater depth later in this chapter, is a particularly useful technique of performance reading (Forsythe, 1995; Liu, 2000; Martinez et al., 1998; Millin & Rinehart, 1999; Rinehart, 1999, 2001; Worthy & Prater, 2002).

Building Motivation

Both oral reading fluency (Adams, 1990; Allington, 1983; Nathan & Stanovich, 1991; Samuels, 1994; Schreiber, 1991; Stanovich, 1980) and motivation (Baker & Wigfield, 1999; Gambrell, 1996; McKenna, et al., 1995; Turner & Paris, 1995; Wigfield, 2000; Worthy et al., 2002) play important roles in the development of successful readers. Good reading instruction influences students' achievement of positive motivational dispositions and specific competencies in code-based skills (Guthrie and Wigfield, 1997). While oral reading fluency is enjoying renewed interest as a result of the findings of the National Reading Panel (2000), motivation to read is frequently overlooked. A 1992 poll conducted by the National Reading Research Center showed that teachers considered the development of reading motivation in students to be the most important issue affecting education (Sweet, 1997).

Research studies on building students' reading motivation are often grounded in Vygotsky's social constructivist theory (1978). Vygotsky believed that cognitive development is promoted mainly through social interactions, particularly those interactions in which students' performance is scaffolded by more competent others. Following Vygotsky's logic, it is clear that the classroom environment or culture significantly affects how a student perceives literacy tasks. These tasks, such as reading and writing, make sense to a student when they occur in daily, authentic settings. Turner (1995) describes literacy as being "socially constructed by teachers and students as they engage in activities and participate in classroom discourse" (p. 413). Turner connects the Vygotskian notion of social context in learning environments to the development of intrinsic motivation in students. She contends that students who are actively engaged in the classroom environment develop intrinsic motivation and assign a deeper value to literacy activities. She also believes that the type of reading program a school follows is not nearly as important as the actual daily tasks a teacher plans. According to Turner and Paris (1995), motivation is derived from the interaction between students and the environments from which they acquire knowledge of literacy. Worthy et al. (2002) also stress Vygotsky's belief in the value of social interaction in developing motivation, emphasizing that students' interactions with others influence students' reading motivation and interest in reading for pleasure.

Gambrell (1996) delineates several distinct ways educators and clinicians can provide an instructional culture that motivates students to read. These guidelines complement Turner's (1995) idea that authentic, engaging tasks help develop motivation. Gambrell recommends that class libraries be rich with a wide variety of books. Students should have ample opportunities to choose books to read and discuss. Like adults, students will often read a book because a friend recommends it. Indeed, the reading practices of clinicians themselves may play a role in building students' motivation, as student will often mimic the reading choices of the adults in their lives.

Promoting Fluency and Motivation through Readers Theatre

School-based professionals are under daunting expectations to develop the social, emotional, and academic growth of all students while meeting state standards and the demanding regulations of the No Child Left Behind Act (2002). Quality time to teach is a valuable commodity in today's schools, given the high-stakes contexts associated with state and federal standards. When possible, educators and specialists plan academic activities that promote multiple skills. Readers Theatre presents a context to develop a wide array of language and reading skills, including oral reading fluency, motivation to read (Forsythe, 1995; Liu, 2000; Martinez et al., 1998; Millin & Rinehart, 1999; Rinehart, 1999, 2001; Worthy & Prater, 2002), literate vocabulary, expanded phrases, and complex sentence structure. SLPs can select which of these many skills they will focus on as intervention objectives.

Readers Theatre is an interpretive activity in which students practice and then perform a written script (Rinehart, 1999). When working on a Readers Theatre piece, students read and reread a particular text multiple times. Because students become so familiar with the text in Readers Theatre, they are able to read with more automaticity (Samuels, 1994). Rather than concentrating the bulk of their reading energy on decoding words, young readers are able to focus on reading with expression and speed.

Readers Theatre provides students the opportunity to practice repeated reading of text within the context of a group. The support of their peers is an essential component of Readers Theatre, which is consistent with Cole's (2002) emphasis on the importance of peer relationships in promoting students' learning. The socially embedded nature of learning within Readers Theatre is consistent with Vygotskian theory (Worthy & Prater, 2002). These researchers contend that Readers Theatre is an "inherently meaningful, purposeful vehicle for repeated reading...effective performances are built upon positive social interactions focused on reading, in which modeling, instruction, and feedback are natural components of rehearsals" (p. 295). Readers Theatre is an ideal strategy for applying a Vygotskian approach. It requires that students interact with one another. Through the process of preparing a Readers Theatre performance, students constructively critique one another. The clinician provides necessary support and modeling as well.

Readers Theatre shows promise for helping a wide range of ages and abilities. In the Martinez et al. (1998) study, second-grade students showed gains in fluency and motivation from 10 weeks of daily Readers Theatre. Millin and Rinehart (1999) and Rinehart (1999) utilized Readers Theatre with second-grade students in Title I programs or identified as at-risk for failure, finding that Readers Theatre supported the development of oral reading ability and attitude towards reading and reading instruction. Worthy and Prater (2002) introduced Readers Theatre to middle school students, finding that Readers Theatre led to increased engagement with even reluctant readers. Although Readers Theatre has not been studied specifically for students with communication impairments, its demonstrated effectiveness for supporting low-achieving students suggests its potential for this population. Additionally, the principles that govern implementation of Readers Theatre are consistent with the current evidentiary base regarding fluency interventions (e.g., National Reading Panel, 2000).

The following provides an explicit description of how SLPs can utilize Readers Theatre as a contextualized approach to support fluency and motivation in young learners. First, guidelines for selecting scripts are presented. We include a sample of a script for Readers Theatre, as well as guidelines for matching students with scripts and details on sources for additional Readers Theatre scripts. Second, guidelines for implementing Readers Theatre with students are presented. We provide details on the frequency and duration of lessons, as well as suggestions for promoting peer support and social interaction. Third, guidelines for evaluating learners' progress are detailed. This includes an overview of measures that might be used to track learners' achievements in fluency and motivation.

Guidelines for Selecting Scripts

The use of Readers Theatre is an ideal means to develop oral reading fluency within a contextualized approach. Students' fluency development is targeted within the context of meaningful, whole, and authentic theatrical scripts and dramatic routines. When choosing scripts, clinicians must bear in mind the reading level of the text. It is vital that students read scripts that are on their independent reading level, as this is the level at which students' fluency is able to develop. Materials that are at the student's instructional or frustrational levels will not support fluency development. Instructional level materials can become independent level texts with repeated reading and initial support from a practitioner, and may occasionally be used with Readers Theatre. However, practice with independent level texts is preferred, as it is reading at this level that appears to most readily support fluency development.

Some sources of Readers Theatre scripts provide a reading level for individual scripts while others provide more general guidelines for recommended age groups. Whatever the case, clinicians need to carefully consider the reading level of scripts so that students are provided scripts that are at their independent level. When scripts reflect students' independent levels, these provide structural scaffolds for the students in their quest to become fluent readers.

Clinicians can either create their own scripts or purchase them from a variety of sources. If creating original scripts, stories should include interesting characters who confront issues or problems (Martinez et al., 1998). In addition, if the focus is on particular vocabulary or grammar, then repeated opportunities to practice will need to be provided. Scripts with a poetic rhythm often provide repeated syntactic structures.

For a complete listing of script sources, see *The Fluent Reader* by Tim Rasinski (2003). Clinicians can develop scripts that complement science or social studies topics for a more direct link to aspects of the general curriculum. Likewise, scripts may be based on well-known literature. Some websites offer prepared scripts to download for free or for a small fee. For instance, Aaron Shepard (2002) has adapted a number of poems, such as the classic poem, *Casey at the Bat,* by Ernest Lawrence Thayer (1888) into scripts for Readers Theatre (see http://www.aaronshep.com). The *Casey at the Bat* script is designed to be used by eight or more readers. Each reader is assigned a number of lines, with turns intermixed. To allow for the repeated opportunities required for a therapeutic focus, no more than three or four students should be in a group and thus each may be required to take on more lines.

When selecting scripts that already exist, clinicians should carefully examine their content, including the conceptual difficulty of the text and the vocabulary. For instance, *Casey at the Bat* is a classic poem and contains difficult vocabulary, which might need to be briefly discussed prior to reading. Clinicians also need to review the background knowledge required for students to understand a script and should develop this background prior to the lesson. Students with little know-ledge of sports or baseball may be challenged when reading *Casey at the Bat.* While the scripts are designed to be short, if they contain too much difficult content, they will no longer be independent-level texts. Clearly, the choice of what kinds of scripts to use is an important one.

While clinicians need not use prepared scripts, there are several advantages to doing so. First, clinicians can readily seek scripts on particular topics and for particular group sizes. For instance, to accompany classroom lessons on China, a clinician might select a script that is already prepared for Readers Theatre on a topic associated with China. Likewise, when working with a group of four students, clinicians can readily select scripts that require four actors. Second, it is very important when building fluency that scripts be tailored to a student's independent reading level—that is, text which is read with 98 to 100 percent accuracy, good expression, and excellent reading comprehension. The script is, in essence, manageable to the student. The success of Readers Theatre as a fluency-building activity is derived from the matching of readers to texts. If students read scripts that are much too easy or which they can read with less than 90 percent accuracy, the Readers Theatre lesson will not be effective for fluency development. While some educators and clinicians may feel comfortable matching students to texts, others do not and may wish to rely on Readers' Theatre scripts that are already leveled.

Guidelines for Implementing Readers Theatre

As an instructional strategy, Readers Theatre has proven to be effective in promoting oral reading fluency and motivation to read in students ranging in age from second grade (Martinez et al., 1998; Millin & Rinehart, 1999; Rinehart, 1999) to middle school (Worthy & Prater, 2002). It is particularly appealing as an instructional strategy because it can be adapted to any classroom or clinical setting. In general, Readers Theatre is most effective when it can be utilized daily and when students are placed into small groups of four to six students based on their independent reading levels. While students of mixed abilities could hypothetically be grouped together, it is likely to be difficult to find a script that contains characters whose lines consistently vary over levels (i.e., one character "speaks" at one level whereas another character "speaks" at a different level).

In a recent research study, Martinez et al. (1998) provided an easy-to-follow schedule for implementating Readers Theatre scripts for a one-week period. Figure 11.1 provides a sample weekly schedule for Readers Theatre implementation. During the practice session, the clinician circulates among

Figure 11.1 Five-Day Instructional Plan for Readers Theatre

Pre-Day 1	Clinician chooses scripts for reading groups.
Day 1	Clinician meets with small groups to introduce the scripts.
	Clinician models fluency by reading aloud the first page of the script.
	Clinician and students discuss the story, including the characters and important aspects of the plot.
	Students begin to read personal copies of the script, reading all of the parts.
	Clinician encourages the students to take their scripts home for extra practice.
Day 2	Students meet in small groups (as dictated by their independent reading level).
	Students read the script, taking a different part with each reading.
	Clinician provides modeling and feedback as needed.
Day 3	Procedures are the same as Day 2.
Day 4	Students in each group choose roles for the performance on Day 5.
	Students practice the script, paying close attention to their newly assigned roles.
Day 5	Small groups perform their scripts for an audience.

From "I Never Thought I Could Be a Star:" A Readers Theatre Ticket to Fluency, by M. Martinez, H. Roser, and S. Strecker, 1998, *The Reading Teacher,* 52, p. 331. © 1998 by the International Reading Association. Adapted with permission.

the groups, providing coaching and modeling. The SLP may need to remind students about a particular character's personality. Examples of helpful coaching include comments like:

- "Remember, that character just lost her favorite toy. How do you think she would sound?"

- "Be sure to pause when you get to the comma."

- "The symbol at the end of that sentence is called an exclamation point. That means the character is going to say his lines with lots of feeling."

Over the course of the week, the SLP also provides a model of fluent reading, such as rereading a part for a student who is having trouble capturing the character's feelings. As the students begin to develop more fluent reading, it is important for the SLP to provide positive feedback when students show progress. Peer support should also be encouraged. Students need to praise one another when they notice expressive reading. To effectively promote peer support, the SLP will need to directly model or prompt such support. An SLP may find it useful to spend the last five minutes of each session asking the students to share their thoughts on their peers' reading. In order to maintain a constructive atmosphere, the clinician will need to provide a framework for the students' responses. The response framework can be as simple as: "I thought that *(student's name)* did a great job reading because (e.g., *she read her lines with lots of expression).* I could tell her character was sad because of the voice she used."

Guidelines for Tracking Progress

Fluency intervention is, like many other language and literacy interventions, a data-driven process. Indeed, the collection and use of data in fluency interventions may even be more important than in other types of interventions, as students must be reading books that are carefully tailored to their independent and instructional reading levels. Thus, when building students' reading fluency, clinicians and educators must be comfortable with nearly constant tracking of progress to know when a particular text is no longer instructional and becomes independent. Teachers who work with students in the classroom on reading development are familiar with the concept of *running records,* in which the teacher conducts frequent checks of students' decoding accuracy when reading texts. Clinicians providing fluency interventions need to become accustomed to the use of running records to track students' progress in certain texts. Also, clinicians should monitor students' overall fluency progress to monitor the effectiveness of interventions.

For data-driven monitoring of student's progress through specific texts, the time taken to read a text and the number of errors made when reading can be tracked using *timed repeated readings*. This procedure requires a student to orally read a passage several times, with each reading timed by the SLP with a stopwatch. This strategy begins with an initial oral reading of a passage to obtain a baseline measure of words per minute. The passage is read two more times, with times and errors recorded each time. Students may graph their own times and errors to see their progress. The Appendix on page 502 presents a chart to record times and errors (or times only). A text is considered independent level when it is read with fewer than two percent errors and near perfect comprehension. Times can be checked against the standards presented in Tables 11.2 and 11.3 (pages 484 and 485).

More formal measures can be used to monitor fluency progress irrespective of texts being read in interventions. In addition to the oral reading fluency measure mentioned previously, DIBELS (Good & Kaminski, 2003) also provides measures to assess initial sound fluency, letter naming fluency, phoneme segmentation fluency, nonsense word fluency, and retell fluency. DIBELS measures are available at no cost on the Internet, and their psychometric quality has been well-documented (Institute for the Development of Educational Achievement, 2002). The standardized set of reading passages for each of the early grade levels is particularly helpful for ongoing monitoring of student performance.

In terms of assessing motivation to read, clinicians will find it helpful to use an assessment tool already shown to have acceptable levels of reliability and validity, such as the Motivation to Read Profile (Gambrell, 1996). The progress of students must be tracked periodically as they progress through an intervention program, since without such data it is difficult to know how effective the intervention is.

Conclusion

SLPs are taking an increasingly involved role in helping students develop critical literacy skills. This chapter discusses the importance of fluency and motivation in students' achievement of skilled reading. Background information was provided on reading development. Methods of assessing and developing fluency and motivation were presented. A specific contextualized skill activity,

Readers Theatre, was elaborated as a potential means for developing both fluency and motivation within a single approach. By providing students with opportunities to engage repeatedly with motivating and familiar texts within supportive interactions with peers, clinicians may simultaneously promote two key areas of literacy, namely fluency and motivation.

References

Adams, M. J. (1990). *Beginning to read: Thinking and learning about print.* Cambridge, MA: MIT Press.

Allington, R. L. (1983). Fluency: The neglected reading goal. *The Reading Teacher, 36,* 556–561.

Allington, R. L. (1984). Content coverage and contextual reading in reading groups. *Journal of Reading Behavior, 16,* 85–96.

Allington, R. L. (1998). Introduction. In R. L. Allington (Ed.), *Teaching struggling readers: Articles from the reading teacher* (pp.1–8). Newark, DE: International Reading Association.

American Speech-Language-Hearing Association. (2001). Roles and responsibilities of speech-language pathologists with respect to reading and writing in children and adolescents (position statement, executive summary of guidelines, technical report). *ASHA Supplement 21,* 17–27. Rockville, MD: Author.

Apel, K., & Swank, L. K. (1999). Second chances: Improving decoding skills in the older student. *Language, Speech, and Hearing Services in Schools, 30,* 231–242.

Baker, L., & Wigfield, A. (1999). Dimensions of children's motivation for reading and their relations to reading activity and reading achievement. *Reading Research Quarterly, 34,* 452–478.

Barr, R., Blachowicz, C. L. Z., & Wogman-Sadow, M. (1995). *Reading diagnosis for teachers: An instructional approach* (3rd ed.). White Plains, NY: Longman.

Barr, R., Kamil, M. L., Mosenthal, P., & Pearson, P. D. (Eds.). (1996). *Handbook of reading research: Volume II.* Mahwah, NJ: Erlbaum.

Bear, D. R., & Barone, D. (1998). *Developing literacy: An integrated approach to assessment and instruction.* Boston: Houghton Mifflin.

Bear, D. R., Invernizzi, M., Templeton, S., & Johnston, F. (2004). *Words their way: Word study for phonics, vocabulary, and spelling* (3rd ed.). Englewood Cliffs, NJ: Prentice-Hall.

Beck, I. L., McKeown, M. G., & Kucan, L. (2002). *Bringing words to life: Robust vocabulary instruction.* New York: Guilford.

Bishop, D., & Adams, C. (1990). A prospective study of the relationship between specific language impairment, phonological disorders, and reading retardation. *Journal of Child Psychology and Psychiatry, 21,* 1027–1050.

Boudreau, D. M., & Hedberg, N. L. (1999). A comparison of early literacy skills in children with specific language impairment and their typically developing peers. *American Journal of Speech-Language Pathology, 8,* 249–260.

Bowers, P. G. (1993). Text reading and rereading: Determinants of fluency beyond word recognition. *Journal of Reading Behavior, 25,* 133–153.

Catts, H. W., Fey, M. E., Zhang, X., & Tomblin, J. B. (2002). A longitudinal investigation of reading outcomes in children with language impairments. *Journal of Speech, Language, and Hearing Research, 45,* 1142–1157.

Cole, J. E. (2002). What motivates students to read? Four literacy personalities. *The Reading Teacher, 56,* 326–336.

Cunningham, P. (1990). Explicit versus implicit instruction in phonemic awareness. *Journal of Experimental Child Psychology, 50,* 429–444.

Dowhower, S. L. (1989). Repeated reading: Research into practice. *The Reading Teacher, 42,* 502–507.

Ehri, L. (1991). Learning to read and spell words. In L. Reiben & C. A. Perfetti (Eds.), *Learning to read: Basic research and its implications* (pp. 57–73). Mahwah, NJ: Erlbaum.

Ehri, L. (1997). Sight word learning in normal readers and dyslexia. In B. Blachman (Ed.), *Foundations of reading acquisition and dyslexia: Implications for early intervention* (pp. 163–189). Mahwah, NJ: Erlbaum.

Forsythe, S. (1995). It worked! Readers theatre in second grade. *The Reading Teacher, 49,* 264.

Gambrell, L. (1996). Creating classroom cultures that foster reading motivation. In R. Allington (Ed.), *Teaching struggling readers: Articles from the reading teacher* (pp. 108–121). Newark, DE: International Reading Association.

Good, R. H., & Kaminski, R. A. (2002). *DIBELS oral reading fluency passages for first through third grades* (Tech. Rep. No. 10). Eugene, OR: University of Oregon.

Good, R. H., & Kaminski, R. A. (2003). *Dynamic Indicators of Basic Early Literacy Skills (DIBELS).* Longmont, CO: Sopris West Educational Services.

Good, R. H., Simmons, D. C., & Kame'enui, E. J. (2001). The importance and decision-making utility of a continuum of fluency-based indicators of foundational reading skills for third-grade high stakes outcomes. *Scientific Studies of Reading, 5,* 257–288.

Guitar, B. (1998). *Stuttering: An integrated approach to its nature and treatment* (2nd ed.). Baltimore: Lippincott.

Guthrie, J., & Wigfield, A. (1997). Reading engagement: A rationale for theory and teaching. In J. Guthrie & A. Wigfield (Eds.), *Reading engagement: Motivating readers through integrated instruction* (pp. 1–12). Newark, DE: International Reading Association.

Hasbrouck, J. E., & Tindal, G. (1992). Curriculum-based oral reading fluency norms for students in grades 2 through 5. *Teaching Exceptional Children, 24,* 41–44.

Herman, P. A. (1985). The effect of repeated readings on reading rate, speech pauses, and word recognition accuracy. *Reading Research Quarterly, 20,* 553–565.

Homan, S. P., Klesius, J. P., & Hite, C. (1993). Effects of repeated readings and nonrepetitive strategies on students' fluency and comprehension. *Journal of Educational Research, 87,* 94–99.

Idol, L., Nevin, A., & Paolucci-Whitcomb, P. (Eds.). (1999). *Models of curriculum-based assessment* (3rd ed.). Austin, TX: Pro-Ed.

Institute for the Development of Educational Achievement. (2002). *An analysis of reading assessment instruments for K–3: Final report.* Eugene, OR: Author.

Kamhi, A. G. (2003). The role of the SLP in improving reading fluency. *The ASHA Leader, 8*(7), 6–8.

Koskinen, P. S., & Blum, I. H. (1986). Paired repeated reading: A classroom strategy for developing fluent reading. *The Reading Teacher, 40,* 70–75.

LaBerge, D., & Samuels, S. (1974). Toward a theory of automatic information processing in reading. *Cognitive Psychology, 6,* 293–323.

Leslie, L., & Caldwell, J. (2001). *Qualitative Reading Inventory–3 (QRI–3).* New York: Longman.

Lipson, M. Y., & Lang, L. B. (1991). Not as easy as it seems: Some unresolved questions about fluency. *Theory Into Practice, 30,* 218–227.

Liu, J. (2000). The power of readers theater: From reading to writing. *The ELT Journal, 54,* 354–361.

Martinez, M., Roser, N., & Strecker, S. (1998). "I never thought I could be a star:" A readers theatre ticket to fluency. *The Reading Teacher, 52,* 326–334.

McKenna, M., Kear, D., & Ellsworth, R. (1995). Children's attitudes toward reading: A national survey. *Reading Research Quarterly, 30,* 934.

Merton, R. (1968). The Matthew effect in science. *Science, 159,* 56–63.

Millin, S., & Rinehart, S. (1999). Some of the benefits of readers theater participation for second-grade Title I students. *Reading Research and Instruction, 39,* 71–88.

Morris, D., & Nelson, L. (1992). Supported oral reading with low-achieving second graders. *Reading Research and Instruction, 32,* 49–63.

Nagy, W. E., & Anderson, R. C. (1984). How many words are there in printed school English? *Reading Research Quarterly, 19,* 304–330.

Nathan, R. G., & Stanovich, K. E. (1991). The causes and consequences of differences in reading fluency. *Theory Into Practice, 30,* 176–184.

National Reading Panel. (2000). *Teaching children to read: An evidence-based assessment of the scientific research literature on reading and its implications for reading instruction.* Washington, DC: National Institute for Child Health and Human Development. Retrieved May 6, 2005, from http:www.nichd.nih.gov/publications/nrp/findings.htm

No Child Left Behind Act of 2001, 20 U. S. C. § 6311 *et seq.* (2002).

Palmer, B. M., Codling, R. M., & Gambrell, L. (1994). In their own words: What elementary students have to say about motivation to read. *The Reading Teacher, 48,* 176–178.

Perfetti, C. (1985). Verbal efficiency theory. In C. A. Perfetti (Ed.), *Reading ability* (pp. 99–122). New York: Oxford University Press.

Rasinski, T. V. (2000). Speed does matter in reading. *The Reading Teacher, 54,* 146–151.

Rasinski, T. V. (2003). *The fluent reader.* New York: Scholastic.

Rinehart, S. D. (1999). "Don't think for a minute that I'm getting up there:" Opportunities for readers' theater in a tutorial for children with reading problems. *Journal of Reading Psychology, 20,* 71–89.

Rinehart, S. D. (2001). Establishing guidelines for using readers theater with less-skilled readers. *Reading Horizons, 42,* 65–75.

Ruddell, R. B., Ruddell, M. R., & Singer, H. (Eds.). (1994). *Theoretical models and processes of reading* (4th ed.). Newark, DE: International Reading Association.

Rumelhart, D. E. (1994). Toward an interactive model of reading. In R. Ruddell, M. R. Ruddell, & H. Singer (Eds.), *Theoretical models and processes of reading* (pp. 864–894). Newark, DE: International Reading Association.

Samuels, S. J. (1979). The method of repeated reading. *The Reading Teacher, 32,* 403–408.

Samuels, S. J. (1994). Toward a theory of automatic information processing in reading revisited. In R. Ruddell, M. R. Ruddell, & H. Singer (Eds.), *Theoretical models and processes of reading* (pp. 816–837). Newark, DE: International Reading Association.

Schreiber, P. A. (1991). Understanding prosody's role in reading acquisition. *Theory into Practice, 30,* 158–164.

Scott, C. M. (1995). A discourse approach to syntax teaching. In D. F. Tibbits (Ed.), *Language intervention beyond the primary grades* (pp. 435–464). Austin, TX: Pro-Ed.

Shepard, A. (2002). *Aaron Shepard's RT Page.* Retrieved December 12, 2003, from http://www.aaronshep.com

Shinn, M. R. (Ed.). (1989). *Curriculum-based measurement: Assessing special children.* New York: Guilford.

Singer, H. (1994). The substrata-factor theory of reading. In R. Ruddell, M. R. Ruddell, & H. Singer (Eds.), *Theoretical models and processes of reading* (pp. 864–894). Newark, DE: International Reading Association.

Spear-Swerling, L., & Sternberg, R. J. (1994). The road not taken: An integrative theoretical model of reading disability. *Journal of Learning Disabilities, 27,* 91–103.

Stanovich, K. E. (1980). Toward an interactive-compensatory model of individual differences in the development of reading fluency. *Reading Research Quarterly, 1,* 32–71.

Stanovich, K. E. (2000). Matthew effects in reading: Some consequences of individual differences in the acquisition of literacy. In K. E. Stanovich (Ed.), *Progress in understanding reading: Scientific foundations and new frontiers* (pp. 159–204). New York: Guilford.

Sweet, A. P. (1997). Teacher perceptions of student motivation and their relation to literacy learning. In J. T. Guthrie & A. Wigfield (Eds.), *Reading engagement: Motivating readers through integrated instruction* (pp. 86–101). Newark, DE: International Reading Association.

Thayer, E. L. (1888). *Casey at the bat.* San Francisco, CA: San Francisco Examiner.

Turner, J. C. (1995). The influence of classroom contexts on young children's motivation for literacy. *Reading Research Quarterly, 30,* 410–441.

Turner, J. C., & Paris, S. G. (1995). How literacy tasks influence students' motivation for literacy. *The Reading Teacher, 48,* 662–675.

University of Oregon. (n.d.). *Oral reading fluency: Retell fluency.* Retrieved September 2, 2003, from http://dibels.uoregon.edu/measures/orf.php.

Vygotsky, L. S. (1978). *Mind in society: The development of higher psychological processes.* Cambridge, MA: Harvard University Press.

Walberg, H. J., Strykowski, B. F., Rovai, E., & Hung, S. S. (1984). Exceptional performance. *Review of Educational Research, 54,* 87–112.

Walczyk, J. (2000). The interplay of automatic and control processes in reading. *Reading Research Quarterly, 35,* 554–566.

Wiederholt, J. L., & Bryant, B. R. (2001). *Gray Oral Reading Test–4 (GORT–4;* 4th ed.). Austin, TX: Pro-Ed.

Wigfield, A. (2000). Facilitating children's reading motivation. In L. Baker, M. J. Dreher, & J. T. Guthrie (Eds.), *Engaging young readers* (pp. 140–158). New York: Guilford.

Winne, P. (1985). Steps toward promoting cognitive achievements. *Elementary School Journal, 85,* 673–693.

Worthy, J., Patterson, E., Salas, R., Prater, S., & Turner, M. (2002). "More than just reading:" The human factor in reaching resistant readers. *Reading Research and Instruction, 41,* 177–202.

Worthy, J., & Prater, K. (2002). "I thought about it all night:" Readers theatre for reading fluency and motivation. *The Reading Teacher, 56,* 294–297.

Yaden, D. (1988). Understanding stories through repeated read-alouds: How many does it take? *The Reading Teacher, 41,* 556–560.

Zutell, J., & Rasinski, T. V. (1991). Training teachers to attend to their students' oral reading fluency. *Theory into Practice, 30,* 161–164.

Appendix: Repeated Reading Graph
for Evaluating Reading Fluency

Student Name _____   Date _____

WPM	Time 1		Time 2		Time 3		Errors
	WPM	Errors	WPM	Errors	WPM	Errors	
190							25+
185							24
180							23
175							22
170							21
165							20
160							19
155							18
150							17
145							16
140							15
135							14
130							13
125							12
120							11
115							10
110							9
105							8
100							7
95							6
90							5
85							4
80							3
75							2
70							1

Chapter 12

Text Comprehension: Facilitating Active and Strategic Engagement

Teresa A. Ukrainetz and Catherine L. Ross

Appendices

Introduction

A major activity beyond the primary grades is independent academic reading. Older students have moved beyond the task of learning to decode, to understanding the message carried by print. Each additional year of schooling increases expectations for comprehension of specialized subject matter. This chapter deals with the comprehension sought for reading expository material for informational and evaluative purposes. Locating information, getting the main idea, remembering details, making inferences, evaluating claims, and synthesizing into a coherent whole, are all part of understanding what is read and heard.

The focus of this chapter is on facilitating the understanding of written text, with an emphasis on engaging students in purposeful listening and reading activities, teaching comprehension strategies, and leading students into greater levels of independent performance. The instruction is aimed at students with poor comprehension, regardless of decoding competence, by including oral as well as print methods of text delivery.

What Is Reading Comprehension?

Snow (2002), in a report prepared for the Office of Educational Research Improvement (OERI), defines reading comprehension as "the process of simultaneously extracting and constructing meaning through interaction and involvement with written language" (p. xiii). This comprehension is accomplished in multiple ways (Manzo, Manzo, & Estes, 2001):

- Understanding the author's stated message (reading on the lines)

- Interpreting the message's underlying meaning and implications (reading between the lines)

- Applying the message in meaningful ways (reading beyond the lines)

Within this triadic division, the understanding of stated information can be further delineated. Paraphrasing or summarizing information shows better understanding than recall of the words used. Recall in any form shows more knowledge ownership than recognition. However, even recognition of having read material and knowing where to relocate it has an important role in this information-overloaded world.

Text comprehension involves both bottom-up and top-down processes (Manzo et al., 2001). *Bottom-up processes* are the most intuitive: letters are identified, then corresponding sounds are retrieved, and then they are blended into collections of sounds. These collections of sounds are identified as meaningful words and synthesized along with semantic, syntactic, and discourse knowledge into the progressively larger units of phrases, sentences, paragraphs, and texts. *Top-down processes* also have significant effects on comprehension. While decoding possibilities can be generated in isolation (e.g., *read* is /rid/or /red/), a precise selection cannot be made without at least a phrasal context ("I read now" versus "I read yesterday"). Sentence parsing requires a larger context, such as is needed to interpret "a man eating fish." *Repair* is not a sufficient meaning for the word *fixed* in "The cat got fixed today." Depending on reader perspective, a report on the number of new coal-bed methane wells in Wyoming can be understood as a profitable financial report or alternately as an environmental destruction report. Comprehension in all of these examples is thus affected in a top-down direction by knowledge of the broader sentential, textual, and social contexts.

Text comprehension is clearly a complex, dynamic act affected by many factors. One way of understanding the process and product of text comprehension is in terms of the three primary elements of the reader, the text, and the activity, plus the underlying layers of sociocultural context (Snow, 2002). All these interact to determine comprehension.

The Reader

Readers come to the text with a range of abilities, motivations, expectancies, knowledge, and life experiences. Evidence indicates students need fluent word decoding ability, an oral language foundation, and relevant world knowledge to be successful comprehenders (Snow, 2002). Students' phonological processing abilities will affect both their early word reading progress and their subsequent text comprehension performance (Stanovich, 1986, 2000). Given adequate word reading skill, students can become strategic readers, knowing what, how, and when to apply metacognitive monitoring (Pearson & Fielding, 1991).

There are many cognitive, motivational, and linguistic abilities needed for text comprehension (Snow, 2002). Cognitive processes include selective and sustained attention, working and long-term memory, critical analytic ability, inferencing, and visualization. Motivation involves the immediate purpose for reading, an interest in the content being read, perceptions of self-efficacy as a reader, and a positive stance toward academic learning. In addition, linguistic abilities include vocabulary; domain and topic knowledge; linguistic and discourse knowledge; and knowledge of specific comprehension strategies.

The Text

Text features have a major effect on comprehension. The meaning representations that a reader constructs from text will be affected by the wording of the text, the ideas units representing the meaning, and the text structure (Snow, 2002). Texts can be easy or difficult depending on these features and how they interact with the reader and the activity in which they are embedded. For example, the morphology of chemistry vocabulary allows very precise meaning (e.g., *carbon monoxide* indicates a specific molecular structure), but can make a text difficult for a skilled reader not versed in that lexicon. Bulleted lists are easier to skim for gist than connected discourse, but may leave gaps in comprehension. Elaborated syntactic structures can transmit subtlety of meaning, but may require several readings to parse correctly, such as this sentence from Jane Austen's novel, *Emma:*

> She was not deceived as to her own skill either as an artist or a musician, but she was not unwilling to have others deceived, or sorry to know her reputation for accomplishment often higher than it deserved. (Austen, 1816/1957, p. 32)

The texts students encounter are increasingly diverse (Hiebert, in press; Manzo et al., 2001). Readings were formerly specifically crafted for instructional purposes or very limited selections of books were used. Snow (2002) reports that, "the reading materials that made it into the *canon* did not come close to representing the array of cultures, socioeconomic classes, and perspectives of the wider society" (p. 24). While the greater variety and sophistication of today's vocabulary in school literature is positive, it can negatively impact development of reading fluency (Hiebert). Not only is there a wider diversity and greater opportunity to encounter authentic texts at younger ages, but multimedia and electronic options have increased greatly. The easy access to a flood of information can complicate, as well as enhance, comprehension.

A challenge that has accompanied this increased range of reading materials is that of matching reader to text difficulty. Text readability is often calculated based on Fry's formula (Fry, 1977), which provides a reading grade level based on the average number of syllables and the average number of sentences across three 100-word passages. This provides a rough estimate of difficulty level, but is clearly a limited measure that does not take into account the many factors affecting the text difficulty.

Readability levels do not indicate how much difficulty an individual reader will encounter with text. Even good readers may struggle with advanced or specialized reading materials. The following standard measures of relative text difficulty can be used to equate degree of challenge across different reader skill levels (Johnson, Kress, & Pikulski, 1987; Kletzian, 1991; Manzo et al., 2001). Comprehension is determined by responses to factual, inferential, vocabulary, and evaluative questions. The three reading levels are:

- Independent: Able to decode 99 percent of the words and comprehend at 90 percent

- Instructional: Able to decode 95 percent of the words and comprehend at 75 percent

- Frustration: Able to decode below 90 percent and comprehend below 50 percent

The independent level of reading is the easiest. Readers can decode and understand easily, without assistance. This is the level of reading that is typically most pleasurable and most likely to occur spontaneously. The challenge for the weak reader is to find interesting material that is at an independent level. The instructional level requires an active stance and assistance in reading. It is the level that textbooks are written at; that is to say, a seventh-grade history text is intended for a reader at grade level to read with some effort and assistance (Manzo et al., 2001). At the frustration level, readers struggle to understand the material. Students who are below grade level in reading will experience great frustration with independent reading of their classroom textbooks.

Decoding difficulty level is arrived at by counting the number of words mispronounced while reading aloud. An informal measure of this for independent student use is the five-finger rule: if you make more than five errors reading aloud a page of text, it is too hard (Fry, 1977; Ukrainetz & Trujillo, 1999).

Clearly, the comprehension score will vary with different question protocols due to the nature and distribution of questions posed. In addition, whereas a student can pronounce the words of a passage and not understand it, decoding problems will consistently affect comprehension. Even if the words are successfully decoded, a slow rate of reading will impair the processing of the sentence and the larger passage.

If a student cannot achieve adequate reading comprehension because of slow and inaccurate word decoding, then an estimate of the student's listening comprehension may reveal to what degree his language development is suffering because of lack of exposure to the literate language gained through reading. The passages can be read aloud and the student asked questions orally. This should be considered an additional estimate of comprehension, not interchangeable with reading comprehension. This is best accomplished with short passages because the student must remember the entire passage and because written language has a lexicon, syntax, and discourse organization designed for the eye, not the ear (Scott, 1995).

The Activity

Activity is the context in which reading occurs (Snow, 2002). Consideration of the psychological components of the entire situation is beneficial for planning intervention. This full context has multiple dimensions that cut across reading text and situation: the motivation for reading, the specific purpose, the reigning conditions, and the particular skills and strategies involved in understanding the text (Ukrainetz, 1998).

The underlying motivation to read may be knowledge (to gain further understanding on a topic), application (to learn how to accomplish an act), or engagement (to enjoy or become absorbed into the reading). The purpose of reading will affect the resultant comprehension—knowing why one is reading helps foreground elements, unite them, fill in between, and go beyond. The initial purpose or goal may be externally imposed, such as a class assignment, or internally generated, such as programming a cell phone. This purpose can evolve during the reading, as the reader encounters new information leading to additional questions, or judges the material noninformative. If multiple purposes conflict, this can negatively impact comprehension, such as when an author is reading source material for an article, but is seduced by other topics within the source material, thus losing focus on the initial purpose.

The conscious strategies and unconscious skills involved vary with the purpose of the task. Skimming, careful reading, memorizing, seeking the main idea, or editing all involve different approaches to the task. If the purpose is to gain preliminary information to determine utility, skimming may be required. If the purpose is to memorize content, then studying is required. Skilled readers can adjust the operations easily, and can recognize in what mode they are operating and why. Conditions dictate the choice of strategies. Good students, who formerly read all their materials comprehensively and carefully, upon entering some college programs with heavy reading loads, may need to read differently. Studying may involve skimming materials, seeking recognition knowledge, and prioritizing what should be read more carefully later.

A revealing example of an activity in which the goal and conditions affected the selection of reading strategies and resultant comprehension was presented by Bazerman (1985). The investigator interviewed and observed seven physicists as they perused journal articles. They were asked to reflect on their reading habits and talk aloud as they read. Results of the study showed that the scientists discarded as much as 75 percent of what they initially examined. They considered titles, authors, and abstracts; matching what they read with their research interests and knowledge of the labs from which the articles were generated. They read selectively within the articles, jumping back and forth between parts, looking for specific features or surprising elements. The physicists made judgments constantly about the relative value of reading or learning material versus time and thought investment. Some articles were set aside for reflection and a second reading, with understanding sometimes coming some time after the reading had ceased. This reading activity illustrates how important it is to understand why one is reading, and what facilitations (e.g., background knowledge) and constraints (e.g., many articles with little time) are present to determine how one should approach the reading task.

Learning How to Read to Learn

Students in the early grades focus their reading efforts on learning how to decode words and make sense of sentences. When this reading becomes automatic and fluent, cognitive space is freed to attend to the meanings gained. For academic pursuits, readers must be able to actively and independently engage in text comprehension to achieve learning goals. Reading to accomplish learning objectives can be described in terms of strategic reading and critical thinking.

Strategic Reading

The term *strategy* is heavily used in the comprehension literature. Strategies are, "actions selected deliberately to achieve particular goals" (Paris, Wasik, & Turner, 1991, p. 611). Strategies become more efficient and developmentally advanced as they evolve into skills (see Chapter 1 for further discussion of these activity components). Skills are automatic information-processing operations that "are applied to text unconsciously for many reasons including expertise, repeated practice, compliance with directions, luck, and naïve use" (p. 611). Skills can resurface as strategies when readers must consciously approach unusually difficult tasks. It is as strategies that these processes are open to inspection and modification, and thus as strategies that they are discussed. However, the ultimate goal is to be a *skilled* reader who unconsciously applies effective information-processing techniques, leaving maximal cognitive space for considering the content gleaned. Conscious strategic reading is hard work in which good readers can, but rarely are required to, engage. The aim is for poor readers to enjoy as much effortless reading as good readers.

There are many possible comprehension strategies. A selection is presented in Table 12.1 on page 512. The strategies are organized by use: before, during, or after reading. Readers choose from these strategies to accomplish their purposes within the specific activities. This selection process itself is a skill; it is the conditional *when* and *why* knowledge needed to enact the procedural *how* details of the declarative *what* understanding (Paris, Lipson, & Wixson, 1983).

For example, strategies used before reading include previewing the material by glancing over the text, looking at pictures, or considering the title and subheadings. The purpose of reading can be specified by posing to oneself guiding questions, such as in this self-talk example on a shark project:

- What am I trying to find out? I want to know the habitat and food habits of great white sharks.

- What is the most important information I am seeking? I want to know if sharks eat people and how often. I bet it is exaggerated like bear attacks because people like to be scared.

- How should I read this to find those answers? I'm going to look at the table of contents and find a section on shark diet and a section on danger to people.

Such prereading acts lead to activation of prior knowledge, prediction of the text content, and a plan for reading. The reader thus enters the comprehension act with purpose and preparation.

Reading with purpose and comprehension monitoring are difficult, even for better readers. August, Flavell, and Clift (1984) provided stronger and weaker 5th graders with stories to read. Some of the stories were missing a page. Skilled readers more frequently noticed the missing page or at least showed some awareness as evidenced by slower reading times and look-backs on those stories. However, half the students in both groups did not report a problem, and both skilled and nonskilled readers made nonwarranted inferences to fill in the missing information. Neither seemed aware that reading struggle might indicate a problem with the text. This lack of text awareness was further supported by Garner and Reis (1981). These investigators examined

Some Comprehension Strategies
Table 12.1   **Before, During, and After Reading**

Stage	Strategy
Before Reading	• Look for organizing concepts • Recall related information, experiences, attitudes, and feelings • Decide how easy or difficult the reading selection is likely to be • Set a purpose for reading • Determine a reason for engagement with the reading
During Reading	• Translate ideas into own words • Use prior knowledge • Compare ideas to personal experience • Identify main ideas • Recognize passage and sentence structure • Note important details • Reread for clarification • Jump backwards and forwards • Pause to reflect and make relevant connections to prior knowledge and experience • Consolidate ideas into larger groupings • Notice unfamiliar vocabulary and infer meanings • Form mental pictures • Evaluate the author's purpose, motive, or authority • Invoke study strategies • Manage time to sustain concentration
After Reading	• Check basic comprehension by asking self what has been learned • Organize information into chunks of manageable size • Decide what is important • Try to clarify ambiguous ideas • Relate what has been learned to other experiences • Evaluate new information in terms of previous knowledge and experience • Plan study strategies according to reading purpose and text features • Review material periodically

Sources: Manzo et al. (2001); Paris et al. (1991); Pearson & Fielding (1991); Snow (2002); Tierney & Readance (2000)

look-back behavior in 4th to 10th grade good and poor comprehenders. Test questions were designed to vary on the need for looking back in the text for answers. Older good comprehenders were the most likely to look back for information, but many of both groups did not look back when necessary.

During informational reading, an essential act is identifying main ideas. To do this, readers must understand what they have read, make judgments about relative importance, and synthesize the information. Identifying the main idea and presenting it in a summary (usually combined with one or two supporting points) improves over the later school years, but remains challenging even into college age (Brown & Day, 1983). Brown and Day investigated summarization performance in grades 5, 7, 10, and in college-age students. The two younger groups tended to delete irrelevant and redundant information and report ideas verbatim, retaining the sequence presented. In contrast, older students collapsed and combined information across paragraphs, synthesizing and paraphrasing, with organization presented by idea units. However, even for the older students, only half inferred main ideas that were not explicitly stated.

Strategic reading is a later-developing skill. Readers must learn to monitor their own comprehension. They must go beyond evaluating their understanding of individual words to evaluating their understanding of larger ideas and progressions. They must be able to use multiple standards in an ongoing judgment process as they read. They must have enough cognitive space left over from the act of decoding words to monitor meaning construction, and be aware when they are inferring intended meaning instead of using stated content, when there is a problem with text, and where to find information. In a review of the developmental literature, Paris et al. (1991) determined that these skills are only emerging in later elementary school and that "even 12 year-old good readers do not detect a large number of errors and inconsistencies inserted into meaningful text" (p. 621).

Critical Comprehension

Critical thinking is going beyond understanding the stated message to inferring, evaluating, synthesizing, and applying the information. Critical thinking is broadly considered "reflective and reasonable thinking that is focused on deciding what to believe or do" (Ennis, 1985, p. 45). While critical thinking does not necessarily involve text or language, text comprehension encompasses the processes of critical thinking, applied to verbal material. As such, critical thinking overlaps with strategic reading. However, there are some concepts in the critical thinking literature that can usefully extend the possibilities presented in strategic reading.

One influential approach to classifying thinking skills is known popularly as *Bloom's taxonomy* (Bloom, Engelhart, Furst, Hill, & Krathwohl, 1956). This taxonomy of cognitive educational objectives was originally developed to assist college and university faculty in writing examinations that emphasized higher mental processes. It moved quickly into broader purposes, appearing as a guide in development of general teaching objectives, subject-specific curriculum development, and evaluation of teaching and learning performance. The taxonomy has received continual attention and interest, appearing as a basic reference for educators worldwide across grade levels and subject areas (Bloom, 1994).

According to Bloom (1994), the objectives developed by a team of educators and several hundred reviewers were primarily pragmatic. They were intended to aid educators in systematically evaluating student learning. The objectives were fairly general, allowing educators to employ their own teaching methods, develop their own specific instructional objectives, and construct their own test items based on guiding categories. They were intended as an educational classification system, with internally logical and psychologically consistent categories, but with the greatest emphasis on reflecting how educators view and teach thinking (Bloom et al., 1956). Bloom's taxonomy does not represent any one theoretical view of cognition, but has been found to be consistent with a number of psychological theories (Kreitzer & Madaus, 1994; Rohwer & Sloane, 1994).

Bloom's taxonomy is divided into six hierarchical levels. The first level, dealing with the acquisition and structure of information, is *knowledge recall*, the "remembering of the idea or phenomenon in a form very close to that in which it was originally encountered" (Bloom et al., 1956, pp. 28–29). The remaining five levels involve the exercise of intellectual skills and abilities on knowledge to achieve a particular purpose. They are *comprehension, application, analysis, synthesis,* and *evaluation.* Table 12.2 presents a summary of the objectives as described by Bloom et al. Verbs are included that often (but not always) align with expected learning outcomes.

Empirical investigations have generally supported trained examiners' ability to classify educational exam questions under these objectives, although synthesis and evaluation levels have been least reliably differentiated and are left out of some empirically based modifications of this taxonomy (Kreitzer & Madaus, 1994). There have been difficulties classifying oral questions in the

Bloom's Taxonomy of Cognitive Educational Objectives

Table 12.2

Cognitive Operation	Description	Key Verbs
Knowledge Recall	Remembering, either by recognition or recall, information pertaining to specifics (terminology and facts), ways and means of dealing with specifics (conventions, classifications, and methods), and universals/abstractions in a field (principles and theories)	*choose, identify, label*
Comprehension	Understanding material; includes translation (putting into another language or modality), interpretation (inferencing, generalizing, and summarizing), and extrapolation (making predictions)	*paraphrase, describe, explain*
Application	Use of abstractions and generalizations in particular and concrete situations without specific instruction on how to accomplish this	*construct, simulate, draw, predict*
Analysis	Breaking a whole into constituent elements to detect relationships among parts or to recognize techniques used to convey meaning; includes distinguishing fact from hypothesis, relevant from extraneous material, relationships between ideas, unstated assumptions, and author's techniques and purposes	*classify, distinguish, differentiate, contrast*
Synthesis	Putting together elements to form a whole; recognizing patterns or creating unusual or creative wholes, new ideas, or sets of abstract relations from the given constituents	*combine, integrate, collect, assemble*
Evaluation	Judgments about the value of materials and methods for certain purposes; intended to be reasoned judgments with clear criteria concerning material presented, based on analysis and not impressionistic opinions	*judge, rate, assess, defend, appraise*

Source: Bloom et al. (1956)

classroom, but Furst (1994) suggests that "this is understandable because the scheme is aimed more at the outcomes of instruction than at the language moves a teacher might undertake to probe meanings, opinions, and preferences and otherwise to facilitate discussion" (p. 33).

The clarity of divisions decreases further when the thinking process is examined (Ukrainetz, Shippen, & Roswell, 1998). A correct answer does not necessarily reflect a critical thought process. Nor does a key word in a question reflect the mental demands of the response. Exam questions may sound like they involve analysis or synthesis, but they are only knowledge recall questions if the content was dictated to the students who memorized it for the examination. Students may study in an evaluative or synthesizing way, but they are usually dismayed if they must execute these higher level acts on an exam. In addition, there are multiple processes and varying levels of critical thought involved in any particular thinking task, preventing simple one-to-one assignment of thinking processes to academic tasks or questions. In "Contrast the medical insurance systems of Canada and the United States," *contrast* keys the reader primarily to the process of analysis, but evaluation of the evidence, synthesis toward a conclusion, and application of abstractions to particular situations are involved in the act.

The taxonomic acts are employed within a variety of complex thinking activities such as problem solving, decision-making, argument evaluation, and conceptualizing (Beyer, 1997). The steps involved in each activity reflect the differing goals of the strategy; problem solving involves seeking a good answer to an issue, while in decision-making, the choices are known and the concern is in evaluating the alternatives. Metacognition is present as an overarching strategy that involves the operations of directing one's mental efforts and reflecting on these mental activities.

Finally, affect is often overlooked as an aspect of critical thought. Attitudes or dispositions that drive and support thinking include seeking reasons, using credible sources, taking into account the total situation, seeking precision, keeping in mind the original and basic concern, and being willing to change positions given sufficient evidence (Ennis, 1985). These personality aspects affect critical thinking. For example, a person who is willing to keep an open mind and who is interested in seeking evidence will be a better thinker than one who is not; or a person who is selective about what is considered credible sources will be harder to convince than one who accepts a wide range of "expert" opinion.

Can Comprehension Be Taught?

Reading comprehension is a complex act that can occur with varied degrees of sophistication. Good readers develop skilled comprehension processes fairly independently, but average and weak readers need assistance to become skilled comprehenders (Snow, 2002). There is a large body of evidence on effective methods of teaching text comprehension. However, there has been persisting concern with the infrequency and ineffectiveness of reading comprehension instruction in the classroom (Manzo et al., 2001; Snow). There has been a tendency to assume that if a student can decode adequately, further reading instruction is not needed. Teachers have tended to trust that progress will occur through reading short passages from texts with controlled difficulty and demonstrating comprehension through answering questions, completing workbook pages, or taking tests.

Several comprehensive reviews of the literature (Snow, 2002; Manzo et al., 2001; Paris et al., 1991; Pearson & Fielding, 1991; Tierney & Readance, 2000) have shown satisfactory outcomes with specific methods for expository text instruction, such as identifying discourse structure, producing hierarchical summaries, and constructing graphical maps of ideas such as flow charts and semantic webs. These reviews concur that consistently successful specific methods across the comprehension literature fall into several themes:

- Explicit, systematic attention to text structure and features that indicate how ideas are related to one another

- Graphical representation of ideas and the relations among ideas

- Drawing relationships between students' own knowledge and the content of the reading selection

- Determining and recasting in a summary the most important information

- Transforming ideas from one form to another

In addition, using these methods within the contexts of the following instructional arrangements has been found to be beneficial (Snow, 2002; Manzo et al., 2001; Paris et al., 1991; Pearson & Fielding, 1991; Tierney & Readance, 2000):

- Having students actively involved in their own learning, both through motivated student choice and self-monitoring during reading

- Instructor modeling of thinking and comprehension processes

- Students tutoring each other or studying cooperatively

- Increasing student opportunities to read connected text, including sustained silent reading and repeated readings of a single text

- Connecting strategy instruction to subject matter

- Employing a diversity of authentic text genres

- Assessment of the learning process through observation, think-alouds, and self-reports

Instruction that employs these features will be thoughtful, dynamic, and process-oriented. The most notable aspect of current comprehension instruction is the role of the instructor. According to Pearson and Fielding (1991), traditionally, the teacher has been task director, requiring, supervising, and evaluating recitations, written practice, and study activities about texts. Recent approaches have changed this role in multiple ways. The first change has been in the question-answer recitation which, in addition to evaluating content recall, now deals with text structure, linking background knowledge to text ideas, and prompting students into asking their own questions.

Another change is a greater attention to teachers giving up sustained control and leading students into independence. Third, the teacher role has evolved into that of a cognitive model—providing a mental window into *when, why,* and *how,* not just *what.* This has led to greater student internalization of strategies and reading independence, and resulted in stronger comprehension outcomes on closely linked dependent measures and even on more general measures of comprehension (Pearson & Fielding, 1991). In cognitive modeling, the teacher demonstrates and shares inner thinking processes, gradually turning over responsibility to the students, so they can ultimately operate independently.

The handover of knowledge to allow independent strategic reading is scaffolding. Scaffolding, in contrast to structured explicit instruction, attends to the students' ongoing understanding and text interpretations, and is modified to fit the moment (Pearson & Fielding, 1991). Instructional methods that have attended to this process, with its degrees of support, dynamic responses, and learning cues, such as those of Palincsar and colleagues (Palincsar, 1986; Palincsar & Brown, 1984; Palincsar, Brown, & Martin, 1987) have had marked success.

In the decade since Pearson and Fielding (1991) reviewed the literature, the emphasis has been on further exploring existing methods and how best to apply them in actual teaching situations. Snow (2002) concludes the OERI report with the current need to investigate the following: how much time is needed for comprehension instruction, how this time should be allocated among the many recommended reading instruction practices for various student populations, how to conduct relevant assessments, how explicit instruction can be embedded with inquiry-based methods and authentic reading materials, and how government policies and practices facilitate or impede effective instruction.

The research evidence shows that there is a wide variety of successful text instruction methods. The support for social-interactionist models of instruction provides a solid foundation for application of contextualized skill intervention to text comprehension. The next section details specific instructional procedures and considers how they are best applied within an intervention framework.

Intervention for Text Comprehension

The Intervention Framework

The foregoing recommended practices in text comprehension instruction fit within a contextualized skill framework. Effective intervention consists of teaching through repeated opportunities on an intense schedule with systematic support aimed at a few explicit skills (RISE, see Chapter 1). These occur within purposeful contexts or using authentic texts with support provided through scaffolding.

Structural scaffolding involves choosing, modifying, or presenting meaningful text in ways that simplify and focus learning while retaining the larger whole. One way to provide structural scaffolding is to use short expository selections extracted from a single larger whole that require a minimum of background knowledge and routine interactive structure. Another structural scaffold is is provided by using familiar content; passages are selected from ongoing classroom instruction, so the background knowledge and purposes of reading are provided by the classroom. Other structural scaffolds are provided by the predictable pattern of question asking and text analysis.

Interactive scaffolds are directed, not toward the content to be learned, but toward the purposes of reading and strategies to obtain the desired information. That is to say, if the book to be read is on dinosaurs, the prompts will focus on how to locate, understand, and evaluate particular dinosaur statements, rather than on learning the content or learning more about dinosaurs.

A key aspect of intervention is an explicit task focus, one that is shared by student and speech-language pathologist (SLP). It can be challenging to maintain a primary therapeutic objective during these interactions with meaningful text, but it is imperative that this occurs.

The methods to be described, while not specifically directed towards identified disabilities, have been successfully applied to poor comprehenders who can decode adequately. For students who also have decoding difficulties, these reading limitations can be circumvented through both presenting print materially orally and sharing in the reading (e.g., reading a passage aloud once, then together examining the printed material for specific information). SLPs are particularly adept at finding ways to bypass limited reading to allow for high-level language exchanges.

This is the intervention framework upon which comprehension intervention is erected. Several instructional activities are presented here, with primary attention to the reciprocal teaching method of scaffolding students into independent strategic comprehension. Students are taught how to read purposefully, actively, and reflectively; how to ask themselves questions as they read, "Where does this seem to be going? Maybe I'd better reread that part." As Manzo and colleagues (2001) state, "Thinking is not completely, or even primarily, a function of intelligence. Rather it is a constellation of strategies and cognitive habits or 'habits of mind'" (p. 48).

Specific Instruction Procedures

This section presents specific steps and procedures for developing text comprehension. Instructions deal with the three phases of reading: (1) prereading schema activation, (2) metacognitive monitoring of silent reading, and (3) postreading schema building. Some methods primarily focus on one phase and others support strategies throughout the process. There are a huge number of instructional activities (see Manzo et al., 2001; Tierney & Readance, 2000), most originally developed 20 or more years ago. A selection are presented below.

Text Preview
When a textbook is introduced, a valuable prereading activity is examining the book for organization and content. A formal version of this is the Survey

Technique (Aukerman, 1972) that presents reading-guide questions on the title, the subtitles, the visuals, the introductory paragraphs, and the concluding paragraphs, with the lesson ending by the class deriving the main idea of the text. The application here is intended to be considerably briefer and more informal. Even a cursory consideration of book features provides schema activation and is more like how purposeful readers approach a text initially.

Students should be guided to handle and examine a textbook. They should learn to ask questions such as the following.

- What is this textbook about?
- How is the book organized?
- What are the topics it covers?
- Is there going to be a lot of reading?
- Are there shortcuts to getting an initial idea of the content of a section?

Weak students may not know they should look at books as tools or vehicles for information. Students may not know that books can be evaluated and judged for ease of use and quality of content and organization. They may not know that real people (or committees) write books and that difficulty in understanding material may be due to ambiguities or errors in presentation, not solely due to the students' own limited understanding. Talking about a book as a tool intended to inform, but written by an actual person, helps the student see that books are not omnipotent and foreign writings, but are something they can read, understand, evaluate, use, and even produce themselves.

Expository books vary in their degree of organizational guidance. The front cover, back cover, and inside cover all provide early indicators of the topic and purpose. Tables of content or subheadings provide an indication of how the material is organized. Knowing that there is an index or glossary will be useful at later points in reading. Interestingly, we discovered in perusing a collection of science books related to the ocean to aid a student writing a shark report that most lacked an opening paragraph. Instead, the prose embarked immediately on the first topic. There was a paragraph describing the organization and purpose of the book, but it was entitled "Note to Parents" or "Teacher's Guide." Students should attend to this information despite the section title because it provides useful advance guidance for their own reading.

Listen-Read-Discuss

Listen-Read-Discuss (Manzo & Casale, 1985) is a basic comprehension instruction procedure. It provides advance notice of text content to facilitate comprehension. It consists of the following four steps:

1. Review the reading selection and prepare a brief, organized overview directed at what you want the students to get from the selection.

2. Present the summary orally to students.

3. Have students read the textbook version.

4. Discuss what has been heard and read in relation to the information and ideas for which the students were directed to find.

SLPs should not direct efforts at teaching content, so just using the steps as set out is not recommended. Instead, the focus should be on the fourth step. The follow-up discussion involving locating the summary information in the text teaches the students how main ideas are determined, supporting details are selected, and summaries are composed. The SLP should prepare the summary rather than depending on the author's published summary, so that the clinician is clear on how the summary was composed and how difficult the passage may be to summarize.

Oral Reading

The Oral Reading Strategy (Manzo, 1980) provides steps to guide students where to find the information or lead them into independent strategy use. This simple procedure models thinking strategies for prereading and active silent reading:

1. The clinician reviews the reading selection in advance, considering it from the students' perspective.

2. The clinician notes in the margins the thinking strategies to model while reading the first few paragraphs aloud (e.g., "This paragraph isn't clear, I will reread it and find the main idea").

3. The clinician reads orally to the students and comments on the accompanying thinking process.

4. Students then take responsibility and complete the reading silently.

Interestingly, this procedure lacks the therapeutic support needed to make the jump from the adult model to independent student use. Students should practice reading aloud and saying the strategies aloud as they read (called *think-alouds)*, with prompts from the SLP.

K-W-L⁺

In K-W-L⁺, anticipation-based reading guides are filled on what the students *Know*, what they *Want* to know, and, after the reading, what they have *Learned* (Carr & Ogle, 1987). The final plus element is categorizing the learning and representing relationships among concepts with graphic organizers. This procedure combines prereading strategies and postreading strategies. It provides a mnemonic to activate background knowledge, remind the students about the goal of the reading, and then reflect on what they did or didn't learn and how that relates to the goal.

Graphic Organizers

Graphic organizers are helpful for analyzing text structure. Information is presented in schematic networks that isolate and emphasize key elements. They reflect the text structure or the relationships among ideas. The visual presentation aids in understanding text structure for students of a range of abilities

Figure 12.1

Attribute Guide for Summarizing
What Is a Raptor? Passage

Attribute	Raptor Dinosaur
Scientific Name	
Historical Period	
Size	
Speed	
Diet	
Habitat	
Distinguishing Features	
Varieties	

Semantic Map for What Has Been Learned about Raptor Dinosaurs

Figure 12.2

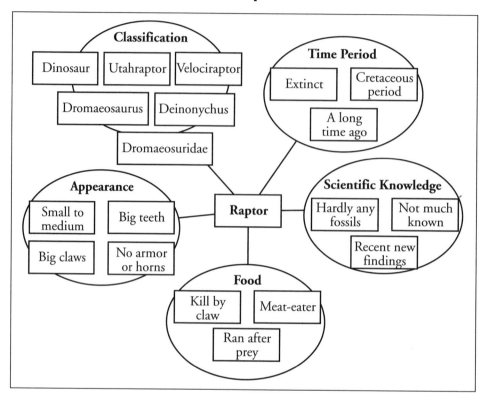

Venn Diagram for Unique and Distinguishing Features between Raptor Birds and Raptor Dinosaurs

Figure 12.3

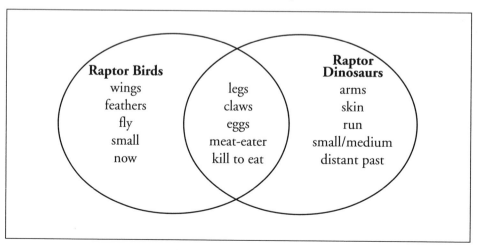

(Idol, 1987; Idol & Croll, 1987). They are more helpful for relational information than factual information (DiCecco & Gleason, 2002). Taxonomic organization is the most common arrangement (e.g., main ideas, subordinate ideas, and supporting details), but the organization can also reflect discourse structure such as the step-wise organization of a procedural text. There are many formats for graphic organizers. Figure 12.1 on page 523 is an attribute guide that organizes information into categories. Figure 12.2 is a semantic map that provides a spatial organization of categorical information. Figure 12.3 is a Venn diagram that emphasizes the common and distinctive information presented on two concepts.

Day's Rules

The process of summarizing, which improves text comprehension, is a complex act itself. Day (1980) derived five rules for summary instruction from observing how students from fifth grade to college age create summaries, then combining this with van Dijk and Kintsch's (1978) macrorules for comprehending and remembering prose. Day's Rules, as referred to by Pearson and Fielding (1991), have been used in many successful summarization instruction studies (e.g., Baumann, 1984; Day, 1986; McNeil & Donant, 1982). A summary is often longer than a single main idea statement, so combining a main idea with one or two supporting details has been used as well (Rinehart, Stahl, & Erickson, 1986). Day's Rules are, in order of difficulty:

1. Delete trivial or irrelevant information.
2. Delete redundant information.
3. Substitute a superordinate term.
4. Find and use stated main ideas.
5. Infer and create your own main idea.

Day's Rules are most applicable to shorter discourse units, such as paragraphs. Consecutive paragraphs provide repeated opportunities to practice Day's Rules. After determining the main idea for a set of paragraphs, the main ideas can be used as headings for creating a larger overall summary in the procedure described next.

Hierarchical Summarization

Hierarchical summarizing instruction involves showing students how to turn headings, subheadings, and topic sentences into prose summaries (Taylor, 1980; Taylor & Beach, 1984). It is a technique for guiding summary construction for longer units of text, such as a book chapter. The technique requires chapters that are organized with headings and subheadings (or creating relevant headings and subheadings can be part of the process). Clinicians model, then provide guided and then independent practice on applying this strategy. In the modeling phase, SLPs think out loud the entire time they are building a summary from the component parts. The clinician and students together talk themselves through the guided practice phase and then the students work alone in the final phase. This has been used as a studying technique, but also teaches summarization itself.

ReQuest

Reciprocal Questioning, or ReQuest, was the earliest educational introduction of mental modeling. The basic procedure is for the SLP and competent peers to model question asking and answering at the outset of reading (Manzo, 1969; Manzo et al., 2001). This is intended to set the purpose for the rest of the silent reading. The reciprocal element is the intention to allow students to set questions based on their own perceptions of what is important (or what they think their classroom teacher will consider important). The questions are not intended to be of the stump-the-class flavor. Rather, they are questions that can be answered by prediction, inference, judgment, evaluation, and experience. The ReQuest process follows these steps:

1. Explain that students will examine the first few sentences of the passage and ask each other questions to improve their ability to set a good purpose for reading.

2. Guide the students in formulating a logical purpose for the subsequent reading. The title and first sentence are shown and the students are told to ask the kinds of questions teachers might on that content.

3. Answer student questions without asking questions back or distracting with elaborate answers.

4. Follow up with additional questions on aspects such as: basic information, translation, inference, personal experience, and evaluation.

5. ·Follow this pattern for four sentences or until a purpose is clear.

6. Then determine possible purposes for the rest of the reading and write these down as predictions.

7. The selection is read silently or aloud.

8. Ask students to look back at the predictions and evaluate whether a good purpose had been set for the reading.

ReQuest questions can be set along three dimensions: *on, between,* and *beyond* the lines. In that case then, rather than the purpose of the reading, the intent is for students to learn to pose factual, inferential, and applied questions and to learn how to locate the information needed. This is a useful way to organize question asking and take it beyond the literal and factual.

Reciprocal Teaching

Reciprocal Teaching (Palincsar & Brown, 1984) takes the basic questioning format of ReQuest, applies it to fundamental comprehension strategies applicable throughout a reading (summarize, question, clarify, predict), and embeds it within a systematic scaffolding format designed along the Vygotskian view that development moves from other-regulation to external self-regulation to internal self-regulation (Vygotsky, 1978).

In this approach, reading comprehension self-questions are taught through all students being teachers. After the adult model, each student, with ongoing support from the SLP, takes a role at asking comprehension questions of the other students about a passage read aloud or silently. Instead of the typical route of choosing the students who have mastered the material, in Reciprocal Teaching, all the students learn through teaching. The students are required to verbalize a question, expecting a real answer from other students. The adult hears the verbalization and can provide assistance when needed. As the students master asking each other the questions, the questions start to become internalized, and they begin asking themselves those questions.

In the early sessions, the role of the instructor is heavy because this activity is challenging: students are accustomed to passive reading, not taking charge, and they do not know how to formulate appropriate questions and respond to peers. It is important that the SLP does not retain more control than necessary. Students with inadequate reading comprehension strategies must be allowed to be the "teachers." This role is of reading the selection (if possible), then asking for the summary and questions, and evaluating the responses is critical to the process of internalizing the SLP-modeled speech so that it will become their own. It may seem unlikely that students can do this, but it is only when students themselves know and act on this knowledge that they will apply it independently in other reading situations.

Choosing Expository Text

All the foregoing procedures must be applied to *something*. To be expository discourse, that something must be bigger than a sentence, but short enough to be analyzed and discussed in detail. Paragraphs and passages may make enough sense to be used in isolation, but if repeated passages can be selected from a larger whole, the semantic and knowledge linkages, as well as common author style, will aid comprehension.

For comprehension instruction, classroom texts can be used. Passages from these texts are motivating for students to use in language intervention because of the immediate applicability to the classroom. The second author, Ross, lets her middle school students choose between history and science reading and the group easily agrees on which is the more important need for that week. The reading for these classes is often at the frustration level for students with language impairments, but can be comprehended with individualized assistance. A caveat in using classroom texts is that strategy must predominate over skill, even if there is pressure to memorize content.

Books that tie into topics addressed within classes or that are on topics that appeal to students independent of the classroom can also be used. These can easily be obtained in regular bookstores or school libraries. In perusing a selection to find the book used as an example text for this chapter, the first author, Ukrainetz, also bought a book about deer, one about bats, and one on "oozing, bubbling, dripping, and bouncing" experiments (VanCleave, 1996). Magazines and manuals are sources of appealing, authentic expository material that is relevant for expository structure production, discourse-based syntax models, and embedded vocabulary, in addition to their uses for reading comprehension. The advantage with using such books is that they can be selected in advance to provide both a meaningful topic and a discourse presentation that is amenable to strategy instruction.

Books that provide coherent, linked paragraphs are needed. This text format is harder to understand and less visually appealing than colorful bulleted notes and boxes spread over a page. For books that are primarily a collection of pictures, subheadings, bulleted notes, points to ponder, and salient facts, students should be guided to sort through and understand headings, boxed notes, and bulleted lists. However, without connected text, there is little opportunity to learn to gain meaning from prose: to understand main ideas, determine supporting points, and evaluate claims in connected expository text.

There is a collection of expository passages available called *QuickReads* (Hiebert, 2003). These are collections of history and science passages, which are intended to promote sight vocabulary and reading fluency through repeated meaningful presentations of controlled difficulty words (in terms of phonotactic and phonemic patterns and word frequencies), written at second-, third-, and fourth-grade independent reading levels. They do not have an overall thematic or logical coherency across selections, and do not have the organization and feel of a "real" book. However, they do provide the convenience of a large array of high interest, easy decoding expository selections that are meaningful in a restricted way. One study (Hiebert, in press) has shown positive results in second-grader reading fluency using these materials compared to uncontrolled literature passages—although there was no advantage demonstrated in comprehension.

Reciprocal Teaching in Language Intervention

There are a variety of methods for teaching comprehension strategies. Reciprocal Teaching stands out from the others—not in the choice of strategies but in the focus on the interaction between instructor and student, and on the use of student-as-teacher as a way into learning. These elements can be applied to ReQuest, K-W-L+, or other comprehension strategy acts. In addition to the focus on scaffolding and internalization, Reciprocal Teaching occurs through oral interactions. It has been applied to listening comprehension, keeps the focus on strategy rather than content, and has an impressive body of evidence supporting its effects. In particular, Palincsar and Brown (1984) reported a randomized group and single-subject experimental treatment study with excellent internal and external validity that should be a model for intervention research.

The research evidence supports Reciprocal Teaching in small groups and classroom settings in teacher-student and peer-tutor arrangements for students of a range of abilities. Although intended for students with decoding fluency and weak comprehension, reciprocal teaching has been successfully applied for young students with limited decoding in listening comprehension formats. Effects, compared to no-treatment and alternate-treatment conditions, have included qualitative improvement in summarizing and question-posing competence within the instructional group conversations, improvements in comprehension of studied materials in both pre- and post-test and repeated measures single-subject comparisons, comprehension improvement on nontrained materials, and improvement on standardized test scores (King & Parent Johnson, 1999; Lederer, 2000; Palincsar, 1986; Palincsar & Brown, 1984; Palincsar et al., 1987).

The process of Reciprocal Teaching is demonstrated in Appendix A on page 553. In this example, the movement from considerable to light scaffolding support for the four strategies (summarize, question, clarify, and predict) is presented. In addition, the clinician models how to find information for a summary and whether answers are explicitly stated in the text. The text used to illustrate is *Raptors!* (Lessem, 1996). This book was bought from the students' section of a regular bookstore. Many students are little experts on dinosaurs and the prehistoric predatory raptor dinosaur was popularized in the movie *Jurassic Park,* resulting in an often impressive store of prior knowledge on this dinosaur. *Raptors!* is written between a fourth- and ninth-grade level (Fry, 1977), with the considerable variation in calculated difficulty depending on the number of scientific names presented (which does not reflect actual difficulty for students with prior dinosaur interests). The book provides factual information with inferential and applied opportunities on an appealing topic. The connected text is a well-formed whole organized into multiple smaller sections that can be presented as individual passages for modeling and teaching dialogues.

The focus of Reciprocal Teaching is on the acquisition process for comprehension strategies. Students must learn how to examine text for reasonable questions, how to form the questions, and how to answer them. The focus is not on gaining content information, but on acquiring strategies for better later content acquisition. As a result, teachers find that little text is "covered" in a Reciprocal Teaching lesson. And strategy acquisition takes time: Palincsar, David, and Brown (1989) caution that, in a classroom situation, students (and teachers) may take 25 sessions to develop competence in strategy use. An additional source of discomfort for teachers is allowing students, especially weak students, to take a leadership role (Palincsar & Brown, 1984; Speece, MacDonald, Kilsheimer, & Krist, 1997). In Reciprocal Teaching, students learn through teaching. The teacher plays a critical guiding role, but students learn through asking questions of each other.

These concerns about Reciprocal Teaching are strengths for language intervention. For the SLP, who is not intending to teach content or cover the curriculum, this focus on strategies in an individual and small group context is ideal. The smaller group setting will allow more learning opportunities per student and thus faster learning. In addition to a skills and strategy focus, the oral conversation, listening comprehension, and individualized scaffolding fit well with the orientation of the SLP. SLPs expect weak students to question and explain. Reciprocal Teaching works well within a language intervention format. The second author, Ross, has used Reciprocal Teaching extensively with students from the upper elementary to high school grades.

Comprehension Intervention Embedded in Projects

Reciprocal Teaching and the other comprehension instruction procedures can be taught within larger projects. The overall purpose aids in student engagement. The steps enable observation of and support for the many comprehension and thinking processes involved. In both units presented here, there is a consistent focus on process over product, and quality of comprehension over correct answers. The major distinctions between the two projects are in the materials collection process and the relative emphasis on analysis and evaluation (debate) versus synthesis (library research project). The projects involve composing text in the form of bulleted notes, so expository structure production and expository syntax could also be targeted within these projects.

Oral Debate

The first project targets critical thinking skills in a process-oriented, contextualized manner. The project is planned for approximately eight sessions (two per week). Scaffolding student performance through models, guiding questions, and demonstrations from other students allows a variety of ability levels to accomplish this activity. It is suited to a group situation with at least four students to allow for two teams. If the group is larger than six, it is best accomplished through a resource classroom so the teacher and SLP can provide sufficient monitoring and scaffolding support. Ross engaged in this project within a high school resource classroom, in collaboration with the teacher.

Ross based this debate project on a critical thinking unit presented in Ukrainetz et al. (1998). In that article, students developed position statements rather than debates. Position statements allow for more nuanced perspectives: students do not have to take a *pro* or *con* position on an issue, but can present arguments in both directions. However, the necessity of clear positions in the debate simplifies the task (less synthesis is required), and provides the social motivation of a good argument.

The overall purpose of the project is that students engage in reasoned and reflective consideration of an issue. The steps enable observation of and support for the many comprehension and thinking processes involved. In this project, consistent with a focus on process over product, there is no "correct" answer. Students are encouraged to make their own conclusions based on careful reasoning. A controversial topic engages the students' interest for the lengthy process of critically evaluating a position. Because the focus here is not on obtaining research sources, a limited number of authentic texts are provided to the students. The issue described here is the controversial rural topic of whether dogs should be allowed to ride in the back of open pickup trucks. It is based on local newspaper articles. It is sometimes difficult to evaluate the credibility of the factual claims from these sources, but that is an example of the real-life evaluations newspaper readers must make.

Bloom's taxonomy is applied throughout this project. Knowledge and comprehension are present in learning new information and recalling it during discussions. Main points and supporting details are determined and unclear material questioned. Literal and inferential comprehension is required. The unit involves the evaluative thinking of analysis and evaluation: students must distinguish between facts and opinions, detect author bias, estimate the factual accuracy of statements, and determine the strength of arguments. Synthesis is present in formulating a position statement. Application occurs in the argument presentation and defense, as well as when skills and knowledge gleaned from this unit are spontaneously and appropriately applied in a new situation. Students' dispositions to learning are engaged and evident during the process. Box 12.1 sets out the steps for developing a debate.

The first step is to determine the main points from the sources provided. The SLP reads each paragraph aloud from an overhead and each student individually highlights the main point on his or her article copy, or if there is no main idea stated explicitly, writes it in the margin. Secondly, the students must agree on the main points. The students collaboratively consider the readings and agree on the main points of each paragraph. They state in a single phrase or sentence the main point. They examine whether main points were explicitly stated or implied and judge how the highlighting and margin comments helped.

The third step is to develop two explicit contrasting position statements, based on the debate statement (e.g., "Be it resolved that dogs should not ride in the back of open pickup trucks"). After developing the position statements, the students are assigned to one of two teams. For the fourth step, each team goes through the recorded main points and stars the points which support their position. The students need to keep referring back to the original position statements (i.e., "We agree that," or "We do not agree that") to remind themselves which position an argument supports. The starred items are then organized into idea groupings and redundant points combined.

The fifth step is to evaluate the strengths of their own arguments. The points are analyzed on three features: (1) fact versus opinion, (2) credible versus doubtful, and (3) relevant versus tangential. Students discuss whether these are all the relevant points and generate others. These are also evaluated on the three argument dimensions. Table 12.3 on page 534 shows an example of the main points, for and against, sorted into facts or opinions. Students must then collate their best arguments: those that are factual, credible, and relevant.

The sixth step of establishing and maintaining debate etiquette is an important part of oral argumentation. The debate process is presented, particularly the concepts of polite disagreement and nonpersonal comments. Examples of polite/impolite and personal/professional comments are role-played, identified, and discussed. This part should not be assumed, because, in our experience, teams may embrace their positions too vigorously, leading to rebuttals that may become heated and sometimes offensive.

Students must then prepare scripts for presenting their positions. They will need guidance for when to write connected text that is read versus when key

Box 12.1   # Steps for Developing a Debate

1. Determine the main points.

2. Agree on the main points.

3. Develop a position statement.

4. Locate and list all points that support a position.

5. Evaluate the arguments on:
   - Fact versus opinion
   - Credible versus doubtful
   - Relevant versus tangential

6. Set debate etiquette.

7. Prepare the scripts.

8. Practice the presentation.

9. Carry out the debate.

10. Reflect on the performance.

Debate Points for Dogs Riding in Open Pickup Trucks

Table 12.3

	Facts	Opinions
Against Dogs in Trucks	• A person saw a dog fall out of a truckbed a few weeks ago. • There is a state law which says it is illegal to carry an animal in a cruel manner. • A national animal rights organization bans dogs from the back of trucks. • States such as Florida and Texas require restraints for dogs riding in vehicles. • A 1988 study of 141 veterinarians found 592 cases of dogs who were launched from the back of trucks.	• Animal rights leaders think that dogs shouldn't be in the back of pickup trucks. • New laws would prevent dogs being injured. • A truck is the dog's territory so it will protect it and maybe bite someone who tries to pet it. • A dog might jump out of a truck and bite someone walking near.
Supporting Dogs in Trucks	• Dogs need to be outside when it is hot. • Dogs need fresh air. • Dogs have good balance. • It is a part of Wyoming culture. • Long leashes in an open truck bed can be more dangerous than a free dog. • Dogs in trucks have rarely bitten people.	• It is no one's business but the dog's owner. • You don't need to pass a law about everything slightly dangerous. • People should make up their own minds about their dogs being in the back of the truck. • The rate of injury is low for all the dogs that travel in trucks. • The town doesn't have time to enforce a ban on loose dogs in trucks. • People should know not to approach dogs in trucks.

phrases are more helpful for more spontaneous commenting. The preparation and subsequent practice are the seventh and eighth steps listed. Both teams practice their half of the debate without the other team. Each team is videotaped and reviewed in terms of content and process to assist in self-evaluation prior to the actual debate.

For the actual debate, the teams should present to a real audience. Ross engaged another resource class for this. Each team states its positions, provides supporting statements, and summarizes with opinions. After both teams present, they are each allowed a rebuttal. The audience, composed of another resource class, rates the debaters using a rubric. The rubric consists of three areas: position statement, supporting points, and rebuttal. Each area is rated on a 1–5 scale with 1 being vague and 5 being clearly presented. The audience then votes for which position was argued most convincingly. Then they voted for which position they supported regardless of strength of argument.

Finally, students reflect on their performance. The videotaped debate is replayed, stopping at intervals to discuss performance. Afterward, the students rate themselves on the performance rubric used by the audience. They discuss what they learned and what should be changed in terms of their own performance. They go through each step of the analysis process and determine whether it was helpful.

Library Research Project

Text comprehension can be part of a larger library research project executed over an extended series of sessions. The second project described is a library research project. Two manageable presentation modalities for this project are a short speech and a poster. Both involve bulleted notes with a minimum of writing. Constructing a research presentation involves generating questions; locating materials; understanding and summarizing text; selecting and evaluating findings; and organizing material into a presentation format. This project is most beneficial for reading comprehension if preceded by an introduction and some concentrated practice in text comprehension. This project is of sufficient duration and complexity that multiple objectives can be addressed, cycling through a primary focus area. The steps in executing a library research project are set out in Box 12.2 on page 536.

The first step involves the SLP presenting a short list of research topics for students to choose from. It is helpful if these topics are centered on a theme, such as Animals of the Yellowstone Ecosystem. Using this example theme as a

Box 12.2   **Research Project Steps**

1. Identify a topic.
2. Determine what is known, not known, and how it all relates.
3. Develop questions to answer.
4. Generate key words for information search.
5. Determine the location of and how to access materials.
6. Skim reference material to determine relevance and quality.
7. Read for understanding of main idea and relevant details.
8. Make paraphrased notes.
9. Relate information from multiple sources.
10. Organize and synthesize the material.
11. Practice oral presentation.
12. Anticipate audience questions.
13. Self-evaluate.

class project, individual students can choose to research a specific animal relating to the theme.

In the second step, students use K-W-L$^+$ in a guided discussion to produce a concept map about their topic that demonstrates what they already know. Figure 12.4 shows a concept map for a project on bears.

The third step is for students to use the concept map to identify questions they would like to answer about their topic, based on what is already known and what other information is needed. The SLP can guide student thinking by having students develop their research questions based on the answers to these questions:

1. What do I already know about my topic?
2. What else do I need to know?
3. What do I want to find out?
4. What else am I wondering about?

As students develop their research questions, they write them in their research project guide. It is helpful to limit the number of research questions to no more than four so that the therapeutic process remains foregrounded rather than the information search.

Figure 12.4 **Concept Map for Project on Bears**

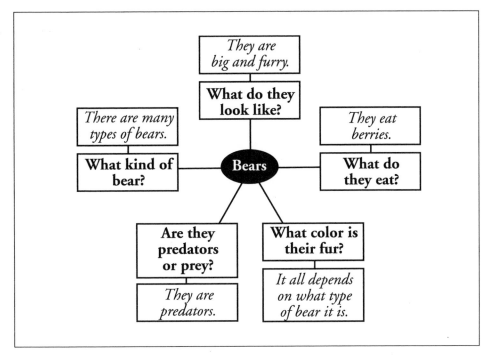

The fourth step is to generate key words for information search. Students identify words from their questions. They brainstorm synonyms for these words, which become additional key words for their research (see Figure 12.5). Some ways to generate additional key words are to look at different spellings, add plural endings, broaden the topic, narrow the topic, and look for related topics. This is a vocabulary knowledge activity with a clear purpose, embedded within the research activity.

The fifth step involves the SLP leading the students in a discussion of possible research tools, how to locate those tools, and how to access the information in the tools. Again, it helps the therapeutic focus to limit the number of research materials to two or three sources (e.g., one book, one interview, and one Internet search). Interviews are particularly valuable because of the opportunity for formal oral interaction. Questions are set up in advance and interviews are role-played and evaluated by peers prior to asking "experts." On the Internet search, the sources will also have to be limited to one to two relevant sites. Students can easily become overwhelmed by the quantity of information available, and lose the critical comprehension focus.

The sixth step is to skim reference material to determine relevance and quality. Determining the relevance and quality of reference materials is a challenging critical thinking skill for both student and clinician. However, skimming is an important skill for working through a large amount of data to obtain information needed. The SLP guides the students to notice the author of the material, the topic, and the claims. Sometimes, the lack of relevance should be obvious, such as when a student of Ross' needed to know the diet of rabbits and searched the Internet for *rabbits + eat,* resulting in the site "Great Rabbit Recipes." Interestingly, this student still needed guiding questions from Ross to determine that this information would not be helpful for his project. Questions can evaluate appropriateness, currency, authority, and reliability. They include:

1. Does the information answer your research questions?

2. Is the information current?

3. What kind of agency published the information? Is the information provided by an expert? How can you tell?

4. Is the information fact or opinion? Is the information clearly biased?

Figure 12.5   **Key Word Generation for Accessing Information Sources**

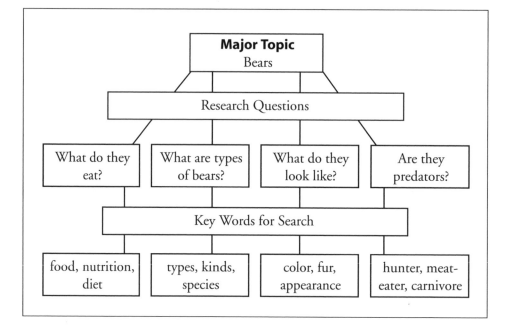

The seventh step is to read for understanding of main idea and relevant details. Students use highlighters to mark main ideas and supporting details to answer their research questions. The SLP reminds the students of learning to identify main ideas and supporting details from previous lessons of Reciprocal Teaching. Next, the students summarize the material with paraphrased notes (eighth step). This is an authentic use of Day's Rules embedded in the research activity. Students paraphrase the highlighted text of main ideas and supporting details. They may use bulleted notes so that the writing process is not so time consuming. Students must then combine information from multiple sources using paraphrased notes to answer research questions (ninth step).

The tenth step is for students to organize and synthesize the material. They make a sketch of the presentation format for the final project. For example, to present a poster, they design and sketch the poster positioning the title, written information, and pictures. Students type final text copy, make graphics, and complete their poster or presentation materials. For oral presentations, students must practice (eleventh step), following guidelines of good speaker qualities including appropriate eye contact, vocal volume, posture, use of visual aids, and clear speaking. Ross uses a formal evaluation form for assessing oral presentations (see Appendix B on page 559).

Students must also consider their audience (twelfth step). This is a critical thinking skill where students must consider vague areas or contrasting positions of the audience to anticipate possible questions. The SLP encourages the students to imagine that they are experts on their topic. This is a good time for students to determine if they need to search for additional information if they cannot answer a question they anticipate may be asked.

Finally, the students reflect on what they have learned. They explicitly consider the specific intervention objectives targeted, but also reflect on their performance in general. In examining both the process and product of learning, they consider the quality of their work and the amount of help they needed. Self-evaluation should happen continuously, as a part of learning, as well as a formal final step. Appendix C, page 560, shows a comprehensive final self-evaluation form that Ross has used with middle school students.

Being Therapeutic and Meaningful for Expository Comprehension

Improving the text comprehension of students with language impairments is challenging. It is easy to either make the activity so contrived that students do not generalize to daily life needs, or so interesting that the instructional focus is lost. The final considerations relate to an explicit skill focus: assessing text comprehension, setting intervention objectives, and collecting data *in situ*.

Text-Based Assessment

Assessment of comprehension involves careful planning and inferencing about internal processes. The SLP must make estimations of what a student understands, what mental route the student used to get there, and what is causing comprehension difficulties. A criterion-based method for estimating these abilities is presented. It combines aspects of the text preview instructional method described earlier in this chapter with items examining passage and word comprehension to provide a helpful assessment procedure.

The Informal Textbook Inventory (ITI) provides evidence of how the student can strategically approach and deal with academic books (Manzo et al., 2001). The SLP selects a classroom text used in several students' classrooms or can select a text considered representative of the types of texts used by the students. The SLP then develops a series of multiple-choice, fill-in-the-blank, matching, or closed-end questions around four dimensions: organization and structure, basic comprehension, applied comprehension, and specialized options. Manzo et al. suggest the following for determining students' strategies:

- Recognizing textbook organization: 3–5 questions on how text is structured, including signaling devices

- Using text organization effectively: 3–5 questions about the index, table of contents, or appendices

- Understanding the main idea: 1–2 questions requiring statements of the main idea

- Noting supporting details: 3–5 questions on specific stated facts

- Understanding vocabulary in context: 3–5 questions about the definitions of key terms

- Understanding graphic or pictorial information: 1–2 questions requiring an interpretation of a graph or chart that adds information not explicitly available in the text

- Drawing conclusions and critical thinking: 1–2 questions that require inferencing and synthesizing

- Evaluating and judging: 1–2 questions that require evaluation and application

- Understanding technical terms: 1–2 questions that require the student to recognize or respond to the use of terminology and graphics

- Understanding passages: 1 cloze passage taken from the text to determine comprehension of connected text

The responses can be oral so that comprehension judgments are not confounded with writing fluency. Likewise, if it is already established that the student has severe word recognition deficits that will interfere with comprehension, the SLP can read the passages orally to the student. This evaluation then provides a sense of what students understand about textbooks and concepts presented without the confound of decoding ability. As an example, the ITI is applied to *Raptors!* in Box 12.3 on page 542. This book does not have many reading aids to examine, such as tables of content, graphs, or glossary—which can be a point of comment in itself.

The questions in the ITI reveal knowledge processes with the requests to locate, use, and infer information. The final element of the Informal Textbook Inventory, Passage Linguistic Comprehension, is tested through a cloze passage with 10 substantive words deleted throughout the text. To make the task easier, print the possible words and some distracter items above the text. This task can reveal reading strategies as part of a postreading interview. Using the completed cloze task, the student reviews each word with the SLP and explains how it was decided what word should be used. The student's answers indicate whether this was fairly random or involved strategies such as key vocabulary, rereading previous text, making inferences, using prior knowledge, and recognizing passage and sentence structure. Additionally, summarization strategies can be examined, such as:

1. Tell the student you are going to ask him or her to summarize what the passage says. Have the student read or listen to a short paragraph.

2. After reading, pause, look expectantly at the student, then say it is time for the answer. But do not ask for the summary immediately.

3. Instead, ask the student what he or she has done to get ready. What did he or she do while reading? What did he or she do after reading?

4. Then ask for the summary. It is important not to ask for the summary until after the reflection because it may interfere with recall of reading strategies.

Box 12.3

Informal Text Inventory
Applied to *Raptors!* Book

Organization and Structure of Text • Locate • Use	**Give the book to the student to handle.** 1. How do you know what this book is about? 2. What tells you the main topics addressed by the book? Show me where to look. 3. Show me a heading and a subheading. 4. Show me the Foreword or Preface. What is it called here? 5. What is the purpose of this Author's Note?
Basic Comprehension • Comprehend and recall • Use graphical or pictorial aids	**Read the first paragraph in the Dromaeosaurus section.** 1. What does Dromaeosaurus mean? 2. Was this the first or last raptor dinosaur to be discovered? **Read the skull description of the Dromaeosaurus.** 3. How was the broad skull helpful for killing other dinosaurs? 4. For what dinosaur is this skull often mistaken? 5. Why was having two eyes facing forward helpful in seeing? **Direct the student to look at the inside covers.** 6. What does the line tell you? 7. What do the pictures tell you?
Applied Comprehension • Infer and synthesize • Evaluate and apply	1. The author said that having both eyes focused forward allowed 3-dimensional vision. What do you guess is meant by 3-dimensional? 2. On the cover, the author calls raptor dinosaurs "nasty." What does this word imply about these dinosaurs? Is it fair to call animals nasty?

Box 12.3—*Continued*

	Applied Comprehension—*Continued*
	3. Why does the author start by talking about the *Jurassic Park* movie?
	4. Was the information presented in this book dependable? Why do you think so?

Specialized Options
 	
• Comprehend terminology
 	
• Comprehend passage
	Show the student the word *Dromaeosauridae.*
	
	1. Pronounce the scientific name for raptor dinosaur.
	
	Say these words for the student.
	
	2. Break up *Utahraptor* and *Velociraptor* into two scientific parts and tell what each part means.
	
	Show the student the sentences.
	
	3. Choose the best answer for each of these sentences.
	
	   a) Velociraptor was especially long _____ and lightly built for a raptor. (winged, legged, ugly)
	
	   b) It was likely the _____ of the raptor dinosaurs, though not nearly as fast (nor as big and smart) as Jurassic Park makes it out to be. (mean, slowest, fastest)
	
	   c) Velociraptor probably did not run quite as fast as the fastest known dinosaur, the ostrich-like ornithomimids, who ran 25 _____. (times, miles per hour, feet per hour)
	
	   d) It may not have run at all! Velociraptor may have _____ like a kangaroo on its powerful hind legs. (run, had eggs, hopped)
	
	   e) However it moved, it was built to be one of the fastest, smartest, and _____ dinosaurs in the world. (big, friendliest, deadliest)

Source: Manzo et al. (2001)

If students can vocalize their thinking processes, this is informative for both correct and incorrect responses—sometimes correct answers can be arrived at through faulty reasoning and vice versa (Ukrainetz et al., 1998). Assessments that do not reveal the process of getting to an answer cannot accurately and fully assess thinking and comprehension skills. For students who cannot express how they arrived at an answer, this will be part of their intervention plan. Learning to use reading strategies involves making their use conscious and explicit—by the end of the year, students should be much better at expressing how they arrived at their responses.

Any criterion-based assessment is most helpful if there is some sense of how typically achieving students fare, particularly given the generally low text-comprehension proficiency of many typically developing students. Administering the assessment to at least three low-average but succeeding students will provide a level of expectation for students in language intervention.

Setting Intervention Objectives and Goals

This section deals with intervention objectives because a clear awareness of objectives assists in providing repeated opportunities for intense, systematically supported, explicit (RISE) intervention. Objectives for the pure Reciprocal Teaching process are fairly easy to set. There is a clear focus on teaching the four comprehension strategies of predicting, summarizing, questioning, and clarifying. Summarizing and questioning are the most frequent activities. Those two can be selected for progress measurement, in terms of both independent performance and accuracy. The objectives can incorporate levels of difficulty from Bloom's taxonomy. Additional instruction, such as K-W-L[+] or Text Preview, can be used during instruction to support one of those four skills without necessitating an additional objective. The objectives are also taught and assessed in the larger oral debate and research projects.

The following examples illustrate level of skill difficulty and the size of the unit from which the information is extracted. A criterion level of 80 percent accuracy in two consecutive sessions may be used.

Easier:

- John will listen to five paragraphs read aloud from a classroom textbook. After each paragraph, he will independently summarize the information orally to include a main idea and two details.

- John will listen to five paragraphs read aloud from a classroom textbook.

After each paragraph, he will independently formulate oral recall/comprehension questions and answers.

More difficult:

- Bill will use a classroom textbook to independently summarize chapters orally to include a main idea and two details.

- Bill will independently formulate oral analysis and application questions and answers for multiparagraph sections he hears read aloud from a classroom textbook.

During extended projects, it is more difficult to delineate the precise skills being taught beyond summarizing and information comprehension and analysis. Both the oral debate and the research project employ a multiplicity of text comprehension and other language skills. The risk in using such motivating and meaningful material is that the therapeutic element may be lost. Target skills should always be kept in the foreground for SLP and student. This means that the SLP's plans do not just target "comprehension skills," but state precisely which skills are being addressed with RISE.

Four objectives that target specific skills addressed in the research project are presented below. Note that only one of these is a direct comprehension objective. The others address vocabulary and syntax within the context of the research project. The wording on the comprehension objective reflects the purpose of summarizing (i.e., to improve note taking). All the objectives include the discourse context to clearly identify how the skills are being taught and used. In these examples, the criteria are specified within each objective.

- Rosita will independently develop two concept maps and key word searches for research topics introduced in class.

- Using concept maps, Rosita will formulate two sets of research questions to guide topic investigation for projects, with no more than two prompts.

- Rosita will show improved note-taking skills by independently summarizing main idea and details for four of five paragraphs read or heard from research materials.

- Rosita will show increased length and complexity of sentences by including multiple clauses and clausal conjunctions in five sentences during her final oral presentation of her research project.

A limited number of comprehension skills should be selected for therapeutic attention. In the example above, Ross identified four objectives as the explicit skill foci that were common difficulties for all the students involved. The students had many areas of weakness, but only a limited number can be addressed repeatedly and explicitly. Other skills used at the students' independent levels may be ignored (e.g., spelling) or compensated (e.g., the SLP reads passages aloud to avoid word decoding problems). The targeted skills are recognized by both the student and SLP as explicit skill foci. During planning, the SLP identifies in advance the repeated opportunities for practice and learning in each stage of the activity and across activities. These skills then receive scaffolded support aimed at handover and internalization of skills.

Intervention objectives aid in planning and maintaining a consistent therapeutic focus. Even though IDEA 2004 removed the requirement for objectives or benchmarks for most IEPs, SLPs should have a clear sense of intermediate objectives. Grouping and synthesizing the individual objectives can provide informative annual goals. Since IDEA 2004 requires annual goals to be measurable rather than a general statement of a target area (§614[d][B][II][aa]), the IEP goal could describe the contextualized performance and expected performance level, as in the following goals:

- Bill will produce 3 chapter summaries and 5 analysis/application questions for each summary, with a rating of 3 or 4 in each category of the assignment rubric.

- John will complete 2 expository writing projects that use concept maps, research questions, and summaries with 80 percent accuracy; and 2 oral presentations on the projects, with a 3 or 4 rating on the scoring rubric.

Tracking Learning

The two projects described above are extended, busy activities with many component skills and strategies required. They take time, planning, and enthusiasm from the SLP. The challenge for the SLP is to maintain an explicit focus on internalizing skills to increase independence levels in future projects and, more specifically, to keep a focus on providing repeated opportunities for the intervention objectives set for each student. There is a lot for a clinician to orchestrate. However, the rewards are ample. Students are motivated and energetic, even those who are not invested in school.

The library research project is the most recent endeavor for Ross. Ross has carried this project out several times with small groups of middle school students. She embedded all of the intervention objectives for each student within this project and assured repeated opportunities to address each objective. The project took six to eight weeks to accomplish. Ross considered this project her most challenging intervention endeavor to date, primarily because she had to keep track of and teach multiple students at a time, with each progressing at an individual rate. But she also considers it her most rewarding enterprise. Ross reported she was continually astounded at the students' good work ethic, focus, and enthusiasm. The students remembered from session to session exactly what they finished the last time and where they needed to start in the next session. Ross reported their increased capacity for self-regulation when they were motivated and understood the process, with questions from the students such as:

- Can I start my Boolean search on the Internet today because I finished identifying my key words last session?

- I have highlighted the answers to my research questions, so today do I get to start taking notes?

- I have typed my research notes. Now can I start my final product design?

- You said we would present our posters to each other here in this group, but I was wondering if I could present mine in reading class because I think Mrs. Smith and the other students would like to see what I've been working on.

In addition, Ross observed that the students learned from and motivated each other. They guided each other on next steps, cointerpreted found information, and showed interest in others' work. They gave advice to each other, such as asking why the other student highlighted a sentence and which research question it answered.

Ross had used Reciprocal Teaching with the students in the previous year, so they were accustomed to the process. She was able to embed it incidentally within the research project, focusing on the comprehension strategies in mini-lessons with each student. Ross found that the students stopped themselves at words with which they were unfamiliar and asked for definitions—they really wanted to be experts on their topic. She contrasted this with reading in their history textbooks, when they just want to skip over unknown words. The students showed limited progress in determining the main idea and summarizing, especially paraphrasing, but were able to find supporting details to answer their personal research questions–but evidence indicates this is a challenging area even for typically achieving students (Brown & Day, 1983).

Keeping data on intervention objectives helps maintain a therapeutic focus in intervention. In the Reciprocal Teaching lessons, data on accuracy levels can be kept fairly easily. There are "correct" and "incorrect" standards for these four skills, so a percent correct is a reasonable criterion–although "partially correct" and "correct with cues" will also need to be considered. For the Reciprocal Teaching, Ross set up a system in which each student received one point for independently summarizing the main idea, another point for the two required details, and another point for a question. This meant three possible "correct" points when the student was taking a turn as teacher. Every time a student answered a question he or she received a point. In a half-hour session, Ross planned for every student to be teacher-student twice. She counted up the possible points and figured a percentage based on "correct"/"incorrect" marks, with notations for items on which the students received assistance.

For the oral debate and library research projects, determining and tracking individual student progress was much more difficult. Objectives had been set at 80 percent independent accuracy, but the interactive and self-regulated format did not lend itself to correct/incorrect data points. Ross had the final projects to examine, but that did not provide intermediate progress data on intervention goals. She decided that what she really needed to measure was student independence towards meeting IEP objectives within the context of the project. The final student self-evaluation asked students to reflect on their performance of the activity and their individual intervention objectives. Appendix C on page 560 provides a rubric for self-evaluation. Ross also used this Likert-style rating scale for tracking progress on each objective during intervention. Appendix D on page 562 provides an example of a rating form for progress on degree-of-independence, and Appendix E on page 563 explains the meaning of each level of independence. Ross has found that students understand this rating system and tell Ross what number they have earned (e.g., "Mrs. Ross, you should give me a 3 today on summarizing because I only needed to ask for help one time and then I worked independently without stopping during the whole session"). Following the instructions at the top of the form, she calculated percentage accuracy for IEP reporting.

Rubrics (e.g., Appendix C) and scoring systems (e.g., Appendix D) result in quantification (i.e., numbers) that may be needed for IEP formats, but they are also consistent with the contextualized skill approach to intervention. A rubric or rating system guides both provision of support for teaching and evaluation of student performance. It helps the SLP provide explicit attention to particular skills. It also leads both the students and the clinician to be aware of how competence on an objective contributes to success in the larger activity. The biggest challenge is to focus on rating progress on specific individual objectives rather than performance on the overall activity and its steps.

Conclusion

This chapter examined the processes involved in text comprehension. Academic reading and listening involve active engagement with meaningful texts. The skills and strategies occur before reading, such as previewing subheadings and looking for organizing concepts; during reading, such as identifying the main idea and rereading for clarification; and after reading, such as reflecting on what has been learned and relating it to prior experiences. Text comprehension also involves critical thinking skills, which include Bloom's taxonomy and a positive disposition toward learning.

Teaching text comprehension involves cognitive modeling within meaningful texts, in which teachers highlight text structure, illustrate how ideas relate, demonstrate reading strategies, and guide students into using those strategies themselves. There are many helpful ways of teaching text comprehension. Reciprocal teaching is presented as one powerful way of scaffolding students into active reading. Comprehension instruction was demonstrated within three purposeful activities that employ authentic texts: sharing a science book, constructing a library research project, and composing an oral debate.

References

August, D. L., Flavell, J. H., & Clift, R. (1984). Comparison of comprehension monitoring of skilled and less skilled readers. *Reading Research Quarterly, 20,* 39–53.

Aukerman, R. C. (1972). *Reading in the secondary classroom.* New York: McGraw-Hill.

Austen, J. (1957). *Emma.* Boston: Houghton–Mifflin. (Original work published in 1816.)

Baumann, J. F. (1984). Effectiveness of a direct instruction paradigm for teaching main idea comprehension. *Reading Research Quarterly, 20,* 93–108.

Bazerman, C. (1985). Physicists reading physics. *Written Communication, 2,* 3–23.

Beyer, B. K. (1997). *Improving student thinking.* Boston: Allyn and Bacon.

Bloom, B. S. (1994). Reflections on the development and use of the taxonomy. In L. W. Anderson & L. A. Sosniak (Eds.), *Bloom's taxonomy: A forty-year retrospective, 93rd yearbook of the National Society for the Study of Education, Part II* (pp.1–8). Chicago: University of Chicago Press.

Bloom, B. S., Engelhart, M. D., Furst, E. J., Hill, W. H., & Krathwohl, D. R. (1956). *Taxonomy of education objectives: Handbook 1, Cognitive domain.* New York: David McKay.

Brown, A. L., & Day, J. D. (1983). Macrorules for summarizing texts: The development of expertise. *Journal of Verbal Learning and Verbal Behavior, 22,* 1–14.

Carr, E. M., & Ogle, D. M. (1987). K-W-L Plus: A strategy for comprehension and summarization. *Journal of Reading, 30,* 626–631.

Day, J. D. (1980). *Training summarization skills: A comparison of teaching methods.* Unpublished doctoral dissertation, University of Illinois, Urbana-Champaign.

Day, J. D. (1986). Teaching summarization skills: Influence of student ability and strategy difficulty. *Cognition and Instruction, 3,* 193–210.

DiCecco, V. M, & Gleason, M. M. (2002). Using graphic organizers to attain relational knowledge from expository text. *Journal of Learning Disabilities 35,* 306–320.

Ennis, R. (1985). A logical basis for measuring critical thinking skills. *Educational Leadership, 43*(2), 46.

Furst, E. J. (1994). Bloom's taxonomy: Philosophical and educational issues. In L. W. Anderson & L. A. Sosniak (Eds.), *Bloom's taxonomy: A forty-year retrospective, 93rd Yearbook of the National Society for the Study of Education, Part II* (pp.28–40). Chicago: University of Chicago Press.

Fry, E. B. (1977). *Elementary reading instruction.* New York: McGraw-Hill.

Garner, R., & Reis, R. (1981). Monitoring and resolving comprehension obstacles: An investigation of spontaneous text lookbacks among upper-grade good and poor readers' comprehension. *Reading Research Quarterly, 16,* 569–582.

Hiebert, E. H. (2003). *QuickReads: A research-based fluency program.* Parsippany, NJ: Pearson.

Hiebert, E. H. (in press). The effects of text difficulty on second graders' fluency development. *Reading Psychology.*

Idol, L. (1987). Group story mapping: A comprehension strategy for both skilled and unskilled readers. *Journal of Learning Disabilities, 20,* 196–205.

Idol, L., & Croll, V. J. (1987). The effects of training in story mapping procedures on the reading comprehension of poor readers. *Learning Disability Quarterly, 10,* 214–230.

Individuals with Disabilities Education Improvement Act of 2004 (IDEA), 20 U.S.C. §1400 *et seq.* (2004).

Johnson, M. S., Kress, R. A., & Pikulski, J. J. (1987). *Informal reading inventories.* Newark, DE: International Reading Association.

King, C. M., & Parent Johnson, L. M. (1999). Constructing meaning via reciprocal teaching. *Reading Research and Instruction, 38,* 169–186.

Kletzian, S. B. (1991). Strategy use by good and poor comprehenders reading expository text of differing levels. *Reading Research Quarterly, 25,* 67–86.

Kreitzer, A. E., & Madaus, G. F. (1994). Empirical investigations of the hierarchical structure of the taxonomy. In L. W. Anderson & L. A. Sosniak (Eds.), *Bloom's taxonomy: A forty-year retrospective, 93rd yearbook of the National Society for the Study of Education, Part II* (pp. 64–81). Chicago: University of Chicago Press.

Lederer, J. M. (2000). Reciprocal teaching of social studies in inclusive elementary classrooms. *Journal of Learning Disabilities, 33,* 91–106.

Lessem, D. (1996). *Raptors!* Boston: Little, Brown.

Manzo, A. V. (1969). The ReQuest procedure. *Journal of Reading, 13,* 123–126.

Manzo, A. V. (1980). Three "universal" strategies in content area reading and language. *Journal of Reading, 24,* 146–149.

Manzo, A. V., & Casale, U. P. (1985). Listen-read-discuss: A content reading heuristic. *Journal of Reading 28,* 732–734.

Manzo, A. V., Manzo, U. C., & Estes, T. H. (2001). *Content area literacy: Interactive teaching for active learning* (3rd ed.). New York: Wiley.

McNeil, J., & Donant, L. (1982). Summarization strategy for improving reading comprehension. In J. A. Niles & L. A. Harris (Eds.), *New inquiries in reading research and instruction* (pp. 215–219). Rochester, NY: National Reading Conference.

Palincsar, A. S. (1986). The role of dialogue in providing scaffolded instruction. *Educational Psychologist, 21,* 73–98.

Palincsar, A. S., & Brown, A. L. (1984). Reciprocal teaching of comprehension-fostering and comprehension-monitoring activities. *Cognition and Instruction, 1,* 117–175.

Palincsar, A. S., Brown, A. L., & Martin, S. M. (1987). Peer interaction in reading comprehension monitoring activities. *Cognition and Instruction, 1,* 117–175.

Palincsar, A. M., David, Y., & Brown, A. (1989). *Using reciprocal teaching in the classroom: A guide for teachers.* Unpublished manuscript.

Paris, S. G., Lipson, M., & Wixson, K. (1983). Becoming a strategic reader. *Contemporary Educational Psychology, 8,* 293–316.

Paris, S. G., Wasik, B. A., & Turner, J. C. (1991). The development of strategic readers. In R. Barr, M. L. Kamil, P. B. Mosenthal, & P. D. Pearson (Eds.), *Handbook of Reading Research, Vol. II* (pp. 609–640). New York: Longman.

Pearson, P. D., & Fielding, L., (1991). Comprehension instruction. In R. Barr, M. L. Kamil, P. B. Mosenthal, & P. D. Pearson (Eds.), *Handbook of Reading Research, Vol. II* (pp. 815–860). New York: Longman.

Rinehart, S. D., Stahl, S. A., & Erickson, L. G. (1986). Some effects of summarization training on reading and studying. *Reading Research Quarterly, 21,* 422–436.

Rohwer Jr., W. D., & Sloane, K. (1994). Psychological perspectives. In L. W. Anderson & L. A. Sosniak (Eds.), *Bloom's taxonomy: A forty-year retrospective, 93rd yearbook of the National Society for the Study of Education, Part II* (pp. 41–81). Chicago: University of Chicago Press.

Scott, C. M. (1995). A discourse approach to syntax teaching. In D. F. Tibbits (Ed.), *Language intervention: Beyond the primary grades* (pp. 435–463). Austin, TX: Pro-Ed.

Snow, C. (2002). *Reading for understanding: Toward an R&D program in reading comprehension.* Santa Monica, CA: Rand.

Speece, D. L., MacDonald, V., Kilsheimer, L., & Krist, J. (1997). Research to practice: Preservice teachers reflect on reciprocal teaching. *Learning Disabilities Research & Practice, 12,* 177–187.

Stanovich, K. E. (1986). Matthew effects in reading: Some consequences of individual differences in the acquisition of literacy. *Reading Research Quarterly, 21,* 360–407.

Stanovich, K. E. (2000). *Progress in understanding reading.* New York: Guilford.

Taylor, B. M. (1980). Children's memory for expository text after reading. *Reading Research Quarterly 15,* 399–411.

Taylor, B. M., & Beach, R. W. (1984). The effects of text structure instruction in middle-grade students' comprehension and production of expository texts. *Reading Research Quarterly, 19,* 134–146.

Tierney, R. J., & Readance, J. E. (2000). *Reading strategies and practices: A compendium.* Boston: Allyn and Bacon.

Ukrainetz, T. A. (1998). Beyond Vygotsky: What Soviet activity theory offers naturalistic language intervention. *Journal of Speech-Language Pathology and Audiology, 22,* 122–133.

Ukrainetz, T. A., Shippen, D., & Roswell, R. (1998). Who's afraid of the big bad wolf? A critical thinking teaching unit. *Rocky Mountain Journal of Communication Disorders, 12,* 27–36.

Ukrainetz, T. A., & Trujillo, A. (1999). "You know, I just don't know what else you'd do?" Five SLPs' perspectives on children's literature in speech-language intervention. *Contemporary Issues in Communication Sciences and Disorders, 26,* 35–48.

VanCleave, J. (1996). *202 oozing, bubbling, dripping, and bouncing experiments.* New York: Wiley.

van Dijk, T. A., & Kintsch, W. (1978). Cognitive psychology and discourse: Recalling and summarizing stories. In W. U. Dressler (Ed.), *Current trends in text linguistics* (pp. 61–80). New York: de Gruyter.

Vygotsky, L S. (1978). *Mind in society: The development of higher psychological processes.* Cambridge, MA: Harvard University Press.

Appendix A: Sample Scaffolding Progression during Reciprocal Teaching

1. Introduction to Strategies

SLP: You are going to be learning how to understand what you hear and read better. You are going to become *active readers*. We are going to practice four reading strategies that we should all use when we read school material. (List and explain each strategy.)

2. SLP Models the Questions, Answers, and How to Find Them

What is a Raptor? When many of us think of raptors, the vicious human-size villains of the book and movie Jurassic Park leap to mind. In the words of a Jurassic Park guard, raptors are "as smart as chimpanzees and as fast as cheetahs." But the book and film are fiction. Although it is based on science, Jurassic Park makes many dramatic exaggerations about dinosaurs. The real raptor dinosaurs were no smarter than ostriches and no faster than poodles. Some raptors were also smaller than poodles. But other kinds of raptors, which have just recently been discovered, were as big as trucks. (Lessem, 1996, p. 6)

Summarize

SLP: This passage is about how smart and fast raptors are depicted in the movies and how that isn't really true. Let's underline those parts.

Question

SLP: What question can we ask about this paragraph? How big are raptors? Yes, that's what I wonder. Also, how smart are raptors? Let's read it again. The answers aren't here. [group reads passage again]

Clarify

SLP: I don't understand about what chimpanzees and cheetahs have to do with raptors. I'm lost. Let's go back and see. It says, "as smart as chimpanzees." What does that mean? Does that mean the raptor is a chimpanzee?

Predict

SLP: I predict that the next paragraph will tell us what raptors are really like. Let's keep reading.

3. Student Turn, with Heavy Support

The first raptor fossils ever found were discovered more than 80 years ago. But not many raptors have been found since. Raptor skeletons are rare. In any environment, meat-eaters are never as common as plant-eaters, because meat-eaters have a less-abundant food supply. And the bones of raptor dinosaurs, like those of other small dinosaurs, were more likely to be scattered by wind and water than were the heavy bones of larger dinosaurs. (Lessem, 1996, p. 6)

Summarize

SLP: Now one of you tell us what this is about?

Students: Raptor bones were blown away.

SLP: Yes, raptor bones were blown away. That's a detail. Why does that matter?

Students: [silence]

SLP: Let's look. Usually the most important idea is at the beginning of the paragraph. This first sentence says bones were found 80 years ago, a long time ago. Is that what the paragraph is about? No. What else do they say. Let's listen again. [reads again] What do you hear that is a main idea?

Students: Hardly any raptors have been found.

SLP: Yes, why have hardly any been found? Those are details.

Students: Hardly any bones. Hardly any meat-eaters. Wind and water made them go away. Their bones weren't heavy.

SLP: There is a lot in this paragraph. Those are all true. They all tell us what? They tell us why scientists have hardly found any. This paragraph is about why raptor bones are hard to find.

Question

SLP: How about a question, what can you ask?

Students: [silence]

SLP:	Choose a sentence and make a question about it, like on a test.
Students:	[points to short third sentence and reads] Raptor skeletons are rare.
SLP:	Ask a question that this sentence answers about how it is to find skeletons. Why…
Bonnie:	Why are raptor skeletons rare?
SLP:	Joe, can you answer Bonnie's question?
Joe:	There are hardly any skeletons.
SLP:	Yes, skeletons are rare [points to the word], so they are hard to find.
Students:	And they blow away because they are light.
SLP:	Yes, that is another reason they are hard to find. Any other reasons? [points to pertinent sentence]
Students:	Because meat-eaters are never as common as raptors.
SLP:	Wait a minute, think about that. Bonnie, what is the problem?
Bonnie:	Raptors are meat-eaters.
SLP:	Joe, answer again. Why are the skeletons rare?
Joe:	Because meat-eaters are never as common as plant-eaters. And raptors are meat-eaters.
SLP:	Good thinking. Joe asked a question, How hard is it to find skeletons? The answer was, "Difficult, because they are rare." Then you gave two answers to why they are rare.
Students:	There were hardly any meat-eaters and the bones were light and get blown away.

Clarify and Predict

[continuing heavy support and guidance]

4. Student Turn, with Moderate Support

Scientists are still trying to determine what raptors are, where they came from, and what became of them. Spectacular new fossil finds, discovered only in the past few years, have forced scientists to change many of their ideas about how raptors looked and acted. (Lessem, 1996, p. 6)

Summarize

SLP: Now one of you start this. What do you ask first? [circles entire paragraph]

Joe: What's this about?

Sally: Scientists.

SLP: Scientists are doing what? Explain better.

Sally: Finding new stuff about raptors.

SLP: Yes, Joe asked for the main idea. Scientists are discovering new facts about raptors. There are only two sentences in this paragraph, but they are long, with lots of parts. [underlines as says *wh* words] What, where, what became? Scientists are finding new information about raptors.

Question

SLP: How about a question, what can you ask?

Students: About the scientists.

SLP: Ask about the scientists. Bonnie, you be the teacher.

Bonnie: What made scientists change their minds, Joe?

SLP: [points to relevant sentence]

Joe: Spectacular [stretches arms out and exaggerates word] new fossil finds.

SLP: Yes, spectacular!

Clarify

Sally: I don't understand *spectacular*.

SLP: OK, you ask someone to clarify that word.

Sally: Clarify *spectacular*, Joe.

Joe: It means fantastic.

Predict

Bonnie: Now I get to ask someone to predict. Joe, what do you predict?

Joe: I predict that the book will say why the find was spectacular.

SLP: I bet you are right. *Spectacular* is a wonderful word, isn't it. Let's all say it a few times. You could surprise your parents with that word.

5. Student Attempt, with Light Support

Not every raptor is a raptor dinosaur. Confused? The word raptor literally means thief. It's a name scientists usually use to describe birds of prey, such as hawks and eagles. Paleontologists don't use the name raptor to describe the group to which these little dinosaurs belong. They call them the Dromaeosauridae (DROH-me-uh-SORE-ih-day). Dromaeosauridae are all small- to medium-size meat-eaters that lived during the last of the three dinosaur periods, the Cretaceous, which lasted from 144 million to 65 million years ago. (Lessem, 1996, p. 6)

Summarize

SLP:	Bonnie, you be the teacher.
Bonnie:	Joe, what is the summary of this paragraph?
Joe:	Scientists call raptor dinosaurs Dromo-somethings, not raptors. Raptors are birds of prey like eagles.
SLP:	That's a good summary. Let's all practice saying that new long word. DROH-me-uh-SORE-ih-day.

Question

SLP:	Next is a question. What would you like to ask the students about Dromaeosauridae?
Bonnie:	Sally, why do we call them raptors if scientists don't?
SLP:	Good question. I wonder that too. What's the answer? Let's look.
Sally:	The answer isn't here.
SLP:	No, it isn't. We need to keep reading.

Clarify

Bonnie:	We need to think about if anything is confusing.
SLP:	Yes, we need to clarify.
Joe:	The book didn't tell us why the find was spectacular!
SLP:	You are right. The author just assumed we knew why. The author was not clear.

Predict

SLP:	Last strategy.
Students:	Prediction.
Bonnie:	Joe, what is your prediction?
Joe:	I don't know.
Bonnie:	Look at the last sentence, that is usually a clue. "So what makes a dinosaur a true raptor, a member of the Dromaeosauridae?"
Joe:	The book will tell us what is a true raptor, not just a fake one.
SLP:	Good questioning and answering. You all summarized, questioned, clarified, and predicted. You hardly needed me at all. You are being *active readers*.

Appendix B: Speaking Rubric for Oral Presentation

Category	4	3	2	1	Comments
Speaks Clearly	Speaks clearly and distinctly, no pronunciation errors.	Speaks clearly and distinctly, but a few word errors.	Sometimes mumbles or makes word errors that affect understanding.	Often mumbles or cannot be understood.	
Posture	Stands up straight, relaxed and confident.	Stands up straight, but not relaxed.	Wiggles or slouches some of the time.	Wiggles or slouches most of the time.	
Eye Contact	Establishes eye contact with everyone in the room.	Establishes eye contact most of the time.	Establishes eye contact occasionally.	Does not establish eye contact.	
Voice	**Pitch** sometimes does not fit content.	**Pitch** sometimes does not fit content.	**Pitch** is monotone.	**Pitch** is monotone.	
	Volume is loud enough almost all the time.	**Volume** is loud enough almost all the time.	**Volume** is loud enough most of the time.	**Volume** is often too soft.	
	Pauses used effectively at least once.	**Pauses** used effectively at least once.	**Pauses** not effective in improving meaning.	**Pauses** not intentional or appropriate.	
Preparation Telling, not reading	Fluent, presentation shows preparation was rehearsed.	Stilted read, presentation needs a few more rehearsals.	Stilted and awkward, presentation clearly needs more rehearsals.	Difficulty presenting own material; not prepared.	

Appendix C: Final Student Self-Evaluation

Name_____

Grade _____   Date_____

My topic was _____

This is my _____ first _____ second _____ third research project

1. Rate your progress.

Task	Amount of Help Needed			
	1￼ A Lot	2￼ Quite a Bit	3￼ A Little	4￼ Independent
Identify Topic				
Identify Research Questions				
Identify Key Words				
Locate Good Sources				
Read Information and Find Answers				
Take Notes from Sources				
Organize Info for Poster				
Construct Bibliography				
Speak and Use Visuals in Presentation				

B. Rate your product.

My learning objectives for this project were:

a) _____

b) _____

c) _____

I improved on my objectives in the following ways:

a) _____

b) _____

c) _____

I also learned _____.

I still need to improve:

_____

_____

Appendix D: Progress toward Independence on Objectives Form

Before the session: Write the date, task, and IEP objective into a row.

During the session: Place a tally mark in a numbered column under Opportunity Ratings for each student opportunity to perform the objective. Use the Independent Work Rating Rubric to determine the correct column placement (i.e., rating) for each opportunity.

After the session: Add the value of each tally (4, 3, 2, 1) to determine the Tally Total. Determine the Possible Total by multiplying the number of opportunities by 4. Calculate the Percentage Accurate by dividing the Tally Total by the Possible Total.

Date	Task	IEP Objective	Opportunity Ratings				Tally Total	Possible Total	% Accurate
			4	3	2	1			

Appendix E:
Independent Work Rating Rubric

Rating	Rubric
1	Constant guidance is required to achieve the desired performance level or level is outside student's learning zone even with assistance, and so expectations have been lowered
2	A considerable amount of guidance is required, but the student sometimes achieves the desired performance level independently
3	Some guidance is needed, but the student often achieves the desired performance level independently
4	No guidance is required, student achieves the desired performance level independently

Chapter 13

Assisting Students in Becoming Self-Regulated Writers

Anthony S. Bashir and Bonnie D. Singer

Introduction

> The key, of course, is to define our goals, our results, in a way
> that is simple enough to grasp easily, and specific enough to
> be actionable. (Lencioni, 2002, p. 78)

This seems so simple, so self-evident. But for many students with learning disabilities, such task management is far from easy, as this high school student, Jack, expresses:

> Even if I know what I have to do, I don't always know how to
> do it or get there. It's just too much for me to think about and
> do. I get so overwhelmed and feel so lost, I just walk away or
> put it off until it's too late.

How very common it is for students like Jack to speak this way about completing their assignments. We hear these comments often from students when they are given an assignment that requires them to internally control, monitor, and select behaviors that will help them achieve a specific goal (e.g., write an essay, read a social studies text, do an experiment, complete a math problem, or design a project). These students try but are defeated. They seem unable to understand the task and cannot set a clear goal for the assignment. They fail to access and use the strategies and abilities needed for reaching their goal. Their chosen approach is not effective or efficient given the task at hand. They lose the motivation necessary to stay with the work and believe that they do not have what it takes to succeed. They find themselves in a dangerous cycle of perceived helplessness. These students present a considerable challenge to educators, families, and themselves.

In school, much of students' efforts are expected to be self-directed and goal-oriented. As is illustrated by Westby in Chapter 8, this transition to independence occurs gradually during the elementary grades. However, by middle school, students are expected to take a degree of partnership in the learning process, regulating and sustaining their learning. Over time, the average student learns and internalizes the processes needed for planning and setting attainable goals as well as selecting and applying strategies and taking actions that allow them to complete a task successfully (Bronson, 2000). Throughout their academic activities, with teacher guidance (and some external motivation such as grades and rewards), students maintain and facilitate their motivation, enhance their sense of self-efficacy, and regulate the range of feelings and emotions they experience during the course of their work. However, students like Jack do not follow this developmental course and, thus, lack the ability to regulate their own learning.

No single factor explains the difficulties these students encounter in setting and achieving their goals, but it is clear that they are not self-regulated learners, and they lack executive functions necessary for efficient learning. Cognitive, linguistic, metacognitive, affective, and motivational factors interact to constrain their performance. The influence of each of these factors varies across different learning contexts and demands (e.g., from writing a journal entry to developing a research paper, from participating in a book discussion group to presenting a response to an argument, from reading a novel to understanding a social studies text), but all pose problems for these students.

The purpose of this chapter is to consider self-regulated learning and executive functioning as they relate to contextually based language intervention. First, we examine these concepts and their influence on learning. We then explore the importance of accounting for these concepts within language intervention. In doing so, we present a strategic written language intervention approach that specifically supports students who have language-learning disabilities, executive function disorders, and/or self-regulatory difficulties.

Self-Regulated Learning: Knowing What to Do When and How

Teachers and speech-language pathologists (SLPs) share a common goal for their students, namely that they become independent and self-regulated learners. Buttrill, Nizawa, Biemer, Takahashi, and Hearn (1989) reported, from teacher surveys and classroom observations, that the most frequent requirement of older students is to work independently. Teachers expect students to organize their time, complete assignments, do independent seatwork, and study on their own at home. In addition, they must be able to listen and take independent notes from lectures, the most common form of teacher communication. Whether in intervention or classroom settings, there is the hope that students will become learners capable of making wise choices that support their academic achievement and personal sense of success.

General Definition

A number of theoretical perspectives explain self-regulated learning. These perspectives vary widely from each other and include operant theory, phenomenological points of view, social cognitive theory, information processing approaches, volitional and Vygotskian views, and constructivist orientations

(Zimmerman & Schunk, 2001). Such a range of perspectives often results in different explanations of what constitutes a self-regulated learner (e.g., motivation, key processes, self-awareness).

Self-regulated learning is not yet clearly differentiated from such terms as self-control, self-management, self-change, and self-directed behavior (Creer, 2000; Zeider, Boekaerts, & Pintrich, 2000) or from metacognition, volition, self-monitoring, and planning (De Corte, Verschaffel, & Op't Eynde, 2002; Demetriou, 2002). Zimmerman (2002) points out that self-regulation for learning is "not a mental ability or an academic performance skill" (p. 65) per se. He notes that self-regulation is a proactive, self-directed process in which students "transform their mental abilities into academic skills" (p. 65). Pintrich (2000) adds that self-regulated students are "active constructive meaning makers as they go about tasks" (p. 452.). Accordingly, self-regulated learners are metacognitively, motivationally, and behaviorally active participants in their own learning processes (Zimmerman, 1986). Self-regulated learning, therefore, "refers to self-generated thoughts, feelings, and actions that are planned and systematically adapted as needed to affect one's learning and motivation" (Schunk & Ertmer, 2000, p. 631).

Components of Self-Regulated Learning

Pintrich (2000), Puustinen and Pulkkinen (2001), and Zimmerman (1994, 2001) point out that, across different perspectives, there are common elements that define self-regulated learners. It is generally agreed that self-regulated learners engage in the following characteristic behaviors.

- **Establish Attainable Goals**—Self-regulated learners set attainable goals and are aware of the specific processes that can ease and improve their achievement of these goals. As such, self-regulated learners are proactive and internally directed. They invoke and manage the thoughts, feelings, and actions necessary for supporting goal attainment.

- **Use Effective Strategies to Achieve Goals**—Self-regulated learners use effective, task-specific learning strategies. Weinstein and Mayer (1986) suggest that effective strategy use is associated with product (or outcome) goals (e.g., use a mnemonic device, decode a word, use conversational strategies) and with process goals (e.g., planning and organizing a task, managing time, monitoring and managing feelings and attitudes). Successful academic outcomes are associated with the use of different strategies that are orchestrated in a smooth, flexible, and integrated manner. Indeed, work on specific metacognitive strategies is shown to facilitate, for example, reading comprehension (Pressley, 1998; Pressley, et al., 1992) and composing (De La Paz & Graham, 2002; Graham & Harris, 1993; Troia & Graham, 2002). This is especially true when students are taught within meaningful contexts that provide them with an understanding of what a strategy is and how, when, and why to use it to facilitate their academic performance.

- **Self-Monitor and Evaluate**—Self-regulated learners monitor and evaluate their academic work. They use self-appraisal and feedback from others to determine the degree to which a given approach supports them with achieving their goals. New realizations about themselves as learners and doers arise from their attention to and use of internal and external feedback.

- **Maintain Motivation**—Self-regulated learners are motivated to resolve problems and complete academic tasks. Theoretical perspectives differ with respect to understanding motivation and its origins. For some, motivation is a reinforced outcome of task accomplishment (operant perspectives), while for others motivation emerges from the development of self-efficacy and the continued use of regulatory processes to attain goals (social-cognitive perspectives). In addition, motivation also has its basis in how students positively or negatively regard themselves as learners (attributional processes). Across all theories of self-regulated learning, the motivation to succeed is a driving force behind everything a student does.

- **Use Supports**—Self-regulated learners are sensitive to and use social supports effectively. Newman (1994) indicates that self-regulated learners seek assistance from those around them who can help them achieve their goals. Models and mentors lead them gradually to incorporate the regulatory processes essential within a given academic domain.

- **Mediate Performance with Language**—Self-regulated learners use language as a major mediating process that internally guides them toward successful task completion. From adults, students learn what to say to themselves to regulate their own thinking and guide their participation in academic activities (Englert & Dunsmore, 2004; Wertsch, 1998). Differing theoretical perspectives all share the notion that self-regulated learners are actively and internally engaged.

In summary, self-regulated learners are proactive in the learning process and in accomplishing their academic goals. To achieve their goals, students act intentionally (i.e., in a manner that has purpose and direction) and in so doing "attempt to monitor, regulate, and control their cognition, motivation, and behavior, guided and constrained by their goals and the contextual features in the environment" (Pintrich, 2000, p. 453).

Executive Functions: The Central Supervisory System

General Definition

The key components of self-regulated learning are often confused with aspects of executive functioning. However, these terms do in fact refer to distinct, yet complementary, concepts. At the most basic level, the term *executive functions* encompasses a range of control processes necessary to carry out purposeful and goal-directed behavior that students self-regulate. While executive functions are defined differently across disciplines, several processes and associated neurological constructs are generally agreed upon. Stuss and Alexander (2000) argue that there is no single executive function (i.e., no single process that defines executive functioning). Rather, executive functions are a *collection* of distinct but related processes that are activated when one must control behavior within novel contexts that evoke competing responses (Denckla, 1996; Hayes, Gifford, & Ruckstuhl, 1996; Lezak, 1995; Pennington & Ozonoff, 1996; Stuss & Alexander; Stuss & Benson, 1986). Accordingly, executive functions interact to serve as a supervisory system for behavior (Shallice, 1988).

Executive Function Components

Though real differences exist about the components of executive functioning, the following are generally accepted to be components (Barkley, 1995, 1997; Eslinger, 1996; Pennington, Bennetto, McAleer, & Roberts, 1996; Pennington & Ozonoff, 1996; Roberts & Pennington, 1996; Stuss & Alexander, 2000):

- **Inhibition**—Inhibitory processes are at the heart of the executive functioning. In the face of a novel task, students must inhibit prepotent (i.e., incorrect) responses in order to determine the correct course of action. Irrelevant thoughts, comments, and behaviors must be inhibited so that an effective response can occur. Inhibition, then, supports one's ability to maintain attention to a task.

- **Working Memory**—To respond to a new task, students must hold their ultimate goal in mind long enough to choose what they must do or say to reach that goal successfully (Barkley, 1997; Roberts & Pennington, 1996). This requires them to remember and, in the moment, process information needed to complete the task (e.g., remember facts and information while writing a paragraph; recall and organize thoughts simultaneously to develop an argument). Working memory, then, allows the student to maintain a "mental set" while engaging hindsight (i.e., what have I done so far?) and foresight (i.e., what do I need to do next to get to my goal?) in the service of completing a task (Barkley). These processes are fundamental to a student's ability to estimate how much time and work will be necessary to reach academic goals.

- **Plan and Organize**—As Scholnick and Friedman (1993) note, planning involves "the construction of an effective way to meet a future goal" (p. 145). Planning and organizing are intricately related processes and are central to completing any task. Allen's (2001) natural planning model suggests that planning first requires students to envision *what* needs to be done (e.g., write a five paragraph essay). Comparing their vision of something that has yet to happen with what is happening at that moment generates cognitive dissonance, which the student resolves by brainstorming numerous options for what they might need to do (e.g., look at the last essay I wrote, go to the library, talk to my teacher, make an outline). This begins to move students from planning *what* to do to organizing *how* they will do it. In order to organize, students must select the action steps they need to take to complete a task and sequence those actions so that they ultimately achieve their envisioned goal. The ability to plan and organize improves with development; not all components of planning and organization develop in synchrony (Bronson, 2000; Scholnick & Friedman).

- **Manage Affect**—All learners bring a memory of past experiences with them to novel tasks. Prior success creates a "mental template" for how to accomplish a new, but similar, task (Helmus, 2004). Also, prior success creates a positive or negative outlook on one's ability to effectively meet new, but similar, task demands. For example, when Jack sits to write an essay, he immediately recalls the difficulty he always has with writing. This then leads him to feel anxious in the face of a new writing assignment, which limits his ability to effectively engage his executive functions. Alternatively, Jack, recalling his prior success with writing, may approach a newly assigned essay with confidence.

At its core, then, the term *executive functions* refers to a set of supervisory processes that overarch "all contexts and content domains" (Denckla & Reader, 1993, p. 433). These processes allow one to hold a goal in mind in order to plan, organize, and perform a novel task while inhibiting intrusions and diversions. As a supervisory system, executive functions are "the sum of the processes recruited at any moment, for any task" (Stuss & Alexander, 2000; p. 296). Collectively, these processes support one's ability to prepare, act, and sustain attention to a task long enough to complete it. Executive functions develop through childhood into adulthood with noticeable advances around the age of 10, in mid-adolescence, and in the 20s (Anderson, Anderson, Northam, Jacobs, & Catroppa 2001; Denckla, 1996; Denckla & Reader, 1993; Klenberg, Korkman, & Lahti-Nuuttila, 2001).

Most attribute executive functioning to cortical structures in the frontal and prefrontal lobes, subcortical structures, and structures in the limbic system (Denckla, 1996; Helmus, 2004; Lesaca, 2001; Pennington & Ozonoff, 1996; Roberts & Pennington, 1996; Stuss, 1992). Executive function disorders can arise from disruptions in neural networks rather than one brain region (Stuss; Stuss & Alexander, 2000). Executive functions are distinct from domain-specific processes, such as sensation, perception, and many aspects of language and memory (Pennington & Ozonoff). By virtue of their neurological connections to frontal and subcortical structures, language and executive functions influence and constrain one another. For example, language disorders can degrade the degree to which inner speech guides planning and control of behavior (Pennington & Ozonoff; Stuss & Alexander; Vygotsky, 1962). As well, executive function disorders can degrade one's ability to plan and organize oral and written language as well as use strategies to support language processing within relevant contexts (Singer & Bashir, 1999).

Variation in the complexity of a given task can alter the interaction between executive and language systems, thereby influencing performance (Singer & Bashir, 1999; Stuss & Alexander, 2000). Additionally, one's memory of previous failures (e.g., with writing, explaining, studying) can lead to anticipatory anxiety in the face of similar tasks, which then degrades one's ability to mindfully approach them using specific strategies that will lead to success (Helmus, 2004).

Executive Function and Self-Regulation: Subtle Distinctions

The difficulty differentiating executive functions and self-regulation arises in part due to the lack of agreement on what exactly constitutes the two activities and in part due to the different theoretical perspectives from which these terms have emerged (Stuss & Alexander, 2000). While this may be a matter of semantics for some, it does contribute significantly to the different understanding of what constitutes executive functioning and, thereby, clouds both assessment and intervention. The result is a blurring of the distinctions between executive functions and self-regulated learning. With this comes a loss of the subtle, yet unique, contributions each makes when students must act in deliberate and intentional ways (e.g., write a term paper).

In this chapter, we see executive functions as distinct from, but central to and supportive of, self-regulated learning. Table 13.1 on page 574 presents the core components of executive functions and self-regulation. As used in this paper, then, executive functions are the processes invoked in the face of a novel and complex task. At their fundamental level, executive functions are directly involved with planning, organization, attention, inhibition, and working memory (Denckla, 1996). These processes are influenced by long term memory (of success and failure), which is tied to one's emotional history within any given task. As such, executive functions are basic to allowing for goal attainment and the emotional set that influences success with intentional action (Helmus, 2004).

In contrast, we see self-regulation for learning as characterized by students' proactive engagement with their own learning success. Self-regulated learners are aware of how and when to use specific strategies and see these as useful for completing a specific academic goal. Consequently, their process is an active process, and they monitor the effectiveness of the methods and strategies they employ for learning. Students use feedback from their own experiences as well as from teachers, therapists, and peers to develop, shape, and adapt their behavior. For this to happen, students must be self-reflective, which is essential for developing and refining self-knowing and self-valuing. This leads, in turn, to overt changes in behaviors and the timely use of strategies within academic tasks. Finally, students are motivated to stay with a task in spite of its challenges. They select and use the skills and strategies necessary for success. In addition, they monitor their performance as they work toward a goal. Success in reaching that goal fuels, once again, motivation and further intentional action.

Characteristics and Components of
Table 13.1   **Self-Regulation and Executive Functions**

Self-Regulation for Learning	Executive Functions
Establish attainable goals.	Inhibit incorrect responses in the face of a novel, complex task.
Use effective strategies to achieve academic goals.	Engage working memory to hold plans and action sequences in mind long enough to execute a task.
Self-monitor and self-evaluate performance.	Plan task approach and behavior for completing the task.
Maintain motivation to achieve goals.	Organize and sequence behaviors needed for task completion.
Use social and environmental supports proactively.	Maintain mental set and attention while performing a task.
Mediate performance with language.	Manage affective responses associated with recall of prior success or failure with a given task.

Supporting Self-Regulation and Executive Functions within Intervention

We encounter students who are discouraged about learning due to their seeming inability to initiate and apply processes that allow them to control their learning and learning outcomes. The difficulties that they encounter are not explained solely on the basis of their language disorders or attention deficits (Singer & Bashir, 1999). These students hold negative beliefs about their ability to understand and gain control over their school performance. They have difficulty planning; organizing their behavior; directing and sustaining their attention; and remembering what they want to do long enough to get it done without getting distracted or pulled off task.

Happily for these students, well-designed instruction can accommodate and support the development of self-regulated learning and executive functions across different situations. For example, individuals with chronic illnesses (e.g., asthma, arthritis, diabetes) can self-manage and self-regulate their care (Creer, 2000; Zimmerman, Bonner, Evans, & Mellins, 1999). In addition, students can learn to use strategies to enhance performance in many academic domains, such as mathematics, reading comprehension, and writing (Dawson & Guare, 2004; Harris & Graham, 1996; Marlowe, 2000; Pressley, 1998; Singer & Bashir, 2004a; Westby, 2004; Zimmerman, Bonner, & Kovach, 1996). The following two studies demonstrate that it is possible to support executive control and self-regulated learning. These have important benefits for self-efficacy, strategy learning, and effective communication.

Cleary and Zimmerman (2004) developed the *self-regulation empowerment program* (SREP) as a means of helping students develop self-motivational beliefs and use academic strategies. The SREP uses microanalysis of behavior as a diagnostic method. For example, authentic interviews assess students' attitudes toward themselves as learners and determine specific behaviors associated with goal setting and achievement. In addition, the approach engages students in teaching strategies directly through the use of cognitive modeling, coaching, and structured practice.

Cleary and Zimmerman (2004) present the case of Anna who struggles in science and mathematics with goal setting, self-efficacy, the use of effective strategies, and self-reflection. Using the assessment and intervention approach of the SREP, Cleary and Zimmerman demonstrate that Anna (and other students) can become a self-directed problem solver by becoming proactive in goal setting, selecting effective approaches to the task at hand, and reflecting on her performance and choices as a means for adjusting and elaborating her behaviors. Cleary and Zimmerman demonstrate that it is possible to enhance students' beliefs about themselves as learners and teach them effective strategies to address the academic content or task-specific challenges presented in school.

Similarly, Singer and Bashir (1999) explored the reciprocal influence of executive functions and self-regulation on language production. Using assessment information from standardized tests and interviews that identified challenging communication tasks and contexts, Singer and Bashir developed a systematic approach to treating an adolescent, George, with language production deficits.

This approach was designed to address the executive and regulatory problems he had in addition to his communication disorders. Using dialogue as both the object and the medium of direct and explicit intervention, Singer and Bashir assisted George with managing both his speech and his language production. The central goal of intervention was to help George develop the regulatory process of self-observation, self-judgment, and self-reaction (Zimmerman, 1989), while developing a reflective speaking approach. This allowed him to use specific strategies to plan, organize, monitor, and pace his oral and written discourse. Questions, such as those in Table 13.2, were used as an intervention framework intended to support George's ability to self-regulate his expression.

General questions and strategic responses like these were carefully discussed with George. The use of these strategies to organize thinking and language was modeled by the SLP as talk-alouds, and practiced in activities that approximated George's real-life situations. The interventions focused on an understanding of the processes involved in thinking and producing language. George was guided to use those strategies that facilitated his communicative performance flexibly. As a result, George developed new approaches to effectively managing his communication. His increased effectiveness resulted from the use of active problem-solving strategies supported by self-reflection (i.e., self-monitoring, self-evaluation, and behavioral adjustments). His explicit use of strategies allowed for the development of new approaches for regulating his thinking, communication, and problem solving that ultimately promoted his independence as a speaker.

George was able to learn to pause, reflect, and move his narratives and expositions forward by carefully planning, organizing, and monitoring his discourse. George was taught to make use of self-talk to help him self-regulate his language productions (Harris, 1990) and monitor his speaking behaviors. The use of self-talk helped him develop self-guidance (e.g., What do I want to say? How should I organize it? I'm getting lost; what do I want to say and how do I get back on track?). In addition, internalized speech provided George with the verbal mediation needed to control and regulate his communication. Once George was able to manage and control his speech production and spoken and written discourse formulation, noticeable changes occurred in other aspects of his language that were not treated directly. For example, George successfully used more diverse and specific vocabulary, increasingly complex syntax, and a broader range of cohesive devices.

In each of the approaches noted above, teaching the self-regulatory and executive processes required for strategy use, speaking, and writing proceeds in

Examples of Guiding Questions for Self-Monitoring, Self-Evaluation, and Behavioral Adjustments

Table 13.2

Guiding Questions	Examples of Self-Talk
What do I want to say?	I want to compare the characters of Jay Gatsby and Nick Carraway in *The Great Gatsby*.
What kinds of thinking do I need to do?	I need to describe the characters, and I need to tell how they are alike and how they are different from each other.
What can I do to help myself plan and organize the material?	Using my graphic, I need to visualize the structure of my speech and decide how to organize the information about the characters.
How will I monitor my speech during my presentation?	I'm speaking too fast. Use my pacing strategy to slow down so that I have more time to explain myself. I'm not saying what I want to…I'm getting lost…What am I trying to say?
What changes can I make so that I am sure to be understood?	What I need to do is change how I'm talking by slowing down my rate and pausing to give myself time to come up with the right words. I can buy time by saying, "Wait. I need to say that again…" Or, "By that I mean…"

a systematic manner and is embedded within a meaningful and authentic learning context (e.g., Singer & Bashir, 1999). In all of these approaches, the teacher, SLP, and student exercise considerable flexibility over how they go about attaining their goals. Their instruction, intervention, and learning goals are selected on the basis of specific academic or assignment demands.

Composing: Integrating Self-Regulatory and Executive Function Processes

Writing is a deliberate act. As such, it requires intentional effort on the part of writers during the composing process. Singer and Bashir (2004a) have proposed a model of writing that accounts for the integration of self-regulatory and executive functions into the writing process. As can be seen in Figure 13.1, written language involves both writing processes and writing foundations. In order to compose, writers must recruit, manage, coordinate, and monitor multiple processes simultaneously. Much as a juggler keeps several balls in the air, writers must juggle all of the component systems of writing. The key to the juggler's success is keeping all the balls moving along smoothly; this the juggler accomplishes by understanding and mastering the many foundation skills required for juggling. The same principle holds for writing (Flower & Hayes, 1980; Singer & Bashir, 2004a, 2004b).

> By acknowledging the basic processes that must be recruited for composing and the numerous variables that control and constrain those processes, we can begin to understand why writers might struggle one day and generate text with ease the next. (Singer & Bashir, 2004a, p. 561)

Well-developed writers have control over the writing process, yet are capable of self-regulating the process as the content, goals, and outcome requirements change. They flexibly adapt the writing process to each writing task, calling upon specific planning and organizing strategies, selecting appropriate text and linguistic structures, monitoring and evaluating the text as it evolves, and revising it accordingly. They manage motivation and the variety of emotions that arise during the composing process. Faced with many different options for expression, writers choose wisely among them, inhibiting those responses that are irrelevant or off topic and maintaining a forward focus to the composing process. They keep the topic and content of the paper in mind to develop a coherent text. All of these processes are coordinated in real time and are facilitated by working memory and other executive and self-regulatory functions. They use both internal and external resources to achieve the goal of a well-formed text that communicates ideas clearly and meaningfully to an unseen reader. It is difficult work, but they stick with it to get the job done.

For students with language-learning and/or executive function disabilities, writing can be a life-long challenge (Singer & Bashir, 2004b). Why? Because writing demands the integration and coordination of diverse cognitive, executive,

Figure 13.1   **A Model of Text Production**

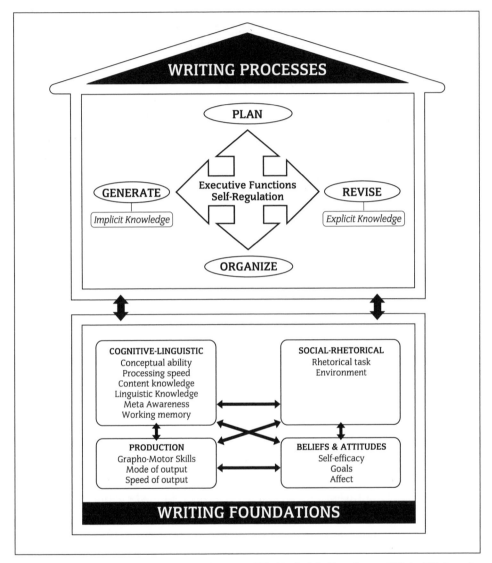

From *Brain Frames: Graphic Strategies to Frame Your Language and Thinking,* by B.D. Singer, in press, Wellesley, MA: Innovative Learning Partners. Reprinted with permission.

memory, linguistic, spatial, motor, and affective systems (Singer & Bashir, 2004a). Each of these systems makes its own contribution to the writing process and the text that is written. Students may struggle with virtually all of the skills that support written expression. If they are not self-regulated and cannot inhibit the intrusion of irrelevant ideas, and if they cannot keep ideas and goals in mind as they write, they are ineffective and inefficient writers (Singer & Bashir, 2004a). They may devote precious cognitive resources to managing only some of what needs to be managed in order to produce a text. They may become frustrated and have diminished feelings of self-worth as well as negative beliefs about their ability to manage the task successfully. Their problems may be confounded by a poor command of language, which renders them "speechless." They may lack sufficient content knowledge to complete the assignment, or they may have deficits in semantic, syntactic, pragmatic, or phonological skills necessary for written expression. Like the novice juggler, they have yet to master the component skills and abilities that writing requires. We have seen this clearly in students who have difficulty with keeping one or more of the following balls in the air:

- Reading their assignments and understanding what they have to do
- Knowing how to get started with the writing task
- Planning, organizing, expressing, and elaborating ideas in writing
- Maintaining motivation and interest in the task at hand

One of the first balls that often gets dropped is the assignment. Students with language and/or executive function disorders have difficulty reading their assignments and understanding what they have to do. Consequently, they cannot set goals, make plans, or organize their approach to writing. As Khema (1987) notes, "Unless we know the direction we are going, it's highly unlikely that we'll get to our destination. We have to know which way to go" (p. 24).

Successful assignment analysis requires insight about language. Embedded within the words of an assignment are clues about what topic(s) must be addressed in the paper, what genre the teacher is looking for, what resources must be recruited to address the topic thoroughly (e.g., curriculum content, texts, etc.), and what discourse moves need to be made within the paper to communicate effectively with the unseen reader. For students with language-learning and/or executive function disorders, this first step can be a major roadblock to success. Many students, faced with a *wall of words* on their assignment sheet, give up before even trying. Rereading the assignment doesn't help because, without strategies to weed the relevant from the irrelevant details, the wall remains impenetrable. Even if students are able to identify the key words that define the writing task, the language of the assignment can, in and of itself, pose another barrier to success.

Consider, for example, the experience of Harry, an intellectually gifted 9th grade student with severe attention and executive function deficits. Harry received the following assignment for homework.

> In *Great Expectations* by Charles Dickens, Pip's foster father, Joe, comes to visit Pip in the city. They are distant and Pip is embarrassed by Joe, even though he realizes all that he has done for him. Analyze a time in your own life when you were embarrassed by a family member. How did it make you feel before, during, and after the incident? Do you think Pip was justified in feeling this way?

Though he had demonstrated in conversation great insight about the novel, Harry's ability to complete this task was thwarted from the very start because he did not understand all of the linguistic elements in the assignment. Therefore, he was not able to identify what he needed to do to initiate and complete the task successfully. Harry struggled with planning and organizing both his approach to this writing assignment and his ideas. He also struggled with recognizing how the language of the assignment directed his planning and organizing efforts. His difficulty making the link between language and purposeful action is evident within the transcript provided in Box 13.1 on page 582, where he is working with his clinician to determine the structural elements required in this paper based on the wording of the assignment.

In Harry, we see a perfect example of the inseparable links among language, executive functions, and self-regulation. Harry was not able to self-regulate writing his paper because he could not plan and organize his approach to this novel task. He immediately recalled the numerous times he has failed with writing due to his disorganization, which left him emotionally vulnerable from the start. He did not believe things would go any differently for him this time, and this made him anxious and fearful of yet another failure. Because he was motivated to (but did not know how to) succeed, Harry sought out and used a mentor. With her guidance, he was able to inhibit the sabotaging inclination to give up without trying, conclude that he is indeed stupid, or divert his attention to his Game Boy.

Instead, Harry employed a specific strategy to figure out the demands of the assignment and how those demands directed his approach with this writing task. In doing so, however, he quickly encountered difficulty. He didn't understand what the language of the assignment was asking him to do in his writing, nor did he understand how the language helped him frame the task at hand (i.e., to analyze). The key action he had to take in the paper—*analyze*—did not evoke an approach to organizing his thinking, a specific text structure, or a set of discourse moves associated with that text structure. No goal for the writing assignment can be set in the absence of understanding the key tasks involved

Transcript of Harry and His Clinician
Box 13.1   ### Analyzing a 9th Grade Writing Assignment

Harry: This one's hard. It sounds like something my English teacher would give me with all these questions!

SLP: Yeah, so do the questions make it hard?

Harry: Well, I don't know. They just tell you to answer, but they don't tell you how to answer it really. I always wish they would simplify it. Well I could just look at it for what it is and take everything literally, but that doesn't always work. "Analyze a time in your own life when you were embarrassed by a family member..."

SLP: So would that be a part?

Harry: So, you have to think. What's analyze mean? Analyze means...what does analyze mean? Does it? Can you just? Would "analyze this" make any sense alone in the assignment, or is analyze a word that means, like, you have to look for analyze? Analyze is a word. But are there any?... Oh, I forget the word.

SLP: Synonyms?

Harry: No, not synonyms, um... like... things that... Are there any specific parts of the assignment that could change the meaning of the word analyze?

SLP: Yes. It depends on what comes after the word analyze.

Harry: Does a word whose verb is analyze ever make sense on its own ...or...in a clause?

in the directive *analyze*. Though he read *Great Expectations* and had an understanding of the novel, he could not show what he knew within an academic task that required him to harness his executive functions (to plan, organize, attend, inhibit, and hold plans, actions, and academic content in mind long enough to write the paper) so that he could regulate his performance (which requires goal setting, selecting strategic approaches, monitoring and reflecting on the work both as it develops and as a whole, evaluating what he has written, maintaining motivation, and adjusting his thinking, language, and actions while he works).

Intervention: Case Study

Over several years, Singer and Bashir (2004b) developed an instruction and intervention approach to teaching expository writing called EmPOWER. Based on the work of Englert and her colleagues (Englert, et al., 1988), EmPOWER evolved into a uniquely different approach to teaching expository writing and intervening with students who exhibit language-learning disabilities and executive function disorders. Similarly, general education students who are simply struggling with self-regulating their writing find the use of EmPOWER an effective strategy for developing expository text.

EmPOWER is a highly explicit, systematic, strategic routine designed for use by both teachers and students to support all aspects of the writing process and expository text development. Specifically, it is designed to teach struggling writers how to coordinate and manage the multiple processes necessary to develop a written text. SLPs and teachers alike will find this approach highly useful for supporting the thinking and linguistic underpinnings of written expression. In addition, they will find that it supports the executive and self-regulatory processes needed for text production. Consequently, the use of EmPOWER allows a close collaboration between teachers and SLPs in teaching writing within highly contextualized settings (Singer & Bashir, 2004b).

Briefly, EmPOWER represents a six-stage writing process: evaluate, make a plan, organize, work, evaluate, rework. Within each stage, specific strategies are taught explicitly to support the numerous cognitive and linguistic subprocesses of writing. A detailed explanation of the EmPOWER approach may be found in Singer and Bashir (2004b). Its elements are illustrated here via the case of Amy, a 7th grade student with coexisting speech, language, and executive function disorders.

Amy: Initial Referral

Amy was referred for language intervention in 4th grade because she was not able to write more than a single sentence without maximum support from a special educator. At that time, she was receiving occupational therapy services in school to address motor planning difficulties that affected her handwriting (dysgraphia). She also had low muscle tone that affected trunk support and manual dexterity. A neuropsychological evaluation in third grade revealed a diagnosis of attention-deficit/hyperactivity disorder and associated executive function deficits affecting planning, organization, sustained attention, and cognitive flexibility. By parental report, she had shown improvement in her ability to sustain her attention with medication, but she continued to demonstrate and experience day-to-day fluctuations.

Upon meeting Amy, it was apparent that she was challenged in many of the systems required for writing. In addition to the aforementioned difficulties, she also presented with markedly impaired speech production (dyspraxia) as well as imprecise articulation associated with her low muscle tone (dysarthria). Reduced executive controls for planning and organizing language also were evident. For example, Amy struggled to formulate her thoughts in an organized way, which rendered her oral narratives difficult to follow. In addition, she had difficulty monitoring "two things at once" when she spoke. Amy's speech articulation became increasingly unintelligible within contexts that placed demands on verbal planning, organization, and formulation (e.g., telling about complex events or explaining what she knew about a topic or how to do something). In contrast to her relative weaknesses with speech and language production, Amy's reading and oral language comprehension abilities were grade appropriate.

Amy: Intervention Using EmPOWER

The EmPOWER strategy formed the backbone of Amy's written language intervention, for it provided a framework for explicitly supporting the range of executive function and self-regulatory systems necessary for writing. In using EmPOWER, the clinician provided Amy with a strategy that helped her to adopt the "internal script" needed to "talk herself through" all of the stages of the writing process. Using EmPOWER, the clinician acted as a mentor. In so doing, the clinician explicitly modeled and instructed Amy how and when to employ strategies designed to support specific cognitive, memory, and linguistic processes within each stage of the writing process. Over time, this resulted in Amy's gradual internalization of language, executive, and self-regulatory processes necessary for writing.

Evaluate

Too often, students do not know how to read a writing assignment to make sense of the information they are provided. Thus, they cannot determine what it is they have to do. Like Harry and Jack, they are often self-defeated from the beginning. The *E* step of EmPOWER—*evaluate*—provided Amy with strategies that helped her to dissect and evaluate the assignment. This allowed her to approach the task and begin to understand what it was asking her to do. She was taught strategies for identifying the "action words" (i.e., words within the assignment that tell her what to do). Based on that evaluation, she was taught to determine how many parts her text would need to include. For example, consider one of Amy's assignments:

> When kids go away for the summer they have all kinds of adventures. Write two paragraphs about an adventure you had this summer. Tell what you did and why you liked it.

In this assignment, Amy identified two action words telling her to do something: *write* and *tell*. She then determined what directives were associated with those words. Finally, she determined that her text would have two parts— one part needed to tell the reader what she did on her vacation, and one part needed to explain why she enjoyed it.

Make a Plan

Even when students read and understand their assignments, they sometimes cannot initiate the writing task. These students lack the planning required to move from direction to action. Like Harry, they may recognize that they must *analyze,* but may not know how that word helps to direct and structure their thinking. With a conscious awareness of her writing goal(s) established within the evaluate step of EmPOWER, Amy was then guided through several prompts to *make a plan* for how she would accomplish the demands of the assignment. These included defining her discourse purpose (i.e., retell, describe, give information, and give her opinion), identifying how she wanted to think about her topic and, given what she knew already, determining whether or not she required additional information.

Organize

The *organize* step of EmPOWER prompts students to display their ideas on paper graphically. Graphic organizers are commonly used to support the planning stages of writing. Typically, these consist of premade graphics students fill in with ideas. Too often, graphics are used that do not look like any specific text structure or any specific thinking process. And all too often, one graphic is used for multiple purposes (e.g., semantic webs are frequently used interchangeably for eliciting brainstormed ideas, categorizing ideas, and/or describing qualities or attributes). As a result, students often find themselves wondering which of the many graphics they have seen would be appropriate for use with a given task. Alternatively, not having found the "one size fits all" graphic helpful, they choose not to use them to support their writing.

Within the organize step of EmPOWER, Amy was taught a set of graphics called Brain Frames (Singer, in press). These evolved from the work of Hyerle (1996, 2000), who identified eight fundamental thinking processes that could be represented visually. Whereas language and cognition are inextricably intertwined (Vygotsky, 1962), Brain Frames were developed to represent the patterns of discourse that share a relationship with fundamental cognitive processes. Each of the Brain Frames depicts a specific cognitive-linguistic process (e.g., *compare/contrast, categorize, sequence*) within a graphic that *looks like* the cognitive-linguistic process it represents and *shows* the spatial/linguistic patterns associated with it (Singer & Heerde, 2004). Amy was not assigned a "graphic organizer" to fill in before writing. Rather, she was first taught to identify the type(s) of thinking and verbal expression that her writing task required. Then, just as an artist frames his artwork, Amy "framed" the words and ideas in her brain by drawing them by hand.

In using the Brain Frames, Amy was not restricted by a preset number of boxes or bubbles on a predrawn graphic. Instead, knowing what kind of thinking and communication she was embarking upon, Amy was empowered to draw as many boxes and bubbles necessary to represent all of her ideas. She arranged words and ideas within graphic patterns associated with a specific cognitive-linguistic process. The Brain Frames, then, supported her working memory by serving as "place holders" for her ideas. With her thinking, words, and ideas anchored on paper, she could step back from and appraise her graphic to determine whether she had retrieved relevant content knowledge for the writing assignment. For the writing assignment about her vacation presented above, Amy decided that she wanted to engage three cognitive-linguistic processes: *telling* (about her vacation), *describing* (her adventures with adjectives), and *showing causes and effects* (regarding her feelings about her adventures).

Work

The transition from planning and organizing using graphics to composing is not one that students with language and executive function disorders make easily. Many students find this transition daunting because composing involves more than just putting ideas into words. Though explicit support with the first three steps of the EmPOWER process was critical for Amy, she also needed assistance with generating language and embedding that language within a text structure. Planning and organization difficulties permeated all aspects of her speech and language system. Thus, although she *knew* a lot about her writing topic, she was not necessarily able to *represent* that knowledge linguistically within age/grade-appropriate text and sentence structures. Therefore, Amy needed additional help with the *work* of writing.

After evaluating task demands, planning her approach to the task, and organizing her thinking, Amy was taught to identify how and where to translate her ideas into written language. In doing so, she used premade templates that represented the elements associated with different text structures. For example, the template for writing an elaborated paragraph elicited a topic sentence, supporting facts, reasons, examples, and details (which became known as FREDs), a place to "say more" about each FRED, and a closing sentence. The multi-paragraph template elicited a thesis statement, topic sentences for each supporting subtopic, FREDs to support each topic sentence, and a concluding statement. An example of Amy's template developed for a two-paragraph text on her summer vacation, is displayed in Figure 13.2 on page 588.

Templates used in the work step of EmPOWER supported various levels of executive functioning. As a place to "hold" Amy's ideas, they served as a stable, external scaffold for working memory. They also supported organizational processes, as they revealed and elicited all text structure elements. The combination of these two functions further supported Amy's organization, as she was able to make conscious choices about which idea to use first, second, third, and so on. Amy was taught to identify and organize the structure of her written discourse separately before drafting her text. By doing so, the burden placed on her to formulate language was supported explicitly.

Amy was now directed to use her completed template to draft her text. At this point, she was able to devote all of her cognitive resources to formulating language because she could refer to her template while she composed. Knowing where she was going with her text, she was free to choose words carefully, craft sentences, weave ideas together with transition words and phrases, and attend to such things as punctuation and spelling. The first draft of Amy's text about her summer vacation is presented in Box 13.2 on page 589.

Evaluate and Rework

At the heart of writing is the capacity to revise and edit, which requires the writer to set goals and adopt evaluative procedures (Bereiter & Scardamalia, 1987; Hayes, 2000). Providing students with procedural supports for evaluating their

Figure 13.2

Amy's Text Structure Template for Two-Paragraph Writing Assignment

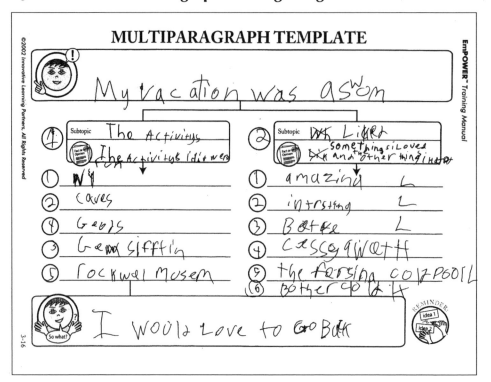

texts makes revising easier (De La Paz, Swanson, & Graham, 1998; Graham, 1997). The final steps of EmPOWER support the development of evaluative systems explicitly. Even though Amy followed her organized multiparagraph template while she drafted, her difficulty developing elaborated text is readily apparent in Box 13.2. The final two stages of EmPOWER then provided explicit scaffolds for her to *evaluate* and *rework* her text.

Amy was guided through these last two steps, using a rubric to self-appraise numerous aspects of her writing (e.g., topic relevance, organization of ideas, complexity and diversity of words and sentences, mechanics). This afforded an opportunity for context-specific intervention that focused on her use of language. For example, Amy was reminded that she needed to "say more" about each kernel idea on her template rather than simply use those kernel ideas to create simple paragraphs. Systematically, she then went through her paragraphs and elaborated key ideas. In addition, she was taught to use a word bank with transition words categorized according to their function (e.g.,

Box 13.2

First Draft of Amy's Text about Her Summer Vacation

Vacation

My vacation was awesome.

The activity's I did were fun. First of all going to NY was sweet. Next I just loved the caves. Then, we went gem sifting and got geodes. Lastly, we went to Rockwell museum.

There are some things I loved and other things I hated. First, at Howe Caverns, the caves were amazing. I loved going in the cold, cold pool. Then at the Secret Caverns it was wet and cheesy.

Some day I want to go back.

---

words that add an idea, tell a sequence, conclude, etc.). She was then guided to analyze the functional relationships between the sentences in her text and make necessary changes to cohesive devices. Amy's revised draft of this assignment is depicted in Box 13.3 on page 590.

While Amy made important changes from her initial draft to her revised draft, her writing still reflects her need for increasingly refined insights about written language. Indeed, appreciating the numerous revisions we routinely make to her writing, she commented that the approach "should be called EmPOWER-ER-ER-ER." After three years of language intervention, Amy still struggled with writing. However, the shifts in her performance in response to the highly explicit instruction EmPOWER offered were impressive. These gains were most pronounced when her teacher also began to use EmPOWER within the classroom, thereby providing her with a consistent strategy to use for writing across home and school contexts.

With a strategic instructional method that scaffolds the use of internal language to mediate the complex behaviors required for writing, Amy was able to recruit numerous skills and strategies to move through each stage of the writing process. Her success is even more impressive when one considers the numerous challenges she has across cognitive, executive function, speech, and language domains. The consistent nature of the EmPOWER approach (i.e.,

Box 13.3

Revised Draft of Amy's Text about Her Summer Vacation

Vacation

My vacation was awesome.

The activity's I did were fun. First of all going to NY was sweet. We went to the mountains in NY and we stayed at Howe Caverns. Howe Caverns motel is so peaceful and seeing the view was amazing. Also I just loved going into the caves at Howe Caverns. Being in the caves just leaves you in awe because of the natural beauty. We went gem sifting and also got geodes. To gem sift you buy a bag of gems get the sifter. Then put a small amount of dirt in the sifter. Next put the sifter in the water carefully and move it back and forth. Additionally we went to the Rockwell museum. The museum has all of Norman's arts. I had a great time.

There are some things I loved and other things I hated. To begin with I loved going in the cold, cold pool at Howe Caverns. My body got use to the water fast. Also at Howe Caverns the caves were amazing. It was beautiful compared to the Secret Caverns which were yuck. Instead at the Secret Caverns it was wet and cheesy. Also being in these caverns did not feel safe. It was originally used as a bomb shelter but is now used for tours. They said you can touch all the rocks but you can't touch the bats, the lights, and the tour guide. Howe Caverns was my favorite.

Someday I want to go back.

the unchanging script for what to say to herself as she sits to write any text) scaffolded Amy's executive function and linguistic processes explicitly so she was able to self-regulate her writing. Over time, the EmPOWER stages, associated visual strategies for representing thinking, language, and text structure, and task-specific linguistic strategies became internalized, thereby affording Amy increased efficiency, success, and independence as a writer. Her successful internalization of the processes and subprocesses of writing can be seen in the spontaneous and independently produced composition summarizing her field trip to see A Christmas Carol, presented in Box 13.4.

Written Language Intervention Guidelines

Many students like George, Harry, and Amy can be found in classrooms across the country. The question for teachers and SLPs then becomes: what do we do to help them develop executive functions and self-regulatory processes for writing? The following are guidelines to assist students in this process:

Box 13.4   **Amy's Independently Produced Composition about a Field Trip**

A Christmas Carol Review

I loved this play a lot. I had a ton of fun.

Today, the 7th grade saw <u>A Christmas Carol</u>. To get there we took coach buses which have TVs, comfy chairs, and a toilet. It took us one hour to get to the North Shore Music Theater. On the way home we watched a movie <u>The Little Rascals</u>.

The theater was the shape of a hexagon. The theater was so beautiful because the scenery was amazing. The scenery was set up all around the stage and on the ceiling. The clocks looked so real just like the city out line on the ceiling.

I was in the fourth seat of our aisle. The characters looked so amazing. They came in the audience at the beginning of the play. Their costumes looked so, so old. Also, the costumes were lovely. Marley's costume was my favorite because it left an indent in my mind his costume had lights on it.

A few things scared me a lot. First was the sound of the thunder when a ghost appeared. Next was the first shot of flames from the floor. Also when Marley's ghost was in midair the flames shot down from the ceiling. I loved how the Ghost of Christmas present's torch would burst in to flames and give off a good smell. Lastly, I was scared when a grave burst into flames while the Ghost of Christmas yet to come was on the top part of the grave.

All of the actors played their parts greatly. The man who played Marley was so good at acting because he could change his emotion fast. Who ever played Scrooge really fulfilled his part because he was never happy.

I would love to go back soon. The Christmas Carol was so fun to watch. Next time I want to sit in the front row. My opinion is go see this play. Also, if you bring someone who is younger hold their hand because they may be scared.

- Understand that different academic tasks demand varying amounts and kinds of executive, self-regulatory, and linguistic control. Accordingly, interventions must be designed flexibly to address the range of academic demands within any given assignment, as well as across grades and curriculum content areas.

- Avoid decontextualized interventions. Situate intervention within authentic learning contexts. Then create goals to address demands that are constraining student performance in that context.

- Use systematic, explicit, and conversational teaching methods to support students' understanding of where, when, why, and how to use strategies to regulate all aspects of the writing process.

- Provide extensive modeling. Modeling involves the SLP demonstrating and talking through the thought process aloud.

- Provide repeated opportunities for apprenticeship. Offer numerous opportunities to practice newly learned skills and strategies within authentic learning contexts, allowing the student to gradually internalize the clinician's models and guidance.

To provide support to students who struggle with writing, teachers and clinicians can:

- Jointly talk through, evaluate, and reflect on student performance. Decide together how best to address difficulties arising within specific writing tasks.

- Help students learn about writing through reading and analyzing texts written by other authors.

- Teach various written language genres and their structural and rhetorical elements directly.

- Help students acquire mindful (not mindless) problem-solving approaches to writing through mentoring, modeling, coaching, and structuring self-evaluations that foster their growth from naive to informed learners.

- Teach students explicit strategies to analyze the language of assignments and, based on that analysis, create action plans that will fulfill assignment goals.

- Teach specific strategies that address the critical components and sub-processes of each stage of the writing process (assignment analysis, planning, organizing, drafting, revising, and editing strategies).

- Use verbal mediation that demonstrates self-talk and provides strategic guidance to students to support executive functions and self-regulation of the writing process.

- Use only graphics that visually represent the structure of text and the patterns of thinking and language that support text development.

- Collaborate with teachers to address relevant student needs, thereby supporting the seamless integration of language intervention and classroom instruction across the curriculum.

Conclusion

Writing requires intentional action. Therefore, learning to write is a difficult task for all students. Writing is supported and constrained by many systems, which must be recruited and coordinated to support fluent production. Among these are: cognitive, linguistic, motoric, affective, social, rhetorical, executive function, and self-regulatory systems (Singer & Bashir, 2004a). Language-learning disabilities alone do not explain all of the problems students may encounter with writing.

SLPs are advised to take into account the interaction of language and executive function disorders and the ways in which they influence self-regulation for learning. When students exhibit executive function disorders and a domain-specific disorder (e.g., language), the result is a failure to compensate for that domain-specific disorder (Denckla, 1996). In other words, students with both language and executive function disorders may have difficulty regulating their language (e.g., oral and written comprehension and production) because the very systems that would allow them to recognize the need to use a strategy in any given context are impaired. Given this, it is no wonder that many students with language-learning disabilities have difficulty becoming self-regulated writers.

For these students, intervention becomes a mentored process that supports students' learning within authentic contexts (i.e., listening, speaking, reading, and writing in school). In writing, for example, students must be supported as they learn to manage the skills and abilities necessary to produce written text. EmPOWER, a strategic approach to teaching and learning writing, was presented as an example of an intervention that guides and scaffolds young writers. EmPOWER offers a framework for teaching students explicitly about all that writing requires. It guides students in assessing writing assignments, planning and organizing their approach to completing those assignments, setting appropriate goals, using language effectively to express their ideas, self-evaluating their writing and language use, and making appropriate changes. Throughout the writing process, students are supported to mindfully choose and use strategies effectively and efficiently. This framework provides a structure in which clinicians can have important conversations with students about writing and address their language needs directly within authentic learning contexts. The overall goal is the development of a writer who integrates executive, linguistic, and self-regulatory processes smoothly throughout the writing process.

References

Allen, D. (2001). *Getting things done.* New York: Penguin.

Anderson, V. A., Anderson, P., Northam, E., Jacobs R., & Catroppa, C. (2001). Development of executive functions through late childhood and adolescence in an Australian sample. *Developmental Neuropsychology, 20*(1), 385–406.

Barkley, R. A. (1995). Linkages between attention and executive functions. In G. R. Lyons & N. A. Krasnegor (Eds.), *Attention, memory, and executive function* (pp. 307–326). Baltimore: Brookes.

Barkley, R. A. (1997). Behavioral inhibition, sustained attention, and executive functions: Constructing a unifying theory of ADHD. *Psychological Bulletin, 121*(1), 65–94.

Bereiter, C., & Scardamalia, M. (1987). *The psychology of written composition.* Mahwah, NJ: Erlbaum.

Bronson, M. B. (2000). *Self-regulation in early childhood: Nature and nurture.* New York: Guilford.

Buttrill, J., Nizawa, J., Biemer, C., Takahashi, C., & Hearn, S. (1989). Serving the language learning disabled adolescent: A strategies-based model. *Language, Speech, and Hearing Services in Schools, 20*(2), 185–204.

Cleary, T., & Zimmerman, B. J. (2004). Self-regulation empowerment program: A school-based program to enhance self-regulated and self-motivated cycles of student learning. *Psychology in Schools, 41*(5), 537–550.

Creer, T. L. (2000). Self-management of chronic illness. In M. Boekaerts, P. R. Pintrich, & M. Zeidner (Eds.), *Handbook of self-regulation* (pp. 601–629). New York: Academic Press.

Dawson, P., & Guare, R. (2004). *Executive skills in children and adolescents: A practical guide to assessment and intervention.* New York: Guilford.

De Corte, E., Verschaffel, L., & Op't Eynde, P. (2002). Self-regulation: A characteristic and a goal of mathematics education. In M. Boekaerts, P. R. Pintrich, & M. Zeidner (Eds.), *Handbook of self-regulation* (pp. 687–726). New York: Academic Press.

De La Paz, S., & Graham, S. (2002). Explicitly teaching strategies, skills, and knowledge: Writing instruction in middle school classrooms. *Journal of Educational Psychology, 94*(4), 687–698.

De La Paz, S., Swanson, P. N., & Graham, S. (1998). The contribution of executive control to the revising by students with writing and learning difficulties. *Journal of Educational Psychology, 90,* 448–460.

Demetriou, A. (2002). Organization and development of self-understanding and self-regulation: Toward a general theory. In M. Boekaerts, P. R. Pintrich, & M. Zeidner (Eds.), *Handbook of self-regulation* (pp. 209–251). New York: Academic Press.

Denckla, M. B. (1996). A theory and model of executive function: A neuropsychological perspective. In G. R. Lyon & N. A. Krasnegor (Eds.), *Attention, memory and executive function* (pp. 263–278). Baltimore: Brookes.

Denckla, M. B., & Reader, M. J. (1993). Education and psychosocial interventions: Executive dysfunction and its consequences. In R. Kurlan (Ed.), *Handbook of Tourette's syndrome and related tic and behavioral disorders* (pp.431–451). New York: Marcel Kekker.

Englert, C. S., & Dunsmore, K. (2004). The role of dialogue in constructing effective literacy settings for students with language and learning disabilities. In E. R. Silliman & L. Wilkinson (Eds.), *Language and literacy learning* (pp. 201–238). New York: Guilford.

Englert, C. S., Raphael, T. E., Anderson, L. M., Anthony, H. M., Fear, K. L., & Gregg, S. L. (1988). A case for writing intervention: Strategies for writing informational text. *Learning Disabilities Focus, 3*(2), 98–113.

Eslinger, P. J. (1996). Conceptualizing, describing, and measuring components of executive function: A summary. In G. R. Lyon & N. A. Krasnegor (Eds.), *Attention, memory, and executive function* (pp. 367–395). Baltimore: Brookes.

Flower, L. S., & Hayes, J. R. (1980). The dynamics of composing: Making plans and juggling constraints. In L. W. Gregg & E. R. Steinberg (Eds.), *Cognitive processes in writing* (pp. 31–50). Mahwah, NJ: Erlbaum.

Graham, S. (1997). Executive control in the revising of students with learning and writing difficulties. *Journal of Educational Psychology, 89,* 223–234.

Graham, S., & Harris, K. R. (1993). Self-regulated strategy development: Helping students with learning problems develop as writers. *The Elementary School Journal, 94,* 169–181.

Harris, K. R. (1990). Developing self-regulated learners: The role of private speech and self instruction. *Educational Psychologist, 25,* 35–49.

Harris, K. R., & Graham, S. (1996). *Helping young writers master the craft: Strategy instruction and self-regulation in the writing process.* Cambridge, MA: Brookline.

Hayes, J. R. (2000). A new framework for understanding cognition and affect in writing. In R. Indrisano & J. R. Squire (Eds.), *Perspectives on writing: Research, theory, and practice* (pp. 6–44). Newark, DE: International Reading Association.

Hayes, S. C., Gifford, E. V., & Ruckstuhl, L. E. (1996). Relational frame theory and executive function. In G. R. Lyon & N. A. Krasnegor (Eds.), *Attention, memory, and executive function* (pp. 279–305). Baltimore: Brookes.

Helmus, A. (2004, November). *Neuropsychological frameworks for understanding executive functions.* Paper presented at the Harvard Conference on Learning Differences, Cambridge, MA.

Hyerle, D. (1996). *Visual tools for constructing knowledge.* Alexandria, VA: Association for Supervision and Curriculum Development.

Hyerle, D. (2000). *A field guide to using visual tools.* Alexandria, VA: Association for Supervision and Curriculum Development.

Khema, A. (1987). *Being nobody going nowhere: Meditations on the Buddhist path.* Boston: Wisdom Publications.

Klenberg, L., Korkman, M., & Lahti-Nuuttila, P. (2001). Differential development of attention and executive functions in 3- to 12-year-old Finnish children. *Developmental Neuropsychology, 20,* 407–428.

Lencioni, P. (2002). *The five dysfunctions of a team: A leadership fable.* San Francisco: Jossey-Bass.

Lesaca, T. (2001). Executive functions in parents with ADHD. *Psychiatric Times, 17,* 11.

Lezak, M. D. (1995). *Neuropsychological assessment* (3rd ed.). New York: Oxford University Press.

Marlowe, W. B. (2000). An intervention for children with disorders of executive functions. *Developmental Neuropsychology, 18,* 445–454.

Newman, R. S. (1994). Academic help seeking: A strategy of self-regulated learning. In D. J. Schunk & B. J. Zimmerman (Eds.), *Self-regulation of learning and performance: Issues and educational application* (pp. 283–301). Mahwah, NJ: Erlbaum.

Pennington, B. F., Bennetto, L., McAleer, O., & Roberts, R. J. (1996). Executive functions and working memory: Theoretical and measurement issues. In G. R. Lyon & N. A. Krasnegor (Eds.), *Attention, memory, and executive function* (pp. 327–348). Baltimore: Brookes.

Pennington, B. F., & Ozonoff, S. (1996). Executive functions and developmental psychopathology. *Journal of Child Psychology and Psychiatry, 37,* 51–87.

Pintrich, P. R. (2000). The role of goal orientation in self-regulated learning. In M. Boekaerts, P. R. Pintrich, & M. Zeidner (Eds.), *Handbook of self-regulation* (pp. 451–502). New York: Academic Press.

Pressley, M. (1998). *Reading instruction that works: The case for balanced teaching.* New York: Guilford.

Pressley, M., El-Dinary, P. B., Gaskins, I., Schuder, T., Bergman, J. L., Almasi, J., et al. (1992). Beyond direct explanation: Transactional instruction of reading comprehension strategies. *The Elementary School Journal, 92,* 513–555.

Puustinen, M., & Pulkkinen, L. (2001). Models of self-regulated learning: A review. *Scandinavian Journal of Educational Research, 45,* 269–286.

Roberts, R. J., & Pennington, B. F. (1996). An interactive framework for examining prefrontal cognitive processes. *Developmental Neuropsychology, 12,* 105–126.

Scholnick, E. K., & Friedman, S. L. (1993). Planning in context: Developmental and situational considerations. *International Journal of Behavioral Development, 16,* 145–167.

Schunk, D. H., & Ertmer, P. A. (2000). Self-regulation and academic learning: Self-efficacy enhancing interventions. In M. Boekaerts, P. R. Pintrich, & M. Zeidner (Eds.), *Handbook of self-regulation* (pp. 631–649). New York: Academic Press.

Shallice, T. (1988). *From neuropsychology to mental structure.* Cambridge: Cambridge University Press.

Singer, B. D. (in press). *Brain Frames: Graphic strategies to frame your language and thinking.* Wellesley, MA: Innovative Learning Partners.

Singer, B. D., & Bashir, A. S. (1999). What are executive functions and self-regulation and what do they have to do with language-learning disorders? *Language, Speech, and Hearing Services in Schools, 30,* 265–273.

Singer, B. D., & Bashir, A. S. (2004a). Developmental variations in writing composition. In A. Stone, E. Silliman, B. Ehren, & K. Apel, (Eds.), *Handbook of language and literacy: Development and disorders* (pp. 559–582). New York: Guilford.

Singer, B. D., & Bashir, A. S. (2004b). EmPOWER: A strategy for teaching students with language learning disabilities how to write expository text. In E. R. Silliman & L. Wilkinson (Eds.), *Language and literacy learning* (pp. 239–272). New York: Guilford.

Singer, B. D., & Heerde, S. M. (2004, November). *Language and spatial skills work together: See what I mean?* Presentation for the American Speech-Language-Hearing Association Convention, Philadelphia, PA.

Stuss, D. T. (1992). Biological and psychological development of executive functions. *Brain and Cognition, 20,* 8–23.

Stuss, D. T., & Alexander, M. P. (2000). Executive functions and the frontal lobes: A conceptual view. *Psychological Research, 63,* 289–298.

Stuss, D. T., & Benson, D. F. (1986). *The frontal lobes.* New York: Raven Press.

Troia, G. A., & Graham, S. (2002). The effectiveness of a highly explicit, teacher-directed strategy instruction routine. *Journal of Learning Disabilities, 35,* 290–305.

Vygotsky, L. V. (1962). *Thought and language.* Cambridge, MA: MIT Press.

Weinstein, C. E., & Mayer, R. E. (1986). The teaching of learning strategies. In M. C. Wittrock (Ed.), *Handbook of research on teaching* (pp. 15–32). New York: Macmillan.

Wertsch, D. J. W. (1998). *Mind as action.* New York: Oxford University Press.

Westby, C. (2004). A language perspective on executive functioning, metacognition, and self-regulation in reading. In C. A. Stone, E. R. Silliman, B. J. Ehren, & K. Apel (Eds.), *Handbook of language and literacy* (pp. 398–427). New York: Guilford.

Zeider, M., Boekaerts, M., & Pintrich, P. R. (2000). Self-regulation: Directions and challenges for future research. In M. Boekaerts, P. R. Pintrich, & M. Zeidner (Eds.), *Handbook of self-regulation* (pp. 749–768). New York: Academic Press.

Zimmerman, B. J. (1986). Development of self-regulated learning: Which are the key subprocesses? *Contemporary Educational Psychology, 11,* 307–313.

Zimmerman, B. J. (1989). A social cognitive view of self-regulated academic learning. *Journal of Educational Psychology, 81,* 329–229.

Zimmerman, B. J. (1994). Dimensions of academic self-regulation: A conceptual framework for education. In D. H. Schunk & B. J. Zimmerman (Eds.), *Self-regulation of learning and performance: Issues and educational implications* (pp. 3–21). Mahwah, NJ: Erlbaum.

Zimmerman, B. J. (2001). Theories of self-regulated learning and academic achievement: An overview and analysis. In B. J. Zimmerman & D. H. Schunk (Eds.), *Self-regulated learning and academic achievement* (2nd ed., pp. 1–37). Mahwah, NJ: Erlbaum.

Zimmerman, B. J. (2002). Becoming a self-regulated learner: An overview. *Theory into Practice, 41*(2), 64–70.

Zimmerman, B. J., Bonner, S., Evans, D., & Mellins, R. (1999). Self-regulating childhood asthma: A developmental model of family change. *Health Education and Behavior, 26,* 53–69.

Zimmerman, B. J., Bonner, S., & Kovach, R. (1996). *Developing self-regulated learners: Beyond achievement to self-efficacy.* Washington, DC: American Psychological Association.

Zimmerman, B. J., & Schunk, D. H. (2001). *Self-regulated learning and academic achievement: Theoretical perspectives* (2nd ed.). Mahwah, NJ: Erlbaum.

Author Index

Subject Index

f = figure   b = box   t = table

A

academic structure, 323–24, 324f, 325t

actions

    in activity analysis, 14–15, 14t, 22–23, 25t, 26b

    in intervention, 33, 34t, 35

action sequence, 219–20

activity analysis

    in assessment, 21–23, 24–25t, 26b

    components, 13–15, 14t

    in intervention, 29–33, 31t, 34t, 35

activity selection, 19–21

activity theory, 13–15

adult-directed intervention, 9–10

adverbial constructions, 151b, 365, 366–67t

after-school programs, 102–3

    See also writing lab approach

Alexander and the Terrible, Horrible, No Good, Very Bad Day (Viorst), 220

All by Myself (Mayer), 219

assessment. *See* contextualized assessment

attribute guides, 523f

audiences, 118–19, 239

    See also feedback

author chairs, 119

author notebooks, 128

    See also New Word Books

automaticity theory, 476

avoidance strategies, 100

B

balanced teaching, 402–3

Berenstain Bears Go to School (Berenstain & Berenstain), 220

Bloom's taxonomy, 336, 337t, 514, 515t, 516

book selection. *See* text selection

bottom-up processing, 505–6

Brain Frames, 585–86

brainstorming activities, 124–26

Brown Bear, Brown Bear, What Do You See? (Carle), 219

C

Casey at the Bat (Thayer), 492–93

charts, two-column, 128, 129f

child-directed intervention, 9–11

children's literature tools, 218–22, 237–38, 246, 467

classroom assessment

    considerations, 327–29

    curriculum-based measurement, 483–84

    inferential skills, 361, 363

    interviews, 343–44